T0222372

Lecture Notes in Artificial Intelligence   10709

Subseries of Lecture Notes in Computer Science

More information about this series at http://www.springer.com/series/1244

Yunfang Wu · Jia-Fei Hong
Qi Su (Eds.)

Chinese Lexical Semantics

18th Workshop, CLSW 2017
Leshan, China, May 18–20, 2017
Revised Selected Papers

 Springer

Editors
Yunfang Wu
Peking University
Beijing
P.R. China

Qi Su
Peking University
Beijing
P.R. China

Jia-Fei Hong
National Taiwan Normal University
Taipei
ROC

ISSN 0302-9743   ISSN 1611-3349 (electronic)
Lecture Notes in Artificial Intelligence
ISBN 978-3-319-73572-6   ISBN 978-3-319-73573-3   (eBook)
https://doi.org/10.1007/978-3-319-73573-3

Library of Congress Control Number: 2017963757

LNCS Sublibrary: SL7 – Artificial Intelligence

Printed on acid-free paper

This Springer imprint is published by Springer Nature
The registered company is Springer International Publishing AG
The registered company address is: Gewerbestrasse 11, 6330 Cham, Switzerland

Preface

The Chinese Lexical Semantics Workshop (CLSW) held in 2017 was the 18th conference in the series established in 2000. CLSW has been held in different Asian cities, including Hong Kong, Beijing, Taipei, Singapore, Xiamen, Hsin Chu, Yantai, Suzhou, Wuhan, Zhengzhou and Macao. Over the years, CLSW has become one of the most important venues for scholars to report and discuss the latest progress in Chinese lexical semantics and related fields, including theoretical linguistics, applied linguistics, computational linguistics, information processing and computational lexicography. CLSW has significantly impacted and promoted academic research and application development in the field, and acted as one of the most important meetings in Asia for lexical semantics.

CLSW 2017 was hosted by Leshan Normal University, China. This year 176 papers were submitted to the conference. All submissions went through a double-blind review process. Of these, 52 submissions (29.5%) were accepted as regular papers and 43 (24.4%) as poster papers. They were organized in topical sections covering all major topics of lexical semantics, semantic resources, corpus linguistics and natural language processing.

On behalf of the Program Committee, we are most grateful to Shiwen Yu (Peking University), Chu-Ren Huang (Hong Kong Polytechnic University), Xinchun Su (Xiamen University) and the Advisory Committee for their guidance in promoting the conference. We sincerely appreciate the invited speakers: Ming Zhou (Microsoft Research Asia), Meichun Liu (City University of Hong Kong), Diana McCarthy (University of Cambridge), Nianwen Xue (Brandeis University), Yiming Yang (Jiangsu Normal University) and Zhifang Sui (Peking University), for their outstanding keynote talks. Also, we would like to acknowledge the conference co-chairs Hongying Zan (Zhengzhou University) and Dan Hu (Leshan Normal University), as well as the chair of the Organizing Committee, Peng Jin (Leshan Normal University), for their tremendous contribution to this event.

Our gratitude goes to all the Program Committee members and reviewers for their time and efforts in the reviewing process. We are pleased that the accepted English papers are published by Springer as part of their Lecture Notes in Artificial Intelligence (LNAI) series and are indexed by EI and SCOPUS.

Last but not the least, we thank all the authors and attendees for their scientific contribution and participation, which made CLSW 2017 a successful event.

October 2017

Yunfang Wu
Jia-Fei Hong
Qi Su

Organization

Program Chairs

Yunfang Wu	Peking University, P.R. China
Jia-Fei Hong	National Taiwan Normal University, ROC
Maggie Wenjie Li	The Hong Kong Polytechnic University, SAR China

Program Committee

Ahrens Kathleen	The Hong Kong Polytechnic University, SAR China
Xiaojing Bai	Tsinghua University, P.R. China
Minghui Dong	Institute for Infocomm Research, Singapore
Shu-Ping Gong	National Chiayi University, ROC
Kam-Fai Wong	The Chinese University of Hong Kong, SAR China
Donghong Ji	Wuhan University, P.R. China
Minghu Jiang	Tsinghua University, P.R. China
Peng Jin	Leshan Normal University, P.R. China
Huei-ling Lai	National Chengchi University, ROC
Baoli Li	Henan University of Technology, P.R. China
Shih-min Li	National Academy for Educational Research, ROC
Yao Liu	Institute of Scientific and Technical Information of China, P.R. China
Maofu Liu	Wuhan University of Science and Technology, P.R. China
Pengyuan Liu	Beijing Language and Culture University, P.R. China
Chia-Rung Lu	National Taiwan University, ROC
Wei-Yun Ma	Academia Sinica, ROC
Yao Meng	Fujitsu Research and Development Center
Haihua Pan	City University of Hong Kong, SAR China
Likun Qiu	Ludong University, P.R. China
Weiguang Qu	Nanjing Normal University, P.R. China
Xiaodong Shi	Xiamen University, P.R. China
Zuoyan Song	Beijing Normal University, P.R. China
Xinchun Su	Xiamen University, P.R. China
Zhifang Sui	Peking University, P.R. China
Le Sun	Institute of Software Chinese Academy of Sciences, P.R. China
Lei Wang	Peking University, P.R. China
Jun Xia	Shenyang Normal University, P.R. China
Shu-Kai Hsieh	National Taiwan University, ROC
Jiajuan Xiong	Southwestern University of Finance and Economics, P.R. China
Jie Xu	The University of Macau, SAR China

Contents

Applications of Natural Language Processing

Lexical Resources

Corpus Linguistics

Lexical Semantics

On le_2: Its Nature and Syntactic Status[*]

Peicui Zhang[1], Jiyan Li[2], Ru'e Liang[1, 3], Youlong Fu[4], Huibin Zhuang[1]

1 Henan University
2 Yanshan University
3 Zhengzhou University of Aeronautics
4 Weifang Medical University
{zhangpeicui,fuyoulong,huibinzhuang}@aliyun.com,dayanlijiyan@163
.com,lianglele1205@126.com

Abstract. Le_2 has special features in both syntax and semantics, and should not be put on an equal footing with le_1. Based on the framework of split CP hypothesis, this paper discusses the syntactic status of le_2. It finds that le_2 is a Fin element, located outside the clause to mark the overall state of the clause. For this reason, its occurrence will not be affected by the existence of the negative marker in a clause (while le_1 will be affected).

Keywords: le_2, nature, syntactic status, split CP hypothesis

1   Introduction

When discussing le, the previous studies usually divide it into two types. The first one is the suffix le, which appears following a verb, especially between a verb and its object, or inserted into an ionized word. For the purpose of discussion, it is marked as le_1. Examples are shown as follows:

(1) 张三昨天去了北京。
    Zhāngsān zuótiān   qù le   běijīng.
    Zhangsan yesterday go le_1 Beijing
    "Zhangsan has gone to Beijing yesterday."

(2) 张三吃了一大碗米饭。
    Zhāngsān chī le   yī   dà   wǎn   mǐfàn.
    Zhangsan eat le_1 one big bowl rice
    "Zhangsan has eaten a big bowl of rice."

(3) 张三洗了澡才出去。
    Zhāngsān xǐ   le   zǎo   cái   chūqù.
    Zhangsan wash le_1 bath then go.out
    "Zhangsan has taken a bath before going out."

---

[*] All correspondence please address to: Huibin Zhuang, School of Foreign Languages, Henan University, Kaifeng, 475001, China. Email: huibinzhuang@aliyun.com

© Springer International Publishing AG 2018
Y. Wu et al. (Eds.): CLSW 2017, LNAI 10709, pp. 3–16, 2018.
https://doi.org/10.1007/978-3-319-73573-3_1

The second one is the sentence final *le*, which appears at the end of a sentence (especially following the object or the complement). For the convenience of discussion, it is marked as *le₂,* as shown below:

(4) 张三昨天去北京了。

　　　Zhāngsān zuótiān　　qù běijīng　　le.
　　　Zhangsan yesterday　go Beijing　le_2
　　　"Zhangsan has gone to Beijing yesterday."

(5) 张三吃饭了。

　　　Zhāngsān chī fàn　le.
　　　Zhangsan eat meal　le_2
　　　"Zhangsan has had a meal."

Besides, due to the research need, some scholars differentiate a third *le*, which appears mainly after the verb and meanwhile at the end of the sentence. For the convenience of discussion, it is marked as *le₃*. For example, as in (6) and (7):

(6) 张三哭了。

　　　Zhāngsān kū　le.
　　　Zhangsan cry　le_3
　　　"Zhangsan cried."

(7) 张三睡了。

　　　Zhāngsān shuì　le.
　　　Zhangsan sleep　le_3
　　　"Zhangsan slept."

In accordance with the specific context, le_3 can be classified as le_1 or le_2. In fact, it may be the fusion between the suffix *le* and the sentence final *le* (Zhu, 1982:209).

Now, there isn't much controversy on the nature of le_1. Most scholars agree that le_1 is the marker of perfective aspect. The argument about *le* mainly revolves around le_2, which is primarily due to the difficulty to define the nature of le_2. It can be somewhat felt through the comparison between le_1 and le_2. Generally speaking, the differences between le_1 and le_2 are in the following aspects:

First, they are different in syntactic positions. As mentioned above, the syntactic distribution of le_1 and le_2 is different. While le_1 is a suffix and appears at the end of a word, le_2 is a sentence final particle and appears at the end of a sentence.

Second, as mentioned above, le_1 is the marker of perfective aspect, merely indicating the completion of events. In contrast, le_2 denotes not only the completion of events but something that is about to happen, which can be shown in (8) and (9) respectively:

(8)——小王，吃饭了没有？

　　　Xiǎo Wáng, chī fàn　le méiyǒu?
　　　Xiao Wang, eat meal　le_2 have-not
　　　"Xiao Wang, do you have a meal?"

　——吃（饭）了。

　　　Chī (fàn)　le.
　　　eat (meal)　le_2
　　　"(I) have eaten."

(9) A(对室友B说): 我先去洗澡了, 洗完澡还要写论文。

    A (duì shìyǒu   B shuō): Wǒ xiān qù xǐzǎo le,

    A (to   roommate B say):   I   first go bathe *le₂*

                             xǐ   wán   zǎo   hái yào   xiě   lùnwén.

                             wach finish bath still need write   thesis

    "A (to his roommate B): I am going to take a bath first. After the bath I still need to write a paper."

Third, *le₁* and *le₂* are quite different when they are linked with the negative marker *bu*. It is mainly because of the language facts that negative marker *bu* can co-occur with *le₂* (while *bu* cannot co-occur with *le₁*). Take the following sentences as examples:

(10) a. 张三吃了饭。

      Zhāngsān chī le fàn.

      Zhangsan eat *le₁* meal

      "Zhangsan ate."

   b. *张三不吃了饭。

      *Zhāngsān bù chī le fàn.

      *Zhangsan not eat *le₁* meal

(11) a. 张三吃饭了。

      Zhāngsān chī fàn le.

      Zhangsan eat meal *le₂*

      "Zhangsan has eaten."

   b. 张三不吃饭了。

      Zhāngsān bù chī fàn le.

      Zhangsan not eat meal *le₂*

      "Zhangsan is not going to have a meal."

Considering the various traits of *le₂*, it is very necessary to have a further discussion. The content of this paper is as follows: Part Two reviews the nature of *le₂* and the interpretation of its syntactic representation; Part Three introduces the split CP hypothesis, and then probes into *le₂* from this perspective.

2   Previous Research

People have different understandings as for the nature of *le₂*. Lü (1999) points out that *le₂* symbolizes that the state has changed or is about to change; Li & Thompson (1981) hold the view that *le₂* indicates a state that is relevant to one aspect of the current situation; Rong (1999) proposes that *le₂* suggests the beginning of a new situation; Arin (2003) points out that *le₂* indicates the boundness of events; Lin (2003) firmly believes *le₂* indicates a kind of consequence; Jin (2003) believes that *le₂* expresses the temporal-aspectual properties of the emergence of some state; Pan & Lee (2004) points out that *le₂* expresses the assertion operator that the clause proposition is true; Shen (2004) thinks *le₂* is a dynamic aspectual marker; Shi and Hu (2006) discovers that *le₂* is attached to clauses, indicating the entrance into the state described by the clause; and so on.

Among these studies, Shi and Hu (2006) clearly specify the syntactic status of *le₂* — a complementizer C. The syntactic structure they have proposed is as follows:

(13) a. 你吃榴莲了。

    Nǐ chī liúlián le.

    you eat durian le₂

    "You ate durian."

b.

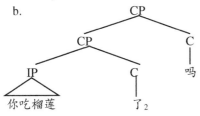

Then, they illustrate the syntactic structure of the co-occurrence of *le₂* and *ma*, which is a question marker in Chinese, as shown in (13):

(13) a. 你吃榴莲了吗？

    Nǐ chī liúlián le ma?

    you eat durian le₂ ma

    "Did you eat durian."

b.

Their solution is very creative. From a whole new perspective, it could solve many tangled problems previous researchers may encounter. However, after further investigation, we find some problems unsettled in this solution.

First, this solution doesn't distinguish between *ma, ne, ba* and *le₂*. Due to the theoretical limitation at that time (Single CP hypothesis), Shi and Hu (2006) have no choice but to put them into one category. In fact, to put *ma, ne, ba* ect., and *le₂* into one category without distinction may undoubtedly cover up the differences between them. It is hard to clarify their level differences[1]; and meanwhile it will unavoidably lead to confusion and misdirection in interpretation.

Second, it doesn't clarify the nature of *le₂*, and merely mark off one kind of *le₂* which is attached to clauses, indicating the entrance into the states described by the clauses. In fact, whether the reference time appears or not does have an impact on the interpretation of *le₂*, such as:

---

[1] Maybe it is due to this that Shi and Hu (2006) have to adopt semantics to exclude some sentences like *Ni chi liulian le ma?*

(14) 既然他不着急洗澡，我就先去洗澡了。

    Jìrán   tā bù zháojí xǐzǎo, wǒ jiù xiān qù xǐzǎo le.

    now.that he not hurry bathe, I then first go bathe le

    "Now that he is not in a hurry to take a bath, I will take a bath first."

(15) 昨天他不着急洗澡，我就先洗澡了。

    Zuótiān   tā bù zháojí xǐzǎo, wǒ jiù xiān xǐzǎo le.

    yesterday he not hurry bathe, I first first bathe le

    "Yesterday he was not in a hurry to take a bath, so I took a bath first."

Indeed, (14) indicates that it is *about to* enter the state described in the clause, that is, into the state of "taking a bath". Shi Dingxu and Hu Jianhua (2006) are quite insightful at this point. However, (15) is different, which contains a time reference of "yesterday". It means, at the point of yesterday, it is about to enter the temporary state of taking a bath; and at the point of the present, this process should have been completed. Look at another example:

(16) 刚才你一直磨磨蹭蹭不洗澡，我先洗了。

    Gāngcái nǐ yīzhí mómócèngcèng bù xǐzǎo, wǒ xiān xǐ le.

    just.now you always dawdle not take a bath, I first wash le

    "Just now you always dawdled and didn't proceeded to take a bath, so I bathed first."

Obviously, (16) can be interpreted as "I have taken a bath" rather than "I am going to take a bath". Perhaps, here *le* can be interpreted as *le₃* (Shi Dingxu , Hu Jianhua, 2006:106) . However, if the phrase *just now* is taken away, then it will definitley be regarded as *le₂*. This is evidently unsatisfactory. Look at the following examples:

(17) 我去北京了.

    Wǒ qù běijīng le.

    I go Beijing le

    "I have been to Beijing. / I am going to Beijing."

(18) 昨天我去北京了。

    Zuótiān wǒ qù běijīng le.

    yesterday I go Beijing le

    "Yesterday I went to Beijing."

(19) 明天我（就）去北京了。

    Míngtiān wǒ (jiù) qù běijīng le.

    tomorrow I (right away) go Beijing le

    "Tomorrow I am going to Beijing."

It is clear that there is only one interpretation in (18), *I have been to Beijing (now I am back)*; and this is true of (19), which can solely be interpreted as *I am going to Beijing tomorrow*. However, there can be two interpretations in (17), that is, *I have been to Beijing (now I come back)*, and *I am going to Beijing*. If so, it is not enough to simply take le_2 as going into the states described in the clause. Therefore, the assumption that le_2 is a marker indicating the starting or ending of the state described in the clause (whether it is starting or ending is determined by the reference time) becomes necessary.

Third, it doesn't take the fact into consideration that *Méiyǒu* (have-not) can negate le_1 and it can negate le_2 within a given reference time, such as (19) and (20). Hence some le_2 are taken as special ones (as *le* in 20), marking them as le_3.

(20)　昨天去北京了。

　　　　Zuótiān qù běijīng le.

　　　　yesterday go Beijing le

　　　　"Yesterday (I) went to Beijing."

(21)　昨天没有去北京。

　　　　Zuótiān méi yǒu qù běijīng.

　　　　yesterday have-not go Beijing

　　　　"Yesterday (I) didn't go to Beijing."

In fact, *le* in (20) is a typical le_2, expressing the completion of the state described in the cause, that is, the state of going to Beijing yesterday.

Now let us turn back to discuss why (22) is not correct.

(22)　*没有去北京了。

　　　　*Méiyǒu qù běijīng le.

　　　　*have-not go Beijing le_2

　　　　Intended reading: "have not gone to Beijing."

Obviously, the le_2 in (22) is contradictory with the nature of marking the starting or ending of the event. What is described in the clause of (22) ('not gone to Beijing') is not a state, so it cannot be further defined with le_2. If a time period is added to the clause of *not gone to Beijing*, just like (23), then the definition of le_2 will be acceptable, as in the following example,

(23)　他很长时间没有去北京了。

　　　　Tā hěn cháng shíjiān méiyǒu qù běijīng le.

　　　　he very long time　　have-not go Beijing le_2

　　　　"He hasn't been to Beijing for a long time."

Considering the above problems, it is necessary to study le_2 deeper and make a further clarification of its syntactic status. We will introduce an important hypothesis—split CP hypothesis (Rizzi 1997, 2004), under whose theoretical framework we will develop a qualitative analysis and discussion on le_2.[2]

---

[2] Shi and Hu (2006: 104–105) have noticed the application prospect of split CP Hypothesis. But they don't make any attempt to apply this approach, which is quite regrettable.

3   Split CP Hypothesis

Before Rizzi's the split CP hypothesis, the syntactic analysis is mainly based on the hypothesis of the complementiser phrase (CP). It is true that CP hypothesis is successful in analyzing the left periphery structure. However, it is difficult to deal with the embedded clause in (24).

(24) I am absolutely convinced [that no other colleague would he turn to].

We know that *wh*-phrase usually moves to the sentence-initial position through *wh*-movement. In fact, it is not merely *wh*-phrase but also other elements that may appear in the sentence-initial position. Just like (24), *no other colleague* originally is the object of *to*, but it appears in the sentence-initial position; meanwhile *would* is raised. Here comes the problem: how to determine the syntactic status of *no other colleague* and *would*? If we put *would* in the position of C (*no other colleague* is located in Spec, CP), it'll be hard to deal with *that*. The reason is, generally speaking, *that* is complementiser, occupying the position of C. But if *that* is placed in the position of C, there would be no position for *no other colleague* and *would*. In this way, the only feasible option is to allow two Cs to exist in the sentence, but it does not conform with the usual practice of the syntax, as in (25):

(25) I am absolutely convinced *[$_{CP}$ [$_{C}$ that [$_{CP}$ no other colleague [$_{C}$ would] [$_{TP}$ he [$_{T}$ t$_{would}$] [$_{VP}$ [$_{V}$ turn] [$_{PP}$ [$_{P}$ to] t $_{no\ other\ colleague}$]]]] (Rizzi, 1997)

Due to these reasons, Rizzi (1997, 2001, 2004) proposes to split CP into Force Phrase (ForceP), Topic Phrase (TopP), Focus Phrase (FocP)[3], and Finiteness Phrase (FinP) etc.. Rizzi（1997: 297）goes on to illustrate their orders in the tree diagram, as shown in (26), (TopP* indicates several topics can co-occur):

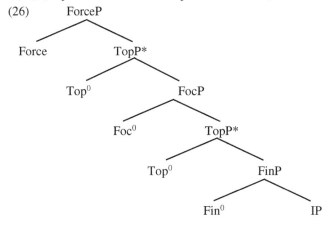

---

[3] According to Radford (2004), the distinction between TopP and FocP is that, from the perspective of the discourse, a focused element represents new information, while topics (the preposed object) represent old information which has already been mentioned previously.

With the split CP hypothesis, let's look at the embedded clause in (24). The analysis is shown in (27) (Rizzi, 1997; Radford, 2004: 328）:

(27)

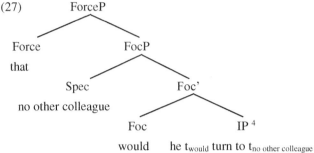

From the above figure, it can be seen that *that* occupies the head position of ForceP; FocP *no other colleague,* which originally is the object of *to,* moves to the position of Specifier within FocP; the auxiliary *would,* which originally occupies the position of T, moves to the head position of FocP.[5]

However, it involves only two projections in sentence (27): CP and FocP. To make a better understanding of split CP hypothesis, let's look at another example:

(28) He had seen something truly evil – prisoners being ritually raped, tortured and mutilated. He prayed that atrocities like those, never again would he witness.

In the underlined part of sentence (28), the preposed object *atrocities like those* is the object of verb *witness.* It is supposed to occupy the position of object following *witness,* but it appears at the beginning of the overall sentence. In accordance with Radford (2004: 329), from the perspective of discourse, the focus element usually represents new information, but here obviously the preposed object *atrocities like those* represents old information, that is, the information which has already been mentioned in the previous discourse. Therefore, this kind of preposed elements should be marked as the topic of the sentence (Rizzi, 1997; Haegeman, 2000), and the relevant movement operation is called topicalization.

According to Rizzi (1997), *that* in (28) should occupy the position of head within the ForceP; *atrocities like those* originally occupies the position of object of the verb *witness,* and becomes the topic of the sentence after the preposed movement (it refers

---

[4] For the convenience of the layout, the part of IP is not unfolded further. If necessary, readers can unfold it based on the previous discussion.

[5] It is worth noting that, as for the internal motivation of the movement, Radford (2004:328) makes some explanation within the framework of Minimalist Program, "suppose that the head Foc of FocP carries an [EPP] feature and an unexplainable focus feature. The two features together attract the focused object *no other colleague* (which itself contains a matching interpretable focus feature) to move into spec-FocP, and Foc is a strong head carrying an affixal [TNS] feature which attracts the auxiliary *would* to move from T into Foc."

back to the *rape, torture* and *mutilation* in the previous clause); the preposed negative adverbial phrase *never again* is a focus element, occupying the position of Spec, FocP; and the auxiliary *would*, which is preposed due to the inversion, occupies the head position within a FocP. Thus, the structure of this part can be illustrated as follows:

(29)

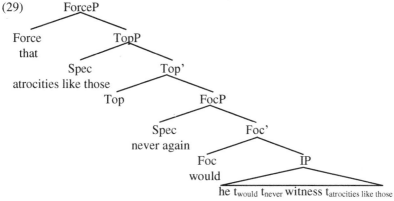

Apart from the three projections-- namely, ForceP, TopP, and FocP, there is a Finiteness Phrase (FinP). In fact, the FinP that Rizzi (1997) proposes is based on Italian data. In Italian, there is a prepositional element *di* as an infinite clause marker to introduce infinite clauses (finite clauses are introduced by *che*), as shown in the following examples:

(30) a. Credo che loro apprezzerebbero malto il tuo libro.
  "I believe that they would appreciate your book very much."
  b. Credo di apprezzare malto il tuo libro.
  "I believe 'of' to appreciate your book very much."

(31) a. Credo che il tuo libro, loro lo apprezzerebbero molto.
  "I believe that your book, they would appreciate it a lot."
  b. * Credo, il tuo libra, che loro lo apprezzerebbero molto.
  "I believe, your book, that they would appreciate it a lot."

(32) a. * Credo di il tuo libro, apprezzarlo molto.
  "I believe 'of' your book to appreciate it a lot."
  b. Credo, il tuo libro, di apprezzarlo malto.
  "I believe, your book, 'of' to appreciate it a lot."

The specialty of *di* lies in that it is different from *che* (equivalent to the English word *that*) which introduces finite clauses in the syntactic position: when there are some preposed syntactic elements, *che* always precedes this preposed element, as shown in (31). When *il tuo libro* (your book) is preposed, *che* can only occur before it rather than after it; however, *di* always follows this preposed element, just like (32).

When *il tuo libro* is preposed, *di* appears after it rather than before it. It indicates that *di* and *che* shouldn't be classified as the same category of the element.

Such analysis not only poses a challenge to the CP hypothesis of single projection, but also shows the necessity for the split CP hypothesis to set up a ForceP of high position and a FinP of low position: the Force of high position contains the complementiser *che*, while Fin of the low position is used to mark the clause whether it is finite or non-finite so as to contain such elements like *di*.

Interestingly, Radford (2004) points out that in English (both Middle English and Modern English), there are counterparts of infinitive particles like Italian *di*. Take Modern English as an example:

(33) SPEAKER A: What was the advice given by the police to the general public?

SPEAKER B: *Under no circumstances* **for** anyone to approach the escaped convicts.

Radford (2004) thinks that the structure of the response in (33) is like what is shown in (32), where *for* takes the position of Fin (Radford, 2004: 334).

Split CP hypothesis succeeds in solving many syntactic problems. So since it is proposed, it has been widely used in cross-language research (such as Frascarelli, 2000; Munaro, 2003; Newmeyer, 2009; Munakata, 2006; van Craenenbroeck, 2010; Darzi & Beyraghdar, 2010; Wakefield, 2011; Zhuang Huibin, 2013).

(34)

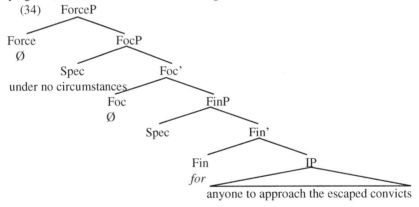

4   Further Discussion on the Syntactic Status of *le₂*

Now, we will adopt the split CP hypothesis proposed by Rizzi (1997, 2003) to reanalyze the syntactic status of *le₂*. First, through syntactic tests, it is found that the position of *le₂* is lower than that of Top and Foc. Look at the following example:

(35) 他吃苹果了。

Tā chī píngguǒ le.

he eat apple le₂

"He ate an apple."

We might as well topicalize and focalize the *apple* in (35), which gives us a clue, as illustrated in (36) and (37) respectively (where # indicates that it is quite different from its basic structure in semantics and pragmatics):

(36) #苹果他吃了。

　　　Píngguǒ tā chī le.

　　　apple he eat le₂

　　　Intended reading: "As for the apple, he ate."

(37) #他苹果吃了。

　　　Tā píngguǒ chī le.

　　　he apple eat le₂

　　　Intended reading: "As for the apple, he ate."

Obviously, the basic structure that corresponds to both (36) and (37) should be "他吃了苹果 (he ate apples)," rather than "他吃苹果了 (he has eaten apples)."

But how to explain the differences on semantics and pragmatics between (36), (37), and (35) within syntax? If *le* of (35) is placed in the position of Fin, this problem may be explained easily, as shown in (38):

(38)a.他吃苹果了

　　　tā chī píngguǒ le.

　　　he eat apple　le₂

　　　"he ate apples."

b.

In this way, the problems of (36) and (37) can get explained. The answer is that *apple* is originally within the scope of *le*, but after topicalization or focalization, it moves out of the scope of *le*, which naturally brings about semantic and pragmatic differences.

The research of negation provides further support. In the previous parts, it has been seen that *le₁* should be regarded as an aspectual marker, which is without any doubt. *Bu* cannot co-occur with *le₁*, mainly because the trace *le₁* has left after lowering cannot get appropriate head government (Zhuang & Liu, 2011). Hence, if *le₁* is an aspectual marker, *le₂* definitely isn't an aspectual marker. The primary reason is that *le₁* cannot co-occur with the negative marker *bu*, while *le₂* can co-occur with it. Look at the following examples:

(39) 我不吃晚饭了。（不饿或者闹情绪等）

Wǒ bù chī wǎnfàn le. (bù è   huòzhě nàoqíngxù)

I   not eat dinner le₂ (not hungry or   in.a.mood)

"I am not going to have dinner." (in the situation of being not hungry or being in a mood)

(40) 我不能吃晚饭了。（已经吃饱了）

Wǒ bù néng chī wǎnfàn le. (yǐjīng chī bǎo le)

I   not can eat dinner le₂ (already eat full le₂)

"I cannot have dinner." (in the situation of being full)

(41) 我很久不吃晚饭了。（正在减肥）

Wǒ hěn jiǔ   bù chī wǎnfàn le. (zhèngzài jiǎnféi)

I   very long.time not eat dinner le₂ (being   on.diet)

"I do not have dinner for a long time." (being on diet)

(42) 我将再也不吃晚饭了。（下决心要减肥）

Wǒ jiāng zàiyěbù   chī wǎnfàn le. (xiàjuéxīn yào jiǎnféi)

I   will   no.longer eat dinner le₂ (determined to.be on.diet)

"I won't have dinner any more." (to be determined to be on diet)

According to the above analysis, *le₂* is not an aspectual marker, for sure. It is likely to occupy a position higher than the T element (pay attention to "将 (jiang)"in (42), which is considered as a tense marker, see Li (2007), Zhuang & Liu (2011)), but lower than the Foc (comparing (35) with (36-37)). Thus, it can only be a Fin.

5   Conclusion

In conclusion, *le₂* is the marker showing the *starting* or the *ending* of a state described by the clause. In this case, whether it is the starting or the ending, it is related to the function of Fin. Therefore, it is justified to take *le₂* as a Fin whether from the perspective of function or syntactic structure.

Acknowledgments

We would like to express my sincere gratitude to Zhenqian Liu, Tian Li, Baopeng Ma, and the two anonymous CLSW reviewers for their inspiration, guidance, comments and/or revision of the argument and language in this paper. The usual disclaimers apply. The study is jointly supported by the Humanities and Social Sciences by the Ministry of Education (14YJC740115), Social Science Foundation of Henan Province (2017BYY003), and The University Program for Cultivating Young Scholars in Henan Province (2016GGJS-025).

References

1. Arin, M. L. (2003). *Aspect, Tense and Mood: Context Dependency and the Marker le in Mandarin Chinese*. Doctoral dissertation, Lund University, Lund.
2. Darzi, A. & Beyraghdar, R. M. (2010). A minimalist approach to the landing site of Persian topics. *Journal of Researches in Linguistics, 2*(1):1-18.
3. Frascarelli, M. (2000). *The Syntax-Phonology Interface in Focus and Topic Constructions in Italian*. Dordrecht/Boston/London: Kluwer Academic Publishers
4. Haegeman, L. (2000). Inversion, non-adjacent inversion and adjuncts in CP. *Transactions of the Philological Society, 98*:121-60.
5. Jin, Lixin. (2003). 'S le' de shiti yiyi ji jufa tiaojian. [The Grammatical Meaning of "S+le" Structure and Its Syntactic Requirements]. *Yuanyan jiaoxue yu yanjiu [language Teaching and Linguistic Studies]* (2):38-48.
6. Li, C. N. & Thompson S. A. (1981). *Mandarin Chinese: A Functional Reference Grammar*. Berkeley: University of California Press.
7. Li, Mei. (2007). *Xiandai hanyu foudingju yanjiu [Negation in Chinese]*. Shanghai: Shanghai Foreign Language Education Press.
8. Lin, Jo-wang. (2003). Aspectual selection and negation in Mandarin Chinese. *Linguistics, 41*(3):425-59
9. Lü, Shuxiang. (1999). *Xiandai hanyu babai ci [Eight Hundred Words in Modern Chinese Language]*. Beijing: The Commercial Press.
10. Munakata, T. (2006). Japanese topic-constructions in the minimalist view of the syntax-semantics interface. In C. Boeckx (Ed.), *Minimalist Essays*. Amsterdam / Philadelphia: John Benjamins Publishing Company. 115-159.
11. Munaro, N. (2003). On some differences between interrogative and exclamative wh-phrases in Bellunese: further evidence for a split-CP hypothesis. In C. Tortora (Ed.), *The Syntax of Italian Dialects*. Oxford / New York: Oxford University Press.137-151.
12. Newmeyer, F. J. (2009). On Split CPs and the "perfectness" of language. In B. Shaer, P. Cook, W. Frey & C. Maienborn (Eds.), *Dislocated Elements in Discourse: Syntactic, Semantic, and Pragmatic Perspectives*. London: Routledge. 114-140.

13. Pan, Haihua & Lee, Peppina. (2004). Mandarin sentence Final -le is an assertation Operator. Paper presented at the 12th Conference of the International Association of Chinese Linguistics, Tianjin, June 18-20, 2004.
14. Radford, A. (2004). *Minimalist Syntax*. Cambridge: Cambridge University Press.
15. Rizzi, L. (1997). The fine structure of the left periphery. In L. Haegeman (Ed.), *Elements of Grammar*. Dordrecht: Kluwer Academic Publishers. 281-337
16. Rizzi, L. (2001). On the Position "Int(errogative)" in the Left Periphery of the Clause. In G. Cinque & G. Salvi (Eds.), *Current Issues in Italian Syntax*. Amsterdam: Reed Elsevier Group PLC. 287-296
17. Rizzi, L. (2004). Locality and left periphery. In A. Belletti (Ed.), *Structures and Beyond: The cartography of syntactic structures* (Vol. 3). Oxford: Oxford University Press. 223-251
18. Rong, Xin. (1999). Putonghua zhong le biaoda de shijian fanchou ji shitai [Time Category and Tense of le in Mandarin]. *Zhongguo yuyanxue luncong [Studies on Chinese Linguistics]*, first series:49-66.
19. Shen, Li. (2004). Aspect agreement and light verb in Chinese: a comparison with Japanese. *Journal of East Asian Linguistics, 13*(2): 141-179.
20. Shi, Dingxu & Hu, Jianhua. (2006). Le$_2$ de jufa yuyi diwei [Syntactic and Semantic Status of le$_2$]. *Yufa yanjiu yu tansuo [Grammar Research and Exploration]*, (13):94-112.
21. Simpson, Andrew & Wu, Zoe. (2002). IP-raising, Tone Sandhi and the creation of S-final particles: evidence for cyclic spell-out. *Journal of East Asian Linguistics, 11*: 67-99.
22. van Craenenbroeck, J. (2010). *The Syntax of Ellipsis*. Oxford: Oxford University Press.
23. Wakefield, J. (2011). *The English Equivalents of Cantonese Sentence-final Particles: a contrastive analysis*. Doctoral dissertation, Hong Kong Polytechnic University, Hong Kong.
24. Zhu, Dexi. (1982). *Yufa jiangyi [Lectures on Grammar]*. Beijing: The commercial Press.
25. Zhuang, Huibin. (2013). 'Wangmian sile fuqin' jushi de CP fenlie jiashuo jieshi [The Study of 'wangmian sile fuqin' on Split CP Hypothesis]. *Waiguo yuyan wenxue [Foreign Language and Literature]*, (4):242-250.
26. Zhuang, Huibin & Liu, Zhenqian. (2011). Negative marker bu in Chinese: its nature and features. *International Journal of Asian Language Processing, 21*(3):107-160.

A Study on the Counter-expectation and Semantic Construal

Strategy of Implicit Negative Adverbs

Jinghan Zeng[1,2] and Yulin Yuan[2]

[1]Department of Modern and Classical Languages and Literatures, University of Rhode Island, Kingston 02881, USA
[2]Department of Chinese Language and Literature, Peking University, Beijing 100871, China
E-mail: woshijinghan@126.com

Abstract: This paper examines the meanings, expressive functions, and semantic construal strategy of the adverbs *bai* (白), *gan* (干), *xia* (瞎), *kong* (空), *xu* (虚), *tu* (徒), and *wang* (枉) in Mandarin. We begin by discussing the original meaning of the adverbs through which their implicit negations are then depicted. Then, we explore the counter-expectative function of the implicit negative adverbs and match them with different verbs. The counter-expectation of these implicit negative adverbs were classified and categorized based on the speakers'intentions, which mainly discusses the semantic condition and construal strategy of implicit negative adverbs. Finally, the construal formula in logic and construal process is analyzed. We conclude that *bai, gan, xia, kong, xu, tu,* and *wang* in Mandarin have implicit meanings, which negate the felicity condition of an event. The implicit negative adverbs can express the counter-expectation of the speaker, indicating that the actual situation is different from what the speaker expected. Additionally, the semantic construal of the counter-expectation relates to the evaluative function of the event, which corresponds to the optimistic orientation of human beings. The semantic construal of the implicit negation in Mandarin can help process negative information in both machine translation and teaching Chinese as a foreign language.

Key words: implicit negation adverbs, counter-expectation, construal strategy, hypothetical inference, optimistic orientation

© Springer International Publishing AG 2018
Y. Wu et al. (Eds.): CLSW 2017, LNAI 10709, pp. 17–26, 2018.
https://doi.org/10.1007/978-3-319-73573-3_2

1   Introduction：the implicit negation and negative adverbs in Mandarin

In Mandarin, a number of adverbs do not have negative formats but can convey negative meaning, as in (1-3):

(1) *Yi-xie ren   dong-bu-dong jiu   yi   ge-zhong li-you shou-fei, huo-zhe bai*(白) *chi bai*(白) *he*.
   some people often   Adv·[1] use-Prep. Various reason charge   or *bai*   eat *bai*   drink
   Some people often charge others for various reasons, or they will eat and drink for free.
   (*bai* means getting something without pay)
   (*bai chi bai he* → eat and drink without paying)

(2) *Wo-men yuan-lai   zuo-meng dou   xiang   bao jin-wa-wa,   dan que xin-xi,   mei xiang-mu, gan*(干) *zhao-ji, wu men-lu*.
   We   originally dream   Adv. want-Aux hold   golden dolls   but lack message
   Neg. project *gan*   worry Neg. way
   We all dream of holding the golden doll first, but we lack messages and projects, are worried but cannot do anything and cannot find any way out.
   (*gan* means doing something in vain)
   (*gan zhaoji* → worried but cannot do anything and with no result)

(3) Yao *diao-dong ke-xue   he   jiao-yu   gong-zuo-zhe de ji-ji-xing, kong*(空) *jiang bu xing, hai-yao gei   ta-men chuang-zao tiao-jian*.
   want arouse scientific and-Conj. educational   worker   Stru. enthusi-asm *kong* tell   Neg. can   still-Adv. give they   create   condition
   In order to arouse the enthusiasm of scientists and educators, it is not enough to speak formally, but also create good conditions for them.
   (*kong* means doing something without practical actions)
   (*kong jiang*→ only tell the theory but do not take action)

The adverbs *bai, gan*, and *kong* in (1-3) are not negative adverbs like *not* or *no* but have negative meanings which can entail negative sentences. They do not negate the prepositional meaning of VP but only negate the premise or result of the event which VP predicates. As a result, the semantic core of these adverbs can be described as *do something with the premise or result which should have but do not have in reality* and the negative meaning of the adverbs are implicit. Zeng and Yuan (2015a, 2015b)

* This paper gets the foundation from the the national basic research program (973 Project): *The Neural Mechanism of Language Cognition* (2014CB340502). I would like to extend my sincere thanks.

[1] Aux- auxiliary verb, Conj- conjunction, Def- definite article, Indef- indefinite article, Neg- negation, Prep- preposition, Stru-structural auxiliary.

proposed this implicit negation and defined it as follows: if a component can entail dominant negative structures to form an implication, then it has implicit negation. As a matter of fact, adverbs like *bai, gan,* and *kong* can be called implicit negative adverbs. In addition to *bai, gan,* and *kong,* other adverbs like *xia*(瞎), *xu* (虚) , *tu* (徒) , and *wang* (枉) also have similar meanings. There are several papers studying adverbs like *bai* such as Liu, Ye (2001) and Zhang, Yisheng (1993,1994,1999,2000,2003) which connected the function of *bai* with negating presupposition. In this study, we investigate these implicit negative adverbs in terms of their pragmatic functions and semantic construal strategy. By analyzing the expressive function, different speakers' intentions, and construal strategies, we hope to clarify the underlying rules regarding how different strategies are adopted.

2   Counter-expectation and construal strategy of implicit negative adverbs

2.1   Counter-expectation of implicit negative adverbs

As the core meaning of implicit negative adverbs is *do something with the premise or result which should have but do not have in reality,* i.e., a situation that should occur in people's expectation but fail to happen in reality, they can express coun-ter-expectation of the speaker in the text. The expectation is a kind of felicity condition for the event that VP predicates in order to accomplish. It also points to a consensus or common sense in the speaker and the listener's epistemic world. In this way, coun-ter-expectation also expresses a kind of subjectivity that the true situation goes against the speaker's intention, as in (4-6):

(4)   *You-de   ren   yiwei zhe   shi bu-lao-er-de,   bai*(白)   *na-qian, xin-li*

　　　guo-yi-bu-qu.

　　　　some   people   think this   is getting without pay   *bai*   take money   in the heart

　　　　fell sorry

　　　Some people thought this was getting things without pay and taking money without putting in effort and they felt sorry about this.

(5)   *Guo-ran da-le yi-ge-yue   hai   mei-you da-xia-lai,   di-ren de   da-pi yuan-bing   gan-dao, kong*(空)   *fu-chu yi-da-dui   shang-wang.*

　　　surely   fight   one-month   still-Adv. Neg.   win   enemy Stru.   large amount   reinforcements come   *kong*   pay   great amount   casualties

　　　Sure enough, they did not win the war a month later. The enemy came and they sacrificed in vain.

(6)   *Ru-guo   xue-ruo   guo-you-jing-ji,   zhi-neng   tu*(徒)   *you she-hui-zhu-yi   shi-chang jing-ji   zhi   ming,   shi-wei zi-ben-zhu-yi shi-chang-jing-ji zhi shi.*

　　　if   decrease   state-owned economy   only   *tu*   have   socialism

market economy   Stru. Name actually capitalism   market economy Stru.
reality

If there is a decline in state-owned economy, then we would only have the name of
state-owned economy in socialism but actually be a capitalist market economy in
reality.

The adverb *bai* in (4) modifies the predication of *na-qian* i.e. *receiving money.*
The event of taking money has a premise that one should have labored or worked
before being paid. However, the subject does not apply any labor and still gets money.
Bai in (4) means getting something for free. The result of the event goes against the
speaker's expectation, forming the counter-expectation. The adverb *kong* in (5) means
doing something in vain. The modified VP is *fuchu yidadui shangwang,* which means
sacrificing. In the event of a war, the expected result of sacrificing should be a win.
However, the reality is *da-le yi-ge-yue hai mei-you da-xia-lai,* which means that the
subject still did not win despite fighting for a month. *Kong* in (5) means paying but
receiving no expected result and expresses the counter-expectation of the speaker. The
adverb *tu* in (6) means completing something without expecting a result or doing
something in vain. The VP modified by *tu* predicates an event where a state-owned
economy has the appearance of a socialist market economy, which should result in
state-owned economy's growth in the speaker's expectation. However, the result is that
state-owned economy has been declining, which goes against the speaker and the
listener's expectations and forms a counter-expectation.

However, identifying the counter-expectation of the speaker is not the ultimate
purpose. To understand the real purpose of a speech in a conversation, we must consider the intention and expectation that the speaker wants to express using implicit
negative adverbs. Although the core meaning of implicit negative adverbs can be
described as two types–getting something for free and doing something in vain–the
speaker's intention in natural language goes beyond these two types. We will now
explore the CCL corpus of Center of Chinese Linguistics of Peking University, and
analyze the subjectivity and intention of the speaker with respect to the event predicated by the VP in the next section.

2.2   Semantic construal strategy of the implicit negative adverbs

By analyzing the types of counter-expectation in the adverb *bai*, Zeng and *Yuan*
(2015) concludes that there are five types of intentions of the speaker: (a) the speaker
thinks that the VP should have effects, such as in *bai pao yi-tang*; (b) the speaker
thinks that the action in VP should not be performed, or hopes that the VP does not
occur, such as in *bai zao-ta dong-xi*; (c) the speaker does not expect the VP to have an
effect, such as in *bai jie-gei ni zhu*; (d) the speaker believes that to realize the VP, the
speaker must pay the price, such as in *bai chi, bai zhu, bai wan yi-tang*; and (e) the
speaker thinks that he or she would be rewarded after the realization of the VP, such
as in *bai na-qian que tou-lan*. However, the speaker's intentions with respect to other
implicit negative adverbs, i.e., *bai, xia, kong, xu, tu,* and *wang*, indicate a dichotomy,
which is determined by the characteristics of their modified verbs. Firstly, when the
semantic feature of the modified verb is negative, the VP would have positive or neu-

tral meaning in semantics, and the speaker's intention in VP modified by the implicit negative adverb is the same as (a). This means that the speaker thinks that the VP should have effects, as in (7-12).

(7) *Ta qi-zi ye-shi dang-yuan, ye he da-jia yi-yang, zai li-tang gan(干) deng-le ta yi-ge-lai xiao-shi, gan dong-le yi-ge-lai xiao-shi.*

his wife is   Party-member too   Conj.   others   the same   in   auditorium *gan*   wait   him

one-more hour   *gan*   freeze   one-more hour

His wife is also a Party-member, waiting for him and freezing in cold air for more than one hour with other people.

(8) *Wo kan-shu ye-shi xia（瞎）kan, zui-hao zhao ge ruan-pan shu jin-qu.*

I   read   am   *xia* read   better   find   Indef. floppy disk   type   in

I always read without any experience. It is better to find a floppy disk to type in.

(9) *Bie-you ji-tuo de you-yi, bu-shi zhen-zheng de you-yi, dao-tou-lai kong（空）shou wu yi.*

Neg.   expected Stru. friendship Neg.   true   Stru.   friendship   in the end *kong*   get   Neg.   good

Do not have expectations in friendships. If it is not true friendship, you would not benefit from it in the end, in spite of being friends.

(10) *You-de bu-men cai-yong xu（虚）zeng li-run de shou-duan lai pian-qu gong-zi.*

some   department   use   *xu*   increase profit Stru. measure   Prep. cheat for   salary

Some departments take measures to increase false profit in order to cheat to get more salary.

(11) *Zhuan-li shen-qing de fan-lan dao-zhi qi-ye tu（徒）jiao nian-fei er wei-chi-zhe mei-you yong de zhuan-li.*

patent   apply   Stru.   spread   lead to company   *tu*   pay annual fee   but

maintain   Neg.   usage Stru. patent.

The increase in patent applications means that many companies pay the annual fee but obtain useless patents.

(12) *Ru-guo ta wang（枉）dan-le gui-xiu zhi ming, jiu gu-fu-le ta si-qu-de die.*

if   she   *wang*   undertake   lady   Stru. fame   then-Adv. disappoint   her dead   father.

If she undertook the fame of being a lady but didn't do what a lady should do, then she would disappoint her dead father.

In (7-12), the speaker expects to be benefit from VP or rewarded after the VP–represented by *Deng-ta yi-ge xiao-shi* or *dong yi-ge xiao-shi, kan-shu, shou-you-yi(i.e. receiving friendships), li-run zeng-zhang, jiao nian-fei,* and *dan gui-xiu zhi-ming,* respectively–occur, while actually this does not happen. As a result, the thing represented by the VP is to no avail and brings the counter-expectation of the speaker in the text.

Secondly, when the semantic feature of the verbs modified by *bai, gan, xia, kong, xu, tu,* and *wang* is positive, the VP would have a negative semantic meaning or mean losing and expending, and the speaker's intention of the VP modified by the implicit negative adverb would become a deontic modality instead of a kind of expectation. This means that the speaker does not expect VP to occur. *Zao-ta, pei, duan, duan-song, liu-shi, hao, shu, fa, fei-jin, zhe-teng, mang, mang-hu, mang-huo,* and *cao-xin* are verbs of this type, as in (13-18).

(13) *Yu-qi   wo-zai   chang-zi-li   gan（干）hao,   bu-ru   suo-xing*
      chuang-chu-lai   yi-tiao   xin lu.

      rather than   in   factory   *gan*   consum   better   simply break

      Indef.   new   path

      It is better to break a new path than be in factory wasting time.

(14) *Yu-qi   bu   ta-ren   hou-chen,   xia（瞎）zhe-teng,   bu-ru   nu-li*
      kai-chuang   zi-ji-de   ming-pai   chan-pin.

      rather than walk   others step   *xia*   toss   better   take-effort create

      own   famous-brand   product.

      It is better to create your own famous brand of products than following in others footsteps.

(15) *Wo   ru-guo   bu   shou,   ni   yi-ding   yao   gen   wo zheng,   kong（空）*
          fei   jing-shen

      I   if   Neg. take   you Aux.   Aux.   Prep.   me   fight *kong*   waste   energy.

      If I had not taken it, then you would fight with me for it, which is a waste of energy.

(16) *Xu（虚）hao   xia-ji   de   guang-yin, shi   hen   bu-dui-de.*

      xu   waste   summer   Stru. time   is   very   wrong

      It is absolutely wrong to waste summer time.

(17) *Lin-wen-cha   ren-wei   tuo-xia-qu   tu（徒）hao   liang-xiang, hui   bu zhan   zi   kui.*

          Lin-wen-cha   think   dragged down tu   cost   food   Aux. Neg. fight   oneself lose

      Wencha lin thinks that only costing of food and money but with no other actions would lead to losing the war before fighting.

In (13-17), the speaker intends to express that the VP should not be realized because there are no expected rewards, or that it is better that the VP does not happen, rather than expecting rewards after realizing the VP, represented by *hao-shi-jian, zhe-teng, fei jing-shen, hao guang-yin, hao liang-xiang,* and *fei xin-yi,* respectively. In this case, there are common indicative words that show the speaker's intention in the sentence, such as the predicate *bu-dui* in (16) and the auxiliary verb *hui* in (17).

3   The logical construal strategy of counter-expectation: a hypothetical inference based on Pollyanna Hypothesis

3.1   The hypothetical inference in logic

By pairing the verb types modified by an implicit negative adverbs with the intentions of the speaker, it is suggested that the intention of the speaker tends towards *should not do something* with a modified verb of negative meaning and *should have results for something* with a neutral or positive modified verb. Such a tendency on intentions could be explained in terms of logic, which denotes that the intention of a speaker is formed based on a simple, hypothetical inference with optimistic principles.

Hypothetical inference is the derivation based on the logical characteristics of the hypothetical proposition. The hypothetical proposition is related to the consideration of the conditional event in the objective world. Similar to material implication, the hypothetical proposition can be represented by P→Q, meaning, if P, then Q. As a result, denying the consequences of the hypothetical proposition would lead to the denial of its antecedent; that is, ¬Q ∧(P→Q) →¬P(if P→Q, then ¬Q →¬P) . This process can be described as follows:

| If P, then Q; | If it rains, then the ground would get wet. |
¬Q	The ground is not wet.
¬P	Therefore, it did not rain.

The deduction above, where the condition P leads to the consequence Q, is what the speaker expected before the event occurs, and constitutes the prior common sense of people when viewing and evaluating an event. However, usually, there is always a gap between reality and people's expectation. When the actual consequent Q deviates from the expectation, the ideal condition P is correspondingly denied, making P an event that should not happen.

3.2   The logical construal strategy of implicit negative adverbs

Let us consider the examples of *bai, gan,* and *xia.*

:

i.   *bai chi bai he*

| If P, then Q; first. | If eating and drinking, then one should pay |
¬Q	The subject did not pay any cost.
¬P	Therefore, eating and drinking should not have happened. (As the subject gets something that he should not have had, then he felt lucky)

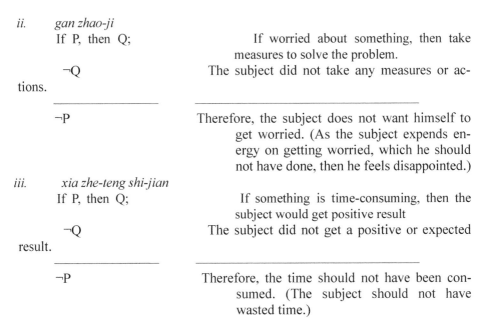

ii.   *gan zhao-ji*
　　　　If P, then Q;   If worried about something, then take measures to solve the problem.

　　　　　¬Q   The subject did not take any measures or actions.

　　　　　¬P   Therefore, the subject does not want himself to get worried. (As the subject expends energy on getting worried, which he should not have done, then he feels disappointed.)

iii.   *xia zhe-teng shi-jian*
　　　　If P, then Q;   If something is time-consuming, then the subject would get positive result

　　　　　¬Q   The subject did not get a positive or expected result.

　　　　　¬P   Therefore, the time should not have been consumed. (The subject should not have wasted time.)

Consequently, the semantic construal strategy of the implicit negative adverbs become relative to a kind of optimistic principle in people's mind, i.e., when meeting good things, people always expect the effects and results, and when meeting bad things, people's expectation is not to let them happen (Yuan, 2014a, 2014b). Using a series of psychological experiments, Boucher and Osgood (1969) proved a kind of Pollyanna Hypothesis, concluding that people always hope to view the positive or good facet of life, rather than the negative or bad facet, which relates to the optimistic principle. Though people usually have wonderful expectations, the facts are sometimes against what we desire. When reality is different from the expectation, the speakers use implicit negative adverbs to express the counter-expectations in their minds. When reality fails to fulfill their expectations, speakers use implicit negative adverbs to express the counter-expectation with an aim to obtain positive results and avoid bad results.

Conversely, the optimistic principle can also be utilized to speculate on and interpret the expectation of the speaker using implicit negative adverbs. In addition to the implicit negative adverbs, the interpretation of other implicit negative components could be relative to the optimistic principle, too (Yuan, 2012). The examples in this study directly demonstrate the optimistic orientation of people when interpreting the meaning of a word.

4   Conclusions

This paper investigates the implicit negative adverbs in Mandarin, *bai*, *gan*, *xia*, *kong*, *xu*, *tu*, and *wang*, and studies the counter-expectation and the semantic construal strategies of such adverbs from a semantic and pragmatic perspective. First, these adverbs are found to have implicit negative meanings, and could be used to entail negative statements with dominant negative markers, whose core meaning is *do something with the premise or result which should have but do not have in reality*. The implicit negative adverbs can express the deviation of reality from the expectation, and can result in a statement that has a counter-expected meaning. Meanwhile, the counter-expectation is a kind of evaluation made by people when viewing an event. Thus, they perform modal functions to display the speaker's subjectivity and intention to the reality, such as feels lucky or disappointed. The process of construaling the counter-expectation of the implicit negative adverbs is relative to the semantic types of the verb modified by the implicit negative adverb. When the meaning of the verb modified terms to be negative, the intention of the speaker is usually that *he or she should not fulfill the event*; when the semantic meaning of the modified verb is neutral or positive, the intention of the speaker is *hoping the event would have effects*. The nature of this process of semantic construal is that people are happy to observe or talk about good results, but abandon bad ones, which reflects the optimistic trend in human beings' minds. The results of this study can be useful in teaching Chinese as a foreign language, as well as in Chinese information processing. The semantic description of the implicit negative adverbs could significantly help mark adverbs meanings. Moreover, while building search engines or during product evaluation, the semantic construal mechanism of the implicit negative adverbs could help the machine accurately ascertain the intention of users.

5   Referrences

1.   Boucher, J & C. E. Osgood. The Pollyanna Hypothesis[J]. Journal of Verbal Learning and Verbal Behavior..1:1-8.(1969).

2.   Levinson, S. C. Presumptive Meanings: The Theory of Generalized Conversational Implicature. Cambridge: The MIT Press, (2000).

3.   Liu, Ye. A Semantic Analysis on Subjectivity of Adverbs of Negative Presupposition *"Bai"* and *"Xia"* Journal of Zhejiang Ocean University (Humanities Sciences). Vol. 28, No. 2, 75-80 (2011). [in Chinese]

4.   Yuan, Yulin. On the semantic levels and overflow conditions of the implicit negative verbs in Chinese. Studies of The Chinese Language. 347, 99-113 (2012). [in Chinese]

5.   Yuan, Yulin. Conception-driven and syntax-directed constructions and construal of sentences: A case study of the interpretation of sentences with the adverb *bai*. Studies of The Chinese Language. Vol. 362, 402-417 (2014a). [in Chinese]

6.   Yuan, Yulin. Optimistic orientation in construing Chinese lexical meanings: Striking a balance between the extensive semantic range and the prominent semantic facets. Contemporary Linguistics. Vol.16, No. 4, 379-395(2014b). [in Chinese]

7.   Zhang, Yisheng: The semantic feature of the adverb *"bai"* and other similar adverbs and their potential connotations. Journal of Jiangsu Normal University (Philosophy and Social Sciences Edition).Vol. 3, 128-132 (1994). [in Chinese]

8.   Zhang, Yisheng: the adverb *"bai"* and *"bai-bai"* in Mandarin. Journal of Huaibei Normal University (Philosophy and Social Sciences). Vol. 1, 113-120 (1993). [in Chinese]

9. Zhang, Yisheng: The study of presupposed negative adverbs in Proto-Mandarin. Research in Ancient Chinese Language. Vol.42, 27-35 (1999). [in Chinese]

10. Zhang, Yisheng: The study of adverbs in Mandarin. Academia Press, Beijing (2000). [in Chinese]

11. Zhang, Yisheng: A Further Discussion of Modal Adverbs "*bai*" in Modern Chinese--A Simultaneous Study of Grammatical Pat terns and Inner Differences of Adverb "*bai*". Journal of Leshan Normal University. Vol. 18, No. 1, 1-10 (2003). [in Chinese]

12. Zeng, Jinghan & Yuan, Yulin. The study on the implicit negative meaning of *bai* in Chinese. Macao Journal of Linguistics. Vol. 46, No. 2, 4-14(2015a). [in Chinese]

13. Zeng, Jinghan & Yuan, Yulin. The implicit negation and Counter-Expectation of *bai* in mandarin Chinese[A]. Qin Lu and Helena Hong Gao (eds.), Chinese Lexical Semantics[C], Berlin: Springer-Verlag Press.47-61.(2015b).

Sentence Patterns of "有(You)" in Semantic Dependence Graphs

Yanqiu Shao[1*], Cuiting Hu[1], LiJuan Zheng[1]

[1] Information Science School, Beijing Language and Culture University, Beijing, China
yqshao@blcu.edu.cu, 1457167081@qq.com, lijuanzhengzai@126.com

Abstract. With the development of natural language processing research, automatic semantic analysis has attracted much more attention. After a full study on the semantic structure characteristics of Chinese sentences, this paper presents an architecture of semantic dependency graphs and builds a semantic dependency graph corpus containing 30,000 sentences. On the basis of semantic dependency graph corpus, this paper focuses on "有(you)" sentences, and summarizes the sentence patterns and rules corresponding to "有(you)" sentences to provide rule support for the automatic semantic analysis model.

Keywords: sentence patterns · semantic analysis · semantic dependency graphs · "有(you)" sentences

1   Introduction

Semantic analysis is a key technology for natural language understanding, and it is an important way to understand semantics in the whole text. As is known to all, syntax and semantics are closely related, and the two parts complement each other. And semantic structure research is an important part of semantic study, whose main task is studying semantic structure of sentences thoroughly so as to clearly explain the various formats and rules of the sentences formed by predicates, as well as enriching and perfecting the theory of "the Three Planes of Grammar Study". Before analyzing the semantic structure of sentences, the observation and analysis of the syntactic structure is beneficial to the description and induction of the semantic structure. At the same time, there is also a certain correspondence between the sentence model which expresses the syntactic structure and the sentence pattern which expresses the semantic structure. This correspondence is not a one-to-one mapping, but a one-to-many reflection. The study on the sentence patterns of Chinese special sentence styles promotes a more systematic studies on sentence patterns, and also makes it easier to comprehensively understand the special sentence styles in Chinese, as well as clarifying its structure and providing better support for natural language processing.

In practical application, the study about semantic structure and sentence patterns of special sentence types in Chinese is beneficial to making computer understand semantic structure of sentences and helping computer to realize automatic semantic

Y. Wu et al. (Eds.): CLSW 2017, LNAI 10709, pp. 27–40, 2018.
https://doi.org/10.1007/978-3-319-73573-3_3

analysis of Chinese sentences, and providing relevant knowledge for the development of automatic syntactic-semantic analyzer. In addition, the study of sentence patterns based on corpus can also help to know about the use state of various semantic structures and provide data reference for automatic semantic analysis. Besides, for the non-native language learners, the study about the semantic structures and sentence pattern types of special sentences in Chinese can also deepen the understanding on Chinese special sentence styles, thus helping them to make good use of Chinese and improving the learning efficiency and the learning ability so as to promote the development of Foreign Chinese Teaching.

2   Background

2.1   Previous Study On Sentence Semantic Analysis

Chinese semantic resources mainly include Chinese PropBank (CPB)[1], Chinese FrameNet[2] and Chinese NomBank[3] and so on; the well-known semantic resources in English: FrameNet[4], PropBank[5] and NomBank[6].

With respect to research methods, sentence semantic analysis methods mainly include shallow semantic analysis and deep semantic analysis. Shallow semantic analysis is represented by the semantic role labeling study[7-8], and the deep semantic analysis is to formalize the whole sentence as a kind of semantic representation, such as the expression of the predicate logic or the combination semantic representation[9] based on dependence. Moreover, the division and quantity of semantic roles are also what linguists concern about.

Semantic analysis of sentences has developed a lot up to now, but there are still some problems. For example, semantic role labeling can only recognize the predicate and predicate-argument structures, but neither can express the semantic relation within argument structures, nor can analyze the semantic of the non-predicate components. In addition, in the semantic role labeling corpus, semantic roles are roughly divided into core roles (Arg0 ~ 5) and affiliated roles (time, place, etc.). Also, the number of semantic roles is small and the semantic meaning of these semantic roles tags is not uniform.

2.2   Study of Sentence Patterns

Sentence patterns refer to structure types of sentences on semantic-plane[10]. For example, the sentence pattern of "黄曼昨天在教室里告诉我一个秘密(Huang Man told me a secret in the classroom yesterday.)" is: [Agent] + [time] + [place] + [tell] / [spread] + [object] + [content]. Besides, sentence patterns can be divided into simple sentence patterns and complex sentence patterns[11]. Simple sentence pattern is a kind of sentence pattern that only contains one verb-core structure, while complex sentence pattern is a kind of sentence pattern that contains two or more verb-core structures.

With the promotion of three-plane theory by Hu Yushu and Fan Xiao's[12], which includes syntactic theory, semantic theory and pragmatic theory, the study on sentence pattern has attracted more and more attention. Fan Xiao[10], Zhu Xiaoya[13], Xu Changhuo[14], Chen Changlai[15] and Lu Chuan[16] have made outstanding contributions to the study of sentence patterns. Among them, Fan Xiao makes a strict definition to sentence patterns, and thinks that "The object of sentence patterns research is the verb-core structure, and sentence pattern is a kind of configuration mode, which is produced by verb-core structure formed a sentence and the sentence semantic component"[10]. Xu Changhuo believes that "Sentence pattern research is studying the relation semantic of sentences on semantic plane"[14], and stresses that valence research is the fate of sentence pattern research. Chen Changlai[15] constructs the sentence semantic structure modes through predicate verbs, and inspects the constituents of semantic structures, namely semantic components. Lu Chuan[16] proposes a predicate case-frame analysis system and divided the modern Chinese sentence patterns into 26 categories. He deeply studies every category and finally forms 128 basic sentence patterns. Tian Zhendu[17] and Kang Shiyong[18] also make outstanding contributions to sentence pattern research. Tian Zhendu[17] focuses on the Chinese sentence pattern system and the frequency of sentence patterns, sentence patterns are divided into single sentence forms and complex sentence forms, and the single sentence form patterns are divided into simple sentence patterns and complex sentence patterns according to the number of verb-core structure in sentence. On the basis of large-scale labeling of corpus, Kang Shiyong[18] establishes the Chinese syntactic system, and inspects the correspondence between sentence patterns and sentence models and counts the frequency and distribution states of sentence patterns.

So far the study about sentence pattern has gained more fruitful results, but there are still some problems. Some studies are too detailed so that the semantic differences are reflected in the systematic analysis of the semantic structure while others are too general so that they can't completely cover the complex and changeable Chinese sentence semantic structures. Both of them may lose the significance of sentence pattern research. In addition, the study about sentence patterns of special sentence types in Chinese is either not enough or to avoid it. Therefore, further discussion and analysis are needed in these areas.

2.3   Research on the Sentence Patterns of "有(you)" Sentences

There are always two controversies about the research scope of "有(you)" sentences: one means "有(you)" sentences in a narrow sense which refer to the sentences with verb "有(you)" or "没有(meiyou)" as the predicate or the predicate center of the sentence; the other one is a generalized "有(you)" sentence that sentence contains the word "有(you)" or "没有(meiyou)". Here, we define "有(you)" sentences with the latter.

The main researchers on the semantics of "有(you)" sentences include Fan Xiao[19], Zhang Yufeng[20-21]. Fan Xiao[18] has conducted some researches about the syntax, semantics and pragmatic of "有(you)" sentence in narrow sense. He not only analyzes the syntax characteristics of "有(you)" sentences, but also divides "有(you)" sentences into basic "有(you)" sentences and extended "有(you)" sentences. Zhang Yufeng[20-21] also puts forward an opinion about the study of "有(you)" sentences, and determines the new way of "有(you)" sentences. In addition, Lu Chuan[16] also does some research on "有(you)" sentences for a more formal induction and summary, and proposes that "有(you)" sentence semantic structures exist in the different basic sentence patterns, such as existence class sentence patterns, possession class sentence patterns and so on.

Study on semantic of "有(you)" sentences is gradually developing formalized, laying the foundation and pointing out the direction for the study of future generations. At the same time, there are some deficiencies in previous studies, which also leave progressive space for future research. For example, previous studies only concerned about the situation with the word "有(you)" as the predicate in a sentence, they barely start a systematic study for "有(you)" sentences in which the meaning of the word "有(you)" is not clear such as "树干有碗口那么大(The trunk is as big as the rim of a bowl.)".

3   Semantic Dependency Graphs

3.1   Semantic Dependency Tree

Semantic dependency tree uses the dependent tree to analyze the semantics of sentences, which is simple and clear. The dependency tree requires that each node has only one parent node and can't cross between the dependent arcs. But this representation method makes the semantic analysis not comprehensive enough. As is shown in Figure 1, there should be a layer semantic association between the node "妹妹(sister)" and the node "能干(competent)", but using the dependency tree method can't show this relationship.

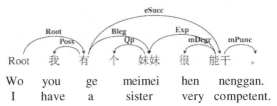

Fig. 1. Semantic Dependency Tree Demonstration

3.2   Semantic Dependency Graphs

The semantic dependency graphs is a directed acyclic graph. The nodes in the graph are composed of words, and sides stand for semantic relations between word pairs. Each side has a semantic label, which means the semantic relations between the dependent word (child nodes) and the core word (parent node). The semantic dependency graph is the inheritance and extension of the dependent tree structure, which is taking into account the characteristics of the dependent tree. At the same time, it breaks some of the original limitations and makes the semantic expression more advantageous than the dependent tree. Taking the sentence in graph 1 for an example as follows:

Advantage 1: allowing that a node can have multiple parent nodes. As long as actual semantic relations exist between words, they will be connected. As is shown in Figure 2, "妹妹(sister)" has two parent nodes, namely "有(you)" and "能干(competent)", but they belong to different semantic roles, which respectively are belongings and experiencer This can be clearly demonstrated using semantic dependency graphs.

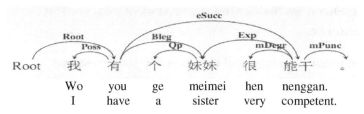

Fig. 2. Semantic Dependency Graphs Demonstration1

Advantage 2: semantic dependency graphs allow non-projection phenomena, which means that dependency arcs can cross each other. As is shown in Figure 3, "他成绩比我好(His grade is better than me.)", there is a semantic relationship between the two word pairs (他，我)(he, I) and (好，成绩)(good, grade) appearing a cross arc because the sentence omits "成绩(grade)", such a representation can better show the semantic relations within the sentence.

Fig. 3. Semantic Dependency Graphs Demonstration2

3.3   Semantic Relations Set and Dependency Graphs

This paper draws on the idea of semantic unit hierarchy and semantic combination and its classification of semantic relations in the Lu Chuan's book *Paralympic Network of Chinese Grammar*[15]. Besides, we also learn from Dong Zhendong's division method of semantic relations and construct a set of cleaner semantic relations system based on the characteristics and advantages of dependency grammar. At the same time, the original semantic dependency system is improved, and a set of new semantic role label sets is determined. An important extension of the system includes the opposite relationship, nested relationships and event relationships. The opposite relationship is used to describe the verb as a modifier to modify the core word and the nested relationship mainly deals with the degradation of the event into a concept in a sentence. Due to the limited space, we do not repeat here.

According to the identified semantic dependency frame and semantic roles, we establish a semantic dependency corpus containing 30,000 sentences which come from different fields, including news corpus (10068), primary and secondary school textbooks (10038), Sina Weibo corpus (5000) and corpus for machine translation (4900). Among them Sina Weibo corpus labeling results still need to be further optimized.

4   Research on the Sentence Patterns of "有(you)" Sentences

4.1   Automatic Extraction and Results of "有(you)" Sentences

"有(you)" sentence is the basic sentence which is often used in modern Chinese, and it is also the high-frequency sentence in a large scale corpus. In view of this, by observing the marked "有(you)" sentences corpus and combining with the prominent characteristics of "有(you)" sentences, which contains the word "有(you)" or "没有(meiyou)", we have designed automatic extraction algorithm for "有(you)" sentences, just as is shown in Figure 4. According to the algorithm, we use the example sentence automatically extraction program to extract 3183 "有(you)" sentences from the corpus. The third step of the algorithm is to check out whether the words "没有(meiyou)" is just as a negative mark. For example, the sentence "他没有来(He did not come.)" is not included in our study because the word "没有(meiyou)" is just as a negative mark. On the basis of these "有(you)" sentences, we analyze the syntactic and semantic features of these "有(you)" sentences, focusing on the summary and summarization of the semantic structure of "有(you)" sentences.

Input: Sentences
Output: To determine whether the sentence is a "有(you)" sentence
Algorithm:
1. See if the sentence has the verb "有(you)" or "没有(meiyou) ".
2. If the sentence has the verb "有(you)", then the sentence is a "有(you)" sentence.
3. If the verb "没有(meiyou)" is used, it is further to determine whether "没有(meiyou)" is marked as a negative mark "mNeg" in the corpus, and if so, the sentence is not a "有(you)" sentence, otherwise it is a "有(you)" sentence.

Fig. 4. "有(you)" Sentence Automatically Extract Algorithm

According to the syntactic characteristics of "有(you)" sentences, we count the frequency and proportion of "有(you)" sentences in corpus. As can be seen from Table 1, the basic type of "有(you)" sentences, namely simple "有(you)" sentences, which is used up to 77.63% in the daily life.

Table 1. The Frequency and the Proportion of the "有(you)" Sentences in the Corpus

Type	Basic type	Extended type
Frequency	2471	712

Proportion	77.63%	22.37%

4.2   The Sentence Patterns and Classifications of "有(you)" Sentences

Sentence patterns have a close relationship with the meaning and nature of the predicate verb, so sentence patterns of "有(you)" sentences and the meaning of the word "有(you)" are inextricably linked. The Chinese word "有(you)" has many meanings, and different meanings will appear in different syntactic structures Even different meanings of some words near the word "有(you)" may affect the semantic structure of the whole sentence. In fact, the semantic structure of "有(you)" sentences is more complicated in the real corpus.

According to the distribution of "有(you)" sentence in the corpus, we divide "有(you)" sentences into five categories. After statistics, the frequency and proportion of the five types in the corpus is shown in Table 2:

Table 2. The Frequency and Proportion of the "有(you)" Sentences of Five Types

Type	Frequency	Proportion
"有(you)" sentences of possessive relationship（YL）	1160	36.44%
"有(you)" sentences of existential relationship（YC）	1065	33.46%
"有(you)" sentences of virtualization dealing（YX）	246	7.73%
"有(you)" sentences of subjective-object relationship（YJ）	607	19.07%
"有(you)" sentences of serial verb relationship（LY）	105	3.30%

We found that in the use of daily language for communication, simple "有(you)" sentences take absolute advantage, accounting for 77.63%. While in the simple "有(you)" sentences, the number of sentences expressing possessive relationship is as much as that express existential relationship. Relatively speaking, "有(you)" sentences that express possessive relationship is slightly dominant. Thus as all we can see, simple "有(you)" sentences account for most of "有(you)" sentences. However, in the complex "有(you)" sentences, the using frequency of the "有(you)" sentences which indicates subjective-object relationship is far more than that "有(you)" sentences which indicates serial verb relationship.

By summing up and summarizing the 3183 "有(you)" sentences, the specific sentence patterns of "有(you)" sentences are shown below:

YL: "有(you)" sentences of possessive relationship

YL 01:[possessor]+ 有(you) + [belongings]

This is the basic sentence pattern of "有(you)" sentences, and its syntactic structure can be expressed as: A + 有(you) + B. Here the meaning of the word "有(you)" is that something belongs to somebody or a part belongs to a whole. For example:

（1） 这块表有三个指针。
Zhekui biao you sange zhizhen.
This watch has three pointers.

（2） 卡罗尔终于有了一只自己的小猫。
Carroll zhongyu you le yizhi ziji de xiaomao.
Carroll finally had his own kitten.

In addition, the above situation has a variant, namely, 有(you) + [belongings]. In this situation, there is no possessor roles or possessor roles do not appear here. For example:

(3) 不管做什么工作，都该有一个认真的态度。
Buguan zuo shenme gongzuo, dou yinggai you yige renzhen de taidu.
No matter what job you do, should you have a serious attitude.

YL 02:[possessor]+[belongings]+有(you)

We can see that, this situation is also a variant sentence pattern of the basic sentence pattern because belongings roles is to forward in basic sentence patterns of "有(you)" sentences. For example:

(4) 我什么东西都没有了。
Wo shenme dongxi dou meiyou le.
I have nothing.

YC: "有(you)" sentences of existential relationship

YC 01:[space]+有(you)+[experiencer]

YC 02:[time]+有(you)+[experiencer]

Here the word "有(you)" means possessing. What is more, it means existence, appearance or occurrence, which means that sometime or somewhere exits somebody or something or somewhere appears or occurs a situation. We can find that the noun on the subject position is used by the location noun or the time noun in these sentences. For instance:

(5) 我们班有位叫英子的同学。
Women ban you wei jiao yingzi de tongxue.
Our class has a student called Yingzi.

(6) 今天下午有零星阵雨。

Jintian xiawu you lingling zhenyu.
There are scattered showers this afternoon.

YC 03:有(you)+[experiencer]

This situation is also a variant of basic sentence patterns, and the use frequency is very high. According to the statistics, the total number of occurrences reached 329 times in corpus, accounting for 30.89% of the total number of such patterns.

(7) 有人吗？
You ren ma?
Anyone there?

YX: "有(you)" sentences of virtualization dealing

The word "有(you)" in these sentences represents comparison and does a reference in order to understand quickly for listener, the meaning is more virtual. For example:

(8) 小王有他爸爸那么高。
Xiaowang you ta baba name gao.
Mr. Wang is as tall as his father.

YX01:[experiencer]+ 有 (you)[virtualization]+[comparison]+[character adjective]

YX02:[experiencer]+有(you)[virtualization]+[quantity phrases]+[character adjective]

Here the meaning of the word "有(you)" just means estimation and subjective guess, in fact, we do not know the specific situation. Just like the sentence:

(9) 这个洞穴有三米深。
Zhege dongxue you sanmi shen.
This cave has three meters deep.

YX 03:[nested experiencer]+ 有(you)[virtualization]+[time course]
Here the word means period, for example:

(10) 他住在这里有三十年了。
Ta zhu zai zheli you sanshi nian le.
There has been thirty years since he lived here.

YX 04:有(you) [virtualization]+[time]+basic sentence pattern
Here the word means indefinite time. At present, scholars generally think that this kind of "有(you)" sentences contain two predicates: one is "有(you)" and the other is the core predicate of the sentence. The word "有(you)" plays the role of the

function word in such sentences here. Just like the following example, "一天(one day)" represents an uncertain day.

(11) 有一天，他出去后再也没有回来。
You yitian,ta chuqu hou zai ye meiyou huilai.
One day, he went out and did not come back again.

XJ: "有(you)" sentences of subjective-object relationship

The word "有(you)" in this kind of sentences is a subjective-object language verb, so this kind of sentences is subjective-object sentences. After a study and analysis, we have a simple and regular classification to this kind of "有(you)" sentence patterns is as follows:

XJ01:[space]+有(you)+[experiencer]‖[experiencer]+【v2】+[classification]
Here the word "有(you)" means existential, for example:

(12)   山上有一座著名的古寺叫寒山寺。
Shanshang you yizuo zhuming de gusi jiao hanshansi.
There is a famous temple on the mountain called Han Shan Temple.

YJ 02:有(you)+[experiencer]‖[affection]+【v2】+[content]
Here the word "有(you)" represents the existence of the properties of the object, for example:

(13)   很少有人能够真正喜欢坐几个小时以上的火车。
Henshao youren nenggou zhenzheng xihuan zuo jige xiaoshi yishang de huoche.
Few people can really like to sit for over a few hours by train.

LY: "有(you)" sentences of serial verb relationship

The word "有(you)" is a serial verb in these sentences, after investigation and analysis, we simply divide the class "有(you)" sentence patterns into two types, as is follows:

LY 01:[possessor]‖[agent]+有(you)+[belongings]+【v2】
Here the word "有(you)" means possessive, for example:

(14) 孩子们有机会上学了。
Haizimen you jihui shangxue le.
Children have conditions to go to school.

LY 02:[possessor]‖[agent]+有(you)+[belongings]+【v2】+[comitative]
For example:

(15) 我们有义务探望年迈的老人。
Women you yiwu tanwang nianmai de laoren.
We have duty to visit old people.

According to the syntactic structure of "有(you)" sentences and the meaning and function of the word of "有(you)", we describe and characterize the sentence patterns of these five categories of "有(you)" sentences, and finally summarize 45 specific sentence patterns from 3183 "有(you)" sentences. The use frequency of the top ten "有(you)" sentence patterns is shown in Table 3, and the top five "有(you)" sentence patterns is :[possessor] + 有(you) + [belongings], [space] + 有(you) + [experiencer], 有(you) + [experiencer], [space] + 有(you) + [experiencer] ‖ [agent] + V2, [possessor] + [prepositions] +[comitative] + 有(you) + [belongings].

Table 3. The Use Frequency of the "有(you)" Sentence Patterns of the Top Ten

The type of "有(you)" sentence	"有(you)" sentence patterns	Frequency	Proportion
YL	Possessor + 有(you) + belongings	1025	32. 20%
YC	Space + 有(you) + experiencer	602	18. 91%
YC	有(you) + experiencer	329	10. 34%
YJ	Space + 有(you) + experiencer ‖ agent + V2	133	4. 18%
YL	Possessor + prepositions + comitative + 有(you) + belongings	88	2. 76%
YJ	Space + 有(you) + experiencer ‖ agent + V2 + content	88	2. 76%
YJ	有(you) + experiencer ‖ experience + V2	67	2. 10%
YC	Experience + 有(you) + quantitative phrase	65	2. 04%
YC	Time + 有(you) + experiencer	47	1. 48%
YJ	有(you) + experiencer ‖ affection + V2 + content	47	1. 48%
		2491	78. 26%

In addition, we compare the initial statistical results with Lu Chuan's sentence patterns, as is shown in Table 4:

Table 4. Comparison between This Article and Lu Chuan's Results

"有(you)" sentence patterns of Lu Chuan	"有(you)" sentence patterns of this paper	
[Space] + 有(you) + [experiencer]	Existential relationship	[Space] + 有(you) + [experiencer]

[Possessor] + 有(you) + [belongs]	Possessive relationship	[Possessor] + 有(you) + [belongings]
[Possessor] + 有(you) + 分事 (fenshi)		
	Virtualiza-tion dealing	[Experiencer] + 有(you) + comparison / quantity phrases + character adjective
		[Nested experiencer] +有(you) + time course
		有(you)[virtualization] + time + basic sentence patterns
	Subjec-tive-object re-lationship	[Space] + 有(you) +[experiencer] ‖ [experiencer] + 【V】 + [classification]
	Serial verb relationship	[Possessor] ‖ [agent] + 有(you) + [belongings] + 【V】 + [comitative]

From the whole point of view, our study about the semantic structure of "有(you)" sentences is more refined in addition to simple sentences such as existential class, possessive class and other common sentence patterns. We also take into account the virtualization dealing "有(you)" sentences, which represents estimated, comparative and indefinite meaning, because such "有(you)" sentences account for a large number in modern Chinese. What is more, they are often used with the high proportion in the dialect such as"这个洞穴有3米深(The cave has 3 meters deep.)" Apart from this, we also analyze the sentence patterns of "有(you)" sentences in complex cases such as subjective-object language class and serial verb class in order to perfect the study of "有(you)" sentence patterns, just like the sentence "山上有座庙叫寒山寺(There is a temple on the hill called Han Shan Temple.)" and "孩子们有条件上学了(The children have condition to go to school.)" Our goal is to set up a large scale model knowledge base in order to help computer to perform automatic semantic analysis.

5   Conclusion

This paper focuses on the research about sentence patterns of "有(you)" sentences in order to help to establish the mapping relationship between sentence models and sentence patterns, so as to promote the development of syntactic and semantic research and help to improve the accuracy of automatic semantic analysis model. At the same time, the description and induction of the "有(you)" sentence can provide the rule support for the automatic semantic analysis model, and provide the corresponding knowledge base for the establishment of the semantic automatic analysis model, thus helping the machine to automatically generate the sentence in line with the norm, which can finally promote the machine translation, automatic question and answer and artificial intelligence and other technology development.

But there are still some deficiencies. First of all, "有(you)" sentences in the actual use of the process is flexible. So using the automatic extraction program can't extract all the examples, and the integrity of the data has been a certain degree of impact. Second, because of the small size of the corpus and low-frequent sentence patterns. Therefore, we also need to do some experiments on a larger scale corpus and enhance the ability of automatically learning and induction in order to enhance the persuasive of sentence patterns description at the same time.

Acknowledgement. This paper is supported by National Natural Science Foundation of China (NSFC) No.61170144 and No.61371129, Major Program of China's National Linguistic work Committee during the twelfth five-year plan (ZDI125-41), and young and middle aged academic cadre support plan of Beijing Language and Culture University (501321303).

References

1. N.Xue,M.Palmer.Annotating the Propositions in the Penn Chinese Treebank[C]. Proceedings of the Second SIGHAN Workshop on Chinese Language Processing, 2003.
2. Liping 有(you), Kaiying Liu. Building Chinese FrameNet Database1[J]. Natural Language Processing and Knowledge Engineering, 2005.
3. Nianwen Xue. Annotating the predicate-argument structure of Chinese nominalizations[C]. Proceedings of the fifth international conference on Language Resources and Evaluation, Genoa, Italy, 2006.
4. Fillmore, Charles J.and Collin F.Baker. FrameNet: Frame Semantics Meets the Corpus[D]. Poster presentation of 74th Annual Meeting of the Linguistics Society of America, 2000.
5. Palmer. M, Gildea. D. and Kingsbury.P. The Proposition Bank: A Corpus Annotated with Semantic Roles[J]. Computational Linguistics, 2005, 31(1).
6. Chang Liu, HweeTou Ng. Learning Predictive Structures for Semantic Role Labeling of NomBank[C]. Proceedings of ACL, 2007.
7. Min Zhang, WanxiangChe, Guodong Zhou, Ai Ti Aw, Chew Lim Tan, Ting Liu and Sheng Li. Semantic Role Labeling Using a Grammar-Driven Convolution Tree Kemel[C]. IEEE Transactions on Audio Speech and Language Processing, 2008, 16(7).
8. WanxiangChe, Min Zhang, Ai Ti Aw, Chew Lim Tan, Ting Liu and Sheng Li. Using a Hybrid Convolution Tree Kernel for Semantic Role Labeling[J]. ACM Transactions on Asian Language Information Processing, 2008, 7(4).
9. Robinson, J.J. Dependency Structures and Transformation Rules[J]. Language, 1970, 46(2).
10. Fan Xiao. Three Plane Grammar View [M]. Beijing: Beijing Language Institute Press, 1996.(范晓. 三个平面的语法观[M]. 北京: 北京语言学院出版社, 1996.).(in Chinese)
11. Fan Xiao, Zhu Xiaoya. Research Methods on Sentences Patterns[J]. Journal of Xuzhou Normal University, 1999, 25 (4).(范晓, 朱晓亚. 论句模研究的方法[J]. 徐州师大学报, 1999, 25(4).).(in Chinese)
12. Hu Yushu, Fan Xiao. On the Three Planes of Grammar Research [J]. Journal of Xinjiang Normal University, 1985, (2).(胡裕树, 范晓. 试论语法研究的三个平面[J]. 新疆师大学报, 1985, (2).).(in Chinese)
13. Zhu Xiaoya. Modern Chinese sentence patterns research [M]. Beijing: Peking University Press, 2001.(朱晓亚. 现代汉语句模研究[M]. 北京: 北京大学出版社, 2001.).(in Chinese)

14. Xu Changhuo. On the Object, Starting Point and Basic Principles of Sentence Patterns Research[J]. Journal of Nanjing Normal University, 1999, (4).(徐昌火. 试论句模研究的对象、起点和基本原则[J]. 南京师范大学学报, 1999, (4).).(in Chinese)

15. Chen Changlai. On the semantic structure of modern Chinese sentences [J]. Journal of Yantai Teachers College, 2000,17 (1).(陈昌来. 论现代汉语句子的语义结构[J]. 烟台师范学院学报, 2000,17(1).).(in Chinese)

16. Lu Chuan. Paralympic Network of Chinese Grammar[M]. Beijing: Commercial Press, 2001.(鲁川. 汉语语法的意合网络[M]. 北京: 商务印书馆, 2001.).(in Chinese)

17. Tian Zhendu.Study on Modern Chinese Sentence Pattern Based on Annotation Corpus [Y]: Yantai: Yantai Normal University, 2002.(田珍都. 基于标注语料库的现代汉语句模研究[D]. 烟台: 烟台师范学院, 2002.).(in Chinese)

18. Kang Shiyong, Xu Xiaoxing. Construction and research of modern Chinese sentence system [J]. Chinese Journal of Information, 2010, (1).(亢世勇, 许小星. 现代汉语句系系统的构建和研究[J]. 中文信息学报, 2010, (1).).(in Chinese)

19. Fan Xiao. Chinese Sentence Type [M]. Taiyuan: Book Hai Publishing House, 1998.(范晓. 汉语的句子类型[M]. 太原: 书海出版社, 1998.).(in Chinese)

20. Zhang Yufeng. Semantic Analysis of "有[You]" sentence[J]. Chinese Language Learning, 1999, (4).(张豫峰. 有字句的语义分析[J]. 汉语学习, 1999, (4).).(in Chinese)

21. Zhang Yufeng. "有[You]" Sentence of Representing Comparison[J]. Chinese language learning, 1999, (4).(张豫峰. 表比较的有字句[J]. 汉语学习, 1999, (4).).(in Chinese)

On the Quantification of Events[*] in *Dou*ₐ（都ₐ） Construction

Hua Zhong

Overseas Education College of Fujian Normal University, Fuzhou, China

jtingshan@163.com

Abstract. In the existing literature, the three aspects of the quantificational adverb *dou*ₐ—the objects of quantification, the properties of quantification and the means by which *dou*ₐ quantifies—are still controversial issues. Therefore in this paper we first try to define *quantify* and construct a quantification system. This quantification system consists of three primary elements including *quantified scope, quantifying unit, quantity value,* as well as two basic quantifying ways including *cumulative sum (forward quantification)* and *distributive division (reverse quantification),* in addition to four main results including *singular, plural, total quantity* and *partial quantity.* On this basis, we define the quantified object of *dou*ₐ as the eventualities expressed by the given sentence; we also redefine *dou*ₐ's properties of quantification as distributive universality. Then we divide the quantification construction of *dou*ₐ into four parts: distributive domain, distributive index, distributive operator and distributive share. Through investigating the syntactic, semantic and pragmatic features of these four parts, as well as the distributive dependency relations between these four parts, we explained how *dou*ₐ quantifies eventualities.

Keywords: *dou*ₐ as a quantificational adverb, quantification system, quantification on eventualities, the quantification construction of *dou*ₐ.

1 Introduction

In the existing literature, although the semantic classifications of the adverb *dou*（都） are different (e.g., trichotomy, dichotomy or univocal), nonethless they all admit that *dou*ₐ （都ₐ） is quantitative[1]. Although *dou*ₐ has been called as a lot of different

---

[*] This article uses this concept "Event" in the wide sense, i.e. what happens in a certain time and place about a thing, how the state of a thing/things is/are being, which property a thing/things has/have, which relationship it has between different things, how many/much the quantity of thing/s is/are, and so on （see Zhan Weidong 2013: 114）. Perhaps the concept *eventuality* of neo-Davidsonian is more suitable， see also Higginbotham （1985、2000） and Parsons （1990、2000）.

[1] In this article *Dou*ₐ is the quantificational adverb *Dou*. If not specified，any *Dou* mentioned below is *Dou*ₐ.

© Springer International Publishing AG 2018
Y. Wu et al. (Eds.): CLSW 2017, LNAI 10709, pp. 41–63, 2018.
https://doi.org/10.1007/978-3-319-73573-3_4

names (e.g., scope adverb, universal quantifier, distributive operator, sum operator, floating quantifier, maximal operator and so on), there has been a consensus that dou_a is a quantificational adverb. But in the existing literature, the three aspects of the quantificational adverb dou_a—the objects of quantification, the properties of quantification and the means by which dou_a quantifies—are still controversial issues.

Therefore, this paper first tries to define *quantify* and to construct a quantification system. Then on this basis, it investigates three aspects of the quantificational adverb *dou* in Mandarin Chinese: the quantified objects, the properties of quantification and the implementation of *dou*'s quantification on eventualities.

2   The Definition and the System of Quantification

To illustrate questions such as the quantified object, the properties of quantification and the means by which *dou* quantifies we must first try to define *quantify* [2] in a precise manner and to construct a primary system of quantification.

It is the writer's opinion that *quantify* is to calculate or measure the number of similar things in a certain field with some quantifying unit; for example, *san tiao yu* (three fishes), *si gongjin shuiguo* (four kilograms of fruit), *yixie xuesheng* (some students), *wubai jiaci feixing* (five hundred sorties).

So the representation of a quantification in a language includes three primary elements: the quantified scope [eg., *yu* (fish), *shuiguo* (fruit), *xuesheng* (student), *feixing* (flight)], the quantifying unit[eg., *tiao* (strip), *gongjin* (kilogram), *jiaci* (sortie)] and the quantity value[eg., *san* (three), *si* (four), *wubai* (five hundred), *yixie* (some), *dabufen* (most of), *meiyige* (everyone), *suoyou* (all of) etc]. Among them, the quantified scope is the scope of the quantified objects, which is a similarity circle of partly similar things (see also Rudolf Carnap 1999: 145-154) . The quantifying unit [eg., *tiao* (strip), *gongjin* (kilogram), *jiaci* (sortie)] is to account for unit of classification, calculation or measurement, that its representation in a language is optional but not enforceable. For instance, the quantifying unit of "*yixie xuesheng/ some students*" should be "atomic individual" which can be expressed as "*ge/wei* (Cl.) " in Chinese, but in this instance of Chinese or English it is implicit. The representation of quantified scope in a language is optional too in different context, for example, in Chinese *yu* (fish) and *shuiguo* (fruit) in "*san* (three) *tiao* (Cl.) [*yu* (fish)]" and "*si* (four) *gongjin* (kilogram) [*shuiguo* (fruit)] " can be implicit or explicit. But the quantity value[eg., *san* (three), *si* (four), *wubai* (five hundred), *yixie* (some), *dabufen* (most), *meiyige* (everyone), *suoyou* (all) and so on.] is a compulsory element and cannot be implicit.

---

[2] Those *quantify* definitions that I can look up are somewhat simple and vague, for example, *Longman English Dictionary* Online writes, "quantify: to calculate the value of something and express it as a number or an amount". *The Contemporary Chinese Dictionary* (Version 6, 2012: 814) defines quantify as: "*lianghua* (quantify): *shi keyi yong shuliang lai hengliang* (can be measured in terms of quantity)."

From an ontological point of view, there are no two identical leaves in the world, and no one can step into the same river twice. Hence, things cannot be repeated and cannot be quantified. But from the perspective of thinking and cognition, human recognition of essential similarities between things is the basis of a "quantified scope" and a "similarity circle", both of which reflect tendency of human beings to seek commonalities between things. When approached from the perspective of "partial similarity", the sun can indeed rise again and things can indeed be repeated and quantified. Each of these quantification is the result of the human tendency to "seek common ground" as well as to "seek differences" within their thought. Without seeking common ground, there can be no "similarity circle" and no "quantified scope". Without seeking difference, there can be no any single object in any quantified scope.

Between the degrees of similarity between quantified objects and the sizes of the similarity circle, the quantification levels, the relation of inverse variation[3] is formed. The higher the degree of similarity, the smaller the size of the similarity circle, and the smaller the extension of a quantified scope, the lower the quantification level. The lower the degree of similarity, the bigger the size of the similarity circle, and the bigger the extension of a quantified scope, the higher the quantification level. For example, in the biological classification system, which usually consists of seven major levels: *Species, Genus, Family, Order, Class, Phylum, Kingdom*, "Species" is the basic unit whose members have the highest degree of similarity, whose similarity circle is the smallest, whose extension of quantified scope is smallest, and whose quantificational level is lowest. The similarity between members of *Genus, Family, Order, Class, Phylum*, and *Kingdom* reduces step by step; meanwhile, their similarity circle, quantified scope and quantification level increase step by step. From a logical point of view, a small "similarity circle" which has a high degree of similarity is really included in a bigger "similarity circle" which has a lower degree of similarity. A categorical proposition whose predication is a small "similarity circle" can entail a categorical proposition whose predication is a bigger " similarity circle " . For instance，"*Mimi shi jiamao* (Mimi is a domestic cat)"entails "*Mimi shi maoke dongwu* (Mimi is a feline animal)". To put it more directly, a small "similarity circle" has the lexical/semantic entailment of a bigger "similarity circle".

There are two ways to quantify the objects in a quantified scope ： One is a cumulative addition (positive quantification), in which thinking mode of "seeking common ground" dominates, and the commonalities of "quantified objects" are highlighted. For instance: *suoyou* (all)，*dabufen* (most)，*ershi* (twenty)，*babai*(eight hundred)，*zongshi* (always)，*tongchang* (usually)，*jingchang* (often)，*zonggong* (in total)，*tongtong* (entirely)，all, most, mostly, twenty, eight hundreds，always, usually, often, totally, together etc. Another is a distributive partition (reverse quantification)，in which thinking mode of "seeking differences" dominates, and the differences of *quantified objects* are highlighted. For

---

[3] This is in complete agreement with the inverse relation of the intension and the extension of a concept.

instance: *mei (yi)* [every (one)], *ge (ge)* [each (Cl)], *gezi* (respectively), *fenbie* (separately), every, each, individually and so on. The results of quantifications can be roughly divided into four kinds: singular, plural, total [universal quantification, e.g., *suoyou* (all), *zongshi* (always), *meiyi* (everyone), all, always, every], partial [existential quantification, e.g., *dabufen* (most), *youxie* (some), *shaoshu* (a few), most, usually, rarely, a few]. Among them, *partial* can be divided into: singular and plural, and *plural* can be divided into: total and partial. In addition, singular and plural can, according to whether the numerical value is certain or not, be divided into: definite number [e.g., *yi* (one), *er* (two)], approximate number[e.g., *geba* (one or two), *yixie* (some), *yidianer* (a little), often, a few]. From this we can construct a primary system of quantification, as shown in the following figure:

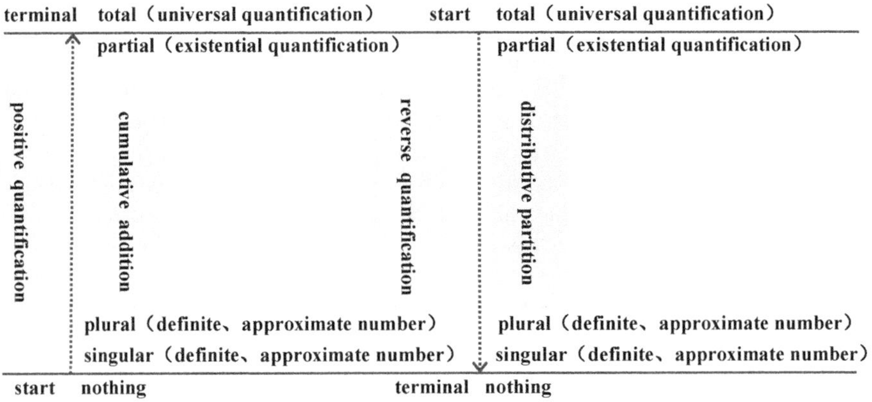

terminal	total (universal quantification)	start	total (universal quantification)
	partial (existential quantification)		partial (existential quantification)
positive quantification	cumulative addition	reverse quantification	distributive partition
	plural (definite、approximate number)		plural (definite、approximate number)
	singular (definite、approximate number)		singular (definite、approximate number)
start	nothing	terminal	nothing

Fig. 1. System of Quantification

3   The objects quantified by *dou*

Speaking of quantification, it is possible that the first thing people think about is that determiners (such as numeral, classifier, quantifier) (see also Liu Danqing 2008: 121, 543) modify nouns or noun phrases, and singular or plural of nouns etc. It seems that quantitative phenomena only occur in the noun domain (Baker 2003: 109-125) ; quantified objects are just the things denoted by nouns. For example:

(1) *san ge xingqi, si liang xiao qiche*
　　 three Cl. week, four Cl. small automobile
　　 three weeks, 　　 four cars

　　 suoyou de haizi, mei ge haizi
　　 all 　　 DE child, each Cl. child
　　 all the children, 　　 each child

hen duo xiangjiao, youxie diannao
very more banana,   some computers
a lot of bananas,   some computers

This viewpoint seems to have become a postulation within grammar studies. It is also the effect of this postulation that *dou* is regarded as a floating quantifier, e.g. Chiu （1990）, Wu（1999） etc, and the plural nominal composition before *dou* is identified as *dou*'s quantified object.

But the theory of event semantics of Davidson （1967）, Higginbotham （1985）, Parsons （1990） etc and the theories of pluractional verb and plural events of Newman （1980, 2000）, Lasersohn （1995）, Bittner & Trondhjem （2008）, Součková （2011） etc, have deepened and expanded our understanding of quantitative phenomena （see also Zhang Qingwen etc 2013）, and have enlightened us regarding the fact that quantitative phenomena not only occur in the noun domain but also in the domains of verbs, adjectives or sentences; the quantified objects are not just the things denoted by nouns but also the action behaviors of verbs, the properties and states of adjectives and the eventualities of sentences.

If X is the quantified object of *Dou*, whether it is a noun (things), or a verb/predicate (actions), or a sentence/proposition (eventualities), it must meet a necessary and sufficient condition, that is: as long as *dou* is used in the sentence, then X is plural; and as long as X is plural, *dou* can be used in the sentence. This is the condition which makes a *dou* sentence tenable. After examining the conditions of a tenable *dou* sentences, it is easy to find that: regardless if the nominal composition before *dou* is singular or plural （see also Yuan Yulin 2005$_b$: 290; Chen Zhenyu, Liu Chengfeng 2008: 337-8）, no matter whether the action/s represented by the verb or the predicate modified by *dou* is/are singular or plural, no matter whether the predicate is a collective predicate or a symmetric predicate, these conditions cannot determine whether a *dou* sentence is ultimately tenable. For instance:

（2）*Tamen dou ba shudian   baowei le.*
    They   all BA bookstore surround LE.
    They   all surrounded the bookstore.
    [*Tamen* （they） is a plural noun]

（3）*Liming he Wangjie dou shi Shandong laoxiang*
    Liming and Wangjie all are Shandong fellow-townsman
    Liming and Wangjie are all from the same town in Shandong province.
    [*Liming and Wangjie* is a plural noun-phrase]

（4）*Ta ba na ge mantou   dou chi le.*
    He BA that Cl steamed bun all eat LE
    He ate the whole steamed bun.
    [*Ta* （he）, *na ge mantou* （that steamed bun） are singular nominal compositions]

(5) *Tamen dou chidao le yi ci / liang ci.*
They all be late LE one time/ two time
They were all late once / twice.
[The action/s of *to be late once / twice* is singular or plural]

(6) *Zhe jitian tamen tiantian   dou ba shudian   bawei   zhe.*
These days they every day all BA bookstore surround ZHE
Recently, they have been surrounding the bookstore every day.
[*Surround* is a collective predicate]

(7) *Zhexie ren   dou shi   fuqi.*
These person all be couple
These persons are all couples.
[*To be a couple* is a symmetric predicate]

The critical condition of a *dou* sentence being tenable is that the eventualities expressed by a *dou* sentence must be plural (see Huang 1996:5, 9), or must be distributive but not collective. For example, the sentences (2/3) that expressed a collective singular eventuality are untenable, and the sentences (4/5/6/7) that expressed distributive plural eventualities are tenable. And what determines whether the eventuality expressed by a *dou* sentence is collective or distributive, is whether the eventuality expressed by a *dou* sentence is plural; it is not just the verb or the predicate modified by *dou* but is the combination of a predicate with a nominal composition (see also Lasersohn 1995: 83, 191; Zhang Yisheng 2003: 393). For instance:

(8) a.*?*Xiaoming ba na di   shui dou he le.*
    Xiaoming BA that drop water all drink LE
    Xiaoming drank that whole drop of water.

    b. *Xiaoming ba na bei   shui dou he le.*
    Xiaoming BA that cup warter all drink LE
    Xiaoming drank that whole cup of water.

    c. *Zhe zhi wenzi   ba na di shui   dou he le.*
    This Cl mosquito BA that drop warter all drink LE
    The mosquito drank that whole drop of water.

(9) a.*?*Zhe tou daxiang ba na ge pingguo dou chi le.*
    This Cl elephant BA that Cl apple   all eat LE
    This elephant ate the whole apple.

    b. *Zhe tou daxiang ba na kuang pingguo dou chi le.*
    This Cl elephant BA that Cl   apple   all eat LE
    The elephant ate all the whole basket of apples.

c. *Ta ba na ge pingguo dou chi le.*
He BA that Cl apple   all eat LE
He ate the whole apple.

Furthermore, from the hierarchies of similarity circles, the predicate which denotes a class of eventualities （see also Parsons 1990:4-5） expresses a larger " similarity circle" than the *dou* sentence, which denotes a part of the class of eventualities but not all of it. Hence the view of Huang （1996: 10, 39）: "*dou* makes the predicate it modifies assert a plurality of minimum events whose size is compatible with the semantics of the predicate," should be revised as: "*dou* makes the sentence assert a plurality of minimum events whose size is compatible with the semantics of the sentence."

Therefore, in light of the condition of a *dou* sentence being tenable, it is not hard to ascertain that the object *dou* quantifies is the eventualities expressed by the sentence.

4   The Quantification Properties/Semantic Functions of *Dou*

In regard to the quantification properties/semantic functions of *dou*, the traditional view is that *dou* is a total or scope adverb. Wang Huan （1983） believes *dou* expresses each of somethings, and Wen Binli （2002） believes *dou* has a distributive reading. These views are straightforward and simple but, at the same time, somewhat ambiguous.

Overseas scholars have used quantification theory （e.g., Lee 1986; Lin 1996, 1998 etc.） to analyze *dou* as a quantificational adverb. In the light of the theory of event semantics Huang （1996, 2005） proposed to explain *dou* as a sum operator on events. Later, Jiang Yan （1998） and Yuan Yulin （2005$_a$, 2005$_b$, 2007） made a further in-depth analysis. These propositions have undoubtedly made remarkable progresses.

But in the existing literature there is no clear definition of *quantify* and no clearly defined framework for a quantification system. Furthermore, the quantified object of *dou* is misjudged as a plural nominal composition, and it is unclear how the semantics of *dou* are divided or compounded. So although each of these theories have undoubtedly achieved something, their achievements are something akin to blind men touching an elephant and taking a part for the whole: there is still lots of confusion as to how the quantification property/semantic function of *dou* is precisely defined and where *dou* should be put in a quantification system.

For example, Huang （1996: 10-13、 39、 65-89） proposed that *dou* is a sum operator that takes the event variable to be its argument. This is a big improvement in the literature of the quantification theory about *dou*, but it is still ad hoc to define *dou* as a sum operator on events.

Although Huang （1996、 2005） did not clearly explain why she defined *dou* as a sum operator on events, it is not hard to conclude that her theory was based on the event semantics of Davidsonism and the reasoning process modeled after the theory on *every*, using the skolem function to logically paraphrase *mei* sentence including *dou*. But the quantification on events of "every-sentence" in English usually is distributive but not cumulative or summing (see also Abusch 1998:22-24; Landman 2000; Champollion 2010a:7-8, 2015, 2016). And as for *mei* sentences in Mandarin Huang (1994, 1996, 2005) mentions two main scenarios:

A. *Dou* is required in *mei* scope, for example:

(10) *Meiyige   ren * (dou)   kan le zheben   shu.*
     Every-MW person dou   read LE this-MW book
     Every person read this book.

(11) *Meiyige xuesheng *(dou) biye le.*
     every-MW student   DOU graduate LE
     Every student graduated.

B. When the object NP in *mei* scope is indefinite as in (12), or the object NP is a reflexive as in (13) or there is an indefinite adverbial phrase within the VP as in (14), *dou* is not required:

(12) *Meiyige chushi   (dou) zuo   yige   cai.*
     every-MW chef   dou make one-MW dish
     Every chef makes a dish.

(13) *Meiyige   haizi (dou) you ziji de chuang.*
     every-MW child dou   has self DE bed.
     Every child has his own bed.

(14) *Meiyige   gexing   (dou) hong le yi nian.*
     every-MW singing-star DOU red LE one year
     Every singing star was popular for a year.

[(10)-(14) are quoted from Huang (1996: 2-3), in (12)-(14) I added (*dou*)]

In B-style *mei* sentences, *mei* and the indefinite phrase containing the numeral-classifier compound or the reflexive pronouns implying the numeral-classifier compound form a numeral-classifier matching construction （see also Yuan Yulin 2008: 117-8）.These sentences, if combined with *dou*, do not produce any semantic change except to make the distribution of the match more prominent. This shows that the *dou* in "*mei...dou...*"sentences can only be distributive.

If you put *dou* in a quantification system and compare it with others, *dou*'s quantification is obviously different from the cumulation of *zonggong* (in total), *yigong* (altogether), *yiqi* (together), *gongtong* (jointly) etc, and is similar to the distribution of *fenbie* (separately), *gezi* (respectively). For example:

(15) a.*Tamen dou kan le zheben   shu.*
         they DOU read LE this-MW book
         They all read this book.

→b.*Tamen fenbie / gezi   kan le zheben   shu.*
   they separately/respectively read LE this-MW book
   They separately/respectively read this book.

→c.**Tamen yiqi / gongtong kan le zheben   shu.*
   they together/jointly   read LE this-MW book
   They together/jointly read this book.

(16) a.*meiyige chushi dou   zuo   yige   cai.*
   every-MW chef DOU make one-MW dish
   Every chef makes a dish.

→b.*meiyige   chushi fenbie /gezi   zuo   yige   cai.*
   every-MW chef separately/respectively make one-MW dish
   Every chef separately/respectively makes a dish.

→c.**meiyige   chushi zonggong/yigong/yiqi /gongtong zuo   yige   cai.*
   every-MW chef in total/altogether/together/jointly make one-MW dish
   Every chef in total/altogether/together/jointly makes a dish.

Of course, we have also noticed that the proposal to define *dou* as a sum operator has won the approval of Jiang Yan（1998）, Yuan Yulin（2005$_b$）etc. As Yuan Yulin（2005$_b$:293）writes, this proposal to define *dou* as a sum operator is quite consistent with the traditional sense that *dou* is a total adverb. However, in traditional Chinese grammar the proposal to define *dou* as a total/scope adverb, is based on that the quantified object of *dou* is a plural nominal composition in the sentence. But since the quantified object of *dou* is not a plural nominal composition in the sentence, thus the proposal that *dou* is a total/scope adverb should not be tenable.

Beyond this, Wang Huan (1983) discovered that if *dou* were defined as sum total, it would very easy to think of *dou* as expressing the whole of plural things and look at these things as a total. For example:

(17) *Xiaozhang、Xiaowang dou chi le sange pingguo*
   Xiaozhang、Xiaowang DOU eat LE three-Cl. apple
   Xiaozhang、Xiaowang both ate three apples.

If *dou* summed the total of *Xiaozhang* and *Xiaowang*, then sentence（17）would be misread as *Xiaozhang and Xiaowang ate three apples in total*. Therefore Wang Huan (1983) concluded that *dou* meant not the total of the things but each of the things. Later, Lee（1986:57-61）, Lin（1998）explained that *dou* was a distributive universal quantifier from the perspective of formal semantics. Although Wang Huan, Lee, Lin all misjudged the quantified object of *dou* as a plural nominal composition, we can be sure that *dou* means a distributive universal quantification (see also Yuan Yulin 2008: 106-7).

In conclusion, having identified the quantified objects of *dou*, it is not difficult to determine the quantification properties of *dou* in comparison with the above-mentioned quantification system. Roughly corresponding to the distributive universal quantifier *mei* of the noun domain, the quantification properties of *dou* are distributive and universal. It expresses a total, plural, approximate quantity value. However, the objects quantified by *dou* are eventualities, and the objects quantified by *mei* are things.

5   The Implementation of *Dou*'s Quantification on Eventualities

Having identified the quantified objects, the quantification properties of *dou*, we now, with reference to the distribution theory of Choe (1987:31, 89-95), divide the quantification construction of *dou* into four parts: distributive domain, distributive index, distributive operator, distributed share. Among them "*distributive domain* and *distributive index*" are, in the words of Choe (1987), sometime called as sorting key. Then to show the implementation of *dou*'s quantification on eventualities, we, under the framework of the quantification system mentioned above, investigate the syntactic, semantic and pragmatic characteristics of each component, and the distributive dependency relation of these components.

5.1   The Components and the Compound Mode of *Dou* Quantification Construction

Having investigated a large number of corpora, we find that *dou* quantification construction consists of four components: A distributive domain + B distributive index + C distributive operator + D distributed share. For instance:

(18) *Women liandui meiyige ren（ban/pai） dou fa le yiting jiqiang.*

A	B	C	D
Women liandui	*meiyige ren（ban/pai）*	*dou fa*	*le yiting*

Our company every-Cl person（squad/platoon） DOU deliver LE one-Cl *jiqiang.*
machine-gun.
Every person（squad/platoon）of our company was delivered a machine gun.

Among them, A is the distributive domain which defines the distributive scope; B is the distributive index which indicates the semantic category of the distributive domain, the unit or condition that the distributive domain is divided, and so on（see also Gillon 1987; Schwarzschild 1996: 69-71; Yuan Yulin 2008:106-10）, thus expressing a certain difference between the quantified eventualities; D is the distributive share which expresses the commonality of the similarity circle of eventualities that are quantified by *dou*, in other words, which is the upper similarity circle that denotes a kind of eventualities in the higher level（see also Parsons 1990: 4-5）; C is the distributive operator *dou* which establishes a distributive dependency relation between "*sorting keys (distributive domain + distributive index) + distributive share*" through the distributive operation.

The complete *dou* construction can be made in the form "A+ B+ C+ D" such as （18）sentence，but also in some inclusive forms，for example：

（19）　*Meige qinfen de xuesheng zou guo de lu dou shi xiangsi de.*

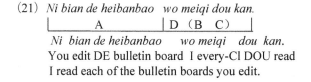

Meige　qinfen　de xuesheng zou guo　de　lu　dou　shi　xiangsi de.
Every-Cl diligent DE student　walk GUO DE way DOU is　similar DE
Every diligent student has a similar experience.

（20）　*Qianhou zong you ershi duo ci,　meici tamen dou zheme dafu.*

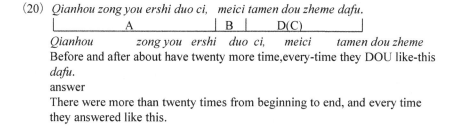

Qianhou　　　　zong you　ershi　duo ci,　meici　　tamen dou zheme
Before and after about have twenty more time,every-time they DOU like-this
dafu.
answer
There were more than twenty times from beginning to end, and every time they answered like this.

（21）　*Ni bian de heibanbao　wo meiqi dou kan.*

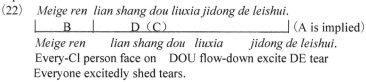

Ni　bian de heibanbao　　wo meiqi　dou kan.
You edit DE bulletin board I every-Cl DOU read
I read each of the bulletin boards you edit.

In sentence（19）B　（*meige*）is included in A [（B）*qinfen de xuesheng zou guo de lu*]. In sentence（20）C（*dou*）is included in D [*tamen*（C）*zheme dafu*]. In sentence（21）BC（*meiqi dou*）is included in D [*wo*（BC）*kan*].

Of course，certain contextual factors might cause A or B，or A and B is/are implied，then the *dou* quantification construction is going to be a incomplete form（see also Xu Jie 1985:11-2；Yuan Yulin 2005$_a$:107，2005$_b$:300-2，2007）. For example：

（22）　*Meige ren　lian shang dou liuxia jidong de leishui.*

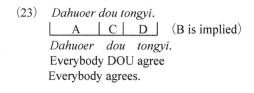

Meige ren　　lian shang dou　liuxia　　jidong de leishui.
Every-Cl person face on　DOU flow-down excite DE tear
Everyone excitedly shed tears.

（23）　*Dahuoer dou tongyi.*

| A | C | D | (B is implied)

Dahuoer　dou　tongyi.
Everybody DOU agree
Everybody agrees.

(24)   *Dou shi ni moceng，yaobu wo ye buhui chidao.*

| C | D | (A and B are implied)

   Dou shi ni moceng，   yaobu   wo ye buhui chidao.
   DOU are you dillydally   otherwise I also cannot late
   The reason I was late was because of your dillydallying.

In addition, the *dou* quantification construction may have more than one A or/and B like a compound classifier [e.g., *jiaci* (sortie)] of the noun domain. For example:

(25)   *Naxie rizili，women yijia sankou，meitian wanshang dou bu kan dianshi le，jizhong zai keting kanbao.*

| A₁ | A₂ | B₁| D （C） |

   Naxie rizili， women yijia   sankou，   meitian wanshang dou bu kan
   Those days   our   a family three people   everyday night   DOU not watch
   dianshi le，   jizhong zai ketingli   kan bao.
    TV   LE   gather in living-room read newspaper
   Those days, the three of us in our family gathered every night, not to watch
   TV, but to read the newspaper together in the living room.

(26)   *Zai jintian zhege shidai，shishi chuchu dou zaifasheng rixinyueyi de bianhua.*

| A | B₁ | B₂ | C | D |

   Zai jintian zhege shidai，shishi   chuchu   dou zaifasheng
   In today   this   age   everywhen everywhere DOU   happening
    rixinyueyide   bianhua.
   with-each-passing-day change
   In today's world, there are new changes everywhere with each passing day.

(27)   *Niannian、yueyue、tiantian、shishi、chuchu，dou zaiguafeng、xiayu.*

| B₁ | B₂ | B₃ | B₄ | B₅ | C | D |

   Niannian、yueyue、   tiantian、shishi、   chuchu，   dou
   every-year every-month every-day everywhen everywhere DOU
   zai   guafeng、xiayu.
   being windy   rainy
   Every year, every month, every day,   everywhere is being windy and
   rainy.

5.2   The Distributive Dependency Relation Between The Components of *Dou* Quantification Construction

To implement *dou*'s quantification on eventualities, *dou* establishes a distributive dependency relation between "(*distributive domain* + *distributive index*) + *distributive share*" through a distributive operation. And the distributive dependency relation has many restrictions and requirements for syntax, semantics and pragmatics on *distributive domain*, *distributive index*, *distributive operator* and *distributive share*.

5.21   The Syntactic Requirements That Distributive Dependency Relation Has on Each Component of *Dou* Quantification Construction

In a *dou* quantification construction *distributive domain* only occurs before *dou* but not after it; it is usually in the position of subject or adverbial modifier or object of the preposition in a prepositional phrase (such as prepositions" *ba/ dui/ rang/ shi/ jiang/ ...+NP* "). The most common forms are the plural NP and some coordinate phrases and clauses. For example:

(28) a. *Dahuoer   dou tongyi.*
　　　 Everybody DOU agree
　　　 Everybody agrees.

　　 b. *Zhexie xuesheng wo dou xihuan.*
　　　 These students I DOU like
　　　 I like all of these students.

　　 c. **Wo dou xihuan* *zhexie xuesheng.*
　　　 I   DOU like   these students
　　　 I like all of these students.

(29) a. *XiaoWang、XiaoLi he XiaoZhao, wo dou tongzhi tamen le.*
　　　 XiaoWang   XiaoLi and *XiaoZhao* I DOU notify them LE
　　　 I notified *XiaoWang, XiaoLi* and *XiaoZhao.*

　　 b. *Xuduo jiaoshi dou zhu zai tongzilouli.*
　　　 Many teacher DOU live in tube-shaped apartment
　　　 Many teachers live in the tube-shaped apartment.

(30) *1985 nian zhijin*   *ta jihu niannian dou yao chuban   yiben*
　　　 1985 year to-this-day he almost every-year DOU might publish one-Cl
　　　 manhuaji.
　　　 cartoons
　　　 Since 1985, he has published a new anthology of cartoons nearly every
　　　 year.

(31) *Xuduo ren dou gandao yiwai.*
　　　 Many people DOU feel surprised
　　　 Many people felt surprised.

(32) *Women ba suoyou de shi   dou gaosu ni le.*
　　　 We   BA   all DE things DOU tell you LE
　　　 We have told you all of the things.

(33) a. *La yangche, deng sanluner, dou gan guo.*
　　　 Pull rickshaw ride tricycle DOU do GUO

Pulling rickshaws, riding tricycles: I've done them all.

b. *Weishenme shangqu le ?   Weishenme xiajiang le ? Dou yao xinzhong*
Why   go-up LE? Why   go-down LE? DOU should in-heart
youshu.
clear
Why did you go up? Why did you go down? You should have a clear
idea about all of these.

As well as a few forms are singular NPs,   for instance：
(34) a. *Naben shu   ta dou   kan wan le.*
That-Cl book he DOU read finish LE
He has finished reading the book.

b. *Xiaoming ba yige   mantou   dou chi le.*
Xiaoming BA one-Cl steamed-bun DOU eat LE
Xiaoming ate up one steamed bun.

c. *Tade zhengge shengming dou zai yunwuzhong   feizhe.*
His whole   life   DOU in clouds-and-mists flying
His whole life was flying in clouds and mists.

The forms of the distributive domain can also be a phrase or sentence that contains coordinative constituents indicating selectional relationship. They are usually connected by a conjunction such as "*wulun* (no matter)/ *bulun* (irrespective of)/ *buguan* (regardless of)/ *renping* (whatever)"etc. For instance：
(35) *Ren he ren   shi zenme bi   daxiao de? Shi ping   nianji daxiao?*
People and people are how compare size de are according age old-young
Hai shi bi   liqi   daxiao?   Dou bu shi.
Or are compare physical-energy more-little DOU not are
How should people be compared? Their ages? Their strength? None of
these.

(36) *Wulun   ta shi ren,   hai shi hu, dou bu kepa.*
No-matter she is human or is fox DOU not scary
No matter whether she is a human being or a fox, she is not scary.

(37) *Bulun   laoshao nanv, dou hui shi yiyang de.*
Irrespective of age sex   DOU will be same DE
Irrespective of age and sex, they will be the same.

(38) *Buguan   ni zhao   bu zhaodedao ta, dou yidingyao kuaidian*
Regardless of you look-for not find could him, DOU must   quickly
huilai.

come-back

Regardless of whether you can find him or not, you must come back
quickly.

（39） *Renping fengchui langda,*　　 *ta dou wanqiang de qianjin.*

Whatever wind-blow waves-beat he DOU doggedly DE go-forward

Regardless of how the wind blew and waves beat, he doggedly went
forward.

In a *dou* quantification construction the distributive index usually occurs before
dou but not after it; it is usually in the position of subject or adverbial modifier or
object of the preposition in a prepositional phrase（such as prepositions"*ba /dui/ rang/
shi/ jiang/* ...+NP "）. The most representative forms are the *mei*-phrase, noun
reduplications, classifier reduplications, some adverbs of time and place（most of
them are reduplication）, some "one + classifier + noun" phrase, some interrogative
pronoun or some phrases/clauses containing interrogative pronoun etc, which
indicate distributive universality and the unit or condition that the distributive domain
is divided into. For example:

（40） *Renqun zhong meige ren dou zai wuyan de chouqi.*

→*Renqun zhong dou meige ren zai wuyan de chouqi.*

Renqun zhong meige ren　　*dou zai wuyan de chouqi.*

Crowd inside every-Cl person DOU -ing whimper DE sob

Everyone in the crowd was sobbing silently.

（41） *Ni bian de heibanbao wo meiqi dou kan.*

→*Ni bian de heibanbao wo dou meiqi kan.*

Ni bian de heibanbao wo meiqi dou kan.

You edit DE bulletin board I every-Cl DOU read

I read each of the bulletin boards you edit.

（42） *Ta he ta jiehun yihou,*　　　*meici huilai,*　　*ta dou rehuhu de*

She and he marry afterwards every-time come-back he DOU warmly DE

wenchangwenduan.

ask-all-sorts-of-questions

Since she married with him, every time she comes back, he always warmly
asks her all sorts of questions.

（43） *Wo ba meiyitiao xiao xiangzi dou zhaobian*　　*le*!

I BA every-Cl small alley DOU search through LE

I have searched through each of the small alleyways.

（44） *Wo shi mei dao yige difang*，*dou ai qu kan dangdide simiao.*

I am MEI arrive one-Cl place DOU like go visit local temple

Wherever I go, I like to visit the local temple.

(45) *Mei dang tiqi   nver,   Ta man lian dou yangyi xiaoyi he zihao.*
Every when mention daughter she whole face DOU filled smile and pride
Whenever she mentions her daughter, her face fills up with smiles and pride.

(46) *Zai ta kan lai, guxiang   chuchu   dou mei,   dou ke rushi*
In he see from, hometown everywhere DOU beautiful DOU can poetic
ruhua;   Renmin gege   dou   qin,   dou shi fumu xiongdi.
picturesque people everyone DOU friendly DOU are parent brother
In his view, everywhere in his hometown could serve as subjects for a poem
    or picture, and everyone is friendly enough to be his parents or brothers.

(47) *Zhexie yundong shi suishi   suidi   dou keyi jinxing de.*
these sports   are anytime anywhere DOU can do   DE
These sports can be played anytime and anywhere.

(48) *Panfu   tuqiang   de daxibei   renmin, niannian yueyue*
Hope-wealthy hope-strong DE northwest people, year-year month-month
dou   zai pan xiu tielu.
DOU -ing hope build railway
Hoping to be wealthy and strong, every month and every year the north-
west people look forward to building a railway.

(49) *Tamen yicici   de kenqiu, dou bei Zhang Shuzhen jujue le.*
They repeatedly DE beg   DOU by *Zhang Shuzhen* refuse LE
They repeatedly begged *Zhang Shuzhen*, but were refused every time.

(50) *Ke he ernvmen   yi shangliang, yigege dou tou fandui   piao.*
But with sons-and-daughters one talk over everyone DOU cast opposing votes
But when he talked it over with his sons and daughters, everyone of them
 voted against it.

(51) *Ta you zhonghou   you cixiang you wenrou, shei dou hui xiangxin*
She and honest-and-tolerant and kindly and gentle who DOU can believe
ta de!
her DE
She is honest and tolerant, kindly and gentle; everyone will believe her.

(52) *Ni wulun   gan shenme dou yiding hui chenggong de.*
You no-matter do what   DOU must can succeed DE
No matter what you do, you will succeed.

(53) *Rujin,   manzu le wenbaoxuqiu   de zhongguoren,*
Nowadays satisfy LE dress-warmly-and-eat-one's-fill DE Chinese

shenme shihou dou youde chi, xiang chi duoshao dou keyi.
what time DOU have eat think eat how many DOU can
Nowadays, with essential needs of food and clothing all met, Chinese people
can eat anytime and as much as they like.

（54）*Hai tai duo le, nali   dou shi hai, changchang shi ba tian chidiao le shide.*
    Sea too more LE where DOU are sea often   are BA sky eat-off LE like
    There is too much sea; everywhere is the sea, it is often as if the sky had been
    eaten up.

The adverbs of time"*yizhi* （all the time）, *changnian* （all the year round）, *yixiang*
（consistently）, *conglai* （ever）, *xianglai* （all along） etc " （see also Yuan Yulin
2005$_a$: 107） can also indicate the semantic category of the distributive domain,   for
example:
   （55） *Wo gangcai yizhi   dou   zai kanzhe ta.*
       I just now all-the-time DOU -ing longking him.
       Just now, I was watching him.

   （56） *Jin   jinian lai, Ningbo de   yixie shangchang   changnian*
       Recent years since, *Ningbo* DE some shopping-mall all-the-year-round
       dou you gouwuquan   huo gouwu cika chushou.
       DOU have shopping-voucher or shopping card sell
       In recent years, some shopping malls in *Ningbo* sell shopping vouchers or
       cards all year round.

In a *dou* quantification construction the syntactic functions of *distributive operator*
and *distributive share* are both simple, as an adverbial *dou* only occurs before the
heart of predicate （see also Yuan Yulin 2005$_b$: 290）. The distributive share is a
predicate （in a words or a phrase or a clause） excluding *distributive domain*,
distributive index and *distributive operator* （see the examples mentioned above）.

5.22   The Semantic Requirements That The Distributive Dependency Relation Has on Each Component of *Dou* Quantification Construction.

Every sentence of *dou* quantification construction is a quantification on eventualities.
Each of the components of *dou* quantification construction has a specific semantic
role, roughly as follows:

The quantity value is expressed as a "total, plural, approximate" by the distributive
operator *dou*, which belongs to the distributive universal quantification. The
quantified scope is the plural eventuality expressed by " sorting key + distributive
share". From the perspective of logic, just like the relationship of concepts in noun
domain organized in a hierarchical structure, the eventualities expressed by the
quantified scope （i.e., the sentence） can entail and be included in the superior
concept or/and the superior "similarity circle" denoted by "D the distributive share"
（i.e., the predicate of the sentence） （see also Davidson 1967）.

Eventualities are volatile or fluid and abstract objects that cannot be observed directly and all sidedly–they can only be observed via their certain constituting elements (see also Součková 2011: 136). And in *dou* quantification construction the quantifying unit is expressed with the help of a sorting key, which is the numeral value of something matching with the size of specific eventuality. Referring to nothing else than the numeral value expressed by the sorting key during the quantification of *dou* the set of eventualities is divided to a individuated eventuality, for instance:

(57) *Women liandui* _meiyige ren (ban/pai)_   *dou   fa   le yiting*
      Our company every-MW person (squad/platoon) DOU deliver LE one-MW
      jiqiang.
      machine gun.
      Every person (squad/platoon) of our company was delivered a machine gun.

In sentence (57), in reference to the quantifying unit expressed by the sorting key "every person (squad/platoon) of our company", the set of eventualities "X of our company was delivered a machine gun" is divided to individuated eventualities.

Having investigated a large number of corpora, we found that the unit of quantifying of eventualities in *dou* quantification construction is usually expressed by reference to three kinds of eventuality constituents: most prominently, their participants, locations and times; this is the same as any other language (see Lasersohn 1995:238-240; Součková 2011:128-9). In addition, the unit of quantifying may be expressed by reference to a certain cause or condition that causes eventuality to occur or exist (see Davidson 2001: 150). Thus by reference to four kinds of sorting keys the quantification of *dou* divides the set of partly similar eventualities to individuated eventualities and then implements the distributive universal quantification.

The first is the participants or agents or related things of eventuality, for instance:

(58) _Women meige ren_   *dou hui lao.*
      We   every-Cl person DOU will old
      Each of us will get old.

(59) _Liuceng gao de jumin lou,_   _meiyidong he meiyidong_ *dou meiyou*
      Six-story high DE resident building every-Cl and every-Cl DOU haven't
      qubie.
      difference
      Each of the six-story residential building has no difference between them.

The second is the time when the eventuality occurs or exists, for instance:

(60) *Ta sihu* _meitian_   *dou   cong zhetiao jie jingguo.*
       She seem everyday DOU from this-Cl street pass
       She seems to pass this street every day.

(61) _Wo meici_   _yanchu_   *ta dou lai, ta dui wo tebie hao.*

I every-time performance he DOU come he to me very kind
He comes whenever I perform, and he is very kind to me.

The third is the location where the eventuality occurs or exists, for instance:
(62) *Zai ta kan lai, guxiang chuchu   dou mei.*
　　 In he see from, hometown everywhere DOU beautiful
　　 In his view, everywhere in his hometown is beautiful

The fourth is the cause or condition that causes eventuality to occur or exist. The most common forms of the causes or conditions is a phrase or sentence that contains coordinative constituents indicating selectional relationship, or contains a interrogative pronoun which indicates distributive universality. These phrases or sentences are usually connected by a conjunction such as "*wulun* （no matter）/ *bulun* （irrespective of）/ *buguan* （regardless of）/*renping* （whatever）"etc. For instance:
(63) *Wulun   ta shi weishenme zhao   ta, ta dou meiyou liyou   tuique.*
　　 No matter she is why   look for him he DOU has-not reason refuse
　　 No matter why she looks for him，he has no reason to refuse.

(64) *Renping zoudao dongxi nanbei, dou rang ren gandao haishi Sichuan de*
　　 Wherever go-to east-west south-north DOU let person feel still *Sichuan* DE
　　 chaguan duo.
　　 teahouse more
　　 Wherever you go，you will feel that *Sichuan* has the most teahouses.

(65) *Buguan   ni zhao   bu zhao dedao ta, dou yidingyao kuaidian*
　　 Regardless of you look-for not find could him, DOU must   quickly
　　 huilai.
　　 come-back
　　 Regardless of whether you can find him or not, you must come back quickly.

5.23　The Pragmatic Requirements That the Distributive Dependency Relation Has on Each Component of *Dou* Quantification Construction

In *dou* quantification construction the distributive dependency relation have four pragmatic requirements on its components:

First, the pragmatic number （see Liu Chengfeng 2007:2） of the distributive domain must be plural, that is, the number of the participants or agents or related things of the eventuality, the time when the eventuality occurs or exists, the location where the eventuality occurs or exists and the cause or condition that causes eventuality to occur or exist must be more than the minimum required by the size of the eventuality in the sentence, which is expressed by the distributive domain. In brief, it is to make the eventuality become plural eventualities. For example:

(66) a.*Xiao Ming de yige   jiejie   (*dou) jiehun le.*
      Xiao Ming DE one-Cl elder-sister (*DOU) marry Le
      One of *Xiao Ming's* elder sisters (*all) married.

    b.*Xiaoming de liangge jiejie   dou jiehun le.*
      Xiao Ming DE two-Cl elder-sister DOU marry Le
      Both of *Xiao Ming's* elder sisters married.

(67) a.*Tamen (*dou) ba shudian   baowei le.*
      They   (*all) BA bookstore surround LE.
      They all surrounded the bookstore.

    b.*Zhejitian tamen tiantian   dou ba   shudian   baowei zhe.*
      These-days tamen everyday DOU BA bookstore surround ZHE
      Recently, they have been surrounding the bookstore every day.

(68) a.*Tamen liangren (*dou) shi dadang.*
      They two-person (*all) are partner
      Both of them are partners.

    b.*Tamen liangren meici   dou shi dadang.*
      They two-person every-time all are partners
      Both of them are partners every time.

(69) a.*Zhetou daxiang ba nage pingguo (?dou) chi le.*
      This-Cl elephant BA that apple   (?all) eat LE
      The elephant ate the whole apple.

    b.*Zhetou daxiang ba nakuang pingguo dou chi le.*
      This-Cl elephant BA that-basket apples all eat LE
      The elephant ate the whole basket of apples.

    c.*Ta ba nage pingguo dou chi le.*
      He BA that apple   all eat LE
      He ate the whole apple.

Sentences (66a)~(69a) only can express singular eventuality; these are tenable without *dou* but untenable with *dou*. Sentences (66b)~(69b) and (69c) express plural eventualities; these are tenable.

Therefore, in *dou* quantification construction the distributive dependency relation requires that the pragmatic number of the distributive domain must be plural. Actually this is one of secondary effects caused by *dou*'s quantification on eventualities. But we cannot think of "sorting key (distributive domain + distributive index)" as the quantified object of *dou*. And just because of the pragmatic requirement, the traditional grammar misjudged the quantified object of *dou* as "sorting key ".

Second， the distributive domain and the distributive index should belong to a same semantic category. Moreover， when the distributive domain is divided in a certain form of the distributive index （see also Schwarzschild 1996: 69-71； Yuan Yulin 2008: 108-11），the numerical value that the distributive domain has been divided into sub-sets is a multiple of the distributive index. For instance:

（70）*Zhexie yifu meiyijian/tao/xiang   dou hen zhijian.*
　　These clothes every-piece/set/case DOU very valuable
　　Every piece/set/case of these clothes is very valuable.

Third， "sorting key (distributive domain + distributive index) " must be definite and must be the topic of the sentence. Regarding the definiteness and the topicality of "sorting key"， there already are some rich discussions in the literature（see Zhang Yisheng 2003: 395； Dong Xiufang 2003； Yuan Yulin 2005$_a$: 106-8, 2007），so I do not expand on it here.

But here is something to add. The internal reason why "sorting key" must be definite and must be the topic of the sentence, is that "sorting key" is the reference of the unit of quantifying on eventualities.

Fourth, *Dou* is the boundary between the non-focus information and the focus information of a sentence. As the distributive operator, *dou* distributes the property of the distributive share to each sub-key covered by the sorting key. The sorting key is the topic， and the distributive share is the comment； the constitutes of the predicate after *dou* express the focus information. Thus *dou* naturally become the boundary （for details see Dong Xiufang 2003， Omitted examples）.

6   Conclusion

In conclusion， acting as the quantifier of nounal things, *dou*'s quantification on eventualities has three primary elements: the quantified scope， the quantifying unit and the quantity value. But *dou* quantification construction consists of four components: *distributive domain + distributive index + distributive operator + distributed share*. Among them " *sorting key + distributive shar* " denotes a quantification domain， that is the quantified object of *dou*， i.e., the eventualities denoted by the sentence/proposition. "*Sorting key （distributive domain + distributive index ）* " denotes the quantifying unit； "*distributive operator*" *dou* denotes the quantity value which is a " total， plural， approximate " ； and the quantification properties/semantic functions of *dou* belong to the distributive universal quantification. The representations of the primary elements and the way of *dou*'s quantification are different with the quantification of things expressed by nouns.

References

1. Zhan Weidong: *On the semantic structure of compound event and the forming conditions of the Verb-Resultative Constructions in Mandarin Chinese*, Research on Chinese as a foreign language, No.1, pp.111-41.(2013) [In Chinese]
2. Higginbotham, James: *On Semantics*. Linguistic Inquiry, No.4, pp.547-593.（1985）
3. Higginbotham, James: On Events in Linguistic Semantics. In J. Higginbotham, F. Pianesi & A. Varzi (Eds.), *Speaking of Events*（pp. 49-79）. New York, Oxford: Oxford University Press.(2000)
4. Parsons, T.: *Events in the Semantics of English*, MIT Press, Cambridge.（1990）
5. Parsons, T.: *Underlying States and Time Travel*. In J. Higginbotham, F. Pianesi & A. Varzi (Eds.), *Speaking of Events* (pp. 81-93). Oxford, New York: Oxford University Press.（2000）
6. Rudolf Carnap: *The logic construction of the world*, interpreted by Chen Qiwei, Shanghai Translation Publishing House. (1999)[in Chinese]
7. Liu Danqing: *A Handbook for Grammatical Investigation and Research*, Shanghai Educational Publishing House.（2008）［In Chinese］
8. Baker, Mark: *Lexical categories: verbs, nouns, and adjectives*. Cambridge: Cambridge University Press.（2003）
9. Chiu，Hui-Chun Bonnie: *A case of quantifier floating in Mandarin Chinese*. The Second North America Conference on Chinese Linguistics. University of Pennsylvania, Philadelphia.（1990）
10. Wu Jianxin: *Syntax and semantics of quantification in Chinese*. PhD diss., University of Maryland at College Park.（1999）
11. Davidson, D.: *The Logical Form of Action Sentences*, in N. Rescher (ed.), *The Logic of Decision and Action*, University of Pittsburgh Press, pp. 81-95. (1967)
12. Newman, P.: *The Classification of Chadic within Afroasiatic*. Universitaire Pers, Leiden.（1980）
13. Newman, P.: *The Hausa Language: An Encyclopedic Reference Grammar*, New Haven & London: Yale University Press.（2000）
14. Lasersohn, P. : *Plurality, Conjunction and Events*, Kluwer, Dordrecht.（1995）
15. Bittner，M. & N. Trondhjem.: *Quantification as reference: Evidence from Q-verbs.* In L Matthewson（ed.），*Quantification: A Cross-linguistic Perspective*（pp.7-66）. Bingley: Emerald.（2008）
16. Součková，K.: *Pluractionality in Hausa*, The Netherlands: LOT.(2011)
17. Zhang Qingwen、Liu Hongyong and Deng Siying: *The semantic properties and realizations of the verbal plurality in Chinese*，Modern Foreign Languages, No.3, pp.246-53. (2013) [In Chinese]
18. Yuan Yulin: *The summative function of* dou（都）*and its distributive effect.* Contemporary Linguistics, No.4,pp.289-304. (2005b)[In Chinese]
19. Chen Zhenyu、Liu Chengfeng: *Pragmatic numbers*, Research and Exploration of Chinese Grammar, Vol. 14, pp.335-54, The Commercial Press, Beijing (2008) [In Chinese]
20. Huang, Shi-Zhe: *Quantification and predication in Mandarin Chinese: A case study of Dou*，PhD diss., University .(1996)
21. Zhang Yisheng: *On the selective restrictions of Chinese adverb* dou（都），Studies of the Chinese Language, No.5, pp.392-98. (2003) [In Chinese]
22. Wang Huan: *All and* Dou, Language Teaching and Linguistic Studies, No.4, pp.24-8. (1983)[In Chinese]
23. Wen Binli、Qiao Zhengwei: *Multiple Specifiers Analysis of Dou-quantification*，Foreign Language Reseach, No.4, pp.70-5. (2002)[In Chinese]
24. Lee, T. Hun-tak.: *Studies on quantification in Chinese*，PhD diss., University of California, Los Angeles. (1986)

25. Lin, Jo-Wang: *Polarity Licensing and Wh-phrase Quantification in Chinese.* Unpublished PhD diss., University of Massachussets. Amherst, MA.(1996)

26. Lin, Jo-Wang: *Distributivity in Chinese and its implication,* Natural Language Semanics No.6, pp. 201-43. (1998)

27. Huang, Shi-Zhe: *Universal Quantification with Skolemization As Evidence in Chinese and English.* New York : The Edwin Mellen Press. (2005)

28. Jiang Yan: *Pragmatic Reasoning and Syntactic/Semantic Characterization of Dou*（都）, Modern Foreign Languages, No.1, pp.11-24. (1998).[In Chinese]

29. Yuan Yulin: *A new explanation of the semantic function and association direction of dou,* Studies of the Chinese Language, No.2, (2005$_a$) [In Chinese]

30. Yuan Yulin: *On the Implicit Negation and NPI Licensing of* Dou(都), Studies of the Chinese Language, No.2, pp.306-20. (2007) [In Chinese]

31. Abusch, D.: *Generalizing Tense Semantics for Future Contexts,* in S. Rothstein (ed.), *Events and Grammar*(pp.13-34). Kluwer Academic Publishers. (1998)

32. Landman, F.: *Events and Plurality.* The Jerusalem Lectures. Dordrecht: Kluwer. (2000)

33. Champollion, L.: *Cumulative readings of every do not provide evidence for events and thematic roles.* In Maria Aloni, Harald Bastiaanse, Tikitu de Jager & Katrin Schulz (eds.), Logic, language and meaning: proceedings of the 17th Amsterdam Colloquium, 213–222. Springer Berlin Heidelberg. http://dx.doi.org/10.1007/ 978-3-642-14287-1_22.(2010)

34. Champollion, L.: *Distributivity, collectivity and cumulativity.* In Lisa Matthewson, Cécile Meier, Hotze Rullmann & Thomas Ede Zimmermann (eds.), *Wiley's companion to semantics.* Hoboken, NJ: Wiley. http://ling.auf.net/lingbuzz/002133. (October 20, 2015)

35. Champollion, L.: *Overt distributivity in algebraic event semantics,* http://ling.auf.net/ lingbuzz/002098. (January 18, 2016)

36. Huang, Shi-Zhe: *Dou as an existential quantifier,* in Proceedings of the 6th North American Conference on Chinese Linguistics ,Vol. 11, pp.114-125. (1994)

37. Yuan Yulin: *On the Coordinate and Restrictive Relation between* mei *and* dou, Journal of Sino-Tibetan language, No.2, pp.105-23.(2008) [In Chinese]

38. Choe，J. W.: *Anti-quantifiers and A Theory of Distributivity.* PhD diss., University of Massachusetts.(1987)

39. Gillon, B.: *The Readings of Plural Noun Phrases in English,* Linguistics and Philosophy Vol.10, pp. 199-219. (1987)

40. Schwarzschild, Roger: *Pluralities,* Kluwer, Dordrecht. (1996)

41. Xu Jie: *The Totalized Objects of Dou-type Adverbs and Their Dis/appearing and Ordering,* Chinese Language Learning, No.1,pp.10-5.(1985)[In Chinese]

42. Davidson, D.: *The Individuation of Events.* in his *Essays on Actions and Events*（pp.137-52）, Oxford University Press Inc., New York.(2001)

43. Liu Chengfeng: *On Pragmatic Number of Modern Chinese,* PhD diss., Fudan University. (2007)[In Chinese]

44. Dong Xiufang: *The position of dou and some related issues,* Chinese Teaching in the World, No.1, pp.495-507.(2003) [In Chinese]

Approximate Constructions Using *duo* 'more' in Chinese

Qiongpeng Luo

School of Liberal Arts, Nanjing University, China
qpluo@nju.edu.cn

Abstract. The approximate constructions using *duo* 'more' in Chinese present some interesting puzzles for compositional semantics. This paper attempts to unveil the lexical semantics of *duo* by investigating its distribution and interpretation in approximate constructions. It is claimed that: (i) the distribution of *duo* is governed by a monotonicity restriction, that is, its domain must be defined by some mereological part-whole relations; (ii) *duo* is an additive particle whose semantics involves the arithmetic operations of addition (+) and multiplication (×). This novel account provides a more motivated account of the seemingly complicated distributional patterns of *duo* approximate expressions.

Keywords: *duo*; Numerical approximation; Classifiers; Count-Mass distinctions; Chinese

1 Introduction

This paper explores the lexical semantics of *duo* in approximate constructions in Chinese. An approximate construction always involves some quantity expression that refers to the number or amount of individuals/entities. Normally, such expressions take the form of either 'numeral+*duo*+classifier+noun' (Num+*duo*+CL+N) sequences or 'numeral+classifier+*duo*+noun' (Num+CL+*duo*+N) ones, as exhibited by (1a) and (1b) below respectively:

(1) a. *shi duo ge ren*
   ten DUO CL person[1]

---

[1] Abbreviations used in this paper are as follows: ASP: aspectual marker *le*; DE: the possessive/relativizer *de*; DUO: *duo*; CL: classifiers;

PER: perfective marker *le*; NEG: negation markers *bu* and *mei*. To distinguish the massifiers from count classifiers, we add a subscript to

CL to gloss massifiers (e.g., *tong* is a massifier and is glossed as CL_{bucket}).

© Springer International Publishing AG 2018
Y. Wu et al. (Eds.): CLSW 2017, LNAI 10709, pp. 64–78, 2018.
https://doi.org/10.1007/978-3-319-73573-3_5

'more than ten persons'
b. *shi bei   duo shui*
   ten CL$_{cup}$ DUO water
   'more than ten cups of water'

Both (1a) and (1b) give rise to some approximate interpretations: (1a) means more than ten persons, and the number is between 10 and 20, and (1b) means more than ten cups of water, and the amount is between 10 cups plus a subpart of one cup, i.e., between 10 cups and 11 cups (the number is between 10 and 11). It should be noted that though both (1a) and (1b) look similar at surface syntax, there semantic interpretations are slightly different.

The approximate constructions involving *duo* have been extensively reported in traditional grammar books such as Lü (1999). However, the internal structure and semantic composition of such expressions (and the lexical semantics of *duo*) have rarely been studied in the theoretical literature. The examples in (1) raise some interesting issues that merit further theoretical exploration. First, what governs the distribution of *duo* is unclear. Lü (1999) reports that *duo* may follow a measure word such as *tong* 'bucket', *jin* 'catty', *xiang* 'basket', *bei* 'cup', but not the individual classifiers such as *ge, ben, zhi, ke*, etc. (following the terminology of Cheng & Sybesma (1999), we dub the former as massifiers and the latter as count classifiers). This is illustrated by the contrast between (2a) and (2b) below:

(2) a. *shi bei   duo shui*
       10 CL$_{cup}$ DUO water
       'ten cups of water and more'
    b. **shi ge duo ren*
        10   CL DUO person
       Intended: 'ten persons and more'

Lü 1957[1984], and Lü (1999) also report that the occurrence of *duo* is sensitive to the type of numerals. *Duo* can follow a round number (i.e., the numbers that are divisible by 10), but not the non-round numbers. Witness the contrast between (3a) and (3b) below:

(3) a. round number: *shi* 'ten'
       shi duo   bei   shui
       10 DUO CL$_{cup}$ water
       'ten cups of water and more'
    b. non-round number: *san* 'three'
       **san   duo   bei   shui*
       three DUO CL$_{cup}$ water
       Intended: 'more than three cups of water

In the literature, *duo* is always glossed as *more*. It should be noted that there is some remarkable difference between them. *More* is not subject to the same constraint as *duo*. For instance, *more* can modify either a round number or a non-round number (*more than ten students/more than three students*).

Second, the internal semantic composition of the approximate constructions using *duo* remains unexplored in the literature. The semantic difference as shown between (1a) and (1b) is still an issue for formal semantics.

Drawing inspiration from recent studies on measurement (Luo et al. 2017), we propose that the distribution of *duo* in approximate constructions is governed by a monotonicity restriction, that is, the semantic domains of *duo* must be defined by some mereological part-whole relations. Semantically, *duo* is an additive particle whose semantics involves the arithmetic operations of addition (+) and multiplication (×). We demonstrate how this novel analysis provides a more motivated account of the seemingly complicated phenomena involving *duo* in Chinese. [2]

The rest of the paper proceeds as follow: §2 lays out some empirical generalizations of *duo* approximate constructions. §3 provides a measurement-based analysis. §4 unveils the internal semantic compositions of the approximate constructions involving *duo*. §5 concludes.

2   Some Empirical Generalizations

2.1 The Distributional Patterns of *duo*

Unlike English *more*, the occurrence of the approximator *duo* in quantity expressions is by no means free. Lü (1957[1984]) observes that its occurrence is subject to a combination of two factors: whether the classifier is an individual one (i.e., the count classifiers such as *ge*, *zhi*, *ben*, *ke*, etc.) or not; whether the numeral denotes a round number or not. The empirical generalizations can be summarized as (4) below:

(4) The distribution of *duo* in quantity expressions:

(i) If the number is a round one: Num+*duo*+{count classifier, massifier}+N;

(ii) If the number is a non-round one: Num+massifier+*duo*+N.

That is, if the classifier is a massifier, *duo* can immediately follow either the numeral or the 'Num+CL' chunk (with different interpretations). However, when the classifier is a count classifier, *duo* can only follow the numeral, not the 'Num+CL' chunk. To illustrate:

(5) a. *shi duo ben shu*

    10 DUO CL book

    'more than ten books'

  b. **shi ben duo shu*

---

[2] To avoid further controversy, *duo* is glossed as DUO, instead of *many/much* or *more*.

(6) a. *shi duo   tong   shui*
      10 DUO CL$_{bucket}$ water
      'ten buckets of water and more'
    b. *shi tong   duo   shui*
      10 CL$_{bucket}$ DUO water
      'ten buckets of water and more'

Likewise, the interpretations of the quantity expressions involving *duo* are open to two different interpretations, depending on whether the accompanying classifier is a count one or a mass one and where *duo* appears relative to the classifier. When *duo* is immediately preceded by a massifier, it appears equivalent to a subportion of the entity measured by means of the measurement unit contributed by the massifier. While (6a) means more than ten buckets of water, where n is any number between 10 and 20, (6b) means ten buckets of water plus a subportion of one bucket of water. In this case, n preferably is a number between 10 and 11, say, 10.5.

2.2 The Interpretations of *duo*

2.2.1 The Approximate Interpretation

The *duo* approximate constructions are used by the speakers to express uncertainty about the precise number or amount of the individuals that satisfy the claim (this is why it is often dubbed as a numeral approximator by traditional grammarians). When asked about how many students are present, the reply in (7a) states that: (a) the speaker is uncertain about the precise number of students who are present; (b) the range of approximation is between 10 and 20, that is, $10<n<20$, and it cannot be more than 20 ($\#n>20$):

(7) a. *You shi duo   ge xuesheng zai xianchang.*
      have 10 DUO CL student   at present
      'There are ten students and more at present.'
    b. **You zhe   shi ge xuesheng zai xianchang.*
      have DEM 10 CL student   at present
      'There are these ten students at present.'

As shown by the contrast between (7a) and (7b), the approximation expressions using *duo* pattern with indefinites in being allowed in existential constructions.

2.2.2 The Comparative Interpretation

Unlike English, Chinese doesn't have a comparative morpheme meaning '-er'. Thus, at surface syntax *duo* is indistinguishable between *many/much* and *more*. When *duo* occurs in quantity expressions expressing approximation, however, the semantic interpretation of this use of *duo* is always comparative:

(8) a. *shi duo ge   xuesheng*
  10   DUO CL   student
  'more than ten students' (10<n<20)
  NOT: 'as many as ten students'

 b. *shi duo   ping   jiu*
  10   DUO CL_{bottle} wine
  'more than ten bottles of wine' (10<n<20)
  NOT: 'as many as ten bottles of wine'

 c. *shi ping   duo   jiu*
  10   CL_{bottle} DUO wine
 'more than ten bottles of wine' (10 <n<11)
  NOT: 'as many as ten bottles of wine'

(8a) means more than ten students, and (8b) means more than ten bottles of wine. (8c) also means more than ten bottles of wine. None of the examples in (8) mean as many/much as N. These facts reveal that taking *duo* to be the counterpart of *many/much* may face challenges: for example, it would yield a wrong reading of 'as many as ten students', rather than 'more than ten students' for (8a).

2.2.3 The Immediacy Constraint

The interpretation of *duo* is regulated by an immediacy constraint: *duo* can only scope over the single unit-morpheme to its immediate left (Zhang 2013). When *duo* is immediately preceded by a numeral N, *duo* appears equivalent to a subpart of N, not the word as a whole. (9) below means more than 70 students, and the number of students is between 70 and 80. That is, *duo* is interpreted relative to *shi* 'ten', the second morpheme of the word *qi-shi* 'seven-ten':

(9) *qi-shi duo ge xuesheng*
 7-ten DUO CL student
 'more than 70 students' (70 <n<80)

A more telling example is due to Lü (1999). In (10a) below, the element that immediately precedes *duo* is the numeral *shi* 'ten'. In this case, the expression means 10 plus a part of 10 (that is, any number between 10 and 20). In (10b), the element that immediately precedes *duo* is the measure word *mu* (a traditional way of measuring area of land in China, 1 *mu* ≈ 666.7 square meters), and the expression means 10 *mu* plus a subportion of one *mu*, that is, any area between 10 *mu* and 11 *mu*, say, 10.5 *mu*:

(10) a. *shi duo   mu di*
   ten DUO mu land

'ten *mu* and more land' (10<n<20)
b. *shi mu duo   di*
   ten mu DUO land
   'ten *mu* and more land' (10<n<11)

2.2.4 The Lower and Upper Bounds

The use of *duo* has both a lower and an upper bound. The following (11) is infelicitous if the speaker expressed a wish to seek a football player whose height is 190cm and more. The sentence is judged to be false if the player turns out to be shorter than 170cm or taller than 180cm. If one day Zhangsan was very thirsty and drank up 5 cups of water, (12) is infelicitous. (11) means someone whose height is between 170cm and 180cm, no more and no less; and (12) means the volume of water is between 3 cups and 4 cups, no more and no less. In both cases, *duo* is associated only with the unit morphemes of the preceding words, not the words as a whole.

(11) *Wo xiang zhao ge   yi-bai-qi-shi   duo   limi   de qiuyuan.*
     I   want find   CL one-hundred-seven-ten DUO centimeter DE player
     'I am looking for a player whose height is more than 170cm.'
     False: if **height (the player)** > 190cm
     False: if **height (the player)** < 170cm

(12) *Zhangsan he-le   san bei   duo shui.*
     Zhangsan drink-ASP 3 CL$_{cup}$ DUO water
     'Zhangsan drank 3 cups of water and more.'
     False: if $\mu_{cup}(\textbf{water}) > 4$
     False: if $\mu_{cup}(\textbf{water}) < 3$

3   A Measurement-based Analysis

As mentioned previously (§1), the *duo* approximation constructions fall into two subtype: (a) Num+*duo*+CL+N; (b) Num+CL+*duo*+N. The interpretations are also different, depending on where *duo* occurs: when *duo* is immediately preceded by a (round-number denoting) numeral, the 'Num+*duo*' is used to count the number (i.e., the cardinality) of individuals; in the other type where *duo* is immediately preceded by a massifier, the 'Num+CL+*duo*' is used to measure the amount of individuals, on the basis of the measuring unit contributed by the massifier. Once we take the cardinality reading to be a special case of measurement (Bale & Barner 2009), the intuitively obvious correlation between the semantics of *duo* and measurement is hard to miss. As pointed out by much recent studies, measurement is subject to a monotonicity restriction, which can be defined by the mereological part-whole relations (cf.

Schwarzschild 2006; Bale & Barner 2009; Wellwood 2015; Luo et al. 2017, a.o.). To illustrate, consider the distribution of *more* in English ((14) is repeated from Bale & Barner 2009: ex. (10)) :

(13) a. *There are more students than professors at the job talk.*

　　b. **There are more student than professor at the job talk.*

(14) a. *Esme has more chairs than Seymour has tables.* (cardinality)

　　b. *Esme has more water than Seymour has juice.* (volume)

　　c. *Esme has more rope than Seymour has string.* (length)

　　d. *Esme has more gold in her ring than Seymour has silver in his necklace.* (purity of materials)

　　e. *Esme has more anger than Seymour has sympathy.* (emotional intensity)

The comparison constructions in (13-14) make use of the semantics of measurement. Many nouns in English have both the count and mass syntax (Bale & Barner 2009). As demonstrated by (14), when they are used as count nouns, they specify comparison by number, however, when they are used as mass nouns, they specify comparison along a variety of dimensions, as long as these dimensions track a mereological part-whole relation (i.e., being monotonic). In mereology, a part-whole relation satisfies reflexivity, transitivity, and antisymmetry (Champollion & Krifka 2016: 377-378):

(15) a. Reflexivity: $\forall x(x \leq x)$

　　b. Transitivity: $\forall x,y,z(x \leq y \wedge y \leq z \to x \leq z)$

　　c. Antisymmetry: $\forall x, y(x \leq y \wedge y \leq x \to x = y)$

The extensions of plural nouns are defined by the part-whole relations. For example, if X denotes a set of professors, and Y denotes another set of professors, then the union of X and Y ($X \cup Y$) also fall within the extension of professors. Both X and Y are subsets of the union of X and Y (that is, $X \subseteq X \cup Y$ and $Y \subseteq X \cup Y$). By contrast, the singular count nouns like *student/professor* denote atomic entities, and atomic entities have nothing except themselves as the parts. The oddness of (13b) demonstrates that applying measuring to them would result in some odd semantics. The contrast between (13a) and (13b) indicates that the distribution of *more* is sensitive to the mereological structure (i.e., part-whole structures) of the entities in question.[3]

　　Wellwood (2015) provides a deeper explanation for the contrast between (13a) and (13b) in terms of measurement. She argues that the semantics of measurement makes use of a measure function μ, and μ is a homomorphism from a structure defined by the part-whole relations ($\leq$) to the domain of degrees and their ordering by $\leq$. μ has some non-trivial structure-preserving property. The structure-preserving property is to be understood in terms of monotonicity. A measure function μ is order-

---

[3] For the notion of mereology and its application to natural language semantics, see Champollion and Krifka (2016).

preserving just in case, for any two things that are properly ordered in a part-whole relation, their measurements are similarly ordered (cf. Schwarzschild 2006; Bale & Barner 2009; Wellwood 2015; Luo et al. 2017, a.o.):

(16) A measure function μ: $D_{\leq Part} \longmapsto D_{\leq Deg}$ is monotonic iff:

for all α, $\beta \in D_{\leq Part}$, if $\alpha < \beta$, then $\mu(\alpha) <^{Deg} \mu(\beta)$.

According to (16), measuring is possible only when it applies to the dimensions that respect part-whole relations. Plural nouns are defined by the part-whole relations (e.g., the denotations of the word *apples* have atomic apples as its subparts). (13b) is out because singular count nouns have nothing but themselves as the subparts. Following this line of thought, I argue that a proper analysis of the comparative *duo* actually depends on the idea that measurement is structure-dependent. That the distribution of *duo* is sensitive to the type of classifiers provides direct support for this claim.

In §2.1, I have mentioned that the distribution of *duo* in quantity expressions is regulated by the type of classifiers: when the classifier is a count (individual) one (such as *ge*, *zhi*, *ke*, *ben*, etc.), *duo* can only follow the numerals alone, not the Num+CL chunks; however, when the classifier is a massifier (e.g., the container classifiers such as *wan* 'bowl', *xiang* 'bucket', *bei* 'cup', etc.), *duo* can be preceded either by numerals or Num+CL chunks. The relevant examples are repeated in the (17-18) below:

(17) When the classifier is a count one:

    (a) Num+*duo*+CL+N (cardinality reading)

       shi duo   ge xuesheng

       10 DUO CL student

       'more than ten students'

    (b) *Num+CL+*duo*+N

       * *shi ge duo   xuesheng*

       10 CL DUO student

(18) When the classifier is a massifier

    (a) Num+*duo*+CL+N, cardinality reading

       shi duo   tong   shui

       10 DUO CL$_{bucket}$ water

       'more than ten buckets of water'

    (b) Num+CL+*duo*+N

       shi tong   duo   shui

       10 CL$_{bucket}$ DUO water

       'ten buckets of water and more'

If *duo* contains a semantic component about measuring, the prediction is that what is measured can either be mass or pluralities. The domains for pluralities and mass are structured in the sense that they are defined by the part-whole relations. In the former case, the measuring is achieved through an order preserving mapping from i-sums to degrees of cardinality. In the latter case, the measuring is achieved through an order preserving mapping from some mass x to a degree of x along a certain dimension. For example, in (18b), the measuring is about volume. The dimension of volume respects part-whole relations:

(19) **volume** tracks a part-whole relation:

$\forall x \forall y [x \leq y \rightarrow$ **volume** $(x) \leq$**volume**$(y)]$

What (19) states is this: if x is a subportion of y, then the volume of x is necessarily a subpart of y (i.e., the measure of x in terms of volume is smaller that of y). It is easy to verify that the dimensions such as weight, height, area, length, etc. are also monotonic, and so is cardinality:

(20) a. **weight**: $\forall x \forall y [x \leq y \rightarrow$ **weight** $(x) \leq$**weight** $(y)]$

   b. **length**: $\forall x \forall y [x \leq y \rightarrow$ **length** $(x) \leq$**length** $(y)]$

   c. **area**: $\forall x \forall y [x \leq y \rightarrow$ **area** $(x) \leq$ **area** $(y)]$

   d. **height**: $\forall x \forall y [x \leq y \rightarrow$ **height**$(x) \leq$ **height** $(y)]$

(21)   Cardinality   is   also   defined   by   the   part-whole   relation: $\forall X,$ $Y(X \subseteq Y \rightarrow |X| \leq |Y|)$ (for any two sets X and Y, if X is a subset of Y, then the cardinality of X is a subpart of that of Y)

This analysis straightforwardly explains why *duo* can follow a massifier but not a count classifier. Massifiers, according to Cheng & Sybesma (1999), contribute units of measurement. For example, *tong* 'bucket' is about volume, and *mu* is about area. Likewise, the other massifiers such as *wan* 'bowl', *xiang* 'basket', *bei* 'cup' all refer to some dimensions that can be defined by the part-whole relations (for more about the dimensionality of classifiers, see Luo et al. (2017) for further details). Hence, the distribution of *duo* is regulated by the type of classifiers is orthogonal to whether the classifier encodes monotonic dimensions.

By contrast, count classifiers name the unit by which the entity denoted the noun naturally occurs (Cheng & Sybesma 1999), or according to Chierchia (1998), they are atomizers that extract atoms from atomless sets. This means the Num+CL chunks denote atomic individuals. As have shown by the oddness of (13b), the domains of atomic individuals are not defined by the part-whole relations. As a result, *duo* cannot follow a count classifier. This is why when the relevant classifier is a count one, *duo* can only follow a numeral, resulting into a cardinality reading.

The following examples (22a) and (22b) illustrate the different domains of count classifiers and massifiers respectively:

(22) a. Count classifier:

   $[\![$ san ge $]\!] = \lambda x.$ **ATOM** $(x) \wedge$ #x=3 $\dashrightarrow$ $\{x'_{AT}, x''_{AT}, x'''_{AT}\}$

   b. Massifier:

⟦ san bei ⟧ = λx. **filled_in_cup** (x) ∧**volume**$_{cup}$(x)=3   ⇢   {x$_{WATER}$, x'$_{WATER}$, x$_{WATER}$ x'$_{WATER}$}

In the following section, we provides a lexical entry of *duo* that makes use of this monotonic measure function μ.

4   The Semantics of *duo* Approximate Constructions

4.1 The 'Num+*duo*+CL+N' Construction

In this construction, *duo* is attached to a numeral that denotes a round number, resulted into a cardinality reading (e.g., *shi duo* means ten and more, and the number is between 10 and 20). I assume that round numbers are like complex numerals which involve some mulplicative operations (×) (see Anderson 2016 and references therein). For example, *shi* 'ten' can be semantically represented as one multiplies ten (10 =1×10), *yi bai* 'one hundred' as one multiplies one hundred (100 =1×100). More examples are provided in (23) below:

(23) a. *qi-shi* '7-ten': 70= 7×10

    b. *qi-bai* '7-hundred': 700=7×100

    c. *qi-qian* 'seven-thousand' 7000=7×1000

The approximator numeral *duo* is essentially an additive particle: it is attached to a numeral and contributes some addition (+) operation. For example, when *duo* follows *qi-shi*, it forms a complex numeral which means 70 and more, and the range is between 71 and 80. This can be semantically represented as (24) below:

(24) a. qi-shi   duo

    7-hundred DUO

    b. ⟦qi-shi duo⟧ = 7×10+10×r

            = 10×(7+r)

In (34b), the ratio number r is a real number between 0 and 1, that is, $r \in [0, ..., 1]$. This representation correctly captures the semantics of the numeral approximation where *duo* is attached to a numeral.

I assume (25) to be the structure for 'Num+*duo*+CL+N' sequences such as *qi-shi duo ge ren*:

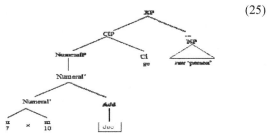

(25)

In (25), the numeral (including *duo*) projects a NumeralP, which is located in the spec of ClP. The ClP is situated above the NP projected by the N. *duo* is an adjunct in NumeralP.

The lexical entry of *duo* is provided as (26) below, and (27) is the step-by-step semantic derivation of (25):

(26) $[\![DUO]\!] = \lambda m \lambda n \lambda x. \mu_{CARD}(x) = m \times (n+r)$

(where: r is a real number between o and 1, $r \in [0, ..., 1]$; μ is a homomorphic map from the i-sums to their cardinality)

(27) a. $[\![qi\text{-}shi\ duo]\!] = \lambda m \lambda n \lambda x. \mu_{CARD}(x) = m \times (n+r)\ (7)(10)$

$\qquad\qquad\qquad = \lambda x. \mu_{CARD}(x) = 10 \times (7+r)$

b. $[\![ge]\!] = \lambda x.\ ATOM(x)$

c. $[\![qi\text{-}shi\ duo\ ge]\!] = \lambda x.\ ATOM(x) \wedge \mu_{CARD}(x) = 10 \times (7+r)$ (via Predicate Modification)

d. $[\![ren]\!] = \lambda x.\ PERSON(x)$

e. $[\![qi\text{-}shi\ duo\ ge\ ren]\!] = \lambda x.\ \lambda x.\ PERSON(x) \wedge ATOM(x) \wedge \mu_{CARD}(x) = 10 \times (7+r)$

In propose, (27e) states that there is a set of atomic individuals whose cardinality is 70 and more, and the number is between 70 and 80. This semantic analysis correctly derives the truth conditions of the numeral approximation constructions where *duo* is attached to a numeral.

Recall that *duo* cannot be attached to a non-round-number numeral such as *er-shi san* 'twenty and three' (# *er-shi san duo*) or *qi* 'seven' (# *qi duo*). Consider:

(28) a. *shi duo   ben shu* (round number)

    10 DUO CL book

    'more than ten books' ($10 < n < 20$)

b. **er-shi san   duo   ben shu* (non-round number)

    2-ten three DUO CL book

    'more than three books'

The explanation for this is straightforward. Consider the cardinal that can be modified by *duo*, such as *er-shi* 'two ten/twenty'. *er-shi* can be decomposed as 2×10, and it can combine with another numeral via addition to form a complex numeral, e.g., *er-shi san* 'twenty and three' ($23 = 2 \times 10 + 3$). If the semantics of *duo* makes use of some addition operation, *er-shi san duo* would be out. As shown by the oddness of (28b), this prediction is borne out.

4.2 The 'Num+CL+*duo*+N' Construction

In this section, I discuss the semantics of the approximate constructions in which *duo* is attached to a massifier. Recall that massifiers contribute units of measurement. I adopt the view that the internal semantics of 'Num+Unit' sequences is essentially a multiplication. For example, *20 meters* is equivalent to 20 times as high as a meter-unit object (Sassoon 2010). Similarly, *shi-bei* '10 CL_{cup}' means (the volume of x) is ten times as much as a cup-unit object. Just like the complex numerals, such constructions also make use of some multiplicative operations (simplifying somewhat):

(29) *shi-mu* '10 CL_{mu}' = $10 \times 1_{mu}$
    shi-bei '10 CL_{cup}' = $10 \times 1_{cup}$
    shi-sheng '10 CL_{lieter}' = $10 \times 1_{liter}$

The syntax for the constructions such as *shi-mu duo di* '10 mu duo land' is given as (30) below. Please be noted that *duo*, as an additive particle, is an adjunct in UnitP:

(30)

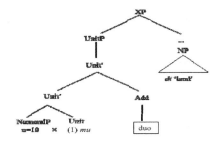

The semantic derivation proceeds straightforwardly, just like 'Num+*duo*+CL+N' constructions:

(31) a. $[\![shi\ mu\ duo]\!] = \lambda m \lambda n \lambda x.\mu_{area}(x) = m \times (n+r)\ (7)(1_{mu})$
        $= \lambda x.\mu_{area}(x) = (10+r) \times 1_{mu}$
    b. $[\![di]\!] = \lambda x.\ LAND\ (x)$
    e. $[\![shi\ mu\ duo\ di]\!] = \lambda x.\ \lambda x.\ LAND(x) \wedge \mu_{area}(x) = 1_{mu} \times (10+r)$ (via Predicate Modification)

The range of *r* is between 0 and 1. The representation (31c) states that the measuring of the area of a certain land is 10 *mu* plus some subportion of one *mu*. Since one *mu* is equivalent to ten *fen* (1*mu* =10 *fen*), this semantics amounts to saying that the measurement of the area in terms of *mu* is between 10 and 11.

The present analysis provides a natural solution to one classic puzzle reported in Lü (1999). Lü (1999) observes that the interpretation of *duo* might be different, depending on its position and the element that precedes it. To repeat some previous examples discussed in §3.3. In (10a) below, the element that immediately precedes *duo* is the numeral *shi* 'ten', and the reading is about 10 plus a part of 10 (that is, any number between 10 and 20). In (10b), the element that immediately precedes *duo* is the measure word *mu*, and the reading is about 10 *mu* plus a subportion of one *mu*, that is, any area between 10 *mu* and 11 *mu*, say, 10.5 *mu*:

(10) a. *shi duo   mu di*
        ten DUO mu land
        'ten *mu* and more land' (10<n<20)
     b. *shi mu duo   di*
        ten mu DUO land
        'ten mu and more land' (10<n<11)

A unified account is in order. Suppose 10 is semantically represented as 1×10. The semantic representation for *shi duo* in (10a) is as (32) below, which states that the number is between 10 and 11.

(32) ⟦*shi duo*⟧ = λmλnλx.μ(x) = m×(n+r) (1)(10)
                = λx.μ(x) = 1×(10+r)

On the present account, *duo* makes use of some arithmetic operation of addition. The difference between (10a) and (10b) can be reduced to what is added: whether it is a subpart of a numeral, or a subportion of one unit (of measurement). Everything else remains the same.

5   Conclusion

This paper has addressed two puzzles that the approximation constructions using *duo* in Chinese poses:

(33) (a) *What governs the distribution of duo? Why the distribution of duo is sensitive to the type of classifiers (duo can follow a massifier but not a count classifier)?*

(b) *What is the internal semantic composition of duo approximation constructions?*

I argue that the lexical semantics of *duo* contains two ingredients: measurement and the arithmetic operation of addition (+). The measurement semantics is realized by a homomorphic map μ and is subject to a monotonicity constraint: two entities that are properly ordered in terms of part-whole relations are similarly ordered in terms of their measurement. A corollary of this constraint is that only those domains that respect the mereological part-whole relations are measurable and accessed by *duo*. This explains why *duo* cannot follow a count classifier. Additionally, an addition operation-based semantics of *duo* has enabled us to explain why *duo* can only follow a numeral that denotes a round number.

The present analysis has some other interesting consequences: first, it provides some deeper motivation for the count-mass distinction of classifiers in Chinese; second, it sheds new light on the internal structure and semantic composition of complex numerals, an area that merits further theoretical exploration on its own.

Acknowledgements. We are grateful to the anonymous reviewers of CLSW 2017 for helpful suggestions and comments. This work was financially supported by the National Social Science Foundation of China under grant No. 16BYY006 and the Ministry of Education (MOE) Humanities and Social Science Fund of China under grant No. 12YJC740074 to Qiongpeng Luo. All errors remain our own.

6   References

1. Anderson, C.: Numerical approximation using *some*. In: Csipak, E. and Zeijlstra, H. (eds.), *Proceedings of Sinn und Bedeutung* 19, 54-70 (2016).
2. Bale, A., Barner, D.: The interpretation of functional heads: using comparatives to explore the mass/count distinction. *Journal of Semantics* 26, 217-252 (2009).
3. Champollion, L., Krifka, M.:Mereology. In: Dekker, P. and Aloni, M. (eds.), *The Cambridge Handbook of Formal Semantics*. Cambridge University Press, Cambridge, UK, 369-388 (2016).
4. Cheng, L., Sybesma, R.: Bare and not-so-bare nouns and the structure of NP. *Linguistic Inquiry* 30: 509-542 (1999).
5. Lü, S.-X: *Zaishuo 'lai' yiji 'duo' he 'ban'* ("Further remarks on *lai* 'about' and *duo* 'many/much', ban 'half'). *Zhongguo Yuwen* (Chinese Philology) (1957). Reprinted in Lü, S.-X: *Hanyu Yufa Lunji* (Papers on Chinese Grammar)(1984). The Commercial Press, Beijing, China. [In Chinese]
6. Lü, S.-X, et al. (eds.): *Xiandai Hanyu Babai Ci* ("Eight Hundred Words in Mondern Chinese") (Revised Edition). The Commercial Press, Beijing, China (1999). [In Chinese]
7. Luo, Q., Hsieh, M.-L., Shi, D.: Pre-classifier adjectival modification in Mandarin Chinese: a measurement-based analysis. *Journal of East Asian Linguistics* 26, 1-36 (2017).
8. Sassoon, G. W.: Measurement theory in linguistics. *Synthese* 174, 151-180 (2010).
9. Sauerland, U., Stateva, P.: Scalar vs. epistemic vagueness: evidence from approximators. In: Gibson, M. and Friedman, T. (eds.), *Proceedings of Semantic and Linguistic Theory (SALT) 17*. CLC publications, Ithaca, NY (2007).
10. Schwarzschild, R.: The role of dimensions in the syntax of noun phrases. *Syntax* 9, 67-110 (2006).

11. Solt, S.: Q-Adjectives and the semantics of quantity. *Journal of Semantics* 32, 221-273 (2015).
12. Welllwood, A.: On the semantics of comparison across categories. *Linguistics and Philosophy* 38, 67-101(2015).
13. Wellwood, A. *et al*: Measuring and comparing individuals and events. *Journal of Semantics* 29, 207-228 (2012).
14. Zhang, N.: *Classifier Structures in Mandarin Chinese*. Mouton de Gruyter, Berlin, Germany (2013).

A Comparative Study on the Definition of Adverbs*

-- Taking *the Dictionary of Contemporary Chinese (the 6th Edition)* and *the Dictionary of Mandarin (Revised Edition)* as Examples

Xiaoyao Zhang, Dekuan Xu**, Shumei Chen

School of Chinese, Ludong University, Yantai 264025
E-mail: 1159676411@qq.com, xudekuan@tom.com, csm620481@sina.com

Abstract: Adverbs play an important role in the research of Chinese vocabulary and lexicography, therefore it is always a focal point in language study. The adverb definition is also the emphasis of the dictionary definition research. Mainly through comparing and analyzing the definition mode of common adverb senses in the Dictionary of Contemporary Chinese (the 6th Edition) and the Dictionary of Mandarin (Revised Edition), this paper summarizes the differences and similarities of definition mode across the Taiwan Straits with a hope to be conducive to the complication of Chinese dictionary and natural language processing.

Keywords: dictionary, adverb, explanation mode, items

1   Introduction

Though there is a common source of language and culture across the Taiwan Straits, the two sides have been separated for years due to political reasons. Therefore, the language and culture across the Straits possess their own characteristics. As the most active part of the language, vocabulary is the most direct form of language difference. Both the Chinese ontology research and the Chinese information processing research must pay attention to these similarities and differences. The purpose of this paper is twofold: on the one hand, the paper studies these similarities and differences, which can help us to understand the actual situation of the meanings of adverbs in two dictionaries; on the other, it is of great significance to promote dictionary compilation, the communication of language and culture and the understanding of language information processing and natural language understanding. Taking *the Dictionary of Contemporary Chinese (the 6th edition)* (hereinafter referred to as "the *Xianhan*")and *the Dictionary of Mandarin (Revised Edition)*, (hereinafter referred to as "*Guoyu*") as research objects, this paper selects the adverb senses that have the same or similar meanings in two dictionaries. The purpose is to find out the different ways in which the dictionaries across the Strait are codified in terms of interpretation and to provide valuable reference for the compilation of dictionaries, the exchange of language cultures and the processing of Chinese language.

We selected 283 adverbs with the same or similar meaning in *Xianhan* and *Guoyu*, totaling 337 items.

* This research is sponsored by the National Natural Science Foundation of China (No. 61572245) and the Student Innovation Foundation of Ludong University (No. ld15w011) and the "13th Five-Year"   Research Project of China's National Language Committee (A Data-mining Based Survey on the Application of Chinese Dictionaries by Overseas Students in China, No. Yb135-41).
** Corresponding author.

Y. Wu et al. (Eds.): CLSW 2017, LNAI 10709, pp. 79–85, 2018.
https://doi.org/10.1007/978-3-319-73573-3_6

The specific selection procedure is: with the adverbs of *Chinese proficiency test in Chinese Syllabus* as the reference items, the common entries in both *Xianhan* and *Guoyu* are retrieved, then adverb senses that have the same or similar meanings in the dictionaries are selected and a comparative analysis is made. This article mainly refers to explanation modes listed in Huang Jianhua's *On Dictionaries*, and the explanation modes are classified into 6 classed and 13 sub-classes, i.e.:

> 1.definition with synonym
>> 1a. synonyms for definition
>> 1b. gloss for additional meaning
> 2. definition with antonym
>> 2a. negative definition
>> 2b. intersectional definition
> 3. morpheme definition
>> 3a. only paraphrase the former
>> 3b. only paraphrase the latter
>> 3c. pre and post morpheme decomposition
> 4. paraphrase of adverbial phrases
> 5. explanatory definition
> 6. compositional definition

This paper intends to analyze the explanation modes from the two respectives: i.e., the overall situation and the sense of correspondence.

2   A General Analysis of the Interpretation of Adverbs

2.1   Distribution of Explanation Methods in *Xianhan*

Through the statistics and analysis of the 283 adverbs, namely 339 items in *Xianhan*, the distribution of the main definitions is shown in table 1.

Table 1. Interpretation and distribution of items in *Xianhan*

Explanation mode	Explanatory definition	Definition with synonym	Compositional definition	Morpheme definition	Paraphrase of adverbial phrases	Definition with antonym	Total Frequency
Frequency	141	130	35	17	9	7	339
Percentage	41.6	38.3	10.3	5.0	2.7	2.1	100

As can be seen from table 1, explanatory definition is the most frequently used interpretation method in *Xianhan*, definition with synonyms is the second, compositional definition, morpheme interpretation and paraphrase of adverbial phrases are descending successively, definition with antonym is the least used in interpretation.

2.2   Distribution of Explanation Methods in *Guoyu*

Through the statistics and analysis of the 283 adverbs, namely 338 items in *Xianhan*, the distribution of the main definitions is shown in table 2.

Table 2. Interpretation and distribution of items in *Guoyu*

Explanation mode	Definition with synonym	Explanatory definition	Compositional definition	Morpheme definition	Definition with antonym	Paraphrase of adverbial phrases	Total
Frequency	180	63	58	27	6	4	338
Percentage	53.3	18.6	17.2	7.9	1.8	1.2	100

From table 2, we can see that in *Guoyu*, definition with synonym is the most frequently used method of interpretation, accounting for 53.3%. Explanatory definition, compositional definition and morpheme interpretation are descending successively. The number of definition with antonym and paraphrase of adverbial phrases is the least with a percentage less than 10.

3   A Contrastive Analysis of the Adverb Items in *Xianhan* and *Guoyu*

The overall situation of the interpretation of the adverbs in the two dictionaries is analyzed above, and the followings are analyzed according to the items.

According to the corresponding situation of the item, the adverbs that we examine are divided into two items corresponding to one and the other. The following analysis will be carried out separately.

3.1   The Two Items Correspond to A Single Item (3)

By two items explaining one item is meant that in the same terms, two items of a dictionary is equal to one item in the other dictionary, thus the explanation mode which in different dictionaries may not be a one-to-one correspondence relationship. In *Xianhan* and *Guoyu*, there are three items which are two items correspond to a single item , i.e., "*zhiguan*", "*chongxin*" and "*buyao*".

Table 3. Two items correspond to a single items in *Xianhan* and *Guoyu*

Lexical entry	Interpretation in *Xianhan*	Explanation mode	Interpretation in *Guoyu*	Explanation mode
只管 *zhiguan* "although"	*zhǐguǎn* 副 （1）尽管：你有什么针线活儿，～拿来，我抽空帮你做。 *Jinguan:ni you shenme zhenxian huor,~nalai,wo choukong bang ni zuo.* （2）只顾：他不会使桨，小船～在湖中打转。 *zhigu:ta buhui shi jiang,xiaochuan~zai hu zhong da zhuan.*	(1)definition with synonym (2)definition with synonym	*zhǐ guǎn* 只顾、儘管。儒林外史˙第三十六回：「你作速料理你的事去，不必只管講話了。」 *Zhuigu、jinguan. Rulinwaishi.disanshiliu hui:「ni zuosu liaoli de de shi qu,bubi zhiguan jianghua le.」* 紅樓夢˙第四十四回：「裏面鳳姐心中雖不安，面上只管佯不理論。」亦作「只顧」。 *Hongloumeng.disishisihui:「limian fengjie xinzhong sui bu'an,mianshang zhiguan yang bu liyu.」yizuo「zhigu」.*	multiple synonyms for definition

| 重新 chongxin "again" | chóngxīn 副 (1) 再一次：~抄写一遍。 Zaiyici:~chaoxie yi bian. （2）表示从头另行开始（变更方式或内容）：~部署｜~做人。 biaoshi cong tou lingxing kaishi(biangeng fangshi huo neirong):~bushu / ~zuo ren. | (1)definition with synonym (2)definition with synonym | chóng xīn 從頭開始，再一次。初刻拍案驚奇 卷十九：「獻神初畢，就將福物收去，整理一整理，重新擺出來。」Congtou kaishi,zaiyici.chukepaianjingqi.ju anshijiu: 「xianshen yibi,jiu jiang fuwu shouqu,zhengli yi zhengli,chongxin bai chulai.」 | compositional definition (morpheme definition+definitio n with synonym ） |
| 不要 buyao "don't" | bùyào 副 表示禁止和劝阻：~大声喧哗|~麻痹大意。 Biaoshi jinzhi he quanzu:~dasheng xuanhua / ~mabi dayi. | explanatory definition | buù yào（1）禁戒之詞。如：「不要動」。 Jinjie zhi ci.ru: 「buyao dong」. （2）不可。有委婉勸阻的意思。如：「大哥，我的話不要忘了。」buke.you weiwan quanzu de yisi. ru: 「dage,wode hua buyao wang le.」 | (1)explanatory definition (2)compositional definition (definition with synonym+explanat ory definition) |

As can be seen from table 3, "*zhiguan*" has two items in *Xianhan*, namely "*jinguan*"(despite) and "*zhigu*"(only). In *Guoyu*, the two items of *Xianhan* are contained in the item of "*zhigu、jin'guan*". "*Chongxin*"(again) is the same. The item "cong tou kaishi,zai yici"in *Guoyu* summed up "zaiyici"and"biaoshi cong tou ling xing kaishi(biangeng fangshi he neirong)"in Xianhan.

"*Zhiguan*" and "*chongxin*", although both of them are two items correspond to a single item, the interpretation methods of them are different. The explanation mode of "*chongxin*" is defined as explanatory definition and definition with synonym in *Xianhan*, which add up to compositional definition in *Guoyu*. The interpretation mode is two corresponding to one.

The item"*biaoshi jinzhi he quanzu*"(expressing prohibition and discouraging) of "*buyao*"(do not) in *Xianhan* summed up the"*jinjie zhi ci*"(Forbidden words)and "*buke. You weiwan quanzu de yisi.*"(do not. There is a euphemism for discouraging) in *Guoyu*. The corresponding situation of the item amount and interpretation mode is one corresponding to two.

3.2   An Item Corresponds to An Item（334）

By an item corresponding to an item is meant that in the common entry of *Xianhan* and *Guoyu*, one of their meanings is explained by only one item, therefore, the corresponding interpretation is also a one-to-one situation (without considering the different interpretations contained in the compositional definition). This type of corresponding interpretation is the most common one with the number greater than 30.

According to the statistical analysis, there are several corresponding situations in which the meanings of items which in *Xianhan* and *Guoyu* are the same or similar (The former is the interpretation mode of *Xianhan* and the latter is the interpretation mode of *Guoyu*):

3.2.1   Definition with Synonym<=>Definition with Synonym

Ninety-seven items which have similar meanings are explained by definition with synonym in

Xianhan and *Guoyu*. Definition with synonym is the most commonly used interpretation mode of the same adverb in *Xianhan* and *Guoyu*.

Table 4. definition with synonym<=>definition with synonym in *Xianhan* and *Guoyu*

Explanation mode in *Xianhan*		Explanation mode in *Guoyu*	Frequency	Percentage	Sub-total Frequency	Percentage
Definition with synonym	Single synonyms for interpretation	Single synonyms for interpretation	20	20.6	48	49.5
		Multiple synonyms for interpretation	28	28.9		
	Multiple synonyms for interpretation	Single synonyms for interpretation	10	10.3	42	43.3
		Multiple synonyms for interpretation	32	33.0		
Gloss for additional meaning		Single synonyms for interpretation	5	5.2	7	7.2
		Multiple synonyms for interpretation	1	1.0		
		Gloss for additional meaning	1	1.0		
		Total	97	100	97	100

It can be seen from table 4 that 90 items which have similar meanings are explained respectively by definition with synonym in *Xianhan* and *Guoyu*. No matter what kind of synonyms are used, the definitions of these adverbs are mostly the same. The difference lies in the special words used in dictionary. For example, in "Single synonyms for interpretation<=>Single synonyms for interpretation":

- 【将】《现汉》：将要。　　《国语》：快要。
  【jiang】Xianhan: jiangyao　　　Guoyu: kuaiyao
  "will   xianhan: be about to　　guoyu: be going to"
- 【大都】《现汉》：大多。　　《国语》：大多數。
  【dadou】Xianhan: daduoGuoyu: daduoshu
  "mostly, Xianhan: for the most part　　Guoyu: the bulk"

"Jiang" in "jiangyao" and "kuai" in "kuaiyao" have similar meanings and they all indicate the imminent time, "daduoshu" adds a "shu" to "daduo" and emphasizes the number.

3.2.2   Explanatory Definition<=>Definition with Synonym

By "explanatory definition<=>definition with synonym" is meant that the same adverbial item is explained by explanatory definition in *Xianhan*, and is explained by explanatory definition in *Guoyu*. There are 57 adverbs in *Xianhan* and *Guoyu* that use this form of interpretation mode.

Table 5. explanatory definition<=>definition with synonym in *Xianhan* and *Guoyu*

Explanation mode in Xianhan	Explanation mode in Guoyu	Frequency	Percentage
Single synonyms for interpretation	Single synonyms for interpretation	26	45.6
	Multiple synonyms for interpretation	31	54.4
Total		57	100

As can be seen from table 5, "explanatory definition<=>multiple synonyms for interpretation" more than "explanatory definition<=> single synonyms for interpretation". This is because multiple synonyms for interpretation in *Guoyu* are much more than single synonyms for interpretation. Therefore, when compared with different interpretation mode, the number of multiple synonyms for interpretation is more than single synonyms for interpretation.

3.2.3   Explanatory Definition <=>Explanatory Definition   （46）

The frequency of this combination of interpretation methods is 46. They are used to explain the usage of words and make interpretation more concrete.

> • 【凡是】《现汉》：总括某个范围内的一切。   《国语》：屬於某範圍的一切。
> 【*fanshi*】《*Xianhan*》：*zongkuo mouge fanwei nei de yiqie.*
>   "*Xianhan: Sum up everything within a certain scope.*"
> 《*Guoyu*》：*shuyu mou fanwei nei de yiqie.*
>   "*Guoyu: All that belongs to a certain sphere.*"

3.3   A Brief Summery

Firstly, explanatory definition, definition with synonym and compositional definition are the main explanation modes of adverbs in *Xianhan* and *Guoyu*. One kind of interpretation method often fails to clarify the usage and meaning of adverbs. According to different adverbs, flexibly choosing two or several kinds of interpretation ways to complement each other is what should be paid attention to in lexicographic editing.

Secondly, definition with synonym<=>definition with synonym has an absolute advantage over all the other interpretation modes, explanatory definition<=>definition with synonym is the second. We should pay more attention to the grammatical relation expressed by adverbs when compiling a dictionary. In explaining adverbs, we should choose the interpretation mode that can express the usages of adverbs and their grammatical functions better.

Thirdly, *Xianhan* is inferior to *Guoyu*in in comprehensive interpretation of some adverb meanings. The reason lies in that besides explain the meanings of the current modern Chinese language, *Guoyu* also contains some items that are often used in ancient Chinese but are not used or seldom used in modern times. As a modern Chinese learning tool in the mainland, *Xianhan* serves as an important tool in transmitting modern cultural civilization. At the same time, we should pay attention to the inheritance of the traditional culture. Some words and sentences should be included to cater for the needs of the times and changes.

4   Conclusion

Both *Xianhan* and *Guoyu* are the most popular and representative dictionaries in mainland and Taiwan respectively and they also have differences. This paper makes a comparative study in terms of explanation mode. We hope that our research can provide a beneficial assistance in the fields of lexicography, the exchange of language cultures across the Straits and Chinese processing. Due to limitation in length, this paper only gives a descriptive analysis. The reasons that cause the similarities and differences of the definitions in the two dictionaries and the practical application of these similarities and differences of the definitions in language and cultural communication and information processing will be the focus of further research.

References

1. Beijing language and culture university Chinese proficiency test center. HSK syllabus. Beijing: Modern press, 1998.
2. Jianhua Huang. On Dictionaries. [M]. Shanghai:Shanghai Lexicographical Press, 2001.
3. Baorong Su. The study of word meaning and the definition of dictionary. [M]. Beijing; commercial press, 2000.
4. Mingyang Hu . Manual of Lexicography[M]. Beijing：Renmin University of China press，1982.
5. Wei Liu, Zhiyi Zhang. A study of definition with synonym of the Dictionary of Contemporary Chinese (the 6th Edition). Lexicographical Studies,2015,(01):19-28+9.
6. The Dictionary of Mandarin (Revised Edition)[OL].[1994]. http:// dicit.revised.moe.edu.tw.
7. Borong Huang, Xudong Liao. The Dictionary of Contemporary Chinese [M]. Beijing：Higher Education Press, 1997.
8. Jun Liu , Dekuan Xu , Mengjia Ma, Shumei Chen.A Comparative Study on the Definition of verbs-- Taking the Dictionary of Contemporary Chinese (the 6th Edition) and the Dictionary of Mandarin (Revised Edition) as examples[J]. Chinese Journal of information,2014,(01):94-99.
9. Yunqin Sun. The study of explanation of adverb in active Chinese foreign learners' dictionaries ——take three active Chinese foreign learners' dictionaries for example. [J]. Yantai: 2012.
10. Yemei Zhang. Study of paraphrase of polysyllable adverbs in Modern Chinese Directory. [J]. Yantai. 2008.

Temporal Behavior of Temporal Modifiers and Its Implications:

The Case of *běnlái* and *yuánlái* in Mandarin Chinese

Wu, Jiun-Shiung

Institute of Linguistics, National Chung Cheng University
168, University Road, Minhsiung, Chiayi County, Taiwan
Lngwujs@ccu.edu.tw

Abstract In this paper, I argue that contrast is an essential and indispensable part of the semantics of *běnlái* and *yuánlái*, in addition to the temporal semantics argued in [1] and [2], based on the discourse function of these two temporal mdofiers. Due to the close interaction between lexical semantics and discourse function, I propose that examining a lexical entry in discourse will give us a more complete and satisfactory picture of the semantics of the lexical entry.

keywords: benlai, yuanlai, lexical semantics, discourse function, temporality

1   Introduction

Examining the semantics of a lexical item, many linguists focus, alone, on the sentences where the lexical item appears and proceed accordingly. While this approach seems reasonable, I would like to argue that research on lexical semantics needs to go beyond the sentence level. Moreover, I argue that the effect of a lexical entry on the inter-sentential relation, i.e. discourse relations or rhetorical relations in terms of [3], [4], [5], [6], etc., plays a significant role in accurately and completely understanding the semantics of the lexical entry.

I base my argument on the temporal/discourse function of two temporal modifiers in Chinese: *běnlái* and *yuánlái*. In a series of research on temporal relations in Mandarin Chinese (hereafter, Chinese), e.g. [7], [8], [9], [10], [11], etc., I argue that a lexical entry influences the temporal relation between two sentences/clauses indirectly through rhetorical relations, based on the semantics of the lexical entry, following [3]'s proposal that the temporal relation between two sentences is determined by the rhetorical relation connecting these two sentences.

[1] proposes a temporal semantics for *běnlái*. [2] revises the temporal semantics for *běnlái* proposed in [1] and suggests a temporal semantics for *yuánlái* when it is not interchangeable with *běnlái*. Since *běnlái* and *yuánlái* have temporal semantics, following the lines of [7], [8], [9], [10], [11], etc., it seems reasonable to suggest that a sentence/clause containing *běnlái/yuánlái* serves as a temporal background for another clause. However, the examination of the Sinica Corpus data reveals otherwise. If it

© Springer International Publishing AG 2018
Y. Wu et al. (Eds.): CLSW 2017, LNAI 10709, pp. 86–96, 2018.
https://doi.org/10.1007/978-3-319-73573-3_7

is on the right track that the semantics of a lexical entry influences the temporal/discourse function of the clause with the lexical entry, then, to provide a complete semantics for *běnlái* and *yuánlái*, their discourse function should be taken into consideration.

This paper is organized as follows. In Section Two, I report descriptive studies on *běnlái* and the temporal semantics of *běnlái* and *yuánlái* proposed in [2] and [1]. In Section Three, I present data retrieved from the Sinica Corpus to demonstrate the discourse functions of these two modifiers. I also discuss the implications of the discourse function of *běnlái* and *yuánlái*. Section Four concludes this paper.

2   Temporal Semantics of *běnlái* and *yuánlái*

There are abundant descriptive studies on *běnlái*, e.g. [12], [13], [14], [15], [16], [17], etc. Basically, all of these studies agree that *běnlái* expresses contrast, even for *běnlái jiù*, which seems to show no contrast at all. See the examples below.

(1)   a. Zhāngsān běnlái hěn xǐhuān Xiǎoměi.
          Zhangsan BĚNLÁI very like   Xiaomei
          'Zhangsan previously liked Xiaomei very much.'
       b. Zhāngsān běnlái jiù hěn xǐhuān Xiǎoměi, (xiànzài gèng xǐhuān le[1]).
          Zhangsan BĚNLÁI JIÙ very like   Xiaomei (now   more like Prc
          'It has long been the case that Zhangsan likes Xiaomei. (Now, he likes her more.)'

The literature such as [12], [13], [14], [15], [16], [17], and so on, suggest that (1a) shows a contrast between Zhangsan not liking Xiaomei and Zhangsan liking Xiaomei. Moreover, (1b) is also suggested to show a contrast: a contrast in the degree how much Zhangsan likes Xiaomei.

While these studies can explain the semantic behavior of *běnlái*, they share a major problem: if *běnlāi* expresses contrast, how can it be distinguished from other discourse connectives serving a similar function, such as *dànshì* 'but', *dàn* 'but', *què* 'but', etc.?

[1] discusses the semantics of *běnlái*. *Běnlái* is interesting in that it can describe a proposition which was true at a past time and is not true at a later time or a proposition which was true at a past time and remains true at a later time.

Let's look at (1). In (1a), *běnlái* indicates that the (tenseless) proposition *Zhangsan like linguistics* was true at a past time but is not true at a later time, presumably the speech time. On the other hand, in (1b), *běnlái* describes that the proposition *Zhangsan like linguistics* was true at a past time and remains true at a later time. (1b) needs

---

[1]   The abbreviations used in this paper include: ASSO for an associative marker, CL for a classifier, Disp for a disposal marker, PASS for a passive marker, Pfv for a perfective aspect marker, Prc for a sentential particle, Prg for a progressive aspect maker, Q for an interrogative marker.

to be uttered in a context where it can be inferred or understood that the proposition *Zhangsan like linguistics* was not true at a past time.

Given the diverse temporal readings expressed by *běnlái*, a reasonable question to ask is whether *běnlái* has a unified semantics. [1] argues that *běnlái* has a unified semantics and propose the following:

(2)   *běnlái(p)* is true at a time t iff $\exists t'$, $t' \prec t$, p is true at t' and whether p is true at the time of utterance depends on whether contrastive information is available concerning whether p holds at different times.

[2] finds that *yuánlái* is interchangeable with *běnlái* in some cases to express readings as discussed for (1), and not in the others. When *yuánlái* cannot substitute for *běnlái*, it expresses 'it turn out that'. See the example below.

(3)   Zhāngsān   yuánlái   xǐhuān   yǔyánxué!
       Zhangsan   YUÁNLÁI   like   linguistics
       'It turns out that Zhansan likes linguistics!'

Yuánlái in (3) indicates that the speaker acquires a new piece of information: Zhangsan likes linguistics. When uttering this sentence, the speaker either assumes that the proposition *Zhangsan like linguistics* was not true at a past time or at least was not aware of it being true. Since *yuánlái* in (3) describes acquiring new information, the sentence usually expresses a surprise for the speaker.

[2] summarizes the temporal readings of *běnlái* and *yuánlái* as follows. *Běnlái* can express two temporal readings: (i) a proposition p was true at a past time, but not true at the speech time, and (ii) p was true at a past time and remains true at the speech time. In addition to the two temporal readings shared with *běnlái*, *yuánlái* has a third one: (iii) p was not true or at least was not known to be true at a past time and is (known to be) true at the speech time.

Based on the above summary, [2] proposes that *běnlái* allows for one-way contrast while *yuánlái* two-way, as shown below:

(4)

	Past time	Speech time
běnlái	+	−
yuánlái	+	−
	−/?	+

(4) says the following. In addition to the reading where a proposition was true and remains true, *běnlái* shows one-way contrast: true at a past time and false at the speech time, whereas for *yuánlái* the contrast is two-way: true at a past time and false at the speech time or vice versa. But, note that here contrast here actually refers to different truth values of a proposition at different time intervals.

In sum, [1] and [2] focus on the temporal semantics of *běnlái* and *yuánlái* and argue for a semantics based on the truth of a proposition at different time intervals.

While [1] and [2] mention contrast, much more attention is paid to different truth values of a proposition at different times.

3   Temporal Relations Revealed by *běnlāi* and *yuánlái*

In this section, I discuss the temporal relations between a sentence/clause with *běnlái/yuánlái* and another sentence/clause. [3] argue that temporal relations are determined by rhetorical relations. That is, rhetorical relations come before temporal relations. Following this idea, I show that, instead of *Background*, *běnlái* and *yuánlái* specify *Contrast* as their default rhetorical relation. As for the unique reading of *yuánlái*, a sentence/clause with *yuánlái* of this reading indicates *Explanation*. Other rhetorical relations are possible, as long as there is an explicit indication in the context, e.g. a cue phrase, an observable relation between situations, etc.

As argued in [7], [8], [9], [10], [11], which follows [3]'s proposal that temporal relations are determined by rhetorical relation, the semantics of a lexical item, such as aspect markers or modal expressions, or of a situation, such as a telic one or an atelic one, indicates a default rhetorical relation. Let's look at two examples.

(5)   a. Suǒzhǎng Guō Fēngmù shuài yuánjǐng gǎnfù xiànchǎng,
       Lt.   Guo Fengmu lead   police   rush.to scene
       'Lt. Guo led police officers and rushed to the scene.'
    b. yòng dāngjià jiāng shāngzhě táiddào gōnglù pang,
       use stretcher Disp wounded carry.to road side
       '(they) carried the wounded, with stretchers, to the side of the road.'
    c. yóu jiùhùchē sòng yī   jíjiù.
       by ambulance send hospital E.R.
       '(the wounded) were sent to the E.R. by ambulances.'

In (5), there is no cue phrases or other information to decide the temporal relations between the clauses. The situation types kick in to help with the decision. The situation types of the events described by (5a, b) are both telic. Since a telic event is inherently specified to come to an end, it is only natural for another event to occur after a telic event. Hence, as argued in [7], a telic event is defeasibly connected to a following clause by *Narration*, which indicates that the temporal sequence of events matches the order of their descriptions. That is, for (5), because there is no information specifying an appropriate rhetorical relation to connect the clauses, (5a) is connected, by *Narration*, to (5b), which in turns is attached to (5c) by the same rhetorical relation. Based on the temporal relation indicated by *Narration*, (5a) occurs before (5b), which in turns occurs before (5c). This result is consistent with native speakers' intuition of the temporal relations manifested in this example. This is how the semantics (event structure) of a telic event helps to determine a rhetorical relation.

Another example demonstrates how an atelic eventuality behaves in terms of rhetorical relations and temporal relations. See below.

(6)   a. Xiǎomíng zài yóuyòng.
          Xiaoming Prg swim
          'Xiaoming was swimming.'
       b. Xiǎohuá kàndǎo le.
          Xiaohua see   Prc
          'Xiaohua saw (that).'
       c. rěnbùzhù jiāo-le   tā jǐ   zhāo.
          can't.help teach-Pfv he a.few move
          '(Xiaohua) couldn't help but teach him a few moves.'

(6a) is atelic because the event is presented by the progressive aspect marker *zài*. An progressive event such as (6a) describes an ongoing event, which has not come to an end yet. Hence, such an event can only provide the time when the event is ongoing for another situation. Therefore, [8] argues that a progressive event is by default connected to a following clause by *Background*, which indicates temporal overlapping. Because there is no information revealing what rhetorical relation connects the clauses in (6), the default rule for a progressive event argued in [8] applies. (6b, c) are attached to (6a) by *Background*, which specifies that the events described by (6b, c) temporally overlap with (6a).

Given the studies on the temporal relations in Chinese, such as [7], [8], [9], [10], [11], since *běnlái* and *yuánlái* are argued to have temporal semantics, as in [1] and [2], it is reasonable if *běnlái* and *yuánlái* indicate, as a default rhetorical relation, *Background*, which specifies that a sentence/clause provides a temporal frame in which another sentence/clause occurs.

However, the data retrieved from the Sinica Corpus suggest otherwise. I find that, when *běnlái* and *yuánlái* are interchangeable, a clause with one of the two temporal modifiers is defeasibly connected by *Contrast* to another one. That is, when there is no indication at all, *běnlái/yuánlái* indicate *Contrast*. Let's look at a few examples.

(7)   a. Wǒ běnlái/yuánlái   méi yǒu shíyù,
          I   BĚNLÁI/YUÁNLÁI not have appetite
          'I previously did not have any appetite.'
       b. Jīng tá yì tíxǐng, jiāshàng fàncài xiāngwèi, tūrán   ràng wǒ
          after she one remind plus   food   fragrance suddenly make I
          jī'ènánnài.
          starving
          'Her reminder and the fragrance of food suddenly made me starving.'
(8)   a. Dāngdì shíwù zài   nánchī dōu chī.
          Local   food   however nasty all eat
          'As for local food, however nasty it tastes, I eat them anyway.'
       b. Xiàng qǐshì, wǒ běnlái/yuánlái   pèng dōu bú pèng, xiànzài
          like   cheese I BĚNLÁI/YUÁNLÁI touch all not touch now
          gānzhīrúyí.
          taste.as.good.as.candy
          'Such as cheese, I previously did not even touch it. But, now, it tastes as

good as good as candy.'
(9)   a. Shān   lǐ běnlái jiù hěn nán   jiàodào jìchéngchē.
         mountain in BĚNLÁI JIÙ very difficult call   taxi
         'It has been very difficult to get a taxi in the mountain.'
      b. hékuàng   shì yèlǐ ne?
         not.to.mention be   night Q
         'Not to mention (how difficult it is to get one) at night.'

In examples such as (7) and (8), *běnlái* and *yuánlái* indicate that the clause containing one of the two temporal modifiers is connected to another clause/sentence by *Contrast*. Because there is no information in the context to specify so, *Contrast* is the default rhetorical relation specified by *běnlái* and *yuánlái*. As proposed in [12], *běnlái jiù* shows a contrast in degree, which can be observed in (9), where the degree of difficulty is contrasted. Again, there is no indication for *Contrast* in this discourse.

[3] propose the *Contrast* does not specify a temporal relation. In (7)-(9), the temporal semantics of *běnlái* and *yuánlái* kicks in and help to identify an appropriate temporal relation. Given the temporal semantics of *běnlái* and *yuánlái*, what is contrasted with the proposition taken by the temporal modifiers is true at a later time. This is an accurate description of the temporal relations in (7)-(9).

As mentioned in Section Two, *yuánlái* has a unique reading, which *běnlái* does not share, i.e. the *it turn out that* reading. [2] also gives it a temporal reading: a proposition was known to be false (or at least was unknown to be true) at a past time, but is known to be true at a later time.

But, this unique reading of *yuánlái* does not enable a sentence/clause with this *yuánlái* to serve as a temporal background. Instead, such a sentence is by default connected to another sentence/clause by *Explanation*! Let's look at an example.

(10)   a. Wǒ wěndào yì-gǔ shāo jīmáo- de   wèidào.
          I   smell one-CL burn chicken.hair- ASSO smell
          'I smelled burned chicken hair.'
       b. zhēng yǎn yí kàn,
          open   eye one look
          '(I) opened my eyes and took a look.'
       c. yuánlái   shì Báibǐ-de   tóufà bèi lúhuǒ   shāozháo le.
          YUÁNLÁI be Baibi-ASSO   hair PASS stove.fire burn   Prc
          'It turned out that Baibi's hair was burned by the stove fire.'

In (10), (10c) explains (10a) because (10c) CAUSEs (10a). That is, to put it in [3]'s terms, (10a) is connected to (10c) by *Explanation*, because of the CAUSE relationship between these two situations. Again, there is no information in the discourse indicate this rhetorical relation and therefore I argue that *Explanation* is the default rhetorical relation specified by *yuánlái*, when it expresses *it turn out that*.

The reason why *yuánlái* of this reading indicate *Explanation* is because in this usage *yuánlái* emphasizes on finding *new* information. Finding new information naturally can help to explain what has happened previously. Moreover, [3] suggests that for

Explanation the result cannot occur before the cause. Hence, for (10), (10c) cannot occur before (10a, b). This inference matches native speakers' intuition about (10).

Běnlái and *yuánlái* are compatible with other rhetorical relations if explicit information in the discourse specifies so. Let's look at a few examples.

(11) a. Rìběn   zhèngfǔ   zài èrcìdàzhàng cǎi   nánjìn   zhèngcè.
      Japan government at WWII   adopt south.ward policy
      'The Japanese government adopted a south-ward policy at WWII.'
   b. Suǒyǐ zǒngdūfǔ   běnlái/yuánlái   yào shèzāi   Kaohsiung
      so   governor.office BĚNLÁI/YUÁNLÁI will located.at Kaohsiung
      Dàbèi.
      Dabei
      'The governor's office previously would be located at Dabei,
      Kaohsiung.'

(12) Rúguǒ   tā běnlái/yuánlái   xǐhuān yǔyánxué, huòxǔ kěyǐ
     if   he BĚNLÁI/YUÁNLÁI like   linguistics maybe can
     wènwèn wèisheme bù xǐhuān le.
     ask   why   not like   Prc
     'If he previously like linguistics, maybe we can ask why he does not
     like linguistics   now.'

(13) a. Yuánlái Lǎozhāng zài jiǎnféi.
      yuánlái Lazhang Prg lose.weight
      'It turns out that Laozhang is trying to lose weight.'
   b. Nánguài   tā zuìjin chī-de-shǎo.
      no.wonder he recently eat-DE-little
      'No wonder he recently eats little.'

In (11), (11b) is connected to (11a) by *Result*, which is decided by the cue phrase *suǒyǐ* 'so'. For *Result*, again, the result cannot occur before the cause. That is, the cause cannot occur before the result, i.e. (11b) cannot occur before (11a). The two clauses in the conditional (12) are connected by *Defeasible Consequence*, which is specified by the connective *rúguǒ* 'if'. For *Defeasible Consequence*, a premise must hold before the consequent. Hence, the *if* clause must hold before the matrix clause in (12). (13a) and (13b) are attached together by *Result*, because of *nánguài* 'no wonder', which indicate a result of natural consequences. In this examples, the temporal relations between the clauses do not contradict the one encoded by the temporal semantics of *běnlái* and *yuánlái* and hence are allowed by these two temporal modifiers.

In short, (11) to (13) show that *běnlái* and *yuánlái* are compatible with rhetorical relations other than the default ones they specified, as long as there is explicit information in the discourse indicating so and these rhetorical relations do not specify a temporal relation contradictory.

Following [3], [7], [8], [9], [10], [11], I propose two default rules to determine the rhetorical relations for *běnlái* and *yuánlái* and a temporal constraint on rhetorical relations that connect clauses with *běnlái* or *yuánlái*.

(14) a. $(?(\alpha, \beta, \lambda) \wedge$ *běnlái/yuánlái*$(p)(\alpha)) > Contrast(\alpha, \beta, \lambda)$
      b. $(?(\alpha, \beta, \lambda) \wedge$ *yuánlái*$(p)(\alpha)) > Explanation(\alpha, \beta, \lambda)$
      c. (*běnlái/yuánlái*$(p)(\alpha) \wedge R(\alpha, \beta, \lambda)) \rightarrow \neg(\beta \prec \alpha)$

(14) are based on the formalism proposed in [3]. α and β are labels for sentences. λ is the label for the (mini-)discourse consisted of α and β. $?(\alpha, \beta, \lambda)$ represents an underspecified rhetorical relation. That is, α and β are connected together to form a (mini-)discourse labeled as λ. But, it is underspecified which rhetorical relation connects α to β, represented by ?. > stands for a defeasible inference. Now, we can explain what (14a, b, c) mean.

(14a) says that: if α is connected to β by an underspecified rhetorical relation and α is presented by *běnlái* or *yuánlái* (i.e. the examples where *běnlái* and *yuánlái* are interchangeable), then by default it is *Contrast* that connects α to β.

(14b) says that: if α is attached to β by an underspecified rhetorical relation and α is presented by *yuánlái* (i.e. the examples where *běnlái* and *yuánlái* are not interchangeable), then it is defeasibly *Explanation* that attaches α to β.

(14c) represents the temporal constraint for *běnlái* and *yuánlái*, when they are interchangeable. It says that: if α is a sentence containing *běnlái* or *yuánlái* and α is connected to β by a rhetorical relation R to form a (mini-)discourse λ, then β cannot occur in the past of α.

The research on the temporal behavior of *běnlái* and *yuánlái* reveals several interesting points. First, while *běnlái* and *yuánlái* are proposed to have temporal semantics, as in [1] and [2], contrast is also an essential part of the semantics of these two temporal modifiers. Second, when rhetorical relations do not determine a temporal relation, such as *Contrast*, the temporal semantics of *běnlái* and *yuánlái* kick in and help to decide a temporal relation. Third, *běnlái* and *yuánlái* are compatible with rhetorical relations other than their default ones, as long as these rhetorical relations specify a temporal relation convergent with the temporal semantics of these two temporal modifiers.

A very interesting point about the discourse function of *běnlái* and *yuánlái* is that they indicate *Contrast*, rather than *Background*, as their default rhetorical relation, even though they are proposed to describe the different truth values of a proposition at different times.

[7], [8], [9], [10], [11] argue that the semantics of a lexical item or of a situation influences temporal relations indirectly through rhetorical relations in two ways: First, a default rhetorical relation is identified so that a temporal relation is decided by the rhetorical relation. Second, a constraint is put on what rhetorical relation is compatible.

Since the data under examination show that *Contrast* is the default rhetorical relation specified by *běnlái* and *yuánlái*, it is insufficient to consider the different truth values of a proposition at different times, concerning the semantics of these two temporal modifiers.

Instead, contrast must be taken into consideration and be identified as an indispensable part of the semantics of *běnlái* and *yuánlái*. Otherwise, it would be extremely difficult to explain the discourse behavior of these two temporal modifiers.

[18], [19], [20], [21], etc. propose dynamic semantics, where semantics is no longer truth-condition, but context-change potential (CCP). That is, the semantics of a proposition is how the proposition changes the information state of the speaker and the addressee. [22] proposes a theory that can model discourse. [3] takes a step further and take discourse relations and discourse structure into consideration. These studies emphasize on the importance and necessity to consider context effects when examining semantics.

My proposal is more conservative. While dynamic semantics has attracted the attention of many semanticists in the last two decades, it still requires more study to know to what extent semantics is dynamic. That is, does every lexical item require dynamic semantics? Much attention has been devoted to modal expression, such as [20], [21], [23], etc. How about other lexical entries?

Although I agree with the ideas of dynamic semantics, I would like to drawn a more conservative conclusion from the research on the semantics of *běnlái* and *yuánlái* and on their discourse/temporal behavior. If the proposal is on the right track that the semantics of a lexical entry affects temporal relations through rhetorical relations, then, in order to get a complete, satisfactory picture of the semantics of *běnlái* and *yuánlái*, it is mandatory to take their default discourse function, i.e. contrast, into consideration. Otherwise, it would be difficult to explain how these two temporal modifiers behave in terms of the specification of default rhetorical relations. It may be insufficient to explore lexical semantics solely based on how a lexica entry behaves with the boundary of a sentence. Looking at how a lexical entry behaves in discourse may shed more light on its lexical semantics. Specifically, I argue that a satisfactory examination of lexical semantics cannot be achieved without taking rhetorical relations into consideration.

4   Conclusion

In this paper, I argue that contrast is an essential and indispensable part of the semantics of *běnlái* and *yuánlái*, in addition to the temporal semantics argued in [1] and [2], based on the discourse function of these two temporal modifiers. It has been demonstrated in [7, 8, 9, 10, 11] how lexical semantics influences discourse function/relation. When *běnlái* and *yuánlái* are interchangeable without affecting the reading of the sentence, the sentence is connected to its neighboring one by *Contrast* (and possibly another appropriate rhetorical relation). While *yuánlái* denotes 'it turn out that', the sentence where *yuánlái* is located is attached to an adjacent one by *Explanation*. While the temporal semantics of *běnlái/yuánlái* still help to determine or to set a constraint on the temporal relation between the sentence with *běnlái/yuánlái* and an adjacent one, their lexical semantics have a significant contribution to deciding what rhetorical relation connects the sentence with *běnlái/yuánlái* to its neighboring sentence. Due to the close interaction between lexical semantics and discourse function, I propose that examining a lexical entry in discourse will give us a more complete and satisfactory picture of the semantics of the lexical entry.

Acknowledgements

This study is part of the research financially supported by Ministry of Science and Technology under the contract number MOST 104-2410-H194-066. I am grateful to my research assistants Hsuan-hsiang Wang and Yi-ling Su for their assistance in conducting this research. I also thank anonymous reviewers and the audience of CLSW 2017 for enlightening comments and discussions. All remaining errors are mine.

References

1. Wu, J-S, Kuo J Y-C (2012) *Benlai* as a Relative Past Marker – Contrastive Semantics, Anchor Time and Discontinuity Readings. Language and Linguistics 13: 351-389
2. Wu, J-S (2012) One-way Contrast vs. Two-way Contrast: On the Semantics of *běnlái* and *yuánlái* in Mandarin Chinse. Cahiers de Linguistique- Asie Orientale 41: 163-271
3. Asher, N, Lascarides, A (2003) Logics of Conversation. Cambridge University Press, Cambridge
4. Mann, WC, Thompson, SA (1988) Rhetorical Structure Theory: toward a functional theory of text organization. Text 8:243-281
5. Taboada, M, Mann, WC (2006a) Rhetorical Structure Theory: looking back and moving ahead. Discourse Studies 8: 423–459
6. Taboada, M, Mann, WC (2006b) Applications of Rhetorical Structure Theory. Discourse Studies 8: 567–587
7. Wu, JS (2007a) Temporal and Atemporal Relations in Mandarin. Taiwan Journal of Linguistics Monograph Series No. 2. Crane Publishing Company, Taipei
8. Wu, JS (2007b) Semantic Difference between the Two Imperfective Markers in Mandarin and Its Implications on Temporal Relations. Journal of Chinese Linguistics 35: 372-398
9. Wu, JS (2009) Aspectual Influence on Temporal Relations: A Case Study of the Experiential *Guo* in Mandarin. Taiwan Journal of Linguistics 7: 1-24
10. Wu, JS (2010) Interactions between Aspect and Temporal Relations: A Case Study of the Perfective *le*. Language and Linguistics 11: 65-98
11. Wu, JS (2011) How *Jingran* and *Guoran* Influence Temporal Relations in Mandarin Chinese: A Case of Semantics-Pragmatics Interface. International Journal of Asian Language Processing 21: 161-184
12. Fan, SY (2001) Xiandai hanyu "...benlai jiu...' geshi tanjiu [Studies in the grammatical pattern of *benlai jiu* in Modern Chinese]. Nanjing shida xuebao [Journal of Nanjing Normal University], Year 2001, Issue 1: 120-124
13. Mao, X, Li, L, Jiao, HY (2008) 'Benlai' yu 'yuanlai' zuo xingrongci de yongfa tantao [An exploration on the adjective usages of *benlai* and *yuanlai*]. Wenjiao ziliao [Information on Literacy Education] 444: 276-278

14. Zhang, J (2006) "Benlai" he "yuanlai" de yongfa bijiao [A comparison on the usage of *benlai* and *yuanlai*]. *Yuyan wenzi yingyong* [Applied Linguistics], Year2006, Issue S2.
15. Zhao, CQ (2007) Benlai he yuanlai de qubie [The distinction between *benlai* and *yuanlai*]. *Lilunjie* [Theory Horizon], Year 2007, Issue 11: 216-217
16. Zhu, XJ (2008) "*benlai*" de yufahua [Grammaticalization of *benlai*]. *Jiaozuo daxue xuebao* [Journal of Jiaozuo University], Year 2008, Issue 1: 21-23.
17. Zhu, XJ, Shu, YY (2007) "*benlai*" de yufahua [Grammaticalization of *benlai*]. *Keji wenhuai* [Technology and Culture], Year 2007, Issue 2: 38.
18. Groenendijk, J, Stokhof, M (1990) Dynamic Montague grammar. In Papers from the Symposium on Logic and Language. Eds. Kalman, L, Polos, L. Adak_emiai Kiad_o. Adakemiai Kiado, Budapest
19. Groenendijk, J, Stokhof, M (1991) Dynamic Predicate Logic. Linguistics and Philosophy 14: 39-100
20. Veltman, F (1996) Defaults in Update Semantics. Journal of Philosophical Logic 25: 221-261
21. Yalcin, S (2007) Epistemic Modals. Mind 116: 983-1026.
22. Kamp, H, Reyle, U (1993) From Discourse to Logic: Introduciton to Modeltheoretic Semantics of Natural Language, Formal Logic and Discourse Representation Theory. Kluwer, Dordrecht
23. Portner, P (2009) Modality. Oxford University Press, Oxford

Distributive Quantifier *měi* in Mandarin Chinese

Hua-Hung YUAN [1(✉)]

[1] Department of Applied Foreign Languages, National Taipei University of Business, Taiwan
`yuan.huahung@gmail.com`

Abstract. This paper aims to understand the function of the distributive quantifier *měi* (每) in the [*měi*-Numeral-NP V Numeral-NP] construction. *Měi* is viewed as a marker of plurality over plural entities, seen as a set denoted by Numeral-NP, and marks the sorting key for a distributive dependency in the sense of Choe (1987). Without *měi*, the structure [Numeral-NP V Numeral-NP] can induce either a distributive dependency or a proportional relation between the two numeral NPs. We account for the implausibility of the sequence [**měi-yī*-NP]. *Měi* involves the notion of unit, which is distinct from the notion of singular number expressed by the numeral *yī* 'one'.

Keywords. *měi* (每)· quantifier· distributivity · distributive dependency· Mandarin Chinese· plurality marker· unit· arithmetic value

1   Introduction: *měi* in Chinese

In this paper, we are interested in the distributive quantifier *měi* (每), especially when it quantifies over a nominal domain. It is often labelled as 'each' or 'every' in English. The quantifier *měi* can be situated along different positions in a sentence: within an NP/DP, or as a modifier to a VP or a CP. Within an NP/DP, *měi* is a determiner before a [Num[1]-Cl N] sequence, as in (1). *Měi* can also occur before a VP, specifically gé (隔), as in (2), and as a modifier to VP *féng* (逢) 'meet' in a CP, marked by a temporal subordinator (*de*)*shí*(*hòu*) ((的)時(候)) 'while', as in (3).

(1)   a. 每一個人都有一本書
      měi   yī-gè   rén   dōu yǒu yī-běn shū

---

[1]Abbreviations: Acc.: Accomplished aspect; Accus.: Accusative case; Cl: Classifier; de: relator *de* (的); loc.: Locative; M.O.: Marker of object *suǒ* (所); Neg.: Negation marker; Nom.: Nominative case; FP.: Final particle.

ⓒ Springer International Publishing AG 2018
Y. Wu et al. (Eds.): CLSW 2017, LNAI 10709, pp. 97–111, 2018.
https://doi.org/10.1007/978-3-319-73573-3_8

every one-Cl person all have one-Cl book
'Everyone has a book.'

b. 每三個學生交一份報告
měi   sān-gè   xuéshēng jiāo   yī-fèn   bàogào
every three-Cl student   hand in one-Cl report
' Students hand in a report per group of three.'

(2)   每隔三公尺
měi   gé   sān-gōngchǐ
every separate three meter
'every three meters'

(3)   每逢春節((的)時(候))
měi   féng chūnjiē   ((de)shí (hòu))
every meet spring festival while
'Every time when it is Chinese new year..,''

Here, we focus on the quantifier *měi* in a NP, especially *měi* alone, without the co-occurrence of *dōu* (都). When *měi* takes a numeral larger than one in the subject position of predicate, it has to co-occur with a numeral NP in the object position, as (1b) and (4) illustrate.

(4)   *每三個學生交報告
měi **sān-gè   xuéshēng jiāo   bàogào*
every three-Cl student   hand in report

1.1   Distributive quantifier *měi* in the literature

In the literature, distributive quantifier *měi* is considered as expressing distributivity between the NP subject and the NP object such as in Huang [1] (2005:35), Li [2] (1997:160), Lin [3] (1997:230) and Yuan [4] (2011:214), while some authors like Xing [5](2008:36) and Zhang [6] (2015:13) treat *měi* in this structure as a universal quantifier, which is the same as in *měi-dōu* construction (1a).

However, *měi* alone is distinct from *měi-dōu* construction. Li [2](1997:160) shows *měi* alone, with the meaning of *per* in English is used in different ways from *měi-dōu* co-occurrence in the following respects : (i) possible omission of *měi* (5a); (ii) its usage in a conditional sentence (5b); (iii) selection of a numeral larger than one to combine with *měi* (5c). Also, Lin [3] (1997:232-233) points out *měi* alone can be uttered in an imperative (5d).

(5)   a. (每)一棟房子(*都)賣二十萬   (example (42a) in (*ibid*:161))
       *(měi) yī-dòng fáng zǐ (*dōu) mài èrshí   wàn*
       every one-Cl house   all   sell twenty ten-thousand
       'Every house is sold at two hundred thousand.'

       b. (第一組有十個人)每個人抬兩個箱子，一共抬幾個箱子？
       (Dì-yī-zǔ yǒu shí-gè rén)   měi-gè rén tái liǎng-gè xiāngzǐ,
       First group have ten-Cl person every-Cl person carry two-Cl box
       yīgòng tái jǐ-gè xiāngzǐ?   (example (44) in (*ibid*:161))
       altogether carry how many-Cl box
       '(There are ten people in the first group.) Everyone carries two
       boxes. How many boxes can they carry?'

       c. 每五個孩子(*都)分一個西瓜   (example (45b) in Li [2] (*ibid*: 162), slightly
          touched) *měi wǔ-gè háizǐ   (*dōu) fēn   yī-gè   xīguā*
                   every five-Cl child   all   share one-Cl melon
                   'Every five children share one melon.'

       d. 每個人做一百下伏地挺身！   (example (48a) in Lin [3] (1997:232)
       měi-gè   rén   zuò yībǎi-xià   fúdìtǐngshēn !
       every-Cl person do one-hundred-Cl push-up
       'Everyone do one hundred push-ups!'

In addition, the VP in this *měi* construction cannot be suffixed by aspect
markers (6), which means this construction does not refer to episodic sentences, as indicate.

(6)   *昨天，**每三個**學生交了兩份報告
       zuótiān , měi sān-gè xuéshēng jiāo -le   liǎng-fèn bàogào*
       yesterday every three-Cl student hand in Acc. two-Cl   report
       Intended: 'Yesterday, each group of three students handed in two
       reports.'

Nevertheless, compared with (5a), even the omission of *měi* is possible but
the presence of *měi* makes (7) unacceptable. How do we account for (7)? Why
is it that *měi* cannot appear here?

(7)   (***每**)五顆蘋果賣 100 元
       (***měi) wǔ-kē píngguǒ mài 100 yuán*
       every   five-Cl apple   sell 100 dollar
       Without *měi*: 'The five apples are sold at 100 dollar.'

We think that the distributive relation between the two numeral NPs should be studied in more detail and explained in a systematic way.

1.2 Research question

We aim to analyze the function of the quantifier *měi* in the construction [*měi*-Num-NP V Num-NP]. How do we explain the quantifier *měi* in the above construction in terms of distributivity?

The distributivity expressed in the *měi* construction without *dōu* refers to the distributive relation between the numeral NP subject and the numeral NP object, one paired to another, as shown in Yuan [4] (2011:211). When the sentential negation operates over the construction (8a), according to its wide or narrow scope, it is either both the NP subject and the object that is negated or only the NP object that is negated, as in (8b).

(8)   a. 不是每個學生交兩份報告
     Bù shì měi gè xuéshēng jiāo   liǎng-fèn bàogào
     neg. be every Cl student   hand in two-Cl   report
     'It is not the case that every student hands in two reports.'

   b. 是每兩個交一份／是三份
     shì měi   liǎng-gè jiāo   yī-fèn / shì sān-fèn
     be every two-Cl hand in one-Cl   be three-Cl
     'It is not the case that each group of two (students) hands in one report./It is three reports (that should be handed in).'

We will analyze the type of distributivity involved in the *měi* construction according to the framework of Choe [7] (1987). In section 2, we will present the notion of distributive dependency in Choe [7](1987). In section 3, we will analyze the structure of [*měi*-Num-NP V Num-NP] and understand how the quantifier *měi* functions.

2 Choe (1987): Distributive dependency

We propose to analyze *měi* as a marker of plurality over NP, playing a role of sorting key in the sense of Choe [7] (1987). This will be shown in section 2.1. In section 2.2, we will show the notion of unit involved in the sorting key discussed in Choe [7] (1987) and relate it to our data in Chinese.

2.1 Conditions for the distributive dependency

Choe [7] (1987) points out that the distributive dependency relation is necessarily available between the two NPs when the two morphemes, NP-*ssik* in Korean (9a) and post-nominal *each* (9b) in English are used.

(9)   a. [Ai –tul – i]   [phwungsen-hana-**ssik**-ul] sa-ess-ta
          child Pl Nom ballon   one-*ssik*-Accus.- buy-past.
          'The children bought a balloon each.'   (Choe 1987:49 (8a))

      b. The children bought a balloon **each**.

Choe [8] (1987:31-32) claims: "the distributive dependency is defined to be a relation between (two) co-arguments. It consists of 'Sorting Key (SrtKy) and 'Distributed Share (DstrShr)." He describes the necessary conditions for the projection of a distributive dependency relation between co-arguments:

(10)   Conditions for distributive dependency
          (a) SrtKy is semantically plural.   (b) DstrShr is indefinite.
          (c) Accessibility of co-arguments, i.e., arguments of the same
          predicate, are accessible to each other for distributive dependency.
          (Choe [8]1987:99)

Choe [7] (1987:34) explains that the distributive dependency of the co-argument NPs in (8b) is brought about by the post-nominal *each*, which marks morphologically/syntactically DstrShr and there is a Srtky (i.e., a (distributive) antecedent) available in the given domain (i.e., among its co-arguments). In other words, when the two morphemes, NP-*ssik* in Korean (8a) or post-nominal *each* (8b) in English marks the SrtKy or the DstrShr, it means the NP subject or object denotes necessarily plural entities so that the distributive dependency is triggered. Choe [7] (1987:142) indicates that semantically plural, SrtKy denotes plural entities and these entities are viewed as a set of entities, which is seen as a unit (*i-part operation* in Choe [7] (1987)'s terminology) and a unit must be a singular entity. For example, in (8b), 'the children' denotes a plurality of children, which forms a unit/a set and this allows each child to be distributed over a balloon.

2.2   Unit in Srtky

The rule of a unit denoted by SrtKy being singular can be seen more clearly in the distributive relation in B *per* A construction in English. Choe [7] (1987:137) shows that B *per* A construction , like *one hat per child* in (11) is seen as realized distributivity, in which *one hat* and *a child* corresponds to DstrShr and SrtKy respectively. It's impossible that SrtKy takes two entities, like *per two children*.

(11)   The children bought **one hat per child** / *per <u>two</u> children yesterday.

However, Choe [7] (1987:142) indicates a counterexample in Korean, (12) which is equivalent to the *per* construction in English and in which a locative *–ey* marks SrtKy and the *–ssik*, distributive element marks DstrShr.

(12)   *Chwuyenca tul-I   twul-ey noray han-kok-**ssik**-ul pwul-ess-ta*
        Performer Pl-Nom. two-loc.-song-one-Cl- *ssik*-Accus. sing-past
        'The performers sang a song per group of two.'

Choe [7] (1987:142) cannot explain why the SrtKy, *twul-ey* 'two' in (12) violates the principle that the unit in SrtKy must be singular. Let's see the equivalent example in Chinese (13). Similar to a Korean case, *měi* is able to take two entities as a unit of SrtKy which triggers the distributivity between the DstrShr, *yī-shǒu gē* 'one song'.

(13)   歌手們**每**兩個人唱一首歌
        *Gēshǒu-men **měi**   liǎng-gè rén   chàng yī-shǒu gē*
        singer-Pl   every two-Cl   person sing   one-Cl song
        'Singers sang a song per group of two.'

How do we explain that in Chinese, the SrtKy marker can take a plural entity as a unit? We'll show in the next section our analysis on *měi*.

3   Our analysis

For us, under the framework of Choe [7] (1987), we can identify the quantifier *měi* as a SrtKy marker according to the conditions for a distributive dependency described in (10). In the next section, we will show how the quantifier *měi* is able to mark SrtKy.

3.1   *Měi* marks SrtKy

We claim that *měi* marks SrtKy because it pluralizes over a set which contains plural entities. This triggers necessarily the distributive dependency between the two Num-NPs in the structure [*měi* Num-NP V Num-NP].

Měi pluralizes over a set denoted by Num-NP. Without *měi* , the structure [Num-NP V Num-NP] can have two readings, distributive and non-distributive, as (14) illustrates. However, when *měi* is used, as in (1b), the NP subject denotes necessarily multiple sets of three entities, which means the distributive reading of the Num-NP subject.

(14)   三個學生交一份報告
        sān-gè   xuéshēng jiāo   yī-fèn bàogào
        three-Cl student   hand in one-Cl report
        (a) Distributive Reading: 'Students hand in a report per group of three.
        (b) Non-Distributive Reading: 'The three students are to hand in a report.'

In the following examples (15)-(17), *mĕi* aggregates plural entities expressed by a numeral larger than one into a single set, i.e a unit and *mĕi* multiplies a set of plural entities while without *mĕi*, the pluralization over the set is not necessarily induced by the structure.

(15) (每)五個同學用三隻筆
     (mĕi) wŭ-gè tóngxué yòng sān-zhī bĭ
     every five-Cl student use   three-Cl pen
     With *mei*: ' Each group of five students uses three pens.'
     Without *mĕi*: 'The five students use three pens (together).' (branching reading)

(16) (每)六公尺種一棵樹
     (mĕi) liù- gōngchĭ zhŏng yī-kē   shù
     every six meter   plant one-Cl tree
     With *mei*: ' There is a tree planted every six meters. (average reading)
     Without *mĕi*: 'Plant a tree every six meters.'

(17) (每)十個人中有三個人得流感
     (mĕi) shí-gè rén   zhōng yŏu sān-rén   dé liúgăn
     every ten-Cl person among have three person gain flu
     With *mei* : ' Three out of ten persons caught the flu. (average value)
     Without *mĕi*: 'There are three persons out of ten (of these people) who caught the flu.'

Therefore, following the framework of Choe [8] (1987), we can easily identify the quantifier *mĕi* as the SrtKy since it pluralizes over a set, seen as a unit containing plural entities denoted by the subject [*mĕi*-Num-NP]. The object [Num-NP] is indefinite, as an unmarked DstrShr. The subject NP is a co-argument with the NP object, as (5a)-(5c), (13), (15) and (17) illustrate.

Since the unit formed by Num-NP is viewed as singular, it can resolve the puzzle that Choe [8] (1987) had, which is the Korean SrtKy marked by *-ey* taking plural entities in it. A unit is always singular. We name it *singularity* of a unit.

We observe the structures appear in a conditional sentence, (18)-(19) where *mĕi* not only pluralizes over a unit of multiple entities but also enumerates those units. When *mĕi* is not used in (18)-(19), the pluralization of a unit of multiple entities is induced due to the presence of a total number, as a domain of quantification in the main clause, but the enumeration of units is absent.

(18) 如果(每)五個同學用三支筆，三十個同學一共用多少支筆呢？
     Rúguŏ (mĕi) wŭ-gè tóngxué yòng sān-zhī bĭ,
     If   every five-Cl student use three-Cl pen

sānshí-gè tóngxué yīgòng yòng duōshǎo - zhī bǐ ne?
thirty –Cl student totally use   how-many- Cl pen FP.
'If each group of five students use three pens, how many pens will
thirty students use?'

(19) 如果(每)六公尺種一棵樹，三十棵樹可以種幾公尺呢？
       Rúguǒ (měi) liù-gōngchǐ zhǒng yī-kē shù ,
       If   every six meter   plant one-Cl tree
       sānshí-kē shù kěyǐ zhǒng jǐ   gōngchǐ ne?
       thirty-Cl tree can plant   how-many meter   FP.?
       'If one plants a tree every six meters, how long can thirty trees plant for?'

In the above examples, the structure [Num-NP V Num-NP] co-occurs with
a domain of quantification, like a total numbers of entities so that the distributive dependency is necessarily triggered. This is because the domain of quantification forces the total number to be divided into plural units composed of
plural entities denoted by the Num-NP subject. Since the plural units, as a
SrtKy are available, the distributive relation between the two Num-NPs are
induced.

In this vein, the statement of Li [2] (1997:160) is right because the quantifier *měi* in [*měi*–Num-NP V Num-NP] can be omitted. [Num-NP V Num-NP]
can trigger the distributive dependency.

In this section, we show that *měi* is a plurality marker at unit level and it
marks the SrtKy in the distributive dependency of the two Num-NPs in the
structure [*měi*–Num-NP V Num-NP]. Without *měi*, the pluralization of units
is not necessarily available. Therefore, the distributive dependency is not necessarily triggered in [Num-NP V Num-NP] structure, which can give rise two
readings, distributive or non-distributive readings of the Num-NP subject.

However, the explanation above cannot account for the two types of [*měi*–
Num-NP V Num-NP] structures. The first type is referred to *měi* combined
with a numeral larger than one as in (7) and (20). The second types is that *měi*
takes the numeral *yī* 'one' as (21), which is a conditional sentence.

(20) (*每)五公斤豬肉賣 500 元
       (**měi*) *wǔ gōngjīn zhūròu mài 500   yuán*
       every five-kilo   pork   sell five-hundred dollar
       With *měi*: **impossible reading.**
       Without *měi*: 'A pocket of five kilos of pork is sold at 500 dollars.'

(21) 如果(??每)一棟房子賣二十萬，五棟房子就可以賣一百萬了。
       Rúguǒ (??měi) yī-dòng fángzǐ mài èrshí wàn ,
       If   every one Cl house sell twenty ten-thousand
       wǔ-dòng fángzǐ jiù   kěyǐ mài yī-bǎi   wàn   le

five-Cl   house   then can   sell one-hundred ten-thousand FP.
'If every house sells at two hundred thousand, five houses can be sold
at one million.'

(5a) is acceptable according to Li [2] (1997:160). However, according to
us, it is acceptable only when the numeral *yī* 'one' is focused like a response
to the question: how many houses per group[2]. When (5a) is integrated into a
conditional sentence, as in (21), native speakers may feel uneasy to hear the
sequence *měi yī* 'every-one' because *měi* enumerates a unit of one single entity expressed by *yī* 'one'. The sentence is completely acceptable when *měi* is
omitted in (21). The following examples shows also the presence of *měi*
makes sentences inacceptable and only the numeral *yī* 'one' in the Num-NP
subject is allowed to indicate the unit includes one single entity.

(22)   (*每)一個人唱一首歌
       (**měi**) *yī-gè   rén   chàng yī-shǒu gē*
       every one-Cl person sing   one-Cl   song
       Without *měi*: 'One person sing a song!'

(23)   (*每)一公斤葡萄賣 80 元
       (**měi**) *yī-gōngjīn pútáo mài 80   yuán*
       every one-Kilo   grape sell eighty dollar
       Without *měi* : 'One kilo of grapes is sold at 80 dollars.'

How do we explain the above two types of structures of *měi*? Why cannot
měi quantify over a unit containing one single entity? To answer this question,
we will begin to deal with the structure [Num-NP V Num-NP] in the next section.

3.2   Structure [Num-NP V Num-NP]

We propose that structure [Num-NP V Num-NP] induces a proportional relation between the two numeral in the co-argumental position of the predicate.
   We have showed that the quantifier *měi* can enumerate units that it pluralizes. Now we integrate (7) and (20) respectively into a conditional sentence,
as in (24a) and (24b). When *měi* is used, the enumeration of units is expressed
because of *měi* pluralization over the Num-NP subject so that (24a) and (24b)
which are considered unacceptable. However, the two sentences can be plau-

---

[2] The question is :
(i) 每多少棟房子賣二十萬 ？
   Měi   duōshǎo dòng fangzǐ mài èrshí   wàn ?
   every how-many   house sell twenty ten-thousnad
   'How many houses per group to sell at two hundred thousand?'

sible only if they are interpreted in a special way: the entities are packed as unit concretely by bags, as the intended translations in (24) indicate. Without *měi*, (24) are perfect sentences.

(24) a.如果(??**每**)五顆蘋果賣 100 元，這 100 顆蘋果可以賣多少錢？
Rúguǒ (??měi) wǔ-kē píngguǒ mài 100   yuán ,
If   every five-Cl apple   sell 100 dollar
zhè   100-kē píngguǒ kěyǐ mài duōshǎo   qián?
This 100-Cl apple   can sell how-many dollar
With *měi*: Intended: 'If the apples are sold with a package of five at one hundred dollars, how many dollars can these one hundred apples be sold at?'
Without *měi*: 'If five apples are sold at 100 dollars, how many dollars can these 100 apples be sold at? '

b.如果(??**每**)五公斤豬肉賣 500 元，100 公斤豬肉可以賣多少錢？
Rúguǒ (??měi) wǔ-gōngjīn zhūròu mài 500 yuán,
If   every five kilo   pork   sell 500 dollar
100 gōngjīn zhūròu kěyǐ mài duōshǎo   qián?
100 kilo   pork   can sell how-many dollar
With *měi*: Intended: 'If the pork here are sold with a package of five kilo at 500 dollars, how many dollars can one hundred kilo sell at?'
Without *měi*: 'If pork of five kilo is sold at 500 dollars, how many can 100 kilo be sold at?'

According to us, the distributive dependency induced by *měi* blocks the interpretation of (24). The structure [Num-NP V Num-NP] presents a proportional relation between the two numerals, like 5:100 in (24a) and 5:500 in (24b). In the same way, we can analyze (15)-(17). Without the pluralization of *měi* at unit level, the structure [Num-Cl-N V Num-Cl-N] reveals a proportion relation, like 5:3 in, 6:1 in (15) and 10:3 in (16), named proportional reading. For these sentences, the distributive dependency reading is also an available choice, especially a domain of quantification, a total number of entities is overtly expressed. In other words, both Num-NPs in the structure show a pure quantity or a value and they don't take any function, like pluralization in charge so that the distributive relation is not necessarily triggered unless the domain of quantification is overtly defined. In the same way, when the numeral in the Num-NP subject is *yī* 'one', as in (22)-(23), we can also interpret the [Num-NP V Num-NP] structure, without *měi* as proportional reading: 1: 1 in (22) and 1: 80 in (23).

In this section, we explained that structure [Num-NP V Num-NP] conveys a proportional reading between the two numerals, which can be a ratio between two quantities denoted by the two Num-NPs.

In the next section, we'll return to the quantification of *měi*.

3.3   Unit in the pluralization of *měi*

In 3.1, we have mentioned that *měi* pluralizes over a unit which includes plural entities and the unit is viewed as singular, which is called *singularity* of unit. Nevertheless, how do we analyze *měi*–Num-NP in which the number of entities is one, i.e only one single entity in the unit?

We find that when the number of entities in the unit denoted by *měi*-Num-NP is one, the numeral *yī* 'one' is not allowed to be used and the well-formed sequence is [*měi*-Cl-N], as illustrate (25)-(26).

(25)   **每個人**唱一首歌
       měi-gè   rén   *chàng yī-shǒu gē*
       every Cl person sing one-Cl song
       'Everyone has to sing a song!'

(26)   **每公斤葡萄**賣 80 元
       měi-gōngjīn pútáo *mài 80   yuán*
       every Kilo grape   sell 80   dollar
       'Grapes are sold at 80 dollars per kilo.'

(27)   每公斤豬肉賣 100 元
       měi   gōngjīn zhūròu mài 100 yuán
       every kilo   pork   sell 100 dollar
       'One kilo of pork is sold at 100 dollars'

This shows the default number of entities in the unit in the *měi* –Num-NP is one. When the number of entities in the unit is one, it fits the idea that the unit is the SrtKy is viewed as inherently singular. The overt expression of the numeral *yī* 'one' is redundant. Thus, only when the number of one single entity is focused, the numeral *yī* 'one' can be used in the *měi*–Num-NP, as in (21), as we mentioned in the section, 3.1.

We can describe the distributive dependency triggered by *měi* again and more completely, as (28) indicates.

(28)   *měi* -[Num-Cl-N]$_{unit}$ V [Num-Cl-N]$_{unit}$, Num >1 in the Num-NP in the
       subject position. When Num=1, as the default value in the unit,
       Num=1 is not realized formally in the structure. Num ≥ 1 in the Num-
       NP n the object position.

In the structure [*měi*–Num-NP V Num-NP], *měi* pluralizes over a set, i.e a unit containing one or plural entities denoted by the Num-NP subject. *Měi* marks SrtKy because it makes pluralization of units ((1b), (15)-(17)). When the unit includes only one single entity, as the default number, it is not needed to express the quantity by the numeral *yī* 'one' ((25)-(26)). When the unit contains more than one entities, the number of entities is expressed overtly by equivalent numerals.

Until now, we showed that [*měi*–Num-NP] denotes a unit which can include one or more than one entities. However, we fail to explain why cannot *měi* pluralize a unit contain only one entity expressed overtly by the numeral *yī* 'one', as in (22)-(23)? In the next section, we will analyze the two notions involved in the unit denoted by [*měi*–Num-NP].

3.4   The two notions involved in the quantifier *měi*

In the previous sections, we analyzed that [*měi*–Num-NP] denotes plural units containing one or more than one entities. This shows the two notions involved in the quantifier *měi*, one is the notion of unit and the other is the notion of singularity of a unit, i.e. the unit being inherently singular. We will show more in detail the two notions related to *měi* by distinguishing *měi* with the numeral *yī* 'one' which indicates a singular number.

The notion of unit of *měi* and the singular number of *yī* 'one'

In 3.1, we showed that [*měi*–Num-NP V Num-NP] denotes necessarily a distributive dependency between the two Num-NPs while [Num-NP V Num-NP], gives rise to a proportional reading can also denote a distributive relation, when the domain of quantification indicated by a total number of entities.

The domain of quantification can be shown with a restriction by a locative. In (29), *měi* and the numeral *yī* 'one' can be replaced by each other and the distributive dependency is triggered between one unit of mooncake and its value of fifteen dollars.

(29)   這家店 小月餅每/一個十五元
    zhè jiā diàn, xiǎo yuèbǐng   **měi** / **yī** *-gè*   *shíwǔ yuán*
    this-Cl store small moon-cake every one -Cl fifteen dollar
    'In this store, each mooncake costs fifteen dollars.'

However, according to us, *měi* and the numeral *yī* 'one' do not convey the same meaning: *měi* indicates the plurality of units composed of one mooncake while the numeral *yī* 'one' indicates the value of fifteen dollars over one single entity.

Moreover, the notion of unit involved in *měi* is indeed distinct from the notion of singular number, denoted by the numeral *yī* 'one'. The unit of *měi* implies the notion of the *arithmetic mean* which is defined as the sum of a collection of numbers divided by the number of items in the collection. However, the notion of singular number cannot necessarily be used to express the arithmetic mean. It is not surprising that in (30a), *měi* is served to indicate the average price over the total volume of vegetables while the singular number expressed by *yī* 'one' cannot rightly convey the average meaning. With the help of the adverb *píngjun* 'average', as in (30b) which explicates the division of the totality of kilos, the singular number *yī* 'one' is able to express the unitary meaning, as *měi* does.

(30) a.蔬菜到貨量 1280 噸,價格**每**/⁇一公斤 19.6 元
   *Shūcài dào-huò-liàng 1280 dūn,   jiàgé **měi** / ⁇yī gōngjīn 19.6 yuán*
   Vegetable volume-of-goods-arrived 1280 ton price every one kilo   19.6 dollar
   'The volume of goods arrived of vegetables is 1280 tons. The (unitary) price is 19.6 dollars **per** kilo.'

   b. ....., 價格平均 ᴼᵏ**每**/ᴼᵏ一公斤 19.6 元
   .... jiàgé píngjun ᴼᵏ**měi** / ᴼᴷ*yī   gōngjīn 19.6 yuán*
   .... price average   every   one kilo   19.6 dollar
   '... The average price is 19.6 dollars **per** kilo.'

This shows the notion of unit and singularity of *měi* can co-occur with the explicit expression of arithmetic values by the adverb *píngjun* 'average'. Therefore, we can find more examples of *měi* being used to express the notion of value of per unit, especially a notion defined by the value obtained with the division of the total numbers or total volume, as the definition of the density, in (31) and the unitary price of a share, in (32). The singular number expressed by *yī* 'one' conveys only a pure quantity which is one, instead of the quantity in a unit over a totality of numbers or volume.

(31) 物質**每**/*一單位體積內所含有的質量，稱為該物質的密度
   *Wùzhì   **měi** / *yī dānwèi tǐjī   nèi   suǒ   hányǒu de zhìliàng ,*
   Substance every one unitary volume inside MO. contain de weight
   chēng wéi gāi wùzhì   de mìdù
   call   as this substance de density
   'The weight **per** unit of volume of a substance is called the density of that substance.'

(32) 漢光電子**每**/*一股淨回升到 5.24 元
   *Hànguāng diànzǐ **měi** / *yī gǔ   jìng huíshēng dào 5.24 yuán*
   H.G   electronics every one share net return raise to 5.24 dollar
   'The value **per** share of Hangugang electronics net raised back to 5.24 dollars.'

Last but not least, the difference between the notion of unit in [*měi*–Num-NP] and the singular number by *yī* 'one' can be captured by the presence of the relator *de* (的), which performs predicative function of a structure of

[Num-Cl-N] (C.f. Paris [8] (1981:87)). We return to our examples, (23) and (26) and see the differentiation in (33) and (34).

(33) *每公斤(重)的葡萄賣 80 元
      ***měi**-gōngjīn (zhòng) de pútáo mài 80 yuán
      every Kilo   weight de grape sell 80 dollar

(34) 一公斤(重) 的葡萄賣 80 元
      yī -gōngjīn (zhòng) de pútáo mài 80 yuán
      every Kilo weight de grape sell 80 dollar
      'The grapes weighted one kilo are sold at 80 dollars.'

Since *měi*-Num-NP is referred to the unit of a total numbers, it cannot be an expression of pure quantity which is the weight of the concerned entities. Therefore, *měi*-NP rejects the presence of the relator *de* before the N and a predicate *zhòng* 'to weight' as well. However, the Num-NP, *yī-gōngjīn* 'one-kilo' expressing the singular number in (34) is able to be transformed into a [V-de NP] structure, which is meant to indicate the weight of the entity.

Therefore, instead of the notion of unit, the numeral one in the structure [Num-Cl-N V Num-Cl-N] is served as a quantity to express a proportional relation between the quantity and its value. Now we return to see (26), which indicates the unitary price of grapes and the numeral one in (23), which is referred to a proportional reading.

The quantifier *měi* and the numeral *yī* 'one' function at different levels. *Měi* takes the Num-NP as unit of pluralization while the numeral *yī* 'one' indicates the existence of a single entity. We are able to explain why [*měi-yī*-NP] is ill-formed. When the number of entities in the unit is one, and if the numeral *yī* 'one' were used, like [*měi-yī*-NP], the functions of *měi* and the numeral *yī* 'one' would be confused. According to the singularity of notion of *měi*, a unit is singular and the only one single entity can be pluralized at unit level. In [*yī*-NP V Num-NP], the numeral *yī* 'one' shows the pure quantity, which is one single entity and the structure express the ratio between one entity and the numeral in the NP object. Due to the pluralization of *měi*, if *měi* and the numeral *yī* 'one' co-occur, like [*měi-yī*-NP], the relation between the two Num-NPs at the co-argumental position become ambiguous between two interpretations, distributive relation or proportional relation.

The table below summarizes the types of structure [Num-NP V Num-NP] with(out) the co-occurrence of the quantifier *měi* and the relations between the two Num-NPs, distributive or proportional.

co-occurrence of *mei*	Structure **Num-NP V Num-NP**	Relation between the two Num-

		NPs
Yes	***Měi-Ø -gè rén chàng yī-shŏu gē*** 'Everyone has to sing a song!'	Distributive
Yes	***Měi wŭ-gè tóngxué yòng sān-zhī bĭ*** 'Each group of five students uses three pens.'	Distributive
No	*Ø wŭ-gè tóngxué yòng sān-zhī bĭ* 'Students, get into groups of five and use three pens!' 'The five students use three pens (together).'	Distributive Proportional
No	*Ø wŭ-kē pínggŭo mài 100 yuán* 'The five apples are sold at 100 dollar.'	Proportional

4   Conclusion

We have shown the quantifier *měi* is a marker of plurality over a set denoted by Num-NP in the structure [*měi*–Num NP V Num NP] and it marks the SrtKy for the necessary conditions for a distributive dependency in the sense of Choe (1987). This quantifier pluralizes NP at the unit level because it pluralizes over a unit containing plural entities denoted by Num-NP, where the numeral is larger than one. Without *měi*, the structure [Num-NP V Num-NP] can denote a proportional reading between the two numerals and it can also trigger the distributive relation between the two Num-NPs. Also, *měi* is associated with the notion of unit, which is different from the singular number expressed by the numeral *yī* 'one'.

Huang [1] (2005:35), Li [2] (1997:160), Lin [3] (1997:230) and Yuan [4] (2011:214) Xing [5](2008:36) and Zhang [6] (2015:13)

References

1. Huang, Shi-Zhe: Universal Quantification with Skolemization as Evidenced in Chinese and English, Lewiston: Edwin Mellen Press (2005).
2. Li, Xiao-Guang : Deriving Distributivity in Chinese. Ph.D. Dissertation, University of California, Irvine (1997).
3. Lin, Tzong-Hong: "On *Ge* and other related problems", in *The Referential Properties of Chinese Noun Phrases*, Xu,L-J (ed.), Collection des Cahiers de linguistique-Asie Orientale 2, 209-253. Paris: EHESS (1997).
4. Yuan, Hua-Hung: Quelques aspects de la quantification en chinois mandarin: pluralité et distributivité, PhD dissertation, Université Paris-Diderot (2011).
5. Xing, Feng Xiang: 'Mei' and some Sentences Relative to it, MA Thesis, Henan University. (2008)(邢凤翔 每及相关句式 河南大学硕论).
6. Zhang, Nan Xi: The Related Research of 'Mei+Number' Structure, MA Thesis, Jilin University(2015)(张楠溪 "每+数量" 结构的相关表达研究 吉林大学硕论).
7. Choe, Jae-Woong: Anti-Quantifiers and a Theory of Distributivity. Ph.D. dissertation, University of Massachusetts, Amherst (1987).
8. Paris, Marie-Claude: Problèmes de syntaxe et de sémantique en linguistique chinoise. Paris : Collège de France, Institut des Hautes Études Chinoises (1981).

On the semantic functions and denotations of *jīngcháng* (經常) and *chángcháng* (常常)

Daniel Kwang Guan CHAN [1] and Yuan Hua-Hung [2]

[1] Centre for Language Studies, National University of Singapore, Singapore 117572
`daniel.chan@nus.edu.sg`
[2] Department of Applied Foreign Languages, National Taipei University of Business, Taiwan
`yuan.huahung@gmail.com`

Abstract. *Jīngcháng* and *chángcháng* are two adverbs which have been classified in the same category of frequency adverbs in the Sinologist literature. While there are clear similarities between the two (e.g. both denote a multiplicity of 'occasions', can be treated as markers of verbal plurality operating at the occasion-level in the sense of Cusic [2], and induce the pure frequency and relational readings in the sense of de Swart [6], they present differences in two aspects: (i) their semantic functions (habituality vs. iterativity) and (ii) their denotations in the view of temporal intervals between two occasions.

Keywords. Verbal plurality, Frequency adverbs, Mandarin Chinese, Pure frequency reading, relational reading, Habituality , Iterativity , Reduplication, Temporal interval.

1. Introduction

In this paper, we analyse two frequency adverbs in Mandarin Chinese, *jīngcháng* (经常) and *chángcháng* (常常), which consist of the morpheme *cháng* (常) both. Previous analyses by Ding [3], Guan [4], Shi and Hu [5], and Zhou [9], have put them in the same category of "adverbs of medium frequency", together with *shícháng* and so on, without indicating how these individual frequency adverbs differ from each other. Those authors indicate that the two frequency adverbs show iteration of events or situations, and as Zhang and Liu [8] notice, both adverbs denote the iteration of events with regularity.

Few differences between the two adverbs have been cited in the Sinologist literature. Some authors, like Guan [4], Zou [10] and Zou [11] mention that *jīngcháng* can be negated by *bù* while *chángcháng* can be negated by *méi* only. Zou [11] indicates that *bù jīngcháng* implies fewer occurrences of an event and a lower frequency but he does not explain why it is so and what *méi chángcháng* (Neg. + *chángcháng*) triggers, and other authors do not do so either. Only in Guan [4] is the negation form *bù jīngcháng* related to the scalarity of frequency adverbs.

© Springer International Publishing AG 2018
Y. Wu et al. (Eds.): CLSW 2017, LNAI 10709, pp. 112–123, 2018.
https://doi.org/10.1007/978-3-319-73573-3_9

1.1 Research questions

From the above, it is clear that more differences between the two adverbs should be explored. We notice that *chángcháng* can be easily combined with frequency adverbials expressing absolute frequencies, *sān tiān...yī cì* (every three days) and *yī tiān...sān cì* but *jīngcháng* can co-occur only with the latter.

(1) 李四{^{??}**经常/常常**}三天洗一次澡.

   Lǐsì ^{??}***jīngcháng*** /*chángcháng*   sān-tiān xǐ   yí-cì   zǎo
   Lisi jīngcháng   chángcháng   three-day wash   once   shower
   'Lisi ^{??}regularly/often showered once every three days.'

(2) 李四{**经常/常常**}一天洗三次澡.

   Lǐsì ***jīngcháng*** /<ins>*chángcháng*</ins>   yì-tiān xǐ   sān-cì   zǎo
   Lisi jīngcháng   chángcháng   one-day wash   thrice   shower
   'Lisi regularly/often showered thrice per day.'

On the other hand, *jīngcháng* (rather than *chángcháng*) can be used to express generalisations about a person's habits:

(3) 一般来说，玛莉**经常**/*****常常**会看书.

   <u>Yìbān lái shuō</u>,   Mǎlì **jīngcháng** /[*]***chángcháng*** huì kàn shū.
   generally speaking Mary jīngcháng chángcháng   will read books
   'Generally, Mary reads books regularly/often.'

With respect to the two similar looking adverbs, we would like to answer the following research questions:

   (i) What are the actual similarities between *jīngcháng* and *chángcháng*?
   (ii) What are the actual differences between *jīngcháng* and *chángcháng*?
   (iii) In what ways should these adverbs be analysed to account for their properties and uses?

We will discuss the semantics of frequency adverbs under Cusic's notion of "verbal plurality" [2]. We will hypothesise that since *jīngcháng* and *chángcháng* consist of *cháng*, the semantic denotations of both adverbs are revealed by their morphological compositions, which are *jīng+cháng* and *cháng+cháng*.

In Section 2, we examine the two possible readings of *jīngcháng* and *chángcháng*, i.e. pure frequency and relational readings, following the insights of De Swart [6].

In Section 3, we will show how *jīngcháng* and *chángcháng* are formed using the same simple morpheme, *cháng*, which is by itself also a frequency adverb. Following Bertinetto and Lenci [1], we will show that both mark iterativity but *jīngcháng* has another feature, regularity. We will also discuss the semantic denotations of the two adverbs and explain why they are different.

2. Verbal plurality markers

In this paper, we analyse both *jīngcháng* and *chángcháng* as markers of "**verbal plurality**" [2], a broad semantic category for describing the multiplicity of actions. In Yuan and Chan [7], frequency adverbs *cháng* and *chángcháng* are considered as markers of verbal plurality at the occasion-level. As a result, *jīngcháng* is treated in the same manner as *chángcháng* because both adverbs denote multiple occasions of an event, as (4)-(5) show.

(4)   他{**经常/常常**}抓着我的手 (每次都抓得我好痛).
    *Tā **jīngcháng** /**chángcháng** zhuā-zhe wǒ-de shǒu.*
    he *jīngcháng chángcháng* grab-Dur.[1] my   hand
    (*méi-cì   dōu zhuā dé   wǒ hǎo tong*).
    every-time all grab until me very pain
    'He grabbed my hand often. (Every time, I was in pain from the grabbing.).'

(5)   他抓着我的手. (#每次都抓得我好痛).
    Tā zhuā-zhe wǒ-de shǒu, (#méi-cì   dōu zhuā dé wǒ hǎo tong).
    he grab-Dur. my   hand   every-time all   grab until me very pain
    'He grabbed my hand. (#Every time, I was in pain from the grabbing.)'

The pluralisation at occasion-level can be seen in (6), where two frequency adverbs co-occur with a temporal subordinate introduced by *(de)-shí(hòu)* '*de*-time, while', an overt marker of occasions. In (6), the only interpretation possible is that there are different speeches (i.e. different occasions) that are being referred to.

(6)   他听演讲(的)时(候),   {**经常/常常**}点头.
    *Tā tīng   yánjiǎng (de)-shí(hòu), **jīngcháng** /**chángcháng** diǎn tóu.*
    he listen speech   while   *jīngcháng* /*chángcháng*   nod head
    'He <u>regularly</u>/ <u>often</u> nodded while listening to a [different] speech.'

Since *jīngcháng* and *chángcháng* are both markers of verbal plurality at the occasion level, they induce two possible readings, pure frequency and relational readings in the sense of De Swart [6]. In this way, the two adverbs share similarities. In the following section, we will present the two readings.

2.1 Pure frequency vs. relational readings

The readings of our two adverbs are similar to those of the French frequency adverb *souvent*. Consider (7) and (8).

(7)   Jeanne se plaint **souvent**.
    'Jeanne often complains.'
    (a) **Pure frequency reading**: There are <u>many situations per unit time</u> in

---

[1] Abbreviations: De: Gentive marker *de* (的) ; Dur.: Durative aspect; Neg.: Negation markers.

which Jeanne complains.

(b) **Proportional reading**: <u>Many of the</u> relevant situations within a certain time period are situations in which Jeanne complains.

In its **pure frequency** reading, it is the high number of complaining events per unit time that is being considered, while the **proportional (relational)** reading looks at the proportion of situations in which Jeanne complains out of the [implicitly or contextually] given set of situations within a certain time period. The determined context can be made explicit with an antecedent clause:

(8)   Quand il était malade, Paul consultait un médecin souvent.
        'When Paul was ill, he often went to see a doctor.'
        (a) **Pure frequency reading**: At the time that Paul was ill, he went to see a doctor many times, i.e. There were <u>many situations per unit time</u> in which Paul went to see a doctor.
        (b) **Proportional (relational) reading**: In <u>many of the situations</u> in which he was ill, he went to see a doctor, i.e. the <u>proportion of situations</u> in which he went to see a doctor is high.

In other words, pure frequency (weak) readings of *souvent* can be paraphrased as "there are x situations such that...", where x is an undetermined number. Proportional (strong) readings are not concerned with the actual number of situations, but the proportion of a set of situations in relation to another determined set of situations.

Returning to our two adverbs, the pure frequency and the relational readings are both available:

(9)   玛莉<u>生病(的)时(候)</u>，**经常/常常**看医生.
        *Mǎlì <u>shēngbìng (de)-shí(hòu)</u> **jīngcháng/ chángcháng** kàn yīshēng.*
        Mary ill while   jīngcháng chángcháng   see doctor
        'When Mary is ill, she regularly/often sees a doctor.'
        (a) **Pure frequency reading**: 'When Mary is /was ill, she sees /saw a doctor on multiple occasions.'
        (b) **Relational reading**: 'Many of the situations in which Mary is/was ill are /were those in which she sees / saw a doctor.'

The two readings can be presented schematically as follows, where the period of time that Mary is ill is represented by the space between the two square brackets [ ] and each of the doctor consultations is represented by the letter 'x':

(10)   Relational reading:

(11)   Pure frequency reading:

[x   x   x   x   x   x   ]   ➤ t

For *jīngcháng*, the pure frequency reading is preferred, and for *chángcháng*, the relational reading is preferred. However, when the antecedent clause refers to a period of time that can only occur once, then both frequency adverbs only have the pure frequency reading.

(12)   玛莉**那次**生病(的)时(候)，**经常/常常**看医生.
        *Mǎlì **nà-cì** shēngbìng (de)-shí(hòu),* **jīngcháng /chángcháng** *kàn yīshēng.*
        Mary that-time   ill   while   *jīngcháng chángcháng*   see doctor '**At
        that time** when Mary was ill, she regularly/often saw a doctor.'
        ➔ **Pure frequency reading only**: 'When Mary was ill that time, she saw a
        doctor multiple times.'

Another way of introducing a single temporal interval is by using a predicate like being 'young', which can only apply once in a lifetime to an individual. In this case, *chángcháng* marks the fact that the situation in the main clause (i.e. seeing a doctor) occurred multiple times, and *jīngcháng* expresses the habit of Mary in the past, i.e. only the pure frequency reading is possible:

(13)   玛莉年轻(的)时(候)，**经常/常常**看医生.
        Mǎlì niánqīng (de)-shí(hòu), **jīngcháng /chángcháng** *kàn yīshēng.*
        Mary young   while   *jīngcháng   chángcháng* see doctor 'When
        Mary was young, she regularly/often saw a doctor.'
        (a) **Pure frequency reading only**: 'When Mary was young, she saw /used to
        see a doctor multiple times.'
        (b) **NOT**: #In many situations where Mary was young, she saw a doctor.'

Therefore, the two frequency adverbs can both induce two readings, the pure frequency reading and the relational reading. However, this distinction between readings cannot account for their difference. We propose to analyse their representation of verbal plurality.

We now have two ways to look at those verbal plurality markers. One is that those adverbs pluralise the occurrence of an occasion, viewed as a point in time. The other is that they pluralise the temporal interval between two occasions. The two ways result in the interpretation of a multiplicity of occasions.

2.2 Representation of verbal plurality at the occasional level

Before proving which way those adverbs function, we have to see how *cháng* is different from *jīngcháng* and *chángcháng* and why the two adverbs are hypothesised as being formed based on *cháng*, the simple morpheme.

In Yuan and Chan [7], it is shown that *chángcháng* and *cháng* are used respectively in particular (episodic) sentences and characterising (generic) sentences. Specifically, on one hand, *cháng* is a marker of habituality denoting a generic property like in an individual-level predication, which explains why it can occur as part of the VP in the *shi* VP *de* construction; on the other hand, *chángcháng* is unacceptable in this construction due to its denotation of an episodic property, like in a stage-level predication. Therefore, since *jīngcháng* cannot appear in the VP part in the *shi* VP *de* construction, as in (14), it is not associated with generic property denotation.

(14) 玛丽是 ^{OK}常/*经常/*常常弹钢琴的
      Mǎlì shì ^{OK}*cháng /*jīngcháng /*chángcháng* <u>*tán gāngqín*</u> *de*
      Mary be   often   *jīngcháng*   *chángcháng* play piano *de*
      With *cháng*: 'It is often that Mary plays piano.' / Mary OFTEN plays piano.'
      (characterising property)
      With *jīngcháng* / *chángcháng*: impossible.

It is obvious that *cháng* can be differentiated from *jīngcháng* and *chángcháng* because the former is intensional and the latter two are not intensional. We propose that there is one more difference: *cháng* is associated with scalarity while *jīngcháng* and *chángcháng* are not. *Cháng* can be modified by degree adverbs such as comparative adverb *bǐ* (比) or *hěn* (很), as in (15)–(16), while it is impossible to do so with *jīngcháng* and *chángcháng*.

(15) 小明<u>比小李</u>常/*经常/*常常迟到
      Xiǎomíng <u>*bǐ Xiǎolǐ*</u> *cháng/*jīngcháng /*chángcháng chídào*
      X.M   compare X.L often *jīngcháng chángcháng*   late 'Xiaoming is
      more often late than Xiaoli.'

(16) 小明<u>很</u>常/*经常/*常常迟到
      Xiǎomíng <u>*hěn*</u> *cháng/*jīngcháng /*chángcháng chídào*
      X.M   very often   *jīngcháng*   *chángcháng* late
      'Xiaoming is often late .'

Moreover, when *cháng* is negated by *bù*, to form a constituent *bù cháng*, it can also be modified by the comparative adverb, *bǐ* (比) and the degree adverb and *hěn* (很), as in (17)–(18). This is not possible for *jīngcháng* and *chángcháng*.

(17) 小明<u>比小李</u>不常/*不经常/*不常常迟到
      Xiǎomíng <u>*bǐ Xiǎolǐ*</u> *bù cháng/*bù jīngcháng/*bù chángcháng chídào*
      X.M compare X.L neg. often neg. *jīngcháng* neg. *chángcháng* late
      'X.M is less often late than X.L.'

(18) 小明<u>很</u>不常/*不经常/*不常常迟到
      Xiǎomíng <u>*hěn*</u> *bù cháng/* bù jīngcháng/* bù chángcháng chídào*
      X.M   very neg. often neg. *jīngcháng* neg. *chángcháng* late
      'X.M is not often late.'

If we adopt the definition of *frequency* given by De Swart [6] for frequency adverbs, which is *the number of occurrences over a unit time*, the unit time involved in frequency adverb is shown as the temporal interval between two occurrences of an action. Thus, *hěn cháng* 'very often' indicates that the temporal intervals between two occurrences are shorter than the [contextually determined] standard length of time on a scale of shortness of intervals. *Bù cháng* 'not often' indicates that the temporal intervals are longer than the standard length on the temporal scale. If *cháng* pluralises over a single occurrence viewed as a point in time, we cannot explain (17)–(18) and there is the morpheme *shǎo* (少) which conveys a low quantity as in (19).

(19)　小明比小李/很少迟到
　　　Xiǎomíng bǐ Xiǎolǐ / hěn   shǎo chídào
　　　X.M   compare X.L   very few late
　　　'X.M came more rarely late than X.L.' 'X.M is rarely late.'

Therefore, we assume that *cháng* denotes a plurality of temporal intervals between two occasions and leads to a scalarity of temporal interval lengths. According to the morphological compositions of *jīngcháng* and *chángcháng*, we hypothesise as follows:

Jīng expresses regularity and when *jīng* combines with *cháng*, it conveys the notion of regular temporal intervals between two occasions. *Chángcháng* is reduplicated form of *cháng* and give a meaning of iterated temporal intervals. Neither *jīngcháng* nor *chángcháng* is scalar as (15) shows and both concern an implicit quantity.

In the next section, we will show the difference between *jīngcháng* or *chángcháng* in view of the difference between "habituality" and "iterativity", as defined by Bertinetto and Lenci [1]. After that, we will analyse this difference with our hypothesis.

3.　Differences

We will show their differences in two ways: (i) habituality vs. iterativity and (ii) the different types of temporal intervals between two occasions.

3.1 Habituality vs. iterativity

Bertinetto and Lenci [1] indicate that "habituality consists of attributing a property to a given referent, rather than asserting anything specific about the pluractional event itself" (*ibid.*: 857). Iterativity, on the other hand, is only a component of habituality, since the semantics of habituality is a presupposition of a "more or less regular iteration of an event" (*ibid.*:852). In other words, habituality involves iterativity, and iterativity is a component of habituality.

Bertinetto and Lenci [1] highlight that there are four features that distinguish habituality from iterativity: (i) numerical specifiability, (ii) temporal localisation, (iii) timeframe, and (iv) determinability of the framing adverbial. The four properties that distinguish habituality from iterativity are summarised below:

Table 1. Properties of habituality and iterativity

	Iterative	Habitual
Numerical specifiability	+ specifiable	– specifiable

Temporal localisation	only past- and future-referring	all temporal domains
Time-frame	strictly delimiting	vaguely delimiting
Determinability of framing adverbial	potentially determinable	non-determinable

We show how *jīngcháng* and *chángcháng* are differentiated from each other. **Firstly**, in the presence of the modal verb *huì*, only *jīngcháng* can co-occur with a habituality adverb:

(20) 按他的习惯，保罗**经常**/***常常**<u>会</u>到户外跑步。
    *àn tā-de xíguàn, Bǎoluó **jīngcháng** /***chángcháng** huì dào hùwài pǎobù.*
    according to one's habits Paul *jīngcháng chángcháng* will go-to outdoor jog
    '**According to his habits**, Paul regularly goes outdoors for a jog.'

Secondly, the multiplicity of occurrences is numerically specifiable in an iterative sentence but not in a habitual sentence:

(21) 保罗｛#**经常**/**常常**｝去法国。他总共去了**二十**次。
    *Bǎoluó #**jīngcháng** /**chángcháng** qù Fǎguó. Tā zǒnggòng qù-le **èrshí** cì.*
    Paul   *jīngcháng chángcháng* go France he in-total go-Acc. **twenty** times
    (a) With *jīngcháng* (**Habitual**): #<u>[impossible numerical specification]</u>
    (b) With *chángcháng* (**Iterative**): 'Paul often went to France.
      'He has gone there a **total of 20 times**''

Thus, *jīngcháng* does not imply numerical specificity and it is not purely iterative like *chángcháng* is.

Thirdly, when the sentence is framed by an adverbial of strict time frame, the habitual adverb *jīngcháng* cannot easily be used, while the sentence with iterative *chángcháng* is completely acceptable (*ibid.*: 858):

(22) 从一月一号到六月三十号，保罗｛??**经常**/**常常**｝在家下厨。
    Cóng yī-yuè yī-hào dào liùyuè sānshí-hào,
    From January first to June thirtieth,
    *Bǎoluó {?? **jīngcháng** /**chángcháng**} zài jiā xiàchú.*
    Paul   *jīngcháng /chángcháng* at home cook
    (a) With *jīngcháng* (**Habitual**): **??**
    (b) With *chángcháng* (**Iterative**): '**From 1/1 to 30/6,** Paul often cooked at home.'

Fourthly, a time adverbial such as *nà-duàn shíjiān* 'that period of time' or *xiǎo-shíhòu* 'when-young' can be interpreted differently: either as a reference time when it co-occurs with the habituality-inducing *jīngcháng*, or as a strict time adverbial when it co-occurs with the iterativity induced by *chángcháng* (*ibid.*: 857):

(23) <u>那段期间</u>/ <u>小时候</u>，保罗｛**经常**/**常常**｝画画。
    <u>*Nà-duàn shíjiān*</u> /<u>*Xiǎo-shíhòu*</u>, *Bǎoluó **jīngcháng** /**chángcháng** huàhuà.*

That-Cl. period /When-young, Paul *jīngcháng* /*chángcháng*   paint
  (a) With *jīngcháng* **(Habitual)**: 'During that period of time/When he was
young, Paul used to paint.
  (b) With *chángcháng* **(Iterative)**: 'During that period of time/When he was
young, Paul often painted.

In this section, we showed how *jīngcháng* and *chángcháng* are different with regards
to habituality and iterativity: *jīngcháng* expresses habituality while *chángcháng* indicates iterativity. The summary of the four tests that served to distinguish the two frequency adverbs is given in the table below:

Table 2. Tests of the difference between *jīngcháng* and *chángcháng*

	chángcháng (Iterativity)	*jīngcháng* (Habituality)
Numerical specifiability	Yes	No
Strictly delimiting time-frame	Yes	No
Determinability of framing time adverbial	Potentially determinable	Non-determina-ble
Co-occurrence with adverb expressing habit	No	Yes

We hypothesise that the regular temporal intervals of *jīngcháng* allow it to co-occur
with habituality adverbs. In other words, regularity is what helps to express habituality
while pure iterativity alone (without regularity) does not suffice to express habituality.

3.2 Two types of representations of verbal plurality

We claim that *jīngcháng* and *chángcháng* are formed using the simple morpheme,
cháng, indicating plurality of temporal intervals between two occasions,. *Jīngcháng*
denotes a cluster of regular temporal intervals between two occasions according to its
morphological composition, while the reduplicated form *chángcháng* denotes to a multiplicity of clusters of temporal intervals between two occasions because the simple
morpheme *cháng* iterates and makes temporal intervals repeat. This is illustrated in
(24)–(25) below:

(24) Temporal intervals between two occasions denoted by *jīngcháng*

(25) Temporal intervals denoted by *chángcháng*:

We now provide several tests to support our hypothesis. Firstly, when the negation
marker *bù* co-occurs with *jīngcháng*, the negation is scoped over regularity, while *chángcháng* cannot be negated by this negation marker:

(26) 小葛**不经常**/*不常常游泳
       Xiǎogě **bù**   **jīngcháng** /*bù **chángcháng** *yóuyǒng*
       Greg   neg. *jīngcháng*   neg. *chángcháng* swim
       (a)With *jīngcháng* : 'Greg does **not** swim **regularly**.'
       (b)With *chángcháng*: (intended: '#Greg does not swim often'.)

Secondly, only *chángcháng* is able to co-occur with the explicit frequency adverb, *sān tiān…yī cì* (every three days), as in (1) above. This shows that the regular temporal intervals denoted by *jīngcháng* are not compatible with explicit regular temporal intervals. However, both *jīngcháng* and *chángcháng* can co-occur with *yī tiān…sān cì* (trice per day) as in (2). We can see that the regular temporal intervals denoted by *jīngcháng* is compatible with the short interval *yī tiān* 'one day' viewed as a point in time, just like the iterated temporal intervals denoted by *chángcháng*.

The regular temporal intervals denoted by *jīngcháng* are continuous ones on the time axis without interruption while the clusters of iterated temporal intervals denoted by *chángcháng* are discontinuous, with interruption. The negation marker *méi (yǒu)* which negates over an event, as in (27), takes scope over all the constituents on its right including the explicit frequency adverbs *yì-tiān…sān-cì* 'thrice per day', seen as a point in time. As a result, the number of the occurrences within the point in time can be negated by *méi (yǒu)*, as shown in (28).

(27) 李四没(有){**经常/常常**}一天洗三次澡.
       Lìsì méi (yǒu) **jīngcháng** /**chángcháng**   *yì-tiān xǐ* <u>*sān-cì*</u> *zǎo*
       Lisi neg. have *jīngcháng chángcháng* one-day wash thrice   shower
       'Lisi did not regularly/often shower thrice per day.'

(28) 但{**经常/常常**}一天洗<u>两次</u>澡
       dàn **jīngcháng** /**chángcháng** *yì-tiān xǐ*   <u>*liǎng-cì*</u> *zǎo*
       but *jīngcháng /chángcháng*   one day wash twice   shower
       'But he often showered twice per day.'

However, as shown in (29), when the explicit intervals marked by *měi* which are continuous ones appear, only the predication with *chángcháng* can be negated by *méi (yǒu)* and the negation scopes over the explicit temporal intervals, *sān tiān* 'three days', indicating a negation over the length of temporal interval, as in (30).

(29) 小葛没(有)[**常常**/*经常每三天游一次泳**]
       Xiǎogě méi (yǒu)[*chángcháng* /* *jīngcháng* <u>*měi sān-tiān*</u> *yóu* <u>*yī-cì*</u> *yǒng*]
       Greg   neg. have *chángcháng jīngcháng*   every three-day swim once swim
       'Greg didn't often swim once every three days.'

(30) 但常常<u>每四天游一次</u>
       dàn chángcháng <u>*měi sì-tiān*</u>   *yóu* <u>*yī-cì*</u>
       but *chángcháng* every four-day swim once
       'But he often swam once every four days.'

As we showed in 3.1, *jīngcháng* marks habituality while *chángcháng* marks iterativity. If our analysis is on the right track, we can attribute the habituality expression of *jīngcháng* to its denotation of regular temporal intervals between two occasions and the iterativity expression of *chángcháng* to its denotations of the plurality of clusters of temporal intervals.

An adverb which denotes regular temporal intervals between occasions is apt to describe a habit, for example, *tiāntiān* 'day-day', which sets the interval length between occurrences as one day. It can be used in an intensional context, like in a subordinate clause marked by *de huà* 'if' of a conditional complex sentence in which the iterative adverb *lǚlǚ* 'repeatedly' expressing repeated events is not acceptable:

(31)   [^{OK}天天/*屡屡/吃维生素 C 的话]，不容易感冒
    [^{OK}*tiāntiān*/ **lǚlǚ   chī wéishēngsù C de huà], bù róngyì gǎnmào
    day-day repeatedly eat vitamin C   if   neg. easy catch-cold
    'If one takes vitamin C everyday/[#]repeatedly, it is hard to catch a cold.'

In the same way, we can understand how *jīngcháng,* which indicates a regularity of continuous temporal intervals, expresses a habit and its possibility to be used in a subordinate clause of a conditional sentence, like in (32). The denotation of clusters of temporal intervals which are discontinuous of *chángcháng* cannot be served in such an intentional context.

(32)   [^{OK}**经常**/*常常吃维生素 C 的话]，不容易感冒
    [^{OK}**jīngcháng**/**chángcháng chī wéishēngsù C de huà], bù   róngyì gǎnmào
    jīngcháng   *chángcháng* eat vitamin   C   if   neg. easy catch-cold
    'If one takes vitamin C regularly / often, it is hard to catch a cold.'

4.   Conclusion

In this paper, we have presented the semantic functions and denotations of the two frequency adverbs, *jīngcháng* and *chángcháng*. While both denote the pure frequency and relational readings, they are different in their semantic functions: *jīngcháng* marks habituality while *chángcháng* marks iterativity. Their semantic denotations are also different: *jīngcháng* denotes regular temporal intervals which are continuous but *chángcháng* denotes multiple clusters of temporal intervals, which allow discontinuity between clusters.

References

1. Bertinetto, P. M., Lenci, A: Habituality, pluractionality, and imperfectivity. In: Binnick, Robert I. (ed.) The Oxford Handbook of Tense and Aspect. Oxford University Press, New York (2012)
2. Cusic, David: Verbal Plurality and Aspect, Unpublished PhD dissertation, Stanford University, Stanford (1981)
3. Ding, Shu Juan : *The Studies of Frequency Adverbs in Chinese* MA thesis, Yanbian University (2004). (丁淑娟. 现代汉语频率副词研究, 延边大学)

4. Guan, He Zhai: *A Study on the Frequency Adverbs in Modern Chinese*, PhD dissertation, Jilin University (2015)(关黑拽. 现代汉语频度副词研究, 吉林大学博论)
5. Shi, Jin Sheng and Hu, Xiao Ping: Types of Adverbs of Verbal Quantification and their selection, *Linguistic Research* 2004 (2):9-14. (2004). (史金生, 胡晓萍. 动量副词的类别及其选择性, 语文研究 2004(2):9-14)
6. de Swart, Henriëtte: *Adverbs of Quantification: A Generalized Quantifier Approach*. PhD dissertation, University of Groningen. New York: Garland (1993).
7. Yuan, Hua Hung and Chan, Daniel Kwang Guan：Verbal Plurality of Frequency Adverbs in Mandarin Chinese, *Chinese Lexical Semantics, 17th Workshop, CLSW 2016, Revised Selected Papers*, ed. Dong, Minghui, Lin, Jingxia, and Tang, Xuri, Cham/Heidelberg: Springer (2016).
8. Zhang, Yuncui and Liu, Pengyuan: The Semantic Features of 'changchang', 'jingchang', 'wangwang, and 'tongchang',- A Corpus-Based Perspective, *Chinese Lexical Semantics, 16th Workshop, CLSW 2015, Revised Selected Papers*, ed. Q. Lu and H.H. Gao , p.148-159 Cham/Heidelberg: Springer (2015).
9. Zhou, Xiao Bing: Classification of Frequency Adverbs and usage rules. *Journal of East China Normal University(Humanities and Social Sciences)* 1999 (4):116-119. (1999) 周小兵. 频度副词的划类与使用规则 华东师范大学学报(哲学社会科学版)
10. Zou, Hai Qing.: The scope and types of frequency adverbs. Chinese Teaching in the World 77, 36–45 (2006). (邹海清:频率副词的范围和类别, 世界汉语教学) (in Chinese)
11. Zou, Yun: *The Comparative Study of the Frequency Adverbs Containing the same Morphem "chang"*, MA thesis, Jilin University. (2009) (邹运. 含有同一语素"常"的频度副词对比研究 吉林大学硕论)

On the Grammaticalization of Chinese Prefix Di

Mengbin Liu*

School of Foreign Languages, Sun Yat-sen University,
No. 135, Xingang Xi Road, Guangzhou, 510275, P. R. China
liumb5@mail.sysu.edu.cn

Abstract. The origin and development of Chinese prefix *di* which indicates ordinal numbers are very important in Chinese ordinal number system. However, in current studies, it is still a controversial issue whether prefix *di* originated from a nominal *di* "order" or a verb *di* "arrange the order" and when it became grammaticalized. This paper provides a detailed analysis about the controversial data in Archaic Chinese from the perspective of generative syntax and semantics, and argues that the prefix *di* indicating ordinal numbers is grammaticalized from the nominal *di* "order/rank" which was frequently used before the numerals. *Di* was first used as a prefix in *Han* Period. The theory and way of analysis of generative syntax and semantics are very helpful for the studies of the historical grammar of Chinese.

Keywords: Chinese; Prefix *di*; Grammaticalization; Syntactic analysis

1   Introduction

The origin and development of Prefix *di* 第 which indicates ordinal numbers are very important in Chinese ordinal number system. Ōta, T. (1987:142) claims that Prefix *di* 第 was originally a noun meaning "order". Wang (1980:258) argues that *di yi* 第一 "the first" originally had the meaning of "rank first place", in which *di* 第 was used as a verb and it was used as a prefix in Han Dynasty. However, Wang (1990:29) puts forward a different claim that "*di* 第 was originally a noun meaning 'order', indicating the rank of nobility, and it was used as a prefix in later than *Jin* 晉 Dynasty (maybe earlier than *Jin* 晉)". Example (1) was used in Ōta, T (1987:142) to support his claim.

(1) 蕭何*第*一，曹參次之。（《史記·蕭湘國世家》）
  Xiaohe di   yi, caocen ci zhi *(Shiji, Xiaoxiangguo shijia)*
  Xiaohe rank first, Caocen next him
  "Xiaohe ranked first, and Caocen the second."

Two similar examples were used to support Wang's claim in both books, as illustrated below:

(2) (平陽侯)......功最多，宜*第*一。（《史記·蕭湘國世家》）

  (Pingyang hou)   gong   zuiduo, yi di yi. *(Shiji, Xiaoxiangguo shijia)*
  (Pingyang minister) contribution most should rank first
    "The minister of Pingyang made the most contribution, so he should be ranked the first place."

© Springer International Publishing AG 2018
Y. Wu et al. (Eds.): CLSW 2017, LNAI 10709, pp. 124–132, 2018.
https://doi.org/10.1007/978-3-319-73573-3_10

(3) 於是孝文帝乃以絳侯勃為右丞相，位次*第一*；平徙為左丞相，位次*第二*。
（《史記·陳丞相世家》）

Yushi xiaowen di   nai yi jianghoubo wei you chengxiang,
Then Xiaowen emperor then Prt Jianghoubo be right premier,

weici di   yi; pingxi wei zuo chengxiang, weici di er. *(Shiji, Chenchengxiang shijia)*

rank rank first Pingxi as left premier   rank rank second

"Then the Emperor Xiaowen assigned Jianghoubo to the position of Right Premier, ranking the first place, and assigned Pingxi to the position of the Left Premier, ranking the second place."

Sentences (1)-(3) are actually similar and they seem to support two opposite arguments.

Liu (1992:193) provides another interesting point. He considered *di* 第 as a verbalized noun when followed by numerals. It was grammaticalized to be a prefix through historical development.

Whether prefix *di* 第 originated from a nominal *di* 第 "order", a verb *di* 第 "arrange the order" or a verbalized noun *di* 第? When it became grammaticalized? For lack of detailed syntactic analysis and evidence, we may conclude that different linguistic intuition resulted in different opinion about the same examples in the literature. This paper provides a detailed syntactic analysis about these examples, including more other data in Archaic Chinese. Through the syntactic analysis and investigation about its historical development, this paper argues that prefix *di* 第 originates from the noun "order". It became grammaticalized and was used as a prefix in *Han* 汉 Dynasty.

Most of the data are selected from the corpus of Taiwan's Academia Sinica and Peking University Chinese Corpus.

2   Analysis about Examples in Previous Studies

In this section, two groups of examples will be discussed. In the first group, *di* 第 is used in the construction: NP (+ADV)+*di yi* 第一, in which *di yi* 第一 means "rank the first place" and surfaces as the predicate of the sentence, and may be modified by an adverb, as shown in (1)-(3) above. In the second group *di* 第 is used in the construction: NP+*yu* 欲/*ling* 令+NP+ *di yi* 第一, in which *yu* 欲 means "want" and *ling* 令 means "cause" or "command", as shown in (4) and (5) below. Sentences in the second group are also frequently used as evidence for arguing that prefix *di* 第 was grammaticalized from a verb. Therefore, they are worthy of discussion.

(4) 上已橈功臣，多封蕭何，至位次未有以復難之，然心欲何*第一*。（《史記·蕭湘國世家》）

Shang yi   rao gong   chen,   duo feng xiaohe, zhi
emperor already hurt contribution minister more award Xiaohe regarding
weici wei you yi fu   nan zhi, ran xin yu   he   di   yi.
rank not have Aux again argue them but heart want Xiaohe rank first.
(Shiji, Xiaoxiangguo shijia)

"The Emperor had already hurt other meritorious ministers because of granting more rewards to Xiaohe, so the Emperor didn't argue in terms of the ranking although he wished that Xiaohe should rank the first place."

(5) 高祖曰："善。"於是乃令蕭何*第一*（《史記·蕭湘國世家》）

Gaozu yue: "Shan." Yushi nai ling xiaohe di   yi *(Shiji, Xiaoxiangguo shijia)*
Gaozu say fine   then then make Xiaohe rank first

"The Emperor Gaozu said: 'Fine'. Then he made Xiaohe rank the first place"

2.1   NP (+ADV)+*di yi* 第一

This paper argues that *di* 第 in this construction, as shown in (1)-(3), cannot be used as the evidence for the argument that Prefix *di* 第 originated from the verb. *Di* 第 is fine to be analyzed as a noun for three reasons.

First, *di yi* 第一 in these sentences can be understood as a nominal phrase which behaves as the predicate of the sentence. It is very common to see a nominal phrase functioning as the predicate in Archaic Chinese, as illustrated below:

(6) 蟹六跪而二螯。（《荀子》）
  xie liu gui er   er ao. (*Xun Zi*)
  crab six leg Conj two claw
  "The crab has six legs and two claws."

(7) 其中多何羅之魚，一首而十身。（《山海經》）
  Qi zhong duo heluo zhi yu, yi shou er   shi shen. (*Shan Hai jing*)
  it   in many Hehuo Prt fish one head Conj ten body
  "In the river there are plenty of fish called Heluo, with one head and ten bodies."

In (6), *liu gui er er ao* 六跪而二螯 "six legs and two claws" functions as the predicate of the subject "crab". In sentence (7), *heluo zhi* yu 何羅之魚 "Heluo fish" and *yi shou er shi shen* 一首而十身 "one head and ten bodies" are nominal phrases which both function as the predicate.

Second, *yi* 宜 "should" can modify nominal phrases in Archaic Chinese. In (2), *di yi* 第一 "rank first" is modified by an adverb *yi* 宜 "should". According to He (1985:686), the basic function of *yi* 宜 "should" is to modify a verb or an adjective. At first glance, we may intuitively feel *di yi* 第一 should be a verbal phrase. However, it is also common to see *yi* 宜 "should" modifying nominal phrases, as illustrated below:

(8) 我國家禮亦宜之。（《尚書》）
  wo guo   jia   li   yi   yi zhi. (*Shang Shu*)
  my country home courtesy also should Pro
  "The courtesy of our country should be like this. "

(9) 宜兄宜弟，令德壽豈。（《詩經》）
  yi   xiong yi   di,   ling de   shouqi. (*Shi Jing*)
  should brother should brother, noble moral longevity
  "(Your majesty and the servants) should be friendly like brothers, and they wish you noble moral and long and happy life."

In (8), the pronominal *zhi* 之 is modified by *yi* 宜 "should", and in (9), the nouns *xiong* 兄 "brother" and *di* 弟 "brother" are modified by *yi* 宜 "should".

Third, sentences in this group can also be understood as existing an empty auxiliary verb φ. It can be spelt out as *shi* 是 "is" or *wei* 為 "is". One piece of evidence comes from the property that in Chinese, the verb can be empty. We can see more apparently through the examples in Mandarin Chinese with the help of the aspect marker *le* 了.

(10) 你這次考試都 φ 第一名了。
  ni zhe   ci kaoshi dou diyi ming le.
  you this CL exam even first place Prt
  "You got the first place in the exam this time."

(11) 你都 φ 大姑娘了。
  ni dou   da   guniang le.
  you already young girl   Prt
  "You are already a lady now."

In both (10) and (11), an auxiliary verb *shi* 是 "is" can be added.

Another piece of evidence comes from generative semantics. According to the theory of type-driven interpretation in generative semantics (cf. Pan & Jiang 1998, Heim & kratzer 1998), in the construction "NP+*shi* 是/*wei* 为+NP", the predicate *shi* 是/*wei* 为 "is" is of type $<<e, t>, <e, t>>$. It need input a nominal phrase of the type $<e, t>$, and the output is also a nominal phrase with the type $<e, t>$, which manifests that *shi* 是/*wei* 为 "is" has no contribution in semantics. It only connects the subject and predicate. Therefore, it can be optional in the level of syntax.

As discussed above, it is pretty good for *di yi* 第一 in (1) − (3) to be analyzed as a nominal phrase rather than a verbal phrase. It lacks evidence for *di* 第 to be analyzed as a verb. Therefore, *di* 第 in these sentences cannot be used as evidence for the argument that prefix *di* 第 originated from a verb.

2.2   NP+*yu* 欲/*ling* 令+NP+*di yi* 第一

According to Zhao (1979), verbs like *jiao* 叫 "ask", *shi* 使 "cause", *xihuan* 喜欢 "like" and *yao* 要 "want" frequently form pivotal construction. In (4) and (5), *yu* 欲 "want" and *ling* 令 "command" seem to be the former verb in a pivotal construction and *di* 第 seems to be the latter verb meaning "arrange the rank". Accordingly, some scholars may claim that the prefix *di* 第 originated from a verb. However, *di* 第 is not necessarily a verb and it is fine to be analyzed as a noun. *Yu* 欲 "want" and *ling* 令 "command" can function as a main verb of a sentence and do not have to form a pivotal construction, as illustrated below:

(12)倒之顛之，自公令之。（《詩經》）
dao zhi dian zhi, zi gong *ling* zhi.
busily Prt busily Prt from duke order them
"(The laboring people) were so busy because of the command from the Duke."

(13)是師也，唯子玉欲之。（《國語》）
shi   shi   ye, wei ziyu *yu*   zhi (*Guo Yu*)
this battle Prt only Ziyu want it
"As to this battle, only Ziyu want to be like that."

(14) 天下之王公大人，皆欲其國家之富也。（《墨子》）
tianxia zhi wang gong   daren, jie *yu*   qi guojia zhi fu   ye. (*Mo Zi*)
world Prt official official   official all want Prt country Prt wealthy Prt
"The officials all want the country to be wealthy."

(15)募民欲財物粟米。（《墨子》）
guamin *yu*   cai   wu   su   mi. (*Mo Zi*)
people want money good rice rice
"The common people want money and grain."

In (12) and (13), *ling* 令 "command" and *yu* 欲 "want" are main verbs of the clause, followed by pronouns *zhi* 之 "them" and *zhi* 之 "it" as the object respectively. In (14), *yu* 欲 "want" is followed by a nominal phrase *qi guo jia zhi fu* 其國家之富 "the wealth of their country" and in (15), *cai wu su mi* 財物粟米 "money and grain" is the object of *yu* 欲 "want".

As a result, *di* 第 in (4) and (5) is not necessarily a verb either. Therefore (4) and (5) cannot serve as the evidence for the argument that Prefix *di* 第 comes from a verb.

3 Analysis about Other Verb-like Usages of *di* 第

This part will discuss some other sentences in which *di* 第 appears like verbs, as illustrated below:

(16)遷有司之吏而*第*之。（《管子》）

qian yousi zhi li er *di* zhi (*Guan Zi*)

appoint official Prt official Conj rank them

"Adjust the appointment of the officials and arrange their rank."

(17)禹遂因而*第*之以成九類常道。（《洪範》）(*Hong fan*)

yu sui yin er *di* zhi yi cheng jiu lei chang-dao

Yu then reason Conj order them Conj become nine CL category

"Then Yu classified them into nine categories according to their order."

(18)武宗即位，*第*功，封越王。（《元史》）

wuzong jiwei, *di* gong, feng yue wang (*Yuan Shi*)

Wuzong enthrone rank contribution assign Yue king

"After the emperor Wuzong is enthroned, he made all of his officials in the right rank according to their contributions, and assigned someone King of Yue."

(19) 長曰恭，舉進士未*第*。（《唐文拾遺》）

zhang yue gong, ju jinshi wei *di* (*Tang Wen Shi Yi*)

eldest name Gong examine candidate not rank

"The eldest was named Gong. He took the imperial examination and he failed to pass it."

(20) 已*第*者聞之多怒。（《歸潛志》）

yi *di* zhe wen zhi duo nu. (*Gui Qian Zhi*)

already rank Prt hear it much anger

"Those who had already passed the imperial examination were very angry."

In these sentences, it seems fine to analyze *Di* 第 as a verb. However, a question arises: does the verbal meaning really come from *di* 第? I argue that the verb meaning does not necessarily come from *di* 第. Let us divide these examples into two groups and discuss respectively. The first group consists of sentences such as (16)-(18) in which *di* 第 is followed by a nominal phrase as its object, described as: …+*di* 第+NP. The second group consists of sentences such as (18) and (19), in which *di* 第 is not followed by anything but it is modified by an adverb, described as: …+ADV +*di* 第.

3.1 …+*di* 第+NP

This paper argues that *di* 第 in these sentences is a noun in nature and is used in causative constructions, and the verbal meaning in such kind of sentence comes from a zero causative verb and a light verb *you* 有 "have". The definition and syntax of causative constructions have been widely studied (cf. Masayoshi. S. 1976, He & Wang 2002 and many others). I assume that a light causative verb featured -*v* exists in this kind of *di* 第 construction. Since it lacks an overt causative verb, the noun *di* 第 moves upwards to combine with the light verb -*v*. If an overt causative verb *shi* 使 "make" existed, then (16) and (18) should appear in the surface as (21) and (22) respectively.

(21) 遷有司之吏而*使之有第*

qian yousi zhi li er *shi* zhi you *di*

appoint official Prt official Conj make them have rank

"Adjust the appointment of the officials and make them in right rank."

(22)武宗即位，*使功有第*，封越王。

wuzong jiwei, *shi* gong you *di*, feng yue wang

Wuzong enthrone make contribution have rank assign Yue king

"After the emperor Wuzong is enthroned, he made all of his officials in the right rank according to their contributions, and assigned someone the King of Yue."

As mentioned before, Liu (1992:193) considers *di* 第 as a verbalized noun often followed by numerals and through grammaticalization it became an affix. My analysis to some extent verifies his argument. The difference lies in that in my analysis *di* 第 is a noun in essence and in deep structure a covert causative verb *−v* exists.

Two pieces of evidence come from the data in classical Chinese. First, it is common to see this kind of usage in classical Chinese, as illustrated below:

(23) a. 夫子所謂生死而*肉*骨也。（《左傳·襄公22年》）

fu zi suo wei sheng si er   *rou*   gu ye *(Zuozhuan·Xianggong 22 nian)*
Prt you Prt say live dead Conj flesh bone Prt

"He is the one who you said that he can make the dead alive and the bone grow with flesh."

b. 夫子所謂使死者生而*使骨長肉*

fu zi suo wei shi   si zhe sheng er   *shi* gu zhang *rou*
Prt you Prt say make dead Prt alive Conj make bone grow flesh

"He is the one who you said that he can make the dead alive and bone grow with flesh."

(24) a. 纵江东父兄怜而*王*我 （《史记·项羽本纪》）

zong jiangdong fu   xiong lian   er   wang wo *(Shiji·Xiangyu benji)*
if   Jiangdong father brother sympathize Conj king me

"Even if the people in Jiangdong sympathize me and make me be the king"

b. 纵江东父兄怜而*使我为王*

zong Jiangdong fu   xiong   lian   er   *shi* wo wei *wang*
if   Jiangdong father brother sympathize Conj make me become king

"Even if the people in Jiangdong sympathize me and make me be the king."

(23a) and (24a) can be analyzed in the same way. Without an overt causative verb, the noun *rou* 肉 "flesh" moves to the position of a causative light verb *−v* for phonological interpretation and surfaces as a lexical causative verb. The corresponding syntactic causative form with an overt causative verb is illustrated by (23b). *Shi wo wei wang* 使我为王 "make me be the king" in (24a) behaves as the underlying structure of *wang wo* 王我 in (24b).

Second, since *di* 第 in (16)-(18) is essentially a noun and a covert causative light verb exists, I assume that the verbal property of *di-v* should be weak and may not be modified by negative adverbs and time adverbs. *Wei* 未 "not", *yi* 已 "already" and *jiang* 将 "will" are used to test the property of *di* 第. As predicated, I cannot find a case in which *di* 第 is at the same time both modified by anyone of these adverbs and followed by an object in the corpus of classical Chinese. As shown below, (25a, b) sound strange.

(25)???a. *wei/jiang/yi di zhi* 未第之 "not/will/already make them in the right rank"

???b. *wei/jiang/yi di gong* 未第功 "not/will/already make their contribution in the right rank"

3.2 ...+ADV +*di* 第

Di 第 in (19) and (20) looks like a verb at first glance because *di* 第 seems to be modified by adverbs *wei* 未 "not" and *yi* 已 "already". However, the question is: does this verbal meaning really comes from the word *di* 第? It is not necessarily so. We assume that an empty verb *ji* 及 "achieve" exists in (19) and (20). It is well-formed when *ji* 及 "achieve" is added, as shown below.

(26) 舉進士未及第
ju   jinshi   wei   *ji*   *di*
examine candidate not achieve rank
"He took the imperial examination and failed to achieve the first rank."

(27) 已及第者聞之多怒。（《歸潛志》）
yi   *ji*   *di* zhe wen zhi duo nu. (*Gui Qian Zhi*)
already achieve rank Prt hear it much anger
"Those who had already achieved the first rank were very angry."

As predicated, there are quite a few of examples in classical Chinese with an overt main verb *ji* 及 "achieve" before the object *di* 第, as shown below:

(28) 及第後知聞，或遇未及第時題名處 （《唐摭言》）
    ji   di hou zhi wen,   huo yu wei ji   di shi   ti-ming chu
achieve rank after know know or see not achieve rank when autograph place
(*Tang Zhi Yan*)
"After successfully achieving the first rank in the imperial examination, when he got to know or ran across the place of his autograph, he… "

(29) 穀未及第時 （《堯山堂外紀》）
gu wei ji   di   shi (*Yaoshantang Waiji*)
Gu not achieve rank when
"When Gu didn't achieve the first rank in the imperial examination,…"

What is more, if the assumption that there exists an empty verb *ji* 及 "achieve" in (19) and (20) is right, *ji* 及 "achieve" should be a transitive verb and *di* 第 "rank" /"place" should behave as its object. Therefore, an additional object should not be allowed in principle. The assumption of this paper is verified by the facts in classical Chinese, because I cannot find any case which allows another object in this construction. Sentences such as (30) and (31) cannot be found in the corpus.

(30) *舉進士未第之
ju   jinshi   wei *di zhi*
examine candidate not rank it
"He took the imperial examination and failed to achieve the first rank in it."

(31)*已第之者聞之多怒。
yi   *di zhi* zhe wen zhi duo nu.
already rank it Prt hear it much anger
"Those who had already achieved the first rank in the imperial examination were very angry."

4   Proposal

As discussed above, the argument that prefix *di* 第 was grammaticalized from verb *di* 第 lacks independent syntactic evidence. I argue that prefix *di* 第 was grammaticalized from noun *di* 第 "rank" because it was frequently followed by numerals. At least two pieces of evidence are provided below.

First, according to various dictionaries about classical Chinese, *di* 第 was derived from *di* 弟. In *Shuo Wen Jie Zi Zhu* 說文解字注，*di* 弟 is considered as a noun first used to indicate the order of the inequable bunches of the reed in Archaic Chinese and then used to indicate the order of other things. Through the development of Chinese, *di* 弟 was specified to indicate the order of the brothers, referring to younger brother specifically. When indicating the order or rank of other things, it was gradually replaced by *di* 第. We can see the distinctive difference between these two words in modern Chinese.

Second, there are many nouns indicating order in Archaic Chinese, and it is quite common for us to see an ordinal prefix or morpheme grammaticalized from a noun through historical development, as *tou* 头 "head" and *shou* 首 "head" shown in (32):

(32) a. *tou* 头 "head" →*tou* 头 "ordinal"

     eg., *tou* santian 头三天 "the first three days", *tounian* 头年 "the first year", *touhui* 头回 "the first time"

     b. *shou* 首 "head" → *shou* 首 "ordinal"

     eg., *shouci* 首次 "the first time", *shoufei* 首飞 "the first flight", *shouchuang* 首创 "the first success"

In terms of the time when *di* 第 was first used as a prefix, I agree with Wang (1980:258) that *di* 第 was first used as a prefix in *Han* 汉 Dynasty. The criterion I adopt is that in *Han* period, the construction "*di* 第+ Num+ Noun" began to appear, as shown in (33) and (34).

     (33) 有男四人，使相工相之，至*第二子*，其名玄成。（《史記·張承相列傳》）

     ... zhi *di'er* zi , qi   ming   xuancheng.

     till second son, Pro name   Xuancheng

     "When goes to the second son, whose name is Xuancheng, ..."

(34) 光武帝，建平元年十二月甲子生於濟陽宮後殿*第二內中*。（《論衡》）

Guang wudi, jianping yuan   nian shi'er   yue   jiazi sheng yu qiyang gong

Guang wudi   Jianping begin year   twelve   month hour born at Qiyang palace

houdian *di'er* neizhong .

backyard second room

"The Emperor Guangwu was born at the second room of the backyard of the palace Qiyang at Jiazi on December in the year Jianping."

In sentences (33) and (34), 第二 *di'er* is followed by another noun *zi* 子 "son" and *neizhong* 內中 "room" respectively, which indicates that 第二 *di'er* itself is not a phrase but a numeral modifying the noun.

Di 第 was frequently followed by numerals from Archaic Chinese. However, it is hard to decide whether *di* 第 is a noun or a prefix in Archaic Chinese. Both understandings are possible. What is more, many of "*di* 第+Num" constructions appeared in the title and they may be added by the editors in the later periods. Therefore, it is much clearer that in "*di*+ Num+ Noun" construction, *di* 第 is a prefix rather than a noun.

5   Conclusion

As discussed above, according to the syntactic analyses about the *di* 第 sentences in Archaic Chinese, this paper argues against the view that the prefix *di* 第 indicating ordinal numbers came from the verb *di* 第 "arrange the rank", and argue that prefix *di* 第 was grammaticalized from the noun *di* 第 "order/rank" which was frequently used before the numerals. *Di* 第 was first used as a prefix in *Han* Period. The theory and way of analysis of generative syntax and semantics are very helpful for the studies of the historical grammar of Chinese.

Acknowledgments. I benefited a lot from discussing the idea and details of my analysis with Prof. Paul.S.Law in City University of Hong Kong. I would also like to express my gratitude to Prof. Pan Haihua and the anonymous reviewer for their valuable suggestions. The paper is funded by the 61th China Postdoctoral Science Foundation Grant (2017M612784).

References

1. Duan, Y. C.: Annotation to the Origin of Chinese Characters [*Shuo Wen Jie Zi Zhu*]. The publisher of Hanjing Culture Ltd. [*Taibei: Hanjing wenhua shiye*] (1983) [In Chinese]
2. He, L. S., Ao. J. H.: On the Explanation of Functions Words in Ancient Chinese [*Gudai hanyu xuci tongshi*]. The Publisher of Beijing [*Beijing Chubanshe*] (1985) [In Chinese]
3. He, Y. J., Wang L. L.: *The Syntax of Causatives in Chinese*, Chinese Language Learning (4), (2002) [In Chinese]
4. Heim, I., Kratzer, A.: *Semantics in Generative Grammar*, Blackwell, UK (1998)
5. Liu, S. Z.: Historical Grammar of Weijin Nanbei Chao [*Weijin Nanbei Chao Lishi yufa*]. The Publisher of Nanjing University (1992) [In Chinese]
6. Masayoshi. S.: Syntax and Semantics. New York: Academic Press, vol.6(1976.)
7. Ōta, T.: Chinese Historical Grammar [*Zhongguoyu Lishi Wenfa*]. The publisher of Peking University (1987) [In Chinese]
8. Pan, H. H., Jiang, Y.: Introduction to Formal Semantics. China Social Sciences Press (1998) [In Chinese]
9. Tang Y. M.: on the Origin of Ancient Chinese Momentum Marking [*Guhanyu dongliang biaojifa tanyuan*]. Research in Ancient Chinese Language [*Guhanyu yanjiu*] (1), (1990) [In Chinese]
10. Wang. L.: History of Chinese Grammar [*Hanyu yufashi*]. The Publisher of Shandong Education (1990) [In Chinese]
11. Wang. L.: History of Chinese [*Hanyu shigao*], Zhonghua Shuju Press (1980) [In Chinese]
12. Zhao. Y. R.: A Grammar of Spoken Chinese [*Hanyu kouyu yufa*].Commercial Press (1979) [In Chinese]

The Degree Usage of *Cai* and Relevant Issues

Lei Zhang

Chinese Language and Literature School, Northeast Normal University

Zhangl1120@nenu.edu.cn

Abstract. This paper investigates the degree usage of 才 [*cai*] and some relevant issues. It is argued that in this case *cai* and the sentence final particle 呢 [*ne*] form a discontinuous constituent, which modifies the element surrounded by it. "才···呢" [*cai···ne*'] requires that the element modified by it has the gradable property. Thus only qualified VPs, AdjPs and NegPs can co-occur with '*cai···ne*'. Some characteristics of '*cai···ne*' are shown by comparing it with other degree adverbs. Moreover, the syntactic structure and semantic interpretation of '*cai···ne*' are given.

Keywords: The degree *cai*· Discontinuous constituent· Co-occurrence restriction

1   Introduction

One usage of the multi-functional adverb 才[*cai*] is to indicate that the relevant degree is high, as shown in (1). However, most studies are devoted to either the unified account of the adverbial *cai* or the case that *cai* serves as a focus particle. Detailed analysis on the case that *cai* signals high degree is short. This paper attempts to explore the degree usage of *cai* and some relevant issues.

(1) a. 那　孩子　才　漂亮　呢![1]
      that child CAI pretty　SFP
      'That child is very pretty!'
  b. 这　孩子　个子　才　矮　呢!

---

[1] In the case of '*cai···ne*', there is another possibility, namely *cai* serves as an exclusive adverb and *ne* expresses mood. In this paper, without special illustration, *cai* takes the degree usage in '*cai···ne*'.

Y. Wu et al. (Eds.): CLSW 2017, LNAI 10709, pp. 133–146, 2018.
https://doi.org/10.1007/978-3-319-73573-3_11

this child height CAI short SFP
'This child is very short!'

The rest of this paper is organized as follows. Section 2 puts forward that in the degree usage the adverbial *cai* and the particle 呢 [*ne*] form a discontinuous constituent. Section 3 explores the restrictions of the discontinuous "才…呢" [*cai…ne*] 'the degree is high' on VPs, AdjPs and NegP. Section 4 makes a comparison among commonly used degree adverbs which indicate high degree. Section 5 provides the syntactic structure and semantic interpretation of '*cai…ne*'. The last section concludes this paper.

2   The Discontinuous Constituent '*Cai…Ne*'

Previous studies such as Lü (1980) have mentioned that, in the case of implying the degree is high, the adverb *cai* should co-occur with the particle *ne*. This paper argues that in the degree case *cai* and *ne* form a discontinuous constituent. The supporting evidences are shown below.

2.1   The Obligatory Co-occurrence of *Cai* with *Ne*

In the case that *cai* taking the meaning 'the degree is high', the appearance of the particle *ne* is generally obligatory. When the particle *ne* is deleted, the relevant sentences become ungrammatical or their basic meanings are changed, as shown in (2), which are gotten by omitting *ne* from the sentences in (1).

(2) a. 那   孩子   才   漂亮!
    that child CAI pretty
    'That child is pretty!'
  b. 这   孩子   个子   才   矮!
    this child height CAI short
    'This child is short!'

In the case that *cai* serves as an exclusive adverb, sentences in (2) are acceptable. For instance, under the influence of the semantics of the focus adverb *cai*, (2a) expresses that 那孩子[*na haizi*] (that child) but no other alternatives can satisfy the open sentence 'x is pretty'. Otherwise, these sentences are unacceptable.

Generally speaking, when *cai* is omitted, the sentences under consideration will become ungrammatical, as seen in (3), which are derived by deleting *cai* from (1).

(3) a. *那   孩子   漂亮 呢!
    that child pretty SFP
  b. *这 孩子 个子 矮   呢!
    this child height short SFP

Since deleting either *cai* or *ne* makes the sentences considered become ungrammatical or change their basic interpretations, it is suitable to treat '*cai...ne*' as a discontinuous constituent.

2.2   Two More Degree Expressions with *Ne*

Besides the discontinuous constituent '*cai...ne*', two expressions "可···呢" [*ke···ne*][2] and "着呢" [*zhene*] containing the particle *ne* can be used to signal 'the degree is high', which shows that *ne* has the capability of co-occurring with another adverb to indicate that the relevant degree is high.

The Discontinuous '*Ke···Ne*'. The adverb *ke* usually co-occurs with a sentence-final particle like *ne* to indicate that the degree denoted by the predicate surrounded by them is high, as illustrated in (4).

(4) a. 长春　　的 冬天 可 冷 呢!
　　　　Changchun DE winter KE cold SFP
　　　　'Changchun's winter is very cold!'

　　 b. 这 条 鱼 可 大 呢!
　　　　this CL fish KE big SFP
　　　　'This fish is very big!'

In a similar fashion, subtracting *ne* will make the relevant sentences either change their interpretations or become marginal, as shown in (5).

(5) a. 长春　　　的 冬天 可 冷!
　　　　Changchun DE winter KE cold
　　　　'Changchun's winter is cold indeed!'

　　 b. 这 条 鱼 可 大!
　　　　this CL fish KE big
　　　　'This fish is big indeed!'

Omitting *ke*, the relevant sentences usually become unacceptable, as shown in (6).

(6) a. ?? 长春　　　的 冬天 冷 呢!
　　　　Changchun DE winter cold SFP
　　　　'Changchun's winter is very cold!'

　　 b.?? 这 条 鱼 大 呢!
　　　　this CL fish big SFP
　　　　'This fish is very big!'

---

[2] The particles *le* and *la* can play the same role, namely '*ke···la/le*' can signal the degree is high, either.

The Combination of *Zhe* and *Ne*. The combination of the two particles *zhe* and *ne* can indicate that the degree is high, either. Look at (7).

(7) a. 他　开心　着　呢!

    he happy PRT SFP

    'He is very happy!'

  b. 她　长　得　好看　着　呢!

    she look DE beautiful PRT SFP

    'She is very beautiful!'

After deleting the particle *zhe* in (7), the corresponding sentences in (8) will become ungrammatical.

(8) a. *他　开心　呢!

    he happy SFP

    'He is very happy!'

  b. *她　长　得　好看　呢!

    she look DE beautiful SFP

    'She is very beautiful!'

Similarly, omitting *ne*, the sentences considered either change their meanings or become unacceptable, as shown in (9).

(9) a. ??他　开心　着!³

    he happy PRT

    'He is very happy!'

  b. *她　长　得　好看　着!

    she look DE beautiful PRT

    'She is very beautiful!'

2.3　Other Discontinuous Expressions with High Degree

Similar to *cai*, to get the high degree reading the adverb 老[*lao*] (very) often relies on the presence of another particle. The degree adverb *lao* chooses the particle 的[*de*] or 了[*le*] and then they form the discontinuous "老…的/了" [*lao…de/le*]. Consider below.

(10) a. 她　的头发老　长　了。

    she DE hair LAO long SFP

    'Her hair is very long.'

  b. ??她　的 头发　老　长.

    she DE hair LAO long

    'Her hair is very long.'

---

³ When *zhe* functions as a mark of progressive aspect，the relevant sentences may become better.

(11) a. 这 湖 老 深 老 深 的。
　　　this lake LAO deep LAO deep DE
　　　'This lake is very deep.'
　　b. *这 湖 老 深 老 深。
　　　this lake LAO deep LAO deep
　　　'This lake is very deep.'

In addition, in the cases of modifying the adjective phrases or verb phrases, the degree adverbs 太[*tai*] (very, too) and 多[*duo*] (very) usually co-occur with the modal particles *le* and 啊 [*a*] respectively. See (12) and (13).

(12) a. 这 支 花 太 美 了!
　　　This CL flower TAI beautiful SFP
　　　'This flower is very beautiful!'
　　b. 这 支 花 太 美!
　　　This CL flower TAI beautiful
　　　'This flower is very beautiful!'

(13) a. 多 可爱 的 孩子 啊!
　　　DUO lovely DE child SFP
　　　'It's a very lovely child!'
　　b. (?)多 可爱 的 孩子!
　　　DUO lovely DE child
　　　'It's a very lovely child!'

Although sentence (12b) is acceptable, its basic reading has been changed, which means that 'this flower is too beautiful, which is excessive'. (13b) is grammatical, but is seldom used.

It turns out that, in addition to using degree adverbs alone, using discontinuous constituents is another usual way to express the degree is high.

3   Restrictions on Modified Elements

As pointed out by previous studies such as Lü (1980), the elements that can occur in the discontinuous constituent of '*cai*···*ne*' are restricted. It is observed by Lü (1980) that, the constituents compatible with the degree usage of *cai* are usually adjective phrases or negation phrases which take verb phrases as their complements.

In this section, the relevant researches are first introduced briefly and my own analysis is then given.

3.1   Previous Studies

Zhang B. S. (2003) provides an explanation on why in a sentence with the emphatic *cai* the verb tends to take the negative form.

Zhang assumes that *cai* is used to express small subjective quantity. Furthermore, he adopts the opinions of Shi (1992) and Shen (1999) on the relation between quantity and positive/negative sentences. They both consider that particles such as 一点儿 [*yidianr*] (a little) and 丝毫 [*sihao*] (a bit) indicating minimal quantity are compatible with verb phrases with the negative form, but do not co-occur with verb phrases holding the positive form. See (14) and (15).

(14) a. 一点儿 不 生气   b. * 一点儿 生气
        a little NEG angry   a little   angry
        'not angry at all'   'a little angry'
(15) a. 丝毫   不   相信   b. * 丝毫相信
        a-little NEG believe   a little believe
        'not believe at all'   'a little believe'

Following their analyses, Zhang illustrates that an action denoted by the relevant verb has a quantity, which is usually expressed by a verbal measure word or a temporal measure word. The negative form of the verb indicates 'no quantity', which is close to 'minimal quantity'. Hence they are compatible with *cai*. However, in the case that a verb phrase expresses the existence of a quantity but does not show the amount, the verb considered is incompatible with *cai*.

It is a pity that Zhang's analysis holds some limitations. First of all, *cai* does not always indicate small subjective quantity, as seen in (16). Given *cai* associates the asserted value 三个人[*san ge ren*] (three people), in (16) *cai* signals the asserted value is more than what is expected/stipulated. Secondly, the negation of a verb phrase does not guarantee 'no quantity', for example, sentences like (17) does not mean 'he did not borrow any book'. Finally, the emphatic *cai* is compatible with verbs with the positive form in some cases, as shown in (18).

(16) 三 个 人   才 能抬起这 张 桌子.
        three CL person CAI can lift up this CL desk
        'It takes three people to lift up this desk.'
(17) 他 没   借   三 本 书.
        he NEG borrow three CL book
        'He did not borrow three books.'
(18) 这 项   工作 才   花 时间 呢!
        this CL   work CAI spend time SFP
        'This work takes much time!'

Hole (2004) puts forward that in the emphatic use type one emphatic kind of *cai*'s usage is to identify 'a particular high degree up to which a gradable property may be ascribed to a referent'. This opinion is insightful.

3.2   An Alternative Account

It is argued that, the discontinuous constituent '*cai...ne*' requires the element surrounded by it to take the gradable property, which makes sure that this element can be modified by a degree adverb, especially by a degree adverb that expresses high degree. To be more specific, the element that can be modified by '*cai...ne*' can introduce a degree scale indirectly on which the alternative degree values are ordered from low to high.

Restrictions on Verbs. Without the help of negation, which kinds of verbs are compatible with the discontinuous '*cai...ne*'? In what follows, the compatibility of '*cai...ne*' with different types of verbs is explored.[4]

Following Xing (1997), verbs can be classified into six semantic categories: (a) action verbs; (b) mental verbs; (c) duration verbs, which is related to the progress of actions, such as 开始[*kaishi*] (start), 停止[*tingzhi*] (stop) and so forth; (d) assertive verbs (断事动词), which refer to verbs that convey the meaning of 'right or wrong', 'have or not have', 'be like' and so on, including the verbs such as 是[*shi*] (be), 有[*you*] (have), （存）在 [(*cun*)*zai*] (exist); (e) causative verbs, which mean 'command' or 'require', such as 叫[*jiao*] (let), 请[*qing*] (ask) and the like; and (f) auxiliary verbs, mainly including modal verbs and directional verbs.

According to my observation, in general duration verbs and directional verbs cannot co-occur with '*cai...ne*', as shown in (19); some action/causative/assertive verbs taking the objects are compatible with '*cai...ne*'. The contrasts are shown in (20)-(22), respectively; and (c) most mental verbs are compatible with '*cai...ne*', because these mental verbs are gradable, as in (23).

(19) a. *比赛　才　　进行　　呢!
　　　　game CAI be-in-progress SFP
　　　*'The Game is in progress very much!'
　　b. *　小明　　才　上来　呢!
　　　　Little Ming CAI come-up SFP
　　　*'Little Ming came up very much!'

(20) a. 这　部 小说　才　贴近 生活　呢!
　　　　this CL novel CAI close-to life　SFP

---

[4] Here the verbs in question are allowed to take a complement.

'This novel is very close to life!'
  b. *张三   才 喝 酒 呢!⁵
     Zhangsan CAI drink wine SFP
     Intended: 'Zhangsan drinks very much!'
(21) a. 他 才 叫 人   操心 呢!
     he CAI let person worry SFP
     'He lets people worry about him very much!'
   b. *张三   才 请 李四 喝   酒 呢!
      Zhangsan CAI ask Lisi drink wine SFP
      Intended: 'Zhangsan asks Lisi to drink very much!'
(22) a. 张三   才 有 品味 呢!
      Zhangsan CAI have taste SFP
      'Zhangsan has very good taste!'
    b. *这里 才 存在   机会   呢!
       here CAI exist opportunity SFP
       *'There are very opportunity here!'
(23) 他 才 害怕 李 老师 呢!
    he CAI be-afraid Li teacher SFP
    'He is afraid of Miss Li very much!'
  In a word, the verbs that can be modified by a degree adverb, especially by the
degree adverb 很[hen] (very) can co-occur with 'cai···ne'.

Restrictions on Adjectives. What kinds of adjectives can appear in the discontinuous
'cai...ne'? To answer this question, I examine the compatibility of this discontinuous
constituent with adjectives listed by Zhang G.X. (2006). The result shows that, the
adjectives that can co-occur with 'cai···ne' have the gradable property. In general,
qualitative adjectives can introduce a degree scale, and thus they are compatible with
'cai···ne'; whereas descriptive adjectives like 漆黑[qihei] (pitch-dark) have inherent
degree meaning, and thereby no degree scale is available. As a result, they are incompatible with 'cai...ne'. The contrasts are seen below.
(24) a. *那 本 书 才   崭新   呢!
      that CL book CAI brand-new SFP
    *'That book is very brand-new!'
    b. 那 本 书 才 新 呢!
       that CL book CAI new SFP

---

⁵ When *cai* associates with the subject 'Zhangsan', (20b) is grammatical, which means that
  'Zhangsan but not other alternatives drinks'. Similarly, in (21a), (22a), (23a), *cai* has another
  possible function, namely it acts as an exclusive adverb, but no longer a degree adverb.

'That book is very new!'

(25) a. *天　才　漆黑　　呢!
　　　　sky CAI pitch-dark　SFP
　　　* 'It is very pitch-dark!'

　　b. 天　才　黑　呢!
　　　　sky CAI dark SFP
　　　'It is very dark!'

Restrictions on Negation. Negation can introduce a scale where alternative degrees are ordered according to the degree of negation and the actual value denoted by '*cai...ne*' is located in the high position of the relevant degree scale. Therefore, '*cai...ne*' is compatible with a negation phrase and the strengthened negation reading is gotten. Consider (26).

(26) 他　才　不　　　讲　　礼貌 呢!
　　　He CAI NEG pay-attention polite SFP
　　　'He is very impolite.'

4　A comparison among Degree Adverbs Expressing High Degree

In Mandarin Chinese, monosyllabic degree adverbs that can signal the degree is high mainly include the following seven: *cai*, *ke*, *tai*, *duo*, *lao*, *hen* and 好[*hao*] (very). In this section, a comparison among these degree adverbs is made from the following two aspects.

4.1　Dependency on Particles

The dependency of these degree adverbs on the occurrence of modal particles is different.

As illustrated above, in the high degree case, the co-occurrences of *cai* with the modal particle *ne* and *ke* with *ne/la/le* are obligatory. They all form discontinuous constituents.

The degree adverb *lao* often need the appearance of the particle *le* or *de*. In some cases, the particle is optional, as seen in (27).

(27) 太阳　　已经 升 得 很 高（了）。
　　　The sun　already rise DE HEN high SFP
　　　'The sun has risen very high.'

It is optional that the adverb *tai* co-occurs with the particle *le* and *duo* with 啊[*a*] (modal particle). In exclamatory sentences, these two adverbs usually co-occur with the corresponding particles to indicate that the relevant degree is high. See also (12).

The degree adverb *hao* holds the inherent exclamatory mood, and thus the presence of the particle *a* is optional even in exclamatory sentences. Look at (28).

(28) 这 个 房间 好 舒服 (啊)!
    this CL room HAO cozy SFP
    'This room is very cozy!'

The relation of the degree adverb *hen* with a modal particle is very loose. In corpora such as CCL, modal particles seldom appear in sentences with *hen*, as shown in (29).

(29) 他 很 健康。
    he HEN healthy
    'He is very healthy.'

4.2   The Compatibility with Negation

In what follows, the compatibility of these degree adverbs with negation is examined. Let's first look at the cases that negation precedes the degree adverbs considered.

Generally speaking, the negative verbs 不 [*bu*] (no) and 没 [*mei*] (no) are incompatible with '*cai···ne*', '*ke···ne*', *hao* and *lao*. Consider below.

(30) a. 丽丽 才 大方 呢!
      Lili CAI generous SFP
      'Lili is very generous!'
    b. *丽丽 不/没 才 大方 呢!
       Lili NEG CAI generous SFP

(31) a. 好   难受 啊!
      HAO unwell SFP
      'It is awful!'
    b. *不/没 好   难受 啊!
      NEG HAO unwell SFP

(32) a. *这 个 菜 可 香   呢!
      this CL dish KE delicious SFP
      'This dish smells very delicious!'
    b. 这 个 菜 不/没 可 香   呢!
      this CL dish NEG KE delicious SFP

(33) a. 老   好 吃 了!
      LAO good eat SFP
      'It is very delicious!'

b. *不/没 老　好　吃　了!

   NEG LAO good eat SFP

It is worth noting that, when the adjective 大 [*da*] (big) is inserted between *lao* and the constituent modified by *lao*, and the particle *le* is deleted, the sentences such as (34) derived from (33) will become good.

(34) 不　老　大　好　吃。

   NEG LAO big good eat

   'It is not very delicious.'

The adverb *duo* can be negated by *mei*, but cannot by *bu*, as shown in (35). In (35c), the high degree denoted by *duo* is reduced due to the semantics of *mei*.

(35) a. 多　　美　（啊）!

    DUO beautiful SFP

    'It is very beautiful!'

  b. *不　　多　美。

    NEG DUO beautiful

  c. 没　　多　美。

    NEG DUO beautiful

    'It is not very beautiful.'

The degree adverb *tai* is compatible with *bu*, but cannot be negated by *mei*. Consider (36).

(36) a. 他　太　开心　了!

    he TAI happy SFP

    'He is very happy!'

  b. 他　不　太　开心。.

    he NEG TAI happy

    'He is not very happy.'

  c. ?(?)他　没　太　开心。

     he NEG TAI happy

     'He is not very happy.'

The adverb *hen* can be negated by both *bu* and *mei*. When *hen* is negated by *bu*, the relevant degree denoted by *hen* is reduced; whereas when it is negated by *mei*, the sentence considered means '*hen*+AdjP/VP' did not happen. See (37).

(37) a. 他　不　很　努力。

    he NEG HEN strive

    'He works not very hard.'

  b. 他　没　很　努力。

    he NEG HEN strive

    'He did not work very hard.'

Next turn to the cases that the negation follows the degree adverbs. In the case of '*cai*…*ne*', '*ke*…*ne/la/le*', *duo*, *tai*, *lao*, or *hen*, *bu* is utilized to modify VPs/AdjPs after it. The degree adverb in question modifies '*bu*+VP/AdjP', as shown in (38). In the case of the degree adverb *hao*, in most cases *haobu* roughly equals to *hao*. Consider (39).

(38) 他 可　不 开心　了!
　　he KE NEG happy SFP
　　'He is very unhappy!'

(39) 丽丽 好 不　容易 完成　了　作业。
　　Lili HAO NEG easy finish ASP assignment
　　'Lili finished her assignment with great effort.'

5   The Syntactic Structure and Semantic Interpretation of '*Cai⋯Ne*'

In the case of discontinuous '*cai⋯ne*', the degree adverb *cai* is adjacent to the predicate and can be treated as one part of the adjunct of X', in which X mainly refers to Adj, Neg or V; *ne* is the other part of the adjunct of X'. Consider (40a), whose tree diagram is demonstrated in (40b).

(40) a. Changcheng　　*cai* chang　*ne*!
　　　The Great Wall CAI long SFP
　　　'The Great Wall is very long!'

　　b.

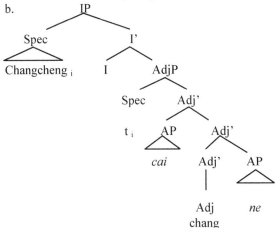

The element surrounded by '*cai⋯ne*' induces a relevant degree scale. In which the reference point is the conventional degree and the asserted value is located higher than the reference point on the scale, as demonstrated in (41).

(41)

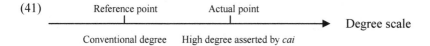

6   Concluding Remarks

This paper has explored the degree usage of *cai*. It is argued that, in this case *cai* and *ne* form a discontinuous constituent to signal the relevant degree is high. Moreover, it has proved that using discontinuous constituents is a usual way to indicate the relevant degree is high. '*Cai⋯ne*' requires that the constituent modified by it has the gradable property, which guarantees that this constituent can be modified by degree adverbs.

To show the similarities and differences of '*cai⋯ne*' with other degree adverbs, a comparison has been made and the results are shown in the following two tables.

Table1 : Dependency on particles

obligatory	mostly	usually	sometimes	seldom
cai (⋯*ne*) *ke* (⋯*le/la/ne*)	*lao*	*tai, duo*	*hao*	*hen*

Table 2: Negation precedes the degree adverbs

	cai⋯ne	*ke⋯ne*	*hao*	*duo*	*tai*	*hen*	*lao*
bu	-	-	-	-	+	+	-/ *bu lao da*
mei	-	-	-	+	-	+	-

In syntax, '*cai⋯ne*' is the adjunct of XP. In semantics, it is located in a high position on the degree scale considered.

Acknowledgments. This paper is supported by the Fundamental Research Funds for the Central Universities and the Funds for Young Team Projects of Northeast Normal University (Project No. 14QT009). The author thus acknowledges these generous supports. Thanks also go to the anonymous reviewers for their invaluable comments. The author alone is responsible for all potential errors which may exist in the paper.

References

1. Bai, M.L. (Paris): A Semantic Study on Modern Chinese *Cai* and *Jiu* (Xiandai Hanyu Cai he Jiu de Yuyi Fenxi). Studies of the Chinese Language (Zhongguo Yuwen), 5, 390-398 (1987). (In Chinese)
2. Biq, Y.O.: From Focus in Proposition to Focus in Speech Situation: *Cai* and *Jiu* in Mandarin Chinese. Journal of Chinese Linguistics. 16, 72-108 (1988).
3. Biq, Y.O.: The Semantics and Pragmatics of *Cai* and *Jiu* in Mandarin Chinese. PhD dissertation. Cornell University (1984)
4. Grade 1955 and 1957, the Class of Language, Department of Chinese Language, Beijing University: Exemplification of Functional Words in Modern Chinese. The Commercial Press, Beijing (1980). (In Chinese)
5. Hole, D.P.: Focus and Background Marking in Mandarin Chinese—System and Theory behind *Cai, Jiu, Dou* and *Ye*. Routledge Curzon (2004).
6. Lai, H.L.: Rejected Expectations: The Scalar Particles *Cai* and *Jiu* in Mandarin Chinese. PhD Dissertation. The University of Texas at Austin (1995).
7. Lai, H.L.: Rejected Expectations: The Scalar Particles *Cai* and *Jiu* in Mandarin Chinese. Linguistics, Vol. 37. 4, 625-661 (1999).
8. Lü, S. X: Eight Hundred Words in Modern Chinese (Xiandai Hanyu Babai Ci). The Commercial Press, Beijing (1980). (In Chinese)
9. Xing, F. Y.: Chinese Grammar (Hanyu Yufaxue). Northeast Normal University Press, Changchun (1997). (In Chinese)
10. Zhang, B. S.: The Subjectivity of the Adverb *Cai* (Fuci *Cai* de Zhuguanxing). Explanations in Chinese Grammar (12), 429- 442. The Commercial Press, Beijing (2003). (In Chinese)
11. Zhang, G.X: A Functional and Cognitive Study of Modern Chinese Adjectives. The Commercial Press, Beijing (2006). (In Chinese)
12. Zhang, L.: A Semantic Study of the Adverbs *Cai* and *Jiu* in Mandarin Chinese. Northeast Normal University Press (2013).

A study on the third interpretation of 'V+ Duration Phrase' in Chinese from the perspective of qualia structure

Wei Chin[1] and Changsong Wang[2(✉)]

[1] Beijing Language & Culture University, Beijing, China
verachinbeijing@kimo.com
[2] Beijing Institute of Technology, Beijing, China
cswang@bit.edu.cn

Abstract. Duration Phrase (i.e. *shifenzhong* 'ten minutes', *santian* 'three days') in "V + Duration Phrase" normally refers to a duration of a certain action or duration since the completion of an event in Chinese. In this article, a less-discussed third interpretation of "V + Duration Phrase" has been put forward to discuss, which refers to the duration of a span (i.e. shelf life of a cake), with the action of the verb being discontinuous in the whole process. It is pointed out that the V in this third reading of "V + Duration Phrase" is not fully lexical, and can be substituted by a semi-lexical verb *yong* 'use' or a light verb as USE. In line with the qualia structure analysis under the framework of generative lexicon theory, this semi-lexical/light verb is found to function as a Telic role of an involved noun of the sentence.

Keywords: duration phrase, duration of an action, duration since the completion of an event, duration of a span, Telic role

1   Introduction

This study originated from our experience in shopping cakes. Once we went to buy a bag of small cakes at a bakery in Beijing. Not knowing the shelf life of the cakes, we asked the shop assistant *zhe dai dangao keyi chi duojiu*, which literally means 'How long can this bag of cakes be eaten?', as shown in (1A). To our surprise, the assistant hesitated a bit and replied as in (1Ba). Her answer made us laugh and realize the ambiguous interpretations of the question with "V + duojiu" 'V+ how long', as shown in (1A): we wanted to ask the shelf life of the cakes, as the interpretation in (1Aa), and the expected answer should be (1Bb). However, the assistant didn't tell us the shelf life of the cakes and showed us the other interpretation in her answer, as shown in (1Ba), which seems to be too obvious to answer. The good thing is that she reminded us, though indirectly, that there are actually different interpretations of "V duojiu" 'V+how long' in Chinese, as exemplified in (1A). The shelf life reading, as *chi wu tian* 'eat five days' in (1Bb), is widely used in our daily life. However, to the best of our knowledge, this reading is less discussed in the literature. Therefore, we aim to explore this third interpretation of "V+ Duration Phrase" (henceforth "V+DurP") in this article, which consists of four sections. We will first introduce the third interpretation of "V+DurP"

© Springer International Publishing AG 2018
Y. Wu et al. (Eds.): CLSW 2017, LNAI 10709, pp. 147–158, 2018.
https://doi.org/10.1007/978-3-319-73573-3_12

in Section Two and make a detailed analysis from qualia roles in Section Three.[1] The last section comes to the conclusion.

(1) A: 这袋蛋糕可以吃多久？

zhe dai dangao keyi chi duojiu?
this CL cake   can   eat how.long
a. 'How long can this bag of cakes hold for eating?'
b. 'How long is it to eat this bag of cakes?'

B: a. 每个人不一样。有的人吃得快，十分钟就吃完了。

mei ge ren   bu yiyang, youde ren   chi de kuai, shi fenzhong jiu chi wan   le, each one person not same   some person eat DE fast, ten minute then eat finish ASP

有的人吃得慢，可以吃三天。

youde ren   chi de   man, keyi chi san   tian.
some   person eat DE   slowly may eat   three   day
'Each person is different. Some eat very fast and finish it within ten minutes; while others may eat slowly and finish it within three days.

b. 这袋蛋糕可以吃五天。

zhe dai dangao keyi chi wu tian.
this CL cake   can   eat five day
'This bag of cakes can hold five days for eating.'

2 The ambiguous interpretations of 'V+ DurP' in Chinese

2.1 The duration of an action and the duration since the completion of an event

As shown at the beginning of this article, there are two possible interpretations involved in (1A), as shown in (1Aa) and (1Ab). Accordingly, two possible answers are available, as respectively shown in (1Ba) and (Bb), in which *shi fen zhong* 'ten minutes' and *santian* 'three days' are often named *shiliang duanyu* 'time-quantity phrase' in the circle of traditional Chinese grammar.[2] Because this time-quantity phrase normally denotes a period of continuous time, it is dubbed as "Duration Phrase" in the literature of generative grammar.[3][4][5][6] In this article, we follow this tradition and adopt the term "Duration Phrase". In previous literature, two main interpretations of 'V + DurP' have been discussed: one is the duration of a certain action, i.e. (*chi*) *shifenzhong* '(eat) ten minutes' in (1Ba); the other is the duration since the completion of an event [5], i.e. *lai meiguo sannian* 'arrive U.S. three years' in (2). Unlike the "(eat) ten minutes" in (1Ba), "three years" in (2) does not refer to the duration of the action *lai* 'arrive', as 'arrive' is an achievement verb and cannot be continuous in nature. Instead, it denotes 'the duration of the state of being three years after his arriving'. The literature on these two readings, mainly thriving in 1970s and 1980s, focus on exploring the different semantic interpretations of duration phrases and their corresponding syntactic structures. [3][4][5] [6] The following comes to the brief review of those analyses which might be involved in our analyses.

(2) 他来美国三年了。

    ta lai   meiguo san nian le.
    he come US   three year SFP
    'It has been three years since he arrived at U.S..'

Ma[2], for instance, unearths the semantic features of 'V+ DurP' in Chinese, and puts forward a classification system for verbs. This is shown in (3).

(3)

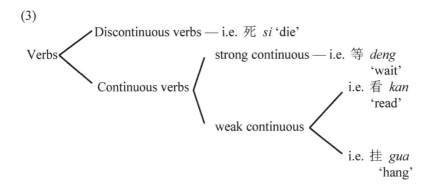

In this classification of verbs, *si* 'die' belongs to the dis-continuous type, because 'die' cannot co-occur with a duration phrase if no other word(s) is/are added, as the ungrammaticality shown in (4a). The *lai* 'arrive' in (2) is also a discontinuous verb. However, *deng* 'wait', *kan* 'read', and *gua* 'hang' can collocate with a duration phrase without the help of others, as shown in (4b), (4c), and (4d). According to Ma's classification, the *deng* 'wait" type of verbs belong to strong continuous verbs, and the duration phrase following these verbs indicate the continuous duration of the action. This is shown in (5a, b). Unlike the *deng* 'wait' type of verbs, the *kan* 'watch' type of verbs belong to weak continuous verbs, as they are ambiguous in meaning. This is shown in (6a) and (b). In (6a), *bange zhongtou* 'half an hour' may refer to the duration of the action of reading, meaning 'Someone has been reading something for half an hour'; or it may refer to the duration since the completion of reading, which roughly means "Half an hour has passes since someone read something". Similarly, both interpretations are available in (6b). Besides the two possible readings involved in weak continuous *read* 'read', as shown in (7a), the weak continuous verb *gua* "hang" can also refer to the duration of a state with the help of *-zhe*, as in (7b).

(4)   a. *死三天   b.（你在这儿）等三天
                *si san tian   (ni zai zher) deng san tian
                die three day   you in here   wait three day
                '*die for three days'   '(You) wait here for three days.'

c. （这本书）看三天
(zhe ben shu) kan   san tian
this CL book read three day
'(You) read this book for three days'

d. （地图在这儿）挂三天
(ditu zai zher) gua san tian
map at   here hang three day
'(The map should) be hanged here
for three days.'

(5)   a. 等了三天了
deng le san tian le
wait ASP three day SFP
'(Someone) has waited for three days'

b. 睡了半天了
shui le   ban tian le
sleep ASP   half day SFP
'(Someone) has slept for half a
day'

(6)   a. 看了半个钟头了
kan le   bange zhongtou le
read ASP half   hour   SFP
'Someone has been reading (sth.)
for half an hour.'
'Half an hour has passed since
finishing reading.'

b. 吃了半个钟头了
chi le   bange zhongtou le
eat ASP half   hour   SFP
'Someone has been eating (sth.)
for half an hour.'
'Half an hour has passed since
finishing eating.'

(7)   a. 挂了三天了
gua le san tian le
hang ASP three day SFP

'(Something) has been hung for three days.'

'Someone has been hanging something
for three days.'

b. 墙上挂着一幅画
qiangshang gua zhe yi fu hua
wall.up hang ZHE one CL
picture
'There is a picture attached
on the wall.'

Tai[3] and Teng[4] apply a higher predicate analysis into the duration phrase which denotes the duration since the completion of an event. For instance, they analyze *san nian* 'three years' in (2) as a predicate, and *ta lai meiguo* 'his arriving at U.S.' as the subject of the predicate and the whole syntactic structure of (2) is shown in (8a). On the contrary, Ernst[5] argues against this higher predicate analysis and provides evidence to show that *sannian* 'three years' in (2) cannot be analyzed as the predicate of the main sentence, instead it should be analyzed as a component of the predicate VP (i.e. an adjunct or complement, which is not specified there), which is predicated over the subject *ta* 'he'. This is shown in (8b). On the contrary, Li[6] argues that the evidence presented in Ernst[5] is not valid enough to deny the analysis shown in (8a). In addition, Li[6] persuasively argues that both analyses in (8a, b) might be possible structures for (2). Due to the limit of space, we will not review the details of Li's analysis. Instead we will focus on the third reading of 'V+ DurP' in the following subsection.

(8) a. [s[s他来美国][vp三年了]]
[s [s ta lai meiguo] [vp san nian le]]
he come U.S.   three year SFP

b. [s[NP他][VP来美国三年了]]

    [s [NP ta] [VP lai meiguo san   nian   le]]

    he   come U.S. three year   SFP

    'It has been three years since he arrived at U.S..'

2.2   The Duration of a Span

As discussed in the above sub-section, different interpretations of 'V + DurP' (e.g. 6) have been discussed in the literature, as in Ma[2], Teng [4], Ernst [5], Li [6], etc.; however, to the best of our knowledge, the shelf life interpretation of 'V + DurP', as listed in (1Bb), has never been discussed seriously in the literature though this usage is quite common in our daily life. Therefore, we will focus on this reading first. In line with the classification of Ma[2], we find that most verbs involved in shelf life reading may be typed into the type of weak continuous verbs in line with Ma[2], as *chi* 'eat' and *he* 'drink' in (9). However, some strong continuous verbs can also occur with this reading. It is worth noting that at this situation this strong continuous verb does not refer to the duration of an action any longer, as shown in (10a), which asks the shelf life of the mattress, and in (10b), which asks the shelf life of the chair. Normally speaking, the answer to (9a)(=11A) should be (11B), which indicates that the shelf life of the cakes is "five days".

(9)   a. 这袋蛋糕可以吃多久?

    zhe dai dangao keyi <u>chi</u> duojiu?

    this CL cake   can <u>eat</u> how.long

    'How long can this box of cakes hold?'

    b. 这种茶叶可以喝多久?

    zhe zhong chaye keyi <u>he</u> duojiu?

    this CL tea can <u>drink</u> how.long

    'How long can this type of tea hold?'

(10)   a. 这个床垫可以睡多久?

    zhe ge chuangdian keyi <u>shui</u> duojiu ?

    this CL mattress can <u>sleep</u> how.long

    'How long can this mattress hold for sleeping?'

    b. 这个椅子可以坐多久?

    zhe ge   yizi keyi <u>zuo</u> duojiu ?

    this CL chair can <u>sit</u> how.long

    'How long can this chair hold for sitting?'

(11)   A: 这袋蛋糕可以吃多久?

    zhe dai dangao keyi <u>chi</u> duojiu?

    this CL   cake   can <u>eat</u> how.long

    'How long can this bag of cakes hold for eating?'

    B: 这袋蛋糕可以吃五天。

    zhe dai dangao keyi <u>chi</u>   wu tian.

    This CL cakes can   <u>eat</u>   five day

    'This bag of cakes can hold five days for eating.'

When an agent, i.e. *ni* "you", is introduced into (11A), as shown in (12A), the shelf life interpretation may be shifted into another interpretation, as the answer shown in (12Bb), which is not an answer to the shelf life interpretation. In this new interpretation in (12Bb), the duration phrase does not emphasize the continuous action of eating as a whole, but focuses on 'how long can the cakes be used for my own eating?'. One thing to note is that the exact duration in this reading has no direct relation with the shelf life of the cakes. Normally, it should be within the limit of shelf life; however, this is not the only option, as it is also possible to go beyond the shelf life, i.e. to eat the cakes for 7 days in spite of the fact that the shelf life of the cakes is just 5 days. Of course, we cannot deny the possibility that the action of eating in (12Bb) is continuous in each interval. For instance, I bought a bag of cakes and ate it within 3 days. Each day I spent 15 minutes in consuming these small cakes. That is to say, in the 15 minutes of the three days, the action of eating is continuous. However, this doesn't mean the eating of these cakes lasts for three whole days without any intervals. In this respect, this new reading in (12Bb) is different from the event duration interpretation, as in (12Ba), in which *shi fenzhong* 'ten minutes' denotes the duration of the activity of eating with no intervals. The two answers to (12A), as in (12Ba) and (12Bb), echo back to the assistant's answer shown in (1Ba). To distinguish from the "shelf life" reading in (11B), we temporarily dub this new reading in (12Bb) as the "time range" reading, which may cover several intervals.

(12)   A: 这袋蛋糕你可以吃多久？
           zhe dai dangao ni   keyi <u>chi</u> duojiu?
           this CL   cake you   can   <u>eat</u> how.long
           'How long do you need to finish this box of cakes?'
     B: a. 我可以吃十分钟（就把它吃完）。
              wo keyi <u>chi</u>   shi fenzhong (jiu   ba   ta chi wan).
              I   can   <u>eat</u>   ten minute   just BA   it eat finish
              'I can finish eating it within ten minutes.'
           b. 这袋蛋糕我可以吃三天。
              zhe dai dangao wo keyi   <u>chi</u>   san tian.
              this CL cake   I   can   <u>eat</u>   three day
              'This bag of cakes can last three days for me to eat.'

Many more similar examples could be found easily. The shelf life reading is available in *kai duojiu* 'drive how long' in (13), in which the shelf life of a car, i.e. how many years can the car be used for driving is questioned. However, if an agent is introduced, as in (14A), the shelf life reading disappears and the duration of action reading, as in (14Ba), and the time range reading, as in (14Bb), appear. The action of eating and driving involved in (12Bb) and (14Bb) is not continuous but intermittent, though each may be continuous in each interval. Take (14Bb) as an example. The action of 'drive' is not continuous in the past three years. It consists of many intermittent intervals in which action of driving may be continuous, as driving for "x hours", "y hours" and "z hours" in (15b). The total hours of driving the car in (15b) is 10 hours, which is the sum of $(x + y + z)$ hours. Obviously, the 10 hours has nothing to do with the "time range of three years", as illustrated in (15b). In this line, "driving three years" in (14Bb) should be differentiated from the duration of continually driving for three hours in (14Ba), as illustrated in (15a). Similarly, *santian* 'three days' in (12Bb) refers to the time range in which the cakes can be consumed. There might be several intermittent events of eating, each of which lasts a certain period, i.e. 15 minutes , and the whole time spans over three days.

(13)   这辆车可以开多久？

zhe liang che keyi <u>kai</u> duojiu

this CL car can   <u>drive</u> how.long

'How long can this car be used for driving?'

(14)   A: 这辆车他开了多久了？

zhe liang che ta <u>kai</u>   le duojiu   le?

this CL   car he <u>drive</u> ASP how.long SFP

'How long has he been driving this car?'

B：a. 这辆车他开了三个小时，一分钟都没休息。

zhe liang che ta <u>kai</u> le san ge xiaoshi, yi fenzhong dou mei xiuxi

this CL car he drive ASP three CL hour one minute even not rest

'He has been driving for three hours with no rest at all.'

b. 这辆车他开了三年，但才跑几百公里，

zhe liang che ta <u>kai</u> le san nian, dan cai pao le ji bai gongli,

this CL car he <u>drive</u> ASP three year but only run ASP few hundred km.

加起来才十个小时。

jiaqilai cai shi xiaoshi.

add.up only ten hour

'He has driven this car for three years. However, it doesn't run too many kilometers. Actually the maximal time he drove this car in total is just 10 hours.'

(15)   a.

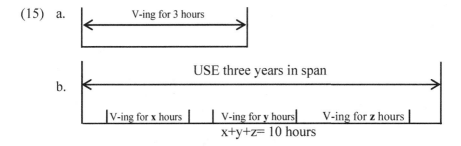

b.

$$x+y+z= 10 \text{ hours}$$

The shelf life reading and the time range reading discussed above are different in some aspects. As pointed out by an anonymous reviewer, the shelf life reading of a duration phrase may be difficult to achieve if a deontic modal verb like *keyi* 'may' (as in 11, 13) is not available. However, this deontic modal is not compulsory in the time range reading of a duration phrase, as shown in (12Bb) and (14Bb). Sometimes, a perfective aspect marker *-le* is involved in the time range reading, as in (12Bb) and (14Bb). For their detailed structure, please refer to Wang & Chin[7].

In spite of these differences, the duration of time range reading involved in (12Bb) and (14Bb) can be regarded as similar with the shelf life reading in (11) and (13), as neither of them denotes the duration of a action or a state since the completion of an event. Instead, they simply refer to the duration of a certain period on how long a product can be used or has been used, without considering whether the action of the verb is continuous as a whole or the action of the verb has been accomplished. In the shelf life reading and the time range reading, the verbs involved are not so lexical in meaning but bleached semantically as a verb like *yong* 'use' or *chixu* 'last', which will be discussed in Section 3.3. For easy composition, we will use "the duration of a span" to cover both these two readings, though this term is not so distinctive from the duration of an action and the duration since the completion of an event, as the latter two also refer to a span. As there is no better way to address it, we temporarily dub the third reading "the duration of a span" to emphasize its coverage of a span, rather than the duration of an action or state.

In the following section, we will first brief introduce the qualia structure in generative lexicon theory, and then analyze how the third interpretation of 'V+DurP' is derived.

3   Qualia roles and the third interpretation of "V+DurP"
3.1   Introduction to Qualia Structure

The theory of generative lexicon, systematically presented by Pustejovsky[1], assumes that lexicon is also generative and a generative lexicon is a computational system which consists of at least four levels of representations: argument structure, event structure, qualia structure, and lexical type structure. In this subsection, we will mainly review the qualia structure [1:85-104], [7].

According to qualia structure [1: 85-86], a lexical semantic structure is defined with four basic roles: Constitutive role, Formal role, Telic role and Agentive role. Constitutive role describes the relation between an object and its constituents or proper parts, which may include material, weight, parts and component elements. For instance, a "book" consists of a cover and many pages. Formal role "distinguishes the object within a larger domain", such as orientation, magnitude, shape, dimensionality, color, and position. For instance, a "book" is different from a CD in its shape and color. Telic role refers to a purpose and function of an object. For example, a book's Telic role is to "read". Agentive role concerns the factors involved in the origin or "bringing about" of an object. It may include creator, artifact, natural kind and causal chain. How does a book come into being? It is achieved through writing and therefore its Telic role is "write".[1],[8] A good example to show how qualia roles are related to a noun is shown in (16), in which different modifiers can be associated with different qualia roles [1], [8: 193]. In (16), "large" is a Formal role of "arrow"; "carved" is an Agentive role of "arrow"; "wooden" is a Constitutive role of "arrow"; and "useful" is a Telic role of "arrow". [8: 193-195]

(16)   a <u>large</u> <u>carved</u> <u>wooden</u> <u>useful</u> arrow

3.2   Selective binding of qualia roles

In discussing the generative mechanism involved in semantics, Pustejovsky proposes Selective Binding [1: 127-131] to explain the polysemy of certain words, as "beautiful" in (17), in which "beautiful" can either refer to "her looking", meaning 'She looks beautiful', or denote the verb "dance", meaning "She dances in a beautiful manner". Pustejovsky proposes that this kind of ambiguous sentences can be interpreted from the perspective of qualia roles. Contra traditional views, it is proposed that an adjective, being a modifier, is able to impose some selections on its head noun. To be specific, an adjective can select a certain qualia role in the qualia structure of its head noun[1:128]. In this line, when "beautiful" selects the Formal role of "dancer", it refers to the appearance of the dancer; when "beautiful" selects the Telic role of "dancer", it modifies "dance" and refers to the manner of dancing. In (18), "fast" seems to modify a noun "typist/drivers" in surface; however, it is actually used as an adverb, denoting the manner of typing/driving. This form-meaning mismatch can also be explained with the qualia roles' selective binding. In (18a), "fast" selects the Telic role of the noun "typists", that is, "type". In this way, "fast" modifies the verb "type" instead of the noun "typist". Similarly, "fast" in (18b) selects the Telic role of "drivers", that is "drive". In this line, it modifies the verb "drive" instead of the noun 'drivers'.

(17)   She is a <u>beautiful</u> dancer.
(18)   a. John is a <u>fast</u> typist.
       b. <u>Fast</u> drivers will be caught and ticketed.

Song[8] shows how selective binding of qualia roles works in Mandarin Chinese. She points out that both *hongde* 'red' in (19a) and *shufude* 'comfortable' in (19b) seem to modify *yizi* 'chair' in form; however, it is not the real case. The 'red', being a color, is a Formal role of 'chair' in (19a). Instead, *shufude* 'comfortable' in (19b) is a Telic role of 'chair' and it modifies the function of the chair, denoting "a chair which is comfortable to sit".

(19)   a. <u>hongde</u> yizi   b. <u>shufude</u> yizi   (adapted from e.g. 5, Song [8: 194])
          red   chair   comfortable chair
          'red chair'   'a chair which is comfortable to sit'

To sum up, qualia roles help us better understand the relations between a modifier and its head noun. Contra traditional views on modifiers, generative lexicon theory assumes that a modifier is no longer subordinate and passive in nature, instead it may impose a selection on the qualia roles of its head noun. In the following subsection, we will explain how the third interpretation of "V+DurP", that is the duration of a span, can be explained with a Telic role.

3.3   Telic role and the duration of a span interpretation in "V+ DurP"

In Section 2, we have discussed the third reading of "V + DurP": the duration of a span. First we note that the shelf life reading is involved in (11), here repeated as (20). Similarly, the *kai duojiu* 'drive how long' in (13) inquires of the expected life of a car. Similar with the shelf life reading, *chi santian* 'eat three days' in (12Bb) and *kai sannian* 'drive three years' in (14Bb) cover the time range of eating and driving. Here

(12Bb) is repeated as (21). Being different from the duration of an action interpretation, as shown in (12Ba, 14Ba), and the duration since the completion of an event, as shown in (2), we classify the shelf life reading and the time range reading as the third interpretation of "V+DurP", that is the duration of a span interpretation. An immediate question about this new third reading is: why does "V+DurP" in (20)-(21) not denote the duration of an action (i.e. 12Ba, 14Ba) or the duration since the completion of an event (i.e. 2))? Where does this third reading come? In the following, we will show the V in "V + DurP" is distinct from a normal action verb and it is related to the Telic role of a noun in the involved sentence.

(20)   A: 这袋蛋糕可以吃多久？

    zhe dai dangao keyi <u>chi</u> duojiu?
    this CL   cake   can <u>eat</u> how.long
    'How long can this bag of cakes hold for eating?'
    B: 这袋蛋糕可以吃五天。
    zhe dai dangao keyi <u>chi</u>   wu   tian.
    This CL cake   can   <u>eat</u>   five day
    'This bag of cakes can hold five days for eating.'

(21)   这袋蛋糕我可以吃三天。

    zhe dai dangao wo keyi   <u>chi</u>   san   tian.

    this CL cake   I   can   <u>eat</u>   three day
    'This bag of cakes can last three days for me to eat.'

Though the verb *chi* 'eat' in (20) and (21) look like an action verb; however, they are not so lexical in meaning, as *chi* 'eat' in (20) and (21) show some restriction in being modified by a manner adverb, as respectively shown in (22) and (23). This is quite weird if *chi* 'eat' in (20) and (21) act as a real action verb, as normally an action verb can be modified by a manner adverbial, as *yong chazi chi* 'eat with a fork'. Meanwhile, *chi* 'eat' in (20A) and (21) can be substituted for by a semantically bleached verb *yong* 'use' or light verb 'USE' [9]. This is respectively shown in (24) and (25). All of these may suggest that the verb in the third reading of "V+DurP" is not so lexical as it seems to be. For more detailed evidence of these bleached verbs, please refer to Wang & Chin[7].

(22)   *这袋蛋糕可以用叉子吃多久？
    *zhe dai dangao   keyi **yong chazi**   <u>chi</u>   duojiu?
    this CL   cake   can   with fork   eat   how.long
    'How long can this bag of cakes hold for eating with a fork?'
(23)   ??*这袋蛋糕我可以用叉子吃三天。
    ??*zhe dai dangao wo keyi **yong chazi**   <u>chi</u>   san   tian.
    This CL cake   I   can   with fork   eat   three day
    'This bag of cakes can hold for three day for me to eat with a fork.'

(24)   这袋蛋糕可以用多久？

    zhe dai dangao keyi yong duojiu?

    this CL cake   can   USE how.long

    'How long can this bag of cakes hold for eating?'

(25)   这袋蛋糕我可以用三天。

    zhe dai dangao (wo) keyi yong   san   tian.

    this CL cake   I   can   USE   three day

    'This bag of cakes can be used for five day for me.'

Why action verbs in (20, 21) can be replaced by a semantically bleached or light verb USE? Are there any rules behind it? We find that the selection of the semantically bleached very *yong* 'use' or light verb "USE" is related to a Telic role of a certain noun in the involved sentence, such as *chi* 'eat' is a Telic role of the "cake" in (1A, 9a, 12Bb, 20, 21), and *kai* 'drive' in (13, 14Bb) is a Telic role of 'car'. Similarly, *he* 'drink', *shui* 'sleep', and *zuo* 'sit' are Telic roles of *chaye* 'tea', *chuangdian* 'mattress' and *yizi* 'chair'. All of these show that the selection of the semantically bleached *yong* 'use' or light verb "USE" in the third interpretation of "V+ DurP" is not arbitrary, but to meet with the Telic role of a certain noun in the related sentence. According to Ma's verb classification system [2], the "USE" involved in the interpretation of a span should be a strong continuous verb like *shiyong* 'use'. This also explains why the durational phrase in the third interpretation covers a whole span even though the involved action embodied by V is not continuous but intermittent if V is interpreted semantically. The reason is that the real verb is not the V as it seems to be. On the other hand, the real verb is a semantically bleached verb *yong* 'use' or a light verb as USE. The V in "V+DurP" seems to denote a manner of the semantically bleached verb *yong* 'use' or light verb USE.[7],[10] This is something like the verb involved in a flip-flop sentence in Chinese, as argued in Wang & Chin [11].

One thing to note is that the duration of an action or duration since the completion of an event interpretation does not require that the V in "V+DurP" to be a Telic role of a noun in the sentence, as *deng* 'wait', *shui* 'sleep' in (5) are not Telic roles of *tian* 'day'. Neither is *lai* 'come' in (2) is a Telic role of *ta* 'he' or *meiguo* 'U.S.'. Of course, these two readings don't exclude the possibility that the V might be a Telic role of a noun, as *chi* 'eat' in (12Ba). Contra these two interpretations, the third interpretation of "V+DurP" normally requires the verb to act as a Telic role of a noun in the sentence.

4   Conclusion

The interpretations of "V + DurP" in Chinese might be ambiguous. Besides the interpretation of the duration of an action and the interpretation of the duration since the completion of an event, a third reading, that is the interpretation of the duration of a span (i.e. shelf life of a product), is explored in this article. In line with the qualia structure analysis under the framework of generative lexicon theory, it is proposed that the action verb in the third reading of "V+DurP" is an imposter, as it is barred from being modified by a manner adverbial and it could be replaced with a semantically bleached verb *yong* 'use' or light verb USE. It is further pointed out that this semantically bleached or light verb USE in the third interpretation of "V+DurP" associates with a Telic role of a noun involved in the related sentence.

Acknowledgement. We thank two anonymous reviewers and the participants in the 18th Chinese Lexical Semantics Workshop (CLSW 17) (Leshan Normal University, May 18-20, 2017) for their comments and revision suggestions. Meanwhile, we want to thank the financial support from the National Social Science Fund (Grant No. 17BYY157).

References

1. Pustejovsky, James (1995) *The Generative Lexicon.* The MIT Press, MA.
2. Ma, Qing-Zhu (1992) Shiliang bingyu he dongci de lei [Time-quantity objects and types of verbs] In *Hanyu Dongci he Dongcixing Jiegou,* ed. Ma Qingzhu, pp 1-12. Beijing Language and Culture University Press, Peking.
3. Tai, James (1973) A derivational constraint on adverbial placement in Mandarin Chinese. *Journal of Chinese Linguistics,* vol 1, no.3. pp 397-413.
4. Teng, Shou-Hsin (1975) Predicate movements in Chinese, *Journal of Chinese Linguistics,* vol 3, no.1, pp 60-75.
5. Ernst, Thomas (1987) Duration adverbial and Chinese phrase structure. *JCLTA,* vol 22, no.2, pp 1-11.
6. Li, Y.-H. Audrey (1987) Duration phrases: distributions and interpretations. *JCLTA,* vol 22, no 3, pp 27-65.
7. Wang, Changsong, and Chin Wei (2017) A study on the syntactic construction of duration phrases in Mandarin Chinese from the perspective of distributed morphology. "Workshop on the Spine of Language", May 13-14. Zhejiang University. Hangzhou.
8. Song, Zuo-Yan (2015) S*hengcheng Ciku Lilun yu Hanyu Shijian Qiangpo Xianxiang* [Generative lexicon theory and event coerce in Chinese] Peking University Press, Peking.
9. Lin, T.-H. Jonah (2001) *Light Verb Syntax and the Theory of Phrase Structure.* Doctoral dissertation, University of California, Irvine.
10. Huang, C.-T. James (2006) Resultatives and unaccusatives: a parametric view. *Bulletin of the Chinese Linguistic Society of Japan* 253, pp 1-43.
11. Wang, Changsong, and Chin Wei (2016) Jufa yinxi jiekou shiyuexia de rongnaju yanjiu [A study on flip-flop sentences in Chinese from the syntax-phonology interface]. *Yufa Jiaoxue yu Yanjiu* [Language Teaching and Research], vol 182, no. 6, pp 48-58.

Semantic Classification and Category Expansion of " *Qing*(轻) X " in Modern Chinese

Xufeng Yang

Beijing Language and Culture University
NO.15,Xueyuan Road,Haidian District ,Beijing,100083,China
xufeng_1109@163.com

Abstract. Based on the statistics of the headlines of the People's Daily Online in the past 10 years,we find that the category of the "*Qing*(轻) X " can be divided into five semantic classes,each of which is based on the prototype meaning and gradually expands into the category of "*Qing*(轻) X " in comparison and generalization.The semantic extension model of the "*Qing*(轻) X" category is similar to the extended pattern of polysemous words,which extends based on the family resemblance.And the category of "*Qing*(轻) X "is open, which means the number of members is expanding.

Keywords: "*Qing*(轻) X ",semantic classification,prototype category, family resemblance,category expansion.

1 Introduction

With the development of society,there are many new words appearing.Meanwhile,the new word"*Qing* X"is also increasingly developing.By searching the headlines of the People's Daily Online,we've got plenty of new words"*Qing* X".For example ,

(1)Pudong Times special offer:*qing tubu* (轻徒步) route around Shanghai become popular(Pudong Times,Jan.13th,2016)

(2)Reconsideration of the emerging public opinion ecology gradually forming"*qing meiti*(轻媒体)"(Hunan Red Net,Jan.13th,2015)

The"*qing tubu*"in example(1)refers to a new hiking way which doesn't require too much time and physical force.Besides,the"*qing meiti*"in example(2)is a new smart media which has various channels,and its content of information generated and spread faster,and the topic of information content is easy. Although the meanings of the two "*qing*" differ a lot,they still have certain similar meaning,that is ,few in number or light in degree.What's worth researching is that a morpheme can have different meanings when form various words.

Researchers have been concerned about the study of words which formed by morpheme of strong word formation for a long time, such as "zero(零)X"Zhang,Y., 2003; He, J, 2004), "*Luo*(裸) X" (Shao,C.,2009; Hu,B., 2010), "X gate/door(门)" (Xu,F.,2007;Zhang,Y.,2007;You,Y.,2011),"X *Ge*(哥)"(Tu,H.,Yang ,W.,2001).Till now,few people have ever discribed or explained the"*Qing*(轻) X".In addition, previous studies mainly focus on syllable,semantic,grammar or rhetoric.They have also adopted cognitive model and conceptual integration to state these phenomena.Based on the above,this article will focus on the semantic features of the "*Qing* X"and distinguish different semantic interpretations of the"*Qing* X".On top of this ,we will make use of prototype theory to find out the semantic expansion process of the "*Qing* X".

2   Semantic Classification Analysis of "*Qing* X"

There are nine senses of the"*qing*" in the"Modern Chinese Dictionary" (the seventh edition), but only the first four senses are used to form the new word "*Qing* X", and the word examples of "*Qing* X" formed by the last some senses have not yet been seen. Based on the different of the "*Qing* X"'s semantic classes, the "*Qing* X" can be classified into the following categories.

2.1   Transport, Military Weapons and so on with Small Load, Simple Equipment

The "*Qing* X" of this class includes: *qingka*(轻卡), *qing hujian*(轻护舰), *qing huopao*(轻火炮), etc, among which the armed forces are the main part,and the transportation is the second. Transportation is most abbreviated,"*qingxing-kache*(轻型卡车)" abbreviates "*qingka*". Most of the "*Qing* X" words are the three syllables,in addition to transportation words ,which are the disyllabic words.And part of speech of these words are nouns.

(3) City logistics summon high-end *qingka*(People's Daily Online,Jan.14th,2003)

(4) The Indonesian Navy will buy two *qing hujian* from the Netherlands(Liberation Army Daily,Jan.21th,2004)

The "*qingka*" in example (3) is light-duty truck which has the small vehicle load and the "*qing hujian*" in example (4) means light-duty frigate .

2.2   The Weight, Thickness or the Proportion of the Material is Small

The "*Qing* X" of this class includes: *qing chaiyou*(轻柴油), *qing youtian*(轻油田), etc, the "X" are mainly industrial materials, which are not very close to people's life. But in recent years, there are several words related to people's lives also entering into this class, such as: *qing paiqiu*(轻排球), *qing waitao*(轻外套), etc. In general, the number of these words are small, the "X" of the "*Qing* X" are mostly disyllable, and all of them are nouns.

(5) In the second quarter, quality problems of some automotive *qing chaiyou*, unleaded petrol product are serious(China Automotive News,Aug.3th,2004)

(6) Flying from Guangdong and Hong Kong: the *qing paiqiu* drift to the "the Belt and Road" (Xinhua News Agency,July4th,2016)

The implication of *qing chaiyou* in example(5) infers a class of diesel which has relatively small density. In addition,the "*qing paiqiu*" in example (6) implies a kind of small weight volleyball.

2.3   The Weight, Thickness or the Proportion of the Material is Small

The class of words that indicates "degree and status is shallow" includes: *qing wu*(轻雾),*qing zheng*(轻症),*qing'an*(轻案),*qing chungao*(轻唇膏),etc, involving natural weather conditions, medical, legal, cosmetics and many other areas. Some examples also express the style of home, clothing, music, such as: *qing sediao*(轻色调), *qing zhengqi-pengke*(轻蒸汽朋克). The class of words that indicates "small amount" includes: "*qing shunü*(轻熟女), *qing feixingyuan*(轻飞行员)" which means the people are young; "*qing tubu*(轻徒步)" which means the exercise intensity is small and the exercise time is short; "*qing fuhua*(轻孵化)" which means the incubation needs a short period.

(7) The same situation, but not the same beauty - Maybelline fresh complexion *qing chungao* go home with you(China Internet Information Center,Feb.15th,2015)
(8) Su Huilun successfully turned into a *qing shunü*, and took along with a new album to promote in mainland.(People's Daily Online,Dec.14th,2007)

The "*qing chungao*" in example (7) means that the lipstick's color is pale and thin, while the "*qing shunü*" in example (8) refers to the young and mature women whose age ranges from 25 to 35.

In this class,nouns account for the vast majority. Verbs within the range of the "*Qing* X" mostly focus on this class, such as:*qing huinuan*(轻回暖),*qing fugu*(轻复古). Except the words which indicate the status of natural climate and the degree of legal offense are disyllables, the rest are mostly three syllables, and there are also several words with more than three syllables.

2.4   Lightheartedness of Mind and Body

This class of words is divided into two sub-classes according to whether it contains intellectual factor: first subclass includes "*qing tiyu*(轻体育), *qing xiju*(轻喜剧), *qing yundong*(轻运动)", etc, referring to the style and theme of doing something or events in a relaxed state of mind; the second subclass such as "*qing licai*(轻理财), *qing meiti*(轻媒体), *qing yeyou*(轻页游), *qing yingyong*(轻应用)", etc, which refers to achieving the purpose of easily handle affairs and libertinism through the Internet.

(9) *qing tiyu*: Keeping fit lightly   (Health Times,Jan.2th,2006)
(10) Medical mobile *qing wenzhen* (轻问诊) helps general patients communicate with director of the hospital directly.(People's Daily Online-Anhui channel,May. 19th,2015)

The "*qing tiyu*" in example (9) denotes easy and relaxing sports, which means using all the time, space to do physical exercise more comfortable and happier; the "*qing wenzhen*" in example (10) is a reference to mobile interrogation platform, which is online real-time communication by adding doctor's WeChat.

The involved scope of the "X" in the "*Qing* X" include the aspects of fitness, entertainment and business. Nouns are the majority, and verbs account for a minority, such as: *qing kaohe*(轻考核), *qing chuxing*(轻出行). In terms of syllable, these "*Qing* X"words show a three syllables-based, multi-syllable development trend.

2.5 Simple, Balanced and Moderate Life

The words belong to this class include "*qing shi*(轻食), *qing shenghuo*(轻生活), *qing wancan*(轻晚餐)" and so on which closely related with people's healthy lives. These words reflects that with the improvement of living standards, people start to pursue a natural, moderate, balanced and convenient lifestyle.

(11)*qing shi*: cool refreshing pleasant summer(Guangzhou Daily,Jun.20th,2013)

(12) Healthy living: ten secret tips for living a *qing shenghuo*(People's Daily Online,Dec.19th,2014)

The meaning of "*qing shi*" in example (11) refers to appropriate, nutrient and healthy diet. The "*qing shenghuo*" in example (12) is equivalently the generalization of this kind of words, including *qing shi*(轻食);*qing ti*(轻体)—keep moderate exercise;*qing xin*(轻心)—put down the pressure and keep the mind peaceful;*qing ju*(轻居)—a simple, green way of living and walking, etc.

We have carried out the statistical analysis of 186[1] new words "*Qing* X" searched from the People's Daily news headline, and the specific distribution situation presents clearly in Table 1:

Table 1. the "*Qing* X"semantic class quantity distribution.

Semantic type	Example	Quantity	Proportion
1.transport, military weapons and so on with small load, simple equipment	*qing ka*(轻卡) *qing hujian*(轻护舰)	17	9.1%
2.the weight, thickness or the proportion of the Material is small	*qing chaiyou*(轻柴油) *qing paiqiu*(轻排球)	12	6.5%
3.the degree and status of the matter is shallow or the amount is small	*qing chungao*(轻唇膏) *qing shunü*(轻熟女)	99	53.2%
4.lightheartedness of mind and body	*qing tiyu*(轻体育) *qing wenzhen*(轻问诊)	37	19.9%
5.Simple, balanced and moderate life	*qing shenghuo*(轻生活) *qing wancan*(轻晚餐)	21	11.3%

Observing the number distribution of each semantic class of the"*Qing* X", you can see that in the "*Qing* X" category, the class of words which expresses "the degree and status of the matter is shallow or amount is small" has the greatest proportion, reaching more than half; but the weight of two classes of words which expresses "transport, military weapons and so on small with load, simple equipment" and "material's weight, thickness or the proportion is small" are lower, that's 9.1% and 6.5% respec-

---

[1] 186 new words only include the condition of a single item of the"*qing*" in the"*Qing* X", it's not in the columns that have multiple meanings. In addition, the figures are only rough statistics, and the details are to be examined.

tively. Thus although there are only four items that can be used to form new words in all the meanings of the"*qing*" , there are also difference between their abilities of word formation: the class which expresses "shallow degree, small amount" has the strongest force of word formation; the class which expresses "small load, simple equipment" has the weakest force of word formation. Except for the above statistics, there are several new words' meanings concurrently belong to the above two classes or three classes, such as "*qing xiaoshuo*(轻小说)" ,which refers to novels that young people are the main reading group and content is easy to read; "*qing nü*(轻女)" ,which refers to the young female with healthy body and young mind.

3   Prototype Theory and its Explanation of "*Qing* X"

3.1   The Prototype Theory

The Prototype Theory was proposed by American psychologist Eleanor Rosch et al in the mid-1970s on the basis of the Ludwig Wittgenstein's Family Similarity. Wittgenstein put forward the principle of Family Resemblances through the study of "game": The members of the category are similar to each other but not the same or unanimous, and the similar situation and degree between the members are not exactly the same. "There is a greater degree of similarity among many members of a category or between a large number of members and a prototype sample member, and it is the similar attributes that distinguish one category from other categories.Human beings make generalizations based on whether the attributes among the members have 'similar links' ".(Wang ,Y, 2007:101)The process of generalization and induction is categorization.The two important means in the categorization process are contrasting and generalizing. The result of the categorization is to get cognitive categories(Ungerer&Schmid, 1996 : 2). Zhu, Y (2010) pointed that "Constructing the same morpheme group need use the same language form, which is morpheme, to mark the things that not have the same but different points, and put these things into the category alleged by the morpheme, thus the process of constructing the same morpheme group is a categorical process."

The Prototype Theory states: A category consists of a number of similar members; the prototype[2] is the best and the most typical member that reflects the characteristics of this category in the same conceptual category, while the other members have different degrees of typicality; there are no common features among the members belonging to the same category, and they have overlapping attributes , which means all members enjoy the partial common attributes ,and form family similarity. The boundaries of the categories are vague, and the membership status in the category is not equal. The category around the prototype member continuously expands to the outside based on the degree of typicality, forming a larger category with undeterminable boundary. (Ao, S., 2006)

---

[2] Scholars have two different interpretations of the term "prototype": One refers to the specific typical representative; and the other refers to abstract schema representation, or attribute set. The "prototype" in this article is the first type.

3.2   Prototype Theory's Explanation on "*Qing* X"

The new word "*Qing* X" can also be seen as a category,as is mentioned in example (1) and example (2),"*qing yundong*(轻运动)"*and* "*qing meiti*(轻媒体)" look like two distinct concepts, "*qing yundong*" is a way of walking, "*qing meiti*" is a new-style tool for disseminating information.After a careful analysis, we find that although the two have different meanings, they are similar.They both have the meanings of the small amount and shallow degree, and they are both members of the "*Qing* X" category. The degree of family resemblance in the"*Qing* X" category is different, and there are differences as well as common points.People gradually built the "*Qing* X" category through the comparison and generalization of the members entering the "*Qing*X".

The initial meaning of the"*qing*" is light carriage, and the "Shuo Wen Jie Zi" points out that "*qing* means the *qingche*(轻车)." Duan,Y.noted that "*qing* originally was the name of the car, so its radical is the car. Later people extended its meaning as lightness in weight." With the development and evolution of the word's meaning, the "*qingche*" is not the main meaning of the"*qing*" in modern Chinese, and its extended meaning "lightness in weight" has become the basic meaning which are well-known. When we refer to the meaning of the "*qing*", we often firstly think of "lightness in weight", thus in modern Chinese, "lightness in weight" has become the most typical and prominent meaning of the "*qing*", and the subsequent items of meanings are all extended and developed on the basis of this. The "*qingka*(轻卡)" of the new word "*Qing* X" is developed from "*qingche*" which is the initial meaning of the "*qing* ",and it is a continuation of "*qingche*" meaning in modern Chinese. The "*qing chaiyou*(轻柴油)" is a class of words closest to the basic meaning, and the rest of "*Qing* X"are extended and developed on the basis of the class of words of "*qing chaiyou*(轻柴油)", such as "*qing chungao*(轻唇膏)", "*qingshi*(轻食)" etc. The meanings of these words have similarities with "*qing chaiyou*", some of them have high level of similarity, such as "*qing chungao*(轻唇膏)"; and some of them have very low similarities, such as "*qingshi*(轻食)".

It can be seen that each member of the "*Qing* X" category has the characteristics of family resemblance, within the category of the "*Qing* X", each member has both similarities and difference in varying degrees, and the boundary of the category are fuzzy and even open. The "*Qing* X" category has the characteristics of prototype category, if we take the words formed by "*qing*" as a category, then the new term "*Qing* X" category is the expansion of the category of the original words.[3]Based on the above characteristics of the"*Qing* X", we believe that it is feasible to analyze the "*Qing* X" with the Prototype Theory.

---

[3] Zhu,Y (2010) mentioned that "The creative analogical creation is not a simple copy of the original word pattern, but the result of the developing variation of original word mode. If the word mode is also seen as a category, and the creative analogical creation is the expansion of the scope of the existing word mode, the result of the expansion is to categorization, from the original word mode farther and farther, and the similarity with the original word mode is getting lower and lower."

4 Category Extension of the"*Qing* X" Based on Family Resemblance

4.1 Category Extension of Each Semantic Class of the"*Qing* X"

Through the semantic analysis of the new word "*Qing* X", we generalize the extend relationship of each semantic class into Fig 1. It is not difficult to find from the figure that the semantic extension pattern of the new word "*Qing* X" is similar to the extended pattern of polysemant meaning.They are all take a basic meaning as prototype, to carry out radiation and diffusion, and there is a family similarity between the semantic after the diffusion and the basic meaning.

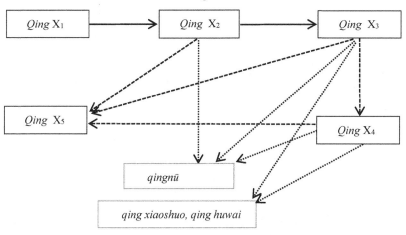

Fig. 1. Semantic class expansion process of the"*Qing* X"[4]

4.2 Semantic Evolution Process of the"*Qing* X"

According to the study of the occurrence time and semantics of the new word "*Qing* X", we roughly defined the semantic evolution process of new word "*Qing* X". The new word "*Qing* X" is a process of gradually categorizing a series of things by using morpheme "*qing*", and this process follows the economic principles of human cognition, which means the most effortless thing in cognition is most likely to be categorized firstly. "*qingche*(轻车)" is the initial meaning of "*qing*", "car is light" means the load of car is small, the equipment is relatively simple, thus the meaning of "the load is small, the equipment is simple" is closest to the origin meaning. The category of words which have the same concept with the car firstly entered the new word "*Qing* X" mode , for example: *qingke*(轻客), *qingqi*(轻气), etc,which omitted the word "car"

---

[4] In this figure,the black solid line indicates the definite extension relation,the bold black dotted line indicates the possible extension relation,and the thin black dotted line indicates the source of the meaning of the marginal word.In addition ,this figure shows the "*Qing* X"semantic development order remains to be further verified.

in the"*Qing* X"; after that, people classified some military vehicles into the model through comparison and summary , such as: *qing hangmu*(轻航母), *qing hujian*(轻护舰), etc;and then the category further extended to military equipment, accouterment and other aspects, such as *qing bubing*(轻步兵), and eventually formed the "*Qing* X₁". On the basis of the initial meaning, "*qing*" developed and extended the meaning "small weight, small density (The opposite of "heavy")", and this meaning became the basic meaning of "*qing*". The new word "*Qing* X₂" which formed on the basis of the basic meaning also becomes the prototype of the "*Qing* X" category. The words firstly entering into the "*Qing* X₂" is the words which belong to industrial material, such as: *qing chaiyou*(轻柴油), and then the words which belong to life material also enter the"*Qing* X₂"category, such as: *Qing waitao*(轻 外 套).The similarity between the"*Qing* X₁" and the"*Qing* X₂" is very high,besides one difference in semantic feature("small load" and "small proportion, small weight"),except for the different attached objects (the"*Qing* X₁" matches with transport, weapons, etc., the"*Qing* X₂" match with materials).

The meaning of "shallow degree, small amount" is extended and developed by the basic meaning and the new word "*Qing* X₃" is also developed by the way. The legal and medical words firstly entered into the"*Qing* X₃" , such as "*qingzui*(轻罪), *qingzheng*(轻症)".After that, the other words related with the daily life also entered the class, for example: *qing luozhuang*(轻裸妆), *qing huinuan*(轻回暖), etc. As the number of the words have access to the"*Qing* X₃" increases, the similarity of members in the"*Qing* X₃" category is decreasing step by step.Some words are more similar than others, for example,*qing huli*(轻护理)and *qing chungao*(轻唇膏) belong to the category of cosmetics, while *qingtai*(轻台), *qing dianping*(轻点评),*qing laohua*(轻老化) can not belong to any class or category, which has great difference. However, they are all able to associate into small class through the contrast and generalization of the members in the"*Qing* X₃". Compared with the"*Qing* X₂", the "*Qing* X₃" turns from quantity to degree,which has high similarity.But the similarity of the"*Qing* X₃" and the"*Qing* X₁" is obviously not as high as the"*Qing* X₂".

The"*Qing* X₄" refers to "easy and happy".It is not yet clear whether it is derived from the"*Qing* X₂" or the"*Qing* X₃", because the meaning of the"*Qing* X₄" is far from the"*Qing* X₂" and the"*Qing* X₃". In terms of the scope of the words entering into "*Qing* X₄", they are all closely related to life, which seemingly close to the"*Qing* X₃", but the similarity of collocation of words cannot be the basis of their similarity, which still need a further research. The"*Qing* X₅" is far away from the typical member "*Qing* X₂" in the"*Qing* X" category,and the gap between the various semantics are relatively large.Furthermore, we can not seen the shadow of the prototype in this semantic class. In addition,there are sporadic language examples in the edge of the"*Qing* X"s each kind, and their meaning comes from a number of small semantic classes.

The extension of the whole "*Qing* X" category starts with the"*Qing* X₁" , while the"*Qing* X₂" as a prototype.The"*Qing* X₃", "*Qing* X₄", "*Qing* X₅" which formed after are all extended on the basis of the"*Qing* X₂" according to the family resemblance . With the categorization of the"*Qing* X", the members within the category become more and more, but the similarity between new members and prototype "*Qing* X₂" is becoming lower and lower with the emerging of some new features . The similarity between the "*Qing* X1", "*Qing* X3" and "*Qing* X2" is highest, while the similarity between the "*Qing* X4", "*Qing* X5" and prototype "*Qing* X2" is lowest. It is precisely because the "*Qing* X" category is carried out with the way of family similarity, and the boundary of its categories is vague and open, so in the later stages of the extension, a word can enter the category which has little similar with the members of the category. The requirements of members to enter in the category are not so strict, the members within the category will show their own characteristics, and the similarity also will be weakened.

5   Conclusion and Discussion

This article studies the new words formation with morpheme "*qing*" and collected the "*Qing* X" in the title of the People's Daily Online in the past ten years as linguistic materials. The words within "*Qing* X" category are divided into five classes, and the mode pattern of the semantic development within the "*Qing* X" category is established. Therefore, the semantic development of the "*Qing* X" is analyzed in detail with prototype category theory, then we find that the semantic development of "*Qing* X" is similar to the development pattern of polysemant meaning, which carries out scope expansion based on the Family Similarity. The "*Qing* X" dates back to "*qingche*", and forms the prototype language example "*qing chaiyou*" and other examples have developed on the basis of family resemblance. The whole "*Qing* X" category is open, each example can enter into this category based on a similar point and the members within the category are still continuing to expand.

But there are some issues worthy of further consideration in the article:

(1) Not all senses of the "*qing*" can constitute a new word, and only four senses can constitute new words. This phenomenon leads us to think: with the same morpheme "*qing*", why some senses can constitute a new word, while others cannot?

(2) For the morpheme "*qing*" which can constitute the "*Qing* X", some of the meaning items constitute a large number of new words, while some of the meaning items constitute a small number of new words. Furthermore, why do some meaning items have strong morphological productivity, but some meaning items have weak morphological productivity?

(3) What are the characteristics of words that can enter the "*Qing* X" category? Why some words cannot enter this category?

To solve these issues, we still need to consider with "*qing*"'s special features and the characteristics of the words which can enter the "*Qing* X" category. According to three formal criteria of identifying the nature adjectives putted forward by Zhang,G.(2006),we think that "*qing*" belongs to the typical character adjective mentioned in this paper, which is simple word-formation, which can be embellished by "the most, more, than and a little" and can used in comparative sentence and also can be marked without the attributive mark "*de*(的)" when constitute attributive-centered relation. From the semantic point of view, although the semantic connotation of "*qing*" is very rich,it's more generic to express "quantity, proportion, weight, degree and other aspects less than the general or less than the comparative object". Therefore, the words constituted by the first three meaning items are more. In the case of the forth meaning item "easy" meaning's morphological productivity, we believe that it is connected with the pursuit of simple and easy lifestyle with the development of the society.

References

1. Ao,S.:An Explanation of the Polysemy in View of the Prototype Theory.Journal of Hubei University (Philosophy and Social Science)4,508-511(2006).(in Chinese)
2. He, J:Get in Touch with"ling X" in Zero-distance.Chinese Linguistics5,46-49(2004).(in Chinese)
3. Hu, B.:Semantic Derivation and Cognitive Model of"*Luo* X（裸X）"Word Family in Contemporary Chinese.Language Teaching and Linguistic Studies3,77-83(2010).(in Chinese)
4. Tu, H.,Yang,W.:Deriving Mechanism of the "X+*Ge*(哥)"Words in Media Language and the Framework of Semantic Relevance.Language Teaching and Linguistic Studies6,24-30(2011).(in Chinese)
5. Ungerer, F.&Hans-Jörg,S.:An Introduction to Cognitive Linguistics.Foreign Language Teaching and Research Press, Beijing(2001).
6. Wang,Y: Cognitive Linguistics. Shanghai Foreign Language Education Press, Shanghai (2007)(in Chinese)
7. Xu,F.:An Analysis of the Development of the "X door(门)"Words meaning.Chinese Language Learning3,38(2007).(in Chinese)
8. You,Y.:Semantic information and cognitive formation mechansim of "X door(门)"Construction.Foreign Language Research4,45-49(2011).(in Chinese)
9. Zhang ,Y.:An Exploration of a Contemporary Neological Word Family of "零（zero）+X".Applied Linguistic1, 96-103(2003).(in Chinese)
10. Zhang, Yi.:The suffix of "～门'（~gate）in Contemporary Chinese.Applied Linguistic4,39-47(2007).(in Chinese)
11. Zhang,G.:Re-analysis of the qualitative adjective.Chinese Teaching in the Word1,5-17(2006).(in Chinese)
12. Zhu,Y:the categorical extensions in the coinage models.Chinese Language2,146-161+192(2010).(in Chinese)

Three Registers behind two Characters: an Analysis of the Words' Formation and their Registers

Jianfei Luo[1] and Jing Xiang[2]

[1]College of Advanced Chinese Training, Beijing Language and Culture University, Beijing, China
[2]School of Foreign Languages and Literature, Wuhan Qingchuan University, Wuhan, China

`nch1980s@163.com, erica.xj@foxmail.com`

Abstract. Three Registers behind two characters, or Two-Character-Three-Register, is a special phenomenon in Chinese word formation, which mainly means that on the premise that a dissyllabic verb consists of two monosyllabic verbs which could be used separately, it represents a picture that three Chinese words belong to three individual registers. 81 groups of such words are exhaustively analyzed in this paper and it is found that (1) the most important function of the Two-Character-Three-Register Phenomenon is to distinguish registers; (2) dissyllabic verbs are mainly laid in formal register, whereas monosyllabic verbs in informal and elegant registers; (3) this can mostly be accounted for through the filling effect of register vacancy.

Keyword: Two-Character-Three-Register Structures, word formation, register, prosody.

1 Introduction

The research object of this study are dissyllabic verbs with both morphemes syntactically applicable in Chinese. According to the Two-Character-Three-Register Theory (Feng, 2015), such verbs are considered as contemporary evidence of Three Register, as exemplified in the following cases:

(1) a. 挖[wa](dig) —挖掘[wajue](dig) —掘[jue](dig)
   b. 帮[bang](help)—帮助[bangzhu](help)—助[zhu](help)
   c. 躲[duo](hide)—躲避[duobi](hide)—避[bi](hide)

In Feng's essay, words on the left are regarded as *informal*, words in the middle as *formal* and words on the right as *elegant*.

On the basis of the Two-Character-Three-Register Theory, the following questions can be discussed:

© Springer International Publishing AG 2018
Y. Wu et al. (Eds.): CLSW 2017, LNAI 10709, pp. 169–179, 2018.
https://doi.org/10.1007/978-3-319-73573-3_14

a. How many verbs with this feature are there in Chinese? More precisely, how many are there in *Modern Chinese Dictionary*?

b. What is the register feature of the morphemes in these verbs when they are used alone? Do they follow the rules of the Two-Character-Three-Register Theory?

c. Do dissyllabic verbs with both morphemes syntactically applicable conform to the Two-Character-Three-Register Theory?

d. What is the proper explanation of this linguistic phenomenon?

Research has been done on the relation between verbs and their register in Chinese. Previous studies have demonstrated that different verbs embody different registers, for which diversity occurs in grammar as well. For example, it is a well-acknowledged grammar rule that verbs cannot be connected with 和[he](and) in coordinate relation. However, if the register of the verb changes, then the rule could be presented in a different way:

(2) a.   *他   买   和   读   了   一   本   书
          ta   mai   he   du   le   yi   ben   shu
          he   buy   and   read   ASP   one   CL   book
          He bought and read a book.

    b.   他   购买   和   阅读   了   一   本   书
          ta   goumai   he   yuedu   le   yi   ben   shu
          he   buy   and   read   ASP   one   CL   book
          He bought and read a book.

The meaning of 购买[goumai](buy) and 阅读[yuedu](read) is almost the same with 买[mai](buy) and 读[du](read). But such monosyllabic verbs cannot be connected with 和[he](and) while dissyllable verbs can be combined with 和[he](and).

Similarly, dissyllabic verbs in *formal* register can be used in the structure [N de V] while monosyllabic verbs in register cannot.

(3) a. 编   教材   --   *教材   的   编
      bian   jiaocai   --   jiaocai   de   bian
      edit   textbook   --   textbook   DE   edit
      to edit a textbook   --   the editing of the textbook

    b. 编写   教材   --   教材   的   编写
      bianxie   jiaocai   --   jiaocai   de   bianxie
      edit   textbook   --   textbook   DE   edit
      to edit a textbook   --   the editing of the textbook

Based on the previous research, it is obvious that disparity in grammar occurs because of prosodic and register features.

By applying "Register Grammar" Theory, this paper will focus on the formation of Two-Character-Three-Register and analyze its distribution, features and patterns.

2   The Collection of Two-Character-Three-Register Verbs

Taking example for the words in (1), this paper studies dissyllabic verbs as well as the correspondent monosyllabic verbs that can syntactically function independently in the entries of *Modern Chinese Dictionary (6th Edition)*, in reference to the fundamental principles of morphology and syntax. The data collection process is depicted below:

Firstly, on the basis of previous research, there are 1093 verbs with similar basic meanings and syllabic duality (monosyllabic/dissyllabic).

Secondly, among these entries, after analysis and discrimination term by term, there are 81 Two-Character-Three-Register verbs that comprise two independent-functioning morphemes in the disyllables.

On whether the morpheme can function independently or not, the standard lies on whether it can be put alone at the terminal node of the phrase (X_0). If it can, it is considered as capable of functioning independently, viz, acknowledged as a word (although it may be required in certain prosodic patterns). Take 赴[fu](to go to) and 寻[xun](to search for) for example:

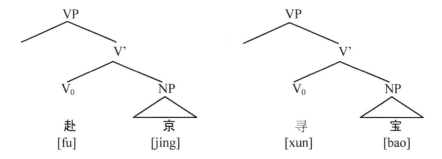

Figure 1: the syntactic analysis of 赴[fu](to go to) and 寻[xun](to search for)

In the cases above, 赴[fu](to go to) and 寻[xun](to search for) are put at the syntactic position V_0. Thus, it is reasonable that these two are regarded as independent components in the phrase, namely, words. This can be questionable because these two are difficult to be used freely. For example, *赴北京[fu Beijing](to go to Beijing), *赴日本[fu Riben](to go to Japan) and *赴美国[fu Meiguo](to go to America) cannot be used conventionally, neither can *寻宝贝[xun baobei](to search for treasure) and *寻宠物[xun chongwu](to search for pets). In this way, morphemes like this are constrained from free use, leading to doubts on whether they can be identified as words. However, in this paper, such constraints are believed to be derived from prosody rather than syntax, leaving no impact on whether these morphemes can be regarded as words, for the reason that syntactically they have taken the position of X_0. By definition of *formal* syntax, all the components that appear at the terminal node of phrases(X_0) should be recognized as words.

Correspondingly, more complicated cases can also be syntactically analyzed and distinguished like 具[ju](possess) as in the structure极具吸引力[ji ju xiyinli](to possess great appeal):

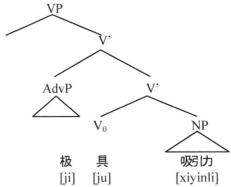

Figure 2: the syntactic analysis of极具吸引力[ji ju xiyinli](to possess great appeal)

3   The Register Identification of Two-Character-Three-Register Verbs

3.1 Informal Register (IR)

The linguistic expression of *informal* register is relatively casual.

(3) a. V什么V[Verb shenme Verb] (rhetorical question):
      去什么去[qu shenme qu](what to go(you'd better not go))
    b. V了个O[Verb le ge Object]
      买了个表[mai le ge biao](to buy a watch)
    c. V什么O[Verb shenme Object] (rhetorical question):
      吃什么饭[chi shenme fan](what to eat(you'd better not eat))
    d. V一V[Verb yi Verb]
      试一试[shi yi shi](to have a try)

The cases above reflect distinct *informal* features. Verbs that are used in such patterns can be identified as *informal*.

3.2 Formal Register (FR)

The essential principle of *formal* register is to distance the *formal* speech from its relevant *informal* speech with the aid of grammar.

（4）a. VO→OV:

编写	教材	→	教材	编写
bianxie	jiaocai	→	jiaocai	bianxie
edit	textbook	→	textbook	edit
to edit a textbook		→	the editing of the textbook	

b. VO→POV:

编写	教材	→	对	教材	的	编写
bianxie	jiaocai	→	dui	jiaocai	de	bianxie
edit	textbook	→	to	textbook	DE	edit
to edit a textbook		→	the editing of the textbook			

c. specific action →abstract action:

编[bian](edit)→编纂[bianzuan](edit)

3.3 Elegant Register (ER)

In *elegant* register, some *informal* speeches are replaced by easily understandable ancient words in order to keep distance.

（5）a. embedded compounding monosyllabic morphemes(ECMM):

不	宜	前往
bu	yi	qian wang
not	appropriate to	go
inappropriate to go		

b. ancient functional word:

乎[hu](interrogative or exclamatory final particle)

4 The Register Feature and the Distribution of Two-Character-Three-Register Verbs

According to these rules, register analysis and annotations have been done on the 81 Two-Character-Three-Register verbs. Based on the categories above, we take 购买[goumai](purchase) as an example of the analytic approach.

看[kan](see) is identified as *informal* for it can be used in all the structures of 3.1, such as 看什么看[kan shenme kan](what to see(you'd better not spectate)), 看了个电影[kan le ge dianying](to watch a film), 看一看[kan yi kan](to have a look)

购买[goumai](purchase) is identified as *formal* for it represents the action solely with no time and spacial implication, e.g.欢迎购买[huanying goumai](welcome to purchase), 拒绝购买[jujue goumai](to refuse to purchase), 谨慎购买[jinshen goumai](to purchase with caution). Its collaborative object is generally abstract like

购买年货[goumai nianhuo](to purchase Spring Festival goods), 购买商品[goumai shangpin](to purchase goods), 购买黄金[goumai huangjin](to purchase gold). This is quite different from the object in phrases like 买一本书[mai yi ben shu](to buy a book), 买二斤茶叶[mai er jin chaye](to buy one kilogram of tea).

购[gou](buy) is identified as *elegant* in the way that it is an ECMM, prosodically bound and syntactically free. It is correct to say 购书[gou shu](to buy a book), 购车[gou che](to buy a car), 购房[gou fang](to buy a house) while improper to say *购书籍[gou shuji](to buy a book), *购汽车[gou qiche](to buy a car), *购房子[gou fangzi](to buy a house), for only the former follows the prosodic rules in classical Chinese.

After analysis, it is clear that the registers of购[gou](buy)-买[mai](buy)-购买[goumai](purchase) are *elegant*, *formal* and *informal* respectively.

Table1. Examples of the Register Identification of Two-Character-Three-Register Verbs

	Group 1			Group 2			Group 3		
	购	买	购买	寻	找	寻找	学	习	学习
	[gou]	[mai]	[goumai]	[xun]	[zhao]	[xunzhao]	[xue]	[xi]	[xuexi]
Informal		+			+		+		
Formal			+			+			+
Elegant	+			+				+	

After identification and classification, the types of the register configuration can be listed as follows:

A1: IR-ER-FR,   A2: ER-IR-FR;
B2: IR-FR-FR,   B2: FR-IR-FR;
C1: ER-FR-FR,   C2: FR-ER-FR;
D1: IR-IR-FR,   D2: ER-ER-FR;
E: others, e.g. ER-IR-ER.

(the left column represents the first morpheme, the middle represents the second, while the right represents the third as in the example of 学[xue](learn)-习[xi](learn)-学习[xuexi](learn))

In Group A, B and C, 1 is the mirror image of 2 while 1 and 2 in Group D form an identical relation. Due to the correspondence and the interrelationship, all the words fall into four groups, as is shown in Table 2.

Table 2. The Distribution of Two-Character-Three-Register Verbs

	A		B		C		D		E
	A1	A2	B1	B2	C1	C2	D1	D2	
Quantity	19	15	7	8	5	1	19	1	6
Ratio	23%	19%	9%	10%	6%	1%	23%	1%	7%
Total	34		15		6		20		6
Total Ratio	43%		19%		7%		24%		7%

5 The Analysis on the Register Feature and Configuration of Two-Character-Three-Register Verbs

5.1 The filling effect of register vacancy

In Group A, the meanings of the Two-Character-Three-Register words (including V_1, V_2 and the dissyllable VV), are quite alike. Take 挖[wa](dig)-挖掘[wajue](dig)-掘[jue](dig) for example. Their explanations in *Modern Chinese Dictionary (6th edition)* are basically the same. Moreover, the examples listed in the dictionary are also similar in various ways. It is difficult to distinguish these three semantically.

Considering this, it is obvious that the value of the Two-Character-Three-Register words does not lie in the distinction of meanings. Let's take another example in terms of register:

(6) a. 挖　　了　　个　　坑
　　　　wa　　le　　ge　　keng
　　　　dig　　ASP　　CL　　hole
　　　　to dig a hole

　　　b. 挖　　什么　　挖
　　　　wa　　shenme　　wa
　　　　dig　　what　　dig
　　　　what to dig(you'd better not dig)

　　　c. 挖　　一　　挖
　　　　wa　　yi　　wa
　　　　dig　　one　　dig
　　　　have a try on digging

(7) a. 挖掘　　文章　　的　　深刻　　思想
　　　　wajue　　wenzhang　　de　　shenke　　sixiang
　　　　dig　　article　　DE　　profound　　meaning
　　　　to dig into the profound meaning of the article

b. 对　　　财富　　　的　　　挖掘
dui　　　caifu　　　de　　　wajue
to　　　treasure　　　DE　　　dig
to dig the treasure

(8)　饮　　水　　勿　　忘　　掘　　井　　人。
yin　　shui　　wu　　wang　　jue　　jing　　ren
drink　　water　　not　　forget　　dig　　well　　people
Do not forget the well digger when you drink from this well.

The phrases in (6) are typical grammatical structures in *informal* speeches. In these structures, 挖[wa](dig) is flexible in use while 挖掘[wajue](dig) and掘[jue](dig) are not. The phrases in (7) are typical in*formal* register structures, which prefers 挖掘[wajue](dig) to 挖[wa](dig) and 掘[jue](dig). The phrases in (8) are relatively *elegant*. In this case it is more fluent and natural to use 掘[jue](dig).

Accordingly, the main difference between the three words in 挖[wa](dig)-挖掘[wajue](dig)-掘[jue](dig) exists in their register, rather than their meanings. These words share similar meanings but belong to different registers. Therefore, the main function of the three different expressions is to make up for register vacancy so that people are able to choose the proper word out of their need for particular register.

5.2 The shift between formal and informal register

The VV structure in Group B and C is *formal* in register. But the correspondent V_1 and V_2 do not fall into *informal* and *elegant* register respectively. In Group B V_1 is *informal* while V_2 is *formal*. Meanwhile, V_1 in Group C is *formal* while V_2 is *elegant*. This does not conform to the Two-Character-Three-Register Theory. There is quite a few of this type, amounting to 19% and 7% separately. Let's take 亲[qin](kiss)-吻[wen](kiss)-亲吻[qinwen](kiss) for an example. Here is the explanation on *Modern Chinese Dictionary*.

（9）　a. 亲[qin](kiss): *verb*, to touch with the lips as a mark of intimacy or affection.

b. 吻[wen](kiss): *verb*, to touch with the lips as a mark of affection.

c. 亲吻[qinwen](kiss): *verb*, to touch with the lips as a mark of intimacy or affection.

According to the dictionary, the meanings of these three are almost the same. There is no difference in the instrument (lips), the object (human or things), and the implication (showing intimacy or affection). Thus, it is difficult for us to distinguish these three semantically. In terms of register, 亲吻[qin wen](kiss) is a rigorous case of *formal* register and亲[qin](kiss) is typically *informal*. However, 吻[wen](kiss) is not correspondingly *elegant* as it is neither ECMM nor classical Chinese. In the strict sense, it is not *formal* either, as *in formal* phrases like 吻一口[wen yi kou](to have a peck) also exist. But if we contrast 亲[qin](kiss) with 吻[wen](kiss), it is obvious that the registers of these two are different. Take X一口[X yi kou] for example. Here is the frequency of examples in the BCC corpus.

（10）a. 亲一口[qin yi kou](to have a peck): 366 times in frequency

b. 吻一口[wen yi kou](to have a peck): 10 times in frequency

As for *informal* phrases like X一口[X yi kou], although both words can be used, it is more proper to say 亲一口[qin yi kou](to have a peck) than 吻一口[wen yi kou](to have a peck). Correspondingly,吻[wen](kiss) is more *formal* than 亲[qin](kiss). Hence, phrases like 亲[qin](kiss)-吻[wen](kiss)-亲吻[qinwen](kiss) are divided into the group of IR-FR-FR.

Phrases like this do not cover three registers simultaneously, possibly because of insufficient elegance of the action itself or register vacancy due to the fact that this kind of expressions only appears in classical Chinese with no correspondence in modern Chinese. Besides, they share a common feature with Group A, i.e., V1 and V2 fall into different registers.

5.3 The register accordance of the monosyllables

This usually refers to Group D, i.e., V_1 and V_2 has the same register while VV has another (mostly *formal* register).In other words, V_1 and V_2 are either both *informal* or both   *elegant*.   For   the   most   part,   it   is   *informal*.   Take 涂[tu](smear)-抹[mo](smear)-涂抹[tumo](smear) for example.

From the basic explanations in the dictionary, we can find the consistency of their meanings. In regard to register, 涂[tu](smear) and 抹[mo](smear) are both used in *informal* speeches. Then what is the difference between these two? In our opinion, the diversity of their meanings will spontaneously appear in *informal* speeches, as is shown in the other senses in the dictionary.

Judging from the other senses, we can see 涂[tu](smear) is to add something to the object while 抹[mo](smear) is to get rid of something. In this way, these two have opposite meanings in the end.

From what is outlined above, it can be concluded that if V_1 and V_2 have no difference in the register, their distinction will mainly be about their meanings. Furthermore, if they do not have much difference in their basic meanings, there will be dissimilarity between their extended senses.

5.4 Other patterns

In addition to the above, there are some other patterns, e.g. phrases with all the words *elegant*(拂[fu](wipe)-拭[shi](wipe)-拂拭[fushi](wipe)), phrases with both verbs *informal*(认[ren](recognize)-识[ren](recognize)-认识[renshi](recognize)) and phrases with both verbs *elegant*(谙[an](to know well)-熟[shu](to know well)-谙熟[anshu](to know well)). However, these types are too rare to see and are mostly concerned with the trait of the words themselves. No universal rule is involved here. Thus, it will not be covered in this paper.

Based on the analysis above, we can see that there is not much difference in the meanings of the words in Two-Character-Three-Register structures. The distinction mainly exists in their registers. It meets the needs of social communication to have words with the same meaning but different register. People can choose words of different registers on different occasions, which evidently enriches our language and makes it more decent.

6   Conclusion

In summary, this paper has presented three key points:

First of all, there are diverse patterns of the register configuration in the Two-Character-Three-Register structures. Generally speaking, dissyllabic verbs are *formal* while monosyllabic verbs are usually *informal* or *elegant*.

Secondly, there is a universal rule in the constitution of Two-Character-Three-Register structures—words with similar meanings can demonstrate different registers. The reason lies in the need to make up for the register vacancy.

Thirdly, the verbs that do not conform to the Two-Character-Three-Register Theory may result from causes like semantic shift, usage changes, or social influence, which lead to alteration of the register.

Acknowledgement.

This research project is supported by Science Foundation of Beijing Language and Culture University (supported by "the Fundamental Research Funds for the Central Universities") (Approval number: 17YJ080202). The paper: *A Structural and Prosodic Analysis of Trisyllabic New word*, published in the Chinese Lexical Semantics 2016, was supported by Science Foundation of Beijing Language and Culture University (supported by "the Fundamental Research Funds for the Central Universities") (Approval number: 16YJ080207). The paper: *On the Interaction between the Structure and the Prosody of Chinese 1+3 Idioms*, published in the Chinese Lexical Semantics 2015, was supported by Science Foundation of Beijing Language and Culture University (supported by "the Fundamental Research Funds for the Central Universities") (Approval number: 15YJ080207).

The project is also funded by MOE (Ministry of Education in China) Project of Humanities and Social Sciences (Project No. 17YJC740064).

References

1. Chen, Y.: On the Emergence of New Lexical Entries and Their Social Significance (in Chinese). Studies in Language and Linguistics, no. 2, 151-158 (1984).
2. Feng, S.: On mechanisms of Register System and its grammatical property (in Chinese). Studies of the Chinese Language, no. 5, 400-412 (2010).
3. Feng, S.: On Prosodic Words in Chinese Language (in Chinese). Social Sciences in China, no. 1, 161-176 (1996).
4. Feng, S.: On the "natural foot" in Chinese Language (in Chinese). Studies of the Chinese Language, no. 1, 40-47 (1998).
5. Feng, S.: Yuti (stylistic-register) Grammar: A linguistic Exploration on Form-function Correlation (in Chinese). Contemporary Rhetoric, no. 6, 3-12 (2012).
6. Jin, L. & Baek Sujin.: On the Linguistic Status and Research Methodology of Stylistics (in Chinese). Contemporary Rhetoric, no. 6, 23-33 (2012).
7. Liu, D.: From Grammatical Construction to Rhetoric Construction (Part 1) (in Chinese). Contemporary Rhetoric, no. 3, 7-17 (2010).
8. Liu, D.: From Grammatical Construction to Rhetoric Construction (Part 2) (in Chinese). Contemporary Rhetoric, no. 4, 14-23 (2010).
9. Liu, S.: Chinese Descriptive Lexicology (in Chinese). The Commercial Press, Beijing (2006).
10. Shen, M.: An Investigation on Meaning Composition of New Words (in Chinese). Applied Linguistics, no.4, 66-72 (1995).

The Meaning of Polysemous Adjective "*Hao*(Good)"[1]

Wang Enxu , Yuan Yulin

Department of Chinese Language and Literature, Peking University,
No.5 Yiheyuan Road, Haidian District, Beijing 100871, China
wangbush000@126.com, yuanyl@pku.edu.cn

Abstract. It is difficult to explain the meaning of polysemous adjectives. Previous scholars have done a number of researches, but there are still two problems unsolved. First, how to describe the meaning of adjective in "Adj + N" compound word? Second, how to describe the meaning of Adjective in "Adj + N" contextual combination? Taking "*Hao*(Good)" as an example, this paper establishes a framework of semantic analyzing for adjective on the basis of Qualia Structure (see table 1). The research shows that:1) the framework is suitable for analyzing not only the meaning of "*Hao*(Good)" in "*hao*(good)+ N" compound word but also in "*hao*(good) + N" combination.2）The "*hao*(good) + N" might have multiple meanings, but the "to function well" is its basic meaning.

Keywords: *hao*(good), polysemy, "*hao*(good)+N", Qualia role, function.

1   Introduction

In order to interpret the meaning of polysemous adjectives, the previous Scholars have done a great deal researches[1-8], there are still some problems left unsolved. The purpose of this paper will take Chinese word "*Hao*(Good)" as an example to solve the following two problems: firstly, to explain the meaning of "*Hao*(Good)" in "*hao*(good) + N" compound words; secondly, to explain the meaning of "*Hao*(Good)" in "*hao*(good) + N" combination in the context.

---

[1] This paper is supported by the Key Project of Research Institute of Humanities & Social Science of National Ministry of Education "A study of lexical semantic knowledge representation and its computing system under Chinese parataxis grammar framework", the National Basic Research Program of China (2014CB340502), the Project of Chinese Postdoctoral Science Fund (2016M600004), the Research Project of State Language Commission "A study on the interpreting principles and methods of Modern Chinese words", and Shandong Province Social Science Fund (16CZWJ31). The anonymous experts of CLSW2017 have put forward many valuable comments. Here, we wish to express our sincere thanks!

Y. Wu et al. (Eds.): CLSW 2017, LNAI 10709, pp. 180–189, 2018.
https://doi.org/10.1007/978-3-319-73573-3_15

2   The interpretation of "*hao*(good) + N(Noun)" compound words

According to the investigation on the CCL (Center for Chinese Linguistics PKU) corpus, "*Hao*(Good)" can collocate with noun[2],verb and adjective. Collocating with verb and adjective, "*Hao*(Good)" is monosemic; but collocating with noun, "*Hao*(Good)" is polysemous. Why the latter collocation can make the "*Hao*(Good)" become a polysemous word?

2.1   Reason analysis

There are two reasons that cause the " *hao*(good) + N" compound words has multiple meanings:

The first one is the relation between adjective and noun. As for qualitative adjective, reference 9 makes a clear definition in WordNet: what qualitative adjective expressed are not the attributes of things but the values of attributes. For example, COLOR are attributes of robins: the color associated with robins can be described by the adjective red. There is a stable association between the noun color, which denotes attributes, and the adjective red, which provide values of those attributes. Nouns can be said to serve as argument for attribute: COLOR (robin) =red. reference 10 points out there is a valence relationship between attribute nouns and things nouns. For example, "*tanxing*(elastic)", "*piqi*(temper)" are attributes nouns, which belong to things nouns "*suliao*(plastic)", "*yeye*(grandpa)", the latter is the valence components of the former. Based on the above analysis, the relationship between things nouns, attributes nouns and values(adjectives) can be summarized as follows:

Attribute noun (thing noun) = adjective   Abbreviation: $N_{attribute}(N_{object}) = Adj_{value}$

The second one is noun. According to the reference 2 and reference 11, a noun may contain ten Qualia roles: formal (abbr. FOR), constitutive (abbr. CON), telic (abbr. TEL), unit (abbr. UNI), evaluation (abbr. EVA), agentive (abbr. AGE), material (abbr. MAT), action (abbr. ACT), handle (abbr. HAN), orientation (abbr. ORI). Through Qualia roles, we can solve such problem of noun referent as: "what are the referent objects of nouns?" (FOR role), "what are the referent objects of nouns constituted by?" (CON role), "where are the referent objects of nouns from?" (AGE role), "where will the referent objects of nouns go?" (TEL role), etc. All of these can help us to describe nouns semantic knowledge in a systematic way.

If reference 9 and reference 10 demonstrate the relationship that is "Attribute noun (thing noun) = adjective" between things nouns, attributes nouns and values(adjectives)

---

[2] Strictly speaking, the "*hao*(good)" and N which appear in "*hao*(good) + N" compound words should be regarded as "adjective morpheme" and "noun morpheme" rather than adjective and noun respectively. For the purpose of the unity of expression, this paper calls them adjectives and nouns temporarily.

makes a theoretical preparation for the unified analysis of "*hao*(good) + N", the appearance of Qualia Structure theory makes the unified analysis of "*hao*(good) + N" become possible.

2.2 The Qualia Structure of "Adj + N" compound words

Nouns contain ten Qualia roles. But in actual context, it is not all of ten Qualia roles that can be highlighted. For example, in "Adj + N" compound words, the "Adj" mainly highlights six Qualia roles of "N": FOR role, CON role, AGE role, TEL role, HAN role and EVA role:(the meanings of words come from Modern Chinese Dictionary, Sixth Edition)

1. Highlighting FOR. "Adj" highlights the semantic information of "N", which are size, shape, dimension, color, etc. For example:

（1）【大地】广大 (形式角色) + 的 + 土地$_N$。

（【*dadi* (broad ground)】*guangda*(broad) $_{FOR}$ + *de* + *tudi*(ground) $_N$。）

【远洋】距离大陆远 (形式角色) + 的 + 海洋$_N$。

（【*yuanyang* (distant sea)】*juli dalu yuan*(distant) $_{FOR}$ + *de* + *haiyang*(sea) $_N$。）

2. Highlighting CON. "Adj" highlights the semantic information of "N", which are quality, attribute, material, weight, whole, component, etc. For example:

（2）【好人】❷没有伤、残、病 (构成角色) + 的 + 人$_N$。

（【*haoren* (healthy person)】❷*meiyou shang, can,bing*(Not injured, disable or ill) $_{CON}$ + *de* + *ren*(person) $_N$。）

【大班】幼儿园里由五周岁至六周岁儿童组成 (构成角色) + 的 + 班级。

（【*daban* (top class)】*you`eryuan li you wuzhousui zhi liuzhousui ertong zucheng* (be made up of children between age five and six) $_{CON}$ + *de* + *banji*(class) $_N$。）

3. Highlighting AGE. "Adj" highlights the semantic information of "N", which are manufacture, existence, the relationship of cause and effect, etc. For example:

（3）【新书】将出版或刚出版 (施成角色) + 的 + 书$_N$。

（【*xinshu* (new book)】*jiang chuban huo gang chuban* (to be published or just published) $_{AGE}$ + *de* + *shu*(book) $_N$。）

【熟食】经过加工做熟 (施成角色) + 的 + 饭菜$_N$。

（【shushi (cooked food)】*jingguo jiagong zuo shu* (cooked) $_{AGE}$ + *de* + *shiwu*(food) $_N$。）

4. Highlighting TEL. "Adj" highlights the semantic information of "N", which are function, value, purpose, etc. For example:

（4）【冷布】防蚊蝇、糊窗户等用 (功用角色) ＋的＋很稀疏＋ 的 ＋ 布N。

（【*lengbu*(gauze)】 *fang wenying, hu chuanghu deng yong* (to be used for preventing mosquitoes entering or mounting window) TEL + *de* + *hen xishu* (very sparse) + *de* + *bu* (textile) N。 ）

【黑市】暗中进行非法买卖(功用角色)＋ 的 ＋ 市场N。

（【*heishi*(blackmarket)】 *anzhong jinxing feifa maimai* (to be used for buying or selling illegally in secret) TEL + *de* + *shichang*(market) N。 ）

5. Highlighting HAN. "Adj" highlights the semantic information of "N", which are habitual action, behavior, influence, etc. For example:

（5）【肥田】❶采用施肥等措施 ＋ 使 ＋ 田地N ＋ 肥沃 (处置角色)。

（【*feitian* (fertile land)】 ❶*caiyong shifei deng cuoshi* (to take some measures such as apply fertilizer to cultivated land) + *shi*(cause) +*tiandi*(cultivated land) N + *feiwo*(fertile) HAN。 ）

【美发】梳理修饰 (处置角色) ＋ 头发N。

（【*meifa*(hairdressing)】 *shuli xiushi* (to groom) HAN + *de* + *toufa*(hair) N。 ）

6. Highlighting EVA. "Adj" highlights the speaker's emotional or subjective evaluations to which the "N" refers to. unlike other Qualia roles, the evaluation role is a semantic role based on the speaker's position. In theory, speakers can evaluate any Qualia roles of a noun, which can form different types of evaluation; but in fact, the most common evaluation types are as follows: EVA-FOR, EVA-CON, EVA-TEL, EVA-HAN, EVA-AGE. For example:

（6）【美景】美好 (评价形式角色) ＋ 的 ＋ 景色N。

（【*meijing* (beautiful scenery) 】 *meihao* (beautiful) EVA-FOR + *de* + *jingse*(scenery) N。 ）

【好人】❶品行好 (评价构成角色) ＋的＋人N；先进 (评价构成角色) ＋ 的 ＋ 人N。

（【*haoren* (good person) 】 ❶*pinxing hao* (good morality and good behavior) EVA-CON + *de* + *ren*(person) N; *xianjin* (good idea) EVA-CON + *de* + *ren*(person) N）

【好话】❶有益 (评价功用角色) ＋ 的 ＋ 话N。

（【*haohua* (good word) 】 ❶*youyi*(beneficial) EVA-TEL + *de* + *hua* (word) N。 ）

【软食】容易咀嚼和消化 (评价处置角色) ＋ 的 ＋ 食物N。

（【*ruanshi* (soft food) 】 *rongyi jujue he xiaohua* (easy to chew and digest) EVA-HAN + *de* + *shiwu* (food) N。 ）

【大片儿】指投资大、制作成本高 (评价施成角色) ＋ 的 ＋ 影片N。

（【*dapianr*(blockbuster)】 *touzi da, zhizuo chengben gao* (big investment and big production cost) EVA-AGE + *de* + *yingpian* (movie) N。 ）

Based on the above analysis, we establish a framework of semantic analysis for Chinese adjectives:

Table 1. the framework of semantic analyzing for adjective on the basis of Qualia Structure

		Qualia roles	example
Adjec-tive	describe noun	FOR: size, shape, color, etc.	【大地】广大 $_{(FOR)}$ + 的 + 土地$_N$.
		CON: quality, attribute, component, etc.	【肥水】含有营养成分 $_{(CON)}$ + 的 + 水$_N$.
		AGE: manufacture, ex-istence, cause, etc.	【新书】将出版或刚出版 $_{(AGE)}$ + 的 + 书$_N$.
		TEL: function, value, purpose, etc.	【冷库】冷藏食物或药品 $_{(TEL)}$ + 的 + 仓库$_N$.
		……	……
	evaluate noun	FOR: size, shape, color, etc.	【美景】美好 $_{(EVA-FOR)}$ + 的 + 景色$_N$.
		CON: quality, attribute, component, etc.	【好人】品行好 $_{(EVA-CON)}$ + 的 + 人$_N$.
		AGE: manufacture, ex-istence, cause, etc.	【大片儿】指投资大、制作成本高$_{(EVA-AGE)}$ + 的 + 影片$_N$.
		TEL: function, value, purpose, etc.	【好话】有益 $_{(EVA-TEL)}$ + 的 + 话$_N$.
		……	……

The framework of semantic analysis for adjective has two advantages as follows:

Firstly, it will contribute to distinguish different meanings of the same adjective in the same collocation. Taking "haoren (good person)" for example, according to Modern Chinese Dictionary, has two senses: ❶ *pinxing hao de ren* (person with good morality and good behavior); ❷ *meiyou shang, can, bing de ren* (person who is not injured, disable or ill). To distinguish the two meanings, scholars might take the method as fol-lows: Because "*hao* (good)" is a double-function adjective, it can highlight not only the psychological meaning of "*ren* (person)" but also the physical meaning of "*ren* (per-son)" when it collocates with "*ren* (person)". Such explanation is valid for "*haoren* (good person)", but it does not work when we encounter "*xinshu* (new book)". Because "*xinshu* (new book)" also has two meanings: ❶ *zhanxin de shu*(new book) ; ❷ *jiang chuban huo gang chuban*(to be published or just published) *de shu*(book).What's more, both of them are physical meanings. They cannot be distinguished by the method of double-function adjective. At this time, if we replace the method of double-function adjective with the method of this paper, it will be easier to distinguish the different meanings of "*hao*(good)+N" than before. For example, "*haoren* (good person)" ❶ and "*haoren* (good person)" ❷ are different: the former highlights the EVA-CON role of "*ren* (person)", the latter highlights the CON role of "*ren* (person)". Similarly, "*xinshu* (new book)" ❶ and"*xinshu* (new book)" ❷ are different: the former highlights the FOR role of "*shu* (book)", the latter highlights the AGE role of "*shu* (book)".

Secondly, it will contribute to distinguish the different meanings of the same adjective. The meaning of an adjective will change with its collocation object，which scholars have noticed and have proposed some methods to explain. Taking "*da* (big)" for example, its meanings in "big mouse" and "big elephant" are different. reference 3 pointed out: "a big mouse is not really big when compared to a small elephant. The interpretation of 'big' depends on the relevant comparison class, and thus the relevant size standard, which have to be made salient by context....But how do you understand 'a big mouse' when no comparison class has been explicitly provided by context (for example, 'a big mouse is sitting on the rubbish bin')? Apparently, you understand is as saying that some mouse is big as far as mice go, not as far as elephants go (and not even as far as rubbish bin s go)." Maybe the explanation of reference 3 will contribute to distinguish the two "big" between "big mouse" and "big elephant", but it doesn't help to distinguish the three "*da*" (big) between "*dadi* (broad ground)", "*daban* (big class)" and "*dapianr* (blockbuster)". If we use the method of this paper, the three "*da* (big)" can be distinguished easily: the "*da* (big)" of "*dadi* (broad ground)" highlights the FOR role of "*di* (ground)", the "*da* (big)" of "*daban* (big class)" highlights the CON role of "*ban* (class)", and the "*da* (big)" of "*dapianr* (blockbuster)" highlights the EVA-AGE role of "*yingpian* (movie)".

3   The interpretation of "*hao*(good) + N(Noun)" combination

The meaning of "Good" will change with its collocation objects [1]. When "Good" collocates with umbrella, its meaning is "to function well "; when "Good" collocates with meal, its meaning is "tasty"; when "Good" collocates with teacher, its meaning is "to perform some act well" [2]. This is also true to the Chinese "*hao*(good)". Then, where does these meanings of come from, and what is the formation mechanism of polysemous "*hao*(good)"?

3.1   The formation mechanism of polysemous "*hao*(good)"

According to the observation of this paper, there are two factors that cause "*hao*(good)" polysemy:

One is the noun. If nouns have 10 Qualia roles, and "*hao*(good)" can evaluates any Qualia roles of nouns. As a result, it will form 10 kinds of evaluations. Accordingly, "*hao* (good) + N(Noun)" will have 10 meanings. But in fact, none of "*hao* (good) + N(Noun)" have so many meanings. For example, "*haoshi* (good thing)" has only 7 meanings, "*haoren* (good person)" has only 4 meanings, and "*haohua* (good words)" has only 3 meanings (Great Chinese Dictionary, 2011 edition). So, is it what that caused the quantitative discrepancy between the possible evaluation and the actual evaluation of "*hao* (good)"? The answer is: the speaker's psychological expectation.

The other is the speaker's psychological expectation. Before speaking or doing somethings, people always have some psychological expectations. As for a "*dao* (knife)", people usually expect it "to function well"(such as sharp, good feeling, to cut well). Therefore, when we say that a "*dao* (knife)" is a "*haodao* (good knife)" has only one meaning, which is "a '*dao* (knife)' to be function well". As for the "*san*(umbrella)", in addition to expecting that if functions (such as comfort, rain-proof) well, people expect tant its appearance and construction are good, too. Therefore, when we say that a "*san*(umbrella)" is a "*hao san* (good umbrella)" which often contains multiple meanings, which is "a '*san*(umbrella)] with good quality ", "a nice looking '*san*(umbrella)'", "a '*san* (umbrella)' to function well", etc. For example: (The evaluation data of "*hao dao* (good knife)" and "*hao san* (good umbrella)" originates from Jingdong mall: https://www.jd.com/)

（7）"*hao dao*"(total evaluation ≥18000) and "*hao san*"(total evaluation ≥8100)

3.2   The formation mechanism of polysemous "*hao*(good)"

reference 1 points out that there is no semantic theory that can describe the meaning of "good" in detail. The comments of reference 1, on the one hand, illustrate the difficulty of describing "good" meaning and, and on the other hand, illustrate the lack of semantic theories that appropriate to describe Chinese "*hao*(good)" meaning. The first part of this paper proves that the Qualia Structure is suitable for describing the meaning of Chinese "*hao*(good)" in compound words. This section will prove that the Qualia Structure is suitable to describe the meaning of Chinese "*hao*(good)" combination in the context, too. The discussion in this section is divided into three aspects:

3.2.1   Theoretical meaning and practical meaning

Theoretical meaning is all of the possible meaning of what "*hao*(good)" has in theory. The number of   theoretical meanings that "*hao*(good)" has depends on the number of meaning that the corresponding noun has. How many meanings does a noun have, does how many meanings "*hao*(good)" have. The practical meaning is the meaning of what "*hao*(good)" has expressed in practical use. Influenced by psychological expectations, when people evaluate something with "*hao*(good)", they usually pay attention to no more than 3 facets (≤3) instead of all facets of things. The asymmetry between "*hao*(good)" theoretical meaning and its practical meaning is not only common in "*hao*(good) + N(Noun)" compound words but also common in "*hao*(good) + N(Noun)" combination. For example:[3]

（8）*hao dao* (good knife) （kitchen knife, total evaluation ≥18000）
    Theoretical meaning:10;

---

[3] The evaluation data originates from Jingdong mall(https://www.jd.com/) and Autohome (http://www.autohome. com.cn/)

Practical meaning:1, which is "a '*dao*(knife)' to be function well";
Key words: sharp, good feeling, to cut well, and so on.
（9） *hao zao* (good jujube) (*Hetian* Jujube, total evaluation ≥12000)
Theoretical meaning:10;
Practical meaning:2, which are "nice looking '*zao*(jujube)'" and "tasty '*zao*(jujube)'";
Key words: big/full grains, good taste, convenience to eat, and so on.
（10） *hao che* (good car) (family car with price of 80000-180000 Yuan, total evaluation ≥7400)
Theoretical meaning:10;
Practical meaning:3, which are "nice looking '*che*(car)'","A car with excellent performance" and "A car with good configuration";
Key words: nice looking, easy to operate, powerful, low fuel consumption, big space, good interior, and so on.

3.2.2   Evaluative meaning and descriptive meaning

Evaluative meaning is the most common and basic meaning of "*hao*(good)". In addition to the evaluative meaning, sometimes "*hao*(good)" has also descriptive meaning. Evaluation meaning is the default, unmarked meaning of "*hao*(good)". Relatively speaking, descriptive meaning is the marked meaning of "*hao*(good)". When "*hao*(good)" expresses descriptive meaning, it often appears with another descriptive "Adj+N". For example:

（11） "*haoren*(healthy person)"-"*bingren*(patient)"   "*haoyan*(healthy eye)"-"*xiayan*(blind)" "*haofan*(qualified meal)"-"*soufan*(spoilage meal)" "*haoma*(healthy horse)"-"*bingma*(sick horse)" "*haoxie*(undamaged shoes)"-"*poxie*(damaged shoes)" "*haoshui*(clean water)"-"*zangshui*(dirty water)" "*haozhi*(tidy paper)"-"*lanzhi*(waste paper)"   "*haoer*(healthy eye)"-"*longer*(deaf ear)"   "*haobi*(undamaged pen)"-"*huaibi*(unusable pen)" "*haopingguo*(good apple)"-"*lanpingguo*(bad apple)" "*haoshouji*(good phone)"-"*huaishouji*(unusable phone)"   "*haoboli*(intact glass)"-"*suiboli*(cullet)" "*haoshibei*(intact stele)"-"*duanshibei*(broken obelisk)" ……

3.2.3   monosemic and polysemous

When "*hao*(good)" collocates with nouns, it is usually polysemous, e.g., "good cars", "good umbrella", "good date" and "good apple". Only in a few cases, it is monosemic. For example:

（12） monosemic "*hao*(good) + N(Noun)"
a. *hao***(good) + creatures** (such as insects / crows / foxes / spiders / bacteria / weasels, etc.): Highlighting the specific benefits to mankind;
b. *hao***(good) + tools** (such as knife / pliers / explosives / detonator / spade / steel, etc.): Highlighting the specific function of tools;

c. *hao*(**good**) + **medical care** (such as drug / medicine / Chinese medicine / plaster / prescription / recipe / antibiotic / sunscreen / stimulant / eye drops / vitamin / Hair Coloring /Cleansing Cream / sunscreen / whitening cream, etc.): Highlighting the specific function and effect of medical care;

d. *hao*(**good**) + **career** (such as driver / teacher / chef / policeman / doctor / forward / postman, etc.): Highlighting the duties of career.

With the above analysis, we can explain why "*hao*(good)" sometimes is polysemous and sometimes is monosemic when it collocates with nouns. The reason is the speaker's psychological expectation: 1) if the speaker has multiple psychological expectations on what the noun refers to, "*hao*(good)" will have a variety of meanings. For example, "*hao che* (good car)", in addition to expecting it "to function well"(Performance Excellence), the speaker also hope that its appearance and configuration to be good, too. 2) if the speaker has only one psychological expectation on what the noun refers to, "*hao*(good)" will have only one meaning, which usually is "to function well". For example, "*hao dao* (good knife)" usually means "to cut well", "*hao siji* (good driver)" usually means "to drive well". 3) if the speaker has no psychological expectation on what the noun refers to, he will not say "*hao*(good) + N(Noun)". For example, the speaker rarely says "*hao jinxing* (good Venus)", "*hao shuicao* (good waterweeds)", "*hao xueshan* (good snowberg)" and so on.

4   Conclusion

reference [12:322] generalized the English "good + N" into four meanings: "First of all, for what it habitually does or can do (good₃)....Second, something (or somebody) can be called good on the basic of what can be done with it, what it is good for (good₄) ... Third, somebody (or something) can be called good because of what he actually does, did, or will do(good₅). Finally, what simply happens, or is the case, may be called good(good₅)." From the view of Qualia Structure, the four meanings can be generalized into one, that is "to function well".

Similarly, the main meaning of Chinese "*hao*(good) + N(Noun)" is also "to function well": if "*hao*(good) + N(Noun)" has more than one meaning, there is at least one meaning is "to function well"; if "*hao*(good) + N(Noun)" has only one meaning, which must be "to function well"; if "*hao*(good) + N(Noun)" is nonsense, what the N(noun) refers to maybe has no value to human beings. There is no need to evaluate them (such as "Venus / waterweeds/ snowberg" and so on). Just as what Aristotle said in *Nicomachean Ethics*: "in general, for all things that have a function or activity, the 'good' and the 'well' is thought to reside in the function"(quoted from reference [12:330]).

References

1. Katz JJ (1964) Semantic Theory and the Meaning of "Good". The Journal of Philosophy 61: 739-766.
2. Pustejovsky J (1995) The generative lexicon. MIT Press, Cambridge.

3. Rakova M (2004) The Extent of the Literal: Metaphor, Polysemy and Theories of Concepts. Peking University Press, Beijing. [photocopy edition]
4. Lakoff G, Johnson M (1999) Philosophy in the Flesh: The Embodied Mind and Its Challenge to Western Thought. Basic Books, NewYork.
5. Zhang Hui, Fan Ruiping (2008) The meaning construction of noun and noun combinations. Journal of Foreign Languages 4:38-49. [In Chinese]
6. Perrin L-M (2010) Polysemous Qualities and Universal Networks, Invariance and Diversity. Linguistic Discovery 1:259-280.
7. Yuan Yulin (2013) On the Relationship between the Meaning of Adjectives and Their Syntactic Characteristics in Mandarin. Journal of Chinese and Tibetan Languages 7:147-165. [In Chinese]
8. Zhang Nianxin, Song Zuoyan (2015) Semantic Construction of Adjective-Noun Compounds in Mandarin: Based on Qualia Structure and Conceptual Blending Theory. Journal of Chinese Information Processing 5:28-45. [In Chinese]
9. Miller GA (1998) Nouns in WordNet. In: Fellbeum C (ed) WordNet: An Electronic Lexical Database.The MIT Press, Cambridge & MA, pp 23-46.
10. Yuan Yulin (1994) A cognitive study of monovalent nouns. Studies of the Chinese Language 4:241-253. [In Chinese]
11. Yuan Yulin (2014) On a descriptive system of qualia structure of Chinese nouns and its application in parsing complex Chinese grammatical phenomena. Contemporary linguistics 1:31-48. [In Chinese]
12. Vendler Z (1970/2002) Linguistics in Philosophy. translated by Chen Jiaying. HuaXia Press, Beijing, pp 291-331.

The (Dis) appearance of Affected Role "lìng/shǐ…" in the Causative Adjective-Noun Composition

Qiang Li

Department of Chinese Language and Literature, Shanghai University, Shanghai 200444, China

`leeqiang2222@163.com`

Abstract. The adjective-noun composition of "emotional value + emotional initiation" has causal meaning, which can be indicated by adding the affected role "lìng/shǐ…" before adjectives. However, "lìng/shǐ…" cannot be added before some adjective-noun compositions. On the basis of some literature, this paper discusses this issue, pointing out that the (dis)appearance of the affected role "lìng/shǐ…" can be preliminarily explained through the semantic relation between the adjectives and nouns referring to things or participants in events.

Keywords: adjective-noun composition; affected role; participant; (dis)appearance

1 Introduction

In the adjective-noun compositions, the structure of "emotional value + emotional initiation" is special, and the emotional adjective acts as the emotional value. Emotion is a mental feeling that occurs within the subject, and is generally triggered by visual or auditory stimuli, which can cause the subject to produce various emotional experience [1]. This type of composition contains a causative relation, and the thing or event as a reason can make the subject produce certain emotion. Meanwhile, the causative relation can usually be explicitly reflected in language forms: adjective plus a noun referring to person, then "lìng/shǐ…" is added before it, so the causative relation among the emotional attribute, property owner and property initiation can be expressed [2]. However, in some compositions, "lìng/shǐ…" must appear in the surface form. Otherwise, the adjective-noun structure cannot be tenable or natural. See the contrast between the two sets of examples below.

(1) a. 令/使人悲哀的消息 —— 悲哀的消息
     b. 令/使人悲哀的决定 —— ? 悲哀的决定
(2) a. 令/使人愉悦的话题 —— 愉悦的话题
     b. 令/使人愉悦的问题 —— ? 愉悦的问题

© Springer International Publishing AG 2018
Y. Wu et al. (Eds.): CLSW 2017, LNAI 10709, pp. 190–197, 2018.
https://doi.org/10.1007/978-3-319-73573-3_16

This paper will discuss the differences between the two sets of examples. On the basis of Li [3], I would like to point out some unexplained phenomena, and try to put forward my own view, hoping to make a preliminary explanation about the (dis) appearance mechanism of the affected role "lìng/shǐ…" in adjective-noun compositions.

2   Existing research and problems

Li [3] had a discussion on the (dis) appearance mechanism of the affected role in the compositions of same adjectives and different nouns. Specifically, she argues that the roles highlighted in the scenes of "消息" (xiāoxi, *message*) and "决定" (juédìng, *decision*) in the above example (1) are different. "消息" activates an event of delivering message, and only the "receiver" is highlighted, while the "sender" is not be highlighted, so when we use the "＿ + de + CAU" structure, it is easy to identify the affected role in event scene, and the "receiver" has the mood or emotion represented by adjective. Hence, there is no need to use "lìng/shǐ rén…" to distinguish which one is the affected role, and "悲哀的消息" (*the sad news*) is established. "决定" (juédìng, *decision*) activates an event of decision, and not only the "decider" can be highlighted, but the "receiver" can also be highlighted. When the "＿ + de + CAU" structure is used, it is not easy to identify the affected role in the event scene, and "lìng/shǐ rén…" is needed to distinguish which one is the affected role. Hence, "悲哀的决定"(*the sad decision*) cannot be established, but "令人悲哀的决定"(*the decision that causes sad emotion*) should be said. In addition, she argues that the (dis) appearance of "lìng/shǐ rén…" in example (2) is relevant to the affected role. Specifically, in the framework of "话题"(huàtí, *topic*), people tend to think that all the "talkers" produce emotion or feeling represented by psychological adjectives, so there is no need to use "lìng/shǐ rén…" to distinguish which one is the affected role. Hence, "愉悦的话题"(*a happy topic*) is tenable. While in the framework of "问题"(wèntí, *problem*), it can be considered that the "questioner" or "answerer" produces the emotion. Therefore, there is a need to use "lìng/shǐ rén…" to distinguish which one is the affected role. "愉悦的问题"(*a happy question*) is not established.

The above explanation is reasonable but also has some problems. First of all, for the interpretation of example (1), I find some examples that contradict her conclusion. For instance:

(3)   a. 令人疲惫的工作 —— ? 疲惫的工作
       b. 令人惊讶的消息 —— ? 惊讶的消息
       c. 令人羞耻的姿势 —— ? 羞耻的姿势
       d. 令人反感的动作 —— ? 反感的动作

If follow the standard of "whether to highlight", I can also think that in example (a), the noun "工作"(gōngzuò, *job*) highlights the "worker", and the object is arguably quite clear, so it is easy to identify participants in the event scene. Therefore, "疲惫的工作"(*an exhausting job*) should be tenable, but actually not, "令人疲惫的工作" is established. In example (b), if the noun "消息"(xiāoxi, *news*) activates "receiver", the object is the only. The same with (1a), "惊讶的消息"(*a surprising news*) should be tenable, but the actual situation is not so, "lìng rén..." must be put before the adjective. In example (c) and (d), the nouns "姿势"(zīshì, *posture*) and "动作"(dòngzuò, *action*) highlight the behavior implementer, and the object is definite, but adjectives cannot be combined directly with nouns. More importantly, from the perspective of the salient object, adjectives do not directly modify the behavior implementer represented by head nouns, but modify the behavior spectator. For the example (2), if in accordance with the relevant interpretation, since "问题"(wèntí, *problem*) can make "questioner" or "answerer" produce feelings of pleasure, such a situation may also exist: a question can make the "questioner" and "answerer" both happy. In such case, there is absolutely no need to distinguish who is the affected role, but why "lìng/shǐ..." must be used?

In view of the above two points, I think that it is necessary to make a deeper investigation on the (dis)appearance of the affected role "lìng/shǐ..." and propose a solution that can explain the above examples in a unified way.

3   Event object referred by nouns and function of specifying object

In the context of Generative Lexicon Theory, nouns are with two opposite semantic attributes. According to the standard of "whether people participate", nouns can be divided into natural type and artifactual type [4, 5]. The biggest difference between the two types is whether they are correlated with the agentive role or telic role in qualia structure. Natural type nouns, such as "stone, water, rabbit, sky", are primary natural things, which are not influenced by human factors, so they have no agentive role. In addition, they do not meet people's needs, so telic role does not exist. Artifactual type nouns, such as "computer, chair, table, knife", are produced through certain means, whose purpose is to meet people's specific needs. Therefore, all these nouns have agentive role and telic role.

With this semantic classification of nouns, in the adjective-noun composition which contains causative relation, adjectives represent psychological emotion or feeling, which is caused by external stimulation and the stimulation is bearded by event or thing referred by nouns. Hence, the event or thing referred by nouns can have a certain impact on someone. From this perspective, in the adjective-noun composition which contains causative relation, artifactual nouns are likely to appear, because they always involve human factors. People may have some emotion or feeling, which is triggered by events or things that nouns refer to.

Events or things referred by artifactual nouns are produced by certain means (agentive role, [6]), and can have a certain impact on people (telic role, [6]); in addition, people can handle them (disposal role, [7]). When artifactual nouns appear in the adjective-noun composition with causative relation, it tends to bring emotional stimuli to two kinds of people: one is the initiator or handler of events or something, namely activated by agentive role and disposal role; one is the passive influenced side of events or things, namely activated by telic role. In my opinion, the (dis)appearance of "lìng/shǐ…" with a causative relation is related with the fact that adjectives semantically modify the initiating handlers or influenced person. If an adjective can semantically describe the emotional attributes of any role, "lìng/shǐ…" cannot appear, because the speaker and listener do not have to distinguish between the two roles. If the adjective semantically describes only the emotional attributes of one specific role, "lìng/shǐ…" must appear, because only in this way can the hearer make the object clear.

This can explain the situation in the above example (1-3). In "悲哀的消息"(*a sad news*), the noun "消息"(xiāoxi, *news*) involves two roles: sender and receiver, who can produce the sad emotion. Therefore, since the object of sorrow is not specified, "lìng rén" cannot appear. On the contrary, in "悲哀的决定"(*a sad decision*), the noun "决定" (juédìng, *decision*)involves decider and person influenced by the decision. As the decider, since he makes a decision, he will not feel sad. A sad emotion can only be produced by a person who is affected by the decision, so it is necessary to use "lìng rén" to specify the object of the adjective "悲哀"(bēi'āi, *sad*). In "愉悦的话题"(*a happy topic*), the two sides in the topic can both produce happy emotion, and speaker does not need to distinguish objects, "lìng rén" cannot appear; while in "愉悦的问题"(*a happy question*), the noun "问题"(wèntí, *question*) involves "questioner" and "answerer". Generally speaking, the pleasant or unpleasant emotional experience is produced in the case of the situation that answerer does not know the question. When the questioner asks the question, he does not have a pleasant or unpleasant emotional attribute. Therefore, since the owner of the emotional attribute is needed to be made clear, "lìng rén" must appear. "令人羞耻的姿势"(*a shameful posture*) and "令人反感的动作"(*a disgusting action*) are the same, "姿势/动作"(zīshì/dòngzuò, *posture/action*) is related with "behavior initiator" and "people affected by behavior". Only the latter will produce "shameful/disgusting" emotion. Therefore, the speaker must use "lìng rén" to specify the object.

In addition to the difference in adjective-noun compositions (1-3), the above explanation can also indicate the difference between the following adjective-noun compositions:

(4)　?　疲惫的工作——令/使人疲惫的工作——工作令/使人疲惫
　　　满意的工作——令/使人满意的工作——工作令/使人满意

(5)　?　惊讶的消息——令/使人惊讶的消息——消息令/使人惊讶
　　　快乐的消息——令/使人快乐的消息——消息令/使人快乐

The noun "工作"(gōngzuò, *work*) always involves two roles: One is the person who arranges the work, and the other is the person who does the work. In "令人疲惫的工作"(*an exhausting work*), the person who arranges the work cannot be tired, while the person who does the work is tired. Hence, both sides need to make clear the object of "疲惫"(píbèi, *exhausted*) between the two roles, and "lìng/shǐ rén" is used. In "满意的工作"(*a satisfactory job*), the object of "满意"(mǎnyì, *satisfactory*) can be the person arranging the work or person doing the work. Therefore, there is no need to make a distinction between the two sides, and "lìng/shǐ rén" wouldn't be there. However, in a specific context, the object of "满意"(mǎnyì, *satisfactory*) is usually explicit. For example (if there is no special account, the following examples are derived from CCL modern Chinese corpus of Peking University):

(6)   a.各级领导干部要努力做出党和人民满意的工作。

b.凭借自己过硬的素质完全可以找到满意的工作。

In sentence (a), "满意"(mǎnyì, *satisfactory*) modifies the person who arranges the work, namely "党和人民"(*the party and the people*), while in sentence (b), "满意"(mǎnyì, *satisfactory*) modifies "the person who does the work", namely "自己"(zìjǐ, *himself*).

The noun "消息"(xiāoxi, *message*) in example (5) always involves two roles: the person who sends and spreads the message and the person who listens to and receives the message. In "令人惊讶的消息"(*a surprising news*), as a news disseminator, which means that he has known the news, he will not be surprised. Only the recipient who does not know the content of the message will be surprised. Therefore, the speaker needs to use "lìng rén" to specify the recipient object. In "快乐的消息"(*a happy news*), both the news sender and the receiver may produce happy feelings, so there is no need to make a distinction between the two. "lìng/shǐ rén" does not need to appear. But in the concrete context, the object that "快乐"(kuàilè, *happy*) modifies is sometimes definite. For instance:

(7)   a.他极其兴奋地告诉了大家这个快乐的消息。

b.这些快乐的消息传到他耳边，让他兴奋不已。

"快乐"(kuàilè, *happy*) in sentence (a) cannot only describe the mood of message sender-"他"(tā, *he*), but can also describe the emotion of message recipient – "大家"(dàjiā, *everyone*). The default object that "快乐"(kuàilè, *happy*) in sentence (b) describes is the mood of message recipient - "他"(tā, *he*).

Of course, in the corpus, I also find the situation that although the object that adjective indicates is definite, but in the actual text "lìng/shǐ…" does not appear. Such as:

(8)   a.无论如何我们通过质量追踪和售后服务都必须给用户一个满意的答复。

b.? 无论如何我们通过质量追踪和售后服务都必须给一个满意的答复。

c.无论如何我们通过质量追踪和售后服务都必须给一个令用户满意的答复。

(9)   a.吃吃喝喝是群众反感的事情，新班子一上台就弄了两个有关吃喝的规矩。

b.? 吃吃喝喝是反感的事情，新班子一上台就弄了两个有关吃喝的规矩。

c.吃吃喝喝是令群众反感的事情，新班子一上台就弄了两个有关吃喝的规矩。

It can be found that although sentence (a) in the above two sets of examples does not have "lìng/shǐ…", the object that adjective describes is clear in the sentence, which helps the hearer to identify it. In this case, "lìng/shǐ…" can be omitted. On the contrary, as shown in sentence (b), if the sentence neither has "lìng/shǐ…" elicit the object, nor the object noun appears, then the hearer does not explicitly know who is the described object referred by adjective, and the acceptability of this sentence is not good. Sentence (c) with "lìng/shǐ…" is semantically equivalent to the sentence (a).

Similar to the above case, the adjectives "感动"(gǎndòng, *moved*) and "感人"(gǎnrén, *moving*) are semantically similar. However, "感人的事迹"(*a moving deed*) can be said, but "感动的事迹"(*a moved deed*) cannot. "事迹"(shìjì, *deed*) relates to two roles: the person who does the deed and the person who is affected by the deed. The subject of "感动"(gǎndòng, *moving*) is only be the person who is affected, and the object is single and clear, so it must be "令人感动的事迹"(*a moving deed*). Because the semantic structure of adjective "感人"(gǎnrén, *moving*) already contains the affected object, it can be directly combined with "事迹"(shìjì, *deed*).

Therefore, here we need to do a little adjustment on the conclusion: if adjectives can semantically illustrate the emotional attributes of any participation in the event referred by nouns, "lìng/shǐ…" may not appear, because it is not necessary for speaker and hearer to distinguish the two roles. If adjectives semantically describe the emotional attributes of one specific participation, "lìng/shǐ…" usually appears, because only in this way can the hearer specify the object described by adjectives. If an object noun appears in a specific text environment, its function is equivalent to "lìng/shǐ…", and to a certain extent, the object noun can cancel the function of specifying object of "lìng/shǐ…", therefore "lìng/shǐ…" may not appear.

Other examples in the corpus can further help us understand the subtle semantic difference caused by the (dis)appearance of "lìng/shǐ…". Such as:

(10)　a.因此，他觉得自己旅途中这番淡淡<u>哀愁的谈话</u>，仿佛触动了她生活中的创伤，不免后悔不已，就好像自己欺骗了她似的。

　　　　b.因此，他觉得自己旅途中这番淡淡<u>使人哀愁的谈话</u>，仿佛触动了她生活中的创伤，不免后悔不已，就好像自己欺骗了她似的。

(11)　a.你如果把这段<u>伤心的故事</u>照实说给人家听，听到的人一定要下泪的。

　　　　b.你如果把这段<u>令人伤心的故事</u>照实说给人家听，听到的人一定要下泪的。

(12)　a.你把这个<u>悲哀的消息</u>告诉他，他也许会来抢救已被赫克托耳剥去铠甲的尸体。

　　　　b.你把这个<u>令人悲哀的消息</u>告诉他，他也许会来抢救已被赫克托耳剥去铠甲的尸体。

The above three sentences (a) are from the corpus, and sentences (b) are added with "lìng/shǐ rén…" on the basis of the original sentence. Two sentences in each case are the same meaning, but there are some subtle differences. Specifically: "哀愁"(āichóu, *sad*) in (10a) can semantically modify both "他"(tā, *he*) and "她"(tā, *she*), while "使人"(shǐ rén) is added in (10b), that the impact of the incident referred by the head noun on the others will be emphasized. In this case, "哀愁"(āichóu, *sad*) is inclined to describe "她"(tā, *she*). "伤心"(shāngxīn, *sad*) in (11a) can both describe the emotion of "你"(nǐ, *you*) and "人家"(rénjiā, *others*)(*the hearer must tear*), while "令人"(lìng rén) is added in (11b), "伤心"(shāngxīn, *sad*) will be more inclined to describe "人家"(rénjiā, *others*). "悲哀"(bēi'āi, *sad*) in (12a) can both modify "你"(nǐ, *you*) and "他"(tā, *he*), and "令人"(lìng rén) can more deliberately describe the influence of "消息"(xiāoxi, *news*) on "他"(tā, *he*), making "悲哀"(bēi'āi, *sad*) more inclined to describe "他"(tā, *him*). That is to say, adjectives in adjective-noun composition without "lìng/shǐ *rén*···" can modify any role, while adjectives in adjective-noun composition with "lìng/shǐ *rén*···" tend to highlight the objects described by adjectives.

In addition, the specifying object function of "lìng/shǐ···" is more clear in the following example:

(13)   a. 他不太相信眼前这个秀丽的姑娘会做出<u>让**他**不满的事情</u>来。
        b.*他不太相信眼前这个秀丽的姑娘会做出<u>让**她**不满的事情</u>来。
        c. 他不太相信眼前这个秀丽的姑娘会做出<u>不满的事情</u>来。

Usually, that a person does something will affect others. Adjective "不满"(bùmǎn, *dissatisfied*) can only explain the feelings of others, but not the people who do the things. Therefore, in the sentence(a), both the person who does things (姑娘, *girl*) and the affected person (他, *he*) appear, "让···"(ràng···) must be used to indicate that the object of "不满"(bùmǎn, *dissatisfy*) is "他"(tā, *he*) rather than "姑娘"(gūniang, *girl*), therefore sentence(b) is untenable. Although "不满的事情"(*an unsatisfied thing*) appears in sentence(c), the whole structure does not express the semantic relation of "emotional value + emotional initiation": something leads to her dissatisfaction. Hence, it is different from the adjective-noun composition discussed in this paper, and is not a counterexample to our relevant conclusion.

4   Conclusion

In sum, I agree with what Li [3] argues, namely, "lìng/shǐ···" has the function of specifying object, but my view is different from hers on the concrete (dis)appearing mechanism. In my opinion, it's not a good idea to judge the salient role, and it's not accurate enough with the explanation of scene activated by nouns. From the perspective of the semantic relation between adjectives and participants in the event referred by nouns, the (dis)appearing mechanism of "lìng/shǐ···" in adjective-noun composition can be preliminarily explained: in a number of participants who are activated by nouns, when the adjective semantically modifies a definite participant, "lìng/shǐ···" usually appear; when the modified object is not clear, namely, the adjective can indicate the emotional attribute of any participant, whether "lìng/shǐ···" emerges is free.

Finally, another case should be referred to. "痛苦的体验/回忆"(*a painful experience/memory*) can be established, because the object involved in "体验/回忆"(tǐyàn/huíyì, *experience/memory*) is usually the person. "痛苦"(tòngkǔ, *painful*) describes the subject, so it is clear and unique, and "lìng/shǐ" may not appear. It is different from the above example (3) in the second section. "姿势/动作"(zīshì/dòngzuò, *pos-*

ture/action) activates behavior subject, while "羞耻/反感"(xiūchǐ/fǎngǎn, *shameful/disgusting*) does not describe the subject, but the observer of posture and behavior, so "lìng/shǐ" is specially needed to anchor this case.

References

1. Zhao, C.: A study of adjective noun combination in modern Chinese. Jinan University Press, Guangzhou (2012) (现代汉语形名组合研究. 广州: 暨南大学出版社,2012) [In Chinese]
2. Liu, D.: Co-occurrence of adjectives and nouns and orientation of adjectives. Journal of Nanjing Normal University. 3, 56-61(1987) [In Chinese]
3. Li, Y.: A syntactic and semantic study of psychological adjectives. MA thesis of Peking University (2010) [In Chinese]
4. Pustejovsky, J.: Type Construction and the Logic of Concepts. In Pierrette Bouillon & F. Busa (eds.), The Language of Word Meaning. Cambridge University Press, 91-123(2001)
5. Pustejovsky, J.: Type theory and lexical decomposition. Journal of Cognitive Science. 6, 39-76(2006)
6. Pustejovsky, J.: The Generative Lexicon. Computational linguistics. 4, 409-441(1991)
7. Yuan, Y.: On a descriptive system of qualia structure of Chinese nouns and its application in parsing complex Chinese grammatical phenomena. Contemporary linguistics. 1, 31-48[In Chinese]

The Study of Content Restriction of Mandarin *yǒu* Measure Construction

Shaoshuai Shen

School of Foreign Languages, Henan University, Kaifeng, China

wps2005@163.com

Abstract. This paper investigates mandarin *yǒu* measure construction, which consists of a main verb *yǒu*, a Measure Subject, and a Measure Object. This construction has been studied by many researchers. However, its content restriction has not been systematically summarized. Based on Autonomous/Dependent Alignment Model in Cognitive Grammar, this paper aims to shed some light on this topic. It is found that there are four rules governing its content restriction, which is motivated by the interaction of the Measure Subject and the Measure Object at the cognitive level.

Keywords: *yǒu* measure construction, content restriction, Autonomous/Dependent Alignment Model

1 Introduction

As a core aspect of *yǒu* construction, *yǒu* measure construction has been discussed by many scholars [1-8], which have shed some light on this phenomenon. In the literature, however, the content restriction of *yǒu* measure construction has not been systematically studied. This paper aims to revisit this topic by using the Autonomous/Dependent Alignment Model(A/DAM) [9] from the Cognitive Grammar perspective, in the aim of systemically discovering its rules for content restriction and the cognitive mechanism behind.

Section 2 introduces the features of *yǒu* measure construction. Section 3 is a brief introduction of A/DAM. In section 4, we present a detailed analysis of content restriction in this construction. Section 5 presents our conclusions.

© Springer International Publishing AG 2018
Y. Wu et al. (Eds.): CLSW 2017, LNAI 10709, pp. 198–209, 2018.
https://doi.org/10.1007/978-3-319-73573-3_17

2   The Features of *yǒu* Measure Construction

For the *yǒu* measure construction, please observe the following sentences:

(1) 目前有污染的乡镇企业占40%，其中重度污染的有10%。

   Mùqián yǒu wūrǎn de xiāngzhèn qì yè zhàn 40%, qízhōng zhòngdù wūrǎn de yǒu 10%.

   'Currently, polluted township enterprises account for 40%, of which the heavily polluted are of 10%.'

(2) 钓上的鲤鱼有三斤重。

   Diào shàng de lǐyú yǒu sān jīn zhòng.

   'The carp trolled from water has a weight of 1.5 kilograms.'

(3) 康柏的iPAQ，软件由微软提供，屏幕只有巴掌大。

   Kāng bǎi de iPAQ, ruǎnjiàn yóu wēiruǎn tígōng, píngmù zhǐ yǒu bāzhang dà.

   'As for the Compaq iPAQ, its software is powered by Microsoft, and its screen is only as big as a palm.'

(4) 巨石加上运石卡车的重量有150吨左右。

   Jùshí jiā shàng yùn shí kǎchē de zhòngliàng yǒu 150 dūn zuǒyòu.

   'The huge rock plus transport truck has a weight of about 150 tons.'

(5) 这个神秘的铁盒子的高度有50厘米。

   Zhège shénmì de tiě hézide gāodù yǒu 50 límǐ.

   'This mysterious iron box has a height of 50 cm.'

(6) 卫东走进戏水大厅，这里面积有足球场大，空间则有七、八层楼高。

   Wèi dōng zǒu jìn xì shuǐ dàtīng, zhèlǐ miànjī yǒu zúqiú chǎng dà, kōngjiān zé yǒu qī, bā céng lóu gāo.

   'Weidong entered the swimming hall, in which the area was as large as a football field and the space was about seven to eight stories high.'

The above examples illustrate the syntactic and semantic features of *yǒu* measure construction. Syntactically, this construction consists of three parts: measure subject(MS), *yǒu* and measure object (MO). The MS is expressed by noun phrases such as 重度污染的 *zhòngdù wūrǎn de* 'the heavily polluted', 鲤鱼 *lǐyú* 'the crap', 屏幕 *píngmù* 'the screen', 巨石加上运石卡车的重量 *jùshí jiā shàng yùn shí kǎchē de zhòngliàng* 'the weight of huge rock plus the transport truck', 铁盒子的高度 *tiě hézide gāodù* 'the height of the iron box', 面积 *miànjī* 'the area', 空间 *kōngjiān* 'the space'. *Yǒu* is the link verb. MO is expressed by numerical phrases, such as 10%, 150 吨*150 dūn* '150 tons', 50厘米*50 límǐ* '50 cm', or by adjective phrases 三斤重 *sān jīn* *zhòng* '1.5 kilogram in weight', 巴掌大 *bāzhang dà* 'as big as a palm', 足球场大 *zúqiú chǎng dà* 'as big as a football field', 七、八层楼高 *qī, bā céng lóu gāo* 'as high as seven or eight stories building'. Semantically, this construction represents a measure relation in which the MS stands for an entity to be measured, the MO a value used for measure, and *yǒu* a connector for the two.

Xing points out that in MO "the numbers is obligatory", but "the adjectives are sometimes optional" [1], as in examples (7-8). Zhang also discusses that this construction "expresses a measure value by comparing, so the following adjectives cannot be omitted" in MO [5], as in examples (9-10).

(7)   这条鱼有三斤重。
      Zhè tiáo yú yǒu sān jīn zhòng.
      'This fish has a weight of three pounds.'

(8)   *这条鱼有重。
      Zhè tiáo yú yǒu zhòng
      *'This fish has weight.'

(9)   晶片只有半个米粒那么大。
      Jīngpiàn zhǐ yǒu bàn gè mǐlì nàme dà.
      'The chip has a size as big as half a grain of rice.'

(10) *晶片只有半个米粒。
      Jīngpiàn zhǐ yǒu bàn gè mǐlì.
      *'The chip has half a grain of rice.'

However, these studies do not fully explain the rules of content restrictions in this construction, which will be explained in the following sections.

3   Autonomous/Dependent Alignment Model

The nature of an autonomous/dependent relation lies in the asymmetry between autonomous and dependent structures. Langacker defines the autonomous structure as "a semantic or phonological structure that 'exists on its own,' not presupposing another structure for its manifestation" [10], which means that it can appear independently, such as a vowel of a syllable and a participant of a relation. Langacker defines the dependent structure as "a semantic or phonological structure that presupposes another for its manifestation" [10], which means that its conceptualization must depend on another relevant component, such as the consonant's dependence on vowel in an CV syllable, and a relation's dependence on its participants. Langacker defines the autonomous/dependency relation as "one structure, D, is dependent on the other, A, to the extent that A constitutes an elaboration of a salient substructure within D" [10].

In line with the discussion of autonomous/dependent relation in Cognitive Grammar, Niu develops the Autonomous/Dependent Alignment Model (A/DAM) to analyze the semantic construction process of language expressions [9], [11]. Niu defines Autonomous/Dependent Alignment as "by virtue of autonomous/dependent relation, an autonomous structure can integrate with a dependent structure by means of semantic profiling and correspondence relation to form a relatively autonomous composite structure" [11], which can be illustrated by the following figure:

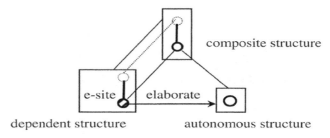

Fig. 1. Autonomous/Dependent Alignment

As shown in Fig.1, the dependent structure profiles a relation, the autonomous structure profiles a thing, which integrate to form a composite structure. The shadowed circle in the dependent structure represents a profiled sub-structure, which provides an elaboration-site (e-site). The bold circle in the autonomous structure represents the profiled sub-structure, which can interpret the e-site in the dependent structure and make the autonomous structure correspond with the dependent structure. The composite structure inherits the profile from the dependent structure, representing a more specific relation. The dependent structure is a profile determinant.

The core notions in A/DAM include: e-site, elaboration, correspondence, profile determinant, and constituency, which is introduced briefly in the following. The e-site is defined as "a schematic element elaborated by another component" [12]. Elaboration refers to the characterization "in finer grained detail" [12]. Correspondence "pertains to conceptual reference" [12], which indicates that the prepositional landmark and the nominal profile refer to the same entity. This notion, by revealing the conceptual overlap between constituent structures, provides the basis for integration between component structures, and shows the semantic contribution of component structure to the composite structure. Profile determinant stands for "the component structure that 'bequeaths' its profile to the composite structure" [12]. Constituency is "one manifestation of hierarchical organization" that can be "observed in symbolic assemblies when a composite structure at one level of organization functions in turn as component structure with respect to a higher level" [12].

The flow chart of A/DAM is shown in Fig.2, in which it begins with the profiling of the autonomous and dependent structure, then goes the elaboration of the e-site by profiled sub-structure in autonomous structure, finally follows the integration of the autonomous and dependent structures into a composite structure.

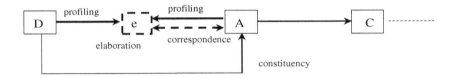

Fig. 2. Autonomous/Dependent Alignment Model [9]

The operation of A/DAM can be illustrated through the analysis of the example *under the table*. In this phrase, *under* is the dependent structure D, profiling a static spatial relationship in which trajector (tr) is above the landmark (lm). The conceptualization of *under* presuppose the existence of participants of a relation. Its lm functions as an e-site e, enclosed by the dotted box, profiling a schematic spatial configuration. *Table* is the autonomous structure A, profiling a specific spatial configuration that elaborates the e-site. By virtue of the elaborating relation, the correspondence relation can be established between the schematic e-site and the specific profile of *table*, as shown by the dotted double arrow. Hence the conceptual entity [UNDER] can integrate with another entity [TABLE] to form a relatively autonomous composite structure [UNDER THE TABLE], as shown by C, which represents a static spatial relations taking [TABLE] as its lm. The ellipsis after C indicates that such a composite structure is capable of integrating with other components to form more complex composite structures.

4   The Analysis of Content Restriction in *yǒu* Measure Construction

This section aims to formulate the rules of content restriction in *yǒu* Measure Construction through the analysis of the semantic anomalies caused by measure subject (MS) or measure object (MO).

(11) ？这所房子有三米。

    Zhè suǒ fángzi yǒusān mǐ.

    ?'The house has three meters.'

The acceptability of (11) is in question. Through the analysis with the help of A/DAM, we can explain the reason for this semantic anomaly. The MS of this construction is NP 这所房子 *zhè suǒ fángzi* 'this house', 有 *yǒu* is the verb, and the MO is QP 三米 *sān mǐ* 'three meters'.

According to the autonomous/dependent relation, the conceptual entity [这所房子] is the autonomous structure, designating a thing with measure feature. It is a three-dimensional spatial configuration, whose measure features have varied dimensions, including height, width, and length. [有三米] is the dependent structure, designating an equivalent measure relation which is stable in conceived time t. Its lm profiles a bounded measure value that is of spatial feature, takes meter as unit, and locates on three in a scale axis. In the dependent structure, the measure feature of lm is unspecific, and can be of any dimensions such as height, width, length, thickness. Thus, the lm of [有三米]is a bounded but unspecific measure value. The schematic tr profiled by [有三米] functions as an e-site, designating a schematic measure feature or an entity with measure feature. The profile of [这所房子] elaborate the schematic tr of [有三米] as a spatial configuration with the shape of a house. Hence [这所房子] establishes a correspondence relationship and integrates with [有三米] to form a composite structure [这所房子有三米], which designates an equivalent measure relation stable in conceived time t whose tr is specific but whose lm still remain unspecific. Therefore, the MO in this construction represents a value with unspecific dimensions, i.e. whether it expresses height, width, or length remains unclear. It cannot boundarize the measure feature of MS. "This unbounded structure makes the whole structure unbounded, destroying its integrity, and ultimately leading to the expression to be unacceptable" [13].

Remedies can be made in (12-13),

(12) 这所房子有三米高。

    Zhè suǒ fángzi yǒusān mǐ gāo.

'The house is three meters high.'

(13) 这所房子的高度有三米。

 Zhè suǒ fángzi de gāodù yǒusān mǐ.

 'The height of this house is three meters.'

 In (12), the MO consists of the QP三米 *sān mǐ* 'three meters' and the adjective 高 *gāo* 'high'. Compared with MO in (11), it has an extra adjective to show the specific dimension of the measure value.

 According to the autonomous/dependent relation, there are two conceptual entities in MO of (12), i.e. [三米] and [高]. [三米] is the autonomous structure, designating a bounded measure value that is of spatial feature, takes meter as unit, and locates on three in a scale axis. [高] is the dependent structure, designating a specific unbounded dimension of height. In the integration process, [高] profiles a schematic sub-structure as e-site which can be elaborated by the specific bounded value of [三米]. Hence the composite structure [三米高] designates a bounded measure value that takes height dimension as spatial feature, takes meter as unit, and locates on three in a scale axis. In this way, the MO of (12) represents a bounded value with the specific dimension of height, and can boundarize the MS of the composite structure.

 Example (13) is another way of remedy, by giving a specific measure dimension to the MS. In the process of its semantic construction, the conceptual entity [这所房子的高度] is the autonomous structure, designating the specific height dimension of a specific spatial configuration with the shape of house. [有三米] is the dependent structure, designating an equivalent measure relation which is stable in conceived time t. The lm of [有三米] is a bounded but unspecific measure value. The schematic tr profiled by [有三米] functions as an e-site, designating a schematic measure feature or an entity with measure feature. The profile of [这所房子的高度] elaborate the schematic tr of [有三米] as the specific height dimension of a specific spatial configuration with the shape of house. Hence [这所房子的高度] establishes a correspondence relationship and integrates with [有三米] to form a composite structure [这所房子的高度有三米], which designates an equivalent measure relation enabling the bounded value of MO to describe the specific height feature of the MS.

 Then, please look at the omission of the adjective in MO as shown in (14),

(14) 昨天来广场的人有8万。

 Zuótiān lái guǎngchǎng de rén yǒu 8 wàn.

 'The people in the square yesterday were 80,000.'

As mentioned above, the adjective is required in MO. However, (14) is well acceptable without a required adjective in MO. We can use A/DAM to explain the reason. The MS of this construction is NP 昨天来广场的人 *zuótiān lái guǎngchǎng de rén* 'the people in the square yesterday', 有 *yǒu* is the verb, and the MO is QP 8万 *8 wàn* '80,000'.

In the autonomous/dependent relation, the conceptual entity [昨天来广场的人] is the autonomous structure, designating a collection of units. Its measure feature has only one prominent dimension, i.e. quantity. [有8万] is the dependent structure, designating an equivalent measure relation which is stable in conceived time t. Its lm profiles a bounded measure value that is a numerical value to express quantity, and locates on eight in a scale axis. Thus, the lm of [有8万]is a bounded numerical value. The schematic tr profiled by [有8万] functions as an e-site, designating a schematic measure feature or an entity with measure feature. The profile of [昨天来广场的人] elaborate the schematic tr of [有8万] as a collection of people with prominent quantity feature. Hence [昨天来广场的人] establishes a correspondence relationship and integrates with [有8万] to form a composite structure [昨天来广场的人有8万], and designates an equivalent measure relation stable in conceived time t in which the unbounded quantity feature of MS is boundarized by the bounded numerical value of MO. By virtue of the prominent quantity feature of MS and MO, the adjective expressing measure feature is not obligatory in MO.

Example (15) illustrates a similar case,

(15) 这条鱼有五斤。

    Zhè tiáo yú yǒu wǔ jīn.

    'This fish has a weight of 2.5 kilograms'.

In (15), the MS is NP这条鱼 *zhè tiáo yú* 'this fish', *yǒu* is the verb, and the MO is QP 五斤*wǔ jīn* '2.5 kilograms'. In the autonomous/dependent relation, the conceptual entity [这条鱼] is the autonomous structure, designating a thing with multi-dimensional measure feature, such as height, width, weight, etc. [有五斤] is the dependent structure, designating an equivalent measure relation which is stable in conceived time t. Its lm profiles a bounded measure value that is only used to express weight, takes 斤 *jīn* (1/2 kilogram) as unit, and locates on five in a scale axis. Thus, the lm of [有五斤]is a bounded and specific measure value. The schematic tr profiled by [有五斤] functions as an e-site, designating a schematic measure feature or an entity with measure feature. The profile of [这条鱼] elaborate the schematic tr of [有五斤] as a fish with certain measure feature. Hence [这条鱼] establishes a correspondence relationship and integrates with [有五斤] to form a composite structure [这条鱼有五斤], and designates an equivalent measure relation stable in conceived time t in which the unbounded measure feature of fish is boundarized by the bounded numerical value 2.5 kilograms. Therefore, the adjective is not obligatory in MO.

The following are two more examples about the omission of adjectives. The MOs here are different from those mentioned above, for they express comparison values instead of numerical values.

(16) *永暑岛有两个马尔代夫首都。

　　　*Yǒng shǔ dǎo yǒu liǎng gè mǎ'ěrdàifū shǒudū.

　　　*'Yongshu Island has two capitals of Maldives.'

(17) 永暑岛有两个马尔代夫首都大。

　　　*Yǒng shǔ dǎo yǒu liǎng gè mǎ'ěrdàifū shǒudū dà.

　　　'Yongshu Island has a size as big as two capitals of Maldives.'

The MS of (16) and (17) are both 永暑岛 *yǒng shǔ dǎo* 'Yongshu Island'. The MO of (16) is 两个马尔代夫首都 *liǎng gè mǎ'ěrdàifū shǒudū* 'two capitals of Maldives', and that of (17) is 两个马尔代夫首都大 *liǎng gè mǎ'ěrdàifū shǒudū dà* 'as large as two capitals of Maldives'. Hence the semantic anomaly in (16) is attributed to the omission of adjective in MO, which can be explained through A/DAM.

In the MO of (16), the conceptual entity [两个马尔代夫首都] designates a thing, which can serve as participants in a relation or as an entity with measure features, such as area, size, width, population, economic aggregate, etc. Without an adjective to specify the measure feature, the MO cannot represent a bounded value, no matter specific or unspecific, thus it fails to boundarize the measure feature of the MS.

In (17), the MO has an extra adjective 大 *dà* 'large'. In the autonomous/dependent relation, the conceptual entity [两个马尔代夫首都] designates a thing with measure features, such as area, size, width, population, economic aggregate, etc., which can elaborate the unbounded measure feature profiled by [大]. [两个马尔代夫首都] can establish a correspondence relation and integrate with [大] to form a composite structure [两个马尔代夫首都大] which designates a bounded and specific value, indicating the size dimension with the reference of the size of two capitals of Maldives. Therefore, [两个马尔代夫首都大] as a bounded and specific value can boundarize the measure feature of conceptual entity [永暑岛] via the measure relation designated by *yǒu*. The composite structure [永暑岛有两个马尔代夫首都大] at the top level designates an equivalent measure relation in which the size of Yongshu Island is measured by the size of two capitals of Maldives.

With respect to the above analysis, we can formulate a set of rules that provides a reasonable explanation to the observation by the two scholars [1], [5]:

i) When MS is a measure feature, the adjective is optional in MO. For example,

(18) 总字数有27万。

Zǒng zìshù yǒu 27 wàn.

'The total number of words is 27 million.'

(19) 海拔高度足有1430米。

Hǎibá gāodù zú yǒu 1430 mǐ.

'The altitude is 1430 meters.'

ii) When MS is an entity with a measure feature, and MO expresses a mono-dimensional value, the adjective is optional in MO. For example,

(20) 下洋镇的篮球队有四个。

Xià yáng zhèn de lánqiú duì yǒu sì gè.

'The number of basketball teams in Xiayang Town is four.

(21) 一个套丝机就有三百多斤。

Yīgè tào sī jī jiù yǒu sānbǎi duō jīn.

'A threading machine has a weight of about three hundred *jīn*.'

iii) When MS is an entity with a measure feature, and MO expresses a multi-dimensional value, the adjective is obligatory in MO to specify the dimension. For example,

(22) 小巷两侧的石壁大约有二十英尺高。

Xiǎo xiàng liǎng cè de shíbì dàyuē yǒu èrshí yīngchǐ gāo.

'The stone walls on both sides of the alley are about twenty feet tall.'

(23) 这张桌子有一米五宽。

Zhè zhāng zhuōzi yǒuyī mǐ wǔ kuān.

'This table is 1.5 meters wide.'

iv) When MS is an entity with a measure feature, and the measure feature is not clearly expressed in MO, the adjective is obligatory in MO to specify the dimension. For example,

(24) 普通晶洞结构一般只有手掌大小。

Pǔtōng jīng dòng jiégòu yībān zhǐyǒu shǒuzhǎng dàxiǎo.

'Generally an ordinary crystal hole structure is only as large as a palm.'

(25) 考试的卷子足有一本书那么厚。

Kǎoshì de juànzi zú yǒuyī běn shū nàme hòu.

The examination paper is as thick as a book.'

5   Conclusion

Yǒu measure construction is a distinctive phenomenon in mandarin. As a hotspot as it is in researches, the rules for its content restriction has yet been discussed deeply. With the help of Autonomous/Dependent Alignment Model, this paper has analyzed the semantic anomaly of this construction, and formulated a set of rules that governed the content restriction, which is based on an interaction between the MS and MO.

References

1. Xing, F. Y.: On "quantitative structure + adjective" (in Chinese). Studies of the Chinese Language, no. 1, pp. 34-36 (1965).

2. Zheng, Y. D.: On "*you*" sentence expressed comparison. Grammar research and exploration, vol. 8. pp. 175-183 (1994)

3. Zhang, Y. F.: On "*you*" sentence expressed comparison (in Chinese). Language Studies, no. 4, pp. 13-18(1998)

4. Liu, Y. H., Pan, W. Y., Gu, W.: Practical modern Chinese grammar (in Chinese). Commercial Press, Beijing (2001)

5. Zhang, B.: Modern Chinese description grammar (in Chinese). Commercial Press, Beijing (2010)

6. Yang, Y. L.: From "adjective + numeral + measure word" to "numeral + measure word + adjective" (in Chinese). Studies of the Chinese Language, no. 6, pp. 499-513(2011)

7. Wen, S. L.: *You* (有) as an informational focus marker in the construction of '*you* + quantitative phrase' (in Chinese). Studies of the Chinese Language, no. 1, pp. 29-37(2012)

8. Xiong, Z. R.: A Syntactic Analysis of Degree Construction with You in Chinese (in Chinese). Language Teaching and Research, no. 4, pp. 46-55 (2016)

9. Niu, B. Y.: Introduction to Construction Grammars (in Chinese). Shanghai Foreign Language Education Press, Shanghai (2011)

10. Langacker, R. W.: Foundations of cognitive grammar: Theoretical prerequisites. Stanford University Press, Stanford (1987)

11. Niu, B. Y.: Autonomous/Dependent Alignment: An Analytical Model of Cognitive Grammar (in Chinese). Foreign Language and Foreign Language Teaching, no. 1, pp. 1-5 (2008).

12. Langacker R. W.: Cognitive grammar: A basic introduction. Oxford University Press, Oxford (2008)

13. Liu, C. D. Structure and boundary: A cognitive study on linguistic expressions (in Chinese). Shanghai Foreign Language Education Press, Shanghai (2008)

14. Shen, S. S.: A Study of Mandarin *yǒu* Measure Construction: Based on A/D-alignment Model (in Chinese). Henan University, Kaifeng (2016)

Metaphors in Chinese Accompanying Gesture Modality and Cognition

Dengfeng Yao[1,2] , Minghu Jiang[2] , Abudoukelimu • Abulizi[2] , Renkui Hou[3] , Lifei Shu[4]

[1] Beijing Key Lab of Information Service Engineering, Beijing Union University, Beijing, 100101, China
[2] Lab of Computational Linguistics, School of Humanities, Center for Psychology and Cognitive Science, Tsinghua University, Beijing, 100084, China
[3] Department of Chinese and Bilingual Studies, the Hong Kong Polytechnic University, Hung Hom, Kowloon, Hong Kong
[4] Special Education College, Beijing Union University, Beijing, 100101, China
jiang.mh@tsinghua.edu.cn

Abstract. Chinese accompanying gestures are a common phenomenon in life, and native speakers of Chinese use gesture modality to express metaphors. This study analyzes metaphors in Chinese accompanying gesture modality from the perspective of cognitive linguistics and cognitive neuroscience rather than the multimodal metaphor theory. Both spoken language and accompanying gesture modalities of metaphors are integrated into discourse, indicating that metaphor creation is based on general cognitive rather than linguistic features. The case study of Chinese accompanying gestures shows that conceptual metaphors can be cognitively activated when they are not expressed in oral modality. The close interaction between modality and language indicates that metaphors are a dynamic attribute rather than a static in the physical and interactive context. The study of metaphors in accompanying gesture modality provides a specific case for further studies on metaphors and offers support for creating a non-literal language cognitive model.

Keywords: Chinese accompanying gestures, metaphor, cognitive linguistics, cognitive neuroscience.

Previous researches about non-literal language cognitive models focus on the aspect of oral and written modalities while ignoring pictures, comics, body postures, gestures, and other modalities and failing to consider the complete symbol resource of the Chinese language. Various modalities play important roles in the expression of thought and culture because these modalities can develop into the interconnected semantic networks in the human brain [1] and then provide the background and framework to convey meanings. Chinese accompanying gestures represent one of the most important modalities, but the accompanying gesture research has received little attention. Most scholars do not think that sign languages, as well as spoken languages, possess a complex grammatical structure. They also do not find metaphor expressions in gestures. Compared

© Springer International Publishing AG 2018
Y. Wu et al. (Eds.): CLSW 2017, LNAI 10709, pp. 210–223, 2018.
https://doi.org/10.1007/978-3-319-73573-3_18

with spoken language, the accompanying gestures are spontaneously produced, their duration is shorter, regularities are difficult to obtain, the requirements of recording (such as a video camera, etc.) are higher, and the available reference materials are fragmentary. These factors continue to hinder the research into metaphors in Chinese accompanying gestures. The previous literatures mainly explain from the perspective of multimodal metaphors that gestures must be collocated with other modalities to achieve metaphors. The present work attempts to discuss metaphors in a single Chinese accompanying gesture modality by using the theory of cognitive linguistics and cognitive neuroscience.

Chinese accompanying gestures are fairly common, and we use gesture modalities to express metaphors. Fig.1 is a common statue of Chairman Mao in mainland China. The statue gesture to extract Chairman Mao had the classic speech with gesture, that is, his right arm stretches forward, his fingers folded and forward, he points straight ahead, with the metaphors being "forward," "victory," and "toward the bright future of communism." Even interpreted by the west as the call of a religious leader [2], these common metaphors in gesture modality are also the conceptual metaphors mentioned by Lakoff. In a certain environment, the spontaneous use of Chinese accompanying gestures indicates that in metaphorical expressions, the accompanying gestures of spoken language represent an important modality of human language.

Fig.1 Statue of Chairman Mao

1   What are metaphors in accompanying gesture modality?

Chinese accompanying gestures are different from Chinese sign language. Chinese speakers are accompanied by gestures that are unconsciously or subconsciously when Chinese speakers are speaking in Chinese. Many studies have shown that 90% of the accompanying gestures are generated while speaking, with the remaining 10% appearing during pauses, but speaking is also followed closely [3]. Given that the accompanying gestures are similar to sign language gestures, several scholars hold the view that some accompanying gestures can be regarded as sign language gestures in essence, i.e., which also have gestures attributes such as location, direction, and so on; thus, these attributes can be superimposed in some sign language gestures [4]. Chinese sign language involves accompanying gestures as well, which generally occur between sign language and actual accompanying gestures. Fig. 2 is an example of accompanying gestures in Chinese sign language. In Fig. 2a, a person describes a fountain by signing a circular shape with her hands and then dropping her hands down to her waist, and then moving them up again to show the fountain. In Fig. 2b, the gesturing person raises her left hand from her thigh to above her head. This action uses the height of the space to analogously describe the abstract concept of "senior." In this image, we can observe that this is the "senior" metaphor mapped to "upward." However, some scholars disapprove the independent accompanying gestures generated by the present of sign language, which can only represent "gestures which interrupt sign language flow" [4]. Therefore, accompanying gesture modality of Chinese sign language remains an open research topic.

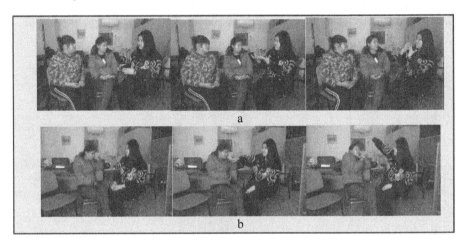

Fig. 2 a. Gestures to describe "fountain", b. Gestures to describe "senior"

Generally speaking, the metaphors in the accompanying gesture modality are usually regarded as representing or instructing the hand movements of the metaphorical source domain [5-7]. And the scholar who recognizes the accompanying gestures of spoken language can be used in metaphors is Psychologist Wilhelm Wundt. He calls the accompanying gestures as a transfer concept from one domain to another "symbolic gestures", and provides an example that expresses the concept of time by using spatial gestures, similar to the aforementioned example of the statue of Chairman Mao [8]. Geneviève Calbris also began earlier to study the metaphors in accompanying gesture modality, she thought, in some extent the accompanying gestures demonstrated that metaphors are a physical representations from concrete objects to abstract objects [2]. For example, two hands face to face and apart, the accompanying gesture indicates the width of a specific path in a certain context, whereas in another context indicates the scope of work that needs to be done. In addition, metaphors in the accompanying gesture modality can also be applied to two concrete entities, for example, the hourglass shape is used to describe the characteristics of a woman's body, or to orally explain various objects according to some parts of the body, such as the foot of a mountain, legs of a table, and armrests of a chair. As a result, we refer to the metaphorical gestures as something that has the potential to use an active cross domain mapping, that is, according to something to understand the cognitive process of another thing [6].

For a long time, people regarded the accompanying gestures only as a supplement to spoken language. It wasn't until the 1980s to the 1990s that with the turn of cognition the accompanying gestures of spoken language began to be regarded as a valuable research phenomenon. Adan Kendon and David McNeill made significant contributions by pointing out that the speech generation process is performed by two forms of synchronous activity: behavior as the vocal organs and body movements [9-10]. The whole accompanying gestures and spoken language can be included in a unified concept, with the accompanying gestures as a part of the psychology, and there is not essential difference in the spoken language itself [10].

2   Accompanying gesture modality and metaphor

Accompanied by gestures as an accompanying speech act, it involves different modalities of spoken language, and thus providing another source of evidence for conceptual metaphors. In particular, the accompanying gesture data can support the opinion of using conceptual metaphors in the thinking process of speaking. Such evidence refutes the view that "Linguistic evidence itself is suspect, because it assumes that there is a pattern in spoken language that directly reflects the conceptual structure" [11]. The accompanying gestures provide another window to understand how we construct concepts and how we use these structures when we speak.

For the relationship between metaphors in accompanying gesture modality and metaphors in spoken language modality, the view of multimodal metaphor theory indicates that metaphors in accompanying gestures can be expressed orally in semantics simultaneously and be separated from spoken metaphors briefly. The metaphor in accompanying gestures has already been expressed before the generation of corresponding spoken metaphor, and it overlaps with spoken metaphors after the utterance. Accompanying gestures and spoken language seem to share a communicative load to express metaphors and share the same metaphors. Hence, metaphors are not limited in verbal expressive media. In other words, it can be multimodal, which is represented as a type of metaphor in verbal–accompanied gesture modality [6]. For example, a Hong Kong news reported in 2015, when the situation in Syria was "tangled," an anchorperson unconsciously used his both hand palms constant transformation, this is clearly an abstract concept of the intricacies of Syria with a specific "twining" gesture.

Actually compared with spoken Chinese, accompanied by gestures flexibility, can directly reflect Chinese spoken language, and cannot reflect the spatial relations, movement, path, shape, and other features. Accompanying Gestures clearly play a huge potential role during the process of language generation and comprehension for the cognitive process [12-13]. For example, a high school teacher in the teaching of language lesson "Last lecture" from Chinese mainland, read "After the news of reactionaries assassinating Mr. Lee came out......, I wonder what they think, what their mind is, and how their hearts grow--!" At this time the teacher thumped the table with a clenched fist, the gestures are metaphor in the fateful bang, effective match the verbal metaphor of Wen Yiduo's detest evil, righteously tall image; make the classroom teaching effect better has been enhanced. Thus, metaphors can clearly be expressed by the accompanying gestures instead of spoken Chinese. And even in some situations, a metaphor can be expressed through verbal modality, and the target domain is realized through the source domain of accompanying gestures. For example, when a secretary of a committee for disciplinary inspection from Chinese mainland talks about a police chief black and white take all, he uses his longitudinal palm to make a cutting gesture, as if in the split space; such is a color metaphor in verbal language, which is embodied in the accompanying gesture as a spatial metaphor. However, two features of the target domain are agglomerated in these two source domains. They can constitute different features of the same scene, that is, two spatial regions are clearly defined: one is black, and one is white. However, in this example, the source domain of spoken language cannot use black and white accompanying gestures as a spatial representation. Whether different expressions of verbal and accompanying gestures only occurs in this situation, or in some cases, the potential accompanying gestures are not used in the source domain in verbal expression to support different source domains, it remains to be seen. In sum, the independence of the content expressed between the accompanying gestures and spoken language is not limited in the accompanying gesture modality and spoken language modality, which proves that Goldin–Meadow's the accompanying gestures are not matched the spoken language. He studied the performance of children in trying to solve the Piaget conservation task and math problems, and found evidence that children can understand some conceptual accompanying gestures before they can express the same thoughts orally [13].

The situation in which a metaphor in accompanying gesture modality is independent of the metaphor in spoken language is a common pipe metaphor. Some people think that understanding this metaphor is a simple problem for extracting semantics from the container of language. Lakoff and other scholars pointed out that some metaphorical concepts play important roles, for example, language expression is the container, thought is the object, and communication is the medium of delivery [14]. Even without the statement about metaphors in spoken language, the metaphor "cartoon is the object" appears in accompanying gestures. This type of accompanying gesture modality is more common and is actually divided into several groups. In addition to the above mentioned expressive media as the container, another pipe metaphorical accompanying gesture focuses on the content of the metaphorical containers, that is, thoughts. These accompanying gestures express the thought, i.e., the metaphor of an object. Müller studied the accompanying gesture of palm up and hands open, indicating that the core of its function is to express the thoughts of the speaker, just as it is an object in the flat, open hands that can be used for inspection [15]. The metaphor of "To know is to see" proposes a universal means of seeing objects that appear to be accompanied by gestures, that is, it offers the sharing knowledge through metaphors. We can understand that this is the point of view shared on two senses of the word (a visual angle and a particular way of understanding it). For example, when we talk about some points, someone, something, and other referents in Chinese, we always hold hands in the shape of a balloon and slightly shake them up and down. In fact, the metaphorical reference of this gesture is not in light of a specific word in discourse but instead of a target reference. This accompanying gesture is responsible for performing a different function; in the function, it is related to the meta narrative level, and it reflects a fact, that is, an idea is being proposed rather than reflecting the uniqueness of the thought itself. In this way, it can be considered as a pragmatic application of metaphorical accompanying gestures.

Metaphors in accompanying gesture modality independent of verbal modality occur in another situation. When we talk about a logical relationship, its logical relationship is expressed as a type of spatial opposition with accompanying gestures. For example, when a researcher explains the finding of artemisinin by female scientist Tu Youyou, he thinks that her success comes from her personal efforts and also from the collective cooperation of her team. When mentioning personal efforts, he puts his vertical hands on the left part of his chest and then takes it back. When mentioning her team, he puts his vertical hands on the right part of his chest. These two accompanying actions lay down two conditions in his point of view, that is, the space in front of him. This type of accompanying gestures can also be used to distinguish independent spaces as different points of view. For example, the different parts of the space in front of speakers can be set up to represent different moral status of different people, similar to describing a "good person" and a "bad person."

Calbris noticed that in the following context, metaphors are expressed through accompanying gestures rather than spoken language in the common expression; when the speaker says a word with an abstract meaning, the speaker sometimes performs an accompanying gesture to reflect the specific source of the word [2]. For example, when expressing "no, retraining will be charged," the gesture involves making a vertical circle with the hand to reflect the word "again," which does not refer to "ring" in French; in fact, it is derived from the Greek word kuklos, which means "circle" [2]. Conceptual metaphors obviously promoted a word in the abstract domain, but it can still be activated in one's culture and continue to constitute an imagistic way, even if it is no longer transparent in the word form itself. Such observations can be proved in accompanying gestures. Lakoff and others discussed this issue in the context of rejecting the so-called "dead metaphor theory" [16]. In their opinion, metaphors may seem to die at the linguistic level, but they have the potential to be conceptually activated. They no longer point to literal meanings, and as a result, "understand" is no longer used as the meaning of "master" in Latin, but the conceptual metaphor of "to understand is to master" is a living metaphor that can be activated in modern English (such as "master what others say") [16].

Metaphors can reflect this fact via accompanying gestures and offer support to the following statement, that is, the metaphorical creation is based on general cognitive characteristics rather than linguistic characteristics [5][6][14]. The evidence of accompanying gesture modality shows that when spoken language is not used to express, conceptual metaphors can be activated in cognition. Therefore, the conceptual metaphors are independent of spoken and written modalities, and are also independent of the accompanying gesture modality. Conceptual metaphors can be used as an effective cognitive structure, even though they do not trigger metaphorical expressions in spoken language. Therefore, we should consider taking metaphors out of concrete modalities and making a concrete analysis. Metaphors are instantiated not only by accompanying gestures but also by pictures [17], of course, the spoken language and written language, and the combination of the two modalities: picture and text metaphors [17], verbal gesture metaphors [6], and different metaphors in spoken language and accompanying gesture combined modality [5]. Metaphors can also be realized at the linguistic level, can also be realized at the picture and gesture levels [5-6]. Furthermore, we have proved that there is no other metaphor expect the accompanying gesture metaphor for the expression of spoken language [5]. Finally, the use of accompanying gesture modalities in the conceptual metaphors of the source domain indicates that the function of conceptual metaphors is widely used as an important and productive basis for metaphorical expression. Metaphorical expression is thus conceived as a universal cognitive principle, which leads to various modalities of metaphorical expression and the creation of new metaphors.

3   Metaphors in accompanying gesture modality and brain processing

How is the brain processed with the accompanying gesture modality metaphor? Earlier studies stated that the accompanying gestures and spoken language belong to different brain areas and perform independent functions. For example, a lot of literature has presented pathological evidence to show that speech and gestures are separate. In the case of ideomotor apraxis, for example, one cannot express meanings by using conventional gestures under the request, but many aphasia patients do not experience such difficulty. Aphasic patients with left handedness can recover, but other aphasia patients cannot. The studies on language acquisition also support the hypothesis that gestures and spoken language are independent. The research has shown that gestures are closely related to object manipulation, similar to the case of a 13-month-old baby using gestures more than spoken language for expression, and using symbolic play before corresponding with words. These phenomena show that language and gestures are independent cognitive processing systems.

In recent years, an increasing number of scholars have agreed that accompanying gestures and spoken language belong to the same cognitive system. Because if the accompanying gestures and spoken language come from the same communication system, then they should be based on the similar or identical physiological basis. Thus, the patients with brain injury should show synchronous delays or failures with the accompanying gestures and spoken behavior. The accompanying gestures mostly appear with non-literal language and more involve the semantics and pragmatic functions. The meaning of pictographic gestures and are closely related to the meaning of spoken vocabulary, although metaphors in the accompanying gesture modalities are indirectly related to the meanings of corresponding words. At present, the studies on aphasia find that it also influences the use of spoken language and accompanying gestures. For example, aphasic patients whose Broca's areas are impaired can perform complex pictographic and metaphorical gestures, but they lack rhythmic gestures; even the rhythmic gestures have no content. In sum, the function is to express similar pragmatic functions with spoken language. Patients with aphasia and damage to the Wernicke's area can generate empty and meaningless spoken language, as well as rhythmic gestures without content, but they nearly never use the pictographic and metaphorical gestures. Even with pictographic and metaphorical gestures, such gestures are difficult to understand. Language acquisition research also explains that the children's spoken language and accompanying gestures are developed together. Children from 2 to 3 years old more express specific objects and situations; they refer to gestures in action and imitate a hand wave to greet or say goodbye. The expression of complex statements, rhythmic gestures, and metaphorical gestures develops later. The researchers found that autistic children exhibited developmental delays and abnormalities in language, as a result of developmental defects in the brain neural system that supports imitation behavior and gesture actions [19]. Other scholars also revealed that left brain injury can cause serious motor imitation failures, rather than an action understanding deficits [20]. As reported in recent studies, the experimental data show that patients with aphasia and Alzheimer's disease had their gesture defects that are highly related to naming defects; that is, understanding and generating a combination of meaningful actions are closely related to the brain auditory comprehension area. Other brain neuroimaging data show that the Brodmann area 44 (BA44) of the brain is responsible for verbal pronunciation and control of hands or arms movements. Several experimental results revealed that the Broca region (BA44) plays an important role in speech processing and behavior cognition (action representation). Combining the aforementioned evidence, some scholars pointed out that the accompanying gestures and spoken language all belong to phonemic clauses, tone units, or syntagma [21] and thus exhibit a psychological structure with both sides of one body [12].

According to the above statement, when the speaker expresses "the future is in front of you," the common accompanying gestures are the five fingers together and stretch the arm forward. The gesture maps to the time domain, and the stretch forward metaphor extends from the beginning of time to the future. To make this gesture, you need to simulate the scene in your mind beforehand. The object location of the space is mapped to the physical gesture space to express the concept of a metaphor. Realizing the simulation relies on the mirror neurons to achieve a preview. For example, the accompanying gesture of "future" requires mirror neurons to simulate forward movement, thus activating the neurons of the anterior motor region to control the finger movements. Then, the mirror neurons form a convergence zone that is responsible for the connection integration of sensory information and motor information, that is, the sensory information from the parietal cortex and the motor information from the premotor cortex. At this point, the knowledge of spoken language and accompanying gesture modalities can work together through the neurons. In this way, when two modal neurons integrate into a neural network, the neural binding occurs. Meanwhile, the Broca's region adjacent to the anterior motor cortex connects the neurons of speech and hearing.

Thus, when a speaker shouts "future," the Broca region also activates the neurons that controlling conceptual structure.

In neuroscience, the interpretation of metaphors remains in the initial stages, but the above analysis of brain processing for metaphors in accompanying gesture modality can explain the physiological basis of metaphors and its psychological reality.

4   Psychological process for metaphors in accompanying gesture modality

Although the most existing studies revealed that accompanying gestures and spoken language belong to the same generation process, modality is only a different expressive modal. The relationships of the cognitive psychology between the spoken language and accompanying gestures, the different scholars have different views.

The lexical retrieval model holds the view that the accompanying gestures are regarded as auxiliary words and compensate for language expression. The accompanying gestures occur only when the speaker's brain has difficulty extracting words, in the case the function of accompanying gestures is lexical access, activation of the lexical semantic network, and extraction of the vocabulary needed by the spoken modality. As a result, these scholars viewed that gestures precede speech and generate spatial imagery in working memory, and that this situation is only activated when speaking [22]. As for others, even the concepts of expression conveyed via accompany gestures and spoken language are similar and basically belong to different types of cognitive structures, i.e., language equates to analytical thinking, whereas accompanying gestures equate to spatio-motoric thinking [23].

Other scholars contended that accompanying gestures and spoken language are inseparable parts of language, share the same cognitive source, and are thus equal in status [12][24][25][26]. The output of language generation comes in two forms, that is, the synchronous output of the vocal organs and body movements [27]. Kita and others explained that gestures are influenced by language thinking, and also are influenced by visual spatial characteristics. These two independent forms of thinking originate from the same cognitive system and interact with each other in the process of encoding [23]. De Ruiter believed that the accompanying gestures and spoken language belong to the same communicative intention and cognitive process [24]; on the basis of the Levelt language generation model [28], a sketch model proposed by using the gesture processing and other multimodal elements, including a conceptualizer which is designed to convey the speaker's idea, and collect and sequence messages, ready to be expressed in the spoken modality, and initiate the message conveyance by using the gesture. Gestures are generated through three stages: first the information to be expressed through a gesture is selected, then the action program is activated to prepare the action, and finally, the action is performed. McNeill and others noticed that gestures and language come from the same growth point, which combines the think components of imagery and linguistic content [29]. Butterworth and others also agreed with the notion that gestures and language are closely connected and are closely related to the brain processing phase. For example, in the generation stage the meaning of vocabulary will dominate the use of pictographic and metaphorical gestures, while the stage of assigning sentence stress will affects the organization of rhythmic gestures, and so on [30].

At present, the former two theories, namely, the interface theory proposed by Kita and the sketch theory model proposed by DeRuiter, are internationally accepted. As for the similarities and differences of these theories, domestic scholars have made comparisons [31]. For the psychological processes of metaphors in the accompanying gesture modality, it can be explained from the pragmatic psychology of non-literal language, that is, contextual information plays an important role. According to the research from Bavelas et al., the function of an interactive gesture is beyond the content of lexical semantics and it mainly expresses the interaction between the speaker and his audience in an actual situation [32]. Gestures can also represent topic change and information status [33], and the pragmatic gestures are related to the sentence structure or language behavior [34]. When Chinese speakers talk about a certain topic, the generation of their accompanying gestures requires to combine the contextual information, including the fluency of speech and whether the speaker wants to convey the thematic or non-thematic information, old or new information, and whether the information is worth paying attention to, and so on. As McNeill said, the accompanying gestures are a part of discourse and chapters [3]. Thus, from the point of view of gesture modality, the accompanying gestures can provide more evidence for psycholinguistics and have theoretical and empirical significance.

5   Suggestions for future work

At present, the research about the metaphors in accompanying gesture modality is limited. To further explore this research area, we need to use the accompanying gesture modality as a separate special case, and further to analyze the factors which influence the accompanying gestural modal metaphors and cognitive theory.

5.1   Wide use of the corpus and statistical analysis method

At present, the study of linguistics widely uses the corpus in the analysis of linguistic phenomena. Linguists use large-scale, intuitive, and credible sentences as research data, which includes the communication of natural spoken language, existing written text, or large corpora. The accompanying gestures are one of the advantages of using corpus available ready-made spoken corpora, because the accompanying gestures are spontaneous behavior in spoken language. However, the drawbacks of accompanying gestures are casual, and they lack standards and specifications. For example, when the Chinese text is used in transfer of the accompanying gestures, Chinese text itself involves the problems about accepting and rejecting detail, which need to be clearly addressed by researchers. Moreover, sign language gestures can be based on the native language when writing comments, but the accompanying gestures cannot be recorded due to the unconventional relationship between their form and meaning.

5.2   Further delimit the scope of metaphors in the accompanying gesture modality

In spoken language and accompanying gestures, the scope of what is considered as a metaphorical expression should vary according to the objectives of the research project. Some projects may be broader than other, including any potential metaphorical expressions, whereas others may focus more on the metaphorical expression of speakers in real time. The most important factor is that the methods for metaphorical cognition should be clear and appropriate. How to recognize the expression of a metaphor in accompanying gesture modality in spoken discourse and written text may require us to develop reliable procedures or guidelines to identify the metaphors that accompanying gesture modality. Video spoken corpora, for example, use what physical attributes, the metaphors occur in which context, the role of metaphorical functions and physical attributes or the use of certain metaphors in the interactions among interlocutors can help to study other issues of metaphor research. These guidelines should help us study other issues in metaphor research. For example, Müller distinguished four expression patterns of accompanying gestures [35] that are not only used to describe specific activities, specific objects, or the properties of specific objects, but also to represent abstract metaphorical concepts. This fact supports the hypothesis of cognitive linguistics, that is, metaphors are based on concrete actions [36].

5.3   Further explicit describing the metaphorical forms in accompanying gesture modality.

In the framework of conceptual metaphor theory, "the target domain is the source domain," metaphor marks the cross-domain mapping of the related words does not involve any problems. By contrast, the accompanying gestures and spoken language make the potential problems of this approach more obvious. Hence, the accompanying gesture forms of words or phrases need to be explained, and the concepts need to be characterized. However, it is extremely difficult to capture the specific behavior of the source domain that contains words or phrases. One solution is to follow the cognitive grammar model [37], uses charts during the analysis process according to Cienki's suggestion [38].

6   Conclusions

Obviously, the metaphors in accompanying gesture modality help us to deepen the understanding of metaphors and cognition. By analyzing accompanying gestures and spoken language, we find that metaphor is a universal cognitive principle that is not limited in language itself. Observations of spoken language and the accompanying gesture metaphors are integrated into discourse patterns. Through these patterns, we can reveal how metaphors are classified. Therefore, metaphors are dynamic and non-static attributes. In addition, the metaphors in accompanying gesture modality, as a necessary component of discourse, contain necessary information to fill the gaps in lexical and syntax. If a metaphor in accompanying gesture modality also gains the attention of speakers and listeners, and uses the same source domain as the metaphor in spoken expression, then it is regarded as the foreground. Thus, the brains of speakers and potential speech perceivers have higher the level of cognitive activation. Therefore, the close interaction between this modality and language, and the interaction between body and context show that metaphor is a dynamic attribute rather than a static one, that is, it is not only dynamic in gesture movement, but also in cognition [6].

Metaphorical construction is a cognitive activity that occurs in the brain during the speaking process. Metaphors are clearly not limited to language, nor is it a specific linguistic principle, or a poetic principle [39]. However, the facts proved that the metaphor is a way of thinking organized, and is mainly embodied in its spoken modality. Spoken modality metaphors are always regarded as a unique phenomenon of language and poetry. Combining spoken language with accompanying gestures can reveal that metaphors can be instantiated in various modalities, especially under circumstances that do not always use the same conceptual metaphors. The imagery of the thought interaction during the speaking process, concrete and suggested modality, and accompanying gestures can trigger new verbal metaphorical expressions. Furthermore, the careful analysis of the syntax, semantics, prosody, and context of spoken language and accompanying gesture metaphor expression reveals that the metaphor is a dynamic attribute and is not a static one in linguistics. Study on the metaphors in accompanying gesture modality provides a more concrete case for further research, which provides support and thinking for the establishment of a broader model of non-literal language cognitive theory.

Acknowledgements This work was supported by the National Natural Science Foundation of China (NSFC) under grant no. 61433015; 91420202; 61602040, the National Social Science Foundation of China under grant no. 14ZDB154, the Humanities and Social Sciences Project of the Ministry of Education in China (MOE) under grant No. 14YJC740104, the key project of the National Language Committee (ZDI135-31), the support plan for high level teacher team construction in Beijing municipal universities (IDHT20170511), the Science and Technology project of Beijing Educational Committee (KM201711417006), and Tsinghua University Self-determination Project (20161080056).

References

1. Hu Zhuanglin. Multimodalization in Social Semiotics .Language Teaching and Linguistic Studies(in Chinese). 1 (3): 1-10(2007).
2. Calbris G. The semiotics of French gestures. Indiana Univ Press (1990).
3. McNeill D. Hand and mind: What gestures reveal about thought. University of Chicago Press (1992).
4. Okrent A. A modality-free notion of gesture and how it can help us with the morpheme vs. gesture question in sign language linguistics (or at least give us some criteria to work with). Modality and structure in signed and spoken languages, 175-198(2002).
5. Cienki A. Metaphoric gestures and some of their relations to verbal metaphoric expressions. Discourse and cognition: Bridging the gap, 189-204(1998).

6. Müller C. Metaphors. Dead and alive, sleeping and waking. A cognitive approach to metaphors in language use. Unpublished Habilitationsschrift, Freie Universität Berlin, Germany (2004).

7. Núñez R, Sweetser E. Spatial embodiment of temporal metaphors in Aymara: Blending source-domain gesture with speech//7th International Cognitive Linguistics Conference. 249-250(2001).

8. Wundt W M. Völkerpsychologie; eine untersuchung der entwicklungsgesetze von sprache, mythus und sitte: Bd. Die Kunst. W. Engelmann (1908).

9. Kendon A. Gesticulation and speech: Two aspects of the process of utterance. The relationship of verbal and nonverbal communication, 25: 207-227(1980).

10. McNeill D. So you think gestures are nonverbal? Psychological review, 92(3): 350(1985).

11. Murphy G L. Reasons to doubt the present evidence for metaphoric representation. Cognition, 62(1): 99-108(1997).

12. McNeill D. Language and gesture. Cambridge University Press (2000).

13. Goldin-Meadow S. Hearing gesture: How our hands help us think. Harvard University Press (2005).

14. Lakoff G, Johnson M. Metaphors we live by. University of Chicago press (2008).

15. Müller C. Forms and uses of the Palm up Open Hand: A case of a gesture family. The semantics and pragmatics of everyday gestures, 234-256(2004).

16. Lakoff G, Turner M. More than cool reason: A field guide to poetic metaphor. University of Chicago Press (2009).

17. Forceville C. Pictorial metaphor in advertising. Psychology Press (1996).

18. Feyereisen P. Gestures and speech, interactions and separations: A reply to McNeill (1985).

19. Charman T, Swettenham J, Baron-Cohen S, et al. Infants with autism: an investigation of empathy, pretend play, joint attention, and imitation. Developmental psychology, 33(5): 781(1997).

20. Halsband U, Schmitt J, Weyers M, et al. Recognition and imitation of pantomimed motor acts after unilateral parietal and premotor lesions: A perspective on apraxia. Neuropsychologia, 39(2): 200-216(2001).

21. Kendon A. Gesture and speech: How they interact. Nonverbal interaction, ed. by JR Wiemann & Randall Harrison. Beverly Hills (1983).

22. Krauss R M, Chen Y, Gotfexnum R F. 13 Lexical gestures and lexical access: a process model. Language and gesture, 2: 261(2000).

23. Kita S. How representational gestures help speaking. Language and gesture, 162-185(2000).

24. De Ruiter J. The production of gesture and speech. Language and gesture (2000).

25. Kendon A. Gesture: Visible action as utterance. Cambridge University Press (2004).

26. Kita S, Özyürek A. What does cross-linguistic variation in semantic coordination of speech and gesture reveal? Evidence for an interface representation of spatial thinking and speaking. Journal of Memory and language, 48(1): 16-32(2003).

27. Kendon A. Some relationships between body motion and speech. Studies in dyadic communication, 7: 177(1972).

28. Levelt W. JM (1989). Speaking. From intention to articulation. MA: The MIT Press, Cambridge (1981).

29. McNeill D, Duncan S D. Growth points in thinking-for-speaking. Language and Gesture (1998).

30. Butterworth B, Hadar U. Gesture, speech, and computational stages: a reply to McNeill. Psychological Review, 1: 168(1989).

31. Chen Hua, Gu Yan, Zuo Han. Theories on the Relationship between gesture and speech -- also on Implications for cognitive linguistics. Journal of Foreign language (in Chinese), (5): 50-58(2013).
32. Bavelas J B, Chovil N, Lawrie D A, et al. Interactive gestures. Discourse processes, 15(4): 469-489(1992).
33. McNeill D, Levy E T. Cohesion and gesture. Discourse processes, 16(4): 363-386(1993).
34. Kendon A. Gestures as illocutionary and discourse structure markers in Southern Italian conversation. Journal of pragmatics, 23(3): 247-279(1995).
35. Müller C. Redebegleitende Gesten: Kulturgeschichte, Theorie, Sprachvergleich. Spitz (1998).
36. Gibbs Jr R W, Berg E A. Mental imagery and embodied activity. Journal of Mental Imagery (2002).
37. Langacker R W. Foundations of cognitive grammar, vol. 2. Descriptive application (1991).
38. Cienki A. Metaphor in the "Strict Father" and "Nurturant Parent" cognitive models: Theoretical issues raised in an empirical study. Cognitive Linguistics, 16(2): 279-312(2005).
39. Cienki A, Müller C. Metaphor, gesture, and thought. The Cambridge handbook of metaphor and thought, 483-501(2008).

Competition and Differentiation of a Pair of Morpheme-inverted Words in Mandarin Chinese: Dòuzhēng and Zhēngdòu

Wensi Li

[1] The institute of Chinese Information Processing, Beijing Normal University, Beijing, 100875
zjklws@163.com

Abstract. A large number of morpheme-inverted words are unique elements in Chinese vocabulary, which is an important lexical phenomenon occurred in the history of the development and evolution of Chinese vocabulary. As a corpus driven study, this paper discusses a pair of morpheme-inverted words *dòuzhēng* (斗争) and *zhēngdòu* (争斗) from microscopic perspective. Based on the statistics and analysis, this paper explores the origin, occurrence time, evolution process, service conditions and the reasons of semantic changes of *dòuzhēng* (斗争) and *zhēngdòu* (争斗). And this study aims at providing some reference for the study of morpheme-inverted words from microscopic perspective.

Keywords: morpheme-inverted words, *dòuzhēng* (斗争), *zhēngdòu* (争斗), evolution.

1 Introduction

1.1 Morpheme-inverted words and its definition in Mandarin Chinese

Morpheme-inverted words are a kind of special words with prominent characteristic in Chinese vocabulary system. If a pair of morpheme-inverted words are both compound words with two same syllables (word morphemes) while the order of the morphemes in these two words are different, then these two compound words are named a pair of "morpheme-inverted words". The morpheme-inverted words are very important in Chinese vocabulary, therefore, there is a necessity to study them in detail and in depth, which is of great significance to the study of development of Chinese vocabulary and lexical semantics.

The definition of the morpheme-inverted words should be focus on "morpheme", "inverted" and "word" respectively.

First, the form of morphemes of two words should be the same, and more significantly, the meaning and part of speech of the morphemes are the same. For example, the meanings of the morpheme *jin*(金) are different in "*jinjiang*(金奖)" and "*jiangjin* (奖金)", so these two words are not morpheme-inverted words though they seem like this kind of words in formation. Then, the two morphemes of a pair of morpheme-inverted words are reversed while the way of word formation remains the

Y. Wu et al. (Eds.): CLSW 2017, LNAI 10709, pp. 224–234, 2018.
https://doi.org/10.1007/978-3-319-73573-3_19

same. There is a counter example: "*fanxin* (烦心)" is in a predicative-object structure and "*xinfan* (心烦)" is in a subject-predicate structure instead. That is, inverting the morpheme position leads to a change in word formation, so that these two words don't meet the definition of morpheme-inverted words. Finally, the area of the study are words rather than phrases, so "*kaihua* (开花)" and "*huakai* (花开)" are not morpheme-inverted words and are not in the scope of this study because "*huakai* (花开)" is not a word after morpheme-inverting.

1.2   Research status

The phenomenon appeared in the pre-Qin period in ancient China that the order of the morphemes of two words are different while the meanings of the words are similar or related. And because of the special formation feature of the morpheme-inverted words, some authors did a lot of work from different aspects. Cen Shifu (1956) has discussed the pair of words "*hehuan*(和缓)" and "*huanhe*(缓和)" and the normative use of them. He noticed that words in modern Chinese are often combined with two similar word-building elements in word formation to form compound words, forming a combined form of coordinate structure, and he also indicated that the order of the combining forms is not fixed, which have no influence to the meaning of some words while do have influence to the meaning of some other words in different eras and regions.

From the perspective of using in different historical periods, Zheng Dian (1964) studied the swap of two characters of ancient disyllabic words and classified the words according to the ancient and modern usage before and after inverting the character order. Zhang Yongmian (1980) studied the meaning and using rules of 85 pairs of morpheme-inverted words in modern Chinese. Cao Tingyu (2000) studied the use age, morphological structure, part of speech and semantic development of some modern Chinese morpheme-inverted words in depth. What's more, there are many concurrent analysis and research. Ding Mianzai (1957) explored the relationship between the structures and meanings of the words in 1950s, and Tan Ruwei (1995) discussed the definition, part of speech, word meanings and structures of morpheme-inverted words. In addition, Zhang Qiyun (2002) classified the morpheme-inverted words in modern Chinese according to the compositions and structures. These studies have contributed to the study of the history of Mandarin Chinese, indicating that the emergence of morpheme-inverted words is not by accident. However, most of these studies only classify morpheme-inverted words in some different aspects, and the surface phenomena are described in a macro way, but there is seldom detailed discussion of specific similarities and differences of the pairs of morpheme-inverted words.

Some studies are for specific works or authors and regard the whole book or the works of the author as the research scope and then focus on the morpheme-inverted words appearing in the book or the works. For example, Han Chenqi (1983) and Wang Sen & Wang Yi (2000) enumerated the words in *Shih Chi* and the *Golden Lotus* and counted them respectively, and gave descriptions of the usage of words and the development of the meanings of words from the perspective of syntax and semantics. It is of great significance to study the works, but it is difficult to analyze morpheme-inverted words deeply and systematically.

The morpheme-inverted words in different dialects have also attracted the attention of scholars. Zhang Wei (2007) did a diachronic study of the morpheme-inverted words in different dialects and analyzed them in optimization theory. In addition, there are also some studies focusing on the causes, usages and rhetorical functions of morpheme-inverted words.

All of these studies have achieved notable results in certain areas, however, most of them analyze morpheme-inverted words from a macro perspective, and then characterize and classify them according to the formation of words and whether the meanings are the same. The authors seldom focus on the origin, occurrence time, evolution process, service conditions and reasons of semantic changes or do research in detail. So there is a certain deficiency in the study of certain morpheme-inverted words from the micro perspective.

1.3   The significance of microscopic study of morpheme-inverted words

The focus of current studies of morpheme-inverted words is mainly on the vocabulary system, and these studies describe the evolution of words in the process of production and development from a macro perspective, and summarize the evolution rules of the morpheme-inverted words. However, the rules cannot apply to all the morpheme-inverted words pairs, at the same time, there are few detailed studies of morpheme-inverted words from a microscopic perspective. In addition, the definition of "the same morpheme", "inverted" and "word" is not clear enough.

I take the morpheme-inverted words *dòuzhēng* (斗争) and *zhēngdòu* (争斗) as an example, study the origin, occurrence time, evolution process, service conditions and reasons of semantic changes in different eras of this pair of morpheme-inverted words.

2   Dòuzhēng (斗争) and Zhēngdòu (争斗) in Ancient Chinese

Based on the definition of the morpheme-inverted words, *dòuzhēng* (斗争) and *zhēngdòu* (争斗) are a pair of morpheme-inverted words. First, *dòuzhēng* (斗争) and *zhēngdòu* (争斗) are both compound words with two syllables; then, they are both made up of two identical morphemes: *zhēng* (争) and *dòu* (斗) in a different order; third, *zhēng* (争) and *dòu* (斗) are related in meaning and make up two two-syllable juxtaposed compound words: *dòuzhēng* (斗争) and *zhēngdòu* (争斗), which have the same word formation; finally, *dòuzhēng* (斗争) and *zhēngdòu* (争斗) are both verbs and only have this one part of speech so that they are not conversion words. Above all, *dòuzhēng* (斗争) and *zhēngdòu* (争斗) are a typical pair of morpheme-inverted words.

Dòuzhēng (斗争) and *zhēngdòu* (争斗) appeared in pre-Qin period in *Lǔ's Commentaries of History* (《吕氏春秋》):

故凡斗争者，是非已定之用也。（战国《吕氏春秋》）

Gu fan douzheng zhe, shifei yi ding zhi yong ye. (zhanguo, Lü shi chunqiu)

So, as long as it is a struggle, it is a measure of right and wrong that has been determined.

争斗之所自来者久矣，不可禁，不可止。（战国《吕氏春秋》）

Zhengdou zhi suo zi lai zhe jiu yi, bu ke jin, bu ke zhi. (zhanguo, Lü shi chunqiu)

The origin of the struggle is very old. It cannot be banned or stopped.

So the original time of the two has no difference. However, *zhēng* (争) and *dòu* (斗) can be morphemes in a word, and they can also be used as a word alone, what's more, most of words were monosyllabic words in ancient Chinese language, and they used to combine to make up phrases whose orders of components are not fixed. So the question is, whether they were double syllable words from the very beginning or they were phrases composed of two single-syllable words and then were gradually fixed in the course of the long evolution process forming disyllabic words? According to the meanings of these two morpheme, *zhēng* (争) means a struggle, and *dòu* (斗), written as "鬥" in ancient Chinese language, describes the case that two men stood opposite each other and the weapons are behind them. The two words were similar in meaning originally and both can be used alone as a word independently. Moreover, it is common that *zhēng* (争) and *dòu* (斗) appear at the same time. For example:

齐庄公好勇，不使斗争，而国家多难，其渐至于崔杼之乱。（《淮南子》，西汉）

Qi Zhuanggong hao yong, bu shi douzheng, er guojia duo nan, qi jian zhi yu Cui Zhu zhi luan. (Huainanzi, Xi Han)

The king of Qi liked martial activities, and although he didn't let the people fight, the country was always so troubled that someone named Cui Zhu killed him.

朝有变色之言则下有争斗之患。（《册府元龟》，北宋）

Chao you bian se zhi yan ze xia you zhengdou zhi huan. (Ce fu yuan gui, Bei Song)

There is an argument in the court, and there is a scourge of strife.

Dòuzhēng (斗争) and *zhēngdòu* (争斗) included in these sentences have been used in combined formation as a word. Besides, based on the retrieval results obtained from the corpus of Center for Chinese Linguistics PKU, I have noticed that there are 17 sentences including *zhēngdòu* (争斗) from the warring states period to the Song dynasty, and 16 sentences including *dòuzhēng* (斗争), that is, the number of language data is similar.

In the perspective of syntactic function, if some function words are inserted between *zhēng* (争) and *dòu* (斗) and separate them, then it is easily to judge whether the syntactic functions and meanings of the words have changed. For example:

民不争而斗，衡无所用也。（《道德真经疏义》，宋）

Min bu zheng er(and) dou, heng wu suo yong ye. (Dao De zhen jing shu yi, Song)

The people don't fight, and the measurement is useless.

有盐井之利，故好*斗而争*。（《东江家藏集》，明）

You yan jing zhi li, gu hao dou er(and) zheng.

There is the benefits of salt wells, so (they) would like to fight.

According to these materials, we can see that the functions and meanings have no differences from the original ones after inserting the function words between the two characters. So we know that *zhēng* (争) and *dòu* (斗) were still used in combined structures as phrases during Ming and Qing dynasties. Further on, we can infer that *dòuzhēng* (斗争) and *zhēngdòu* (争斗) were not fixed compounded words with two syllables at the very beginning, instead, they were phrases made up with two independent words *zhēng* (争) and *dòu* (斗) and fixed in the evolution of ancient Chinese.

In the early stages, *dòuzhēng* (斗争) and *zhēngdòu* (争斗) are phrases composed by two one-syllable words and they are the same in the meaning which is the same as *zhēng* (争) and *dòu* (斗) that refers to the conflicts between people, looting and other phenomena resulting from small contradictions. And they were widely used to describe the conducts and relationship between people of a small country, residents and neighbors in a block, noting that they describe the ordinary people such as "*min* (民)", "*xia* (下)", "*ren* (人)", "*xiangdang* (乡党)" or someone who are specific. The retrieval results obtained from the CCL Corpus and BCC Corpus show that *dòuzhēng* (斗争) and *zhēngdòu* (争斗) were roughly the same and had not changed until Song dynasty when *dòuzhēng* (斗争) was first seen be used to describe relation between countries and politics.

边境宴然，苍生蒙福，义同一家，靡有兵革*斗争*之事。（《大金吊伐录》，北宋）

Bianjing yanran, cang sheng meng fu, yi tong yi jia, mi you bing ge douzheng zhi shi. (Da Jin diao fa lu, Bei Song)

The border is peaceful, and the people are happy living like a whole family, and there is no war.

以太子之事托宋公，后虽有*斗争*，宋公必能定乱。（《周朝秘史》，明小说）

Yi Taizi zhi shi tuo Songgong, hou sui you douzheng, Songgong bi neng ding luan. (Zhou chao mi shi, Ming dynasty, novel)

(He) trusted him with the crown prince, and then, ever if there is a struggle, he would be able to calm the mess.

But the word *zhēngdòu* (争斗) has not been seen to describe other objects.

In addition, in the data of the Ming and Qing dynasties retrieved by CCL Corpus, there were nearly 200 *dòu* (斗) in the corpus, and only 7 words of *zhēng* (争) appeared. The word *zhēng* (争) had been widely used in Ming dynasty and Qing dynasty in novels, stories and classics, especially popular novels. And novel was the typical form of literature in Ming and Qing dynasties, rising and developing with the prosperity of the economy of urban commercial, generating from the folk , circulating in oral form in the early stage, with the content including the historical romance, saga, God evil spirit novel and traditional case-solving stories. So the stories in Ming-Qing novels were secular and closed to ordinary people's life. The word *zhēng* (争) had been fixed in the Ming and Qing dynasties, and was used to describe activities about the life of the lower classes.

In the period of the republic of China, the use of *zhēng* (争) continued.

皇子继承者目标选定，围绕立皇子在宫中展开了更为激烈的斗争。（《武宗逸史》，民国）

Huangzi jicheng zhe mubiao xuan ding, weirao li huangzi zai gong zhong zhankai le gengwei jilie de douzheng. (Wuzong yi shi, Minguo)

The imperial heir to the throne was chosen, and there was a more intense struggle in the palace.

夫人就设法在她们中间挑拨、构陷，务必使其互相争斗，两败俱伤。（《古今情海》，民国）

Furen jiu shefa zai tamen zhongjian tiaobo, gouxian, wubi shi qi huxiang zhengdou, liangbaijushang. (Gujin qing hai, Minguo)

In the period of the republic of China, few number of sentences containing the word *dòuzhēng* (斗争), and there is only one sentence which is the example above in CCL Corpus retrieval results. But the number of the sentences containing data for *zhēngdòu* (争斗) is 48, so the numbers of frequency of the two words varies widely.

Thus, we can see that the words *dòuzhēng* (斗争) and *zhēngdòu* (争斗) began to be divided in semantics and gradually be fixed. The meaning of *zhēngdòu* (争斗) has not changed, and *dòuzhēng* (斗争) could be used in the same way as *zhēngdòu* (争斗) to express the struggle between ordinary people, but also for the upper business and political occasions of governments and countries. In other words, after the Song Dynasty, *zhēngdòu* (争斗) was used to represent the daily life of the lower people, and *dòuzhēng* (斗争) was used in cases involving the state affairs.

3   Dòuzhēng(斗争) and Zhēngdòu(争斗) in Modern Chinese

This pair of morpheme-inverted words *dòuzhēng* (斗争) and *zhēngdòu* (争斗) formed in ancient times and gradually fixed down, being divided from the same word meaning to different meanings. In modern Chinese, *dòuzhēng* (斗争) and *zhēngdòu* (争斗) have inherited their meanings in ancient Chinese, and are still verbs. However, in modern Chinese, according to search results in the CCL Corpus, the usage frequency of *dòuzhēng* (斗争) is significantly higher than *zhēngdòu* (争斗). The numbers of sentences containing two words retrieved in CCL modern Chinese corpus are showed here:

	Modern Chinese	Contemporary Chinese
Zhēngdòu (争斗):	41	1178
Dòuzhēng (斗争):	213	36755

The numbers of search results are in sharp contrast to the numbers of search results in ancient Chinese corpus. This means that the word meanings of the two words may have changed.

In the Modern Chinese Dictionary, the meaning of *Zhēngdòu* (争斗) does not differ from the meanings formed in ancient Chinese, and there are two specific items: a)fight; b) refers to the opposing party trying to overcome the other side; struggle. *Dòuzhēng* (斗争)has the following three terms: a) the contradictory parties are in conflict with each other and one party tries to win over the other; b) the masses against reasoning, exposing, prosecution, etc. against hostile elements or bad guys; c) work hard. At the same time, the changes of the semantic terms can be observed from the data of this period：

革命的阶级则通过教育宣传革命思想，提高群众觉悟，使其奋起斗争。

Geming de jieji ze tongguo jiaoyu xuanchuan geming sixiang, tigao qunzhong jue-wu, shi qi fenqi douzheng.

The revolutionary class propagates revolutionary ideas through education, and en-hances the consciousness of the masses to fight.

生产力的发展，生产力与生产关系的矛盾，经济基础与上层建筑的矛盾，只有通过阶级矛盾、阶级斗争和暴力革命表现出来。

Shengchanli de fazhan, shengchanli yu shengchanguanxi de maodun, jingjijichu yu shangcengjianzhu de maodun, zhiyou tongguo jieji maodun, jieji douzheng he baoli geming biaoxian chulai.

The development of productive force, the contradiction between productive force and production relations, the contradiction between economic base and superstructure, can only be manifested through class contradictions, class struggles and violent revo-lutions.

It can be seen that in addition to the same meaning of *dòuzhēng* (斗争) and *zhēng-dòu* (争斗), the *zhēngdòu* (争斗) maintains the original meaning, and in addition to describe the upper and national issues, *dòuzhēng* (斗争) also derived a special mean-ing: the masses against reasoning, exposing, prosecution, etc. against hostile elements or bad guys. This requires us to look for answers from the social and historical back-ground, because language is a reflection of social life and, to some extent, a record of social life. Looking back at China's modern history, China has experienced arduous anti-imperialist and anti-feudal process, and the Chinese people made unremitting efforts to pursue liberation. Later, there were some mistakes in the socialist revolu-tion, construction and reform period, and then carried out the adjustment and chaos anyway.

In the period of the new-democratic revolution, the Chinese people, under the lead-ership of the Communist Party of China, overthrew the three great mountains of im-perialism, feudalism and bureaucratic capitalism, and achieved the victory of the new democratic revolution. During this period, the usage frequency of *dòuzhēng* (斗争) is significantly exceeded *zhēngdòu* (争斗). The contradiction between the Chinese peo-ple and imperialism, the confrontation between communism and bureaucratic capital-ism inevitably led to the struggle against imperialism and the struggle of the proletariat against bureaucracy and bourgeoisie. *Dòuzhēng* (斗争) evolved this special meaning based on its two original terms of meaning. Since the original meaning of *dòuzhēng* (斗争) can be used for both the conflict and the competition between the lower people and the hostility at the upper level, the *dòuzhēng* (斗争) can go through the upper and lower strata, and the social contradictions in the period of the new democratic revolution conflict permeates the social dimensions from the upper to the lower. Thus, this special meaning is borne by the word *dòuzhēng* (斗争) rather than by *zhēngdòu* (争斗) because of the limited meaning of *zhēngdòu* (争斗).

After the founding of the People 's Republic of China, Chinese society has entered a period of modern history. At the early years, Chinese society experienced long-term unrest and disputes, and social contradictions are still sharp with social and economic depression and political turmoil. And people experienced many historical events. China made achievements during that time but also made some mistakes. In modern Chinese history, especially in the 1960s and 1970s, the frequency of *dòuzhēng* (斗争) was significantly higher than that of other periods, and the number of frequency in one year reached 30000, resulting in a sharp increase in the frequency of this word. Figure 1 shows the frequency of *dòuzhēng* (斗争) from 1949 to 2015.

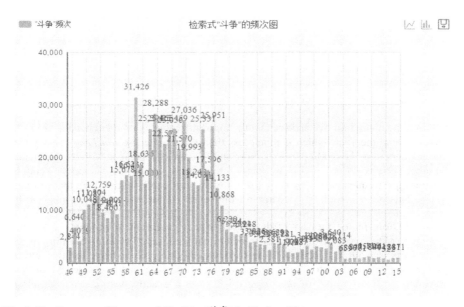

Fig. 1. The Frequency Diagram of *dòuzhēng* (斗争) in Modern History.

In contrast, in the same historical period, the frequency of *zhēngdòu* (争斗) is much less, and the frequency is shown in Figure 2.

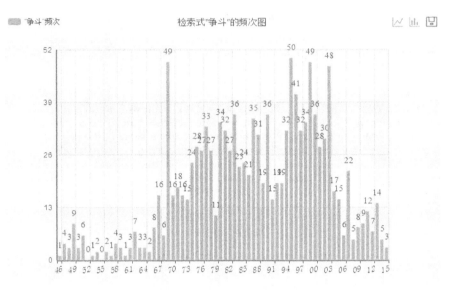

Fig. 2. The Frequency Diagram of *zhēngdòu* (争斗) in Modern History.

From the histogram, we can see that the highest frequency of *zhēngdòu* (争斗) is 50 times in a single year, which is much less than the number of *dòuzhēng* (斗争). But the frequency of *zhēngdòu* (争斗) is more stable keeping a balance with the frequency in other periods. What's more, we can see that in the late 1960s and early twentieth century, the frequency of *dòuzhēng* (斗争) was significantly higher than that of other years. This phenomenon is inseparable from social contradictions and is bound to be affected.

In addition, in the process of development and evolution, *dòuzhēng* (斗争) and *zhēngdòu* (争斗) have differentiated in emotional tendency. The same meaning of the two words is neutral, and there is no obvious emotional color here. In other terms, *zhēngdòu* (争斗) refers to "fight" with a negative and spontaneous tendency, and the meaning of "hard work" of *dòuzhēng* (斗争) has a exactly positive and conscious tendency. Because the context of *zhēngdòu* (争斗) has been the daily life of the lower people since ancient time and there has been no change, it makes the secular and vul-gar features to be consolidated and highlighted. In the process of meaning differentia-tion, *dòuzhēng* (斗争) is used in serious and formal political occasions, involving the national honor and the common ideals of the whole people. In the long-standing Chinese culture of respect for morality, the regime is sacred and the people are the masters of the country and the fundamental purpose of politics is to safeguard the fundamental interests of the people, so the use of the term *dòuzhēng* (斗争) is mostly positive.

4   Conclusion

This paper makes a microscopic study of a pair of morpheme-inverted words: *dòuzhēng* (斗争) and *zhēngdòu* (争斗) from diachronic perspective. First of all, it clarifies the importance of studying morpheme-inverted words from the microcosmic level, and then defines the scope of the morpheme-inverted words. Then, the concepts of *dòuzhēng* (斗争) and *zhēngdòu* (争斗) were confirmed by the definition of morpheme-inverted words, and the diachronic analysis was carried out in ancient Chinese period and modern Chinese period respectively.

As a corpus driven study, this paper got the following conclusions with the help of the CCL Corpus of Peking University and BCC Corpus of Beijing Language and Culture University:

1) *Dòuzhēng* (斗争) and *zhēngdòu* (争斗) were appeared in the pre-Qin period as phrases made up with two independent words with only one syllable. In the ancient Chinese stage, they were gradually stabilized and then formed a closed structure and evolved into words with fixed meaning.

2) *Dòuzhēng* (斗争) and *zhēngdòu* (争斗) were the same in the meaning at the very beginning. It was about in Song dynasty, *dòuzhēng* (斗争) was used for the upper business and political occasions of governments and countries. And zhēngdòu (争斗) still described activities about the life of the lower classes. Thus, in Song dynasty, the meaning of them began to become divided.

3) In ancient Chinese period, there was little difference between *dòuzhēng* (斗争) and *zhēngdòu* (争斗). But with the changing of dynasties and the development of literary forms, the frequency of *zhēngdòu* (争斗) is significantly higher than *dòuzhēng* (斗争). And the frequency of *zhēngdòu* (争斗) was very high in Ming-Qing novels.

4) In modern Chinese period, the *dòuzhēng* (斗争) has been extended, and the *zhēngdòu* (争斗) is fully inherited from the ancient Chinese period, which has not changed much. The *dòuzhēng* (斗争) has formed a fixed special item because of the special causes of social history and politics.

5) Social life and historical politics have influence on vocabulary greatly and profoundly, by which the word *dòuzhēng* (斗争) and *zhēngdòu* (争斗) are influenced in modern Chinese.

6) Because of the differentiation, evolution, consolidation and strengthening of the meaning, some terms of *dòuzhēng* (斗争) and *zhēngdòu* (争斗) tend to be different in emotional colors. The emotional color of *dòuzhēng* (斗争) is positive, while the emotional color of *zhēngdòu* (争斗) is negative.

This paper studied the generation, the differentiation and the competition of *dòuzhēng* (斗争) and *zhēngdòu* (争斗) from microscopic perspective, hoping to provide some reference for the microscopic level research for morpheme-inverted words.

5   Acknowledgment

This work was supported by the Hi-Tech Research and Development Program of China (2012AA011104), and by China State Language Affairs Commission "Twelfth Five" Scientific Re-search Project (YB125-124).

References

1. Cao Tingyu: A Study on the Same–Morpheme and Contrary–Order Synonym of Modem Chinese. Jinan Journal (Philosophy & Social Science Edition) (05), 57–64 (2010).
2. Cen Shifu: "Gentle" or "Ease". Chinese Knowledge, (1956).
3. Ding Mianzai: Ding Mianzai: The Structure and Meaning of the Same Words.Academic Monthly (02), (1957).Academic Monthly (02), (1957).
4. Han Chenqi: The Disyllabic Words Inversing the Word Order in the Historical Records. Studies of the Chinese Language (03), (1983).
5. Lin Yan: Reverse order with the prime word "calculation–calculating" research. Central China Normal University (2011).
6. Tan Ruwei: Tan Ruwei: Four Aspects of the morpheme-inversed words. A New Study of Lexical Studies. Language Press, Beijing (1995).
7. Wang Sen, Wang Yi: Disyllable Words of Different Arrangement in Jin Ping Mei Ci Hua. Journal of Lanzhou University (06), 125–135 (2000).
8. Xun Endong, Rao Gaoqi, Xiao xiaoyue, Zang Jiaojiao: The construction of the BCC Corpus in the age of Big Data. Corpus Linguistics (1), (2016).
9. Zhang Dexin: Talk about the Inverted Words. Chinese Language Learning, (06), 18–22 (1995).
10. Zhang Qiyun: A Unified Study of Chinese Words in Modern Chinese. Studies in Language and Linguistics (01), 72–82 (2002).
11. Zhang Wei: Studies on morpheme-inversed words in dialects. Tangdu Journal, (03), 117–120 (2007).
12. Zhang Wei: A Study on the Morpheme-inversed Words of Middle Chinese. Fudan University (2005).
13. Zhang Yongmian: The Disyllabic Words with Inversed Characters in Modern Chinese, Studies of the Chinese Language (03), (1980).
14. Zhang Zhiyi, Zhang Qingyun: Lexical Semantics. The Commercial Press, Beijing (1992).
15. Zheng Dian: The Disyllabic Words in Ancient Chinese. Studies of the Chinese Language (06), (1964).
16. Modern Chinese Dictionary. The Commercial Press, Beijing (2005).
17. Center for Chinese Linguistics PKU, http://ccl.pku.edu.cn:8080/ccl_corpus/, 2017/6/30

The Polylexicalization and Grammaticalization of *Zhiyu*

Xin Kou

Department of Chinese Language and Literature, Peking University, Beijing, China

e-mail: snjdkx@163.com

Abstract. *Zhiyu* can be used as a conjunction and an adverb in Mandarin Chinese. This research focuses on the polylexicalization and grammaticalization of this word. The conjunction *zhiyu* derives from the "verb +preposition" construction "*zhi+yu*", which means "arrive at/in", while the adverb *zhiyu* comes from the same construction means "result in". According to the development of these homographs, the mechanism of polylexicalization is the differentiation of morpheme meanings. Additionally, texts also provide conditions for meaning change. When *zhiyu* became two different words, the grammaticalization progresses of both words happened separately.

Keywords: *Zhiyu*, Polylexicalization, Grammaticalization

1 Introduction

In Mandarin Chinese, the word *zhiyu* can be divided into two lexicons. *Zhiyu1* is a topic-marker [1][2], which transfers the old topic of the discourse to a new topic and demonstrates that the new topic contrasts with the old one. *Zhiyu2* functions as an adverb [3][4], which means "to a certain degree". Besides, this lexicon is usually used in negative sentences or in rhetorical question mood.

Zhiyu1 and *zhiyu2* share the same form, and their meanings are related. Therefore, it is no doubt that the both lexicons stem from the construction "*zhi* (v.)+*yu* (prep.)" in ancient Chinese. The development of *zhiyu1* is discussed by numerous documents [5][6], while the study about the evolution of *zhiyu2* is still defective. Hence this research focuses on how the construction "*zhi+yu*" developed into *zhiyu1* and *zhiyu2* with the perspectives from grammaticalization and lexicalization.

2 *Zhiyu1* and *Zhiyu2* in Modern Mandarin Chinese

2.1 *Zhiyu1*

In Mandarin Chinese, *zhiyu1* usually appears at the beginning of a sentence to introduce a new topic. Such as:

    (1) 至于手脚，可以少看或不看。

Y. Wu et al. (Eds.): CLSW 2017, LNAI 10709, pp. 235–242, 2018.
https://doi.org/10.1007/978-3-319-73573-3_20

As to hands and feet, you should ignore them.

(2) 至于谁和谁打，与怎么打，那就一个人一个说法了。

As to who will join into the war and how it will go on, people have different opinions. From (1) and (2), we know that *zhiyu1* locates at the sentence-initial, which can be followed by noun phrases or verb phrases, then a clause. In addition, *zhiyu1* is limited to a certain text. It requires a preceding clause to set up information background. Therefore, *zhiyu1* cannot introduce a totally new topic, which is the difference between it and *duiyu/guanyu*. *Duiyu* and *guanyu* can be used in titles, while *zhiyu1* cannot.

Pragmatically, the topic introduced by *zhiyu1* always has relation with the preceding information, and the relation can be coordination, transition or comparison. Moreover the clause after "*zhiyu1*+X" is usually used to describe the topic X in detail. Xing points out that the two features of conjunctions are (1) the function of the conjunction is coherence, (2) the conjunction is related to two parts. [3]Based on this definition, *zhiyu1* can be recognized as conjunction.

2.2   *Zhiyu2*

According to Hou, the meaning of *zhiyu2* is to some degree which exceeds the expectation of the speaker. [7] In the perspective of syntactic structure, *zhiyu2* can modify verbs and adjectives, and it usually appears in negative or rhetorical question mood. For examples:

(3) 你要是不愿意，可以把话说清楚，不至于为这个坏了咱们的感情。

   If you were not happy to do this, you could tell us. It is not worth to destroying our friendship for this.

(4) 我要是有出息，何至于跑到外边去混饭吃。

   If I had been more competitive, I would not leave my hometown.

In (3) and (4), "destroy our friendship" and "leave my hometown" are not the expectation of the speakers. Furthermore, the examples above can be only expressed in negative mood. The negative 不 (not) cannot be eliminated:

(3') *你不愿意，而且没有把话说清楚，至于为这个坏了咱们的感情。

(4') *我没出息，至于跑到外边去混饭吃。

Besides, *zhiyu2* can become a clause independently, yet it should be still expressed in rhetorical question mood. Such as:

(5) 人家骂你一句你就舞刀动枪，要死要活的，至于吗？

   They just argued with you, you should not so overreact.

And sometimes, *yu* in *zhiyu2* is phonetic reduction. Moreover, if we want to use *zhiyu2* in an affirmative sentence, the form *yizhiyu* should be used.

(6) 体育馆太小了，以至于球队都要在外面的停车场热身。

   The gym was so small that the players had to warm up in the park.

(7) 金字塔表面的石砖拼合得非常紧密，以至于人们很难在其中插入一把刀子。

   The bricks of Pyramid are arranged too closely to put a knife between them.

Related documents hold the view that *yizhiyu* is a conjunction. However, considering the semantics of *yizhiyu*, which means "leading to", it has closer link with *zhiyu2* rather than the conjunction *zhiyu1*.

3   The Historical Evolvement of *Zhiyu*

According to *Shuo Wen Jie Zi*, *zhi* means "birds fly down to the ground", referents to coming. Therefore, *zhi* expressed the meaning of arriving in ancient Chinese. Since *zhi* was an intransitive verb, it always compounded with the preposition *yu*. And the construction *zhiyu* was usually followed by nouns of locations in the pre-Qin period, which meant arriving at some place. Such as:

(8) 至于牛山而不敢登。

   (He) arrived at the Mountain Niu, but did not dare to climb. (*Spring and Autumn Annals*)

(9) 送子涉淇，至于顿丘。

   I accompanied with you to cross the River Qi, and arrived at the Mountain Dun (*The Book of Songs*)

At the same time, the temporal nouns could be the object of *zhiyu*. For example:

(10) 自二月不雨，至于秋七月。 (*Spring and Autumn Annals*)

   It have not rained from Feb. to July.

(11) 自契至于成汤八迁，汤始居亳。(*Jinwen Shangshu*)

   From Chengtang, this dynasty set there capital in Bo.

In (10), zhiyu was combined with the temporal nouns, while in (11), the name Chengtang was a metonymy, which actually referred to a certain period. Besides, *zhiyu* could also indicate expanding scape:

(12) 刑于寡妻，至于兄弟 (*The Book of the Songs*)

   His good affection expanded from widows to brothers.

According to Ungerer & Schmid, the expansion of *zhiyu*'s meaning can be interpreted by metaphor [8]. As expressed the meaning of expanding, this construction could be used in the conceptual domain.

Furthermore, this construction appeared in the structure "*zhiyu*+N+VP", such as:

(13) 至于文武，缵大王之绪。(*Jinwen Shangshu*)

   When it came to Emperor Wen and Emperor Wu, the nation was more powerful.

In this example, *zhiyu*+N was no longer a verb phrase, but introduced a new topic, as the NP *Wen and Wu* was more semantically combined with the VP.

Simultaneously, *zhiyu* could also be followed by adjectives or verbs, which expressed the meaning of leading to some results.

(14) 言既遂矣，至于暴矣。

   As soon as I promised you, you started to treat me badly. (*The Book of the Songs*)

However this phenomenon only appeared once in *The Book of the Songs*. In the later documents such as *Guo Yu*, *zhiyu* could be seen in these structures frequently.

(15) 失威而至于杀。

The emperor lost his majesty so that he was killed by others. (*Guo Yu*)

(16) 智不能匡君，使至于难。

My wisdom is not enough to help the emperor so that the country is trapped. (*Guo Yu*)

In these sentences, *zhiyu* significantly contained the causative meaning, which expressed the effect caused by some force.

In two Han Dynasties, the two meanings of *zhiyu* were both widely used. According to our statistical data, In *Huai Nan Zi*, the examples of *zhiyu* amounted to 42, among which 11 used *zhiyu* with the meaning of leading to.

(17) 是故至于伏尸流血，相支以日。(*Huai Nan Zi*)

Therefore it led to the massacre, and people were hard to survive.

As *zhiyu* with the meaning of leading to was used more frequently, the two lexicons of *zhiyu* were departing with each other. The difference between them was that the change of state was autonomous or caused by force. Moreover, in the Dong Han Dynasty, the bisyllablization of vocabulary of Chinese language was happening, which affected *zhiyu* and made it condenser to be a whole word. When the preposition *yu* integrated into the construction *zhiyu*, the construction "*zhi* (v.) +*yu* (prep.)" formed the verb *zhiyu*.

3.1   The Development of *Zhiyu1*

Zhiyu with the meaning of arriving at was the more frequently used in ancient Chinese. It could express the meaning of arriving at some place or expanding to some scape of conceptual domain. In addition, in syntax, the structure "*zhiyu* +N, VP" was more frequently used. Such as:

(18) 至于封侯，真命也夫！(*Shi Ji*)

As to conferring a dukedom, it is just the destiny tragedy to General Li

In this example, *zhiyu* was used as a new topic marker, which had less meaning of arriving at, but functioned to transfer topics. Therefore, we assume that *zhiyu* had completed the progress from verb to topic marker in Dong Han dynasty. However, the meaning of arriving at in *zhiyu* did not disappear until Ming and Qing period. In Two Song dynasty, the frequency of *zhiyu* with the meaning of arriving at decreased gradually, which was caused by the appearance of *dao* [9]. Finally in Modern Chinese, the meaning of arriving at is almost expressed by *dao* rather than *zhiyu*.

3.2   The Development of *Zhiyu2*

Zhiyu with the meaning of leading to was always used in the causative structures, which resulted in the reanalyzing of *zhiyu*. Because in these structures, *zhiyu* was rarely used by itself, but combined with some conjunctions like *gu*(so), *yi*(in order to) and *er*(so), or combined with the causative verb *shi*(cause). In addition, *zhiyu* with this meaning was used to be modified by negative markers.

(19) 先君与君，自不至于此。(*Shi Shuo Xin Yu*)

Of course our ancestor and your honor would not break up with each other.

(20) 是因其所已知而推之，以至于无所不知也。(*Zhu Zi Jia Xun*)

According to what he knew, he inferred the thing that he did not know. Therefore, he knew everything in the world.

From the examples above, *zhiyu* could be followed by nouns, pronouns or verbs. Semantically, *zhiyu* in all this examples meant leading to, yet there were other words or markers in these sentences to indicate the causative meaning. However, as *zhiyu* could combine with verbs like 无所不知 (knew everything in the world), we can suppose that here *zhiyu* was an adverb rather than a verb. At least, *zhiyu* had the both syntactic features.

Till Minguo period, *zhiyu* was still used as either an adverb or a verb. Such as:

(21) 万一不谨，甚而至于得罪了名人或名教授。(*The Cat, the dog and the rat*)

If I was careless, I might offend the celebrities or famous scholars.

(22) 我就是最提倡开学堂的，可万料不到学堂的流弊竟至于如此之大。(*The soap*)

I advocate to establish schools, however, the drawbacks of schools are unexpectedly tremendous.

In both the examples, *zhiyu* more liked a verb. Nevertheless, in Modern Chinese, the two examples were unusual. Though in Modern Chinese, the part of speech of *zhiyu2* is a difficult problems deserving deeper research, in this paper, what we can determine is that *zhiyu2* derives from the construction verb+ preposition *zhiyu*. Hence, the interpretation to the syntactic features of *zhiyu2* can be contribute to the progress of the grammaticalization of verb *zhiyu* to the adverb *zhiyu*.

4 The Polylexicalization and Grammaticalization of Zhiyu

4.1 The Mechanisms of the Polylexicalization

Polylexicalization is different from the lexicalization in the multiple paths of development. The phrase experienced the polylexicalization can develop into two or more lexicons. [10] The polylexicalization leads *zhiyu* to two lexicons. Since the verb *zhi* had to be added by the preposition *yu* in order to combine with an object, the mass examples made zhiyu become more condensed. In addition, as time passing by, the meaning of *zhiyu* divided, forming the meaning of arriving at and leading to separately. As we pointed out in this paper, the mechanisms of this progress are the incorporation of preposition, the metaphor and the metonymy.

The independent preposition incorporate into another word, then they blend into a new word, which called incorporation of preposition. In ancient Chinese, the construction *zhi+yu* experienced this progress and formed the verb zhiyu. No matter with the meaning of arriving to or leading to, *zhiyu* was frequently used and the arriving meaning of zhi became more and more faded. Therefore, the preposition *yu* decategorized and incorporated into the whole word zhiyu.

Besides, in pre-Qin period, the structure of Chinese syllables changed tremendously. And words experienced bisyllablization, which also promoted the fusion of *zhiyu*.

Cognitive principles can affect the development of words a lot. The change of the meaning of zhiyu was caused by the metaphor projection from space to time then to degree. Hence the meaning is more fade so that zhiyu can no longer be understood if it is divided into zhi and yu.

Similarly, the formation of *zhiyu2* attributed to the change from arriving at to leading to. The force to impel this transform is conceptual metonymy. According to our previous analysis, *zhiyu* with the meaning of arriving at could change to express the meaning of expanding scape, therefore, *zhiyu* could be used to indicate the result or degree. Besides, zhiyu with the meaning of leading to has the internal displacement. And, at first zhiyu is used to describe the objective state, but as time passing by, the meaning of this word is more abstract. It contains more subjective descriptions, so it always appears with subjective adverbs like *jing* (unexpectedly) and *shen* (even).

4.2   The Grammaticalization of *Zhiyu*

After the lexicalization, *zhiyu* with the meaning of arriving at and the meaning of leading to developed separately. Syntactically, the context provide the condition of reanalysis of *zhiyu1*. In the examples above, we can notice that *zhiyu1* developed closer to the NP, is due to the change of the meaning of *zhiyu*. Therefore, at the end of the program, the structure NP1+VP1, *zhiyu*+NP2+VP had formed. Moreover, in this structure, NP2 is easy to be analyzed as a new topic, which led to the interpretation of topic maker for *zhiyu*.

As for *zhiyu2*, reanalysis is also the most important reason of grammaticalization. *Zhiyu2* is usually located before verbs or adjectives so that *zhiyu* gradually lost the features of verbs, and was easy to be regarded as an adverb.

In addition, the subjectivization also promoted the progress of grammaticalization of *zhiyu*. The meaning of *zhiyu1* expanded form space to conceptual domain. In this progress the meaning from real world projected to the abstract world, which can be contributed to subjectivizaiton, while *Zhiyu2* is consistently subjective in semantics. As we pointed out above, this word is always used to express the expectation and opinions of speakers. So the subjectivization is also a factor of grammaticalization of *zhiyu*.

Finally, the conditions for the grammaticalization of *zhiyu1* and *zhiyu2* are frequency. *Zhiyu1* is numerously used after Han dynasty, and the verb meaning is gradually replace by the function of topic marker. In Two-Song period, *zhiyu2* increased in the documents, and the words followed it were almost VP rather than NP. Table1 demonstrates the frequency of *zhiyu1* and *zhiyu2* in different periods.

Table 1. the frequency of *zhiyu1* and *zhiyu2* in different periods

periods zhiyu	*zhiyu*(verb)	*zhiyu1*	*zhiyu2*
The Analects of Confucius	5	1	0

Han Fei Zi	5	2	0
Records of the Grand Historian(Shi Ji)	168	16	0
Bao Pu Zi	30	16	0
Buddhist Records of the Western World (Da Tang Xi Yu Ji)	16	18	2
Zhu Zi Yu Lei（Chap.1—5）	24	26	13
Ancient And Modern Wonders (Gujin Qiguan)	5	11	9
A Dream of Red Mansions	3	15	15

In the end, we use figure1 to present the progress of the grammaticalization of *zhiyu*.

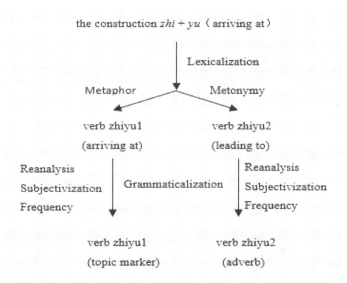

Figure 1. the progress of the lexicalization and grammaticalization of *zhiyu*

5   Conclusion

Zhiyu functions as a conjunction and an adverb in modern Mandarin Chinese. This research studies the polylexicalization and grammaticalization of this word. The conjunction *zhiyu1* derives from the construction "*zhi* (v.)+*yu* (prep.)", which means arriving at/in, while the adverb *zhiyu2* comes from the same construction means resulting in. According to the development of the both words, we analyze the mechanisms of the lexicalization and grammaticalization, which can be concluded as reanalysis, subjectivizaiton and frequently used.

References

1. Wang, R.: The topic mark function and text cohesion function of *duiyu, guanyu* and *zhiyu*, Journal of College of Chinese Language and Culture of Jinan University, No.3, (2004) [In Chinese]
2. Xu, J-Y.: The Study of Topic Marker *guanyu, duiyu* and *zhiyu*, Master Dissertation, Shanghai: Shanghai Normal University, (2010) [In Chinese]
3. Xing, F-Y.: Differentiate and Analysis of Parts of Speech in Chinese. Beijing: The Commercial Press, (2003) [In Chinese]
4. Rao, C-R.: *Zhiyu* and *guanyu* are not perpositions. *Chinese Language Learning*, No.7, (1987) [In Chinese]
5. Dong, X-F.: *Lexicalization: the development of bisyllable words in Chinese*. Chengdu: Sichuan Ethnic Press. [In Chinese]
6. Zhou, G-G.: Lexicalization and grammaticalization of *zhiyu*, Jounral of Yunnan Normal University, No.1, (2013) [In Chinese]
7. Hou, X-C,: The Dictionary of Function Words in Modern Chinese, Beijing: Peking University Press.(1998) [In Chinese]
8. Ungerer. F., Schmid J. *An Introduction to Cognitive Linguistics*, Beijing: Foreign Language Teaching and Researching Press. (2008)
9. Qin, X-H,: The development and substitution of *ge, zhi* and *dao*, *Journal of Hebei Radio & TV University*, No.4, (2010) [In Chinese]
10. Liu, H-N,: The polylexicalization and grammaticalization of *Jiayi*, *Linguistic Science*, No.6, (2011) [In Chinese]
11. Hopper. P, Traugott E. Grammaticalization，Beijing: Foreign Language Teaching and Researching Press.(1993)

Applications of Natural Language Processing

Research on the Recognition of Chinese Autonomous Verbs Based on Semantic Selection Restriction and Natural Annotation Information

Wang Chengwen[1], Xun Endong[1*]

[1]Institute of large data and language education, Beijing Language and Culture University, Beijing, 100083, China
chengwen_wang15@126.com, edxun@126.com

Abstract. Verb has always been an important yet challenging topic in linguistic research. The secondary classification of verbs is of great value for language ontology and language applied research. This paper investigated the computer recognition of autonomous verbs and constructed rules for recognizing such verbs, which is based on the contextual characteristics of automatic verbs and some natural annotation information (mainly punctuations and position information). A rule-based automatic recognition algorithm was thus devised. The F1 value of the algorithm is 86.3% on the manually labeled test data.

Keywords: Autonomous verb, Natural annotation information, Semantic selection restriction, Automatic recognition.

1   Introduction

Different researchers have different definitions of "autonomous verb" since it was first proposed by Ma (1985). They may have used a different term or defined a slightly different intension or extension of the concept. However, their definitions are generally consistent. Ma (1992) pointed out that semantically speaking, an autonomous verb expresses a conscious or an intentional behavior or action, which is subjectively decided and freely controlled by the action-takers. A non-autonomous verb, by contrast, expresses an unconscious or an unintentional behavior or action. Yuan (1991) classified all verbs into human-subject verbs and nonhuman-subject verbs according to the relationship between the verb and the imperative sentence. The human-subject verbs are further classified into controllable verbs and uncontrollable verbs. Generally speaking, autonomous/non-autonomous, controllable/uncontrollable and conscious/unconscious are all used to describe verbs with such particular semantic features. The particularity of the semantic features of the verb often has certain effects on its syntactic combinability.

Y. Wu et al. (Eds.): CLSW 2017, LNAI 10709, pp. 245–254, 2018.
https://doi.org/10.1007/978-3-319-73573-3_21

There are few studies on autonomous verbs. The existing studies mainly focus on two aspects. One aspect is on the classification system of verbs. The verbs are firstly classified into autonomous verbs and non-autonomous verbs. The non-autonomous verbs are further classified into attribute verbs, dynamic verbs, stative verbs and so on (Ma, 1992; Yuan, 1998; Jiang, 2004). The other aspect is on the contextual grammatical features of autonomous verbs and the grammatical and semantic differences of non-autonomous verbs in certain syntax forms (Ma, 1992; Liu, 2010; Qiao, 2009; Gao, 2008; Zhou, 2002; Wang, 2004). As discussed above, current studies on autonomous verbs mostly adopt the perspective of language ontology. Studies combining autonomous verbs with computer research is relatively rare.

Currently, studies in the field of natural language processing in Chinese have mostly focused on the syntactic and semantic parsing and have made considerable progress. However, to improve the research on natural language processing, it is necessary to rely more on formal linguistic knowledge. Insentences in Chinese, predicate serves as the main element of a sentence. To understand the core predicate component, it is imperative to work on a more elaborate classification system of verbs and explore distinguishable formaltagging features. Therefore, the present paper made an attempt to the automatic recognition of autonomous verbs by choosing appropriate formal features, to shed light on applied linguistic research on autonomous verbs.

2   Selection of Autonomous/Non-autonomous Verbs and Preparation of the Test Dataset

The main goal of this paper is to realize the recognition of autonomous verbs with rule-based algorithms. To begin with, appropriate data need to be selected as the test dataset. To our knowledge, there are no publicly available data on annotated autonomous/non-autonomous verbs that are suitable for the present study. Although Kang (2001) included autonomous/non-autonomous verb categories in the project "Modern Chinese New Words Information (Electronic) Dictionary", the autonomous/non-autonomous verbs are only restricted to new words and thus not suitable for the current experimental test. According to previous studies, we decided to sample the autonomous/non-autonomous verbs from "Modern Chinese Dictionary".

Having established the data source, we made a few adjustments when sampling data. Firstly, we selected disyllabic verbs instead of monosyllabic verbs. This is because a large amount of monosyllabic words have multiple meanings, some of which express meanings that can be controlled by human consciousness whereas some others express meanings that cannot be controlled by human consciousness. These polysemousverbs are difficult to be classified into either category. For example, "跑, pao3" is an autonomous verb when it means "to run",but it is non-autonomous when it means "to leak (gas)"; "生, sheng1" is an autonomous verb when it means "to light a stove", but it is non-autonomous when it means "to get rusty". Disyllabic verbs, however, are composed of two morphemes and thus have fewer ambiguities, which makes it relatively easy to classify the disyllabic verbs. Song (2007) found that monosyllabic words are more likely to be polysemous than multisyllabic words, based on data provided by Chinese Synonyms Thesaurus. Specifically, 47.2% of monosyllabic words have multiple meanings, while the proportion is 10.28% for multisyllabic words. Moreover, monosyllabic words have 2.13 possible meanings on average. Secondly, we reduced the number of verbs. Out of 1,653 entries, we randomly selected 950 disyllabic verbs, to ensure a better and more efficient annotation.

The selected verbs were manually annotated as autonomous or non-autonomous. The annotation was primarily based on the grammatical form, accompanied with the semantic judgment when necessary. The grammar judgment was tested in the sentence frame-?[来去]+V+O+?[来去][1] (*?[lai2 qu4]+V+O+?[lai2 qu4], ?[come go]+V+O?[come go]*) proposed by Ma. Verbs that fit the frame were annotated as 1 (autonomous); otherwise they were annotated as 0 (non-autonomous). The following table lists some examples of the annotated data.

Table 1. The annotated data

Verb	autonomous/nonautonomous
讨论,*tao3lun4, to discuss*	1
调查,*diao4cha2, to investigate*	1
研究,*yan2jiu1, to research*	1
分析,*fen1xi1, to analyze*	1
组织,*zu3zhi1, to organize*	1
劳动,*lao2dong4, to work*	1
斟酌,*zhen1zhuo2, to consider*	1
保重,*bao3zhong4, to take care*	1
照顾,*zhao4gu4, to take care*	1
爆发,*bao4fa1, to explode*	0
包括,*bao1kuo4, to include*	0

---

[1]The "?" preceding a modified item indicates that it's (or not) necessary. Only one among the items within "[]" is necessary.

沦亡,*lun2wang2, to be annexed*	0
以为,*yi3wei2, to believe*	0
貌似,*mao4si2, to seem*	0
相似,*xiang1si4, to resemble*	0
好转,*hao3zhuan3, to improve*	0

3   Analysis of the Contextual Features of Autonomous Verb Distribution

Language units with some common characters often have the same distribution in linear language sequences. For example, adverbs often appear before verbs as a decorative element. Based on this assumption, the contextual features of the autonomous verbs are taken into consideration when summarizing the rules. Furthermore, there are significant differences in the compatibilities of verbs withone certain grammatical format. For instance, "看见(*kan4jian4, to see*)" generally does not fit in the sentence of "别看见 (*bie2kan4jian4, don't see*)", while "看(*kan4, to look*)" does. The differences in language unit combinations often reflect the grammatical and semantic differences of different clustering language units. Based on the analyses of the examples above, it is obvious that the verbs that can fit the format of "别 v (*bie2 v, don't v*)" and that are basically semantically self-sufficient are automatous verbs; they are self-controllable by human consciousness and are intentional behaviours or actions. In the meanwhile, in the format of "别 v (*bie2 v, don't v*)", "别 (*bie2, don't*)" has a strong semantic limit to the followed verbs. As a negative adverb, when "别 (*bie2, don't*)" is used before a verb to be a separate sentence, it often has a strong imperative indication. It often indicates don't do something or do something, which is automatously controllable by the listeners.

Based on the distinctivefeatures of semantic selection restriction and the results from previous studies, four preliminary types of distributioncontexts are obtained:

(1) negative adverb + autonomous verb

An autonomous verb is often be preceded by a negative adverb, such as 别看 (*bie2kan4, don't look*), 别讨论(*bie2tao3lun4, don't discuss*), 甭说话 (*beng2shuo1hua4, don't talk*) and so on.

(2) autonomous verb + quantifier phrase

The quantifier phrases are mainly classified into time phrases and momentum phrases, excluding the quantitative phrases. They are complimentary to autonomous verbs, such as

商讨一下 (*shang1tao3yi1xia4, to discuss a bit*), 去一趟 (*qu4yi1tang4, to pay a visit*), 教三遍 (*jiao1san1bian4, to teach three times*) and 整顿一番 (*zheng3dun4yi1fan1, to rectify for a while*).

(3) frequency adverbs like "屡次 (*lv3ci4, repeatedly*)" and autonomous verbs

Frequency adverbs like "屡次 (*lv3ci4, repeatedly*)" mainly indicate the repetition of the actions. Wefocus on examining the collocation restriction between "一再 (*yi1zai4, repeatedly*)" and autonomous verbs.

(4) dummy verb + autonomous verb

The most common dummy verbsare "进行 (*jin4xing2, conduct*)", "给以 (*gei3yi3, to give*)", "予以 (*yu3yi3, to grant*)" and "加以 (*jia1yi3, to add*)".

4   The Recognition of Autonomous Verb Based on Semantic Selection Restriction and Natural Annotation Information

4.1   Summary of Autonomous Verb Recognition Rules

The four contextual features of the autonomous verb distribution are listed above. The summarization of the rules is not entirely based on the distribution characteristics, but with appropriate selection. For (1) negative adverb + autonomous verb, considering that "甭 (*beng2, don't*)" is very colloquial and also has many limitations in the collocation with verbs, the negative adverb "别*(bie2, don't)*", which has less limitations, was selected for the test framework of "别 + v (*bie2 + v, don't v*)". For (2) autonomous verb + qualifier phrase, similarly, compared with "一趟 (*yi1tang4, a visit*)" and "一番 (*yi1fan1, for a while*)", "一下 (*yi1xia4, a bit*)" has relatively less restrictions on the semantic selection and the collocation with verbs. Besides, adding too many rules may cause errors in the recognition of autonomous verbs. In order to avoid this, only "一下(*yi1xia4, a bit*)" was selected. Moreover, the composite test framework was composed by two directional verbs "来 (*lai2, come*)" or "去(*qu4, go*)" and "一下 (*yi1xia4, a bit*)", which were often collocated with autonomous verbs: "v + 一下 (*v + yi1xia4, v + a bit*)", "来 v 一下 (*lai2 v yi1xia4, come v a bit*)", "去 v 一下(*qu4 v yi1xia4, go v a bit*)". (3) We selected "一再 (*yi1zai4, repeatedly*)" to compose the framework with verbs: "v + 一再 (*v + yi1zai4, v + repeatedly*) " or "一再 + v (*yi1zai4 + v, repeatedly + v*)". (4) Compositions of the test framework include "进行+ v (*jin4xing2 + v, conduct + v*)", "给以 + v (*gei3yi3 + v, to give + v*)", "予以 + v (*yu3yi3 + v, to grant + v*)" and "加以 + v (*jia1yi3 + v, to add + v*)".

According to the observations of the examples from Lu (2003), the examples are language units with basic sematic self-sufficiency, e.g., "别喝! (*Bie2he1! Don't drink!*)", "别了解! (*bie2liao3jie3! Don't understand!*)", "进行调查 (*jin4xing2diao4cha2, to conduct an investigation*)" and "进行查找 (*jin4xing2cha2zhao3, to conduct a search*)".

Based on this understanding, the natural annotation information was added into the process of summarizing rules. The concept of natural annotation information comes from the user-generated information in the Internet applications. Natural annotation information was first introduced by Sun (2011) and is used to extract useful information in natural language processing from massive Internet data. In natural annotation information, the punctuation or location information is powerful demarcation information and facilitates extracting the chunk knowledge of language. Therefore, to ensure a higher level of sematic self-sufficiency and independency of the specific exemplar language units in the summarized test framework, the position information was restricted. In the BCC corpus, "w" is a location identifier. "w 吃 (*w chi1, w eat*)" means the query of clauses starting with "吃 (*chi1, to eat*)" and "w 一下 (*w yi1xia4, w a bit*)" means the query of clauses ending with "一下 (*yi1xia4, a bit*)". In orderto have independent language units of examples after recognition based the matching rules,the position identifier "w" was selectively added to the pre-summarized frame. There are two advantages for this design: one is that, as mentioned above, the independency of the identified matching unitis ensured. The other one is that, when searching for a unit beginning with "别 + v (*bie2 + v , don't + v*)", the examples like "分别 + v (*fen1bie2 + v, respectively + v*)" are excluded. The set of rule for recognition is: Rule 1- w 别 vw (*w bie2 vw, w don't vw*); Rule 2 - wv 一下 w (*wv yi1xia4 w, wv a bit w*); Rule 3 - 来 v 一下 w (*lai2 v yi1xia4 w, come v a bit w*); Rule 4 - 去 v 一下 w (*qu4 v yi1xia4 w, go v a bit w*); Rule 5 - v +再三&&再三+v (*v + zai4san1&& zai4san1 + v, v + repeatedly && repeatedly + v*); Rule 6 - 进行 v w (*jin4xing2 v w, to conduct v w*); Rule 7 -给以 vw (*gei3yi3 vw, to give vw*); Rule 8 - 加以 vw (*jia1yi3 vw, to add vw*); Rule 9 -予以 vw (*yu3yi3 vw, to grant vw*).

4.2   Idiographic Flow for Autonomous Verb Recognition

Following the flow for autonomous verb recognition:

(1)   The   machine   reads   the   annotated   autonomous   and   non-autonomous verbssuccessively. In the reading process, the annotated classification information is not read. For example, for "斟酌 1 (*zhen1zhuo2 1, to consider 1*)", only the verb "斟酌 (*zhen1zhuo2, consider*)" is read.

(2) The machine reads all the rules into the program. The language examples composed of verbs and test frames are regarded as search terms. The occurrences of these items in the BCC corpus were recorded automatically. For instance, "w 总结一下 w (*w zong3jie2yi1xia4 w, w to summarize a bit w*)" composed of "总结 (*zong3jie2, to summarize*)" and "wv 一下 w (*wvyi1xia4 w, wv a bit v*)" occurred 2,295 times in the BCC corpus.

(3) The items that successfully matched rules (i.e. items can be found in the corpus) are annotated with 1; otherwise, annotated with 0.

(4) The annotated data are exported to the specified files.

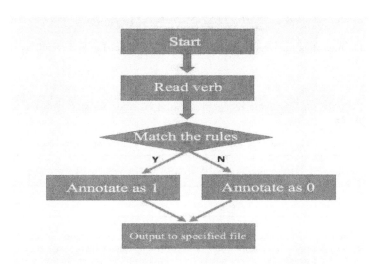

Fig. 1. Automatic recognition flow chart

5   Results and Discussion

5.1   Experiment Evaluation

It is necessary to evaluate the validity of recognition algorithm based on rules. In the present study, we employed the evaluation criteria that are widely used in the field of natural language processing (word segmentation, Part-of Speech tagging, syntactic analysis, etc.): precision, recall and F1 measure. We will introduce the criteria respectively as follows:

Precision is the percentage of elements that are correctly tagged among all the tagged elements in machine analysis, as shown in Formula (1):

$$P = \frac{\text{Frequency of correct tagging}}{\text{Total frequency of tagging}} \times 100\% \quad (1)$$

Recall is the percentage of elements that are correctly tagged among the number of tokens in the sample, as shown in Formula (2):

$$R = \frac{\text{Frequency of correct tagging}}{\text{Number of units in the sample}} \times 100\% \quad (2)$$

F1 value measures the overall result based on both precision and recall, as shown in Formula (3):

$$F1 = \frac{2*R*P}{R+P} \times 100\% \quad (3)$$

The results of the automatic recognition based on rules are shown in the following table (Table 2).

Table 2. The results of automatic recognition of verbs tagged as 1 (autonomous verb)

	Precision	Recall	F1
Tagged as 1	79.2%	94.3%	86.3%

As shown in Table 2, the recall performance of the set of rules is good, but the precision is only around 80%, with almost 20% of the instances incorrectly recognized.

5.2   Experiment Analysis

The precision level is relatively low. We investigated the errors manually. The statistical results are shown in Table 3.

Table 3. The statistics of the tagging results

	Test set	Machine tagging	Errors
Tagged as 1	630	786	156

As shown in Table 3, 630 verbs were manually tagged as 1 in the test set. However, the number of verbs tagged as 1 was 786 in automatic tagging. We found that most verbs that were manually tagged as 0 were tagged as 1 in automatic tagging, which affected the precision.

In order to explain the tagging errors, we investigated the 156 verbs that were incorrectly tagged as 1 in an exhaustive manner. Specifically, we looked into the performances of verbs and language examples composed of some testing frames in the corpus. We focused on the occurrences of verbs that were classified as non-autonomous but incorrectly tagged as 1 in the corpus. We found that the occurrences of the linguistic examples that matched these verbs were few in the corpus. For instance, "感觉, *gan3jue2, feel*" only occurred 20 times after being matched with the testing frame "wv 一下 w, *wv yi1xia4 w, wv a bit w*". The verb "包括, *bao1kuo4, including*" only occurred 14 times after being matched with a certain testing frame. This low occurrence was common among the 156 verbs that were investigated, with most verbs occurring less than 100 times. The low occurrences were not very persuasive in a large data corpus. In other words, the combination of the verbs and the testing frames does not comply with the language usage facts, suggesting that the verbs cannot be applied in these testing frames.

Therefore, it can be concluded that the 20% tagging errors are mostly attributed to the fact that the restrictions of previous searching process for the matching rules were too general. Specifically, if the verb and testing frame composed an example that had occurred in the corpus, the verb was recognized as an autonomous verb. This kind of recognition was too general.

6   Implications for Future Studies

The automatic recognition of matching rules presented in the current study is not detailed enough. In the present study, the verb is recognized as an autonomous verb if the combination of the verb and a certain testing frame (i.e. a language example) occurs in the corpus. There are no scientific restrictions on the occurring frequencies or the coordination between rules. In the meanwhile, the instances of abnormal single-action compacting (e.g., "百度一下, *bai3du4yi1xia4, searching a bit using Baidu*", "文艺一把, *wen2yi4yi1ba3, being arty a bit*") were not taken into sufficient consideration. A few things need to be improved in future studies:

(1) Through the statistics of the occurrence frequency of language examples, a Value can be chosen as a reference standard. For example, for verb v_1, if the occurrence frequency of "wv_1 一下 w, *wv_1 yi1xia4 w, wv_1 a bit w*" in the corpus is higher than the Value, the verb is considered successfully matched with the rules.

(2) Different rules in the rule set contribute differently to the recognition of autonomous verbs. Due to the time limit of the present study, it is not yet experimentally determined whether the validity of rules of different types is of equal value. In future studies, different weights can be assigned to different rules in identification and then the total score is evaluated, e.g. Score=αR1+βR2+γR3+δR4. Finally, the tagging of 1 or 0 is based on the Score.

(3) The experimental testing data are selected after the cross validation of the manual tagging by two linguistic students. The testing data may be scientifically inaccurate. Therefore, it is necessary to improve the approach of tagging testing data.

Acknowledgement

This paper is supported by the Fundamental Research Funds for the Central Universities, and the Research Funds of Beijing Language and Culture University(17YCX141).

References

1. Ma, Q.: The Chinese verb and verbal constructions (in Chinese). Peking University Press, Beijing (2004).
2. Ma, Q.: Autonomous verbs and non-autonomous verbs (in Chinese). Journal of Chinese Linguistics 3, 157-180 (1988).
3. Yuan, M.: A further discussion on the classification of non-autonomous verbs (in Chinese). Studies of the Chinese Language 4, 262-268 (1992).
4. Jiang, W.: On verbs of sensation or feelings (in Chinese). The Northern Forum 5, 61-63(2004).
5. Liu, C.: "N de A" phrase and non-autonomous verbs (in Chinese). Applied Linguistic Research7,35-36(2010).
6. Qiao, Q.: The research on semantic category of Chinese verb "Autonomous/non-autonomous" (in Chinese). Journal of Jilin Architectural and Civil Engineering 26, 117-120 (2009).
7. Gao, P.: Research on verb's restrictions in the format of "V + Yi-xia" (in Chinese). Journal of Gansu Radio& TV University 18(2), 16-18 (2008).
8. Zhou, X., Deng, X.: A comparative analysis on "Yizai" and "zaisan" (in Chinese). Chinese Language Learning 1, 61-64 (2002).
9. Wang, Z.: The choice of autonomous and non-autonomous verbs by passive expressions (in Chinese). Chinese Language Learning 6, 17-22 (2004).
10. Kang, S.: The development and application of modern Chinese new words information (electronic) dictionary (in Chinese). Lexicographical Studies 2, 55-63 (2001).
11. Lu, J.: Modern Chinese grammar research tutoria (in Chinese). Peking University Press, Beijing (2003).
12. Song, R.: On the fundamentality of language knowledge in NLP (in Chinese). Xiyuan Press, Beijing (2007).
13. Sun, M.: Natural language processing based on naturally annotated web resources (in Chinese). Journal of Chinese Information Processing 25(6), 26-32, (2011).
14. Xun, E., Rao, G., Xiao, X., Zang, J.: The construction of the BCC corpus in the age of big data (in Chinese). Corpus Linguistics 3(1), 93-109 (2016).

Disambiguating Polysemous Word Senses Based on Semantic Types and Syntactic Collocations: A Case Study of "*Zhongguo*+N"

Lulu Wang[1] and Meng Wang[2]

1. Department of Linguistics, Communication University of China, Beijing, China
e-mail: lulu.wang@cuc.edu.cn
2. School of Humanity, Jiangnan University, Wuxi, China
e-mail: wangmengly@163.com

Abstract. This paper deals with the polysemous words in noun compounds and investigates the relationship between their senses and the semantic types of the co-occurrent nouns. Taking "*Zhongguo*+N" as a studying case, we first review the senses of *Zhongguo* that are defined in Chinese Wordnet, WordNet and HowNet. Then we claim an innovative way of distinguishing the senses by integrating the semantic types based method and collocation based method. Afterwards, we focus on the noun compounds of "*Zhongguo*+N" and investigate the relationships between the semantic types of the collocating nouns and the different senses of *Zhongguo*. It turns out that the senses of the polysemous words are related to the semantic types of the co-occurrent nouns. In detail, the sense of culture highly relates to artificial objects, and the sense of location has more collocating nouns, while the sense of organization has the lowest frequency. These results show that the collocation information is the solid evidence for the sense distribution.

Keywords: Noun compounds, Polysemy, Word sense disambiguation, Semantic type, Syntactic collocation

1 Introduction

Polysemous words are words with multiple senses that are related with each other. It is not a challenge for people to distinguish the senses within a certain context, since the word sense is disambiguated automatically with the context. In contrast, it is an open problem of natural language processing, which is known as word-sense disambiguation (WSD). The solution to this problem impacts the result and the efficiency of other implementation tasks, such as noun compounds interpretation. For example,

(1) a. 99 届 的　　12 个 哈佛　MBA　　　　中国　学生　中，
99 year PART 12 CL Harvard MBA　　　China　student of
有　6 个 已　　回　　国。
have 6　CL already return country

© Springer International Publishing AG 2018
Y. Wu et al. (Eds.): CLSW 2017, LNAI 10709, pp. 255–262, 2018.
https://doi.org/10.1007/978-3-319-73573-3_22

"Of the twelve graduated Chinese students from the 1999 MBA class of Harvard, six have already came back to China."

b. 中国　国务院　　副 总理　　兼 外长　　　　　　　　　　钱 其琛

China State-Council vice premier and Minister-of-foreign-affairs Qian Qichen

率领　的　　中国 代表团　　出席 会议。

lead   PART China delegation attend meeting

"The Chinese delegation, which is headed by Chinese Vice Premier and Minister of foreign affairs Qian Qichen, attended the meeting."

c. 魏 明伦　说 《图兰多》是 "外国人 臆想　的　　中国 故事"。

Wei Minglun say Turandot COP foreigners imagine PART China story

"Wei Minglun said 'Turandot' is the 'Chinese story' that foreigners had imagined."

In (1a-c), "中国" (*Zhongguo*) is ambiguous. According to Chinese Wordnet, "中国" in (1a) refers to the name of the country. But the one in (1b) denotes either to the country, or the Chinese government. While the one in (1c) refers to the country or the Chinese culture. To admit that, the latter one is more appropriate in this context, in which "中国故事" (*Chinese stories*) refers to the stories featured with Chinese Culture. These three senses of the word "中国" are easy for people to understand. Since the senses appear in different contexts and thus the ambiguity issues resolve automatically. However, it is difficult for the computing systems to identify which sense of the word is used in a sentence. Especially, some disambiguation methods face the challenges of data sparsity with rare words or senses [1-2]. Moreover, it is not easy to acquire the context information. To solve this problem, a syntactic collocation method is more effective than the traditional way [3]. As noun compounds are very productive and easy to obtain, we could use noun compounds as the context for the polysemous words.

Previous studies of noun compounds focus on the interpretation issue [4-5], but lack the considerations on polysemy problems. Some researchers have noticed that some noun compounds have ambiguous meanings [6]. For example, "中国电影" (*Chinese movies*) is interpreted as "the movie produced/shoot/made in China" or "the movie from China". Obviously, "中国电影" is analyzed as a locative noun, which refers to the name of the country as (1a). In fact, "中国电影" can also be interpreted as "the movie featured with Chinese culture". It is necessary to investigate deeper to the polysemous relation in noun compounds.

Recent studies on word-sense disambiguation tasks include vector-space based word sense induction [1] and concept based neural language models [7]. In the latter case, it discovers the shared concepts among senses. For instance, the senses of *apple* are presented as two concepts: fruit and company. Here, the concepts are also known as the semantic types. Similar to the studies in noun compounds, there is a relationship between the semantic types of the nouns and the interpretation patterns [6]. Following this idea, we investigate the relation between the senses of the polysemous words and the semantic types of the co-occurrent nouns in noun compounds.

This paper is organized as follows: we first review the senses of *Zhongguo* that are defined in the three representative lexical resources, including Chinese Wordnet, Word-Net and HowNet. Then we claim a new way of distinguishing the senses by integrating the semantic types based method and collocation based method. In section three, we focus on the noun compounds of "*Zhongguo*+N" and investigate the relationships between the semantic types of the collocating nouns and the different senses of *Zhongguo*. Based on the statistical data, we further generate the semantic types distribution of its senses. Section four is the conclusion.

2   Distinguishing the Senses of Polysemy Words

In traditional dictionaries, a word meaning is represented as a sense or a lexeme. But such defining method is controversial, since there is lack of a unified understanding of the word. In WordNet, the senses are defined as concepts, which are represented as synonymy sets (synsets). These ideas distinguish the words from the semantic perspective. An alternative way is to define the word sense as the occurrences of the word in context [8]. As for our task, these methods have pros and cons. In the following, we take *Zhongguo* as an example and compare its senses in Chinese Wordnet, WordNet and HowNet. Then, we analyze the collocation data of the noun compounds and thus suggest a semantic type and syntactic collocation unified method of word sense disambiguation.

2.1   Senses of *Zhongguo* defined in Chinese Wordnet, WordNet and HowNet

Chinese Wordnet[1] is a natural language processing platform developed by the Central Research Institute of Taiwan, China. It defines the senses based on the empirical evidence from the Sinica Corpus[2]. There are three senses of *Zhongguo* defined in Chinese Wordnet: (1) locative noun: the name of the nation, the country that lies in the eastern Asia, east to the Pacific, north to Russia, the most populous country in the world; (2) proper noun: the government governing China; (3) common noun: Chinese culture.

It is obvious that the senses defined in this way are clear and easy to understand. But it is controversial of the correctness of the definition. Instead, other lexical resources adopt the concept based or the collocation based way to distinguish the word senses.

Wordnet[3], developed by Princeton University, is a lexical database for English, which is also the most notorious concept based corpus. The word senses are defined as

---

[1] http://lope.linguistics.ntu.edu.tw/cwn/

[2] Sinica Corpus (Academia Sinica Balanced Corpus of Modern Chinese) is a large balanced corpus of Modern Chinese, please see: http://www.sinica.edu.tw/SinicaCorpus/

[3] http://wordnet.princeton.edu/

synonyms sets (synsets). To take *China* as an example, its lexical entry is defined as follows:

> S: (n) China, People's Republic of China, mainland China, Communist China, Red China, PRC, Cathay (a communist nation that covers a vast territory in eastern Asia; the most populous country in the world)
>
> S: (n) china (high quality porcelain originally made only in China)

As is shown above, *China* corresponds to two homographs in English, which are *China* and *china*. As for the senses of *China*, the definition is represented as the synonym sets, which includes People's Republic of China, mainland China, Communist China, Red China, etc.

Among the Chinese lexical resources, HowNet and Chinese Concept Dictionary are also based on concepts. In **HowNet**[4], the concept is represented as sememes. The sememes are the smallest units. In defining the words, HowNet focuses on the relationship between concepts and features, which in total is like a concept net. For example, *Zhongguo* is defined as follows:

> DEF={RelatingToCountry|与特定国家相关:RelateTo="China|中国"}
>
> DEF={place|地方:PlaceSect={country|国家},belong="Asia|亚洲",
>
> domain={politics|政},modifier={ProperName|专}}

Such concept based resources can avoid the controversial differences caused by the traditional definition method. Moreover, concepts are more easily to retrieve in NLP tasks, such as the retrieval and cluster issue of concepts [7]. They view the concepts as sets of similar meanings. Then, if we want to locate the proper word sense, we just need to locate the concept that fits in the context. Then we search for other words that belong to the concept. Thus, this method finds a way to acquire the context information, which is very illuminating.

2.2   Collocation Based Method

In data driven methods, some scholars distinguish the word senses by syntactic information, in which the word sense is defined as the occurrences of the word in context [8]. An alternative method is a vector based semantic composition one in a statistical way [9]. Specifically, the word that are not obviously distinguished in traditional dictionaries could be clearly distinguished by syntactic allocations [3]. For example, "发表" (*publish*) has two senses based on the *Modern Chinese Dictionary*: the first one refers to suggesting advices to the community; the second one means publishing articles, painting and songs in published units. When "发表" (*publish*) collocates with "意见" (*comments*), it refers to the first meaning, but when it collocates with "文章" (*articles*), it denotes to the second meaning.

In light of this idea, we use noun compounds as the context of the polysemous words. In the next section, we will investigate the relationships between different senses of *Zhongguo* and the semantic types of the collocating words.

---

[4] http://www.keenage.com/

3   The Collocations of Noun Compounds

We make use of the semantic types from the *Chinese Semantic Dictionary* as the concept types. This dictionary is constructed on WordNet and classify the semantics of nouns into five categories, including concrete entity, abstract entity, process, time and space. There are 1522 annotated senses of 671 polysemous words [10].

Due to the limitedness of the experimental condition, we only investigate the binary noun compounds, which are the most frequently used patterns[5]. We find 500 results of "中国$4的"[6] from the CCL corpus of Chinese texts[7]. Then we select 75 binary noun compounds among them. Adding 38 noun compounds from the literature, we have 113 noun compounds in total. We annotate these noun compounds with the senses of *Zhongguo* and the semantic types of the collocating nouns. Based on this annotated data, we have derived the relationship between the word sense of the first noun of the compound and the semantic type of the second one. To be convenient, we also use the semantic type to denote the senses of *Zhongguo*. According to the previous definition from Chinese Wordnet, we represent them as "处所|机构|文化" (*location | organization | culture*). Afterwards, we make a statistical analysis of the annotated data, and the different senses of *Zhongguo* show different tendencies.

First, in the noun compound of "*Zhongguo*+N", the most frequently used sense is "处所" (*location*), then goes with "文化" (*culture*), while the sense of "机构" (*organization*) is the least frequent.

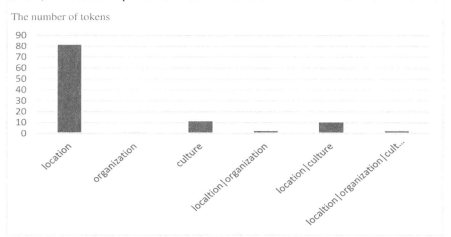

Fig. 1. The senses of *Zhongguo* in "*Zhongguo*+N"

---

[5] According to the statistical results, binary noun compounds are the most frequently used noun compounds (77%) [4].

[6] The sequence means to return the strings of less than four characters between "中国" and "的".

[7] http://ccl.pku.edu.cn:8080/ccl_corpus/index.jsp?dir=xiandai

Second, the collocating nouns with the sense of "处所" (*location*) cover the widest range of semantic types, including concrete entity, abstract entity, process, time and space.

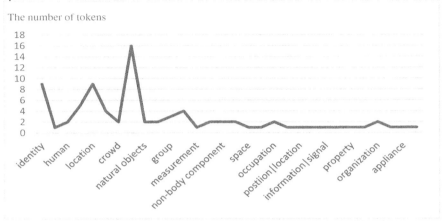

Fig. 2. The semantic types of the nouns collocating with the sense of location

It is shown in the above figure that the most frequent collocating semantic types are domain, identity and location. For example, "史学" (*history studies*) in "中国史学" (*Chinese history studies*) belongs to the semantic type of domain, "学生" (*student*) in "中国学生" (*Chinese student*) corresponds to the type of identity, and "北京" (*Beijing*) in "中国北京" (*Beijing of China*) denotes to the type of location. In contrast, the other types are much less frequent. In addition, figure 1 and figure 2 both illustrate that "处所" (*location*) is the most frequently used sense.

Third, the semantic types that go with "文化" (*culture*) have significant features, most of which belong to the types of artificial objects, construction and tools. Also, the semantic type of consciousness is related to the human factor.

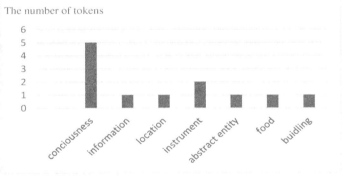

Fig. 3. The semantic types of the nouns collocating with the sense of culture

Fourth, the nouns that collocate with all three senses of "处所|机构|文化" (*location | organization | culture*) belong to the type of vague property, such as "方面" (*aspect*) in "中国方面" (*the Chinese*), "特色" (*characteristics*) in "中国特色" (*Chinese characteristics*), and "形象" (*image*) in "中国形象" (*Chinese image*) all belong to the type of vague feature. Because of this vagueness, there is no strict limitations of the collocating nouns, and thus it could collocate with the word of multiple senses.

5   Conclusion

This paper deals with the relationship between the senses of polysemous words with the collocating nouns in binary noun compounds. We take "*Zhongguo*+N" as the research object, firstly compare the senses of *Zhongguo* in Chinese Wordnet, WordNet and HowNet. We believe that the semantic types based method is more solid that it could avoid the problems of the subjective predictions. Also, the collocation based method is more objective. Thus, we unify the two methods and suggest a semantic type and collocation integrated method as the criteria to distinguish the senses.

Based on the real data, we find out that there are certain relationships between the word senses of *Zhongguo* and the semantic types of the collocating nouns. For example, the sense of culture is highly related to artificial objects, and the sense of location has the widest range of collocating categories, while the sense of organization is the least frequently used. According to these statistical data, we conclude that: on one hand, it is necessary for us to distinguish the different senses in interpreting noun compounds; on the other hand, we can also make use of noun compounds as the context for the syntactic distributions of the different senses, and thus to provide the solid evidence for word sense disambiguation.

The article is just an elementary analysis in disambiguating the polysemous words in noun compounds, which requires much more data to be proved. There are also many other areas that are related to the topic, such as noun compounds interpretation, paraphrasing, and other natural language processing tasks.

Acknowledgments

We would like to thank the anonymous reviewers of CLSW 2017 for the comments. Thanks also go to the Natural Social Science Foundation of China (12&ZD175), the Natural Science Foundation of China (61300152) and the Research Project of Communication University of China (CUC16B09) for the support.

References

1. Reisinger J., Mooney R. J.: Multi-prototype vector-space models of word meaning. In Proceedings of NAACL 2010, 201: 109-117 (2010).
2. Pina L. N., Johnson R.: A Simple and Efficient Method to Generate Word Sense Representations. ArXiv preprint arXiv: 1412. 6045 (2014).

3. Wu, Y-F.: The Principles and Methods of Sense Discrimination for Chinese Language Processing, Applied Linguistics, 2 (2006). [In Chinese]
4. Wang, M.: Linguistic Knowledge Acquisition of Noun for the Construction of Probabilistic Lexical Knowledge-base. Ph.D. Dissertation, Peking University (2010). [In Chinese]
5. Wang, L-L., Wang M.: A Study on the Taxonomy of Chinese Noun Compounds. In proceedings of CLSW 2015 (2015).
6. Wei, X.: Research on Chinese Noun Compound Interpretation for Semantic-Query. Master Thesis. Peking University (2012). [In Chinese]
7. Cheng J-P., Wang Z-Y., Wen J-R., Yan J., Chen, Z.: Contextual Text Under-standing in Distributional Semantic Space. In Proceedings of CIKM 2015 (2015).
8. Kilgarriff, A.: I don' t believe in word senses. Computers and the Humanities, 31: 91-113 (1997).
9. Blacoe, W., Lapata M.: A Comparison of vector-based representations for semantic composition. In Proceedings of EMNLP 2012, 546-556 (2012).
10. Wang, H.: A syntagmatic study on noun senses in contemporary Chinese. Peking University Press (2004). [In Chinese]

Extracting Opinion Targets and Opinion Words with CenterNP and syntactic-semantic features

Jing Wang[1]

[1] Beijing Normal University, Beijing 100875, China
Wangjing1204@foxmail.com

Abstract. Extracting opinion targets and opinion words from online reviews are 2 fundamental tasks in opinion mining. This paper proposed a novel approach to collectively extract them with centerNP and other syntactic and semantic features. Researching on the models of opinion targets and words on their syntactic and semantic features through HNC theory, this paper found that the opinion targets are some special noun phases (NP), and we named them centerNPs which are made up with conceptual categories g,r,z,pw,ww and v, and their syntactic position must be in chunk GBK. So this paper extracted the centerNPs as the candidate of the opinion targets, and introduced other syntactic and semantic features such as syntactic position of opinion targets, the conceptual categories and contextual features of opinion targets and opinion words. The experimental results showed that our approach achieved a good performance.

Keywords: opinion mining, sentiment analysis, centerNP, syntactic-semantic features, HNC theory

1 Introduction

In opinion mining, extracting opinion targets and opinion words are 2 fundamental subtasks. Opinion targets are objects about which users' opinions are expressed, and opinion words are words which indicate opinions' polarities. Extracting them can provide essential information for obtaining fine-gained analysis on customers' opinion. Thus, it had attracted a lot of attentions (Hu and Liu, 2004b; Liu et al., 2012; Mukherjee and Liu, 2012).

To this end, previous work usually employed a collective extraction strategy (Qiu et al., 2009; Hu and Liu, 2004b). Their intuition is: do syntactic analysis for every opinion sentences by some parsers like Stanford Parser; opinion targets and opinion words always co-occur with opinion words in sentences, and there are strong modification relationship between them (called opinion relation in (Liu et al. ,2012)). If a word is an opinion word, other words having opinion relation with it will be its opinion targets. Among the works which employed this widely used approach, almost everyone had defined the nouns /noun phases as the candidate of the opinion targets and the verbs/adjectives as the candidate of the opinion words, and limited the opin-

© Springer International Publishing AG 2018
Y. Wu et al. (Eds.): CLSW 2017, LNAI 10709, pp. 263–274, 2018.
https://doi.org/10.1007/978-3-319-73573-3_23

ion relation to modified or dominated relationship. Although the strategy has been widely employed by previous works, it still has its limitation.

1) Can all the nouns/noun phases be the candidate of opinion targets?

When extracting the opinion targets, almost every previous works set the NP(nouns/noun phases) as the default candidate, (Zhu, Cun-Qing and Zhang,2010; Liu, Xu and Zhao,2014) identifying the NP to extract the opinion targets with some pruning approaches. But NP is a very complex structure with hierarchical attributes which is the largest distraction for opinion targets extraction. For example "*配件的价格*(the price of accessories)", "*ISO感光度的调整功能*(the function of adjustment for ISO sensitivity)" (the words with underline is the attribute of the NP). Jun Zhao (1999) proposed the Chinese base noun phrase called base NP for short which was defined as:

- baseNP →baseNP ＋baseNP
- baseNP →baseNP ＋ noun|noun-verb
- baseNP → limiting attribute ＋ baseNP
- baseNP →limiting attribute ＋ noun|noun-verb
- limiting attribute → adjective|distinguishing words|verb|noun|
              location words|wester words|(numeral + quantifiers)

According to the definition of the baseNP, the attributes of a baseNP contains adjective, distinguishing words, verb, noun and so on, and some of them are not the part of opinion target, sometimes they would be the opinion words.

Summarizing the expression models of opinion targets from their inherent structure in opinion reviews, this paper proposed a conceptual of centerNP as the candidate of opinion targets.

2)   Does the opinion target collocate with opinion words immediately?

Most of the opinion words are adjective or verbs, and opinion targets are NPs, so the previous works always define their opinion relations as modified or dominated relations, like "精致的屏幕(clear screen)", "性价比很高(post performance is high)".

So opinion words and opinion targets were extracted by setting a window, and their distance is 4 to 6 characters around the opinion words to detected whether there were opinion target(Liu&Hu, 2004). But this method ignored the far collocation relationship of the opinion targets and words, like the following sentences:

这个价格对于20x刻录机来讲是相当便宜的。(This price for 20x CD writer is quite cheap.) The opinion word 便宜(cheap) collocates far with the target (price) , they don't modified with each other immediately. So this paper introduced the HNC parser to parse a sentence into several chunks, and set 3 hierarchical detections to recognize the opinion words and targets in order to avoid the drawback of setting windows.

3)   Ignore the semantic feature of the opinion target.

The previous works always took the syntactic features into consideration but always ignored the semantic ones. For example, the semantic conceptual categories of an opinion target always present a "specific object" instead of a humanity concept.

To remedy this defect we introduce the conceptual categories of Hierarchical Network of Concepts (HNC) theory (Huang, 1998; Miao, 2005) in this paper. HNC theory divides the concept in the world into 6 global conceptual categories, they are dynamic concept(V) , abstract static concept(G), specific object concept (W), humanity concept(P), attribute concept(U) and logical concept (L), all of them have sub-concept. Some conceptual categories had been used in this paper to pruning the centerNP that didn't accord with the rules.

Thus, to resolve the problems above, we presented a novel approach with centerNP and the syntactic-semantic features of opinion targets and opinion words. Firstly, we introduced the HNC parser to parse the sentences, and get the categories of every word for the sentences; secondly, researched on the syntactic structures of a parsed sentence, the syntactic features of opinion words and targets with their collocation relations were recognized for their extraction. Thirdly, the candidates of opinion targets were recognized by centerNP with excluding unmatched conceptual categories. At last, an experiment on real-world datasets from different domains were performed, the results showed that the approach we proposed were effective.

2   Related work

There are many significant research efforts on opinion targets/words extraction by statistics method, rule-based method and rule-statistics methods.

For the statistics methods, many works set the opinion words/targets as a linear tagging tasks with some classifier like CRF(Li and Huang, 2010) and SVM(Wu and Zhang, 2009).

For the rule-based method, most works had find the syntactic structures between opinion words and targets after sentences parsing, and then extracted the opinion words and targets, the common parsers are Stanford Parse and LTP of Harbin Institute of Technology. Hu and liu (2004) first put forward the task of opinion targets extraction, after dependency parsing they extracted the opinion targets by association method and divided the opinion targets into common and uncommon types. For the common targets, they extracted them first and extracted all the nearest adjectives as pinion words; for the uncommon ones, they set the adjective as the candidate of opinion words first and extracted the nearest NP as the opinion targets. The limitation of the method is they only selected the adjective as the opinion and ignore the syntactic structures of the opinion words and targets. Liu, Zhao and Qin et al. (2010) improved the pruning method of opinion phrases base on the work of Hu and Liu. They mainly used the word frequency to filter the NP appeared infrequently by PMI algorithm in order to mine the more accurate opinion targets. Wang and Wu (2011) classified the modified structure of opinion words-targets after phrase parsing into 5 types to extract them. But the collocation of opinion words and targets contains are not only modified relation but also the others like govern and be governed, far collocation and so on. Huang and Pu(2011) proposed a phrase tree structure to present the appraisal expression pattern, as well as a method based on approximate convolution tree kernels to calculate the similarity between the structures, and then extracted the opinion expressions. Zhao, Qin and Che et al. (2011) proposed a method that used syntactic paths to automatically recognize the opinion expressions. But the approaches above all concentrated on the syntactic structures but ignored the semantic features.

The method based on the rule-based and statistics always tagged the phrase or dependency parsing results on the opinion corpus, and trained them by the classifier machine like CRF and SVM to extract the relation between opinion words and targets, like in Kolya and Das (2011), Xia and Du (2014). But this approaches only used the syntactic structures without semantic features.

It is concluded that most previous works will introduce the NLP technology like phrase or dependency parsing to solve the task of opinion words/targets, but most works had limited the opinion words as adjective and the opinion targets as NP which didn't accord with the real corpus, and the semantic features in the sentences always were ignored.

3   The method based on CenterNP and syntactic-semantic features

In this section, we proposed our method in details, the CenterNP, HNC Parser with its syntactic structure and HNC semantic features of conceptual categories would get a detail explanation.

3.1   The Introduction of CenterNP

The paper first research on the 1979 opinion targets of camera reviews in Dataset2 of COAE 2008(Zhao, Xu et al., 2008), and summed up their models and distribution, the results are as follows:

Table 1. The models and distrbution of opinion targets

Models	Examples	Num	Frequency
w	白平衡(white balance)	1117	56.44%
w w	按键布局(keyboard arrangement)	681	34.41%
w w w	背景虚化效果(background bokeh effect)	106	5.36%
w DE w	配件的价格(price of attachment)	43	2.17%
w DE w w	白平衡的调节方式 (accommodation mode of white balance)	12	0.61%
w w w w	图像细节捕捉能力 (image detail capture capacity)	8	0.40%
w w DE w	操作按键的布局 (arrangement of operating keyboard)	8	0.40%
w w DE w w	ISO感光度的调整功能	2	0.10%

	(adjustment function of ISO sensitivity)		
w w w DE w	照片写入存储卡的时间 (time of photos writing into SD)	1	0.05%
w + w w	手柄和镜头位置(hand shank and shot position)	1	0.05%

In table 1, "w" presents a word with whose semantic conceptual categories is g, r, z, pw, ww, v and h$g, the meaning of the letters will be explained in the following chapter.

The models of the opinion targets are the parallel, cascade and parallel-cascade with some special conceptual categories. Usually, a NP has poly-attribute, and the most nearest attribute of the head word (the last word of a NP) is nouns or verbs presented materials, property or the scope (Huang and Liao, 2007) which would add the vocabulary semantic elements to the head word, and the combination of this kind of attribute and the head word must be at the center of a NP, so we named it CenterNP, according to the definition of baseNP, we defined CenterNP as follows:

$$\begin{aligned}
&\text{centerNP} \rightarrow \text{centerNP} + \text{centerNP} \\
&\text{centerNP} \rightarrow \text{centerNP DE centerNP} \\
&\text{centerNP} \rightarrow \text{centerNP} \\
&\text{centerNP} \rightarrow \text{w} + \text{word} \\
&\text{centerNP} \rightarrow \text{w (DE) w} \\
&\text{w} \rightarrow \text{SPN|pw|ww|g|r|z|v|qh}
\end{aligned} \tag{1}$$

In equation (1), "+" presents coordination relationship, "DE" presents modification relationship, "|" presents selection, "()" presents not essential. The semantic conceptual category of w has been explained in chapter 3.3.

From the models and distribution of opinion targets, CenterNP can be the candidate of opinion target. But not all the CenterNP can be the opinions; the syntactic and semantic features must be taken into consideration.

3.2   The semantic conceptual categories of CenterNP in HNC parsing

The former chapter had talked about the Generalize Conceptual Categories (GCC) of HNC, and all 6 kinds of the GCC have sub-level Conceptual Categories called CC. Here are the conceptual categories that would be used in recognize the CenterNP:

Table 2. The Conceptual Categories Of A Word In Centernp

GCC	CC	Conceptual categories	举例
SPN	SPN	figure or letter	LCD、MPEG4
W	pw	artificiality	mouse、battery
	ww	lifeless things	menu、photo
G	g	static conception	function、quality
	r	effect	effect

	z	value	speed、 cost performance
V	v	dynamic concept	take (a photo)、 charge (a battery)
QH	qh	affix	card
L	l4	logic sign for 2 object inside a chunk	DE, and

Table 3. The Details Of "Qh"

qh	Details	example
h$g	noun-postfix	-性(-ity)、 -感(-ness)
q$u	adjective-affix	可- （-able）
q$v	verb-affix	预- （pro-）
h$v	verb-postfix	-化(-ize)
h$w	postfix for things	-卡(-card)

3.3   The syntactic analysis of HNC parsing

The HNC parser was a rule-based system developed by Institute of Chinese Information Processing, Beijing Normal University based on the theory of Hierarchical Network Concept. An opinion text can be divided into several big sentences named CS and the punctuations at the end of the sentences like period, and a CS can be divided into several small sentences named SS and the sign for dividing the SS named SST like comma, and a SS can be divided into 3 kinds of chunks ABK, GBK, EK and some logical sign L0 like the word "把"(ba), chunk ABK is the an auxiliary chunk for SS corresponding to the adverbial modifier in the classical linguistics approximately, EK is the essential part of a SS contains the core predicate named E and its adverbial modifier named QE and complement named HE, and the GBK is always the subject and object in a SS. The syntactic analyses of HNC parsing are as follows:

$$TEXT(sentiment) = \sum(CS + funtucations\ at\ the\ end\ of\ a\ sentences) \qquad (2)$$

$$CS = \sum(SS + SST) \qquad (3)$$

$$SS = (ABK, GBK, EK_n, L0) \qquad (4)$$

$$EK = QE_n + E + HE_n \qquad (5)$$

The letter "n" indicated the level of an EK in SS, here is a sentence parsed by HNC Parser:

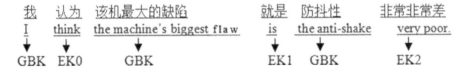

Fig. 1. A sentence parsed by HNC Parser. There are 3 GBK in the SS, and 3 EK with different level,EK0 is the highest, EK1 is the middle one and EK2 is the lowest.

The generalized list of the sentence is:

(CS (SS (GBK 我)(EK0 认为)(GBK 该机最大的缺陷) (EK1 就是) (GBK 防抖性)(EK (QE 非常非常)(E 差)))。)

(CS (SS (GBK I)(EK0 think)(GBK the machine's biggest flaw) (EK1 is) (GBK anti-shake)(EK (QE very very)(E poor))).)

The syntactic features of CenterNP. An opinion targets in a sentence must be a subject or objective ignoring the ABK, so the candidate CenterNP of a opinion target must be in the chunk GBK, it can be the whole GBK or a part of a GBK. For example:

(GBK 这部手机的功能)(EK (QE 很)(E 强大))。 The mobile's function is very powerful.

(GBK 手机的功能)(EK (QE 很)(E 强大))。   A mobile's function is very powerful.

The phrase with emphasis point is a CenterNP as well as the opinion targets in the sentence, the words with underline is the opinion words of the sentences.

Moreover, the conceptual categories of the GBK contains CenterNP must not express the humanity concept.

The syntactic relationship of opinion words with opinion targets. The previous works for extracting opinion targets/words always set a 4-6 size window around opinion targets/words to detect the other. But if the collocation distance between opinion targets and words exceed the window, it would fail to extract the opinion targets and words.

The opinion words usually are adjectives, verbs and some nouns (the Generalized Conceptual Categories are U, V and G), so the opinion words can be in GBK and EK, and the targets are in GBK. This paper researched the syntactic relationship between opinion words and targets in details based on the results of HNC Parser, and summarized the their relative positions in a sentence, and table 4 had listed the syntactic positions and their collocation models.

Table 4. the syntactic position and collocation models of opinion words and targets

Position	Collocation Models	Examples
In the same GBK	OP+centerNP	(GBK *(OP 精致的)*(centerNP 做工)) (delicate work)
		(GBK *(OP 不错)*(DE 的)(centerNP 影像质量)) (good image quality)
	centerNP++OP+centerNP	(GBK (centerNP 做工)*(OP 精致)*(DE 的)(centerNP 手机)) (a mobile with delicate work)
		(GBK 如此 *(OP 强大)* (centerNP 功能) (DE

		的)(centerNP 手动相机))
		(such a manual mobile with powerful function)
In different chunks of a SS	OP ++centerNP	(EK *(OP 喜欢)*)(GBK 这种(centerNP 屏幕))
		(like this kind of screen)
		(GBK (centerNP 开关机速度))(EK 很 *(OP 快)*) (the speed of startup & shutdown is high)
		(GBK (centerNP 开关机速度)(EK 没有)(GBK 一点*(OP 瑕疵)*)(there is no flaw of the speed of startup & shutdown)
In different SS	centerNP++SST++OP	(GBK (centrtNP 短信提示音的铃声选择方面))，仅提供5种 (SST，)(EK (QE 有些)(E *(OP 遗憾)*))。 (about the ring selection of note warning, it only offered 5, which is regreted.)

The relative syntactic positions of opinion words and target can be divided into 3 types, that is all of them in a same GBK, one in GBK and another in EK or different GBK of a SS, in different SS. The "+" presents collocation, "++" presents far collocation relationship, and the collocations between opinion targets and words have several types, here only listed the common ones.

3.4   The arithmetic of extracting opinion words and targets.

From the analysis above, CenterNP is the key of recognizing opinion targets, and it can be the candidate of opinion targets when they in the GBK without expressing humanity concept, and only the candidates were collocated with opinion words can they be extracted as opinion targets. Considering about that, this paper constructed the arithmetic of extracting opinion words and targets:

Parameter definition: OT presents opinion targets, OW presents opinion words, OS presents opinion sentences, Syn(X) presents the syntactic position of X, Sem(X) presents the semantic conceptual category of X;

Input: the set of opinion sentences OSSET

Output: dualistic group <OT, OW>

Step1. Parse every sentences in OSSET and get the GBK;
Step2. For GBKi,while Sem(GBKi) <> P, extract centerNP in GBKi, and get centerNPi;
Step3. Recognize OP,get OPi;
Step4. For every OPi
    IF Syn (OP$_i$) = GBK, detected centerNP$_i$ forward in GBK;
        IF a centerNP$_i$ is detected, then OT = centerNP$_i$, OP=OP$_i$;
        ELSE IF detects backwards, get centerNP$_i$, then OT=centerNP$_i$,OP=OP$_i$;

ESEIF Syn(OP$_i$)=EK and Sem(OP$_i$)=u, then detect cen-
terNP$_i$ in the SS forward;
    IF centerNP$_i$ can be detected, then OT= the most
nearest centerNP$_i$, OP=OP$_i$;
    ELSE IF detects backwards, get centerNP$_i$, then OT=
the most nearest centerNP$_i$, OP=OP$_i$;
    ELSE IF detected backwards crossing SST , find the
nearest centerNP$_i$, then OT=centerNP$_i$, OP=OP$_i$;
    ELSEIF Syn(OP$_i$)=EK and Sem(OP$_i$)=v, then detect cen-
terNP$_i$ in the SS backwards;
    IF centerNP$_i$ can be detected, then OT= the most
nearest centerNP$_i$, OP=OP$_i$;
    ELSE IF detects forward, get centerNP$_i$, OT= the
most nearest centerNP$_i$, OP=OP$_i$;
    ELSE IF detects forward crossing SST, find the
nearest centerNP$_i$, then OT=centerNP$_i$, OP=OP$_i$;
    ELSE detects failed, the OP$_i$ has not its relative
OT.

Step5. End ,output <OT,OP>.

4   Experiments

4.1   Datasets

Dataset for opinion targets extraction. This paper used the dataset2[1] of COAE 2008 as the test corpus which contains Chinese reviews about five products. The corpus has 473 passages and about 3000 sentences in total. Most sentences are subjective and some are objective, the four products are notebook, mobile, digital camera and cars.

    In order to reduce the influence of parsing results, this paper selected randomly 20 passages from every domain to parse and check the parsing results manually. Here are the details of the selected 80 passages:

Table 5. the details of test dataset

domain	Passage number	Sentence number	Opinion target number
Notebook	20	420	402
Mobile phone	20	387	341
Car	20	422	353
Digital Camera	20	250	254

The lexicon of opinion words. This paper constructed a lexicon of opinion words by some common sentiment lexicon used widely, they are: the Chinese sentiment lexicon

---

[1]   http://ir-china.org.cn/coae2008.html

of Hownet[2] (Dong and Dong, 2000), the NTUSD[3] of Taiwan University, emotional word ontology of Dalian University of Technology(Xu, Lin et al., 2008), Chinese appraisal lexicon of Tsinghua University(Guo,1999; Wang, 2001; Shi,2005; Li, 2007). By combining the lexicons above, taking out the repeated words and added some online words like "给力"(powerful), "点赞"(support), we got a lexicon contains 13995 opinion words with 6987 positive words, 6634 negative words and 74 words related to the context. Most words' conceptual categories are U and V, some are G, like "缺点"(flaw).

4.2   The Results and Analysis

This paper extracted the opinion targets/words on the checked results of HNC parsing with the method we proposed, the results are shown in table 6.

Table 6. The Extraction Results of Using CenterNP and Syntactic-Semantic Featurs

domain	results		
	Precision	Recall	F-measure
Notebook	87.50%	60.87%	71.79%
Mobile phone	84.38%	62.79%	72.00%
Digital Camera	**91.18%**	64.58%	**75.61%**
Car	68.85%	**64.62%**	66.67%
average	82.98%	**63.22%**	71.52%

According to table 6, the task of extracting the opinion words and targets got a good result, the average of precision is 82.98%, average of recall is 63.22% and the average of F-measure is 71.52%, among which the results on digital camera get the best precision 91.18% and F-measure 75.61%. It was proved that the method based on CenterNP and syntactic – semantic features we proposed in the paper was effective.

But the table 6 also showed that the results on car domain was lower than the other domains, its F-measure only was 66.67%; and the recall on the 4 domains was lower than precision especially on the digital camera domain. According to research on the corpus, we got the reasons as follows:

1. The models and syntactic position of opinion targets on car are more complex than on digital camera. The opinion targets of car sometimes appear in chunk ABK which wasn't processed specially; and the construction of opinion targets on car is more complex and long than others.
2. The conceptual category g which made up the CenterNP is too broad and covers too many words like "东西(thing)", "事情(thing)" which are widely used and have no actual functions for opinion targets extraction. It is the reason for the low recall.

---

[2]   http://www.keenage.com/html/c_bulletin_2007.htm
[3]   http://www.data-tang.com/data/11837

5   Conclusion

This paper presented a novel method with CenterNP and syntactic-semantic features to co-extract opinion words and targets. We introduced the HNC Parser to parse the sentences based on HNC theory. By researching the models of opinion targets on the real corpus, a new concept CenterNP was proposed as the candidate of opinion targets. Combining the CenterNP with syntactic analysis and semantic conceptual categories, an algorithm of extracting opinion targets and words was proposed, and the results of the experiment showed the method was effective.

References

1. Hu M, Liu B. Mining and summarizing customer reviews[C]//Proceedings of the tenth ACM SIGKDD international conference on Knowledge discovery and data mining. ACM, 2004: 168-177.
2. Hu M, Liu B. Mining and summarizing customer reviews[C]//Proceedings of the tenth ACM SIGKDD international conference on Knowledge discovery and data mining. ACM, 2004: 168-177.
3. Huang B, Liao X. Modern Chinese[J]. the 4th additional edition, 2007:83-92.
4. Huang Y H, Pu X J, Yuan C F, et al. Appraisal expression extraction based on parse tree structure[J]. Jisuanji Yingyong Yanjiu, 2011, 28(9): 3229-3234.
5. Huang Z. The Hierarchical Network of Concepts theory[J]. 1998.
6. Kolya A K, Das D, Ekbal A, et al. Identifying event: sentiment association using lexical equivalence and co-reference approaches[C]//Proceedings of the ACL 2011 Workshop on Relational Models of Semantics. Association for Computational Linguistics, 2011: 19-27.
7. Li F, Han C, Huang M, et al. Structure-aware review mining and summarization[C]//Proceedings of the 23rd International Conference on Computational Linguistics. Association for Computational Linguistics, 2010: 653-661.
8. Liu H, Zhao Y, Qin B, et al. Comment target extraction and sentiment classification[J]. Journal of Chinese Information Processing, 2010, 24(1): 84-88.
9. Liu K, Xu L, Zhao J. Extracting opinion targets and opinion words from online reviews with graph co-ranking[C]//Proceedings of the 52nd Annual Meeting of the Association for Computational Linguistics. 2014, 1: 314-324.
10. Miao C J. HNC (Hierarchical network of concepts) theory introduction[J]. 2005.
11. Moghaddam S, Ester M. On the design of LDA models for aspect-based opinion mining[J]. Cikm, 2012:803-812.
12. Qiu G, Liu B, Bu J, et al. Expanding domain sentiment lexicon through double propagation[J]. International Joint Conference on Artificial Intelligence Proceedings, 2009, 38(4):1199-1204.
13. Wang F, Wu Y, Xu Y, et al. Predicting the Semantic Orientation of Word Collocations[C][D]. The proceedings of the Third Chinese Opinion Analysis Evaluation(COAE 2011).Jinan,2011:5-25.
14. Wu Y, Zhang Q, Huang X, et al. Phrase dependency parsing for opinion mining[C]//Proceedings of the 2009 Conference on Empirical Methods in Natural Language Processing: Volume 3-Volume 3. Association for Computational Linguistics, 2009: 1533-1541.

15. XIA M, DU Y, ZUO B. Micro-blog opinion analysis based on syntactic dependency and feature combination[J]. Journal of Shandong University (Natural Science), 2014, 11: 004.
16. Zhao J, Xu H, Huang X, et al. Overview of chinese opinion analysis evaluation 2008[J]. Proceedings of the First Chinese Opinion Analysis Evaluation, 2008.
17. Zhao Y Y, Qin B, Che W X, et al. Appraisal Expression Recognition Based on Syntactic Path[J]. Journal of Software, 2011, 22(5): 887-898.
18. Zhu Z Y, Cun-Qing L I, Zhang P. Topic Words And Opinion Words Extraction From Chinese Product Reviews Based On Syntax Pattern[J]. Journal of Chongqing University of Technology, 2010.

Acquiring Selectional Preferences for Knowledge Base Construction

Yuxiang Jia, Yuguang Li, and Hongying Zan

School of Information Engineering, Zhengzhou University, China
{ieyxjia,iehyzan}@zzu.edu.cn,liyuguang1993@163.com

Abstract. Selectional preference, or SP, is an important lexical knowledge that can be applied to many natural language processing tasks, like semantic error detection, metaphor detection, word sense disambiguation, syntactic parsing, semantic role labeling, and machine translation. This paper studies semantic class level SP acquisition for knowledge base construction. Firstly, the noun taxonomy of SKCC, a Semantic Knowledge-base of Contemporary Chinese, is adjusted for SP acquisition. Secondly, a MDL-based tree cut model is implemented. Thirdly, SP in SKCC is introduced as the source of gold standard test set to evaluate SP acquisition performance. Three kinds of predicate-argument relations are investigated in the experiments, including verb-object, verb-subject, and adjective-noun relations. For the verb-object relation, the top1 strict accuracy is 24.74% while the top3 relaxed accuracy reaches 75.26%.

Keywords: Selectional Preference, Knowledge Base, MDL, Noun Taxonomy

1 Introduction

Selectional preference, or SP, is an important lexical knowledge. It describes which nouns fit to be a certain role of argument of a predicate and to what extent they fit. For example, animate entities are preferred to be the agent of the literally used verb "eat" while edible entities are preferred to be its patient. SP knowledge can be applied to many natural language processing tasks, like semantic error detection, metaphor detection[1], word sense disambiguation[2], syntactic parsing[3], semantic role labeling[4], machine translation[5], etc. SP knowledge has been integrated into some important lexical knowledge bases, including VerbNet[6] in English and SKCC[7] (Semantic Knowledge-base of Contemporary Chinese) in Chinese. However, handcrafted knowledge bases can't well meet the requirement of large scale real text processing. Automatic SP knowledge acquisition is needed.

For predicate v and its argument role r, SP acquisition is to compute the value $sp_r(v,C)$ (sp for short) for noun semantic class C. The value $sp_r(v,C)$ stands for how well C fit to be the argument role r of the predicate v. Such semantic class level knowledge is easy understood for human beings and convenient for building knowledge bases. Based on WordNet, Resnik[8] uses KL-divergence to compute sp value while Li and Abe[9] utilize MDL (Minimum Description Length) principle for model selection. Jia et al.[10,11] implement the KL-divergence method with HowNet semantic hierarchy for Chinese SP acquisition. They also propose a LDA-based model and neural network models to induce Chinese SP knowledge.

This paper studies Chinese SP acquisition for knowledge base construction. We use the semantic classes of SKCC, and employ MDL-based model and a large scale corpus to determine which semantic classes are proper and compute their *sp* values. We compare the acquired SP knowledge with handcrafted SP in SKCC to test the knowledge acquisition performance.

The rest of this paper is organized as follows. Section 2 describes the noun taxonomy of SKCC and its adjustment. Section 3 introduces the MDL-based tree cut model. Section 4 investigates the SP knowledge in SKCC, the source of gold standard test set to evaluate SP acquisition performance. Experiments and conclusions are given in section 5 and 6 respectively.

2   The Noun Taxonomy

The noun taxonomy in SKCC contains 87 semantic classes. It forms a five-level tree structure excluding the root node 名词 /noun, as is shown in Fig.1. The parent node and child nodes take a hypernym-hyponym relationship. Level 1 has 5 semantic classes, including 过程/process, 具体事物/concrete things, 抽象事物/abstract things, 时间/time, and 空间/space. Level 2 has 16 semantic classes, like 生物/animate, 非生物/inanimate and 构件/component. Level 3 has 17 semantic classes, like 人/human, 动物/animal, 植物/plant and 微生物/bacteria. Level 4 has 32 semantic classes, like 个人/individual and 团体/community. 16 semantic classes in level 5 are leaf nodes, like 职业/occupation, 身份/status, 关系/relation, 姓名/name, 机构/institution and 人群/group.

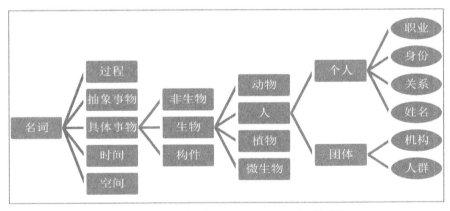

Fig. 1. An example of the noun taxonomy in SKCC

In order to utilize the taxonomy in the SP acquisition model, we require that only leaf nodes contain words directly. All non-leaf nodes should not contain words directly and the words they contain are composed by words of their child nodes. However, non-leaf nodes except the root node in SKCC noun taxonomy do contain words directly. For example, 人/human contains 174 words (like 老百姓/people), 个人 /individual contains 426 words (like 姑娘/girl), and 团体/community contains 99 words (like 家/family). So we adjust the structure of the taxonomy by adding a leaf node for each non-leaf node containing words directly and move the contained words to the added leaf node. Fig.2 gives an example of the taxonomy adjustment. We add a leaf node for each of the three non-leaf node 人/human, 个人/individual and 团体 /community. The name of the added leaf node is composed by the non-leaf node name and the suffix "_G" with the meaning "General".

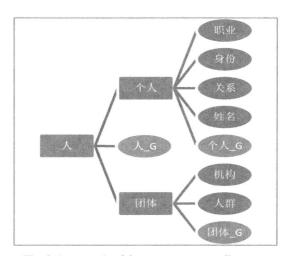

Fig. 2. An example of the noun taxonomy adjustment

There are 22 non-leaf nodes and 65 leaf nodes among the 87 nodes in SKCC noun taxonomy. Among the 22 non-leaf nodes only the root node doesn't contain words directly. We add 21 leaf nodes for the 21 non-leaf nodes containing words directly. After adjustment, the new taxonomy contains 108 nodes, including 22 non-leaf nodes and 86 leaf nodes. In total, 38706 nouns with different senses are contained in the SKCC noun taxonomy.

3   The MDL-based Tree Cut Model

3.1   The Tree Cut Model

The noun taxonomy is a tree of semantic classes. A tree cut is a subset of semantic classes, in which the intersection of each two semantic classes is empty while the union of all semantic classes is the whole vocabulary of the taxonomy. A semantic class is represented as a set of words belonging to that semantic class. A tree may have several tree cuts, among them two are special, i.e., the root node and all leaf nodes. Take the tree shown in Fig.2 as an example. It has 5 tree cuts listed in Fig.3.

Γ	Semantic classes
1	[人]
2	[个人, 人_G, 团体]
3	[职业, 身份, 关系, 姓名, 个人_G, 人_G, 团体]
4	[个人, 人_G, 机构, 人群, 团体_G]
5	[职业, 身份, 关系, 姓名, 个人_G, 人_G, 机构, 人群, 团体_G]

Fig. 3. An example of tree cuts

Let $\Gamma=[C_1,C_2,...,C_k]$ be a tree cut, containing k semantic classes C_1 to C_k. For each $C_i(0\leq i\leq k)$, let $sp_r(v,C_i)$ be $P(C_i|v,r)$, written as $P(C_i)$ for short. Then we get a parameter vector $\theta = [P(C_1),P(C_2),...,P(C_k)]$, satisfying $\sum_{i=1}^{k} P(C_i) = 1$. Γ and θ together make a tree cut model M, written as M = (Γ, θ). This model can well represent the SP knowledge because Γ answers which semantic classes are preferred by the predicate and θ gives the preference values.

3.2   The MDL Principle for Model Selection

The noun taxonomy gives us many tree cuts. For a certain tree cut Γ and its model $\hat{M} = (\Gamma, \hat{\theta})$, $\hat{\theta}$ is the parameter to be estimated. For each predicate v and its argument role r, we can train parameters for each tree cut model and select the best one. The training sample set S is composed of triples (v,r,n) extracted automatically from large scale real texts. We choose MDL principle as the criterion for model selection and select the model with the minimum description length.

Let the total description length of $\hat{M}$ and S be $L(\hat{M}, S)$. It is divided into two parts, as shown in Equation 1.

$$L(\hat{M},S) = L\left((\Gamma,\hat{\theta}),S\right) = L(\hat{\theta}|\Gamma) + L(S|\Gamma,\hat{\theta}) \tag{1}$$

$L(\hat{\theta}|\Gamma)$ is the parameter description length, where $L(\hat{\theta}|\Gamma) = \frac{k}{2} \times \log_2 |S|$, |S| is the sample size, and k is the number of semantic classes in the tree cut.

$L(S|\Gamma,\hat{\theta})$ is the data description length, where $L(S|\Gamma,\hat{\theta}) = -\sum_{n\in S}\log_2 \hat{P}(n)$, $\hat{P}(n)$ is short for $P_{\hat{M}}(n|v,r)$, $\hat{P}(n) = \frac{1}{|C|} \times \hat{P}(C)$, $\hat{P}(C) = \frac{f(C)}{|S|}$, and $f(C)$ is the sum of the frequency of words belonging to the semantic class C which can be counted from S.

We don't compute the description length of each tree cut model and choose the best one, because the noun taxonomy has a great number of tree cuts and the time complexity is very high. Rather we implement a high efficient algorithm based on dynamic programming introduced by Li and Abe[9].

4 SP in SKCC as a Gold Standard Test Set

SP knowledge is integrated into SKCC. For verbs, two argument roles, subject and object, are filled with proper noun semantic classes. For adjectives, one argument role, subject, is filled with proper noun semantic classes. Table 1 gives four SP examples with partial information from SKCC. We can see that each record corresponds to a sense of a predicate, and different senses of a predicate may have different SP knowledge. For example, the literal sense of 吃/eat with sense number 1 has a subject semantic class 人/human and an object semantic class 食物/edible or 药物/medicine.

Table 1. SP examples in SKCC

词语/word	词类/pos	义项/sense	主体/subject	客体/object
吃/eat	v	1	人/human	食物|药物 /edible|medicine
喝/drink	v	-	人/human	食物|药物 /edible|medicine
孤独/lonely	a	-	人|动物 /human|animal	x
美丽/beautiful	a	-	具体事物 /concrete things	x

Table 2 shows some statistics of the three types of predicate-argument relations in SKCC, including the number of predicate senses with SP knowledge, the number of predicates with SP knowledge and the number of preferred noun semantic classes. As can be seen, the numbers of verb-object relation, VerbObj, are smaller than those of verb-subject relation, VerbSub, because only transitive verbs can take object while most verbs can take subject. However, the average number of semantic classes each verb sense takes of VerbObj is over 1.5, which is greater than that of VerbSub. The numbers of adjective-noun relation, AdjNoun, are the smallest because of the small size of adjective vocabulary.

Table 2. Statistics of SP in SKCC

	VerbObj	VerbSub	AdjNoun
Number of predicate senses	8431	20485	3554
Number of predicates	7677	19163	3265
Number of semantic classes	12883	24313	4063

We investigate the distribution of semantic classes for each predicate-argument relation type and list the top5 semantic classes in table 3. We can see that, for VerbObj relation, the top3 semantic classes are 抽象事物/abstract things, 具体事物/concrete things and 人/human. While for VerbSub relation, the dominant semantic classes are 人/human and its hyponym 个人/individual. As for AdjNoun relation, 人/human and 抽象事物/abstract things are the dominant semantic classes.

Table 3. Top5 semantic classes

VerbObj	Percent	VerbSub	Percent	AdjNoun	Percent
抽象事物 /abstract things	16.62%	人/human	52.36%	人/human	27.98%
具体事物 /concrete things	15.11%	个人/individual	10.91%	抽象事物 /abstract things	27.15%
人/human	13.14%	具体事物 /concrete things	5.44%	具体事物 /concrete things	11.67%
事件/event	7.11%	抽象事物 /abstract things	4.88%	空间/space	4.26%
过程/process	3.42%	动物/animal	3.35%	动物/animal	3.50%

We further investigate the node level distribution of these semantic classes in the taxonomy to see how deep human annotators will search down the taxonomy when they choose the preferred semantic classes for the predicates. As is shown in table 4, all the average node levels are smaller than 3 and the average node level for AdjNoun is about 2. Level 0 means that the semantic class is the root node 名词/noun.

Table 4. Level distribution of semantic classes

	VerbObj	VerbSub	AdjNoun
Level 0	0.03%	0.01%	0%
Level 1	39.43%	13.18%	46.96%
Level 2	16.74%	6.27%	9.62%
Level 3	22.05%	58.47%	36.08%
Level 4	17.52%	16.39%	6.67%
Level 5	4.26%	5.68%	0.66%
Average level	2.30	2.95	2.04

5   Experiments

The training sample set is extracted from 60 years' People's Daily corpus. The corpus is parsed by Zpar[12]. Dependency triples of relations OBJ, SUB, and NMOD with adjectives are extracted. We only keep triples with nouns in the SKCC taxonomy and composed of at least two Chinese characters. At last, we get 1,405,072 distinct verb-OBJ-noun samples, 1,395,525 distinct verb-SUB-noun samples, and 189,410 distinct adjective-NMOD-noun samples with frequency of each sample.

5.1   Acquired Selectional Preferences

With the MDL-based tree cut model, the adjusted noun taxonomy, and the extracted training sample set, we can acquire selectional preferences for a certain predicate and a certain argument role. Table 5 shows the learned top10 preferred object semantic classes of the verb 吃/eat ranked in descending order of $P(C)$ and some frequently collocated words belonging to each semantic class. We can see that, the most preferred semantic class 食物/edible is correct for the literal usage of 吃/eat. The word 药/medicine, which usually collocates with 吃/eat is put in the semantic class 食物/edible in SKCC. So the semantic class 药物/medicine is not ranked as one of the top preferred semantic classes.

Table 5. The top10 preferred object semantic classes of the verb 吃/eat

Semantic class	$P(C)$	Example words
食物/edible	0.4730	饭/meal 药/medicine 大锅饭/mess 水果/fruit
自然物_G/natural	0.0649	水/water
事件/event	0.0368	苦头/hardship 年夜饭/new year dinner
抽象事物_G/abstract things	0.0322	东西/thing 回扣/rebate 官司/lawsuit
动物/animal	0.0289	螃蟹/crab 鸡/chicken 虫/bug
事性/property of event	0.0273	定心丸/reassurance
地理/geography	0.0247	山/mountain 海/sea
人工物_G/artifact	0.0216	老本/capital 补贴/subsidy
植物_G/plant	0.0168	水果/fruit 苹果/apple
个人/individual	0.0159	胖子/fatty

The quality of the acquired SP knowledge could be improved by considering the following aspects. Firstly, disambiguate semantic class for nouns. For simplicity, we just equally divide a noun's frequency to all its direct semantic classes right now. Secondly, disambiguate word sense for verbs. Without word sense disambiguation of verbs, we may mix preferred semantic classes of different senses. For example, the verb 吃/eat in "吃/suffer 苦头/hardship" or "吃/live on 老本/capital" does not correspond to its literal sense. Thirdly, text preprocessing including word segmentation, part-of-speech tagging, syntactic parsing and semantic parsing may introduce errors. Lastly, some idioms or metaphorical expressions may bring mistakes when segmented into different parts. For example, when the idiom "靠山吃山/those living on a mountain live off the mountain, 靠海吃海/those living near the sea live off the sea" is parsed, 山/mountain and 海/sea are extracted as the objects of 吃/eat and abstracted into an improper semantic class "地理/geography".

5.2   Evaluation

SP knowledge in SKCC is employed as the gold standard test set. As we don't do word sense disambiguation for predicates, we combine the semantic classes of polysemous predicates firstly. Then each SP record corresponds to a predicate instead of a predicate sense. We employ two metrics to evaluate the acquired selectional preferences, the strict accuracy and the relaxed accuracy. For the strict accuracy, if the acquired semantic class is contained in the corresponding semantic classes in the gold standard data, then it is correct. For the relaxed accuracy, if the acquired semantic class is contained in the corresponding semantic classes or their child nodes, it is correct.

We randomly sample 287 verbs for VerbObj relation, 287 verbs for VerbSub relation and 263 adjectives for AdjNoun relation. Then, we acquire selectional preferences for the selected predicates. We examine those top1~3 acquired preferred semantic classes to see whether there is correct one. Thus, we get top1~3 strict accuracy and top1~3 relaxed accuracy for each predicate-argument relation. It is clear that standard becomes more relaxed from top1 to top3.

Table 6 and 7 show the evaluation results. As can be seen, the top1 strict accuracy is around 20% and the top3 relaxed accuracy is around 70% for all three predicate-argument relations. It performs best on the VerbObj relation, where the top1 strict accuracy is 24.74% and the top3 strict accuracy is 47.04%.

Table 6. Top1~3 strict accuracy

	Top1	Top2	Top3
VerbObj	24.74%	40.42%	47.04%
VerbSub	12.20%	16.38%	20.56%
AdjNoun	20.53%	38.02%	46.39%

Table 7. Top1~3 relaxed accuracy

	Top1	Top2	Top3
VerbObj	61.32%	73.17%	75.26%
VerbSub	62.37%	70.73%	73.87%
AdjNoun	47.53%	64.64%	67.68%

The great improvement from strict accuracy to relaxed accuracy reflects that the model tends to find hyponyms of the correct semantic classes. This point can also be reflected from table 8, where the average level of the acquired semantic classes is deeper than that of the correct semantic classes. This finding offers another chance to improve the quality of acquired SP knowledge by decreasing the level of semantic classes.

Table 8. Average level of semantic classes on the sampled test data

	VerbObj	VerbSub	AdjNoun
Gold standard SP	2.07	2.75	1.80
Auto acquired SP	2.82	3.48	2.70

6   Conclusions

This paper studies Chinese selectional preference acquisition for knowledge base construction. Firstly, the noun taxonomy of SKCC is introduced and adjusted for SP acquisition. Secondly, a MDL-based tree cut model is implemented. Thirdly, SP in SKCC is analyzed and employed as the source of gold standard test set. SP acquisition is carried out on a large scale corpus. Three types of predicate-argument relations are investigated in the preliminary experiments. For the verb-object relation, the top1 strict accuracy is 24.74% while the top3 relaxed accuracy reaches 75.26%. After analyzing experimental results, we put forward ideas to improve the quality of the acquired SP knowledge for our future work.

Acknowledgments. This work is partially supported by grants from the National Natural Science Foundation of China (No.61402419) and the National Social Science Foundation of China (No.14BYY096).

References

1. Jia, Y.X., Yu, S.W.: Unsupervised Chinese Verb Metaphor Recognition Based on Selectional Preferences. In: Proceedings of PACLIC22, pp. 207-214 (2008)
2. McCarthy, D., Carroll, J.: Disambiguating Nouns, Verbs, and Adjectives Using Automatically Acquired Selectional Preferences. Computational Linguistics, 29(4), 639-654 (2003)
3. Zhou, G.Y., Zhao, J., Liu, K., et al.: Exploiting Web-derived Selectional Preference to Improve Statistical Dependency Parsing. In: Proceedings of ACL, pp. 1556-1565 (2011)
4. Wu, S. M., Palmer, M.: Can Selectional Preferences Help Automatic Semantic Role Labeling? In: Proceedings of *SEM 2015, pp. 222-227 (2015)
5. Tang, H.Q., Xiong, D.Y., Zhang, M., Gong, Z.X.: Improving Statistical Machine Translation with Selectional Preferences. In: Proceedings of COLING, pp. 2154-2163 (2016)
6. Schuler, K.K.: VerbNet: A Broad-coverage, Comprehensive Verb Lexicon. University of Pennsylvania, Philadelphia, PA (2005)
7. Wang, H., Zhan, W.D., Yu, S.W.: Structure and Application of the Semantic Knowledgebase of Modern Chinese. Applied Linguistics, 1, 134-141 (2006) (In Chinese)
8. Resnik, P.: Selection and Information: A Class-based Approach to Lexical Relationships. University of Pennsylvania, Philadelphia, PA (1993)
9. Li, H., Abe, N.: Generalizing Case Frames Using a Thesaurus and the MDL Principle. Computational Linguistics, 24(2), 217-244 (1998)
10. Jia, Y.X., Wang, H.S., Zan, H.Y., et al.: Research on Chinese Selectional Preferences Acquisition. Journal of Chinese Information Processing, 28(5), 66-73 (2014) (In Chinese)
11. Jia, Y.X., Xu, H.F., Zan, H.Y.: Neural Network Models for Selectional Preference Acquisition. Journal of Chinese Information Processing, 31(1), 155-161 (2017) (In Chinese)
12. Zhang Y., Clark, S.: Syntactic Processing Using the Generalized Perceptron and Beam Search. Computational Linguistics, 37(1), 105-151 (2011)

Identifying Chinese Event Factuality with Convolutional Neural Networks

Tianxiong He[1], Peifeng Li[1] and Qiaoming Zhu[1]

[1] School of Computer Science and Technology of Soochow University, Key Lab of Computer Information Processing Technology of Jiangsu Province, China

pfli@suda.edu.cn

Abstract: Event factuality describes the factual level of the event expressed by event narrator and is one of the deep semantic representations of natural texts. This paper focuses on identifying Chinese event factuality and proposes an effective approach based on CNN (Convolutional Neural Networks). It extracts factual related information from event sentences and then regards them and their transformation as features. Meanwhile, it transfers the features to word vectors to construct a sentence-level word vector map. Finally, it inputs the word vector map to the CNN model to identify event factuality. Experimental results show that our approach achieves a higher performance by using factual features and CNN model, especially the advantage to tackle the imbalanced data distribution problem.

Keywords: Event Factuality, Factual Features, Convolutional Neural Networks

1 Introduction

Event factuality describes the factual level of the event expressed by event narrator. When people talk about an event, they express not only the subjective attitude of the event, but also the certainty of the occurrence of the event. This level of certainty can be described as "already happen", "probably happen" or "not happen". Event factuality plays an important role in many fields of research and practice. In question answering system, more accurate answer can be selected according to different degrees of factuality contained in those candidate answers. In text semantic analysis, it can be used as an auxiliary information element to provide deep semantic analysis. In sentiment analysis system, it can also be used as a semantic feature to provide auxiliary analysis. In addition, event factuality identification itself can be used as an upper level semantic understanding task, e.g., network public opinion monitoring, news hot spot finding and social phenomenon analysis.

In Chinese texts, there are many factors that affect the factuality of event, i.e., predicates (e.g., "怀疑"(suspect), "证实" (verify)), adjectives or adverbs (e.g., "可能"(may), "必须"(must), "一定"(definite)) and negative words (e.g., "尚未"(not yet), "没有"(no)). The semantic implications of such lexical information affect the factual expression of event in different ways. In this paper, these information are collectively referred to factual information. From the perspective of Chinese linguistics, different types of factual information are not isolated and there is a connection between them. How to understand and excavate this connection from the view of semantic point plays an important role in the task of event factuality identification.

However, in practical applications, there is a large amount of unlabeled text information. It greatly hinders the development of the event factuality identification task. To solve this problem, a convolution neural network method is proposed in this paper. It first uses a series of information extraction methods to extract factual information in event sentence. Then, from the perspective of Chinese linguistics, a series of factual features are processed and transformed based on rules. Finally, the feature words are quantized and added into the convolution neural network CNN (Convolutional Neural Networks) model to recognize event factuality. Experimental results show that the feature information extracted and transformed by our method can improve the task of event factuality recognition. At the same time,

© Springer International Publishing AG 2018
Y. Wu et al. (Eds.): CLSW 2017, LNAI 10709, pp. 284–292, 2018.
https://doi.org/10.1007/978-3-319-73573-3_25

our method using CNN model has more advantages in dealing with imbalanced data distribution.

2   Background

At present, there is only a little related research on the task of event factuality identification, basically focusing on the corpus with all kinds of annotated factual information. Minard [1] annotated a news corpus, MEANTIME, based on event and temporal information. In this corpus, the factualities are divided into five categories: "factual", "counterfactual", "non-factual", "underspecified" and "no factuality", which are mainly expressed by three attributes: certainty, time and polarity. Certainty attribute values are divided into: "certain", "non-certain" and "underspecified". Time attribute values are divided into: "past", "future", "underspecified". Polarity attribute values are divided into "positive", "negative" and "underspecified". Minard [2, 3] designed a model for event factual analysis - FactPro. First, a machine learning-based method is used to extract and transform the certainty, time and polarity of events. Then a rule-based method is used to combine the above three attributes to infer the event factuality. Diab[4] built a small corpus for factuality analysis, which divides factualities into three categories: "committed belief", "non-committed belief" and "not applicable", and then proposed a factuality tagging method based on basic lexical features, POS features, word class features and shallow syntactic features. Kilicoglu [5] proposed a rule-based combination method to recognize event factuality in biomedical field, which focused the connection among predicates in the same coverage domain. Lee [6] used an unsupervised method for event detection and factuality recognition.

Based on the TimeBank corpus, Sauri [7] constructs the FactBank corpus for event factuality analysis. The factualities were divided into seven categories: "certain", "non-certain", "probable", "non-probably", "possible", "non-possible" and "uncertain". Sauri [8,9,10] designed a factuality Analyzer - De Facto from the view of linguistic point. It used the dependency syntax tree of an event sentence to construct a top-down factuality analysis method. Qian [11] focused on the "uncertain" category in the FactBank corpus, which is different to identify from other categories. Firstly, the maximum entropy classification model was constructed based on a series of features to classify the events to "certain" or "uncertain". Then, a rule-based approach is applied to the results of the above stage to subdivide the events to seven categories.

In Chinese, Cao [12] constructed an event factuality corpus based on ACE (Automatic Content Extraction) 2005 corpus, which divided the event factualities into five categories: "factual", "counterfactual", "probable", "not probable" and "not certain". It also proposed a three-dimensional factual representation to identify Chinese events factuality [13]. Using the above corpus, He [14] proposed a method of event factuality analysis based on maximum entropy model and achieved the remarkable results. It used rules to handle features, including the factual features, relation features, linguistic features and rule-based semantic features.

3   CNN-based event factual recognition

The task of event factuality recognition can be regarded as a text classification task. Whether using a rule based approach, a feature engineering approach or even a deep learning based approach, these are all factuality classifications of existing events.

The model of event factuality recognition in this article is shown in figure 1. Firstly, it extracts factual information from text (event selected predicates, negative words, degree words, etc.). Then, it transforms the factual features based on the factual information. Finally, it inputs the word vector map to the CNN model to identify event factuality.

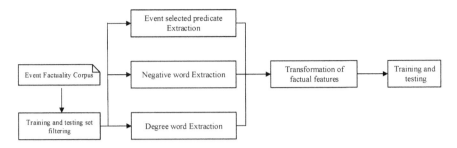

Fig. 1. A framework for event recognition based on Convolutional Neural Networks

In the whole process, the event factuality identification task is organized at levels. The key tasks of this method are factual information extraction, factual features transformation and CNN model training and testing. The relevant information is the foundation of the framework. The processing and transformation of features is to obtain the factual features which closer to the event factuality expression. And the CNN model is used because of its characteristics of feature mining.

3.1 Factual information extraction

In this paper, factual information mainly consists of three categories: event selected predicate, negative words and degree words. As shown in example 1, the event selected predicate is "worried" and its property is judged as "Maybe". The negative word is "not return". The degree word is "might" and its property is judged as "Maybe". The whole event's factuality is "Not Probable".

E1：Prosecutors are worried[ESP/Maybe] that she might[Degree/Maybe] not return[Negative] to Taiwan.

The example above contains factual information exists in most cases. This section will introduce a series of extraction methods to extract three kinds of factual information from raw text. Before extracting, we need to segment the event text.

(1) Extraction of event selected predicates

The event selected predicate is a special predicate with the attitude of the narrator to an incident. So, it is different from the common predicates and more in terms of lexical semantic differences. Therefore, it is difficult to obtain good results when predicate extraction is performed by using common feature engineering methods.

In addition, since event selected predicates are very specific, most event selected predicates are more centralized in common Chinese predicates. After comprehensive consideration, the experiment will be done by formulating the word list to achieve the goal of extraction.

In this paper, the common predicates are classified into three kinds according to attributes. The "证明"(verify) and "报道"(report) are classified as "Certain" class. The "怀疑"(doubt) and "试图"(attempt) are classified as "Maybe" class. The "询问"(ask) and "打探"(inquire) are classified as "Not Certain" class. Then, use the Chinese synonym tree to expand the synonyms. Finally, we use the pre-trained Word2Vec model to further enrich the vocabulary of the three classes of event selected predicates.

As shown in example 1, after the word list matches, the event selected predicate is "worried". And then it is possible to determine its property as "Maybe" according to the category of words.

(2) Extraction of negative words and degree words

In Natural Language Processing domain, the problem of sequence tagging is often encountered. A sequence of states is determined based on the sequence of observations. At present, the method of sequence annotation has been proved to have good effect in word segmentation, POS tagging and named entity recognition. However, the identification of negative words and degree words is also a typical sequence tagging problem.

In this paper, a sequence labeling model based on conditional random field CRF (Conditional Random Field) is used to transform the identification of negative words and degree words into the problem of judging whether the nodes are in the triggering words. The use of corpus annotation is Chen Zhancheng's Chinese negative and uncertain information recognition corpus [15]. Feature template using Unigram template. Features are characters, words and word's POS. At the same time, selecting the appropriate template window to finish the experiment.

As shown in example 1, by training a sequence of tagging models, it is possible to identify negative word "not return" and degree word "might".

After identifying the degree words, it is also necessary to determine its property. First, construct the corresponding degree word list according to the property. And then classify the existing degree words into three categories: "Certain", "Maybe" and "Not Certain". Then the Word2Vec model is used to calculate the similarity between the extracted degree words and the three vocabularies. The word that obtains the maximum similarity of the degree word, and then determines its property according to the category of the word list.

For example, after the extraction of the degree word "might", the word similarity is calculated in turn with the words in the three types of vocabulary. Selecting the maximum similarity of the word category as property. It's able to know "Maybe" is its property.

3.2 Factual Features Transformation

Factual information mainly includes event selected predicates, negative words and degree words. These three kinds of words all influence the factuality of the event. If we only use the independent lexical information as features and ignore their semantic connection, it will be a little insufficient and not conducive to the factual expression of event. Therefore, from the perspective of Chinese linguistic, the degree and polarity properties are transformed into features by making rules. The feature tables used in this article are shown in table 1.

Table 1. Factual features

Feature class	Specific description
Lexical	Event selected predicates, negative words, degree words, etc.
Degree	Transformation feature of event selected predicates and degree words
Polarity	Transformation feature of the number of negative words

(1) Lexical features

Lexical level features are constructed mainly from factual information related words themselves. As shown in example 1, you can get vocabulary level features: "worried", "might" and "not return". The lexical features can be sequentially added into the CNN model while need to be pre-processed in other classifiers due to variable length of features.

(2) Degree feature

Event degree refers to the certainty of event occurrence. It is the basic semantic information makes up the factuality of an event. In factual information, the event selected predicates and degree words both contain degree property. So, the degree feature can be derived from the rank attributes of the two classes of words. Referring to the Chinese event factuality 3D representation method[13], the transformation method of the level dimension is summarized as follows.

Degree conversion rule: Firstly, the default degree feature is "Certain". Then, if the event selected predicates or degree words exist, the property set is transformed according to the priority of "Not Certain" > "Maybe" > "Certain".

As shown in example 1, the default level feature is "Certain", but the event selected predicate and degree word both contain "Maybe" property, so the final level is "Maybe".

(3) Polarity feature

Event polarity is an important factor in determining the occurrence of an event. Polarity is mainly influenced by negative words in the text. Referring to the Chinese event fact 3D representation method[13], the transformation method of the polarity dimension is summarized as follows.

Polarity conversion rule: According to the number of words in the negative sense, if the number is even, the polarity feature is set as "positive". If the number is odd, the polarity feature is set as "negative".

Through the above feature transformation methods, we can obtain the factual features of the event. Namely, lexical level features, degree features and polarity features. Among them, the degree and polarity are fused and transformed after taking into account the relation between factuality and factual information. To a certain extent, these two features have a great effect on the task of event factuality identification.

3.3　Convolution neural network model

Compared with other commonly used machine learning methods (e.g., maximum entropy model), deep learning method has more advantages in feature mining. Through iterative feature learning, with the number of layers increases, the acquired features are more abstract and more representative. This has unique advantages in classification tasks. The CNN model used in this paper corresponds to the input of each neuron in the volume layer to the local accepted domain of the previous layer. After extracting the local feature, this kind of local information feature has a certain effect on the factuality recognition task. In addition, unlike recurrent neural network focusing on time series, the CNN model pays more attention to feature mining in space. The word order between features can be better utilized, and the training of the model is more efficient because of the local connection and weight sharing technology. At present, there are many related methods in the research of sentence classification using CNN model. Among them, Kim[16] proposed a sentence classification method based on CNN model, which used the word vector instead of the word in the sentence. And since sentences are made up of words, a sentence can be represented by a word vector matrix. Kim has proved that this method has good performance in sentence classification.

After the extraction and transformation of all event sentences through 3.1 and 3.2 sections, the factual feature sets of each event sentence can be obtained. In this paper, the CNN model uses $x_i \in R^k$ as the k-dimensional word vector corresponding to the i-th word in the feature sets. A collection of factual features of length n can be represented as the formula (1).

$$x_{1:n} = x_1 \oplus x_2 \oplus ... \oplus x_n \tag{1}$$

In formula (1), $\oplus$ is the concatenation operator. Let $x_{i:i+j}$ refer to the concatenation of features x_i, x_{i+1}, ..., x_{i+j}. In the CNN model, convolution operations need to set a filter $w \in R^{hk}$. The filter uses a window of length h and does a convolution operation at the word vectors in the window. Finally, a feature c_i is generated from a window of features $x_{i:i+h-1}$. As shown in formula (2).

$$c_i = f(\mathbf{w} \cdot x_{i:i+h-1} + b) \tag{2}$$

Here $b \in R$ is a bias term and f is a non-linear function such as the hyperbolic tangent. In a set of factual features, a feature map can be generated by processing the features contained in such a filter. As shown in formula (3).

$$\mathbf{c} = [c_1, c_2, \dots, c_{n-h+1}] \tag{3}$$

After get the feature map $\mathbf{c} \in R^{n-h+1}$, we then apply a max-pooling operation over the feature map and take the maximum value $\hat{c} = max\{\mathbf{c}\}$ as the feature corresponding to this particular filter. The purpose of this method is to select the value (maximum) that can best represent the feature map, and also to solve the feature extraction problem of the indefinite length feature set.

First, a variety of filters (different window sizes) are used to obtain the various feature maps. Then, we can get all kinds of new features after performing the maximum pool sampling operation. Finally, these features form the penultimate layer and are passed to a full connected softmax layer whose output is the probability distribution over labels.

In the CNN model of this paper, regularization is used to reduce the overfitting problem. We employ dropout on the penultimate layer with a constraint on l_2-norms of the weight vectors. Dropout prevents co-adaptation of hidden units by randomly dropping out. That is, Perform operations such as formula (4) on the penultimate layer $z = [\hat{c}_1, \dots, \hat{c}_m]$ (here we have m filters) for out unit y in forward propagation.

$$y = \mathbf{w} \cdot (\mathbf{z} \circ \mathbf{r}) + b \tag{4}$$

In formula (4), $\circ$ is the element-wise multiplication operator and $\mathbf{r} \in R^m$ is a 'masking' vector of Bernoulli random variables with probability p of being 1. Gradients are backpropagated only through the unmasked unit. In addition, we constrain l_2-norms of the weight vectors by rescaling $\mathbf{w}$ to make $||\mathbf{w}||_2 = s$ whenever $||\mathbf{w}||_2 > s$ after a gradient descent step.

4   Experimentual Results and Analysis

4.1 Datasets and experimental setup

The Chinese event factual corpus [12] is used in this paper for evaluation. But in our experiment, we do not use any annotated information. In this corpus, the event factualities are divided into five categories: "Factual", "Counterfactual", "Probable", "Not Probable" and "Not Certain". Table 2 shows the number of individual events in this corpus where most of the events belong to the categories "Factual" and "Probable categories".

Table 2. The number of events in the factual category

Factual category	Factual	Counterfactual	Probable	Not Probable	Not Certain
Event number	2286	298	530	105	46

The experimental performance is evaluated in term of precision, recall, F1-measure, macro-averaging and micro-averaging based on 5-flod Cross Validation. Besides, Jieba word segmentation tool is used to pre-process the data and Word2Vec on Chinese Wikipedia training data is used to obtain the word vector map. In our evaluation, filter windows h is assigned 2, 3, 4 with 80 feature maps each, dropout rate p is assigned 0.5, l_2 constraint s is assigned 3 and mini-batch size is set to 50.

In the experiment, the word set is constructed by using the word list of event related information. And then the WordBag features are processed according to the word frequency. Because of the lack of research in event factuality recognition based on unlabeled raw text, the WordBag features on Maximum Entropy Model (ME) is used as the baseline.

4.2   Results and discussion

The experimental results are shown in table 3 and it shows that the factual features (Factual) have a distinct advantage over the WordBag feature (WordBag). The ME model using factual features raised 4.06% and 2.64% in macro-averaging and micro-averaging F1 values, respectively. The promotion of CNN model using factual features is more significant and the macro-averaging and micro-averaging F1 values are increased by 21.52% and 3.95% respectively, which is due to the improvement of both accuracy and recall.

According to the analysis, factual features strengthen commonalities between similar events and diversities between heterogeneous events. And we also use some advanced level features, such as the degree and polarity feature. The degree feature indicates the degree of certainty of an event's occurrence and the polarity feature indicates whether the event occurred. These two features both play a great role in improving the factual classification of events. At the same time, the great improvement of macro-averaging F1 value indicates that the factual feature is more advantageous in dealing with the classes with a small set of instances.

Table 3. The experimental results using different features and classification models

	Macro-Averaging			Micro-Averaging		
	P(%)	R(%)	F1(%)	P(%)	R(%)	F1(%)
WordBag/ME	53.03	48.22	49.86	76.26	76.26	76.26
WordBag/CNN	47.55	35.53	36.78	76.84	76.84	76.84
Factual/ME	61.32	52.11	53.92	78.9	78.9	78.9
Factual/CNN	66.03	56.28	58.3	80.79	80.79	80.79
Joint /ME	51.18	50.04	49.23	80.7	80.7	80.7
Joint /CNN	**70.52**	**59.14**	**61.82**	**81.81**	**81.81**	**81.81**

In addition, table 3 shows that when using the same WordBag features, the macro-averaging F1 value decreases and the micro-averaging F1 value rises slightly in the model of CNN. It shows that the CNN model is more affected by noise under the semantic features of shallow layer while the ME model is better balanced. When using the factual features, the CNN model improved by 4.38% on macro-averaging F1 value and 1.89% on micro-averaging F1 value compared to the ME model. It shows that the CNN model has a great assistant function in the further feature extraction under the high quality feature model, but the more unsatisfactory classification result under the feature model of poor quality and high noise. As the deep web learning model, CNN model has the greatest advantage of mining existing features. If the current classification features are very close to the event factual expression, the deep feature information obtained after iterative learning can further reflect the information between the classification features. However, if the current classification features deviate from the factual expression, then the CNN model will be used to dig out more information which is not conducive to classification and noise is introduced to reduce the performance of the experiment.

At the same time, it can be seen in table 3 that both the ME model and the CNN model have been improved after fusing the Factual features and the WordBag features to form joint features. This shows that these two types of features are complementary to the factuality classification of events, both of which complement each other and provide more accurate feature information for factual classification tasks. To some extent, both the WordBag features and Factual features are important information mined from event texts. The WordBag features are relatively shallow character to display information compared with Factual features. So the effect of Factual features in the factuality recognition task is better than the WordBag features. But from another perspective, WordBag features contain abundant information but they are difficult to form the expression of event factuality. While the Factual features through feature extraction are more effective features of the classification model but they are not enough. These two types of features combine the advantages of both, and to some extent make up for the shortcomings of both.

Table 4. Experimental results using factual features

	ME			CNN		
	P(%)	R(%)	F1(%)	P(%)	R(%)	F1(%)
Factual	85.71	90.51	88.03	**87.38**(+1.67)	**90.73**(+0.22)	**89**(+0.97)
Counterfactual	62.44	71.5	66.45	**65.73**(+3.29)	**81.88**(+10.38)	**72.83**(+6.38)
Probable	61.55	47.55	53.51	**62.11**(+0.56)	**51.7**(+4.15)	**56.24**(+2.73)
Not Probable	46.02	31.43	36.68	**56.24**(+10.22)	**33.33**(+1.9)	**41.2**(+4.52)
Not Certain	50.87	19.56	24.92	**58.67**(+7.8)	**23.78**(+4.22)	**32.24**(+7.32)

Table 4 gives the performance of different categories of facts in the ME model and the CNN model. The result shows a better performance in use of Factual features of the CNN model compared with ME model in each category. In the "Factual" and "Probable" categories, F1 values were increased by 0.97% and 2.73%. While in the "Counterfactual", "Not Probable" and "Not Certain" categories, F1 values increased significantly and were 6.38%, 4.52% and 7.32%. Table 4 shows that all categories of ascension have benefited from the accuracy and recall rate of synchronous lifting, which further indicates that the CNN model has unique advantages in the event classification task and can improve the overall performance of the system. According to the characteristics of the CNN model, it carries on deeper feature information mining on the basis of the original feature. After several iterative operation, it takes on more effective new features. The Factual features can be further extracted by combining the CNN model which make great contributions to the performance improvement of the system

In addition, the input of features in the CNN model are the word vectors. So when the features of similar meaning (such as event selected predicate "怀疑"(suspect) and "质疑"(query)) are input into the model, their similarities can be mined by CNN model. Meanwhile, the CNN model also takes into account spatial features which deepen the representation of the factual feature model while mining the correlation between features.

At the same time, table 4 shows that the performance of three small classes of "Counterfactual", "Not Probable" and "Not Certain" are greatly improved in the use of CNN model. It also shows that the depth feature mining of CNN model has better performance advantages on dealing with class imbalance problem. And from the overall performance of small classes, the effect still has some room for improvement.

5   Conclusion

In this paper, we focus on identifying Chinese event factuality and propose an effective approach based on CNN. First, a series of information extraction methods are used to extract factual information from the text. Then, we use linguistic rules to deal and transform features from the factual information. Finally, we transfer the features to word vectors to construct the sentence level word vector map and input them to the CNN model to identify event factuality. Experimental results show that the Factual features extracted from this method have important contributions to the event factuality recognition.

Meanwhile, the CNN model improves the system performance after adding Factual features and has more advantages in dealing with unbalanced data.

But from the result of the experiment can be found in small class performance processing, there is still much room for improvement. Uneven distribution of data is a long-standing problem, there are also many existing methods. How to further enhance the factual recognition performance of a class with few instances is worthy of further consideration and discussion.

References

1. Minard A L, Speranza M, Urizar R, et al.: MEANTIME, the NewsReader Multilingual Event and Time Corpus. In Proceedings of the 10th International Conference on Language Resources and Evaluation. 4417-4422 (2016).

2. Minard A L, Speranza M, Caselli T.: The EVALITA 2016 Event Factuality Annotation Task (FactA). In Proceedings of the 3rd Italian Conference on Computational Linguistics & the 5th Evaluation Campaign of Natural Language Processing and Speech Tools for Italian. 26-33 (2016).

3. Minard A L, Speranza M, Sprugnoli R, et al.: FacTA: Evaluation of Event Factuality and Temporal Anchoring. In Proceedings of the 2nd Italian Conference on Computational Linguistics. 187-192 (2015).

4. Diab M T, Levin L, Mitamura T, et al.: Committed belief annotation and tagging. In Proceedings of the 3rd Linguistic Annotation Workshop. 68-73 (2009).

5. Kilicoglu H, Rosemblat G, Cairelli M J, et al.: A Compositional Interpretation of Biomedical Event Factuality. In Proceedings of the 2nd Workshop on Extra-Propositional Aspects of Meaning in Computational Semantics. 22-31 (2015).

6. Lee K, Artzi Y, Choi Y, et al.: Event Detection and Factuality Assessment with Non-Expert Supervision. In Proceedings of the 2017 International Conference on Empirical Methods in Natural Language Processing. 1643-1648 (2015).

7. Sauri R, Pustejovsky J.: FactBank: A Corpus Annotated with Event Factuality. Language Resources and Evaluation, vol. 43. 227-268 (2009).

8. Sauri R.: A Factuality Profiler for Eventualities in Text. ProQuest (2008).

9. Sauri R, Pustejovsky J.: Are You Sure that this Happened? Assessing the Factuality Degree of Events in Text. Computational Linguistics, vol. 38. 261-299 (2009).

10. Sauri R, Verhagen M, Pustejovsky J.: Annotating and Recognizing Event Modality in Text. In Proceedings of the 19th International Florida Artificial Intelligence Research Society Conference. 274-289 (2006).

11. Qian Z, Li P, Zhu Q.: A Two-Step Approach for Event Factuality Identification. In Proceedings of 19th International Conference on Asian Language Processing. 10-16 (2015).

12. 曹媛, 朱巧明, 李培峰.: 中文事件事实性信息语料库的构建方法. 中文信息学报, vol. 27. 38-44 (2013).

13. Cao Y, Zhu Q, Li P.: 3D Representation of Chinese Event Factuality. In Proceedings of the 15th Chinese Lexical Semantic Workshop. 7-13 (2014).

14. 何天雄, 李培峰, 朱巧明.: 一种中文事件事实性识别方法, 计算机科学, vol. 5. 241-244 (2017).

15. Chen Z, Zou B, Zhu Q, Li P.: The Scientific Literature Corpus for Chinese Negation and Uncertainty Identification. In Proceedings of the 14th Chinese Lexical Semantic Workshop. 657-667 (2013).

16. Kim Y.: Convolutional Neural Networks for Sentence Classification. arXiv preprint arXiv:1408.5882 (2014).

Recognizing Textual Entailment Using Inference Phenomenon

Han Ren[1], Xia Li[1], Wenhe Feng[2,*] and Jing Wan[3]

[1] Laboratory of Language Engineering and Computing, Guangdong University of Foreign Studies, Guangzhou 510420, China
[2] School of Computer, Wuhan University, Wuhan 430072, China
[3] Center for Lexicographical Studies, Guangdong University of Foreign Studies, Guangzhou 510420, China
hanren@gdufs.edu.cn, 200211025@oamail.gdufs.edu.cn,
wenhefeng@gmail.com, jingwan@whu.edu.cn

Abstract. Inference phenomena refer to inference relations in local fragments between two texts. Current research on inference phenomenon focuses on the construction of data annotation, whereas there are few research on how to identify those inference phenomena in texts, which will contributes to improving the performance of recognizing textual entailment. This paper proposes an approach, which uses inference phenomena to recognize entailment in texts. In the approach, the task of recognizing textual entailment is formalized as two problems, that is, inference phenomenon identification and entailment judgment, then a joint model is employed to combine such two related subtasks, which is helpful to avoid error propagation. Experimental results show that the approach performs efficiently for identifying inference phenomena and recognizing entailment at the same time.

Keywords: Recognizing Textual Entailment, Inference Phenomenon, Averaged Perceptron, Entailment Judgment.

1 Introduction

Recognizing Textual Entailment(RTE) is a challenging task of judging the inference relation between two statements, that is, given a premise(T) and a hypothesis(H), the task is to decide if H can be inferred from T. As one of the most important research topics in natural language understanding, RTE can be widely employed in many natural language processing applications such as question answering, information extraction and machine reading[1, 2].

Textual entailment involves multiple inference relations, such as hyponymy, apposition, syntactic alternation and coreference. However, current research mainly focuses on designing generic models or features to recognize a variety of inference relations, which may ignore differences of such relations and impact the recognition

---

* Corresponding Author.

Y. Wu et al. (Eds.): CLSW 2017, LNAI 10709, pp. 293–302, 2018.
https://doi.org/10.1007/978-3-319-73573-3_26

performance. To investigate inference relations in RTE tasks, some research efforts have been made to sort inference phenomena in RTE data, and build annotation frameworks as well as resources of such phenomena[3, 4, 5]. Take the following text pair as an example[6]:

> T: *The Hong Kong government said the case was its first successful action against peer-to-peer file sharing.*
> H: *The government acts against peer-to-peer file sharing.*

There are two kinds of inference phenomena in the above example: one is **anaphoric** for *its* in T and *The government* in H, and the other is **nominalization** for *action* in T and *acts* in H. Acquiring inference phenomena is helpful to understand complex semantic relations between T and H, which will contribute to achieving a better performance for RTE.

Current research on inference phenomenon mainly focuses on annotation framework and resource construction, whereas research on recognize entailment in texts using inference phenomenon is very insufficient. This paper proposes an approach, which uses inference phenomena to recognize entailment in texts. In the approach, RTE is formalized as two problems, that is, inference phenomenon identification and entailment judgment, and a joint model is employed to recognize inference phenomenon and textual entailment in a unified way, which is conducive to avoiding error propagation. Also, a feature set including 22 specific features for inference phenomenon and 15 features for entailment recognition are employed, particularly. Experimental results show that the approach performs efficiently for identifying inference phenomena and recognizing entailment.

The rest of the paper is organized as follows. Section 2 gives related work of RTE and inference phenomena. Section 3 describes the joint model in detail. Section 4 gives experimental results and discussion. Finally, the conclusion and the future work are given in Section 5.

2   Related Work

Research on inference phenomenon mainly focus on resource construction, such as [3, 5, 6]. However, current available resources in English are mostly built for exploration purpose, so that they are too small to be experimentally used. To this end, NTCIR RITE-3[7] released a Chinese entailment resource, in which each text pair is annotated the inference phenomenon as well as the entailment class. Although the goal of annotating inference phenomena is to evaluate the performances of the systems in the challenge, such annotated results can also be used for helping entailment judgment, which will be shown in this paper.

There is still few research on identifying inference phenomenon for RTE. Huang et al.[8] showed a preliminary research: they built heuristic rules for 5 contradiction phenomena and used them to identify those phenomena; then the identification results were featured and used in an SVM for entailment judgment. The experimental result showed that the classifier had a comparable performance with those middle-ranked systems in RTE-5. It indicates that inference phenomenon identification may helpful for recognizing entailment in texts.

3   The Approach

This section describes an approach to recognize entailment in texts using inference phenomenon. In the approach, inference phenomenon identification and entailment judgment are viewed as a joint task.

3.1   Inference Phenomenon

Table 1. Inference phenomenon schema.

Name	Value	Feature Description
Abbreviation	T/F	True if an abbreviation exists
Apposition	T/F	True if an apposition exists
Case_alternation	T/F	True if active and passive alternation exists
Clause	T/F	True if T has a clause is not exist in H
Coreference	T/F	True if a pronoun(in T) antecedent exists in H
Hypernymy	T/F	True if the hypernym of a word in T exists in H
Lexical_entailment	[0,1]	The scores of two words(in T and H) that are lexically entails
List	T/F	True if all the coordination constituents in H exist in T
Meronymy	T/F	True if two word(in T and H)have an meronymous relation
Modifier	T/F	True if a modifier in T is missing in H
Quantity	T/F	True if an equivalent quantity exists in T and H
Scrambling	T/F	True if the words in T and H are same but the order is different
Spatial	T/F	True if spatial inference exists in T and H
Synonymy	[0,1]	The similarity value of synonymous words in T and H
Temporal	T/F	True if temporal inference exists in T and H
Transparent_head	T/F	True if a syntactic head in T is replaced by one of its children in H
Antonym	[0,1]	The score of antonymous words in T and H
Exclusion:predicate _argument	T/F	True if predicates and arguments are not identical in T and H
Exclusion:quantity	T/F	True if quantitative contradiction exists in T and H
Exclusion:spatial	T/F	True if spatial contradiction exists in T and H
Exclusion:temporal	T/F	True if temporal contradiction exists in T and H
Negation	T/F	True if a negative word exists either in T or H

The NTCIR RITE-3 challenge[7] defined an Chinese inference phenomenon schema, which contained 19 entailment phenomena and 9 contradiction ones. The following experiments use the schema, except that the following inference phenomena are adjusted:

1)combine *relative_clause* and *clause* as *clause* phenomenon, because two of them describe a clause syntactic constituent that T has but H has not;

2)combine *antonymy*, *exclusion_modality* and *exclusion:modifier* as *antonymy* phenomenon, because all of them describe a antonymous or opposite meaning between T and H;

3)remove *paraphrase*, *inference* and *exclusion_common_sense* phenomena, because all of them do not have a local lexical or syntactic counterpart between *T* and *H* but need to make a global inference analysis.

The inference phenomenon schema in this experiment is list in Table 1.

3.2   The Joint Model

The goal of the approach is to judge entailment in texts using inference phenomena. Intuitively, a pipeline method can be adopted, that is, inference phenomena in texts are identified first, then an entailment classifier using the results of inference phenomenon is used to make binary judgment(entailment or non-entailment). However, such pipeline method may lead to error propagation: if the result of inference phenomena identification for a text pair is incorrect, the final judgment of entailment is probably wrong.

This paper proposes an approach to combine inference phenomenon identification and entailment recognition as one task. By this approach, error propagation is avoided, and such two subtasks can learn each other will benefit the overall performance as well.

Formally, the task is defined as follows, and the goal is to find the optimal solution of (p, c) :

$$(\hat{p}, \hat{c}) = \underset{p,c}{\mathrm{argmax}} \ Score_{joint}(t, h, p, c) \tag{1}$$

where $p = \{(x_i, y_i, l_i) | x_i \in t, y_i \in h\}$ is the inference phenomenon set, in which x_i and y_j are the *i*th token and *j*th token in *t* and *h*, respectively, and l_i is the phenomenon of the two tokens. c is the entailment class of the text pair (t, h). $Score_{joint}(\cdot)$ is a linear model:

$$Score_{joint}(t, h, p, c) = \\ Score_{phe}(t, h) + Score_{ent}(t, h, p) \tag{2}$$

where $Score_{phe}(\cdot)$ and $Score_{ent}(\cdot)$ are the models for inference phenomenon identification and entailment judgment, respectively. Such two models can be defined independently, for example, using two classifiers with different feature sets. The approach in this paper uses an incorporated way is formalized as follows:

$$Score_{joint}(t, h, p, c) = w_{phe \oplus ent} \cdot f_{phe \oplus ent}(t, h, p, c) \qquad (3)$$

where f is the joint vector including all features for two subtasks, and w is the weighting vector. By this approach, the results of inference phenomenon identification can directly guide the entailment judgment, for example, if the inference phenomenon *synonymy* is found in a (*T, H*) pair, it probably means that *T* entails *H*; on the other hand, the result of entailment judgment can also indicates the inference phenomenon identification, for example, if *T* entails *H*, such text pair may have a low probability of having the inference phenomenon *antonymy*.

Algorithm 1 Training Algorithm

Input: training examples (t_i, h_i), $i \in (1, N)$; iteration number T

Output: Parameter vector w

Algorithm:

   $w \leftarrow 0$;

   for $t = 1..T$ do

     for $i = 1..N$ do

       $p_i \leftarrow \text{Gen}(t_i, h_i)$;

       $(p_i, c_i) \leftarrow \text{argmax } w \cdot f(t_i, h_i, p_i, c_i)$;

       if $(p_i, c_i) \neq (\hat{p}_i, \hat{c}_i)$ then

         $w \leftarrow w + f(t_i, h_i, \hat{p}_i, \hat{c}_i) - f(t_i, h_i, p_i, c_i)$;

     end for

   end for

An averaged perceptron is employed in the approach to train and predict inference phenomenon and entailment class. The training algorithm to find the optimal parameter *w* is shown in Algorithm 1, in which the method $Gen(\cdot)$ is to find the set *p* that contains all possible inference phenomenon pairs. The method is straightforward: the value of each token pair in *T* and *H* is computed according to the definition in the inference phenomenon schema; if the value is a binary one and the value is true(or 1), the pair will be picked out, while if the value range of the feature is [0,1] and the feature value is above the threshold(experimental setting is 0.5), the pair will be picked out as the candidate.

Identifying most of inference phenomena needs support from rich background knowledge. Since the dataset of the experiment is a Chinese data collection, several Chinese knowledge bases, including Tongyici Cilin, HowNet, Baidu Hanyu[†], Ciba Hanyu[‡], Wikipedia and a geographic ontology[9] are employed. In particular, a word embedding-based method[10] is used to identify *lexical_entailment* phenomenon. Such

---

[†] http://hanyu.baidu.com/
[‡] http://hanyu.iciba.com/

method trained a 100 dimension word embeddings and used them to build features for recognizing lexical entailment.

Identifying some inference phenomena depends on the results of structural analysis. To this end, the Stanford CoreNLP tool[§] is employed, and the reasons are: 1)it can perform multiple tasks such as syntactic analysis, semantic analysis and anaphora resolution and; 2)it works well in Chinese texts. In addition, heuristic rules are manually made to identify *case_alternation* and *list* phenomenon.

Algorithm 2 Decoding Algorithm

Input: testing example (t, h)

Output: entailment class c

Algorithm:

 for $p_i \in \text{Gen}(t, h)$ do

  $\hat{p}_i \leftarrow \text{argmax} \max(w \cdot f(t, h, p_i, c_E),$

   $w \cdot f(t, h, p_i, c_{NE}))$;

  $p \leftarrow \hat{p}_i$;

 end for

 $c \leftarrow \max(w \cdot f(t, h, p, c_E), w \cdot f(t, h, p, c_{NE}))$

Algorithm 2 describes the decoding procedure, in which the most possible inference phenomenon token pairs are picked out using the joint model,   and scores of the two joint models, which assume the entailment judgment is *entailment* or *non-entailment*, is computed respectively. Finally, an entailment decision is made according to the higher one of such two score values.

3.3   Feature Space

There are two kinds of features used in this approach. One is for inference phenomenon identification and the other is for entailment judgment.

Inference Phenomenon Features The goal of the method $Gen(\cdot)$ is to find the rough identification results of inference phenomenon, while IP features are employed for fine identification. Such features investigate coincidence and similarity of string and structural contexts:

$$C(x, y),\ C(x_{+1}, y_{+1}),\ C(x_{-1}, y_{-1}), C(x_\uparrow, y_\uparrow), C(x^{pos}, y^{pos}),$$
$$C(x^{pos}_{+1}, y^{pos}_{+1}),\ C(x^{pos}_{-1}, y^{pos}_{-1}),\ C(x^{pos}_\uparrow, y^{pos}_\uparrow),\ C(x^{len}_\uparrow, y^{len}_\uparrow),$$
$$C(x^{role}, y^{role}),\ S(x_\downarrow, y_\downarrow),\ S(x_{sib}, y_{sib})$$

where + and - means the left and right word, $\uparrow$ and $\downarrow$ means the syntactic parent and children, *pos* means Part-Of-Speech, *len* means the length to the syntactic root, *role* means semantic constituent, *sib* means the siblings. $C(\cdot)$ judges if the two tokens are

---

[§] http://nlp.stanford.edu/

identical and $S(\cdot)$ computes the similarity of two sets derived from the two tokens. Note that one of the two tokens may missing; in such cases the feature value is 0.

Entailment Judgment Features The goal of these features are used for the overall entailment judgment. Such features are investigated by many researches. In this paper, a feature set named basic features proposed by Ren et al.[11], which includes string, structure and linguistic features, is employed. For joint learning, some additional features are also used: for each token pair in p, if none of the two tokens is missing, replace the token in H by the token in T and build the features in accordance with basic features; otherwise, assign the additional feature values to 0.

4 Experiment

4.1 Settings

The performance of the joint model reported in this paper is evaluated on the dataset in NTCIR RITE-3 challenge, including 581 training data and 1200 test data, each of which contains a premise and a hypothesis annotated with an inference phenomenon and an entailment class of them. Such data are preprocessed as follows:

1)normalize punctuations and half-width characters;

2)for each text pair, do word segmentation, POS tagging, dependency analysis and semantic role labeling;

3)recognize named entities in texts.

The metrics in the experiment are precision, recall and F-1 score.

4.2 Evaluation on Entailment Judgment

In this evaluation, four systems are set: the first one(baseline1) uses only basic features for entailment judgment to classify entailment in texts, not identifying inference phenomena; the second one(baseline2) is similar with the first system, except that the inference phenomenon features generated according to the inference phenomenon schema are incorporated; the third one(pipeline) uses a pipelined way, that is, firstly identify inference phenomena using the inference phenomenon features, then judge entailment using basic features in entailment judgment features; the fourth one(joint-F_{EJ_add}) adopts a jointly simple way, that is, the input of the model is text pairs and the output of the model is the entailment judgment, while features used in the model are the same with the third system; the fifth one(joint+F_{EJ_add}) is a joint model with all the features like the third system, a.k.a., the model introduced in Section 3.2. All the systems uses averaged perceptron for training and prediction. Experimental results are shown in Table 2.

The experimental results show that, in comparison with the performance of the baseline1, the fifth system(this paper's approach) achieves an improving 11.4% of precision, 6.17% of recall and 9.48% of F1 for entailment class, and an improving 5.11% of precision, 12.17% of recall and 9.86% of F1 for non-entailment class. Apparently, the approach in this paper remarkably improve the performance for RTE.

Table 2. Results of entailment judgment.

	Entailment			Non-entailment		
	P	R	F1	P	R	F1
baseline1	0.5119	0.6800	0.5841	0.5583	0.3750	0.4487
baseline2	0.5523	0.6950	0.6155	0.5910	0.4383	0.5033
Pipeline	0.5687	0.7033	0.6289	0.6004	0.4583	0.5198
joint-$F_{EJ\ add}$	0.6030	0.7317	0.6611	**0.6165**	0.4850	0.5429
joint+$F_{EJ\ add}$	**0.6259**	**0.7417**	**0.6789**	0.6094	**0.4967**	**0.5473**

It also can be seen from the experimental results that:

1)It is efficient to improve the performance of RTE by identifying inference phenomena in texts. In comparison with the performance of the baseline1, baseline2 achieves an increasing 4.04% of precision, 1.5% of recall and 3.14% of F1 for entailment class, and an increasing 3.27% of precision, 6.33% of recall and 5.47% of F1 performance for non-entailment class.

2)Fine inference phenomenon identification helps to improve the entailment recognition performance. The pipeline system outperforms the baseline2 in every metric, showing that the performance of RTE can be improved by identifying inference phenomena more precisely.

3)It is a better way to joint two related tasks of inference phenomenon identification and entailment judgment as an incorporated one. In comparison with the performance of the pipeline system, the joint system without additional features for entailment judgment(the fourth system) achieves an increasing 3.43% of precision, 2.83% of recall and 3.22% of F1 for entailment class, and an increasing 1.61% of precision, 2.67% of recall and 2.31% of F1 performance for non-entailment class, showing that joint learning of such two tasks helps to improve the performance of entailment judgment.

4)Although how to incorporate the two tasks of inference phenomenon identification and entailment judgment still needs to be discussed, the system performance proves an valuable exploration for the problem: the performances in nearly most metrics of the fifth system outperform those of the fourth system, and the reason lies in that, the additional features for entailment judgment help to improve entailment judgment according to the results of inference phenomenon identification, which can also be tuned by the result of entailment judgment, just like the example in Section 3.2.

4.3   Evaluation on Inference Phenomenon Identification

This evaluation reports the performances of the pipeline and the joint approach for inference phenomenon identification. Such systems are the third and the fifth one described in Section 4.2. The metric in this evaluation is F1 score. The results are shown in Table 3.

The experiment results show that the performances of joint approach outperform the pipeline one in most cases of inference phenomenon identification. Obviously, just as the discussion in the Section 4.2 points out that, inference phenomenon identification and entailment judgment promote each other to achieve a better performance.

Table 3. Results of inference phenomenon identification.

	Joint	Pipeline
Abbreviation	0.6761	0.6657
Apposition	0.7187	0.6353
Case_alternation	0.3655	0.2641
Clause	0.7240	0.6446
Coreference	0.4295	0.3986
Hypernymy	0.6581	0.6566
Lexical_entailment	0.5103	0.4287
List	0.4730	0.4122
Meronymy	0.5837	0.6268
Modifier	0.6983	0.5487
Quantity	0.6360	0.6049
Scrambling	0.6410	0.6706
Spatial	0.6155	0.6142
Synonymy	0.6843	0.6286
Temporal	0.6433	0.6323
Transparent_head	0.6298	0.7290
Antonym	0.5127	0.3965
Exclusion:predicate _argument	0.5249	0.4420
Exclusion:quantity	0.6449	0.6127
Exclusion:spatial	0.5207	0.5604
Exclusion:temporal	0.6304	0.5984
Negation	0.4081	0.3805
Macro-F1	0.5877	0.5478

It also can be seen that, some inference phenomena are easy to be identified, such as *apposition*, *synonymy* and *modifier*. Those phenomena are lexical ones and easy to be identified since the required knowledge for identification is easy to be acquired. On the other hand, performances of some inference phenomena are very low, for example, *case_alternation*. Identifying such inference phenomena needs fine linguistic analysis as well as richer knowledge support, rather than matching templates that are pre-defined.

5   Conclusion

This paper introduces a joint approach to incorporate inference phenomenon identification and entailment judgment for RTE. In this approach, averaged perceptron is used to build a linear model to predict entailment class and inference phenomena by employing features from such two tasks. The approach not only helps to recognize entailment in texts, which is approved on the experiments, but also contributes to exploring a way to find reasons and explanations for textual entailment.

Acknowledgements

This work is supported by National Natural Science Foundation of China(61402341, 61402119), Bidding Project of GDUFS Laboratory of Language Engineering and Compting(LEC2016ZBKT 001, LEC-2016ZBKT002) and China Postdoctoral Science Foundation funded project(2013M540594).

References

1. Androutsopoulos, I. and Malakasiotis, P.: A Survey of Paraphrasing and Textul Entailment Methods. Journal of Artificial Intelligence Research, 38(1), 135-187 (2010).
2. Dagan, I. and Dolan, B.: Recognizing textual entailment: Rational, evaluation and approaches. Natural Language Engineering, 15(4), i-xvii (2009).
3. Bentivogli, L., Cabrio, E., Dagan, I., Giampiccolo, D., Leggio, M. L. and Magnini, B.: Building textual entailment specialized data sets: a methodology for isolating linguistic phenomena relevant to inference. Proceedings of the International Conference on Language Resources and Evaluation, Valletta, Malta (2010).
4. Kaneko, K., Miyao, Y. and Bekki, D.: Building Japanese Textual Entailment Specialized Data Sets for Inference of Basic Sentence Relations. In proceedings of the 51st Annual Meeting of the Association of Computational Linguistics Sofia, Bulgaria (2013).
5. Sammons, M., Vydiswaran, V. G. V. and Roth, D.: "Ask not what Textual Entailment can do for you...". Proceedings of the Annual Meeting of the Association for Computational Linguistics, Uppsala, Sweden (2010).
6. Garoufi, K.: Towards a better understanding of applied textual entailment: Annotation and evaluation of the RTE-2 dataset. Germany, Saarland University, Master Thesis (2007).
7. Matsuyoshi, S., Miyao, Y., Shibata, T., Lin, C.-J., Shih, C.-W., Watanabe, Y., et al.: Overview of the NTCIR-11 Recognizing Inference in TExt and Validation (RITE-VAL) Task. In Proceedings of the 11th NTCIR Conference (2014).
8. Huang, H.-H., Chang, K.-C. and Chen, H.-H.: Modeling Human Inference Process for Textual Entailment Recognition. Proceedings of the 51st Annual Meeting of the Association for Computational Linguistics, Sofia, Bulgaria (2013).
9. Ren, H., Wu, H., Tan, X., Wang, P. and Wan, J.: The WHUTE System in NTCIR-11 RITE Task. In Proceedings of the 11th NTCIR Conference, Tokyo, Japan (2014).
10. Zhang, Z., Zhou, H., Yao, D. and Lu, X.: Recognition of Chinese Lexical Entailment Relation Based on Word Vector(in Chinese). Computer Engineering, 42(2), 169-174 (2016).
11. Ren, H., Wu, H., Lv, C., Ji, D. and Wan, J.: The WHUTE System in NTCIR-10 RITE Task. Proceeding of the 10th NTCIR Conference, Tokyo, Japan (2013).

Deriving Probabilistic Semantic Frames from HowNet

Yidong Chen[1, 2], Yu Wan[1, 2], Xiaodong Shi[1, 2], Suxia Xu[1, 2, *]

[1] Department of Cognitive Science, School of Information and Engineering, Xiamen University, Xiamen 361005, P. R. China
[2] Fujian Key Laboratory of Brain-inspired Computing Technique and Applications, Xiamen University, Xiamen 361005, P. R. China
[*] Corresponding Author: suxiaxu@xmu.edu.cn

Abstract. Representing knowledge as frames has a long history in artificial intelligence and computational linguistics. However, constructing frame banks that support frame-based processing is quite time-consuming, leading to the unavailability of usable frame banks for many languages, including Chinese. This paper proposed a method for deriving probabilistic semantic frames from HowNet, which is a well-known common-sense knowledge base and has been successfully used in many NLP applications. Unlike most previous HowNet-related work which focused on using HowNet as a lexico-semantic bank, this work viewed the HowNet dictionary as a semantic-annotated corpus. According to the proposed method, governor-role-dependent triples are firstly extracted from the concept definitions of the HowNet dictionary. Then, they are organized into frames by the governors and the probabilities are estimated based on maximum likelihood estimation (MLE). Finally, the probabilistic frames form a frame bank. Moreover, in order to overcome the data sparseness problem, a smoothing method based on HowNet's taxonomy was put forward. To verify the constructed frame bank, we applied it in a task to recognize relationships between Chinese word pairs, which are extracted from the Chinese Message Structure Database of HowNet. The experimental results showed that, even without using context information, the system based on the constructed frame bank achieved an accuracy of 83.74%, which indicates the soundness of the constructed frame bank.

Keywords: Semantic Frames, Probabilistic, HowNet.

1 Introduction

Representing knowledge as frames has a long his-tory in artificial intelligence and psychology. Especially, in the linguistics and computational linguistics communities, frame semantics [1], which uses frames as the central representation of word meaning, has proved to be a useful semantic representation, with the development and applications of FrameNet [2]. Actually, research related to frames (e.g. [3]; [4]) is still one of the hotspots in the field of natural language processing (NLP).

Clearly, FrameNet is a key resource for frame-based NLP tasks. Unfortunately, due to the high cost of manual construction, FrameNet-like resources for most languages,

© Springer International Publishing AG 2018
Y. Wu et al. (Eds.): CLSW 2017, LNAI 10709, pp. 303–314, 2018.
https://doi.org/10.1007/978-3-319-73573-3_27

including Chinse, are not available or small in scale compared with the FrameNet for English [5].

In addition to building FrameNet manually, there were also works on building FrameNet for other languages by mapping frames from English FrameNet based on bilingual resources. For example, [6] and [7] both tried to derive Chinese FrameNet from English FrameNet based on Chinese-English resources. Although these approaches could greatly reduce the human labor, they have two problems. Firstly, they only focus on the mapping of the frames without involving the mapping of the annotated corpus. This leads to the fact that the derived resources are often not sufficient to be used as computational resources, since frames themselves do not contain probability information. Secondly, it is still an open problem whether or not one-to-one correspondences between frames for two different languages exist. Actually, existing research (e.g. [5]; [8]) suggests that the one-to-one assumption may not apply to all situations.

On the other hand, being a common-sense knowledge base, HowNet [9] has been successfully applied in many NLP applications. According to HowNet's philosophy, semantic relation is also an important concept. Actually, HowNet defines common frames for all the Event sememes. For example, according to the HowNet taxonomy, the required frame elements for the {try|尝试} event is defined as `agent` and `content`. Moreover, by carefully observing the HowNet dictionary, we find that the definitions of the concepts actually provide a huge number of instances for semantic relations. For example, the definition of the concept 枪 is expressed as:

```
{weapon|武器:{firing|射击:instrument={~}}}
```

And it is actually an instance of the instru-ment relation, as follows:

```
<firing|射击, instrument, weapon|武器>
```

Therefore, we may regard HowNet dictionary as a semantic annotated corpus, which could be used as a good source for learning probabilistic frames.

In this paper, we proposed a method for extracting frames from HowNet dictionary. To the best of our knowledge, although HowNet has been wildly used, most work focus on using it as a reasoning machine based on its taxonomies, none has been conducted to tackle this point.

The rest of this paper is organized as follows. Section 2 gives a brief introduction of HowNet. Section 3 describes the method for deriving probabilistic semantic frames from HowNet dictionary in detail. Section 4 describes the experiments we conducted for verifying the derived frame bank. Finally, we give a conclusion in section 5.

2   A Brief Introduction to HowNet

HowNet is an on-line common-sense knowledge base unveiling inter-conceptual relations and inter-attribute relations of concepts by means of lexicons of Chinese and their English equivalents [10].

Each concept in HowNet lexicon is defined in a language, called Knowledge Database Markup Language (KDML). The KDML is mainly composed of sememes, which are unseparated semantic units and are organized in hierarchical taxonomies, and semantic roles. Concretely, the KDML uses 2089 sememes, 128 secondary features and 94 semantic roles as its vocabulary and adopts an extended BNF as its syntax. Actually, a KDML expression could be viewed as a semantic graph. For example, the definition for the concept 经理, i.e.

```
{human|人:
        HostOf={Occupation|职位},
        domain={economy|经济},
        modifier={official|官}, {manage|管理:agent={~}}}
```

could be looked on as the following semantic graph (see Fig. 1):

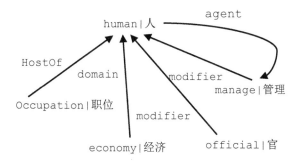

Fig. 1. The semantic graph corresponding to the concept of "经理"

3   Method

This section describes the method of automatically deriving probabilistic semantic frames from the HowNet dictionary. The basic extraction procedure will be addressed, followed by the description of the smoothing method.

3.1   Extracting Frames from the HowNet Concept Definitions

Formally, probabilistic frames could be defined as follows,

```
<Frame> ::= (<FN> <Count> <FE>+)
<FE> ::= (<FEN> <Count> <Prob> <Role>+)
<Role> ::= (<RN> <Count> <Prob>)
<FN> ::= sememe defined in HowNet
<RN> ::= sememe defined in HowNet
<FEN>::= relation defined in HowNet
<Count> ::= Real Values
<Prob> ::= Real Values
```

As shown in the above definition, a frame <Frame> is composed of a frame name <FN> and a set of frame elements <FE>. And, a frame element <FE> consists of a frame element name <FEN> and a set of candidate roles <Role>. Obviously, this definition is very similar to that of FrameNet, except that two additional fields, i.e. <Count> and <Prob> were introduced to represent the counts and probabilities, respectively. Moreover, in this definition, the frame name <FN> and the role name <RN>, are both the sememes defined in HowNet, and the frame element name <FE_Name> is the semantics relation defined in HowNet.

According to this definition, the procedure for extracting probabilistic semantic frames from the concept definitions of the HowNet dictionary can be described in Algorithm 3.1, as follows:

Algorithm 3.1
```
Input: hownet_dictionary
Output: frame_set
frame_set ← φ
foreach def in hownet_dictionary do
   TS ← GetTriples(def);
   foreach <g, r, d> in TS
      IncCounts(frame_set, g, r, d, 1);
   end foreach
end foreach
foreach fr in frame_set do
   fr.fe.prob ← fr.r.count/fr.count;
   fr.fe.r.prob ← fr.fe.r.count/fr.fe.count;
end foreach
frame_set ← CutOffByProb(frame_set);
return frame_set;
```

where GetTriples function recursively gathers all the semantic triples from the given concept definition, which is actually a semantic graph. For example, when given the concept of "带徒弟", as follows:

```
{teach|教:target={human|人:{study|学习:agent={~}}}}
```

GetTriples function will first construct its corresponding semantic graph, as shown in Fig. 2,

Fig. 2. The semantic graph corresponding to the concept of "带徒弟"

and then extract a set which contains the following two semantic triples:

```
<teach|教, target, human|人>
<study|学习, agent, human|人>
```

Moreover, `IncCounts` function increases the count field of frames, frame elements, and roles that match the given triplet, and `CutOffByProb` function removes all frame elements and roles whose probabilities are less than a given threshold, which is set to 0.001 in this paper.

3.2 Smoothing Based on the HowNet Taxonomies

Due to the data sparsity, the semantic frames obtained by Algorithm 3.1 are still problematic. On the one hand, some important frame elements are still missing. On the other hand, the corresponding probabilities estimated are far not accurate. For example, by performing Algorithm 3.1, the following probabilistic frame for the {steal| 偷} will be derived:

```
{steal|偷}
  agent 57.38% (17.50)
    {human|人} 100.00% (17.50)
  location 9.84% (3.00)
    {InstitutePlace|场所} 100.00% (3.00)
  source 6.56% (2.00)
    {facilities|设施} 100.00% (2.00)
  modifier 3.28% (1.00)
    {guilty|有罪} 100.00% (1.00)
```

In this frame, the frame element `possession` was not learned. However, as defined in the Event taxonomy of HowNet, `possession` is a required frame element of the {steal| 偷} event.

However, if we observe the frame for its parent sememe {take| 取} and its sibling sememe {rob| 抢}, as shown below, we may find the learned `possession` frame element. This suggests that the information contained in the frames for {take|取} and {rob|抢} could be borrowed for smoothing the frame for {steal|偷}.

```
{take|取}
  possession 59.65% (17.00)
    {water|水} 29.41% (5.00)
    {information|信息} 17.65% (3.00)
    {lights|光} 11.76% (2.00)
    {place|地方} 5.88% (1.00)
    {letter|信件} 5.88% (1.00)
  manner 31.58% (9.00)
    {fierce|暴} 55.56% (5.00)
    {unlawful|非法} 11.11% (1.00)
    {alone|独自} 11.11% (1.00)
    {SetAside|留存} 22.22% (2.00)
  source 28.07% (8.00)
    {facilities|设施} 62.50% (5.00)
    {computer|电脑} 37.50% (3.00)
  patient 1.75% (0.50)
    {information|信息} 100.00% (0.50)

{rob|抢}
  agent 70.68% (47.00)
    {human|人} 95.74% (45.00)
    {community|团体} 4.26% (2.00)
  location 12.03% (8.00)
    {waters|水域} 100.00% (8.00)
  possession 9.02% (6.00)
    {Power|势力} 33.33% (2.00)
    {aircraft|飞行器} 33.33% (2.00)
    {human|人} 16.67% (1.00)
    {wealth|钱财} 16.67% (1.00)
  domain 9.02% (6.00)
    {royal|皇} 100.00% (6.00)
  source 5.26% (3.50)
    {family|家庭} 85.71% (3.00)
    {human|人} 14.29% (0.50)
  manner 4.51% (3.00)
```

```
   {unlawful|非法} 100.00% (3.00)
 patient 3.01% (2.00)
   {human|人} 100.00% (2.00)
 means 3.01% (2.00)
   {frighten|吓唬} 100.00% (2.00)
 purpose 1.50% (1.00)
   {mating|交配} 100.00% (1.00)
```

Inspired by the observations, we propose a smoothing method based on the HowNet taxonomies. The general idea is that the semantic frames with inheritance or affinity should be similar and can be borrowed for smoothing. Concretely speaking, the following three heuristic rules are used:

Rule 1 smoothing by parent relationship:

If a triple <gov, slot, dep> is observed to occur n times, add $\alpha*n$ occurrence times to the triple <ParentOf(gov),slot,dep>. Here, α is an adjustable parameter and ParentOf($\cdot$) is a function that returns the parent sememe of the given sememe in the HowNet taxonomy.

Rule 2 smoothing by children relationship:

If a triple <gov, slot, dep> is observed to occur n times, add $\beta*n$/ChildrenCount(gov) occurrence times to every triples <cgov, slot, dep> that satisfies gov=ParentOf(cgov). Here, β is an adjustable parameter and ChildrenCount($\cdot$) is a function that returns the children amount of a given sememe in the HowNet taxonomy.

Rule 3 smoothing by sibling relationship:

If a triple <gov, slot, dep> is observed to occur n times, add $\gamma*n$ occurrence times to the triple <sgov, slot, dep> that satisfies ParentOf(gov)=ParentOf(sgov). Here, γ is an adjustable parameter.

By introducing the above three rules in the extraction algorithm, we obtain a more reasonable probability frame bank. As an example, we list the final probabilistic frame for {steal|偷} as follows,

```
{steal|偷}
  agent 53.05% (26.08)
    {human|人} 99.42% (25.93)
  location 9.01% (4.43)
    {InstitutePlace|场所} 98.86% (4.38)
  source 6.19% (3.04)
    {facilities|设施} 99.01% (3.01)
  possession 4.76% (2.34)
    {money|货币} 19.30% (0.45)
    {wealth|钱财} 17.66% (0.41)
    {expenditure|费用} 15.95% (0.37)
    {artifact|人工物} 7.10% (0.17)
    {payment|酬金} 5.38% (0.13)
    {news|新闻} 5.12% (0.12)
    {crop|庄稼} 3.57% (0.08)
    {coupon|票证} 3.06% (0.07)
    {fund|资金} 2.36% (0.06)
  modifier 4.07% (2.00)
    {guilty|有罪} 100.00% (2.00)
  domain 1.27% (0.62)
    {economy|经济} 34.17% (0.21)
    {military|军} 28.84% (0.18)
    {agricultural|农} 13.40% (0.08)
    {police|警} 12.28% (0.08)
```

Clearly, the missing frame elements and roles are now learned after the smoothing. Moreover, the probabilities are more reasonable.

4   Experiments

There are no standard methods for verifying the soundness of semantic frame banks. In this experiment, we used the derived frame bank in a task of recognizing relationships between given Chinese word pairs and verified its soundness by testing the recognition system based on it. This section describes this experiment in detail, including the data, the recognition method, and the results.

4.1 Data

The data used in the experiment comes from the HowNet's Chinese Message Structure Base [11], which contains 268 Message Structure Patterns and 11,000 examples. Concretely, a Message Structure Pattern consists of the following 4 parts:

- A syntax pattern
- A semantic pattern, which shows the semantic categories of the participants, the semantic relationship and the semantic dependency direction.
- A set of query-answer pairs which show the possible questions and answers about this message structure.
- A set of example word pairs.

Below shows an example of a Message Structure:

```
SYN_S = V --> N
SEM_S = (event|事件)-->[possession](thing|万物/part|部件)
Query1: What is event?
Answer1: V + N
Examples: 取-款,取-钱,取-货,换-汇,换-房,换-货,施-惠,...
```

Please note that, we do not use all the examples from the HowNet's Chinese Message Structure Base. Specifically, we removed the following data:

- Examples for the message structures with more than two participating sememes.
- Examples for the message structures related to and relationships.
- Examples for the message structures related to naming entities.
- Examples that contain unknown words.

Finally, 2,933 word pairs were selected, among which 10% were used as developing data and other 90% were used as testing data. Table 1 shows the statistics.

Table 1. The Statistics of the Testing Data

Types	Amount of patterns	Amount of word pairs
Message Structures related to Entity/Part	34	566
Message Structures related to Event	50	1,216
Message Structures related to Attribute	5	227
Message Structures related to Attribute Value	9	805
Message Structures related to Time	1	15
Message Structures related to Space	2	104
Total	101	2,933

4.2   The Recognition Method

Since this method is used to test the capability of the derived probabilistic frame bank, it has a simply framework, which uses probabilistic information in the frame bank to calculate the probability of the relationship and uses the HowNet's taxonomies to measure the similarities. Moreover, similar to most semantic role annotation work, we assume that the syntactical information, i.e. POS information, has already been obtained in advance. And, this method does not use external information such as context.

```
Algorithm 4.1
Input: word1, pos1, word2, pos2
Output: <sem1, sem2, rel, dir>
WS1 ← LookUpHowNet(word1, pos1);
WS2 ← LookUpHowNet(word2, pos2);
score_best ← MIN_VAL;
foreach ws1 in WS1 do
    foreach ws2 in WS2 do
        fs1 ← GetFirstSememe(ws1); fs2 ← GetFirstSememe(ws2);
        fr ← LookUpFrameBank(fs1);
        foreach fe in fr.slots do
            d ← GetMostSimSememe(fr.fe.r, fs2)
            score ← λ₁*Log(fr.fe.prob) +
                    λ₂*Log(fr.fe.r.prob) +
                    λ₃*Log(Sim(d, fs2));
            if score > score_best then
                score_best ← score;
                sem1_b ← ws1; sem2_b ← ws2;
                rel_b ← fe; dir_b ← right;
            end if
        end foreach
        fr ← LookUpFrameBank(fs2);
        foreach fe in fr.slots do
            d ← GetMostSimSememe(fr.fe.r, fs1)
            score ← λ₁*Log(fr.fe.prob) +
                    λ₂*Log(fr.fe.r.prob) +
                    λ₃*Log(Sim(d, fs1));
            if score > score_best then
                score_best ← score;
                sem1_b ← ws1; sem2_b ← ws2;
                rel_b ← fe; dir_b ← left;
            end if
        end foreach
    end foreach
end foreach
return <sem1_b, sem2_b, rel_b, dir_b>
```

Algorithm 4.1 is very simple: by looking up the dictionary and traversing all possible combinations, it finally selects the combination with the highest score as the output. And, score is calculated based on a log-linear model, which contains three features concerning probability information and similarity information. Moreover, the parameters were tuned based on MER method using the developing data.

Although the above algorithm is simple, the recognition results are encouraging. Table 2 lists three examples concerning "吃", which shows that the simple algorithm give encouraging results.

Table 2. Three Examples Concerning "吃"

Inputs	Results
吃 V 烤鸭 N	{eat|吃}, {food|食品}, patient, 1
吃 V 食堂 N	{eat|吃}, {InstitutePlace|场所}, location, 1
吃 V 老本 N	{depend|依靠}, {fund|资金}, partner, 1

4.3 Results

The experimental results are shown in Table 3. From the experimental results, two points could be learned. First, the smoothing method could bring significant improvements. Secondly, the derived frame bank and the probabilistic information contained in it are quite reasonable.

Table 3. The Results

Types	Precision (%)	
	No smoothing	Smoothing
Message Structures related to Entity/Part	68.73	86.04
Message Structures related to Event	60.87	74.16
Message Structures related to Attribute	72.17	84.35
Message Structures related to Attribute Value	77.27	94.04
Message Structures related to Time	80.00	100
Message Structures related to Space	89.42	100
Total	68.87	**83.74**

5   Conclusion

In this paper, we propose a method for automatically deriving probabilistic frames from HowNet. To verify the constructed frame bank, we applied it in a task to recognize relationships between Chinese word pairs extracted from the Chinese Message Structure Database of HowNet. The experimental results showed that, even without using context information, the system based on the constructed frame bank achieved an accuracy of 83.74%.

Acknowledgement

This work was supported by National Natural Science Foundation of China (No. 61573294), National Social Science Foundation of China (No. 16AZD049) and Fujian Province 2011 Collaborative Innovation Center of TCM Health Management.

References

1. Fillmore, C. J.: Frame Semantics. In: Linguistics in the Morning Calm. Hanshin, Seoul (1982).
2. Baker, C. F., Fillmore, C. J., Lowe J. B.: The Berkeley FrameNet Prject. In: Proc. of COLING-ACL 1998, pp. 86-90. Association for Computational Linguistics, USA (1998).
3. Johannsen, A., Alonso, H. M., Søgaard A.: Any-language frame-semantic parsing. In: Proc. of EMNLP 2015, pp. 2062-2066. Association for Computational Linguistics, Portugal (2015).
4. Liu, S., Chen, Y., He, S., Liu, K., Zhao, J.: Leveraging FrameNet to Improve Automatic Event Detection. In: Proc. of ACL 2016, pp. 2134-2143. Association for Computational Linguistics, Germany (2016).
5. You, L., Liu, K.: Building Chinese FrameNet Database. In: Proc. of NLP-KE 2005. IEEE, China (2005).
6. Chen, B., Fung, P.: Automatic Construction of an English-Chinese Bilingual FrameNet. In: Proc. of HLT-NAACL 2004, Association for Computational Linguistics, USA (2004).
7. Chow, I. C., Webster, J. J: Populating FrameNet with Chinese Verbs Mapping Bilingual Ontological WordNet with FrameNet. In: Proc. of ICCPOL 2006, pp. 165-172. Springer, Germany (2006).
8. Ma, H.: A Systematic Study of Frame Semantic in the Domain of Transaction of Chinese. Ph. D Dissertation. Shanghai Normal University, Shanghai (2008).
9. Dong, Z., Dong, Q.: Hownet and the Computation of Meaning. World Scientific, USA (2006).
10. Dong, Z., Dong, Q., Hao, X.: HowNet and Its Computation of Meaning. In: Proc. of COLING 2010, pp. 53-56. China (2010).
11. Dong, Z., Dong, Q.: HowNet's Chinese Message Structure Base of HowNet. http://www.keenage.com, last accessed 2017/5/12.

Semantic Relations Mining in Social Tags Based on a Modern Chinese Semantic Dictionary

Jiangying YU [0000-0003-1822-1461]

Yunnan Open University, Kunming, Yunnan, 650223, China
Beijing Language and Culture University, Beijing, 10083, China
yujiangying2008@qq.com

Abstract. At present, many scholars have studied the semantic relations mining in social tags based on *WordNet*—an English semantic dictionary and have made some progress. There have been few studies to combine modern Chinese semantic dictionary and social tags. The paper selects tag data from *Dòubàn Reading* first, then uses the classification and coding system of *A Thesaurus of Modern Chinese*(TMC), calculates the semantic similarity of tag data and mines the semantic relations in social tags by *WordSimilarity*—a lexical semantic similarity computing system. The results obtained with this method, not so different from the way we think of lexical semantic relations, have a higher accuracy.

Keywords: Semantic Relations, Social Tags, Semantic Dictionary.

1 Introduction

In recent years, with the development and popularization of Web2.0 such as del.icio.us, flicker, Dòubàn, etc, the generation, organization, publishing and sharing of Internet information have been changed, network users have become more and more important and a user-centered social network has gradually formed. Network information users spontaneously choose proper words to describe certain types of resources according to their own understanding of information resources. This free-optional, convenient and flexible way of classification has been welcomed by the network information users, since the markup language is not subject to any restrictions. For folksonomies' labels, on the other hand, there are some shortcomings; for instance, the diversity, fuzziness, and unorganized state of the labels and the lack of semantic relations between words, which not only seriously affect the efficiency of information retrieval, but are difficult to adapt to the requirements of the semantic web. Therefore, we hope to optimize the folksonomy system, improve the efficiency of the network information dissemination and retrieval and construct a semantic network between tags.

Literature research reveals that empirical studies on specialized systems for Chinese characteristics have not been carried out yet in China. A small amount of empirical data basically comes from foreign popular folksonomy websites such as

© Springer International Publishing AG 2018
Y. Wu et al. (Eds.): CLSW 2017, LNAI 10709, pp. 315–320, 2018.
https://doi.org/10.1007/978-3-319-73573-3_28

del.icio.us, and instances are also selected from foreign online dictionary such as WordNet. As Chinese language has its own characteristics, transplanting the results of foreign research simply is not effective. Therefore, this paper tries to mine the semantic relations in social tags by selecting tag data from *Dòubàn Reading* and *TMC*.

2   A Thesaurus of Modern Chinese (TMC)

SU Xin-chun and his team have completed *A Thesaurus of Modern Chinese(TMC)* in 2013. *TMC* inherits the tradition of conceptual classification since *Synonym Dictionary* to reflect conception relations of the whole society and human recognition. It embodies more than 80,000 modern Chinese words with high frequency and constructs a five-level semantic classification system with 9 classes in the first level, 62 in the second level, 508 in the third level, 2,057 in the fourth level and 12,659 fifth-level classifications. This kind of semantic classification emphasizes the governing function from upper semantic levels to subordinate levels, the coverage function of the subordinate semantic levels to the upper levels and the complementary function between the neighboring semantic levels.

Different methods have been respectively used in the five-level semantic classification. Numbers in capital Chinese characters are first-level, lower-case characters are second-level, capital letters are third-level, lower letters are fourth-level, Arabic numerals are fifth-level. Therefore, you can clearly show the semantic class hierarchy and sequence with a set of numbers, and every word has a unique "ID." For example, the word "people" has an ID of "壹一Aa01," while the word "dictionary" has an ID of "叁八Eb29."

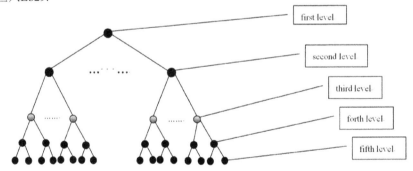

Fig. Five-level semantic classification system of *TMC*.

3   Word Similarity Computation Based on *TMC*

Polysemy is prevalent in the Chinese language. One word may have more than one meaning. This is what we call polysemy, and such a word is called a polysemous word. Multiple meanings of a polysemy are usually placed under the same item of one word in a traditional dictionary, while different meanings of a polysemy are placed under different items in *TMC*. The word "milk," for example, has three IDs: 壹五 Ae08, 壹五 Ca07, and 伍七 Cd02. Therefore, when calculating the similarity of Chinese words, we should consider all the meanings of one word. When calculating the similarity of two words, we first find out different IDs for different meanings of polysemy in *TMC*, then calculate its similarity, and finally take the maximum of the similarity as the similarity of two words. The specific calculation method is to first judge two meanings of polysemy as a leaf node branch from which level in *TMC*, and see the IDs of the two meanings of polysemy differ from which level. Judging from first-level, if IDs are kept the same, multiply this number by 1, otherwise, multiply by the corresponding coefficient from the branch level. In addition, to guarantee the similarity of two meanings' controls in [0, 1], multiply it by a parameter adjustment $\cos\left(n * \frac{\pi}{180}\right)$, then multiply it by a controls parameter $\frac{n - k + 1}{n}$ since the similarity will be directly affected by it to branch from which level. Among them, n is the total number of nodes of branching, k is the distance between two branches, so you can get more precise similarity of different meanings of polysemy.

In addition, we also introduce a word semantic similarity computing system called *WordSimilarity*. The system can calculate the semantic similarity between more than one word at the same time. We will choose this system to calculate the semantic similarity between words tags, which generally fall into two cases:

First, simple words, which have been included in *TMC*. We can directly calculate the semantic similarity between simple words with the *WordSimilarity* system, which can also be used as the credibility of the corresponding matching concept. For instance, the semantic similarity between "literature" and "novel" we calculated is 0.899.

Second, compound words, which are formed by some simple words and have not been included in *TMC*. For compound words, firstly, we complete the compound word segmentation by positive maximum matching method, then calculate the semantic similarity between simple words after the segmentation by *WordSimilarity* system, and finally we take the average value as the semantic similarity between compound words. For example, we calculate the semantic similarity between "literature " and "Chinese literature" like this: firstly, as a compound word, "Chinese literature" has been divided into "Chinese" and "literature," then we get the semantic similarity between "literature" and "Chinese" which is 0.899, then between "Chinese" and "China" which is 1.0 according to the *WordSimilarity* system, and finally we take the average value as the semantic similarity between "literature" and "Chinese literature" which is 0.793.

4   Empirical Studies

4.1   Tag Data

Douban.com (Chinese: 豆瓣; pinyin: Dòubàn), launched on March 6, 2005, is a Chinese SNS website allowing registered users to record information and create content related to film, books, music, and recent events and activities in Chinese cities. It can be seen as one of the most influential web 2.0 websites in China. Unlike Facebook and Renren, *Dòubàn* is open to both registered and unregistered users. For registered users, the site recommends potentially interesting books, movies, and music to them in addition to serving as a social network website and record keeper; for unregistered users, the site is a place to find ratings and reviews of said media.

In order to conduct research, we first extract the top 5 books from the 2016 list of Chinese literature in *Dòubàn Reading*, then extract the five *Dòubàn* members of the most respectively commonly used tags from these books resource tags, and finally we get a sample data set containing 25 labels (see Table 1).

Table 1. Label sample data set from *Dòubàn reading*.

book name	tag 1	tag 2	tag 3	tag 4	tag 5
午夜起来听寂静	poetry	poem	Chinese Literature	Literature	China
重读	essays	Literature	prose	Chinese Literature	writing
走进一座圣殿	essays	life	prose	Literature	China
平原上的摩西	novel	Chinese Literature	China	short story	Literature
台北人	novel	Chinese Literature	short story	Literature	China

4.2   Semantic Relations Mining in Social Tags Based on TMC

As before, we use *WordSimilarity* to calculate the semantic similarity between different tag words. Of these tags, the results for the simple words "poetry, poem, literature, Chinese literature, China, essays, prose, novel, short story, writing, life" can be found in Table 2 below.

Table 2. Semantic similarity between tag words based on *WordSimilarity*.

	poetry	poem	Chinese	Literature	China	essays	prose	writing	life	novel	short story
poetry	1.000										
poem	1.000	1.000									
Chinese	0.622	0.622	1.000								
Literature	0.657	0.657	0.793	1.000							
China	0.586	0.586	0.793	0.586	1.000						
essays	0.678	0.678	0.632	0.678	0.586	1.000					
prose	0.678	0.678	0.632	0.678	0.586	0.765	1.000				
writing	0.100	0.100	0.100	0.100	0.100	0.100	0.100	1.000			
life	0.586	0.586	0.451	0.586	0.315	0.586	0.586	0.541	1.000		
novel	0.657	0.657	0.743	0.899	0.586	0.678	0.678	0.100	0.586	1.000	
short story	0.657	0.657	0.743	0.899	0.586	0.678	0.678	0.100	0.586	0.959	1.000

We can see from the above calculation results:

(1) The semantic similarity between the two labels words "poetry" and "poem" is 1. Then we check the result in TMC and find that the ID of poetry and poem is the

same (叁八\Dd01). Thus, it could be concluded that "poetry" is synonymous with "poem.".

(2) There are several pairs of labels words whose semantic similarity is greater than 0.65 and less than 1 (< literature, poetry/poem >, < literature, Chinese literature >, < literature, essays>, < literature, prose >, < literature, novel >, < the literature, the short story >, < China, Chinese literature >, < essays, poetry / poem >, < essays, fiction >, < essays, short stories >, < prose, poetry / poem >, < prose, novels, essays, short stories >, < novels, poetry / poem >, < novels, Chinese literature >, < short stories, poetry / poem >, < short stories, Chinese literature >, < short story, novel >). These tag words share a high semantic similarity and constitute near-synonymy units.

(3) The semantic similarity between the tag word "writing" and other tag words is 0.1. That is to say, there is no correlation between the tag word "writing" and the other tag words. Then we check the result in TMC and find that the ID of "writing" is 陆五Ea01, which is viewed as clearly different from IDs of other tag words. Therefore, it can be concluded that there are no semantic relations between them.

5   Conclusions

Folksonomy is an important way of information organization in the network age. Semantic relations in mining through social tags can both greatly optimize the classification system of the masses, and provide theoretical support for the next generation of Internet comprehensive implementation. This paper is only a trial study with small sample sizes on semantic relations mining and as the experimental results show, the semantic relations mining based on *TMC* has a good accuracy. It's important to note that the inadequacies of the study are mainly the limitations regarding the research tools and sampling, limiting us from studying the subject further.

References

1. Chklovski, T., Pantel, P.: VerbOcean: Mining the Web for Fine-Grained Semantic Verb Relations. In: Proceedings of Conference on Empirical Methods in Natural Language Processing(EMNLP-04), pp. 33-40. Barcelona, Spain (2004).
2. Miller, G. A.: Wordnet: A Lexical Database for English. Communications of the ACM 38(11), 39–41(1995).
3. Dòubàn Homepage, https://en.wikipedia.org/wiki/Dòubàn, last accessed 2017/03/25.
4. Feng, L. I., Fang, L. I.: An New Approach Measuring Semantic Similarity in Hownet 2000. Journal of Chinese Information Processing21(3), 99-105 (2007).
5. Markines, B., Cattuto, C., Menczer, F., Benz, D., Hotho, A., & Stumme, G. Evaluating Similarity Measures for Emergent Semantics of Social Tagging. In: Proceedings of the International Conference on World Wide Web, pp.641–650. New York, NY, USA (2009).
6. Melnik, S., Garcia-Molina, H., & Rahm, E. Similarity Flooding: A Versatile Graph Matching Algorithm. In: Proceedings of the 18th International Conference on Data Engineering(ICDA), pp.117–128. Santa Barbara, CA, USA (2002).

7. Madhavan, J., Bernstein, P. A., & Rahm, e on Very Large Data Bases, pp.49–58. Morgan Kaufmann Publishers Inc, Italy (2001).
8. Su, X. CH. A Thesaurus of Modern Chinese (TMC). 1st edn. The Commercial Press, Beijing, CHN (2013).
9. Xiong, H. X.: Research Overview on the Combination of Tag and Ontology in Social Tagging System. Journal of Intelligence 32(8), 136–141 (2013).
10. Xiong, H. X., & Wang, X. D.: Research on Mapping between Tag and Ontology in Folksonomy System. Information Science32(3), 121–126 (2014).

Supported by the National Language Committee of China (Grant No. YB125-170).

Lexical Resources

The Study of Indian Domain Ontology Building Based on the Framework of HNC

Huang Jinzhu[1], Zhang Keliang[1,2] and Li Feng[3]

[1] Luoyang University of Foreign Languages Luoyang 471003, China
[2] Center for Computer and Language Information Engineering, CAS, Beijing 100089, China
[3] Logistics Science Research Institute, Beijing 100166, China
hjz_johnsmith@126.com

Abstract: The study applies the theory and method of Hierarchical Network of Concepts (or HNC theory) to Indian domain ontology building, which is approved to be effective. The process of ontology building covers two phases: collection of ontology terms, top-level framework design of ontology. Firstly, the study applies HowNet, TYCCL and Word2Vec to assist collecting India-relevant terms based on word similarity calculation, and then HNC conceptual tree table is applied to build Indian Ontology. The corpus of training Word2Vec models mainly comes from People daily, Wikipedia and Sogou news and then, based on the well-trained models, Word2Vec is applied to assist basic term collection. According to HNC conceptual tree table, the Indian Ontological Knowledge Base (or IOKB) covers seven general fields of India such as politics, economy, military and culture, etc. Currently, IOKB has more than 4350 concepts and instances, 51 object properties and 207 data properties.

Keywords: HNC, Domain ontology, India, Word2Vec

Although ontology-relevant research has witnessed more than 20 years of development and got gratifying achievements, application-oriented domain ontology building is still the focus of many fields especially military field. Under this background, this study applies technology of Deep Learning (or DL) to ontology term collection, which combines the subjective judgments of expertise and statistical information of Word2Vec to make ontology building project easier. Besides, in order to make ontology building project more precise and scientific, ontology researchers try to apply different methods to help design the top-level framework of ontolgy. HNC theory, one of the most important computational linguistic schools, has widely been ac-

© Springer International Publishing AG 2018
Y. Wu et al. (Eds.): CLSW 2017, LNAI 10709, pp. 323–335, 2018.
https://doi.org/10.1007/978-3-319-73573-3_29

cepted by various natual language processing fields. Applying HNC method to help design and implement Indian domain ontology is a kind of meaningful attempt and will undoubtedly better the general quality of ontology.

1   HNC and Ontology

1.1   HNC Theory

HNC theory[1] is created by Huang Zengyang, a well-known professor of Chinese Academy of Sciences. From linguistic conceptual space, HNC tries to supply a set of formalised representations on all entities of our world, which is applicable and meaningful to make machine or computer intelligent enough to understand human languages[1][2][3]. In the framework of HNC theory, the relationships of linguistic concept, language symbol and natural entity are as follows:

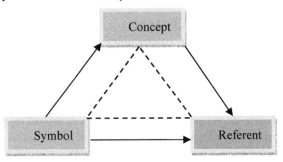

Fig.1. The relationships of concept, symbol and thing

HNC theory covers four different child theories: conceptual element theory, sentence category theory, contextual unit theory and contextual framework theory. In order to conceptualise human languages, HNC designs three semantic networks, elemental conceptual network, basic conceptual network and logic conceptual network, and these networks play an important role in natural language understanding and other NLP projects. This study takes elemental conceptual network and basic conceptual network as guideline to assist designing the top-level framework of IOKB.

1.2   Ontology

The concept of "ontology" firstly comes from philosophy in which ontology is called as entity theory or existential theory that is a systematic description of real entity

---

[1] http://www.hncnlp.com/

of the world [4][5]. In 1993, Gruber gives a widely recognized definition of ontology: ontology is a definite standard explanation of conceptual model [4][5]. As a subclass of ontology, domain ontology is an ontological knowledge base that covers knowledge of specific domain. According to the opinion of Perez, ontology can be organized by the method of classification, and he puts forward five different modeling primitives including class, relation, function, axiom and instance [6]. Ontology has unique ways of formalization and reasoning mechanism, and possessing the characteristics of knowledge sharing, semantic interoperability and reusability, etc [7].

2   Knowledge Resource Preparation for Ontology Building

Knowledge resource preparation is the first step and also the basic step of ontology project. Currently, ontology researchers apply various methods such as rule-based method [8], KB-based method [9] and statistics-based method [10] to collect ontology terms. In order to accomplish the task of building IOKB, the study applies a fusion method which combines HowNet, TYCCL and Word2Vec to help collecting ontology terms. And the general procedure of the study is as follows:

Indian domain ontology project mainly covers three phrases: model training, basic knowledge resource preparation and ontology building. The task of model training involves data crawling, data processing, and Word2Vec training. Then the well-trained models are integrated with HowNet[2] and TYCCL[3] to calculate word similarity. Basic knowledge resource preparation mainly involves three sub-tasks: creation of seed term set, term extension and creation of core term set. In order to make India-relevant terms systematic and authoritative, the study creates a seed term set through extracting terms from current authoritative dictionaries, books, CNKI[4] and Arxiv[5] database. Then, the fusion method is applied to extend the seed term set and, based on the collected terms, an English-Chinese bilingual core term set is built. Consequently, the study applies HNC method to design the top-level framework of IOBK and accomplishes the task of ontology building project.

---

[2] http://www.keenage.com/html/e_index.html

[3] http://ir.hit.edu.cn/demo/ltp/Sharing_Plan.htm

[4] http://www.cnki.net/

[5] https://arxiv.org/

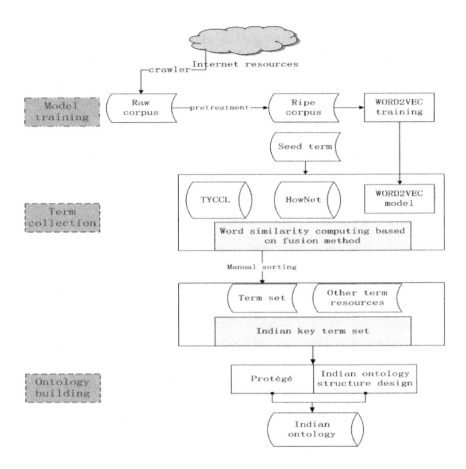

Fig.2. The procedure of Indian domain ontology building

2.1   Ontological Term Collection Based on Fusion Method

2.1.1   Brief Introduction of Word2Vec

Word2Vec [11] is a kind of lexical vector computing tool put forward firstly by Google in 2013. It represents words of texts with real value vectors in the vector space and applies high-efficient vector computing method to calculate semantic similarity of words. The model could apply two Forward Neural Network models: Continuous Bag of Words (CBOW) and Skip-Gram [12]. Different from common FNNM, these two models delete the non-linear latent layer, which improves the speed of calculation while the result is also satisfactory. The structures of two models are as follows:

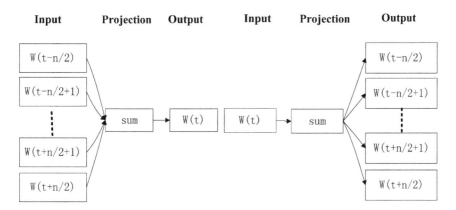

Fig.3. The models of CBOW and Skip-Gram

From the figure, we can find that CBOW model gets occurrence probability of current words through its context:

$$P(Wt \mid W(t - \frac{n}{2}), W\left(t - \frac{n}{2} + 1\right), \dots, W(t + \frac{n}{2} + 1), W(t + \frac{n}{2})).$$

Opposite to CBOW, Skip-Gram model applies current word to predict the occurrence probability of its context:

$$P(Wi|Wt) \qquad\qquad (t - c \leqq i \leqq t + c)$$

$i \neq t$ and c represents the size of window.

2.1.2   English-Chinese Core Term Set Creation

Based on the collected terms, the study makes detailed testing for the definition of relevant parameters in the fusion method. Through comparative analysis, we find that word similarity calculation result of Word2Vec are more stable than that of HowNet-based and TYCCL-based methods, and what's worse, the KB-based methods often gives us some incorrect result generated by the absence of specific words. Therefore, the study takes Word2Vec as the chief tool of the fusion method, and the fusion formula is as follows:

$$Sim_{integ} = p \times W_{sim} + (1 - p) \times \frac{T_{sim} + H_{sim}}{2}$$

In which Sim_{integ} is synthetic word similarity value, W_{sim}, H_{sim} and T_{sim} are word similarity values computed by Word2Vec, HowNet-based method and TYCCL-based method respectively. And the parameter p is the weight of W_{sim} while $(1 - p)$ is the weight of the arithmetic mean value of H_{sim} and T_{sim}. In our experiments, we set the weight of Word2Vec to 1/3、1/2、3/5、7/10 and 4/5 respectively to test and compare Sim_{integ} values so that the parameter p could be properly set. Through comparison and analysis, the parameter p is set to 1/2 consequently.

Based on the fusion method and collected seed terms, the study makes perfect estension upon the seed term set, and gets 3250 India-relevant terms ultimately which will serve as the basic knowledge resource for IOKB building.

3   Ontology Building Based on HNC Conceptual Tree Table

HNC supplies us with detailed information of linguistic concept classification and conceptual hierarchical relationship, which is very meaningful and useful to top-level framework design of ontology. HNC conceptual tree table [2][3] divides all concepts into eight types: politics[a1], economy[a2], culture[a3], military[a4], law[a5], technology[a6], education[a7] and hygiene[a8], in which military concept classification is the most complete. The general conceptual classification system of HNC is as follows:

Therefore, the study, based on the conceptual classsification method of HNC, designs and implements the top-level framework of IOKB by means of borrowing, modification, and extension. Detailed concept classification informatioin of politics and military is as follows:

（1）politics [a1]

---

[6] Function-effect chain of HNC includes six different phases of an action: function, process, transmision, effect, relation and state.

Table 1. Conceptual classification system of HNC

ID	Conceptual type	Category and sub-category			Introduction
1	chief primitive concept (φ)	function-effect chain[6] (0-5)			describing basic rules of all entities of the world.
2	extended primitive concept 1 ($\psi//\varphi$)	spiritual life 1		Psychology (71)	describing current human antivities.
				will (72)	
				Behavior (73)	
				Thinking (8)8	
		Labour 1 (a)			
		spiritual life 3		Pursuit (b)	
				Ideology (d)	
3	extended primitive concept 2 ($q//\varphi$)	Labour 1 (q6)			describing diachronic human antivities.
		spiritual life 2	surface layer (q7)		
			deep layer (q8)		
4	basic concept (j)	basic concept	basic ontological concept (j0-j6)		describing basic topics of philosophy.
			basic property concept (j7-j8)		
5	grammartical logical concept (l)	grammartical logical concept (l)			describing indispensible logical rules of language.
6	pragmatic logical concept (f)	pragmatic logical concept (f)			describing indispensible non-logical rules of language.
7	basic logical concept (jl)	basic logical concept (jl)			describing logical rules that serve as basic precondition for judgement.
8	general logical concept (s)	general logical concept (s)			describing the concept that combines the features of primitive concept, basic concept and logical concept.
9	basic entity concept(jw)	basic entity concept(jw)			describing the feature of all natural entities.
10	attached entity concept(w//p)	attached entity concept(w//p)			describing the feature of entity and human.
11	physical concept(x)	physical concept(x)			describing the feature of entity.

System and policy[a10]
  Social system[a10t]
  Political system[a10n]
  politics[a03:(e2m)]
political activity[a11]
  political agency[a11t]
    government agency[a119]
    parliament agency[a11a]
    judiciary agency[a11b]
  party activity[a117:(e5n)]
administration[a12]
  administrative strategy[a10m]
  political struggle[a13]
diplomatic activity[a14]
  diplomatic policy[a143:(e0m,e6x,ean,m)]
  government diplomacy [a14t]
    envoy activity[a149:(53x,e2n,7)]
    diplomatic negotiations [a14a:(t=a)]
  international diplomacy [a14\k]
    visit[a14\2:(d01,-0|)]
    diplomatic forms[a14m]
conquer[a15]
  whole country conquer[a15e0n]
  regional conquer[a15\k]
  control conquer[a15t]

From the above lists, we can see HNC conceptual tree table supplies detailed description upon political agency, political system and policy while only simple description of political figures, facilities, etc needed for ontology are supplied. Based on the lists, the study designs political top-level framework that covers five classes: party, political agency, political system, national policy, and political activity. In the framework of HNC, diplomacy is a sub-class of politics. In order to highlight the importance of diplomacy, the study extracts diplomacy as a self-independent class which covers five sub-classes: diplomatic agency, diplomatic figure, diplomatic policy, diplomatic relationship and diplomatic activity.

（2）military[a4]
  military activity[a40]
    military research[a409]
    military deployment[a40a]
    military training[a40b]
    military tactics[a409c25]

```
            military strategy[a409c26]
        military agency[a41]
            military agency structure[a41e2m]
                horizontal structure [a41e219]
                vertical structure [a41e21a]
            military figure[a41e5m]
                officer[a41e51]
                soldier[a41e52]
                sergeant[a41e53]
            command agency[a41d01]
                command agency structure[a41d01-0\k=4]
                operation agency [a41d01-0\1]
                equipment agency [a41d01-0\2]
                intelligence agency [a41d01-0\3]
                logistic agency [a41d01-0\4]
            troops[a41t=b]
            military institute[a41i]
        war[a42]
        war effect[a43]
        security[a44]
            public security[a44a]
            counter-terrorism[a44b]
            intelligence combat[a443]
                intelligence collection[a41d01-0\k=4]
                intelligence analysis[a41d01-0\1]
            secret security[a44i]
        armament[a45]
            military facility[a459]
            military equipment[a45a]
        military and technology[a46]
                military technology [a469]
        military and economy [a47]
                heavy industry[a47(n)i]
                economic defence[a470]
```

HNC conceptual tree table supplies very detailed description of military concepts which are key points of both conceptual tree table and IOKB. Based on the lists, the study designs military top-level framework that covers seven classes: military strategy, military agency, military equipment, military facility, military exercise, military personnel and military technology. In the framework of HNC, security is a sub-class of politics. In order to highlight the importance of security, the study extracts security as a self-independent class which covers five sub-classes: security agency, security equipment, security facility, security power and security technology.

The top-level framwork of economy and culture is also designed in the same way. The general top-level framework of IOKB is as follows:

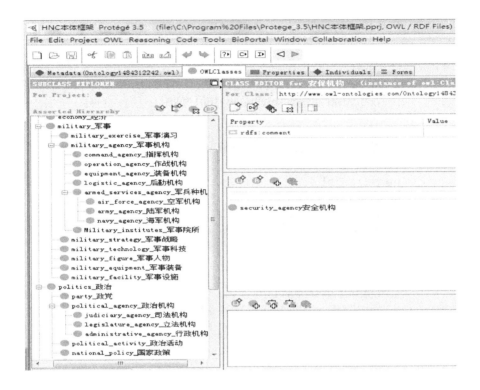

Fig.4. Visualization of Indian ontological knowledge base

Based on the top-level framework and India-relevant term resource, the study carries out the task of building IOKB. Currently, IOKB has more than 4350 concepts and instances, 51 object properties and 207 data properties. In order to ensure the accuracy and conprehensiveness of IOKB, the study applies Pallet reasoner and OOPS![7] Tool [13][14] to test and evaluate IOKB. The detailed evaluation result of OOPS! is as follows:

---

[7] http://oops.linkeddata.es/

Evaluation results

It is obvious that not all the pitfalls are equally important; their impact in the ontology will depend on multiple factors. For this reason, each pitfall has an importance level attached indicating how important it is. We have identified three levels:

- **Critical** ⊘ : It is crucial to correct the pitfall. Otherwise, it could affect the ontology consistency, reasoning, applicability, etc.
- **Important** ⊘ : Though not critical for ontology function, it is important to correct this type of pitfall.
- **Minor** ○ : It is not really a problem, but by correcting it we will make the ontology nicer.

[Expand All] | [Collapse All]

Results for P03: Creating the relationship "is" instead of using "rdfs:subClassOf", "rdf:type" or "owl:sameAs".	1 case | Critical ⊘
Results for P04: Creating unconnected ontology elements.	1 case | Minor ○
Results for P05: Defining wrong inverse relationships.	12 cases | Critical ⊘
Results for P07: Merging different concepts in the same class.	21 cases | Minor ○
Results for P08: Missing annotations.	1034 cases | Minor ○
Results for P10: Missing disjointness.	ontology* | Important ⊘
Results for P11: Missing domain or range in properties.	239 cases | Important ⊘
Results for P12: Equivalent properties not explicitly declared.	1 case | Important ⊘
Results for P13: Inverse relationships not explicitly declared.	43 cases | Minor ○
Results for P21: Using a miscellaneous class.	2 cases | Minor ○
Results for P22: Using different naming conventions in the ontology.	ontology* | Minor ○
Results for P30: Equivalent classes not explicitly declared.	9 cases | Important ⊘
Results for P41: No license declared.	ontology* | Important ⊘
SUGGESTION: symmetric or transitive object properties.	18 cases

Fig.5. The detailed test result of OOPS!

OOPS! supplies 14 critical pitfalls, 258 important pitfalls and 1232 minor pitfalls totally. According to the evaluation result, the study makes some crucial readjustments to correct most of these pitfalls and further perfect the ontology. Consequently, the general quality of IOKB is satisfactory and the hirarchical structure is as follows:

4   Conclusion

The study applies HowNet, TYCCL knowledge bases and Word2Vec to assist ontology term collection, which makes IOKB project easier and more effective. In order to improve the general quality of the ontology, the study applies HNC theory and relevant methods to help design and implement ontology top-level framework. Based on the above works, all terms collected are filtered once again and filled into the pre-built ontology framework according to the specific conceptual classification. Currently, the knowledge of IOKB covers seven general fields of India such as politics, economy, military and culture etc, contains more than 4350 concepts and instances, 51 object properties and 207 data properties. After continuous enrichment of ontology knowledge, IOKB will surely be useful and meaningful to various NLP fields such as India-relelant information extraction, etc.

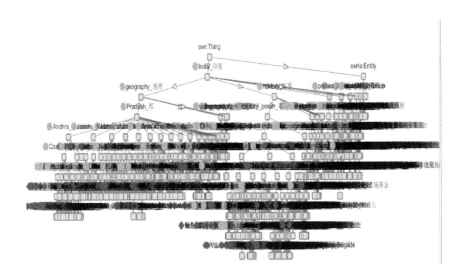

Fig.6. The general hirarchical structure of IOKB

References

1. Zhang, K.L., Ambiguity resolution of syntactic structure based on HNC theory. Chinese Journal of information, 18(6), 43-52(2004).
2. Zhang, K.L., MT-oriented Sentence Category and Sentence Format Transfer from Chinese to English. Henan university press, Kaifeng (2007).
3. Miao, C.J., HNC Introductory Theory. Tsinghua University Press (2005).
4. Gruber, T.R., Toward Principles for the Design of Ontologies Used for Knowledge Sharing.International Journal of Human and Computer Studies, 43(5/6), 907-928(1993).
5. Gruber, T.R., A Translation Approach to Portable Ontology Specifications. Knowledge Acquisition, (5), 199(1993).

6. Perez, A.G., Benjamins V R. Overview of Knowledge Sharing and Reuse Components: Ontologies and Problem-Solving Methods.Proceedings of the IJCAI-99 workshop on Ontologies and Problem-solving Methods (KRR5), 1-15(1999).
7. Kaustubh Supekar, M.S., A Peer-review Approach for Ontology Evaluation.In 8th International Protege Conference, Madrid, Spain (2005).
8. Bourigault, D., Gonzalez-Mullier, I., Gros, L.C., A natural language processing tool for terminology extraction. In Proceedings of 7th EURALEX International Congress. (1996).
9. Zhang, G.P., Diao, L.N., Wang, Y., Aviation term semantic knowledge base building based on HowNet. Journal of Chinese information, 28(5), 92-101(2014).
10. Zhang, Z.Q., Iria, J., Brewster, C., et al. A comparative evaluation of ter recognition algorithms.IN: Proceedings of the Sixth International Conference on Language Resources and Evaluation (2008).
11. Mikolov, T., Karafi, M., Burget, L., et al. Recurrent Neural Network Based Language Model. In Proceedings of Interspeech, 131-138.MIT Press,Chiba, (2010).
12. Mikolov, T., Ilya, S., Kai, C., et al. Distributed Representations of Words and Phrases and Their Compositionality. In Proceedings of NIPS-2013(2013).
13. Poveda-Villalón, M., Suárez-Figueroa, M.C., et al. Validating Ontologies with OOPS!. Knowledge Engineering and Knowledge Management. Lecture Notes in Computer Science, (7603), 267-281(2012).
14. Poveda-Villalón, M., Gómez-Pérez, A., Suárez-Figueroa, M.C. OOPS! (OntOlogy Pitfall Scanner!): An On-line Tool for Ontology Evaluation. International Journal on Semantic Web and Information Systems (IJSWIS), 10(2), 28-35(2014).

Mandarin Relata: A Dataset of Word Relations and Their Semantic Types*

Hongchao Liu and **Chu-Ren Huang** and **Renkui Hou**

CBS,The Hong Kong Polytechnic University
11 Yuk Choi Rd. Hung Hom, Hong Kong
jiye12yuran@126.com
churen.huang@polyu.edu.hk

Abstract

For both the training and evaluation of semantic distributional models, language datasets are needed that are both elaborate in their word level descriptors and readily intuitive to human judgment. The current paper introduces a dataset for Mandarin, Chinese constructed through the combination of word relation pairs from two distinct sources: corpus extraction, and human elicitation. Our results show that while more word relation pairs were gained through the corpus extraction process, human elicited semantic neighbors were almost twice as likely to show agreement with human raters. The current methods created 4091 word relation pairs that span hypernymy, hyponymy, synonymy, antonymy, and meronymy alongside semantic type information. To date, this is the largest collection of human-rated word relation pairs in Mandarin, Chinese.

1 Introduction

One of the many critical tasks in natural language processing, whether by supervised or unsupervised methods, is the measurement of semantic similarity and relatedness between words. Distributional methods, which depend on large corpora of natural text, have proven successful at this task in both practical applications (Grefenstette, 1994), and in modeling cognition (Bellegarda, 2000; McDonald, 2000). However, the struggle to identify word relations is still unsatisfactory due to the requirement of focusing on only one kind of relation at a time (Santus et al., 2015).This difficulty persists in studies that implement supervised (Girju et al., 2006),

semi-supervised (Pantel and Pennacchiotti, 2006) and unsupervised methods (Santus et al., 2014b; Santus et al., 2014a).

Multiple resources have been introduced to serve as benchmarks in the evaluation of distributional semantic models (DSMs). The evolution of such tools implies that an ideal benchmark for the training and evaluation of DSMs must not be too large yet represent a diverse number of relation types. Large datasets of word relation pairs, like WordNet (Fellbaum, 1998), and ConceptNet 5.0 (Liu and Singh, 2004) are unfit for this task in the sense that they are more taxonomic than representative of human judgments (Santus et al., 2015).Task-specific resources that have examined a single relation type on the other hand have served well through question-based elicitation, for both the identification of synonymy (Test of English as a Foreign Language: (Landauer and Dumais, 1997)), and antonymy (Mohammad et al., 2008). More recently, BLESS (Baroni and Lenci, 2011) introduced a dataset that included several relations, including hypernymy, co-hypernymy, meronymy, event, and attribute among others, while simultaneously lacking synonymy and antonymy. On the heels of the demand for greater more elaborated datasets. (Santus et al., 2015) introduced EVALution 1.0 that provided the key relations (hypernymy, synonymy, antonymy, meronymy) plus word level descriptors that included word frequency, POS, and twenty-four semantic types such as whether a word is best categorized as abstract vs. concrete; basic, subordinate or superordinate, etc. More importantly, EVALution 1.0 was tested for reliability by way of human raters in a sentence judgment task.

The current paper introduces a dataset for the training and evaluation of DSMs for Mandarin, Chinese. We sought to benefit from the mix of methods that have been used thus far for the creation

*Great appretiation to president Wang Ailing and other teachers and students of the Second Senior High School of Boxing county for their help on the rating task of the dataset.

© Springer International Publishing AG 2018
Y. Wu et al. (Eds.): CLSW 2017, LNAI 10709, pp. 336–340, 2018.
https://doi.org/10.1007/978-3-319-73573-3_30

Table 1: Example elicitation form

Target word	Relation	Template	Answer
骨头 (gutou, bone)	Synonym	骨头 (gutou, bone) is similar to __.	骨 (gu, bone)
骨头 (gutou, bone)	Antonym	骨头 (gutou, bone) has the opposite meaning with __.	肌肉 (jirou, muscle)
骨头 (gutou, bone)	Hyponym	__ is a kind of 骨头 (gutou, bone).	头骨 (tougu, skull)
骨头 (gutou, bone)	Hypernym	骨头 (gutou, bone) is a kind of __	
骨头 (gutou, bone)	Meronym	__ is a part/member of 骨头 (gutou, bone)	骨髓 (gusui, marrow)
骨头 (gutou, bone)	Holonym	骨头 (gutou, bone) is a part/member of__	身体 (shenti, body)

Table 2: The Collected Simplified Chinese data

Word X	Relation	Word Y	Template	Vote
足球 (zuqiu,football)	Hypernym	球 (qiu,ball)	足球 (zuqiu, football) is a kind of 球 (qiu, ball)	2
熊 (xiong, bear)	Synonym	狗熊 (gouxiong, black bear)	熊 (xiong, bear) is similar to 狗熊 (gouxiong, black bear)	1
拉链 (lasuo, zipper)	Holonym	包 (bao, bag)	拉链 (lasuo, zipper) is a part/member of 包 (bao, bag)	1

Table 3: Sentence Judgement Task Result (part)

Word X	Relation	Word Y	Sentence to be checked	Reliability check result						
膀胱 (pangguang, bladder)	Holonym	尿 (niao,ball)	膀胱 (pangguang, bladder) is a part/member of 尿 (niao, ball)	3	1	0	1	0	0	0
球皮 (qiupi, ball cover)	Synonym	狗熊 (gouxiong, black bear)	球皮 (qiupi, ball cover) is a part/member of 狗熊 (gouxiong, black bear)	4	1	0	0	0	0	0
水牛 (shuiniu, buffalo)	Hypernym	牛 (niu, cattle)	水牛 (shuiniu, buffalo) is a kind of 牛 (niu, cattle)	4	1	0	0	0	0	0

Note: For the "Total votes of judgement", the seven columns represent "totally agree", "agree", "don't know", "disa-gree", "totally disagree", "don't know X" and "don't know Y" respectively.

of benchmarks for the evaluation of DSMs in English. We thus implemented both automatic methods of extraction from existing tools as well as human elicitation of semantic neighbors.

2 Construction of the Dataset

The construction of Mandarin Relata included three basic steps: (1) The collection of word relation pairs; (2) The assessment of reliability for said word relation pairs; (3) Further elaboration of the selected words' semantic information. We will introduce them individually.

2.1 Collection of the Word Relation Pairs

Two methods were used in the collection of raw data. The first method involved the elicitation of semantic neighbors through human volunteers. The second method involved extraction of word relation pairs from Chinese WordNet(CWN, (Huang et al., 2010)).

2.1.1 Elicitation Task

For the goal of eliciting semantic neighbors from human volunteers we chose 100 common nouns. Our volunteers were three linguistics Ph.D. students who were all native Mandarin speakers from Mainland China. Each volunteer completed an elicitation task whereby each target word was featured in a carrier sentence that required the volunteer to fill in a missing word.

The carrier sentences elicited the sought after semantic relations: synyonmy, antonymy, hyponymy, hypernymy, meronymy, and holonymy. As can be seen in Table 1, each answer forms a pair with the target word.

Finally we get the raw relation pairs as in Table 2 which will be judged by human:

From the 100 target words, our three participants produced 1029 semantically related neigh-

bors, excluding repeated items.

2.1.2 Extraction from Chinese WordNet

Our second method of collecting word relation pairs involved the extraction of data from CWN. CWN was created through both corpora analytic methods and translation with English words found in WordNet. The original data is in the traditional Chinese orthography that is in use in Taiwan. The semantic relations that are covered in CWN are: antonym, synonym, hyponym/hypernym, meronym/holonym, nearsynonym, and variant. All of the null value and repeated pairs were removed leaving a total of 10,000 word pairs. To increase the diversity of the words' relation types, we only extracted words that appeared with at least two relations. This reduced our extraction of word relation pairs to 5,471.

Combining both the word pairs extracted from CWN and the word pairs collected from the elicitation task we then had a raw dataset of 6600 word pairs.

2.2 Sentence Judgment Task

In order to assess the word pairs' reliability we then constructed a sentence judgment task. Sixty volunteers, that did not take part in the elicitation task, were asked to check the reliability of the collected/extracted word relation pairs. Each sentence will be judged by five volunteers. Each word relation pair was inserted into carrier sentences like the ones used in the elicitation task. The volunteers were then told to rate the sentences according to five options: "totally agree", "agree", "don't know", "disagree", "totally disagree". If the participants did not know either of the target vocabulary they were given the choice of, "don't know X" and "don't know Y" respectively as in Table 3:

In line with the sentence judgment task used in (Santus et al., 2015), only word pairs that received three or more votes from "totally agree" or "agree" were regarded as positive word pairs. This rule left us with 4091 positive word relation pairs, and 2509 negative pairs as can be seen in Table 4.

Table 4: Numbers of Checking results

Relation	Positive result	Negative result	Total
Synonymy(SimillarTo)	616	449	1065
Antonymy(OppositeWith)	638	607	1245
Hyponymy(KindOf)	1161	842	2003
Meronymy(Part/MemberOf)	1251	77	1328
Nearsynonymy(Raltated)	378	383	761
Variant(DifferentForm)	47	151	198
Total	4091	2509	6600

It should be noted that a large percentage of the negative word pairs came from volunteers choosing the "don't know X" or "don't know Y" categories, which nontrivially came from the CWN data. We believe that this was in part due to the fact that the CWN data was presented in traditional Chinese orthography to volunteers from the Mainland that use simplified Chinese on a daily basis. While translating the traditional to simplified Chinese characters was possible prior to the creation of the judgment task, we opted not to do so for fear of suboptimal translation.

For the word pairs collected from the elicitation task, the rate of reliability (i.e., the percentage of agreement between raw word pairs and positive word pairs from the judgment task) was very high at 94.5%. The rate of reliability for the extracted CWN word pairs was considerably lower at 55.3%.

2.3 Semantic Tagging

To enrich the semantic information of the dataset, we asked three more linguistics Ph.D. students to tag the semantic type of all the relata. Semantic tags included the following:

1. Basic/Subordinate/Superordinate: for example, "flower" can be tagged "Basic", "Rose" as "Subordinate" and "Plant" as "Superordinate" ;

2. General/Specific: "city" can be tagged as "General" while "Washington" can be tagged as "Specific" ;

3. Abstract/Concrete: "sorrow" can be tagged as "Abstract" while "rock" can be tagged as "concrete" ;

4. Event/Action/Time/Space/Object/Animal /Plant/Food/Color/People/Attribute: such that "autumn" can be tagged as "Time" .

The above tags covered the majority of the relata. However, some words, specifically adverbs, resist categorization. The semantic tagging result is as Table 5 (in the last page).

The frequency of the relata is calculated in a combined corpus of Chinese gigaword (Hong and Huang, 2006) and Sinica (Chen et al., 1996). It should be noticed that not all of the relata can be found in the corpus and thus only the ones appeared in the corpus had the frequency information. The PoS tags can be found in (Chen et al., 1996).

3 Conclusion

In this paper we present word relation pairs collected from two distinct sources: an elicitation task with human volunteers, and the extraction of data from CWN. Combined they provide 4091 positive, and 2,509 negative word relation pairs for Mandarin, Chinese in the simplified orthographic script.

Our results showed that the human elicited semantic neighbors were 94.5% reliable when tested in a human judgment task. This was near double that of the words extracted from Chinese WordNet (55.3% reliability). While these current findings strongly suggest that large taxonomic datasets of word relations are not suitable for the creation of task-specific datasets, (as suggested by (Santus et al., 2015)), this should be taken with some caution. It is not possible to know the rate at which the traditional Chinese affected our volunteers' performance, seeing as that was not within the scope of the intended study, but rather an unintended but interesting consequence. And while the current results do not stand definitively against the use of large taxonomic resources such as WordNet and CWN, they do support the use of human elicitation as a data collection method for datasets that intend to behave as benchmarks for the training and evaluation of DSMs.

Although each word relation pairs is validated by five volunteers, the agreement test are not implemented and inner group agreement test items are not set at the beginning of the questionaaire. Inter-group Kappa agreement test is onging. Inner-group agreement test is about to be simulated between similar words within the dataset.

4   Acknowledgement

This paper is supported by National Social Science Foundation(16BYY110).

References

Marco Baroni and Alessandro Lenci. 2011. How we blessed distributional semantic evaluation. In *Proceedings of the GEMS 2011 Workshop on GEometrical Models of Natural Language Semantics*, pages 1–10. Association for Computational Linguistics.

Jerome R Bellegarda. 2000. Exploiting latent semantic information in statistical language modeling. *Proceedings of the IEEE*, 88(8):1279–1296.

Keh-Jiann Chen, Chu-Ren Huang, Li-Ping Chang, and Hui-Li Hsu. 1996. Sinica corpus: Design methodology for balanced corpora. *Language*, 167:176.

Christiane Fellbaum. 1998. *WordNet*. Wiley Online Library.

Roxana Girju, Adriana Badulescu, and Dan Moldovan. 2006. Automatic discovery of part-whole relations. *Computational Linguistics*, 32(1):83–135.

Gregory Grefenstette. 1994. *Corpus-derived First, Second, and Third-order Word Affinities*. Rank Xerox Research Centre.

Jia-Fei Hong and Chu-Ren Huang. 2006. Using chinese gigaword corpus and chinese word sketch in linguistic research. In *The 20th Pacific Asia Conference on Language, Information and Computation (PACLIC-20). November*, pages 1–3.

JR Huang, Shu-Kai Hsieh, Jia-Fei Hong, Yun-Zhu Chen, I-Li Su, Yong-Xiang Chen, and Sheng-Wei Huang. 2010. Chinese wordnet: Design, implementation, and application of an infrastructure for cross-lingual knowledge processing. *Journal of Chinese Information Processing*, 24(2):14–23.

Thomas K Landauer and Susan T Dumais. 1997. A solution to plato's problem: The latent semantic analysis theory of acquisition, induction, and representation of knowledge. *Psychological review*, 104(2):211.

Hugo Liu and Push Singh. 2004. Conceptnet—a practical commonsense reasoning tool-kit. *BT technology journal*, 22(4):211–226.

Scott McDonald. 2000. Environmental determinants of lexical processing effort.

Saif Mohammad, Bonnie Dorr, and Graeme Hirst. 2008. Computing word-pair antonymy. In *Proceedings of the Conference on Empirical Methods in Natural Language Processing*, pages 982–991. Association for Computational Linguistics.

Patrick Pantel and Marco Pennacchiotti. 2006. Espresso: Leveraging generic patterns for automatically harvesting semantic relations. In *Proceedings of the 21st International Conference on Computational Linguistics and the 44th annual meeting of the Association for Computational Linguistics*, pages 113–120. Association for Computational Linguistics.

Enrico Santus, Qin Lu, Alessandro Lenci, and Chu-Ren Huang. 2014a. Taking antonymy mask off in vector space. In *Proceedings of PACLIC*, pages 135–144.

Enrico Santus, Qin Lu, Alessandro Lenci, and Churen Huang. 2014b. Unsupervised antonym-synonym discrimination in vector space.

Enrico Santus, Frances Yung, Alessandro Lenci, and Chu-Ren Huang. 2015. Evalution 1.0: an evolving semantic dataset for training and evaluation of distributional semantic models. *ACL-IJCNLP 2015*, page 64.

Table 5: Semantic Information of the Relata

Relata	TT_freq	Dominent_PoS_freq	PoS_distribution	Total votes for semantic tagging																	
設備	64737	Na_64735	Na_64735|VC_2	1	1	1	2	1	1	2	0	0	3	0	0	0	0	0	0	0	0
山東	4222	Nc_3803	Nb_419|Nc_3803	0	3	0	3	0	3	3	0	0	0	3	0	0	0	0	0	2	0
看來	10310	D_9170	D_9170|VE_881|Dk_259	1	0	2	0	2	0	1	0	0	0	0	0	0	0	0	0	0	0
浮游	247	Nv_173	VA_74|Nv_173	0	3	0	1	0	2	3	0	0	1	0	1	0	1	0	0	0	1
床	6497	Na_4182	Na_4182|Nf_2315	2	1	0	1	0	3	0	0	3	0	0	2	0	0	0	0	0	0
當成	4571	VG_4571	VG_4571	1	1	0	3	0	3	0	3	0	0	0	0	0	0	0	0	0	0
蟹	652	Na_652	Na_652	1	2	0	2	0	2	0	0	0	0	3	0	3	0	0	0	0	0
死	29731	VH_27551	VC_7|Nv_50|VH_27551|Dfb_2122|VJ_1	1	1	0	1	1	2	1	0	3	0	0	0	0	0	0	0	0	1
放出來	172	VB_172	VB_172	1	2	0	2	1	2	1	0	2	0	0	0	0	0	0	0	0	0

Note: TT_freq is the word's total frequency in the corpus, Dominent_PoS_freq is the most frequent PoS for this word, Dominent_PoS_freq is the different PoS's frequency of the word. Basic, Subordinate, Superordinate, General, Specific, Abstract, Concrete, Event, Action, Time, Space, Object, Animal, Plant, Food, Color, People, Attribute.

Quantitative Analysis of Synergetic Properties in Chinese Nouns

Yujie Liu, Pengyuan Liu[1]

School of Information Science, Beijing Language and Culture University, Beijing, 100083

`liuyujieblcu@163.com; liupengyuan@blcu.edu.cn`

Abstract. This paper analyses more than 13000 nouns in contemporary Chinese and investigates their synergetic properties on the basis of word polysemy. HowNet is used in this paper to measure the word polysemy and it proves to be an effective approach. Statistical analysis of the data indicates that the polysemy of nouns abides by the modified Zipf-Alekseev distribution. The results of function fitting with Altmann Fitter show that word polysemy is somewhat related to some linguistic variables including word length, word frequency and polytexuality, which means that each variables in the subsystem of lexicon is still synergetic and Köhler's lexical model proves to be effective for Chinese nouns.

Keywords: synergetic polysemy word length frequency polytexuality

1 Introduction

Synergetic linguistics derives from Synergetics which is proposed by German scholar Hermann Haken. It concentrates on the theory that language is a self-organizing and self-regulating system, thus providing a unique framework in linguistics studying. Köhler (1986) has formulated a synergetic lexical model, which was tested on German by Köhler, and contributes to a new understanding of the lexical subsystem of human language and the interrelationship among the components in lexical subsystem. Hereafter, with the Köhler's model, in-depth explorations have been conducted into the lexical subsystem, and the theory was tested on lexical structures of some languages, such as English(Gieseking, 1998) and Polish(Hammerl, 1991).

Some researchers have conducted quantitative investigations into a variety of languages based on synergetic linguistics on a certain part-of-speech, especially on verbs. Wang L. (2014) tested the synergetic model on data from Chinese and his study demonstrated once more the cross-linguistic validity of the model with respect to a highly analytic language. Songgao et al (2014) analyzed the synergetic properties among the valency and polysemy, word length, frequency and polytexuality, and present a synergetic model of Chinese verb valency. But few people have conducted

---

[1] Corresponding author

© Springer International Publishing AG 2018
Y. Wu et al. (Eds.): CLSW 2017, LNAI 10709, pp. 341–348, 2018.
https://doi.org/10.1007/978-3-319-73573-3_31

research on nouns especially on Chinese nouns. We attach great importance on the testing of the synergetic properties on different languages and subsystem for the fact that the lexical system is made up of many subsystems such as verbs, nouns, adjectives and other parts of speech. As noun is the largest part-of-speech, they play an important role in the lexical system, exploring the synergetic properties of nouns is a significant step to demonstrate the universality of Köhler's lexical model.

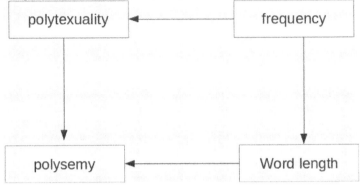

Fig. 1. Hypothetical synergetic lexical model

From Köhler's model, we find that polysemy has always been the focus of the synergetic lexical subsystem. As a result, we proposed a simplified model of each variable in lexical subsystem as figure 1. According to this model, we believe that word polysemy is related to other variables and there exists some systematic correlation among those variables. In the next part of this paper, we focus on the polysemy of Chinese nouns to explore the synergetic properties among polysemy, word length, frequency and polytexuality.

2   Materials and Method

From the *Lexicon of Common Words in Contemporary Chinese* which consists of totally 56008 common words, we extract 313084 nouns. Since sometimes a word has more than one meaning, polysemy is measured by the number of meanings of a word. In previous studies, researchers usually measure the polysemy of words according to the *Chinese Modern Dictionary* (L.Wang, 2014;Song Gao,2014). According to our research, we hold the view that measuring the polysemy of a word with HowNet is much more effective than the *Chinese Modern Dictionary*. We are going to test the proposition in the following part. As a result, the polysemy of a certain word is determined by the number of different definitions in HowNet. Considering that HowNet doesn't exactly consist of all nouns in the *Lexicon of Common Words in Contemporary Chinese,* we finally select the intersection part of them, which consists of 13066 nouns.

Word length is an important parameter in synergetic linguistics theory. In alphabet writing system such as English, German, Spanish, word length is usually measured by the number of syllables or letters. Given the particularity that Chinese is a kind of non-alphabet language, composed of Chinese character, a Chinese character usually carries one syllable. In contemporary Chinese, most words are made of two syllables, so it seems somewhat meaningless to measure the word length in terms of syllables or characters. In this paper, we measure word length by pinyin letters. For example, the pinyin of the word "汉语[Chinese]" is "hanyu", and it consists of five letters "h a n y u", so its word length is five.

Another two important parameters word frequency and polytexuality are computed using ten years' corpora from DCC corpus[2]. Polytexuality is measured by the number of texts in which the given linguistic entity occurs (Köhler, 1986). Another term for this concept is document frequency.

After collecting the required data for Chinese nouns polysemy, word length, frequency, and polytexuality, we are going to discuss the distribution of them and investigate the interrelations among those variables. We fit the data using Altmann Fitter[3] for a comprehensive explanation.

3   Result and discussion

3.1   Distribution of Polysemy of Chinese Nouns

As mentioned above, polysemy is an important property of lexical unit. It is measured by the number of different definitions in HowNet. For example, the word "脸面 [face]" in HowNet has two different definitions, one of which relates to the reputation of one person while the other meaning refers to the skin of human or animal. So the polysemy of "脸面[face]" is two and so on for all the words. In order to prove that using HowNet to measure polysemy is more reasonable, we make a little calculation on the polysemy of words in HowNet for the fact that HowNet is widely used in computing linguistics. The following data is performed on data of the polysemy of all words in HowNet. From the data below we can see the number of words decreases rapidly with polysemy increasing, which means that Chinese words are mainly composed of words with a few meanings. Among more than one hundred and twenty models, the Mixed geometric-logarithmic distribution is demonstrated to have the highest fit level. The results are as follows:

poly-semy	the num-ber of words with x poly-semy	Expected number of words with x polysemy	poly-semy	the number of words with x polysemy	Ex-pected number of words with x polysemy
1	47460	47490.61	12	13	9.67

---

[2] DCC corpus is established by Beijing Language and Culture University. It contains ten-years corpora of eighteen newspapers around China by the end of 2015.
[3] http://www.ram-verlag.biz/altmann-fitte.

2	5867	5853.08	13	8	6.36
3	1164	1196.83	14	3	4.19
4	446	405.07	15	1	2.76
5	213	203.72	16	2	1.82
6	141	123.01	17	4	1.20
7	74	78.94	19	1	0.52
8	44	51.58	21	1	0.22
9	32	33.89	25	1	0.04
10	18	22.30	30	1	0.02
11	8	14.68			

Table 1. the polysemy distribution of words in HowNet

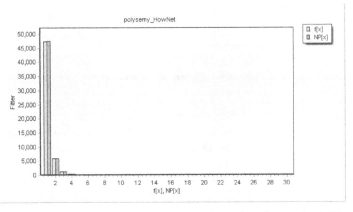

Fig. 2. Fitting the Mixed geometric-logarithmic distribution to the polysemy data in HowNet.

The parameter values in this function are q=0.6585, θ=0.2245, α=0.0505. The fitting result is extremely good with X^2 = 22.69, $P(X^2)$ = 0.0655, DF = 14, C=0.0004, R^2 = 1.000, which seems to be better than fitting result in the paper of Wang (2014), in which X^2 = 336.1304, $P(X^2)$ = 0.0000, DF = 14, C=0.0066, R^2 = 0.9995. As a result, we choose HowNet as the standard in measuring the polysemy of words.

Research shows that the polysemy of verbs fits the positive negative binomial distribution in both German and English (Köhler, 1986; Liu, 2011). As an individual part-of-speech, to test whether the polysemy of nouns is still regularly distributed, we finally select 13066 nouns which are both in the *Lexicon of Common Words in Contemporary Chinese* and HowNet as the final data. The result indicates that the polysemy distribution of Chinese nouns abides by the Right truncated modified Zipf-Alekseev distribution.

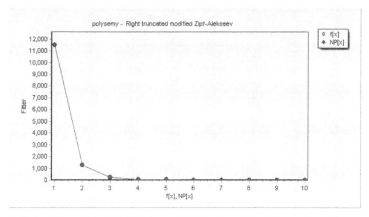

Fig. 3. Fitting the modified Zipf-Alekseev distribution to the polysemy data of nouns.

The fitting result is good with $X^2 = 6.56$, $P(X^2) = 0.2557$, DF =5, C=0.0005, $R^2 = 1.000$, which means the polysemy of Chinese nouns is lawfully distributed. From the data we can see that the largest polysemy is ten and the number of words with one polysemy account for the most nouns. That proves that even for individual part-of-speech, the polysemy distribution is still regular and systematic.

3.2   polysemy and word length

According to Köhler's synergetic model, a longer word tends to have a smaller degree of polysemy (Köhler, 1986, 2012). Some researchers tested it on verbs, such as Liu (2011) collaborated it in English verbs; Čech and Mačutek (2010) and Čech et al. (2010) confirmed it with Czech verbs.

Since the *Lexicon of Common Words in Contemporary Chinese* includes standard pinyin for each word, so we measure the word length of Chinese nouns using the annotated pinyin provided by it. To study the relation between polysemy and word length, we calculate the mean word length with x polysemy. The result shows that it fits the Consul-Mittal-binomial distribution with three parameters n=10, p=0.3571, θ=0.1601. The mean word length decreases with the increasing of polysemy.

polysemy	Mean word length	Number of words with x polysemy
1	6.81	11470
2	6.02	1279
3	4.86	201
4	3.98	65
5	3.78	26
6	3.82	11
7	3.00	7
8	2.00	1

| 9 | 2.75 | 4 |
| 10 | 3.00 | 2 |

Table 2. polysemy and mean word length of Chinese nouns

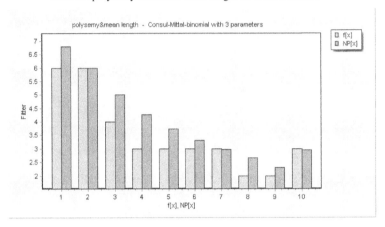

Fig. 4. polysemy and mean word length of Chinese nouns

The data fits the distribution function well with $X^2 = 0.3508$, $P(X^2) = 0.9992$, $DF = 6$, $C=0.0088$, $R^2 = 0.9553$. From the distribution, we can easily conclude that generally the stronger polysemy a noun has, the shorter the word is. Of course it is concluded in general, and we don't rule out individual and special circumstances like word with ten polysemy. As a result, Köhler's hypothesis about the relation between polysemy and word length proves to be reasonable.

3.3   polysemy and polytexuality

Polytexuality is determined by the number of texts that the given word occurs. Generally speaking, polytexuality has a positive relation with word frequency, because a word occurs more frequently, it accordingly occurs in more texts. In our hypothetical model, polytexuality is the function of polysemy. We collect the polytexuality of nouns in ten-years corpora of DCC copurs and fit the data with Altmann Fitter.

poly-semy	polytex-uality	Expected polytexuali-ty	poly-semy	polytex-uality	Expected polytexuali-ty
1	1304.82	1325.04	6	1995.00	2066.71
2	1574.93	1620.07	7	2094.71	2111.26
3	1832.76	1792.81	8	2092.00	2133.62
4	1958.02	1913.03	9	2094.75	2124.43
5	2090.15	2001.57	10	2094.00	2042.61

Table 3. polysemy & mean polytexuality of Chinese nouns

Result indicates that the data of polysemy and polytexuality fits the Negative hypergeometric distribution well. The values of the parameters in this function are k=2.2986, m=1.2317, n=9. And X^2 = 12.5719, $P(X^2)$ = 0.0504, DF = 6, C=0.0007, R^2 = 0.9779, which means there is a systematic connection between polysemy and mean polytexuality. It also proves the validity of the synergetic model.

3.4   word frequency and polytexuality

In Köhler's synergetic lexical model, polytexuality is the function of word frequency. As we get the word frequency and polytexuality of all more than 13000 nouns, we fit the data with power function. Although the result is not that perfect, but it is still acceptable (a=0.161, b=1.8425, R^2 =0.6752). The result indicates that if a word is used more frequently, it tends to occur in more texts, which means its polytexuaity is stronger.

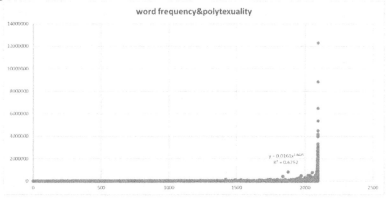

Fig. 5. Fitting the power function with frequency and polytexuality data.

The fitting result of word frequency and polytexuality shows that there exactly exists positive synergetic correlation between them.

4   Conclusion

With Chinese nouns from the *Lexicon of Common Words in Contemporary Chinese* and HowNet, this paper has analysed more than 13000 Chinese common nouns, investigating the synergetic properties of their polysemy and other linguistic variables, including word length,word frequency and polytexuality. Through our study, an important finding is that there exist synergetic properties in Chinese nouns. Though it is only a certain part-of-speech in the whole lexical system, it is also self-organized and systematic. Polysemy of nouns is related to a variety of linguistic factors. Though it is a little part of lexical system, we believe that even a part-of-speech is a self-organized and self-regulated system. Every linguistic variable is to some extent related to others, especially for polysemy of words.

On the basis of previous studies, the application of synergetic approach to Chinese language research has proved feasible and effective. As a fundamental feature of lexicon, word polysemy is put into the central place in this paper. The interrelations between word polysemy and other linguistic variables are discussed. In addition, we propose that measuring word polysemy by HowNet is more effective compared with the *Chinese Modern Dictionary.* What we need to point out, however, is that we don't analyze all nouns in the *Lexicon of Common Words in Contemporary Chinese,* instead we only include about a half of them for the limit of HowNet[4].

In conclusion, this paper is the first attempt to conduct a synergetic study on a certain subsystem, namely nouns, of Chinese lexicon on the basis of word polysemy. Further research should include more Chinse nouns and more linguistic variables or other parts of speech like adjectives, which will facilitate the comparison among different languages and different part-of-speech for further explanation on the synergetic lexical model.

Acknowledgement This paper is supported by the Research Funds of Beijing Language and Culture University(Grant No.17YCX135) and supported by the Major Project of the National Language Committee of the 12th Five-Year Research Plan in 2015 (ZDI 125-55)

Reference

1. Köhler.R. 1986. Zur linguistischen Synergetik. Struktur und Dynamik der Lexik. Bochum: Brockmeyer.
2. Köhler.R. 2005. Synergetic linguistics. In: Altmann, G., Köhler, R., Piotrowski, R.G. (eds.), Handbook of Quantitative Linguistics: 760-774. Berlin: de Gruyter.
3. Köhler.R. 2012. Quantitative Syntax Analysis. Berlin, New York: de Gruyter.
4. Liu, H. 2011. Quantitative Properties of English Verb Valency. Journal of Quantitative Linguistics, 18(3), 207–233.
5. Wang L.2014, Synergetic Studies on Some Properties of Lexical Structures in Chinese, Journal of Quantitative Linguistics, 21(2), 177-197.
6. Wang L. 2014, Quantitative and Synergetic Studies on Lexical Units in Chinese, der Universität Trier Doctoral thesis, January
7. Wang, L. 2012. Word length in Chinese. In R. Köhler (Ed), Studies in Quantitative Linguistics 13 pp. 39–53. Lüdenscheid: Ram-Verlag.

---

[4] For the limit of expenses, we only have the old version of HowNet.

Construction of an Online Lexicon of Chinese Loan Words and Phrases Translated from English

Lei Wang[1,2], Shiwen Yu[1], Houfeng Wang[1]

[1]Key Lab of Computational Linguistics of Ministry of Education, Peking University Beijing
[2]School of Foreign Languages, Peking University Beijing
{wangleics,yusw,wanghf}@pku.edu.cn

ABSTRACT. From Morrison to Pearl S. Buck, Chinese language has been introducing new words from western languages – English as a typical source – for over a hundred years. Generally speaking, this new vocabulary is termed as loan words, which can be traced to two major sources: 1. Introduced by western missionaries having worked in China; 2. Introduced by Chinese intellectuals via Japanese "和制汉辞(hé zhì hàn cí)" that were originally translated from western literature in the early 1900s. From the perspective of Chinese-English equivalence, these new words in Chinese form a one-to-one relation with their English source words for they were directly or indirectly translated from English. Therefore they may translate it into some other expressions. Currently, dictionaries of Chinese loan words serve as the vehicles of this new type of vocabulary, but they have only paper-versions and limited number of entries, which lag behind the fast development of information technology and the growing need of instant acquirement of knowledge. Therefore, to compile a new lexicon for Chinese loan words that have one-to-one correspondence with English will help translators work with a better quality and efficiency.

Keywords: lexicon of loan words and phrases, English origin, one-to-one correspondence

© Springer International Publishing AG 2018
Y. Wu et al. (Eds.): CLSW 2017, LNAI 10709, pp. 349–356, 2018.
https://doi.org/10.1007/978-3-319-73573-3_32

1 Introduction

In China, translation has a history of thousands of years, in which climaxes appeared many a time. From the translation of Buddhist scriptures in Tang Dynasty (618 A.D. – 907 A. D.) to the translation of western literature in modern time, translators have been playing a significant role in the development of Chinese civilization and making great achievements in introducing western science and technology, which provides a dynamic for China's economy and social development. The core of translation lies in its quality, which both translators working in companies and localization enterprises and students learning translation at universities have been paying great attention. However, one of the many reasons that leads to wrong translation is the wrong choice of words or word senses. For example, the Chinese word "沙发(shā fā)" is translated from the English word "sofa" and there are no other equivalents. However, many translators may not know that the Chinese word "出发点(chū fā diǎn)" was translated from the English phrase "starting point" by Japanese translators.

As is known to all, there may be more than one senses of a word in any language of the world. For example, Chinese verb "抄(chāo)" can mean "抄写(chāo xiě, to copy)" or "抄近路(chāo jìn lù, to take a shortcut)" if it collocates with different nouns. Someone estimates English word "get" can have more than twenty meanings when collocating with different objects. Nevertheless, there are some special words in Chinese language – translated words. Originally they are from English or the sense we are using today is from English. During the past century, with the constant collisions of oriental and occidental civilizations the Han-Tibetan language family represented by Chinese and the Indo-Euro language family represented by English have been exerted much influence in the process of translation and introduction. This influence results in numbers of changes on the lexical and syntactic structures of Chinese language. The changes are mainly traced back to the Christian classical texts translated by western missionaries, the Chinese translators' works in late period of Qing Dynasty (1636 A.D. -1911 A.D.) and the introduction of Japanese textbooks. All the above-mentioned factors contributed to the birth of modern Chinese, which shares great similarities in terms of translation with its source language-English from lexical, phrasal and syntactic perspectives.

2   Related Work

Western missionaries in China worked diligently on translating western works into Chinese and created many new words for Chinese with respect to religion, science, technology and literature. Italian missionary Masini(2007) studied the loan words in Chinese in 19th century whereas Shen(2010) uses A. H. Mateer and E. Morgan's books and studies the influence of translation on Chinese vocabulary conducted by western missionaries at the beginning of 20th century.

Zhou(2007) focuses on the books translated by John Fryer and investigates the new vocabulary on modern science and technology. Besides the translation by western missionaries, Japanese scholars also translated many western books and created a lot of "和制汉辞" by using Chinese characters in Japanese language that enriched Japanese vocabulary to a large extent. For the fact that Chinese and Japanese are closely related, Chinese intellectuals represented by Qichao Liang translated many Japanese books and brought these new words such as "民主(mín zhǔ, democracy), 政治(zhèng zhì, politics), 经济(jīng jì, economy),哲学(zhé xué, philosophy), 美学(měi xué, aesthetics)" into Chinese, which made Japanese also one of the sources of the new words in Chinese. Chen(2007) investigates the transformation of vocabulary from Japanese to Chinese in the interaction between China and Japan in the 1920s and Gu(2011) studies in detail the Japanese borrowed words of Chinese in her PhD thesis and provides a list of 2,250 words as such. However, Zhang and Lu(1995) analyzes the Japanese borrowed words in the *Dictionary of Chinese Loan Words* and think that there are only 878 such words in Chinese language.

At present, dictionaries of Chinese loan words are the main vehicles of these words. The earliest one can be traced back to the *Dictionary of Loan Words* published by Shanghai Skyhorse Publishing House in 1936. The later influential ones include: *Dictionary of Chinese Load Words* compiled by Zhengyan Liu, Mingkai Gao, Yongqian Mai and Youwei Shi published by Shanghai Dictionary & Book Publishing House in 1984, *Dictionary of Chinese Borrowed Words* by Qixiang Cen published by The Commercial Press in 1990. The most recent one is the *Dictionary of Modern Chinese New Words* compiled by Hong Kong Chinese Study Association published by Chinese Dictionary Publishing House in 2001. So far there has not been an online version of dictionaries as such and we hope our work can be a breakthrough.

3 The Design of Lexical Entries

Our goal is to construct a Chinese-English dictionary that features in the Chinese words translated from English, i.e. their origins are English and they become Chinese words via translation. The translation methods can be transliteration or free translation, or both. We adopt the method of investigating prestigious dictionaries – mainly influential dictionaries of Chinese loan words – and related lexicons published by researchers to determine the entries for our dictionary. However, we do not choose Chinese words but their equivalent English words as the main key for search primarily because there appeared many a translation for an English word in history. We add a field for these various translations for researchers or linguists who study the history of Chinese language. For example, the words "社会(shè huì, society)" and "资本(zī běn, capital)" had been translated into "群(qún, group)" and "母财(mǔ cái, mother capital)" respectively by Fu Yan. Although his translations have been replaced by Japanese translations eventually, they provide valuable reference for those who study ancient literature.

What we need to do next is to fill up the fields in the dictionary. Both the English and Chinese explanations of the entries are added in order to enrich its content. The English one is from *Oxford Intermediate Learners' English-Chinese Dictionary* (4th Edition, electronic version)(Turnbull 2010) whereas the Chinese one is from *Modern Chinese Dictionary* (electronic version)(Lyu 1996). Both the dictionary are of certain authority and sustain long-term practical use. We induce the content of the two dictionaries into a database and match the entries with the explanations in the dictionaries. The fields of each entry is listed in the following Table 1.

Table 1. The Entries of Our Dictionary

序号	英语源词	汉语翻译词	汉语释义	英语释义	其他翻译	词源
1	democracy	民主	指人民在政治上享有的自由发表意见、参与国家政权管理等的权利。	system of government by the whole people of a country, esp. through representatives whom they elect	德莫克拉西,德先生	日语借词
2	middle school	中学	对青少年实施中等教育的学校	(esp Brit) school for children aged between 9 and 13 years		传教士翻译

| 3 | conta-gious disease | 传染病 | 由病原体传染引起的疾病。如肺结核、麻风、天花、伤寒等 | (of a disease) spreading by contact | | 日语借词 |
| 4 | ... | ... | ... | ... | ... | ... |

4   Loan Words with Affixes

English belongs to the Hindu-European family and has abundant affixes and derivation has been the major formation of its vocabulary. For example, the English Encyclopedia includes over 170 prefixes and 200 suffixes. In the transformation from ancient Chinese to modern Chinese, the phenomenon of affix derivation also emerged. To distinguish them from their counterparts in English, Chinese linguists call them "quasi-affixes". The concept was first proposed by Lyu in *The Analysis of Chinese Grammar* in 1978, which turned a new leaf of study Chinese affixes. For this Xu(1997) also remarked: "In Chinese-Tibetan languages, the derivation that plays an important role in new word creation is not those affixes whose senses are fading and that only serve as formal markers, but those quasi-affixes that retain their certain senses". Because quasi-affixes emerge very fast, many new words have been created in this way, especially in scientific literature and became a part of Chinese lexicon. We also build a lexicon for Chinese quasi-affixes and extract those words from *People's Daily* corpus and then found their translations from LDC lexicon. To do this, we adopt the statistical relational degree of hypothesis-test (Chang 2003) method. Let C be a sentence-level corpus and assume the corpus is consisted of n sentences. Each affix and its root word form a pair represented as (x, y), then the relation of appearance of x and y is based on the following table:

Table 2. The appearance of word pair (x, y)

	x	$\neg x$
y	a	b
$\neg y$	c	d

a, b, c and d stand for:

a: total counts of sentences that include both x and y;

b: total counts of sentences that include x but not y;

c: total counts of sentences that include y but not x;

d: total counts of sentences that include neither x nor y;

In this paper, we use the following three methods to compute the relational degree between word pairs: Mutual Information(MI), χ2 value, Log-likehood(LL). The formulae are as the following:

(1) χ^2 value

$$\chi^2(x, y) = \frac{n \times (a \times d - b \times c)^2}{(a + b) \times (c + d) \times (a + c) \times (b + d)} \quad (1)$$

(2) Mutual Information

$$MI(x, y) = log_2 \frac{n \times a}{(a + b) \times (a + c)} \quad (2)$$

(3) Log-likehood

$$LL(x, y) = 2 \times (a \times log_2 \frac{a \times n}{(a + b) \times (a + c)}$$
$$+ b \times log_2 \frac{b \times n}{(a + b) \times (b + d)}$$
$$+ c \times log_2 \frac{c \times n}{(c + d) \times (a + c)} + d \times log_2 \frac{c \times n}{(c + d) \times (b + d)}) \quad (3)$$

We adopt three methods because when there appear differences between two methods the third method can be applied to make the final decision. We use the above formulae to calculate the collocation of the affix and its root word. Table 3 has the result:

Table 3. Common quasi-affixes in Chinese words

Prefix	Example	Suffix	Example
软-(soft-)	软着陆(soft-landing)	化(-ize)	现代化(modernize)
自-(self-)	自适应(self-adaptive)	度(-ity)	灵敏度(sensitivity)
类-(quasi-)	类词缀(quasi-affix)	门(-gate)	伊朗门(Iran gate)
后-(post-)	后现代(post-modern)	性(-ity)	灵活性(flexibility)
...	...	...	...

By the current standards of Chinese word segmentation, loan words with affixes will be either segmented into different words or treated as one, as can be seen from the following Figure 1.

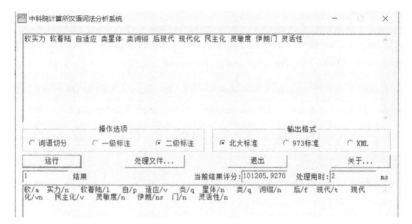

Figure 1. Segmentation result of loan words with affixes

Thus, there is not a consensus on how to treat this type of words from an NLP perspective. By building the lexicon, we also hope that there will be a new guideline for processing loan words with affixes, which is also able to reflect both their origin and status quo.

5   Conclusion and Future Plan

In our research we adopt an empirical method, combined with literature investigation and textual statistics, to summarize the Chinese vocabulary translated from English and provide persuasive evidence. We compile an online lexicon of such words by computation and verify its content manually. Also we sort Chinese loan words and delete those that are outdated in the paper-version dictionaries such as "运转手" (meaning "driver"), "觉书"(meaning "memorandum"), etc.. By constructing an electronic lexicon, we hope users can share their finding via the Internet. In the near future we plan to further verify the content of our dictionary and bring it into use for translators or students who are learning translation, in the process of which feedback is also expected by questionnaires.

Acknowledgement. Our work is supported by National High Technology Research and Development Program of China (863 Program) (No. 2015AA015402) and the Visiting Scholar Project sponsored by China Scholarship Council.

References

Chang, Baobao, Research on translating equivalent word pairs based on statistical models, in Journal of Computer, vol. 26(5), pp. 616-621, 2003.

Chen Liwei, Transformation of Vocabulary: The Interaction and Share of Knowledge between China and Japan at Modern Time. Website of Academic China, 2007(5) B.

Gu Jiangping, A Study of Japanese Borrowed Words in Chinese, Shanghai Dictionary Publishing House, 2011.

Lyu, S., Ding, S.: Modern Chinese Dictionary, 3rd edn. The Commercial Press, Beijing (1996)

Masisni, translated by Heqing Huang, The Formation of Modern Chinese Vocabulary – A Study of Chinese Loan Words in 19th Cenruty. Shanghai Chinese Dictionary Publishing House. 1997. pp 188-274.

Shen Guowei, Lexical Exchange Between China and Japan at Modern Time: The Creation, Acceptance and Share. Chung Hwa Book Co. Ltd. 2010. pp 428-430

Turnbull. J., Waters. A. ed., Translated by Longbiao Hu. Oxford Intermediate Learners' English-Chinese Dictionary (4th Edition), Shanghai: Commercial Press, 2010.

Xu, Shixuan. The analysis of word creation by derivation in Chinese-Tibetan languages," in National Languages, vol. 4, pp 23-31, 1999.

Zhang Yiming, Bailin Lu, An Investigaton of Japanese Borrowed Words in the Dictionary of Chinese Loan Words. Teaching of Open University, 1995(5). Pp 11.

Zhou Zhenhuan, Western Missionaries and Study of Western History in Late Qin Dynasty. Shanghai Ancient Book Publishing House, 2007

Corpus Linguistics

Study on the Annotation Framework of Chinese Logic Complement Semantics

Kunli Zhang[1], Yingjie Han[1], Yuxiang Jia[1], Lingling Mu[1], Zhifang Sui[2], Hongying Zan[1]

[1] School of Information Engineering, Zhengzhou University, Zhengzhou, Henan 450001, China
[2] Key Laboratory of Computational Linguistics, Ministry of Education, Peking University, Beijing 100871, China
`{ieklzhang,iellmu,iehyzan,ieyjhan}@zzu.edu.cn,szf@pku.edu.cn,`
`iehyzan@zzu.edu.cn`

Abstract. The meaning expressed by elements of negation, degree, tense and aspect, modality and mood in a sentence attached to the basic predicate-centered proposition is called logic complement semantics, which is embodied as semantic constraints of logic semantic operators to the predicate. Logic complement semantics is the effective supplement to the basic logic meaning, and is important for deep understanding of sentence semantics. In this paper, a Chinese logic complement semantics annotation framework aimed for deep semantic comprehension is preliminarily practiced, which constructed a classification system including negation, degree, tense and aspect, and mood on the basis of existing research results, built the operator dictionary, established rules for annotation, and annotated logic complement semantics operators of a sentence which have been tagged with basic propositional arguments. Finally, the statistics of the annotation result are presented, and the problems in annotation process are analyzed.

Keywords: logic complement semantics, negation, degree, tense and aspect, mood, annotation framework

1 Introduction

Since natural language understanding is based on the semantic understanding, digging deep semantic understanding with obvious form will be the breakthrough in natural

Y. Wu et al. (Eds.): CLSW 2017, LNAI 10709, pp. 359–373, 2018.
https://doi.org/10.1007/978-3-319-73573-3_33

language understanding in the future. It is often believed that a sentence is the relatively complete meaning expression unit of natural language. Therefore if someone wants to understand natural language, he/she needs to understand the meaning of the sentence. The semantic structure of a Chinese sentence can be abstracted as "{[<|(proposition component) tense and aspect component)|modal component>mood component] tone component}"[1]. And in this structure, the proposition component and the tense and aspect component can be regarded as the objective semantic expression of the sentence, while the modal component, the mood component and the tone component can be taken as the thought system of a sentence. The proposition component consists of two parts: the basic proposition meaning centered with the predicate in a sentence, and the negative component and the degree component adhered to the predicate. The meaning conveyed by negative components, degree components, modal components and tense and aspect components is an important level for the deep semantic understanding of a sentence.

We take sentence (1) to (7) as examples to illustrate the basic components of the semantic structure of a Chinese sentence. Sentence (1) describes an objective fact "他去北京参加会议(*He went to Beijing to attend the meeting*)". In sentence (2), the word "没有[*meiyou*] (*not*) " expresses the negative meaning of the basic proposition, and therefore, is called negative operator. In sentence (3), the words "已经[*yijing*] (*already*) " and "了[*le*] ( ) " suggest that the fact described by the basic logic meaning is completed, and therefore, are called the tense and aspect operators. Sentence (4) adds the speaker's subjective attitude "可能[*keneng*] (*might*) " which expresses an uncertain judgment that whether the proposition is truth. The meaning expressed by "可能[*keneng*](*might*) " is called modal meaning or modality, and the word "可能[keneng](*might*)" is called modal operator or modal mark. In sentence (5), the modal particle "吗[*ma*] ()" and the punctuation "? " show that this sentence is an interrogative sentence, and the word "吗[ma] ( )" is called the mood operator. In sentence (6), the word "呀[*ya*] ( )" can be regard as the processing of the prosodic features, and therefore, is called the tone operator. In sentence (7), the adverb of degree "很[hen](*very*)" enhances the degree of the word "可能[*keneng*] (*might*)". So it is called the degree operator.

(1) 他去北京参加会议。(*He went to Beijing to attend the meeting.*)

(2) 他没有去北京参加会议。(*He didn't go to Beijing to attend the meeting.*)

(3) 他已经去北京参加会议了。(*He has gone to Beijing to attend the meeting.*)

(4) 他可能去北京参加会议。(*He might go to Beijing to attend the meeting.*)

(5) 他去北京参加会议了吗? (*Did he go to Beijing to attend the meeting?*)

(6) 他呀，去北京参加会议了。(*He went to Beijing to attend the meeting.*)

(7) 他很可能到北京参加会议了。(*He is likely to go to Beijing to attend the meeting.*)

In this paper, the components of negation, degree, tense and aspect, modality, mood, tone, etc., outside the basic logic semantics are categorized as the logic complement semantics which are the supplements to the basic proposition. The modality annotation framework has been described in detail in literature [2], so it will not be depicted in detail here. And the tone component will be discussed separately. Therefore, in this paper we will focus on discussing negation, degree, tense and aspect, mood components from the perspective of semantic comprehension. And we try to establish the annotation framework of the logic complement semantics and annotate the operators of Chinese sentences which have been annotated with basic proposition arguments. The logic semantic annotation mainly aims to annotate the semantic function of the explicit components. As for negative component and degree component, the scope of operators will also be marked in the argument structure.

The rest part of this paper is organized as follows. In Section 2, we review the related research. In Section 3, we introduce the annotation framework of logic complement semantics of Chinese sentence. In Section 4, we present the construction process of the corresponding operator dictionary. In Section 5, we describe the annotation process of logic complement semantics and analyze the result. At last, we conclude the paper and list further works.

2   Related Research

Many researchers have studied the semantic structure of Chinese sentences. Yu [3] referred proposition component as "subject reflecting", and analyzed the constituent function of Chinese auxiliary verbs accordingly. Chen[4] further analyzed the verb-centered construction of Chinese sentences, and discussed the basic rules of mapping verb-centered constructions to syntactic structures. Zhang [5] considered the abstract semantic structure of Chinese sentences as "{[<|(proposition structure) tense and aspect structure)|sentence module structure>modal structure] mood structure}". But from the perspective of semantic comprehension, it may be open to question of putting "sentence module structure" and "proposition structure" in parallel in this hierarchy. In addition, mood structure covers not only functional mood, but also tone. In structure {[<|(proposition component) tense and aspect component)|modal component>mood component] tone component}, Lu[6] pointed out that the subjectivity of modality, mood and tone that all belong to the mind category, gradually increases. Modality is objectively expressed to the "thing" in the sentence, while mood is the core symbol of the communicative unit in the sentence, and is for the communicative object "people". And tone is temporary processing of the prosodic features of the sentence so as to strengthen or weaken the original semantics on the basis of the sentence being as the communicative unit.

For the purpose of deep semantic understanding, both the objective expression and the subjective concept expressed by the speaker should be focused on. In literature [2], Zhang et al have differentiated modality and mood, and studied the annotation framework of modality, which provided basis and criteria for the rest of the semantic structure. As for negation, degree, tense and aspect and mood attached to the basic logic semantics of the sentence, different researchers have analyzed and illustrated from different angles on markers, syntax and semantics, which will be described in further detail later in the following section. But none of them focus on systematical study on the annotation of logic complement semantics of sentences from the aspect of machine oriented processing. Based on annotation of semantic role of predicate in corpus of 973 subtopic *Acquisition and Organization of the Chinese Language Knowledge and World Knowledge that Integrates Three-dimension Space*, we carry out systematic research and annotation of logic complement semantics of the Chinese sentence.

3   Classification System of Logic Complement Semantics

The annotation of logic complement semantics will be taken on the foundation of the annotated basic proposition arguments, and the annotation framework includes a modality classification system based on the existing research, operator dictionaries, and guidelines for annotation. The annotation framework of the four components will be introduced as follows. The classification system of complement semantics is shown in Table 1.

3.1   Negation

The negative semantics, an important part of the logic-semantics relations, is usually done by the negative words in the sentence. The annotation of the negative semantics includes marking the negative word and its scope. The negative words in the sentence are called negative operators (abbreviated as "neg"), which are usually negative adverbs, such as "不[bu](not)", "没[mei](not)", "没有[meiyou](not)", "未[wei](not)", etc. In this section, the scope of negative operators will be discussed, and the construction of the operator dictionary will be described in Section 4.

Table 1. The classification system of the logic complement semantics

Category		Typical operator	Tag	Operator No.
negation		不[bu](not)/d	neg	35
degree	high degree	很[hen](very)/d	dgr_high	95
	low degree	稍微[shaowei](very)/d	dgr_low	48
tense and aspect	future tense	将[jiang](will)/d	tense_fut	19
	past tense	刚[gang](just)/d	tense_past	6
	progressive aspect	着[zhe]( )/u	tense_prog	5
	perfective aspect	了[le]( )/u	tense_perf	19
mood	indicative intonation	的[de]( )/u	intonation_indicative	32
	interrogative intonation	吗[ma]( )/y	intonation_interrogative	19
	imperative intonation	吧[ba]( )/y	intonation_imperative	24
	exclaim intonation	啊[a]( )/y	intonation_exclamation	21
Total				323

In a sentence containing a negative word, all components modified by the negative word constitute the negative scope. In fact, there is only one component in the negative scope that is called the focus of negation. Linguists have conducted a comprehensive study on whether the negation word has a scope and how to determine the scope.

Some scholars believed that negative words do not have a scope. For example, Xu et al [7] considered that the negative words do not have independent scope, but modify the whole sentence. Lv [8] pointed out that "in the sentence, the negative scope of '不[bu](not)' and '没[mei](not)' includes all words after '不[bu](not)' and '没[mei](not)' ". Some scholars hold the opposite view. For instance, Yuan [9] considered that the negative words have their own independent scope, and the negative center can be separated from the focus of the sentence. In the case of the unmarked, the scope of the negative word must be the composition after the negative word. In the case of the marked, the negative scope can be traced back to the component before the negative word.

Lee et al [10] also believed that a negative word has its own scope, that is, the negative word only denies the composition on its right side. Shen [11] discussed the adjacency negation. When there are other adverbial components adjacent to the negative word before the verb, the negative word usually denies the adverbial components adjacent to the negative word, not the verb.

According to the need of deep semantic understanding in this paper, the negative scope is the negative operator and its subsequent verb phrase or adjective phrase. In the annotated corpus, the negative operator will be signed as "neg", and its scope will be marked with "{ }".The annotated example is shown as sentence (8).

(8) 生活 常常 是 {<不[*bu*](*not*)>neg 公平} 的 。(*Life is not often fair.*)

To ensure the integrity of the linguistic components in the negative scope, in such a special case, "verb+不[*bu*](*not*)+complement", the scope will include the verb in front of the negative operator, as shown in sentence (9).

(9) {<没有>neg 我们 {克服<不[*bu*](*not*)>neg 了} 的困难} 。(*There is no difficulty we can't overcome.*)

In addition, the negative word will not be marked when it appears in some collocations, such as "verb 不[*bu*](*not*) verb" , or in the end of the interrogative sentences, as shown in sentence (10) and (11) respectively.

(10) 刘 教授 吃 不[*bu*]( ) 吃 慢头 ? (*Does Professor Liu eat steamed bread?*)

(11) 你们 签订 合同 没有[*meiyou*]( ) ? (*Did you sign the contract?*)

3.2   Degree

The degree meaning refers to the degree restriction to the modified words, and the degree operators in the sentences are mainly degree adverbs. The degree adverbs are a closed collection, and a number of linguists have discussed some of the degree adverbs. Zhang [12] divided 89 adverbs into two categories, named the absolute degree adverbs and the relative degree adverbs. And the absolute degree adverbs are further divided into the highest level, higher level and lower level, while the relative degree adverbs include super level, high level and low level. Lin et al. [13] classified 85 degree adverbs. The categories are the same as the literature [12], and according to the degree from high to low, there are four levels, namely extreme level, high level, middle level and low level. These divided categories and levels are more detailed. From the aspect of annotated feasibility, we merge the extreme level and high level in literature [13] into high degree, and middle level and low level into low degree.

The scope of degree adverbs is easy to determine, because degree adverbs have the characteristics of strong positioning. Except for a few adverbs which can act as complements, such as "很[*hen*](*very*)" and " 极[*ji*](*very*)", degree adverbs are always the adverbial modifier in the verb-adverbial structure. When the degree verb collocates with other verbs, it is close to the center word, and is in the innermost. Only when collocated with "不[*bu*](*not*)", will the degree verb not be close to the center word.

Degree operators (abbreviated as "dgr") are mainly the degree adverbs, such as "很 [*hen*](*very*), 非常 [*feichang*](*very*), 稍微 [*shaowei*](*slightly*), 有点儿 [*youdianr*](*a little*)", which restrict the degree of the main modified predicate. And in terms of the degree, they are divided into two categories, namely high degree (abbreviated as "dgr_high") and low degree (abbreviated as "dgr_low"). The tags (as shown in Table 1) are added as the symbols behind degree operators and "{ }" is used to show their scope. The scope of degree operator is usually the adverb phrase, adjective or adverb behind the operator. Annotated examples are shown as sentence (12) and sentence (13).

(12) 考试 期间 她   {<非常[*feichang*](*very*)>dgr_high 用功}   。 (*During the exam time, she worked very hard.*)

(13) 大家 对于 工资 问题 一般 都 {<比较[*feichang*](*fairly*)>dgr_low 关心}   。 (*We are generally concerned about the issue of wages.*)

In one special case, the scope will include the predicate in front of the degree operator, when the operator containing the word "得[*de*]( )"appears behind the predicate, as shown in sentence (14).

(14) 病人 的 妻子 {伤心 得 <很[*hen*](*very*)>dgr_high}   。 (*The patient's wife was very sad.*)

3.3   Tense and Aspect

Tense and aspect are the semantic elements added to the proposition that have the objective basis. Tense refers to a specific tense, and it indicates the temporal relationships between the time when the behavior takes place and the time when we talk about it. It is generally divided into past tense, present tense, future tense, etc. There is no tense in Chinese, but if necessary, there are time adverbs and tense particles. Aspect is used to describe the process of progression of an action. Shi [14] elaborated that the mark system of aspect is consisted of three verb suffix. They are "了[*le*]( )", "着[*zhe*]( )", and "过[*guo*]( )" and they represent the different stage of an action. "了[*le*]( )" indicates the completion of an action and is called "realized aspect". "着[*zhe*]( )" means a continuous stage of action and is called "durative aspect". "过[*guo*]( )" refers to the end of an action, and is called "perfective aspect".

In this paper, tense includes future tense and past tense. Aspect includes progressive aspect and perfective aspect. The specification of operators of tense and aspect is shown in Table 1. The tense and aspect operators and their types should be annotated on the restricted argument structure in the annotation task of tense and aspect.

1) Future Tense

Future tense means the action and state in the future. It also means the frequent action and state in a certain period of time in the future. It often used in conjunction with future adverbials. For example, "明天[*mingtian*](*tomorrow*)", "下周 [*xiazhou*] (*next week*)", and "将来[*jianglai*](*future*)" and so on. The typical operators are "赶明儿[*ganmingr*](*by the moment*)", "将[*jiang*](*will*)", etc. Examples are shown in sentence (15) and (16).

(15) <赶明儿[*ganmingr*](*by the moment*)>tense_fut 我 长 大了，也 要 当 医生。(*When I grow up, I will be a doctor.*)

(16) 竞赛 <将[*jiang*](*will*)>tense_fut 分区 同时 进行。(*The competition will take place in different regions at the same time.*)

2) Past Tense

Past tense indicates the state of the non-persistent action or the existence of a certain time in the past, and it indicates that the action happens frequently and repeatedly. It is often used in conjunction with the past adverbial, such as "昨天[*zuotian*](*yesterday*)", "昨晚[*zuowan*](*last night*)", "两天前[*liangtianqian*](*two days ago*)", etc. It denotes the ability and nature of the subject in the past. The typical operators are "刚刚[*ganggang*](*just*)", "才[*cai*](*just*)" and so on. The example is shown in sentence (17).

(17) 我 <才[*cai*](*just*)>tense_past 从 上海 回来 不久。(*I just came back from Shanghai.*)

3) Progressive Aspect

Progressive aspect means the ongoing action and the ongoing state. The typical operators include auxiliary word "着[*zhe*]( )" and the adverb "正[*zheng*]( ), 在[*zai*]( ), 正在[*zhengzai*]( )", etc. Sentence (18) is an example.

(18) 红旗 <在[*zai*]( )>tense_prog 飘扬。(*The red flag is blowing.*)

4) Perfective Aspect

Perfective aspect indicates that the action has been completed. Situation will be associated with a reference time in Comrie's opinion [15]. Perfective aspect describes both the inner time structure of the situation and the external time relationship between the situation and the reference time. Mochizuki[16] pointed out that perfective aspect has both inner time structure and the characteristics of time. The operators include auxiliary word "了[*le*]( )", "过[*guo*]( )", etc, adverbs "已[*yi*](*already*)", "已经[*yijing*](*already*)", "曾[*ceng*](*once*)", "曾经[*cengjing*](*once*)", modal particle "来着[*laizhe*]( )", "来的[*laide*]" "了[*le*]( )", etc. Examples are shown in sentence (19) and (20).

(19) 西红柿 <已[*yi*](*already*)>tense_perf 熟 透 了。(*The tomatoes have already matured.*)

(20) 我 整整 干 <了[*le*]( )>tense_perf 八 个 钟头。(*I have been working for eight hours.*)

3.4   Mood

Mood indicates the view and attitudes toward behaviors or things. It is the voice under the control of the emotional movement. In the text, the emotional color of a sentence entirely depends on modal particles. There are three points of view in mood classification. The first one divides mood into indicative, imperatives, interrogative and exclamation. The second one takes all re-expressions of the proposition in the sentence as mood. He [17] and Qi [18] are supporters of this view. The third one is a compromise of the first view and the second one. Sun [19] considered that generalized mood include mood and tone, and mood only includes indicative, interrogative, imperative and exclamation. The authors of this paper adopt the first view and classify modal particle into indicative, interrogative, imperative, and exclamation according to the mood to be expressed. The specification of operators of mood is shown in Table 1.

1) Indicative Intonation

Indicative intonation expresses an objective statement of the facts. It includes affirmative tone and negative tone, and does not express strong feelings. The operators include "的[de]( )", "了[le]( )", "嘛[ma]( )", "呢[ne]( )", "罢了[bale]( )", "也[ye]( )" and "而已[eryi]( )". The example is shown in sentence (21).

(21) 要 干 好 这 项 工作，不 懂 外语 是 不 行 <的[de]( )>intonation_indicative。(*You must master a foreign language in order to do this work better.*)

2) Interrogative Intonation

Interrogative intonation can be divided into two kinds. One is to convey the meaning of trust; the other is to convey the meaning of doubt. Different interrogatives are different in terms of degree. The operators include "吗[ma]( )", "么[me]( )", "吧[ba]( )", "呢[ne]( )", "也[ye]( )" and "乎[hu]( )". Examples are sentences (22) and (23). In sentence (22), interrogative is expressed by "哪儿[nar](*where*)" and "啊[a](*ah*)" is not necessary. The tone is more gentle when there is an "啊[a](*ah*)" in the sentence.

(22) 你 在 哪儿 <啊[a](*ah*)> intonation_interrogative?   (*Where are you?*)

(23) 明天 你 来 <吗[ma]( )>intonation_interrogative?   (*Will you come tomorrow?*)

There are some special occasions that the sentences do not contain mood words. The interrogative mood is expressed by interrogative pronouns or some patterns. Sentence (24) and (25) are the examples. They will not be annotated in our annotation system.

(24) 现在 几 点 钟 了? (*What time is it   now?*)

(25) 你 是 学 英语，还 是 学 日语? (*Do you learn English or Japanese?*)

3) Imperative Intonation

Imperative intonation is used to express the mood of command, request, order, invitation, and supervision and so on. It can also be used to indicate prohibition, permission and advice, etc. The operators include "吧[*ba*](*well*)", "啊[*a*](*ah*)" and so on. Sentence (26) is an example.

(26) 别 再 说话 <啦>intonation_imperative! (*Don't talk any more.*)

There are some imperative sentences that don't include modal particle, such as sentence (27). The imperative sentence without the explicit operator is not considered in our annotation.

(27) 请 打开 灯。 (*Please turn on the light.*)

4) Exclamation Intonation

Exclamation expresses the subjective emotion. A variety of strong emotions, such as praise, surprise, sadness, anger, ridicule, scare, fear or hope and other emotional reactions are expressed from exclamation. The operators are "啊[*a*](*ah*)", "呀[*ya*](*yeah*)", "哇[*wa*](*wow*)" and so on. An Example is shown in sentence (28).

(28) 多 好 的 天 <啊[*a*](*ah*)>intonation_exclamation! (*What a good day!*)

4   The Construction of the Logic Complement Semantics Operator Dictionary

The words in the logic complement semantics operator dictionary are mainly extracted from the literatures on monographic study and on case study, and have been analyzed and selected when they were included in the dictionary. Considering the needs of annotating, we describe operators from different properties such as ID, words, POS, sources, definitions, example sentences, full-pinyin, modality category and annotation tag, etc. It is interesting to note that most negative operators and degree operators are adverbs and the majority of tense and aspect operators and mood operators are auxiliaries, modal particles and adverbs. Fortunately, the existing *Chinese Function word Knowledge Base*, abbreviated as CFKB [21], includes dictionaries of adverbs, conjunctions, prepositions, modal particles, location words and auxiliaries. And the adverbs in CFKB are divided into subcategories, including negative adverbs and degree adverbs, which can be directly used as negative operators and degree operators. So we extract the properties of operators from CFKB, and then take the *Modern Chinese Dictionary* (h), the *Dictionary of Modern Chinese Grammar* (y)[22] and other (z) contents as the supplement to construct the operator dictionary. In order to use the methods and results of usage automatic recognition of CFKB for further automatic annotation, the words from CFKB remain the granularity partitioning of usage in the operator dictionaries, and the ID code is encoded according to coding rules in literature [21] of CFKB. Samples from the corresponding operator dictionaries are shown in Fig. 1.

1	ID	词语	词性	来源	释义	例句	用法	类别	标记	全拼音
2	d_bing4bu4	并不	d	CFKB	表示否定，略带反驳意味	~把这当回事儿<y>|把你的话~当回事	修饰动词。<x>	否定	neg	bing4bu4
3	d_bing4wei4	并未	d	CFKB	表示加强否定语气。<z>	但不少大企业的投资热~刹车，出手仍	修饰动词、形容词，或动词短语	否定	neg	bing4wei4
4	d_bu4_2	不	d	CFKB	表示否定。<b>	~是<b>|你去不去？——~一定<b>|为	用在动词、形容词或个别副词	否定	neg	bu4
5	d_bu4_2m	不	d	CFKB	表示否定。<x>	~怎样<x>|~这样<x>	用在个别的指示代词、疑问代	否定	neg	bu4
6	d_bu4bian4	不便	d	CFKB	表示不恰当，带有委婉语	我~直说<x>|这里太冷，~久坐<x>|他	修饰动词。<z>	否定	neg	bu4bian4
7	d_bu2ceng2	不曾	d	CFKB	对"曾经"的否定。<b>	这种事在历史上也~出现过<b>|老张~	用于动词语或形容词的前面。	否定	neg	bu2ceng2

(a) Negation

1	ID	词语	词性	来源	释义	例句	用法	类别	标记	全拼音
2	d_bi3jiao4	比较	d	CFKB	表示具有一定程度。<b>	从这里走~近<b>|今天~冷<b>|大汶口	修饰形容词，不用于否定句。	程度_低	dgr_low	bi3jiao4
3	d_bi3jiao4	比较	d	CFKB	表示具有一定程度。<b>	我~爱看电影<b>|他~能动脑筋<b>|城	修饰动词，不用于否定句。<b>	程度_低	dgr_low	bi3jiao4
4	d_bu4da4_1	不太	d	CFKB	表示程度较浅的否定，用	~见效<x>|我的话，他总~听<x>|~说	修饰动词或形容词，<x>与时间	程度_低	dgr_low	bu4da4
5	d_da4_1a	大	d	CFKB	表示程度深。<b>	~有问题<b>|~有要打起来的架势<b>	~+有+名词，名词仅限于双音节	程度_高	dgr_high	da4
6	d_da4_1b	大	d	CFKB	表示程度深。<b>	天已经~亮<b>|~喊一声<b>|陪同我的	~+(动词|形容词)，动词、形容	程度_高	dgr_high	da4
7	d_da4_1c	大	d	CFKB	表示程度深。<b>	兄弟俩性格~不相同<b>|他感觉身体~	~+不+(动词|形容词)，限于少	程度_高	dgr_high	da4
8	d_da4_1d	大	d	CFKB	表示规模大，程度深，带	~书特书<b>|~书而特书<b>|~睡特睡	~A[而]特A，A是单音节动词。	程度_高	dgr_high	da4

(b) Degree

1	ID	词语	词性	来源	释义	例句	用法	类别	标记	全拼音
2	d_jiang1_1	将	d	CFKB	表示动作或情况不久就会	中央民族乐团~于2月1日乘机离开	修饰动词或动词短语，用于书	将来时	tense_fut	jiang1
3	d_cai2_1	才	d	CFKB	刚刚，表示事情在前不久	他~走。<b>|我~从上海回来不久。<b	用于单句。<b>；或用于前一小	过去时	tense_past	cai2
4	u_zhe5_1	着	d	CFKB	时间上表示已然，包括过	外面正下~毛呢。<y>|大家正在议论~	双音节动词前边常用"正在"。	进行体	tense_pro	zhe5
5	u_zhe5_3	着	d	CFKB	表示相对的时间，可用于	我俩举~队旗入场，<x>|小王把东西	前边的动词带"着"，表示作	进行体	tense_pro	zhe5
6	u_guo5_1	过	u	CFKB	表示动作完毕。<b>	他吃~晚饭来看的我。<x>|赶到那儿，	用在动词后。这种"动词+~"	完成体	tense_per	guo5
7	u_guo5_2	过	u	CFKB	表示过去曾经有这样的事	这本小说我看~。<b>|去北京的事他	用在动词后，动词前可加副词	完成体	tense_per	guo5
8	u_guo5_3	过	u	CFKB	有同现在相比较的意思。	这地方曾经热闹~一阵子。<x>|他小时	形容词带"过"，一般需要说	完成体	tense_per	guo5

(c)Tense and Aspect

1	ID	词语	词性	来源	释义	例句	用法	类别	标记	全拼音
2	u_de5_t2_5a	的	u	CFKB	表示一定的语气，用在句	他会走~。<b>|我问过老吴~。<b>|我	用在陈述句末尾，表示情况确	陈述语气	intonatio	de5
3	y_ba4le5	罢了	y	CFKB	表示如此而已，有把事情	这不算什么，我不过尽了我的职责~。	用在陈述句的末尾<b>。常跟	陈述语气	intonatio	ba4le5
4	u_zhe5_2	着	u	CFKB	用于祈使句，带命令口吻	你听~！<x>|快把门关~！<x>|稳~点	用于祈使句，带命令口吻，时	祈使语气	intonatio	zhe5
5	y_a5_t1_2	啊	y	CFKB	表示请求、催促、命令、	你可别告诉小邓~！<h>|慢慢说，说清	用在祈使句末尾。<h><b>	祈使语气	intonatio	a5
6	y_a5_t1_3	啊	y	CFKB	表示增强语气。<h>	多好的天~！<h>|他的行为多么高尚~	用在感叹句末。<h>	感叹语气	intonatio	a5
7	y_a5_t1_4	啊	y	CFKB	在有疑问指代词的问句和	是谁~？<b>|你是打哪儿来的~？<b>	用在问句末尾。<b>或用在反问	疑问语气	intonatio	a5
8	y_ba5_t1_2	吧	y	CFKB	使原来的提问带有揣测、	这座房子是新盖的~？<b>|他就是李	用在问句末尾。<b>	疑问语气	intonatio	ba5

(d) Mood

Fig. 1. Examples of logic complement semantic operator dictionary

In the operator dictionaries, multiple semantics of the same word can belong to the same category or to different categories. For example, in Figure 1, "过[*guo*]()" has three semantic meanings ("u_guo5_1", "u_guo5_2" and "u_guo5_3") which all belong to the perfective aspect category, while "着[*zhe*]()" also has three semantic meanings which belongs to the progressive aspect category("u_zhe5_1" and "u_zhe5_3") and the imperative intonation category ("u_zhe5_2") respectively. In the modality operator dictionary, except for the adverbs, a few auxiliary verbs, verbs and phrases are also included. So the modality operators extracted from CFKB account for 62.4% of the total. The operators of the four components discussed in this paper are all derived from CFKB, and have been classified into different categories by differentiating the semantic meanings. So far, four dictionaries contain 323 operators, and the operator number of each category is shown in Table 1.

5 Annotation and Analysis of Logic Complement Semantics

The logic complement semantics annotation mainly aims to annotate semantic function of the corresponding operators in the argument structure. In addition, the scope of negative operators and degree operators are also annotated. "< >label" is employed to mark the operator, and the label represents the corresponding category (as shown in Table 1) of the operator. For negative operator and degree operator, "{}" is added to show their scope, which indicates the range of the verbal composition or adverbial composition dominated by the operator.

We have preliminarily annotated the operators and their scopes in 10,634 segmented sentences which have been marked with basic proposition arguments. The examples are shown as sentences (29) and (30). The number of operators appearing in the corpus, the annotated frequency of the operators and the top 5 high-frequency words are all shown in Table.2. In the annotated corpus, a total number of 125 operators appeared, and accounted for 38.7% of the total operators' number, while the frequency of the top 5 operators accounted for 86.7% of the total annotation frequency. Although it conforms to the law of high frequency of common words, from the aspect of operator coverage, it is necessary to further supplement the corpus.

Table 2. The Statistics of Result

Category	Annotated words No.	Frequency	Top 5 words
negation	13	1,323	<不[bu](not)>neg(895), <没有[meiyou](not)>neg(239), <没 [mei](not)>neg(144), <并不[bingbu] (not)>neg(12), <未 [wei](not)>neg(10)
degree	52	1,298	<很[hen](very)>dgr_high(485), <最[zui](most)>dgr_high(204), <更 [geng](more)>dgr_high(127), <太[tai](too)>dgr_high(112), <非常 [feichang](very)>dgr_high(46)
tense and aspect	26	3,079	<了[le]( )>tense_perf(1857), <着[zhe]( )>tense_prog(197), <已经 [yijing](already)>tense_perf(163), <过[guo]( )>tense_perf(149), <将 [jiang](will)>tense_fut(117)
mood	34	2,138	<了[le]( )>intonation_indicative(1147), <吗[ma]( )>intonation_interrogative(378), <的[de]( )>intonation_indicative(376), <吧 [ba]( )>intonation_imperative(61), <了[le]( )>intonation_imperative(30)
Total	125	7,838	6,794

(29) 劳动者 只有 具备 { <较>dgr_low 高 } 的 科学 文化 水平 、 丰富 的 生产 经验 和 先进 的 劳 动 技术 , { <才>mod_emphasis { <能>mod_ability 在 现代化 的 生产 中 发挥 { <更>dgr_high 大 } 的 作用 } } 。 (*Only if workers have a high level of scientific and cultural, rich experience in production and advanced labor technology, can they play a great role in the modern production.*)

(30) 词典 {< 太 >dgr_high 旧 } < 了 >intonation_indicative ， 再 买 一 本 新 的 < 吧>intonation_imperative ， { <好在>mod_comment_3 也 {<不>neg {<太>dgr_high 贵}} } 。(*The dictionary is too old, and buy a new one, please. Fortunately, it is not too expensive.*)

1) Co-occurrence of negative operators and other operators

The co-occurrence of negative operators and other operators may change the category of logic complement semantics. For instance, when negative operators and other operators co-occur, "可能[*kneng*](*may*)" is of probability modality, and "不可能 [*bukeneng*](*impossible*)" is of certainty modality, while "一定[*yiding*](*must*)" is of certainty modality, and "不一定[*buyiding*](*uncertain*) " is of probability modality. If negative operators (like "不[*bu*](*not*)") and modal operators co-occur, modality and negativity should be annotated separately. Then, corresponding modality can be determined by logic calculation. In sentence (31), "不[*bu*](*not*)" is negative, and "可能 [*keneng*](*may*) " is of probability modality, while "不可能[*bukeneng*](*impossible*) " means certainty modality. In this case, "不[*bu*](*not*)" and "可能[*keneng*](*may*) " will be marked respectively. Annotated result is shown in sentence (31).

(31) 他 {<不>neg {<可能>mod_possibility在六点钟回到家}} 。(*He can not get home at six o'clock.*)

2) Same Word Belongs to Different Categories

In the annotation process of logic complement semantics, there are two types of multi-category words to be distinguished. The first one is the word belonging to verb operator and logic complement operator. For example, the word "没有[*meiyou*](*not*)" can be the head verb or negative operator, so it needs to be distinguished. For example, in sentence (32), "没有[*meiyou*](*not*)"as the head verb will not be annotated as negative operator. The second one is the word belonging to different categories of logic complement semantics. For instance, the word "了[*le*]( )" belongs to tense and aspect and mood according to different contexts. These above two cases need to be focused on in the annotation process.

(32) 你 的 钢笔 没有 墨水 了 。(*There is no ink in you pen.*)

6   Conclusion

Aiming for deep semantic understanding, we firstly integrated the existing research results and constructed the classification system of logic complement semantics. And then we built the logic complement semantics operator dictionary on the basis of the CFKB. Finally, we established annotation rules, and annotated negative operators, degree operators, tense and aspect operators and mood operators and their scopes which appeared in 10,634 sentences.

So far we have only carried out a preliminary discussion of the annotation framework of logic complement semantics, and the annotated words in the corpus only account for 38.7% of all operators. We will try to annotate more typical sentences, and develop machine learning methods to automatically annotate operators on the basis of this annotated corpus. In addition, only the logic complement semantics with explicit marked words has been annotated in this paper, and the study of implicit logic complement semantics should be our further work. It is expected that according to the abstract semantic structure, the study of deep semantic understanding can be conducted on the basis of both explicit and implicit logic complement semantics..

Acknowledgments. We thank the anonymous reviewers for their constructive comments, and gratefully acknowledge the support of National Basic Research Program of China (2014CB340504), National Natural Science Foundation of China (No.61402419, No.60970083), National Social Science Foundation (No.14BYY096), Basic research project of Science and Technology Department of Henan Province (No. 142300410231, No.142300410308) and science and technology project of Science and Technology Department of Henan Province (No. 172102210478).

References

1. Zhang, X.H.: An Initial Study on Modality Category of Modern Chinese. Master Thesis. Sichuan Normal University, Chengdu(2008).(In Chinese)
2. Zhang, K.L., Mu, L.L., Zan, H.Y., et al.: Study on Chinese Modality Annotation Framework. Chinese Lexical Semantics (LNAI10085), 2016:291-305.
3. Yu, K.: Inside-Proposition Elements and outside-Proposition Elements: Taking Chinese Auxiliary Verbs as Examples. Chinese Teaching in the World. Vol.1996 No.1:27-34(1996)(In Chinese)
4. Chen, C. L.: The Semantic Structure of Modern Chinese Sentence. Yantai Teachers University Journal (Philosophy and Social Science Edition), Vol.17 No.1: 67-72+77 (2000)(In Chinese)
5. Zhang, L.: The Semantic Structure of Modern Chinese Sentence. The Northern Forum,Vol.1995 No.5:54-60.

6. Lu, C.: Grammar Subjective Information and Modality Tag of Chinese. China Commercial Press, Beijing(2003)(In Chinese)

7. Xu J., Li Z.Y.: Focus and Two Non-linear Grammatical Categories. Chinese Language. Vol.1993 No.2: 81-92 (1993) (In Chinese)

8. Lv S.X.: Interrogative, Negation and Affirmative. Chinese Language. Vol.1985 No.4: 15-22 (1985) (In Chinese)

9. Yuan, Y. L.: Study on the Focus, Presupposition and Scope Ambiguity of Negative Sentences. Studies of the Chinese Language, Vol.2000 No.2: 99-108 (2000) (In Chinese)

10. Lee, Po-Lun, Haihua Pan. The Chinese Negation Marker Bu and its Association with Focus. Linguistics, 2001,39(4): 703-731.

11. Shen, J.X.: Asymmetry and Markedness. Jiangxi Education Press, Nanchang (1999)(In Chinese).

12. Zhang Y.S.: Modern Chinese Function Word Study. Xuelin Press, Shanghai (2004)(In Chinese)

13. Lin, H.,Guo, S.H.:On the Characteristics, Range and Classification of Adverbs of Degree. Journal of Shanxi University(Philosophy and Social Science), Vol.26 No.2:71-74(2003)(In Chinese)

14. Shi, Y.Z.: The Different Functions of Progressive Aspectual Markers. Chinese Language Learning, Vol.2006 No.3:14-24(2006)(In Chinese)

15. Comrie.B. Aspect. Cambridge University Press,Cambridge,1976.

16. Mochizuki. Perfective Aspect in Chinese. Chinese Language Learning. Vol.2000 No.1:12-16 (2000)(In Chinese)

17. He,Y.: On the Modality System of Modern Written Chinese. Journal of Renmin University of China, Vol.6No.5:59-66(1992)(In Chinese)

18. Qi, H. Y.: Modality Words and Modality System. Anhui Education Press, Hefei (2002)(In Chinese)

19. Sun, R. J.: Four Functions of the Toned Words at the End of Sentences. Journal of Nantong University (Social Science Edition), Vol.21 No.2:76-80(2005)(In Chinese)

20. Zan, H.Y., Zhang, K.L., Zhu, X. F., Yu, S.W.: Research on the Chinese Function Word Usage Knowledge Base. International Journal on Asian Language Processing.Vol.21 No.4: 185-198(2011)

21. Zhang, K.L.,Zan, H.Y.,et al.: A Survey on the Chinese Function Word Usage Knowledge Base. Journal of Chinese Information Processing.Vol.9 No.3:1-8(2015)(In Chinese)

22. Yu, S.W., Zhu, X.F., Wang, H., et al.: Dictionary of Modern Chinese Grammar. Tsinghua Express, Beijing (2003)(In Chinese)

Building A Parallel Corpus with Bilingual Discourse Alignment

Wenhe Feng[1], Han Ren[2,*], Xia Li[2] and Haifang Guo[3]

[1] School of Computer, Wuhan University, Wuhan 430072, China
[2] Laboratory of Language Engineering and Computing, Guangdong University of Foreign Studies, Guangzhou 510420, China
[3] Henan Institute of Science and Tech-nology, Xinxiang, Henan 453003, China
wenhefeng@gmail.com, hanren@gdufs.edu.cn,
200211025@oamail.gdufs.edu.cn, 1181314606@qq.com

Abstract. This paper describes a discourse resource, namely a Chinese-English parallel corpus, based on the idea of bilingual discourse alignment. We introduce a bilingual collaborative annotation approach, which annotates English discourse units based on Chinese ones, and annotates Chinese discourse structure based on English ones subsequently. Such approach can ensure full discourse structure alignment between parallel texts, and reduce cost for annotating texts of two languages as well. Annotation Evaluation of the parallel corpus justifies the appropriateness of the discourse alignment framework to parallel texts.

Keywords: Discourse Analysis, Discourse Structure, Discourse Alignment, Discourse Annotation.

1 Introduction

Bilingual discourse alignment refers to the alignment of bilingual texts with discourse structure, which generally contains discourse unit, connective, hierarchy, relation and nuclearity. The following example demonstrates a parallel Chinese-English text pair annotated with aligned discourse structures, shown in Figure 1. In Figure 1(a), each uppercase letter under a line denotes a discourse unit over the line; slashes indicate discourse hierarchy, and the count of slashes between each two clauses refers to the depth of the discourse relation in the discourse structure tree of the sentence; each word between two clauses with brackets indicates the discourse relation of them; each word with braces is a connective; each label @ in two clauses denotes which one is the nuclear between them.

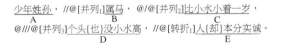

少年姓孙，//@[并列₁]属马，@/@[并列₂]比小水小着一岁，
　　A　　　　　　　　B　　　　　　　　　C
@///@[并列₃]个头{也}没小水高，//@[转折₁]人{却}本分实诚。
　　　　D　　　　　　　　　　　　　E

---

* Corresponding Author

© Springer International Publishing AG 2018
Y. Wu et al. (Eds.): CLSW 2017, LNAI 10709, pp. 374–382, 2018.
https://doi.org/10.1007/978-3-319-73573-3_34

This boy, a member of the Sun family, //
A
@[COORDINATION₁]had been born in the year of the horse.
B
@/@[COORDINATION₂]Although he was a year younger
C
@///@[COORDINATION₃]and a head shorter than Water
D
Girl, //@[TRANSITION₁]he was honest and sincere.
E

Fig. 1(a). Text representation of discourse units and relations

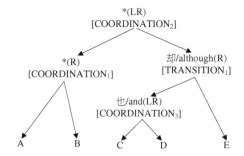

Fig. 1(b). Tree representation of discourse structure and relations

Fig. 1. An example of Chinese-English text pair annotated with aligned discourse structure.

As a detailed explanation, in Figure 1(a), one @ label left adjoining a slash or multiple slashes means a nuclear is on the left side of such slash or slashes, while two @ labels adjoining on both side of a slash or multiple slashes indicate two nucleus are on both side of such slash or slashes. A more clear tree representation of aligned discourse structure of such two texts for the example is shown in Figure 1(b), in which a leaf node denotes a discourse unit, while a non-leaf node represents the discourse relation of its descedents. For example, 却/*although* denotes the connective 却 in Chinese and *although* in English. An asterisk denotes an implicit connective. (R) means a right child is nuclear, while (LR) means both left and right child are nucleus. [COORDINATION] denotes the discourse relation Coordination. Directed edges indicate the discourse hierarchy, namely the direction of an edge is always from a high layer to a low one.

Bilingual discourse alignment shows rich and fine-grained discourse information within bilingual texts, and can be widely used in many cross-lingual natural language processing applications such as Machine Translation[1], Question Answering[2] and Sentiment Analysis[3].

Current research on aligned discourse resources mainly focuses on bilingual parallel corpora, such as [4, 5, 6], most of which focus on paragraph or sentence-level alignment rather than structural alignment that can provide more precise discourse alignment knowledge. Discourse resources such as RST[7] or PDTB[8] as well as non-English discourse resources such as [9, 10, 11, 12, 13, 14] provide rich knowledge of discourse structure and relation, whereas none of them provides parallel discourse texts so that the knowledge of parallel structure in bilingual discourse texts is hard to be captured through such resources.

In this paper, we describe a discourse resource, namely a Chinese-English parallel corpus, based on the idea of bilingual discourse alignment. As a matter of fact, bilingual discourse alignment is a challenging work because it requires a full discourse parsing and alignment analysis for texts of different languages. To this end, we employ a bilingual collaborative annotation approach to deal with bilingual discourse alignment. More specifically, we first annotate each Elementary Discourse Units(EDU, in the corpus is a clause) in texts of source language, then we find the paralleled EDU in texts of target language. After annotating discourse structure of texts of target language based on paralleled EDUs, we annotate paralleled discourse structure of text of source language based on discourse structure of text of target language. Such approach can ensure full discourse structure alignment between parallel texts, and reduce cost for annotating texts of two languages as well.

2   The Discourse Alignment Annotation Framework

2.1   Discourse Representation Scheme

We employ a scheme named Connective-driven Dependency Tree(CDT) proposed by Li et al.[9] for discourse representation. Such scheme takes advantage of the hierarchical structure representation by RST and the connective-argument structure representation by PDTB. More specifically, a CDT describes a discourse hierarchy of a text, while each leaf in the CDT is an EDU(namely a clause) and each non-leaf node is a connective with a nuclearity indicator and a discourse relation type, as shown in Figure 1. Each sub tree in a CDT indicates the governing scope of the root node, that is, a connective. Such scheme has been applied in the construction of Chinese Discourse Corpus[9] and discourse analysis technologies[15, 16].

Although such scheme is used for monolingual discourse analysis, it can be still employed in our bilingual discourse alignment annotation. This idea is based on the assumption that if two texts can be inter-translated, discourse structure and relations of such two texts are also correlated. More specifically, two texts with high inter-translation quality probably have the same discourse relations and the discourse hierarchy. In other words, two inter-translated texts can be projected to one CDT provided that discourse structure for each text would be aligned.

2.2   The Annotation Approach

The overall annotation approach for bilingual discourse alignment describes as follows. First we annotate each EDU in texts of source language, then we find the paralleled

EDU in texts of target language. After that, we annotate discourse structure of texts of target language based on those paralleled EDUs. Then we find each counterpart for each part of discourse structure, such as relations, nucleus and connectives from text of source language. Finally, a CDT is built according to the discourse structure annotated. Such approach can ensure full discourse structure alignment between parallel texts, and reduce cost for annotating texts of two languages as well.

A detailed explanation for discourse structure annotation is shown as follows:

EDU alignment annotation. The strategy of EDU alignment annotation is that, we first annotate EDUs in texts of source language, then we find the counterpart for each EDU in texts of target language. Since our data need to be annotated come from a parallel corpus, it is easy to find the translation counterpart of target language for each EDU of source language.

Hierarchy alignment Annotation. The strategy of hierarchy alignment annotation is that, we first annotate discourse hierarchy in texts of target language, then we employ a tree to represent such discourse hierarchy, each leaf in it denoting a EDU in texts of target language. We replace each EDU with the corresponding EDU in texts of source language, thus we get a tree representing the hierarchy of texts of source language.

Relation alignment annotation. The annotation approach of relation alignment is the same with the annotation approach of hierarchy alignment annotation. For example, if a relation is assigned to two EDUs in texts of target language, it is also assigned to two corresponding EDUs in texts of source language.

Connective alignment annotation. The strategy of connective alignment annotation is that, we find one connective respectively according to each discourse relation in texts of both source and target language, then we combine them as one non-leaf node in their CDT, like the form of 却/although.

Nuclearity alignment annotation. The strategy of nuclearity alignment annotation is the same with the annotation approach of hierarchy alignment annotation: first we annotate nuclear for each text of target language having a discourse relation, then we annotate the same nuclear for the corresponding texts of source language.

3   The Chinese-English Discourse Alignment Corpus

Following the discourse alignment annotation framework, we build a Chinese-English parallel corpus. This section gives a detailed description of annotation process and experimental analysis.

3.1   Data Collection

Our data collection comes from the following government paperwork: The 2012 and 2014 Report on the Work of the Chinese Government, The Report on 18th National Congress of the Communist Party of China, and The Report on Decision of the Central Committee of the Communist Party of China on Deepening The Reform in A Comprehensive Way, which include a total amount of 140,000 words. All documents are parallel texts in Chinese and English with high translation quality.

3.2   Annotation Training

Two student annotators are trained under the supervision of their advisor. The training process contains three steps: first, the advisor gives the instruction on the strategies and criteria of annotation, and annotates five paragraphs as the examples; second, the annotators and the advisor finish the work of ten paragraph annotation respectively; third, each annotator finds the differences between one's annotated results and the advisor's results, and discusses the annotation errors with the advisor.

3.3   Annotation Agreement Evaluation

In the experiment of annotation agreement, we select 2014 Report on the Work of the Chinese Government(the former part), which includes 156 valid paragraphs, as the experiment data for annotation agreement evaluation. Two annotators annotate 816 and 819 discourse relations within the data, respectively.

We evaluate the annotation agreement with the following aspects: EDU, hierarchy, relation, connective and nuclearity. Four agreement metrics are defined in the experiment:

Chinese annotation agreement. The metric computes the ratio of the same annotation contents(EDU, connective, etc.) among all annotation contents in Chinese texts by two annotators.

English annotation agreement. The metric is similar with Chinese annotation agreement except that the annotation texts are English.

Non-alignment annotation agreement. The metric computes the ratio of the same annotation contents among all annotation contents in the parallel texts, regardless of whether they are aligned.

Alignment annotation agreement. The metric computes the ratio of the same annotation contents aligned among all annotation contents in the parallel texts.

Table 1. Annotation agreement evaluation results.

		Chinese	English	Non-alignment	Alignment
EDU		0.968	0.930	0.950	0.909
Hierarchy	partial	0.928	0.881	0.904	0.850
	full	0.709	0.630	0.669	0.636
Relation		0.872	0.860	0.865	0.835
Connective	explicit	0.400	0.950	0.876	0.389
	all	0.278	0.690	0.474	0.205
Nuclearity		0.843	0.843	0.843	0.818

Table 1 shows the agreement evaluation results. In Table 1, EDU means the agreement of same partition positions annotated by the two annotators, *partial* means the agreement of left EDUs or right EDUs of discourse partitions, *full* means the agreement of both left and right EDUs of a discourse partition, *explicit* means the agreement of explicit connectives, *all* means the agreement of all connectives, *nuclearity* means the agreement of nuclearity annotation(left, right or both) in all identical partitions by the two annotators.

Table 1 shows that, there are high agreement results in EDU partition: the agreement rate achieves a 90.9% performance even if it requires that both Chinese texts and English texts have same partition positions. It can be also seen from Table 1 that, the agreement performances of partial hierarchy alignment are better than those of full hierarchy alignment. On the other hand, the agreement performances of English texts are lower than those of Chinese texts, and the reason is that, partition positions always exist at positions of punctuations in Chinese texts, whereas they do not always exist at positions of punctuations in English texts, which may cause more annotated errors in hierarchy annotation of English texts.

Relation alignment shows high agreement performances: the agreement rate achieves a 83.5% performance even if it requires that both Chinese texts and English texts have same discourse relation types. Table 1 also shows that, the two annotators have a high agreement on explicit English connectives, with the agreement rate 95%, whereas they have a big divergence on explicit Chinese connectives, with the agreement rate 40%. The reason is obvious, since explicit connectives in English are much more than those in Chinese, hence the annotators are easier to identify English connectives. On the other hand, implicit connectives are more difficult to be judged, so the agreement performances of all connectives, including implicit ones, are lower than those of explicit connectives.

3.4   Corpus Statistics

Table 2. Statistical results of discourse relations in different languages.

Discourse Relation type	Chinese			English		
	Explicit	Implicit	All	Explicit	Implicit	All
Background	0	13	13	1	12	13
Progression	2	3	5	3	2	5
Comparison	0	0	0	0	0	0
Illustration	0	284	284	3	281	284
Exemplification	1	9	10	0	10	10
Assessment	2	22	24	0	24	24
Deduction	1	1	2	1	1	2
Selection	0	0	0	0	0	0
Parataxis	25	1685	1710	1103	607	1710
Hypothesis	0	1	1	0	1	1
Purpose	19	183	202	185	17	202
Concession	0	2	2	0	2	2
Continuity	0	7	7	6	1	7
Condition	23	53	76	48	28	76
Causality	0	159	159	41	118	159
Transition	6	6	12	12	0	12
Generalization	9	12	21	6	15	21
Total	88	2440	2528	1409	1119	2528

In order to investigate discourse structure and relations in texts with different languages and genres, we count the frequency of each explicit and implicit discourse relation in all data collections, shown in Table 2. It can be seen that, the former eight types of discourse relation have less differences between Chinese and English texts than the latter nine ones. It also shows that, the relation *Parataxis* is the most frequent relation in both Chinese and English texts.

Table 3. Explicit connectives in Chinese and English texts.

	Chinese		English	
	Connective	Frequency	Connective	Frequency
1	也/and	8	and	650
2	但/but	6	,...and	246
3	确保/ensure	6	To	99
4	以/to	6	,...,...and	81
5	其中/in...	4	,...,...,...and	29
6	使/for	4	so as to	26
7	为/for	4	so that	23
8	重点/importantly	4	to	22
9	并/and	3	and	19
10	既..又../not only..but also..	3	thus	17

Table 3 shows the top 10 connectives in Chinese and English texts. We can see that connectives more frequently appear in English texts and in Chinese ones.

Table 4. Nuclearity position distribution in Chinese and English texts.

	Chinese		English	
	Frequency	Ratio	Frequency	Ratio
Left	581	23.0%	614	24.3%
Right	242	9.6%	213	8.4%
Both	1705	67.4%	1701	67.3%

Table 4 shows the position of nuclearities in Chinese and English texts. In this table, *left* means the nuclearity of a text is the EDU that is on the left side of the connective(either explicit or implicit), *right* means the nuclearity is the EDU that is on the right side, while *both* means the nuclearities are both EDUs that are on the left and right side of the connective. It can be seen that, nuclearities are more frequently appear on the left side of the connectives.

4   Conclusion

This paper describes a discourse resource, namely a Chinese-English parallel corpus, based on the idea of bilingual discourse alignment. We employ a bilingual collaborative annotation approach to deal with bilingual discourse alignment, that is, annotating English discourse units based on Chinese discourse units annotated, and annotating Chinese discourse structure based on English discourse structure annotated. Such approach can ensure full discourse structure alignment between parallel texts, and reduce cost for annotating texts of two languages as well. Annotation Evaluation of the parallel corpus justifies the appropriateness of the discourse alignment framework to parallel texts.

Acknowledgements

This paper was supported by Program of humanities and Social Sciences of Ministry of Education (13YJC740022, 15YJC740021), Major projects of basic researches of Philosophy and Sociology in colleges, Henan(2015-JCZD-022), China Postdoctoral Fund (2013M540594), National Natural Science Foundation of China (61402119, 61502149, 61402341) and Bidding Project of GDUFS Laboratory of Language Engineering and Computing (LEC2016ZBKT001, LEC2016ZBKT002).

References

1. Guzman, F., Joty, S., Marquez, L. ı. and Nakov, P.: Using discourse structure improves machine translation evaluation. Proceedings of the 52nd Annual Meeting of the Association for Computational Linguistics, Baltimore, Maryland, USA (2014).
2. Saint-Dizier, P.: Emerging applications of natural language processing: concepts and new research, Chapter 28. IGI Global (2013).
3. Ghorbel, H.: Experiments in cross-lingual sentiment analysis in discussion forums Proceedings of 4th SocInfo conference, Lausanne, Switzerland (2012).
4. Koehn, P.: Europarl: a parallel corpus for statistical machine translation. Proceedings of the 10th Machine Translation Summit, Phuket, Thailand (2005).
5. Ralf, R. S., Pouliquen, B., Widiger, A., Ignat, C., Erjavec, T., Tufiş, D., et al.: The JRC-Acquis: a multilingual aligned parallel corpus with 20+ languages. Proceedings of the 5th International Conference on Language Resources and Evaluation, Genoa, Italy (2006).
6. Tian, L., Wong, D. F., Chao, L. S., Quaresma, P., Oliveira, F., Lu, Y., et al.: UM-Corpus: A large english-chinese parallel corpus for statistical machine translation. Proceedings of the Ninth International Conference on Language Resources and Evaluation, Reykjavik, Iceland (2014).
7. Carlson, L., Marcu, D. and Okurowski, M. E.: Building a discourse-tagged corpus in the framework of Rhetorical Structure Theory. Proceedings of the Second SIGdial Workshop on Discourse and Dialogue, Aalborg, Denmark (2001).
8. Prasad, R., Dinesh, N., Lee, A., Miltsakaki, E., Robaldo, L., Joshi, A., et al.: The Penn discourse treebank 2.0. Proceedings of the Sixth International Conference on Language Resources and Evaluation, Marrakech, Morocco (2008).
9. Li, Y., Feng, W., Sun, J., Kong, F. and Zhou, G.: Building chinese discourse corpus with connective-driven dependency tree structure. Proceedings of the 2014 Conference on Empirical Methods in Natural Language Processing, Doha, Qatar (2014).

10. Prasad, R., Husain, S., Sharma, D. M. and Joshi, A.: Towards an annotated corpus of discourse relations in Hindi. Proceedings of the 6th Workshop on Asian Languae Resources (2008).
11. Rachakonda, R. T. and Sharma, D. M.: Creating an Annotated Tamil Corpus as a Discourse Resource. Proceedings of the Fifth Law Workshop, Portland, Oregon (2011).
12. Xue, N.: Annotating Discourse Connectives in the Chinese Treebank. Proceedings of the Workshop on Frontiers in Corpus Annotation II: Pie in the Sky (2005).
13. Zeyrek, D. and Webber, B.: A discourse resource for Turkish: annotating discourse connectives in the METU corpus. Proceedings of the 6th Workshop on Asian Languae Resources (2008).
14. Zhou, Y. and Xue, N.: PDTB-style discourse annotation of Chinese text. Proceedings of the 50th Annual Meeting of the Association for Computational Linguistics, Jeju Island, Korea (2012).
15. Li, Y., Feng, W., Zhou, G. and Zhu, K.: Research of Chinese Clause Identificiton Based on Comma. Acta Scientiarum Naturalium Universitatis Pekinensis(Chinese), 49(1), 7-14 (2013).
16. Sun, J., Li, Y., Zhou, G. and Feng, W.: Research of Chinese Implicit Discourse Relation Recognition. Acta Scientiarum Naturalium Universitatis Pekinensis(Chinese), 50(1), 111-117 (2014).

NTU-EA: A Graphic Program for Error Annotation

Jingxia Lin[1] and Kang Kwong Kapathy Luke[2]

[1, 2] Nanyang Technological University, Singapore, 637332
`jingxialin@ntu.edu.sg; kkluke@ntu.edu.sg`

Abstract. This paper reports the Nanyang Technological University Error Annotation Program (NTU-EA), a language error annotation program with graphic user interface. Compared with previous studies, the program is featured by being efficient, comprehensive, and flexible for error annotation of Chinese language. The results exported from the program can be readily used for various purposes including error analysis and construction of learner corpora. The NTU-EA program is free for download.

Keywords: error annotation · error types · GUI · learner corpus · NTU-EA

1 Introduction

Learner corpora (or "中介语语料库" in Chinese) consists of language data with naturally occurring errors committed by foreign/second language learners and the contexts where the errors occur. Compared with researchers' personal observations or elicited experimental data, learner corpora with natural language data serves as a rich resource for research on language pedagogy, foreign/second language acquisition, contrastive interlanguage analysis, and even NLP-aided error detection and analysis. Recent years have witnessed an increasing number of studies based on learner corpora, e.g., [1], [2], [3], among many others, on Mandarin Chinese as the target language.

A learner corpus becomes even more efficient and informative for more sophisticated analysis if it is accompanied with error annotations, such as the types of error committed and how the errors can be corrected. Some of the existing error-annotated learner corpora include the Cambridge Learner Corpus (hereafter "the Cambridge corpus", [4]), the Dynamic Corpus of HSK composition (hereafter "the HSK corpus", [5] and the Learner Corpus of Test of Chinese as a Foreign Language (hereafter "the TOCFL corpus", [6]) among others. However, due to the nature of error identification, currently annotation is primarily done manually by trained coders. One practice is for coders to identify and correct errors in the original texts (e.g., a piece of writing by a language learner), and then manually transfer the annotations into corpora, which is time-consuming. Furthermore, when there is a large number of error types, it becomes inefficient not only for coders to select the intended error code, but also for the comparison of annotations by different coders to reach agreement.

This paper reports a graphic user interface (GUI) program that enables coders to detect and annotate errors directly in the interface: the Nanyang Technological University Error Annotation Program ("NTU-EA" in short). Our program not only improves

© Springer International Publishing AG 2018
Y. Wu et al. (Eds.): CLSW 2017, LNAI 10709, pp. 383–391, 2018.
https://doi.org/10.1007/978-3-319-73573-3_35

the speed and accuracy of annotation, but also provides convenient output for construction of annotated corpora and research on errors. NTU-EA is open to all and free for download   upon   request   or   at   the   following   link: http://www.ntu.edu.sg/home/jingxialin/NTU-EA-download.htm.

2   Functions and features of NTU-EA

2.1   A general introduction

The NTU-EA is first featured by a simple but functional GUI which allows direct error annotation in the interface. As shown in Figure 1, the interface consists of four major parts: a tool bar at the top, three text boxes in the middle left showing the text under annotation, a drop-down menu of error types in the middle right, and a table at the bottom displaying a summary of error annotations.

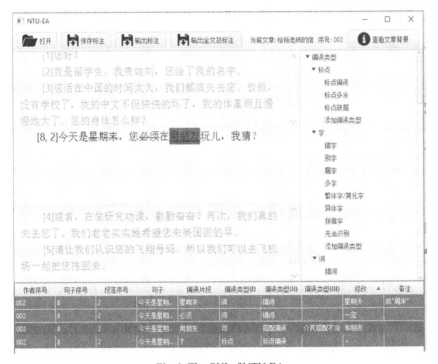

Fig. 1. The GUI of NTU-EA

Secondly, the NTU-EA program develops a set of error annotation schema that is catered to Chinese language. Compared with previous studies, our error system is designed in a way that is relatively structured, comprehensive, and flexible in order to capture all possible error types that may occur in Chinese.

Thirdly, the program exports two kinds of annotated results: one with annotation information only and is thus ready for checking of annotation consistency and error analysis, and the other with the complete annotated texts that is ready for corpora construction.

Other features available in the program include file encryption, so that certain information (e.g., the original/annotated data, or data contributor's profile) is only accessible to authorized users. The rest of this section will introduce in detail the major functions and features of the NTU-EA.

2.2   Data contributors' background information

Background information of data contributors (or language learners for learner corpora) is of no less importance to error analysis than the language data they contribute. A corpus accompanied with contributors' information enables users to construct subcorpora according to different parameters, such as a subcorpus of writings produced by learners whose first language is English, or who are advanced learners of Mandarin Chinese.

The NTU-EA is equipped with options for the input of contributors' profile. In addition to basic information such as gender, age, nationality, and education, users can input details of each contributor's language background, including the proficiency levels (listening, speaking, reading, and writing) of the languages/dialects they speak, preference of the language/dialect used with different groups of people (e.g., with parents, siblings, strangers), the preferred language/dialect when different activities are carried out (e.g., watching TV, sending text messages), and the number of years of learning Chinese. Depending on their needs, users can add additional background information into the program.

The contributors' information can be loaded into the GUI along with their language data, so the information is accessible to authorized users by clicking the command labeled 查看文章背景 'check background' in the tool bar located at the top of the interface (see Figure 1).

2.3   Data loading

When language data (e.g., a piece of writing) is loaded into the interface, the whole text will be automatically segmented into sentences, so coders are able to annotate errors sentence by sentence. As shown in Figure 1, a whole piece of writing is displayed in three text boxes: the sentence to be annotated (in black) is located in the middle, whereas the texts before and after the sentence are displayed (in grey) in the two text boxes above and below the sentence respectively. As such, coders have an overview of the whole text, which is especially helpful when identifying errors beyond the sentence level (e.g., discourse errors). Once the sentence is annotated, a click on the ↓ key on the keyboard leads to the next sentence, i.e. the next sentence will jump into the middle text box and appear in black for annotation. For better tracking of the data, the GUI also numerically marks each sentence in the text. For instance, the eighth sentence in the second paragraph of a writing piece will be marked as [8, 2].

2.4   Annotation of errors

Types of errors. Developing a set of annotation schema that is not only comprehensive but also uncomplicated and unambiguous has been a challenge for constructing learner corpora. Different corpora have adopted different systems and numbers of errors. For instance, the Cambridge Corpus offers up to 88 error codes. Among them, the majority of the codes consist of two sets of letters: the first set represents five general types of errors, e.g., "F" for wrong form, "M" for something missing, and "R" for something needs replacing; the second set of letters represents nine major word classes (i.e. part of speech), e.g., "N" for noun, "V" for verb, and "J" for adjective. The combination of these two sets of letter specifies an error type, e.g., "MN" means that a noun is missing. Each set of letters can also be used in conjunction with other letters for other types of errors. For example, punctuation errors are coded with "P", so the combination of a letter of general error and "P" represents a wrong use of punctuation (e.g., "MP" means that a punctuation is missing). Similarly, the set of letters for word classes can combine with additional types of error, e.g., "C(countability) + word class" and "AG (agreement errors) + word class" represent errors in countability and agreement of a certain word class respectively. Moreover, additional error codes are taken up for extra error types that cannot be captured by the two sets of letters, e.g., "AS" for incorrect argument structure, "S" for spelling error, and "IV" for incorrect verb inflection. The system, while straightforward, is not without drawbacks. Firstly, the system (like other systems do) is sometimes ambiguous. For example, a verb with incorrect inflection can be marked as "FV" (verb in wrong form), "S" (wrong spelling), or "IV" (wrong verbal inflection). Furthermore, the system does not clearly distinguish between errors that occur at different linguistic levels (e.g., punctuation, form, word, and sentence), which may also lead to inconsistent coding. For example, the missing of a noun object may be coded with "MN" (noun missing) or "AS" (incorrect argument structure). In addition, the large number of codes (88 codes) may pose a challenge for coders to efficiently select the appropriate error types.

In contrast to the Cambridge system, the TOCFL corpus uses only 25 error codes under eight broad types (i.e. 词汇 'words', 语法 'grammar', 形式 'form', 语序 'word order', 语义 'meaning', 冗词 'redundant word', 缺词 'missing word', and 话题 'topic'). However, such a simplified categorization is not satisfactory either. For example, it may not be easy to determine what kind of errors belongs to 语义 'meaning', as meaning can be closely related to the two other types, 词汇 'words' and 语法 'grammar'; explanation may also be needed to differentiate 词汇 'words' from 冗词 'redundant word' and 缺词 'missing word'.

Unlike the Cambridge and TOCFL corpora, the HSK corpus adopts a top-down system and classifies error types according to different linguistic levels, ranging from 篇章 'discourse', 句 'sentence', 词 'word', 字 'character', to 标点 'punctuation'. Except for 篇章 'discourse', each of the four other levels consists of subtypes. For example, 标点 includes 错误标点 'incorrect punctuation', 空缺标点 'missing punctuation', and 多余标点 'unnecessary punctuation'. Similarly, sentence errors covers nine subtypes (e.g., 病句 'incorrect sentence', 句子成分残缺 'missing sentential constituent', 语序

错误 'incorrect word order') and some of these subtypes are again further classified. For instance, 病句 'incorrect sentence' covers the major constructions that are often wrongly used by language learner (e.g., 把字句错误 'incorrect BA construction', 被字句错误 'incorrect passive construction', and 比字句错误 'incorrect comparative construction'). In total, the HSK system consists of 51 error types. Coders are required to annotate errors following a top-down priority order. That is, if an observed error can be analyzed as an error at the discourse level (the topmost level of errors), it will be directly marked as a discourse error; if not, the error will be then examined at the next level (i.e. sentence error) or lower until the proper level is identified.

In view of the previous studies, we propose a relatively more comprehensive and flexible system. Given that a differentiation of linguistic levels facilitates both error coding and analysis, we build the schema upon the HSK system. Specifically, we follow the HSK system and classify errors according to different linguistic levels and list subtypes under each error type when necessary.

Some modifications have also been made to present the errors more clearly and to cover more types of errors.

Firstly, the HSK system uses the term 病句 'incorrect sentence' for reference to the frequently used constructions ("句式" or "构式") in Chinese, e.g., the BA/BEI constructions and double object constructions. As the term is broader than it actually covers, NTU-EA changes 病句 into 构式偏误 'construction error' in order to more precisely present the errors under this category.

Secondly, while the HSK system has as many as nine subtypes under 句 'sentence', they still cannot well capture some grammatical errors that may commonly happen in language learning. For instance, the phrase 用朋友玩儿 '(literally) use friends to play' for expression of 'play with friends' is better analyzed as a collocational error between preposition and its object. Therefore, the NTU-EA system adds 搭配不当 'inappropriate collocation' as a new error type, under which six subtypes are available: 主谓搭配不当 'inappropriate subject-predicate collocation', 动宾搭配不当 'inappropriate verb-object collocation', 定中搭配不当 'inappropriate attributive-head collocation', 状中搭配不当 'inappropriate adverbial-head collocation', 述补搭配不当 'inappropriate verb-complement collocation', and 介宾搭配不当 'inappropriate preposition-object collocation'.

Thirdly, the HSK system only provides a broad category 篇章错误 'discourse error' that covers all kinds of errors that may be ascribed to cohesion or coherence. The NTU-EA system follows [7] and adds the commonly observed discourse errors such as 照应 'referencing', 省略 'ellipsis', 替代 'substitution', and 连接 'conjunction' as the subtypes.

Additionally, our program takes into consideration inappropriate expressions due to speaker's cultural misunderstandings. For instance, an expression such as 我贵姓刘 'My respectful surname is Liu' is grammatically correct, but unacceptable by the social-cultural conventions of Chinese (e.g., gender and social class of speakers). Therefore, our program takes 篇章及语用偏误 'discourse and language use error' as a broad error type (cf. 篇章 'discourse' in the HSK system) and adds 文化理解和表达偏误 'error of cultural understanding and expression' as a subtype.

Finally, considering that no error system can be fully comprehensive and new errors may arise out of new findings in theoretical and pedagogical research, the NTU-EA makes available an option of 增加偏误类型 'add new error types', so that new error types can be flexibly added into the system.

Figure 2 presents the major (sub)types of our error system. In the figure, the error types presented in italic are newly added by our program, whereas the others are primarily based on the HSK system. Further classification is also given for some of the subtypes (e.g., 搭配偏误 'inappropriate collocation', 构式偏误 'construction error', and 句子成分残缺 'missing sentential constituent').

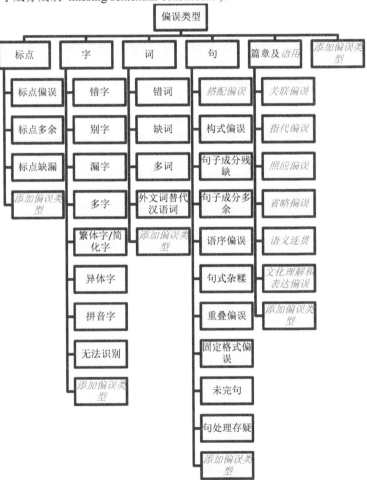

Fig. 2. Error coding system of the NTU-EA program

Annotation of errors. The NTU-EA presents an efficient way for annotation, via which coders can directly mark on the text loaded into the program. Specifically, if an error is observed in the text (the middle text box on the left side of the GUI), the coder can select the erroneous part (arbitrary contiguous text spans, be it as small as a punctuation or as long as a sentence) with the cursor, and then select the corresponding error type from the drop-down error menu on the right side of the GUI. Overlapping text spans are allowed in cases where one error is embedded in another, e.g., when a character error happens in a word error (cf. the HSK system). Once the error type is selected, the table at the bottom of the GUI will record the annotation, including the data contributor's ID, the sentence and paragraph numbers where the error is located, the whole sentence where the error is in, the text span where the error occurs, and the error (sub)types, as illustrated in Figure 1. Moreover, the program provides two textboxes, titled as 修改 'correction' and 备注 'remarks' respectively, where coders can input the corrected form and any other comments. The table also enables coders to make changes to or delete the annotations they make.

During the process of annotation, the errors in the original text (on the right side textboxes of the GUI) are also marked differently depending on their types. For example, a punctuation error is highlighted in blue. That is, if a coder selects the punctuation that is wrongly used, the font color of the punctuation will turn into blue. As illustrated in Figure 3, the two word errors (星期末 and 必须) are marked by a strikethrough, the error at the sentence level (用朋友) is underlined, and the punctuation error at the end of the sentence is shown in blue color. The marking serves as a direct visual assistance for coders.

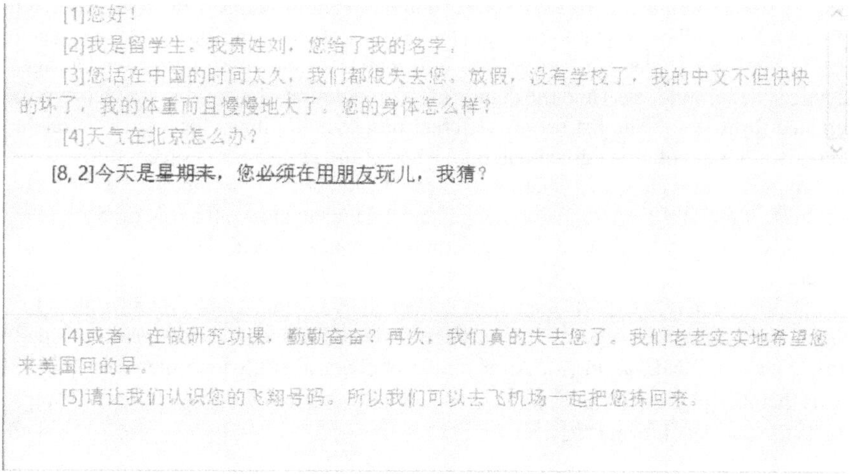

Fig. 3. Error marks in texts

Practical issues and solution. Firstly, as mentioned in Section 2.4.1, coders may find the existing error types insufficient for the errors they may have observed, so our system provides the option of 添加偏误类型 'add error types' at all levels. As such, new types of errors can be flexibly added to the system.

Secondly, given that our system is based on linguistic levels, it is expected that an error may sometimes belong to different levels at the same time. For example, the missing conjunction 还 'but also' in the complex sentence (1) may be analyzed as 关联偏误 'conjunction error' at the discourse level and 缺词 'missing word' at the word level. For such cases, even though it is advisable to tag the error as a 关联偏误 according to the top-down priority principle, coders are allowed to annotate both types of errors. Similarly, when a coder is indeterminate regarding which type an observed error belongs to, the coder can assign all possible types to the error.

(1) 她不但不帮我，[还]笑我。

In addition, as mentioned in Section 2.4.2, embedding is allowed if a text span belongs to two error types. For example, 平 in (2) belongs to both character error and word order error: firstly, it is firstly used for the character 苹, and secondly the direct object 一个平果 where 平 is located is used in a reversed order with the indirect object 他. Our program is designed in a way to display the embedding (see Section 2.5).

(2) 老师给了一个平果他。

2.5   Exporting annotation information

The NTU-EA program exports two types of annotation information. The first is an excel file with a list of all error annotations and the profiles of data contributors. That is, each entry in the list includes the background information of the contributor (gender, age, language background, etc.) and the details of the annotation (the error, error (sub)types, corrected form, etc.). The list serves different purposes. It allows for a more efficient comparison for annotation agreement, e.g., whether the same error is successfully identified by different coders and whether an error is categorized into the same error type. Moreover, it facilitates error analysis, e.g., statistical analysis of all kinds of errors, the kinds of learners for a given error types, and the kinds of errors by a given type of learners.

The program also exports the whole annotated text, which can be readily taken for construction of learner corpora. The output mainly follows the Cambridge corpus that formats texts in XML, as in (3). An example is given in (4), where the code "错词" means that a wrong word (星期末) is used and the word following the symbol "|" represents the corrected form ("周末").

(3) <ERROR CODE>wrong word|corrected word</ERROR CODE>
(4) 今天是<错词>星期末|周末</错词>

When an error is embedded in another, both errors can be annotated. Take (2) as an example again. The output, as in (5), will have the lower level of error (wrong character, coded by "错字") embedded inside the higher level of error (wrong word order, coded by "语序偏误"), and the corrected form of each error is given immediately after the error.

(5) 老师给了<语序偏误>一个<错字>平|苹</错字>他|他一个苹果</语序偏误>。

With the output being XML-tagged, users can freely construct corpora based on different needs, e.g., a corpus with original data only, corrected data only, or a corpus with all annotation information.

3   Conclusion and future development

This paper introduced the NTU-EA program for Chinese language error annotation. The program is free for download. Currently, a corresponding web-based platform is under development for annotation via Internet and will be open for all once completed.

Acknowledgements

The project is supported by Singapore MOE AcRF Tier 1 Fund M4011571. We would like to thank our student assistants Wei Yumou and Khoo Yong Kang for their help.

References

1. Zhang, B.: Jiyu Zhongjieyu Yuliaoku de Hanyu Cihui Zhuanti Yanjiu [Research on Chinese words and phrases based on learner corpora]. Peking University Press, Beijing (2008).
2. Zhao, J.: Jiyu Zhongjieyu Yuliaoku de Hanyu Jufa Yanjiu [Research on Chinse grammar based on learner corpora]. Peking University Press, Beijing (2008).
3. Xiao, X., Zhang, W.: *Shoujie Hanyu Zhongjie Yuliaoku Jianshe yu Yingyong Guoji Xueshu Taolunhui Lunwen Xuanji* [Proceedings of the first international workshop on constructing and applying learner corpora]. World Books Publishing Company, Beijing (2011)
4. Nicholls, D.: The Cambridge learner corpus: Error coding and analysis for lexicography and ELT. *Proceedings of the Corpus Linguistics 2003 Conference*, pp572-581. Lancaster University, Lancaster (2003).
5. Zhang, B., Cui, X., Ren, J.: Guanyu "HSK Dongtai Zuowen Yuliaoku" Jianshe Gouxiang [On constructing the dynamic corpus of HSK composition]. In *Yuyan wenzi yingyong yanjiu lunwenji*. Sino United Publishing (Holdings) Limited, Hong Kong (2004).
6. Chang, L.: TOCFL Zuowen Yuliaoku de Jianzhi yu Yingyong [the construction and application of TOCFL]. *Dierjie Hanyu Zhongjie Yuliaoku Jianshe yu Yingyong Guoji Xueshu Taolunhui Lunwen Xuanji* [Proceedings of the 2nd international workshop on constructing and applying learner corpora], pp141-152 (2012).
7. Halliday, M. A. K., Hasan, R.: *Cohesion in English*. Longman, London (1976).

A Comparable Corpus-based Genre Analysis of Research Article Introductions

Guiling Niu

School of Foreign Languages, Zhengzhou University, Zhengzhou, Henan 450001, China
mayerniu@163.com

Abstract. Research concerning academic genre has attracted an increasing attention from linguistics abroad and at home, ranging from a wide variety of perspectives, but there is still a shortage of research regarding the introduction part of research articles (RA). This paper makes a multi-level comparative analysis of Chinese and English RA introductions by employing the strengths of large corpora in terms of large text, multi-function and rigorous selection of texts, based on our self-compiled large-scale comparable corpus: Chinese-English Comparable Introduction Corpus (CECIC). Studies based on comparable corpora can avoid the "translationese" of parallel corpora. Findings reveal that there is still significant difference between Chinese RA introductions and the international ones and that the irregular *move* distribution feature of rhetorical structure in Chinese RA introductions is still prominent today, indicating that it is still necessary to strengthen Chinese RA writers' genre awareness. That the current research chooses RA introductions, a weak point in academic studies, as the research focus is our positive effort to contribute to world genre analysis, and it will be beneficial to academic variety and theoretical innovation.

Keywords: comparable corpus, genre analysis, paper introduction

1 Genre Analysis and RA Introduction Research

Genre used to be categorized as a literary term, but the range of genre has been considerably expanded since Swales [18] combined the concept of genre with the com-

© Springer International Publishing AG 2018
Y. Wu et al. (Eds.): CLSW 2017, LNAI 10709, pp. 392–407, 2018.
https://doi.org/10.1007/978-3-319-73573-3_36

municative function of text and introduced it to many non-literary fields in the 1980s, but genre is applicable to all text types now [2][11][12].

Compared to the other three levels of text analysis (register analysis, grammatical analysis and rhetorical analysis), which still stay at the superficial description of languages, genre analysis transcends simple description of text features and is meant to interpret the motivation of text construction and to explore the social and cultural factors as well as psychological and cognitive factors behind text structure, and thus reveal the special way to attain the communicational goal and the normalization of text construction. Therefore, genre analysis possesses the attributes of interpretation, linking linguistics, sociology and psychology closely together [1].

Reading research articles (RAs) can facilitate researchers to learn about the history and latest development of the related area, and the relatively fast and efficient way to access information is to read the introductions of RAs. RA introductions have been identified as the vital part of RA texts which serve the persuasive and promotional function to readers [1] [10] [18] [19] [20]. An introduction is located at the beginning of an RA full text, playing the role of leading readers to learn about the detailed information of the subsequent part of the full text and providing an interpretation of the related research perspective, equivalent to the "road map" of the full text clue.

In general, an introduction is an indispensible part of a research article, serving the functions of clarifying research purpose, giving a literature review of the current research situation, pointing out the research gap and producing feasible solutions, and suggesting related assessment criteria, etc. Nevertheless, an RA introduction is also viewed as the most difficult part to write. RA introduction writers are supposed to use standardized drafting approach and structural style to clarify the theme of the article, to include a large amount of research information in a limited text length, and to reflect the research level of the current research in the related field in this part.

The most influential contribution to introduction genre analysis is Swales' CARS (Create a Research Space) Model by using his *move-step* analysis approach and this model has been revised and perfected step by step. Swales [18] first posed "Four-Move Model" of RA introductions and stressed their promotional function. Create-a-Research-Space metaphor privileges an environment in which originality (especially in theory) tends to be highly prized, competition tends to be fierce, and academic promotionalism and boostetism are strong [8][20]. In other words, "it primarily reflects research in a big world, in big fields, in big languages, with big journals, big names, and big libraries."[20] For instance, Lindeberg [8] believed that the research topic is promoted by stressing its significance in move 1 (Claims of Centrality) ; an RA introduction writer tends to present the research gap by pointing out the inadequacy of prior studies and then suggest the future research space (Statements of Knowledge Gaps) in move 2, while in move 3 the writer will promote the current research by predicting its possible contributions (Boosts of Writers' Own Contributions). This model is basically the identical to Swales' CARS model, and thus further proves Swales' conclusion. The three moves in CARS model are divided according to their respective functions and they are cohesive, coherent and supportive to each other and integrated into one complete body. hey achieve the goal of persuading RA readers and promoting their research findings by using brief words and clear and logical rhetorical structure of *moves*.

Based on his "Four-Move Model (Background, Other, Contrast, Aim)", Swales introduced his famous "CARS" Model for the first time in his masterpiece Genre Analysis in 1990 [19], interpreting the communicative procedure of RA introductions form 3 *moves* and 11 *steps* (each *move* consists of several *steps* and the *moves* are carried out through the specific *steps*). The three *moves* are: move 1. Establishing a Territory; move 2. Establishing a Niche; move 3. Occupying the niche, which are Swales' research findings based on his 110-RA paper corpus. Later on, numerous studies have been conducted concerning RA introductions, for instance, Ahmad made a detailed analysis of 20 Malaysian conference article introductions, and Samraj [8] did a comparative analysis of American graduate students' thesis introductions from three disciplines (biology, philosophy and linguistics) . Swales adjusted move 3 in CARS Model from " occupying the niche " into " Presenting the Present Work ", and adjusted the *steps* under the three *moves* accordingly form content to sequence [19][20]. Some required and optional specific *sub-steps* were added to the revised CARS Model under the required *steps*, which further perfected the genre structure analysis model of RA introductions. Swales later on made a descriptive analysis of the rhetorical structure of RA introductions in educational psychology with the new model [20].

There has been a growing number of studies on genre analysis in China in recent years, which have given a rise to plenty of research findings, ranging mainly from three aspects: 1. from different disciplines. With Swales' "three-move" CARS model, Xu et al. [25] investigated English-major graduate students' thesis introductions in six universities of Northern China; Jiang & Xu [5] compared the rhetorical structure traits of Chinese and English legal RA introductions. 2. from different theoretical perspectives. Wang et al. systematically analyzed the functions of RA introductions, contended that an introduction is expected to included 5 elements of two levels, and suggested a basic structural model of these elements and levels, giving rise to the originality and scientific nature of RA introductions [24]; He & Yu [3] adopted functional grammar theory and corpus approach to find the method to realize the Experiential Function of RA introductions [23], and they also summarized and described the register features of RA introductions through quantitative analysis of natural texts.

Compared to research in foreign countries, there is a deficiency in the studies at home concerning genre analysis of RA introductions.

There are more theoretical studies than practical ones, there is a lower percentage of empirical research, and the sample sizes seem to be smaller than what is expected. Some studies have just made theoretical comments on genre analysis of RA introductions but lacked a practical analysis and substantial deeper research is needed. It is true that there is an upward tendency in empirical research in China in recent years, but non-empirical research still takes a dominant position.

The other defect in studies of RA introductions is that most studies are limited to interlingual contrast (generally between Chinese and English), one single discipline or area, and empirical research on RA introductions out of intralingual contrast and interdisciplinary contrast is badly needed.

So far, there is still an obvious inadequacy of research on RA introductions from the perspective of genre analysis, which views RA introductions as an independent genre, and there are even fewer genre studies of RA introductions by using large-scale bilingual corpus approach.

Therefore, it is badly necessary to construct a large-scale comparative corpus or more to make contrastive genre research of RA introductions in different cultural contexts.

2   The Methodological Framework

2.1   The Analytical Model: *Move* and *Step*

Swales' "*move-step*" CARS Model is adopted in this research.

The concept *move* could be termed as "a text made up of a bundle of linguistic features which give the segment a uniform orientation and signal the content of discourse in it" [16] and has been used as "term of art" by Swales [20]. In genre analysis, each *move* starts with textual functions and contexts which are identified and confirmed from the linguistic thread of contexts. If a set of sentences convey the same class of communicative information, they can be identified as the same *move*.

A "move" in genre analysis is a discoursal or rhetorical unit that performs a coherent communicative function in a written or spoken discourse. Although it has sometimes been aligned with a grammatical unit such as a sentence, utterance, or paragraph, it is better seen as flexible in terms of its linguistic realization. At one extreme, it can be realized by a clause; at the other by several sentences. It is a functional, not a formal, unit [20].

Swales & Feak [21] pointed out that a *move* is a set of words accomplishing special tasks, which is a functional rather than grammatical concept. *Moves* have different lengths, and they can be phrases or paragraphs. *Moves* and their constituent elements are partly determined by inferencing from context, but also by reference to linguistic clues in the discourse, for example:

> The methods used to collect data on patients with cervical and prostate concer were identical
> with those reported in our retrospective study of colonic and rectal tumors. (British Medical
> Journal, 30 August, 1986)

In this example, the lexical items "methods", "collect" and "data" provide clues which suggest that the segment of text is presenting information on methods of data collection, indicating that explicit lexical items can signal explicitly the information contained in the *move*.

2.2   The Schematic Structure of Genre Analysis

Swales' CARS Model is comprised of three *moves*, under each of which there are respectively one *step* or more *steps* [20]. CARS Model indicates that researchers can give a full play to their originality on the premise of not destructing the basis genre structure or genre prototype, namely, RA writers can select different *steps* according to different communicative purposes and targets under the "three-move" structure, and each *move* is realized through several optional *steps*.

2.2.1   Swales' CARS Model

Although many scholars have raised some revised suggestions to the definition or interpretation of *move*, Swales' genre analysis based on *moves* is still one of the most widely used methods in analyzing academic texts at present, and this method is also universally used to make research on RA abstracts and RA conclusions or other parts of academic texts [7][14][26].

Table 1. Swales' Macrostructure and Meaning of MOVE and Labels (from: Swales 2004)

MOVE	Typical Labels	STEP(s)
MOVE 1	**Establishing a Territory**	Topic generalizations in increasing specificity
MOVE 2	**Establishing a Niche**	Step 1A Indicating a gap or
		Step 1B Adding to what is known
		Step 2 Presenting positive justification
MOVE 3	**Presenting the Present Work**	Step 1 Announcing present research descriptively and/ or purposively
		Step 2 Presenting RQs or hypotheses
		Step 3 Definitional clarification
		Step 4 Summarizing methods

2.2.2 Annotation Model

Based on our experience of reading a large number of research articles, and on our experimental annotation before formal annotation, we found that many RA introductions didn't follow CARS model and there are mainly the following three conditions: (1) In *move* sequence, some introductions texts are not arranged according to the order of move 1, move 2 and move 3, and sometimes move 1 appears after move 2 or move 3, and in contrast move 3 occurs before move 1 or move 2 occasionally; (2) In *move* content, there isn't a clear dividing line between each two moves and the three *moves* are sometimes interlocked with each other in content; (3) In *move* completeness or integrity, some introductions include all the three *moves* while some other ones only highlight one *move* and fewer words even none are used to the other two *moves*. Besides, there are also some maxims before move 1 in some RA texts which seem to have relationship with the introductions or not and we termed them as "Attracting the Readership".

The features of *steps* under each *move* appear to be more complicated. Considering different characteristics of RA introductions, we experimented and discussed repeatedly, supplemented and perfected our annotation scheme to establish a more applicable annotation model based on Swales' "three-move, 11-sptep" CARS model. We adjusted the rhetorical *move-step* structure of RA introduction as follows (the adjustment to *step* is too intricate and this level will not be shown in the following table and the corresponding detailed discussion will also be left to future research).

Table 2.   Revised Annotation Macrostructure and Meaning of MOVE and Labels

MOVE	Typical Labels
MOVE 1	Establishing a Territory
MOVE 2	Establishing a Niche
MOVE 3	Presenting the Present Work
POSTPOSITION MOVE	Postposition Move
PREPOSITION MOVE	Preposition Move
ATTRACTING THE READERSHIP OPTIONAL OPENING	Attracting the Readership Optional Opening
OTHERS	Others

After having finished annotation, we retrieved data and analyzed the *move* distribution of the Chinese and English RA introductions.

2.3   A brief Introduction of the Corpus

This research aims to make a multi-level comparative research of Chinese RA introductions and international English RA introductions to explore the generic structure features of Chinese and English RA introductions by adopting self-developed Chinese-English Comparable Research Article Introduction Corpus (CECIC), making good use of the privileges of corpora, eg. big text, multi-function, rigid text sampling and the integration of qualitative analysis and quantitative analysis, etc.

A comparable corpus is generally categorized into two types, bilingual/multilingual corpora which are constituted of different languages, and monolingual corpora which are made up of different varieties of the same language. A monolingual comparable corpus is helpful to observe non-native language texts in contrast native language texts, or to analyze the similarities and differences of different varieties of the same language, while a bilingual/multilingual corpus is always used to comparative linguistics or comparative lexicology. Comparable corpora expands the range of research questions and can avoid the influence of translationese of parallel corpora.

Systematic sampling [9] is employed for the corpus construction, that is, to systematically divide the whole into a certain number of groups, and then retrieve samples from the respective groups based on a fixed sampling distance. We set strict criteria to select the journals and theses from which introductions are retrieved to ensure the corpus balance and representativeness and to make the data in the sub-corpora comparable (for future inter- and intra-lingual comparison and interdisciplinary comparison). At the same time, all of the selected research articles were published in 2013 or 2014, which guarantees the timeliness of the RA introduction data.

The corpus CECIC is comprised of two parts: thesis introductions and journal introductions, under each of whom are two sub-corpora: CD for Chinese thesis introductions, , under each of which are two sub-corpora: CD for Chinese thesis introduction corpus and ED for international English thesis introduction corpus; CJ for Chinese journal RA introduction corpus and EJ for international English journal RA introduction corpus. Therefore, in this paper we choose to analyze and compare the data in the four sub-corpora: CD, ED, CJ and EJ, as is shown in **Table 3**.

Table 3. Corpus Size of Four Sub-corpora

Four sub-corpora	CD	ED	CJ	EJ
Number of Words	1,119,767	694,499	270,932	453,001

Corpus size: Statistics show that there are 2,538,199 words (3,318,659 words/ characters) in CEICC.

As is shown in **Table 3**, without complicated statistical computation, there is clearly a difference in the number of words in the four sub-corpora. Despite the same number of introductions in Chinese thesis sub-corpus and International English thesis corpus, it is obvious that there are much more words in Chinese Theses than in International English ones. In contrast, the number of words n Chinese journal RA introductions is 50% short than that in the International English ones. Judging from the data in the above table, we may tentatively conclude that Chinese graduate students tend to use a lot more words in their thesis introductions, while Chinese journal RA writers use a shorter text length to write their introductions, in comparison with the international RA writers.

3   Data Analysis and Discussion

3.1   *Move* Distribution Features of Chinese and English RA Introductions

3.1.1 Move Distribution

Table 4. Normalized Introduction MOVE Distribution (every 10,000 running words)

	Thesis RA Introductions		Journal RA Introductions	
	CD	ED	CJ	EJ
MOVE 1[1]	**17944**	12622	4803	7280
MOVE 2	**8124**	3901	1259	2207
MOVE 3	6579	**8089**	1274	**5018**
ATTRACTING THE READERSHIP OPTIONAL OPENING	34	46	10	42
OTHERS	**28**	1	15	5
TOTAL	32709	24659	7361	14552

Owing to different sizes of the four sub-corpora, the raw frequencies of each *move* in the sub-corpora are not comparable to each other, and therefore, it is necessary to respectively normalize the raw data of each *move* in each sub-corpus, to make it possible to make comparative analysis of the distribution of *moves* in the four sub-corpora.

The three *moves* and their respective *steps* are expected to be closely related to each other, and they are cohesive, coherent and supportive to each other and are integrated into a holistic body. Move 1 is defined as "Establishing a Territory" and serves the function of analyzing the research background and attracting and locating readers' attention to the related research field from macros to micros, making a preparation to point out the importance and necessity of "the current research"; Move 2 is labeled as "Establishing a Niche". It is aimed to summarize the research defects or research gap in "this" field by sorting out the current research situation abroad and at home, and to clarify the significance of a certain study to eke out the defects or fill the gap, and thus it will affirm the niche of "this research" which has not been presented formally; Move 3 is known as "Presenting the Present Work" which naturally and timely introduces "the current research" and for which the previous two *moves* have laid good foundation. In this *move*, it seems logical and natural to sum up the research purpose, approach, methodology and significance of this research so far. The respective *steps* under each *move* assume the function of realizing the general purpose.

---

[1] The frequency of the three independent moves, move 1, move 2 and move 3, all include the number of irregular moves (preposition move and postposition move) , which is applicable in the whole paper.

All data in **Table 4** are normalized accordingly so that the data are comparable. Results indicate that there is different manner in the *move* and *step* distribution between Chinese and English thesis introductions and Chinese and journal article introductions. In the first place, in terms of thesis introductions, there is a higher frequency of move 1 and move 2 in Chinese graduate students' thesis introductions than in international English ones, especially in move 2, the former is as approximately twice as the latter. However, in move 3, there is a moderately lower frequency in Chinese graduate students' thesis introductions than in international English ones. In the second, in terms of journal RA introductions, the frequency of each of the three *moves* in Chinese journal RA introductions is lower than that in international English ones, and in spite of the fact that the number of move 1 and move 2 in the latter is nearly as twice as that of the former, but the difference of corpus size (the number of running words in each sub-corpus) between the two sub-corpora can mainly account for the *move* distribution difference because the *move* distribution ratio (only move 1 and move 2) between the two sub-corpora is nearly the same as the corpus-size ratio. What is abnormal is that the number of move 3 in Chinese graduate students' thesis introductions is largely lower than that in the international English ones, only approximately one-third of the latter.

As is shown in **Table 4**, both Chinese thesis and journal RA introductions use a lot of words in move 1 and move 2 but spend inadequate words in move three to talk about the current research which is expected to be the focus. One of the reasons for the difference in thesis introductions may be that different university employ different thesis templates. The other reason for the difference in *move* distribution is that there is a stronger conventionality in international thesis and journal RA introductions, and their writers are more aware of their writing purpose, have a clearer and stronger genre awareness, consciously use a larger text coverage and longer text length to lead readers to understand the current research and its findings, so as to enhance the credibility and persuasiveness of this research, and thus achieve a better "persuasion" effect to readers. Conversely, Chinese RA writers use a lot of words to introduce the research background of this field but fail to spare more words to illustrate the current research, which weakens the "road-map" function and persuasion power of introductions. After all, readers' attention tend to be more attracted by the writers' own research perspective, purpose, methodology, procedure, findings and conclusion, etc.

A further analysis is needed to interpret the difference.

3.1.2   Difference Analysis of *Move* Distribution

Table 5.   MOVE Distribution and Difference Analysis (Normalized Frequency)

| MOVE | THREE | Thesis Introductions | | | | Journal RA Introductions | | | |
FEATURES	MOVES	CD	ED	X^2 Test	Sig.[2]	CJ	EJ	X^2 Test	Sig.
REGULAR	MOVE 1	17310	11923	78.9888	0.000	4773	7146	2385.6978	0.000
MOVES	MOVE 2	7717	3821	131.0228	0.000	1228	2159	931.2731	0.000
	MOVE 3	5828	7687	1993.3445	0.000	1220	4821	4423.5876	0.000
POSTPOSITION	MOVE 1	632	693	110.3458	0.000	29	134	133.1453	0.000
MOVE	MOVE 2	236	52	49.8669	0.000	19	39	20.5914	0.000
PREPOSITION	MOVE 2	171	28	49.3715	0.000	12	9	0.1862	0.666
MOVE	MOVE 3	751	402	5.6927	0.017	53	197	173.7576	0.000
TOTAL of THREE	MOVE 1	**17944**	12622	119.5668	0.000	4803	7280	2485.0868	0.000
MOVES	MOVE 2	**8124**	3901	174.6922	0.000	1259	2207	947.9515	0.000
	MOVE 3	6579	**8089**	1780.7124	0.000	1274	**5018**	4596.3576	0.000

As is shown in **Table 5**, most RA introductions, Whether in Chinese ones or international English ones, employ Swales' CARS model, which further prove the universality and effectiveness of this model. But in specific application, there is a moderate or significant difference between Chinese RA introductions and the corresponding international English ones, which is embodied in the following aspects:

Data in **Table 5** reveal that, in terms of thesis introductions, there isn't a statistical significant difference（P>0.5）between Chinese thesis introductions and the international English ones only in the use of move 3, and there is a significant difference between Chinese thesis introductions and the international English ones only in move 1, move 2, preposition move or postposition move (P<0.5). While in terms of journal RA introduction, there is a significant difference between Chinese journal RA introductions and the international English ones in all *move* categories, move 1, move 3, preposition move and postposition move (P<0.5) except in move 2（P>0.5）. Therefore, overall, there is a significant structural difference between Chinese RA introductions and   international ones, and the "Chinese-style" RA writing features are still prominent and needs our attention. What are the causes that have led to the significant dif-

---

[2]   sig.: P>0.05 means "insignificantly different"; P<=0.05 means "significantly different".

ference deserves further research, which will be beneficial and meaningful to promote Chinese RA writers' competence and proficiency.

3.2   Text Coverage[3] of Three *Moves* and Irregular *Moves*

Table 6. Text Coverage of Three *Moves* and Irregualr *Moves* (unit: Word)

MOVES	CD	CJ	ED	EJ
MOVE 1	57.89%	67.45%	52.01%	54.99%
MOVE 2	20.04%	14.29%	11.91%	14.87%
MOVE 3	21.89%	18.11%	35.93%	29.95%
POSTPOSITION MOVE	2.06%	0.43%	2.18%	0.81%
PREPOSITION MOVE	2.08%	0.51%	1.11%	0.89%
ATTRACTING THE READERSHIP OPTIONAL OPENING	0.17%	0.16%	0.12%	0.12%
OTHERS	0.10%	0.12%	0.00%	0.05%

Moves in introductions are generally sequenced in such a typical and regular order as: move 1 --> move 2---> move 3. Still, there are always some exceptions, and as **Table 6** unfolds, the phenomenon of irregular sequence *moves* is also universal in both Chinese RA introductions and international English ones.

An RA introduction plays a role of leading readers to learn about the subsequent detailed information of the full text and to provide interpretative perspectives, and it has developed into a strongly procedural and conventional genre, and a "move" in genre analysis is a discoursal or rhetorical unit that performs a coherent communicative function in a written or spoken discourse [17][20]. According to the consensus from researchers abroad and at home who are specialized in EAP research, RA introduction writers are supposed to introduce their research background, make a literature review in related area, find problems and research gap existing at present, and then reasonably point out the significance and reasoning of the current research in solving the problems and filling the gap and afterwards naturally introduce the research methodology. This structure is very helpful and effective in drawing readers' attention to the current research, reasonably and logically, step by step, which will make the introduction in-

---

[3] Text Coverage refers to the percentage of the number of words of one *move* in comparison with the number of words in the whole text, for example. in a sub-corpus.

formative and persuasive, and the function of persuasion and promotion of RA intro-ductions will be well embodied in this way.

Data in **Table 5** and **Table 6** reveal that there are a certain number of irregular *moves* in both Chinese and international English RA introductions and that the data on irreg-ular *moves* also reflect the writers' difference in using irregular *moves*. Overall, there is a lower text coverage in international English RA introductions than in Chinese ones, indicating that the phenomenon of irregular *moves* is more prominent in Chinese RA introductions. On one hand, it is most likely that some Chinese RA introduction writers are too eager to highlight their own research, and at the beginning of the introduction, without making a good foundation in move 1 and move 2 for move 3 in a regular sequence they straightforwardly present their research purpose and methodology in advance which should be included in move 3 at the end of the introduction, which seems abrupt and not convincing enough to readers and thus weaken the convention-ality and procedure of introduction. Besides, it will also add to the difficulty for readers to accept the writers' point of view because of inadequate argument and evidence which should be carried out in move 1 and 2. On the other hand, another phenomenon of irregular *moves* is that some Chinese RA introduction writers introduces research background repeatedly after they have finished all the three *moves* by taking a "move 1 ---> move 2 (--->move 1)---> move 3 ---> move 1 (--->move 2)" structure, and thus irregular *moves* occur. Lack of genre awareness may account for this phenomenon, for some RA introduction writers are not clear about the functions of each *move* and fail to arrange the *move* content in an appropriate order.

4   Conclusion

CECIC is a comprehensive database, which bridges the gap between the genre of introduction and social functions. We believe it will facilitate researchers to make a relatively overall and comprehensive analysis of Chinese and International English RA introductions. Genre analysis can not only provide a description of communicative activities, but is also helpful for students to interpret the implicit meaning in the de-scription. Therefore, genre analysis can serve as important EAP resources [20], and thus effectively enhance ESP/EAP teaching and translation teaching [13][15]. To researchers, An introduction serves the function to lead them to learn about the sub-sequent detailed information of the text in advance and to provide interpretative per-spectives. A high quality introduction will help readers to effectively access the ideas and logic of the whole text and access the most important and necessary information. Compared to Taylor and Chen's research findings in over 20 years ago [22], the irregular *move* distribution feature of rhetorical structure in Chinese RA introductions is still prominent today, indicating that it is still necessary to strengthen Chinese RA writers' genre awareness, and that it is an obligatory approach to affirm the functions and effects of each *move* and *step* in introductions.

The construction of this RA introduction corpus will facilitate a large number of RA readers to select readable research articles and access relevant research information, and will help more Chinese researchers to promote their findings to the world. However, this paper only discusses the usage of RA introductions at CARS *move* level on account of the limitation of this article length, and leaves the expanded research to the future, in which we will further analyze the deep causes of significant difference between Chinese RA introductions and international ones, and will also discuss the usage of RA introductions at CARS *step* level in detail.

Acknowledgements. This work was supported by the Humanities and Social Sciences Research Project of the Education Department of China: "The Theoretical Construction of Diplomatic Translation and Building the Diplomatic Discourse System with Chinese characteristics (No.17BYY006)", Henan Project of Philosophy and Social Science: "The Construction and Application of Chinese-English Comparable Introduction Corpus (No.2014BYY003)" and Henan Provincial Key Scientific and Technological Breakthrough Project: "Diplomatic Machine-aided Translation Model and Corpus Construction in the Context of Modern Information Technology（No.132102210026)".

References

1. Bhatia, V. K.: Applied genre analysis and ESP. In T. Miller (Ed.), Functional approaches to written texts: Classroom applications, pp. 134-149. United States Information Agency, Washington DC (1997).

2. Dudley-Evans, T.: Genre analysis: An approach to text analysis for ESP. In M. Coulthard (Ed.), Advances in written text analysis, pp. 219-228.Routledge, London, England (1994)

3. He, J., Yu, J., A Corpus-based Investigation of Research Article Introductions from the Perspective of Experiential Metafunction. Journal of Guilin Normal College, 03:104-108(2006) (In Chinese)

4. Huang, C., You, X.: Reasoning patterns of undergraduate theses in translation studies: An intercultural rhetoric study. English for Specific Purposes, 41, 68-81 (2016)

5. Jiang, T., Xu, J., A Genre Analysis of RA Introductions in English Legal Articles: From English-Chinese Contrastive Perspective. Social Science Research, 02:203-208(2013) (In Chinese)

6. Liang, M.C., Li, W.Z., Xu, J.J.: Using Corpora: A Practical Coursebook. Foreign Language Teaching and Research Press, Beijing(2010)(In Chinese)

7. Lim, J. M. H.: How do writers establish research niches? A genre-based investigation into management researchers' rhetorical steps and linguistic mechanisms. Journal of English for Academic Purposes, 11:229-245 (2012)

8. Lindeberg, A.C.: Promotion and politeness: Conflicting scholarly rhetoric in three disciplines. Abo Akademi University Press, Finland (2004)

9. Liu R.Q.: Research Methods in English Language Teaching. Foreign Language Teaching and Research Press, Beijing(2016)(In Chinese)

10. Loi, C. K.: Research article introductions in Chinese and English: A comparative genre-based study. Journal of English for Academic Purposes, 9: 267-279(2010)

11. Martin, P. M.: A genre analysis of English and Spanish research paper abstracts in experimental social sciences. English for Specific Purposes, 22, 25-43 (2003)

12. Mirahayuni, N. K.: Investigating textual structure in native and non- native English research articles: Strategies differences between English and Indonesian writers (Unpublished doctoral dissertation). University of New South Wales, Sydney, Australia (2002)

13. Niu G.L.: The Construction and Application of Chinese-English Parallel Abstract Corpus. Intellectual Property Publishing House, Beijing (2013) (In Chinese)

14. Niu, G.L.: A Genre Analysis of Chinese and English Abstracts of Academic Journal Articles: A Parallel-Corpus-Based Study. CLSW 2013, LNAI 8229 proceedings (2013)

15. Niu, G. L.: Structurally and Functionally Comparative Analysis of Lexical Bundles in the English Abstracts of Chinese and International Journals. CLSW 2014, LNAI 8922 proceedings(2014)

16. Nwogu, K. N. The Medical Research Papers: Structure and Function . English for Specific Purposes, 16 (2): 119-138 (1997)

17. Samraj, B.: A discourse analysis of master's theses across disciplines with a focus on introductions. Journal of English for Academic Purposes, 7: 55-67(2008)

18. Swales J. Aspects of article introduction. Birmingham, UK: The University of Aston, Language Studies Unit (1981)

19. Swales, J. M.: Genre Analysis: English in Academic and Research Settings. Cambridge University, Cambridge (1990)

20. Swales, J. M.: Research Genres: Explorations and Applications. Cambridge University Press, Cambridge (2004)

21. Swales, J. M., C. B. Feak. Abstracts and the Writing of Abstracts. Ann Arbor, University of Michigan Press, Michigan (2009)

22. Taylor, G., & Chen, T.. Linguistic, cultural, and subcultural issues in contrastive discourse analysis: Anglo-American and Chinese scientific texts. Applied Linguistics, 12: 319-336(1991)

23. Ventola, E., Mauranen, A.: Non-native writing and native revising of scientific articles. In E. Ventola (Ed.), Functional and systematic linguistics: Approaches and uses, pp. 457-492. Berlin, Mouton De Gruyter, Germany (1991)

24. Wang, W., Yang, C.: Claiming centrality as promotion in applied linguistics research article introductions. Journal of English for Academic Purposes, 20: 162-175(2015)

25. Xu Y., Guo, Li., Xu, T., The Genre-Based Teaching Approach Is Indispensible: Investigation of the Introduction Genre in English Majors' MA Theses in China. China English, 04:47-51+60(2007) (In Chinese)

26. Yang, R., Allison, D.: Research articles in applied linguistics: Moving from results to conclusions. English for Specific Purposes, 22, 365-385 (2003)

Figurative Language in Emotion Expressions

Sophia Yat Mei Lee

Department of Chinese and Bilingual Studies
The Hong Kong Polytechnic University
ymlee@polyu.edu.hk

Abstract. This paper examines the use of figurative language in expressing emotions in social media. Based on the analysis of 300 posts from Weibo.com, we argue that there is a close interaction between figurative language and emotion. It is found that 27% of the posts contain figurative devices such as metaphor, simile, rhetorical questions, and irony. Among the five basic emotions, the emotion of *anger* has the greatest tendency to be expressed via the figurative devices, followed by *sadness*, *fear*, *surprise*, and *happiness*. In addition, the data shows that rhetorical questions are the most frequently used figurative device for evoking negative emotions, i.e. *anger* and *sadness*. We believe that the linguistic account of figurative language in emotion expressions will significantly enhance the effectiveness of the existing automatic emotion classification systems.

Keywords: Emotion Expression, Figurative Language, Social Media.

1   Introduction

Figurative language is the use of words or expressions with a meaning different from their literal interpretation. It is generally believed that emotion expressions are rich in figurative language. However, previous studies mostly focus on the perception of the emotion bearer rather than the textual representation of the figurative devices in emotion expressions. Unlike literal language, figurative expression makes use of linguistic devices such as metaphor, irony, and rhetorical questions to project more complex meanings. This poses a real challenge for emotion detection and classification modelling in the field of Natural Language Processing (NLP). This paper offers a linguistic account of the use of figurative language in expressing emotions in social media, aiming to enhance the robustness of the existing automatic emotion classification systems. It aims to address the following questions:

1) How frequently is figurative language used in expressing emotions in social media posts?
2) What types of emotion are more commonly expressed through figurative devices?
3) How are figurative devices used to express emotions?

Section 2 gives an overview of the previous studies in relation to figurative language and emotion. Section 3 describes the methodology of the present work including data collection and annotation. It also presents the analysis and results. Section 4 discusses

© Springer International Publishing AG 2018
Y. Wu et al. (Eds.): CLSW 2017, LNAI 10709, pp. 408–419, 2018.
https://doi.org/10.1007/978-3-319-73573-3_37

the frequently used figurative devices in emotion expression in social media. Section 5 concludes the paper.

2   Related Work

Previous studies suggested that figurative language is commonly used for emotion expressions (Kövecses, 1990, 2003; Lakoff and Johnson, 1980; Fussell and Moss, 1998; Gibbs et al., 2002). Fainsilber and Ortony (1987) proposed that metaphor was more frequently found in the descriptions of their emotional states than the descriptions of behaviors. Gibbs et al. (2002) also agreed that figurative language such as irony and metaphor is especially useful in emotional communication. This phenomenon may be due to the properties of emotions.

First, figurative language is used because of the complexity and abstractness of emotion. Ekman and Davidson (1994) noted that emotions are complex as they are made up of affective responses, physiological reactions, cognitions, behavioral responses, and the like. Fussell and Moss (1998) considered metaphor and other figurative expressions as devices that may capture these diverse components of emotion. Following Lakoff and Johnson (1980)'s theory of metaphor, emotion concepts are largely constituted by metaphor which is often used to conceptualize abstract entities. Kövecses (1990) also suggested that the abundant use of figurative language (in particular metaphor) in expressing emotions is due to the abstractness of emotion. This is further supported by Fussell and Moss (1998: 113) who claimed that "the subjective nature of emotional experiences appears to lend itself to figurative expression". Without denying the role of figurative language in conceptualizing emotion, Foolen (2012: 359) emphasized the need for expressivity. He suggested that figurative language possesses expressive value due to the property of "strong images" by exemplifying an example as follows: "the word *explosion*→ image of an explosion→ feeling of fear→ impulse to run away".

Apart from complexity and abstractness, the level of emotional intensity is another reason for the use of figurative language. Fainsilber and Ortony (1987) found that figurative language was more often used to express intense emotions than milder emotions. Williams-Whitney et al. (1992) expanded on the findings proposed in Fainsilber and Ortony (1987) by examining the metaphor use in terms of writers' experience. They suggested that both experienced and inexperienced writers used more metaphor for feelings than for actions. However, experienced writers used more metaphor to talk about others' emotion states than those inexperienced ones. Fussell (1992) demonstrated a significant increase in the use of figurative language when describing intense emotions than mild ones, in particular for happiness and sadness. This proves that one of the functions of figurative language is to convey intensity. However, Gibbs et al. (2002) indicated that figurative language conveying intensity may be understood differently from literal expression with intensifiers. For example, the literal phrase *get very angry* is not equivalent to the idiom *blow your stack* since the former fails to capture the subtle nuances of people's experience of being angry. "Thus, an important reason why figurative language is special in emotional communication is because it reflects something about people's ordinary conceptualizations of their complex emotional experiences" (Gibbs et al. 2002: 136).

Fussell and Moss (1998) investigated how people describe others' emotions by showing them movie scenes in which the characters were sad or depressed. Literal phrases such as *sad, angry* or *depressed* were used when talking about all the movie clips, but metaphor and idiom were tailored to specific scenes to capture the specific emotions of the characters. Data shows that figurative language can be used to differentiate a single emotion between complex variations and it may be one way to reduce potential ambiguities in the conventional affective lexicon, such as *depressed* which is loosely used.

As for the relationship between irony and affective responses, Dew and Winner (1995) proposed the "tinge hypothesis", suggesting that ironic criticism automatically reduces the amount of condemnation that listeners experience. However, Colston (1997) argued that ironic criticism actually enhances condemnation and criticism in some cases. Leggitt and Gibbs (2000) examined the particular patterns of emotions that are communicated and evoked by different ironic statements, namely sarcasm, rhetorical questions, satire, understatement, overstatement, irony not directed at the addressee, and non-ironic statements. Gibbs et al. (2002) indicated that people feel different emotions on hearing various types of ironic statements. Sarcasm, rhetorical questions, and overstatement all evoked similar and quite negative reactions whereas understatement and satire evoked relatively neutral reactions. Nonpersonal irony evoked a lower degree of negative and hostile emotions than the other statements. In addition, speakers of sarcasm and rhetorical questions appeared to feel relatively neutral emotions while the participants perceived more positive intentions and a lower degree of negative intent with non-personal irony, and a greater desire to evoke positive emotions with satire. Sarcasm and rhetorical questions were perceived as having very negative intent.

Although the figurative uses of language have been found to have a strong correlation with emotion, figurative expressions represent a great challenge in automatic emotion classification system. A growing body of Natural Language Processing (NLP) research has attempted to process the relationship between sentiments classification and different figurative devices, such as simile (Qadir, 2016), idioms (Citron et al., 2016), and irony (Reyes, 2012). The results seem to be largely encouraging. Nonetheless, these studies almost exclusively focus on English and other European languages. Emotion analysis with figurative expression in Chinese has been under-investigated.

3   Corpus Data

3.1   Dataset and Annotation

The dataset was retrieved from *Weibo.com*, one of the more popular social media platforms in China. After removing posts that contained noise and advertisements, we extracted 4,195 posts for emotion annotation (Lee et al., 2015). Examples (1) and (2) are considered noise posts in that (1) does not convey any emotion and (2) is an advertisement of the cosmetic brand 'Benefit'. Additionally, we also removed short posts that contained less than 10 words.

(1) 我参与了"你最喜欢的明星团体投票"，投给了"SHINee"这个选项

(I participated in "favorite star combination election" and voted for "SHINee")

(2) benefit 贝玲妃˘ 泡沫洁面膏˘ 推荐的洗面奶
(Benefit is a recommended foam facial cleanser)

Following Lee et al. (2013), five basic emotions were annotated in each post, namely *happiness, sadness, fear, anger,* and *surprise*. We then randomly selected 300 posts for the figurative analysis. Annotators identified the use of figurative language, imagery, and symbolism in the posts. Figurative language is the language that uses words or expressions with a meaning that is different from the literal interpretation. A number of types of figurative language that were identified in the posts include rhetorical questions (as in (3), a question that does not require an answer); metaphors (as in (4), where 果 实 (fruit) is metaphorically used to indicate accomplishment); simile (as in (5), where an explicit comparison is made between 我 (I) and 狗 (dog)); personification (as in (6), in which 病魔 (sickness) is attributed with human qualities); hyperbole, as in (7), where the fatigue of the eyes is exaggerated to the degree of blindness; and irony (as in (8), a statement that is contrary to an intended meaning).

(3) 为什么人的年龄就不能刷新呢?
(Why can people's age not be refreshed?)

(4) 收获生命中最美的果实
(Harvesting the most beautiful fruit in life)

(5) 我又得被骂的像狗一样!
(I've been scolded like a dog again!)

(6) 积攒了许久的病魔把我打倒了
(The long-hidden sickness has taken me out)

(7) 眼睛都要逛瞎了!
([My] eyes are almost blind because of [on-line] shopping!)

(8) 你他妈真对得住我。我真的爱死你了
(You are so damn nice to me. I really love you to death)

It is not uncommon that a post is expressed through the use of different figurative devices. For example, (9) involves the use of rhetorical questions, irony and hyperbole.

(9) 你 是 要 笑死 我? 堂堂七尺 男儿 这么 兴师动众 把 我 喊 出来 绕 这么 大 一 圈 就 为了 送 这个 给 我
(Do you want me to die of laughter? You have done all this and gone to such great lengths to ask me out just to give me this?)

Another type of figurative language, namely imagery, has also been annotated. It uses language that engages the five senses: sight, hearing, smell, taste, and touch. For instance, in (10), the depiction of sunshine, warmness, and dancing snowflake create an atmosphere of happiness.

(10) 大年三十，既有温暖阳光，又有飞舞雪 花，好兆头啊 ！
(On New Year's Eve, there is warm sunshine and dancing snowflakes, what good omens!)

Finally, symbolism is the use of a term or a sign that possesses specific connotations in addition to its literal meaning, as in (11), where 汗水 (sweat) represents the efforts that one exerts.

(11) 要付出多少汗水才能走到这一步
(How much sweat [effort] do we need to give to get to this stage?)

3.2   Data Analysis

Of the 300 posts analyzed, the total number of emotions identified is 380. This indicates that more than one emotion may be involved in a post. Figure 1 shows the distribution of emotions in the dataset. The *happiness* emotion has the highest frequency (35%) among the five emotions, followed by *sadness* (23%), *fear* (22%), *anger* (14%), and *surprise* (6%).

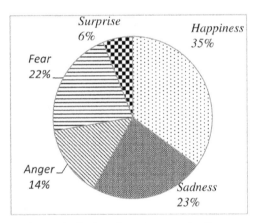

Fig. 1. Distribution of emotion types in all posts

Figure 2 and Table 1 show that the *anger* emotion is the only type of emotion that the majority uses figurative devices. From Table 1, we can see the tendency of figurative devices being used in posts for each emotion in descending order range from *anger* (57%), *sadness* (33%), *fear* (26%), *surprise* (18%), to *happiness* (13%). Overall, 27% of the total emotions contain figurative devices.

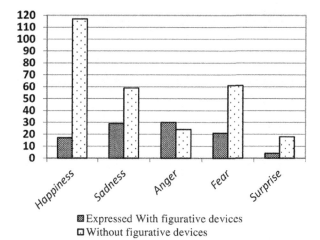

Fig. 2. Emotion using figurative language

Table 1. Emotion using figurative language

Emotion Type	No. of Emotion		Total
	Expressed with figurative devices	Expressed without figurative devices	
Happiness	17 (13%)	117 (87%)	**134**
Sadness	29 (33%)	59 (67%)	**88**
Anger	31 (57%)	23 (43%)	**54**
Fear	21 (26%)	61 (74%)	**82**
Surprise	4 (18%)	18 (82%)	**22**
Total	**102**	**279**	**380**

It is also observed in Table 2 that rhetorical questions are the most frequently used figurative device (over 37%, or 38 out of 102) for emotion expression. It is particularly productive in evoking negative emotions, i.e. *anger* (39%) and *sadness* (29%). Metaphor is the second most common figurative device in expressing emotion; it, however, does not show any preference for a specific emotion type, as can be seen in rhetorical questions. In the next section, we will examine the types and distribution of rhetorical questions and features of metaphors used in the posts.

Table 2. Distribution of each type of figurative language

	Happiness	*Sadness*	*Anger*	*Fear*	*Surprise*	**Total**
Idiom	1	0	0	2	0	**3 (3%)**
Irony	1	1	4	0	0	**6 (6%)**
Personification	3	4	0	0	0	**7 (7%)**
Simile	3	2	0	3	0	**8 (8%)**
Hyperbole	1	3	4	3	0	**11 (11%)**
Metaphor	7	6	11	5	0	**29 (28%)**
Rhetorical Question	1	13	12	8	4	**38 (37%)**
Total	**17** **(17%)**	**29** **(28%)**	**31** **(30%)**	**21** **(21%)**	**4** **(4%)**	**102** **(100%)**

4   Emotion and Figurative Language

4.1   Rhetorical Questions (RQ)

Rhetorical question is a question that is asked without the expectation of an answer. Results show that rhetorical question is the most commonly used figurative device for evoking emotion. It can be roughly classified into two major types – closed question and open question. In Chinese, closed questions can be represented in the form of A-not-A structure, particle, alternative, and echo types. On the other hand, open questions are questions with wh-words such as what, who, and how.

Table 3. Distribution of type of rhetorical questions used

		Happiness	*Sadness*	*Anger*	*Fear*	*Surprise*	**Total**
Close Class Question	A-not-A		1	1	3		**5**
	Alternative		2				**2**
	Echo			3		1	**4**
	Particle	1	1	2	3	2	**7**
Open Class Question	How		1		1		**2**
	How many				1		**1**
	What		1	1		1	**3**
	Who		2				**2**
	Why		5	1			**6**
Series of Q			2	2			**4**
Total		**1**	**15**	**10**	**8**	**4**	**38**

Table 3 shows the distribution of the types of rhetorical question used in the data. As mentioned in Section 3, rhetorical questions tend to be more associated with negative emotions such as *anger* and *sadness*. This association is weakened by the polarity of the emotion. Our observation is that the more negative the emotion is, the greater the tendency to use rhetorical questions, as indicated in Figure 3.

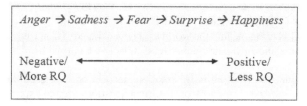

Fig. 3. The interaction between emotion polarity and the use of rhetorical questions

This finding is in line with Roberts and Kreuz (1994) who argued that the discourse goal of the use of rhetorical questions is to show negative emotion. It is also suggested in Gibbs et al. (2002), rhetorical questions were perceived as having very negative intent. Burnkrant and Howard (1984) suggested that rhetorical questions have the potential to motivate an audience to more intensively process the message content. Howard (1990) proposed that rhetorical questions have the potential to enhance the processing of message content to a greater extent. This explains why rhetorical questions are used more frequently when stronger emotion intensity is involved.

Previous research also pointed out that one of the most valuable functions of rhetorical questions is that they enable speakers to make stronger statements, with greater implications than straightforward assertions. (12a) is an example of a rhetorical question collected from the dataset. The same semantic content could be formulated in a statement as in (12b). Comparing (12a) and (12b), it is obvious that the (12a) expresses a stronger intensity of *sadness* emotion than the statement in (12b), by way of raising a rhetorical question.

(12) a. 哪里还有时间和朋友们聊天呢?
   (How can [I] still have time to chat with friends?)
   b. 没有时间和朋友们聊天
   ([I] do not have time to chat with friends)

Studies which investigated the effects of the use of rhetorical questions versus statements generally agreed that rhetorical questions often engaged people's minds more than straightforward statements, and it can enhance audience elaborations on a given message (Ahluwalia and Burnkrant, 2004; Howard and Burnkrant, 1990; Petty et al., 1981; Swasy and Munch, 1985). It has been suggested that rhetorical questions are one of the most effective tools for persuasion (Frank, 1990).

Some instances use a series of rhetorical questions to increase the emotion intensity, as in (13). They tend to indicate the existence of *sadness* and *anger*. Frank (1990:734) mentioned the use of clustering of rhetorical questions as "...in each case the question is re-stated for emphasis, in slightly different form. This makes for a stronger impact on the hearer; a strategy that most likely would be unnecessary if these were simply informational questions, but is a highly effective device for persuasion...". To apply the above observation in our data, rhetorical questions were used intentionally by the writers to draw readers' attention to their strong emotions. The purpose of using a cluster of rhetorical question is clearly for affective, rather than informational, effect.

(13) 老天让我来到这个世界上演悲剧的吗？我投降还不行?! 拜托. 我承受
不了那么戏剧化的生活！ 能让我正常地活下去吗？
(Did God bring me into the world to act out a tragedy? Can I surrender? Please.
I cannot stand such a dramatic life! Can't I live a normal life?)

In terms of question type, all basic emotions tend to be expressed through closed
types, except for *sadness*. Over 70% of rhetorical questions used to express the *sadness*
emotion are open types. This is particularly obvious with the use of the *why* question
word (which comprise one-third of the rhetorical questions for *sadness*). Of the five
why rhetorical questions expressing *sadness*, four appear in the structure of 'why +
negation'. Examples are given in (14) - (16):

(14) 为什么信宜没有 pizza hut！
(Why is there no Pizza Hut in Xinyi?)

(15) <u>为何</u>连答案都<u>不</u>确定正确与否？
(Why can't [we] even decide whether the answer is correct or not?)

(16) <u>为什么</u>人的年龄就<u>不</u>能刷新呢？
(Why can people's age not be refreshed?)

Results show that the *surprise* emotion is highly correlated with the use of rhetorical
question. In the dataset, *surprise* emotion has the least tendency to be expressed with
figurative devices; and rhetorical question is the only figurative device that being used
to express this emotion. It is found that some adverbs such as 难道 and 居然 repeatedly
appeared in the instances with *surprise* emotion, as in (17) and (18). The adverb 难道
has been recognized as a "rhetoric interrogation" marker that serves to manifest the
speaker's emotion in a discourse (Alleton, 1988; Jing-Schmidt, 2008). The connotations of these adverbs typically indicate *surprise*. The high frequency uses of these adverbs lead to a strong correlation between *surprise* and rhetorical question.

(17) 难道有很多韩国人去那游览˜?
(Don't tell me that there are many Korean visiting that place?)
(18) 我爹居然听过 mr.simple!?!?!?!?
(Surprisingly, my father listens to Mr. Simple !?!?!?!?)

4.2   Metaphor

The second most commonly used figurative device in our dataset is metaphor (28%).
Metaphor refers to an implicit comparison between two dissimilar objects. Unlike rhetorical questions, metaphor is more evenly used in evoking different emotions, as in
(19) showing *sadness*; *happiness* in (20) and *anger* in (21). Studies suggested that people often have a conventionalized metaphorical expression for emotions, such as
ANGER IS HEAT and UP IS HAPPINESS (Lakoff and Kövecses, 1987). Yu (1995)
found that Chinese text tends to use more body parts, especially internal organs, in its

metaphor in expressing emotional states. Fainsilber and Ortony (1987:247-248) mentioned that the metaphors produced by their participants on the whole "were disappointingly banal. They used eight times as many frozen, or dead, metaphors as novel ones". However, these observations do not apply in our data. Most of the metaphorical instances found in this study are novel rather than conventional, such as in (19), which makes a comparison between affection and luxury goods to imply that affection is something valuable to the writer but cannot be easily obtained; (20), where the writer compares himself to an athlete with boundless energy in being able to stay out talking with a partner until very late; and (21), where monks are likened to a gold-panning thief in order to express the writer's negative feelings towards them. One potential reason for the difference may be the source of the data. The data from previous studies were mainly drawn from conversations or monologues, while the data in this study were collected from social media. Speakers might tend to produce novel metaphors in conversation due to the time pressure. The written modality in social media allows its users to have sufficient time to formulate metaphorical expressions in a more creative way.

(19) 感情才是我的奢侈品，而物质只是我的日用品。
(Affection is my true luxury good. Material goods are just daily necessities.)

(20) 我是能量满分选手，我们又聊到这么晚才 回家。
(I am such an energetic athlete, we talked until very late again before going home.)

(21) 这两天街上的和尚特别多，都赶上年底出来 淘金的小偷了，看到开车的停下就走过去搭讪。
(There are particularly large numbers of monks on the streets these two days, the same number as the gold-panning thieves that appeared at the end of the year and struck up a conversation with every stopping car.)

In addition to the above, it was found that punctuation can also function to intensify the emotions expressed through figurative devices. First, the repetition of exclamation marks, question marks, or the mix of two in conjunction with rhetorical questions, as shown in (18), expresses a strong emotion of *surprise*. Second, when the punctuation is placed in the middle of a word or phrase, i.e. in an inappropriate position, it is usually for emphasis or more intense emotion, as in (22). The idiom 狗眼看人低 'such a snob' is separated with extra exclamation marks in between each character to show a higher intensity of *anger*.

(22) 不就是有钱么，狗！眼！看人低！
(It's all money. Such! A! Snob!)

5   Conclusion

This paper explores the use of different figurative devices in expressing emotions in social media. Results show that there is a close interaction between figurative language and emotion. We find that about one-third of the posts contain figurative devices such as metaphor, simile, rhetorical questions, and irony. Among the five basic emotions (i.e. happiness, sadness, anger, fear, and surprise), the *anger* emotion has the greatest tendency (54%) to be expressed via the figurative devices, followed by *sadness, fear, surprise*, and *happiness*. In addition, the data shows that rhetorical questions are the most frequently used figurative device (over 30%) for evoking negative emotions, i.e. *anger* and *sadness*. We believe that this linguistic account of figurative language in emotion expressions will enhance the existing automatic emotion classification systems.

Acknowledgements

This work is supported by the General Research Fund (GRF) sponsored by the Research Grants Council, Hong Kong (Project No. 15609715) and a Faculty Research Grant sponsored by the Hong Kong Polytechnic University (Project No. 1- ZEVK).

References

1. Ahluwalia, R., Burnkrant, R. E.: Answering questions about questions: A persuasion knowledge perspective for understanding the effects of rhetorical questions. Journal of Consumer Research. **31**, 26-42 (2004).
2. Alleton, V.: The so-called "rhetorical interrogation" in Mandarin. Journal of Chinese Linguistics. **16**, 278-297 (1988).
3. Burnkrant, R. E., Howard, D. J.: Effects of the use of introductory rhetorical questions versus statements on information processing. Journal of Personality and Social Psychology. **47**, 1218-1230 (1984).
4. Citron, F. M., Cacciari, C., Kucharski, M., Beck, L., Conrad, M., Jacobs, A. M.: When emotions are expressed figuratively: Psycholinguistic and Affective Norms of 619 Idioms for German (PANIG). Behavior Research Methods. **48**, 91-111 (2016).
5. Colston, H. L.: "I've never Seen anything like it": Overstatement, understatement, and irony. Metaphor and Symbolic Activity. **12**, 43-58 (1997).
6. Dews, S., Winner, E.: Muting the meaning: A social function of irony. Metaphor and Symbolic Activity. **10**, 3-19 (1995).
7. Ekman, P. E., Davidson, R. J.: The nature of emotion: Fundamental questions. Oxford University Press (1994).
8. Fainsilber, L., Ortony, A.: Metaphorical uses of language in the expression of emotions. Metaphor and Symbol. **2**, 239-250 (1987).
9. Frank, J.: You call that a rhetorical question?: Forms and functions of rhetorical questions in conversation. Journal of Pragmatics. **14**, 723-738 (1990).
10. Foolen, A.: The relevance of emotion for language and linguistics. In Foolen, A., Ludtke, U. M., Racine, T. P., Zlatev, J. (eds), Moving Ourselves, Moving Others: Motion and Emotion in Intersubjectivity, Consciousness and Language, pp. 349-369 (2012).
11. Fussell, S. R.: The Use of metaphor in written descriptions of emotional states. Unpublished manuscript, Carnegie Mellon University (1992).

12. Fussell, S. R., Moss, M. M.: Figurative language in emotional communication. In Fussell, S. R., Kreuz, R. J. (eds) Social and Cognitive Approaches to Interpersonal Communication, pp. 113-141 (1998).
13. Gibbs, R. W., Leggitt, J. S., Turner, E. A.: What's special about figurative language in emotional communication. In Fussell, S. R. (ed.), The Verbal Communication of Emotions: Interdisciplinary Perspectives, pp. 125-149. Mahwah, New Jersey: Lawrence Erlbaum Associates (2002).
14. Howard, D. J.: Rhetorical question effects on message processing and persuasion: The role of information availability and the elicitation of judgment. Journal of Experimental Social Psychology. **26**, 217-239. (1990).
15. Jing-Schmidt, Z.: The manifestation of emotion: on the Mandarin Chinese NanDao. Journal of Chinese Linguistics. **36**. 211-234. (2008).
16. Kövecses, Z.: Emotion Concepts. New York: Springer-Verlag (1990).
17. Kövecses, Z.: Metaphor and Emotion: Language, Culture, and Body in Human Feeling. Cambridge University Press (2003).
18. Lakoff, G., Johnson, M.: Metaphors we live by. Chicago: University of Chicago Press (1980).
19. Lakoff, G., Kovecses, Z.: The cognitive model of anger inherent in American English. In Holland, D., Quinn, N. (eds), Cultural Models in Language and Thought, pp. 195-221. Cambridge: Cambridge University Press (1987).
20. Lee, S.Y.M., Chen, Y., Huang, C.-R., Li, S.: Detecting emotion causes with a linguistic rule-based approach. computational intelligence. Special Issues on Computational Approaches to Analysis of Emotion in Text. Wiley-Blackwell (2013).
21. Lee, S.Y.M., Wang, Z.: Emotions in code-switching texts: Corpus analysis and construction. In Proceedings of SIGHAN Workshop, the 53rd Meeting of Association for Computational Linguistics (ACL 2015) (2015).
22. Leggitt, J. S., Gibbs, R. W.: Emotional reactions to verbal irony. Discourse Processes. **29**, 1-24 (2000).
23. Petty, R. E., Cacioppo, J. T., Heesacker, M.: Effects of rhetorical questions on persuasion: A cognitive response analysis. Journal of Personality and Social Psychology. **40**, 432-440. (1981).
24. Qadir, A.: Acquiring Knowledge for Affective State Recognition in Social Media. Doctoral dissertation, The University of Utah (2016).
25. Reyes, A., Rosso, P., Buscaldi, D.: From humor recognition to irony detection: The figurative language of social media. Data and Knowledge Engineering. **74**, 1-12. (2012).
26. Roberts, R. M., Kreuz, R. J.: Why do people use figurative language? Psychological Science. **5**, 159-163 (1994).
27. Swasy, J. L., Munch, J. M.: Examining the target of receiver elaborations: Rhetorical question effects on source processing and persuasion. Journal of Consumer Research. **11**, 877-886. (1985).
28. Williams-Whitney, D., Mio, J. S., Whitney, P.: Metaphor production in creative writing. Journal of Psycholinguistic Research, **21**, 497-509 (1992).
29. Yu, N.: Metaphorical expressions of anger and happiness in English and Chinese. Metaphor and Symbol. **10**, 59-92. (1995).

From Linguistic Synaesthesia to Embodiment:
Asymmetrical Representations of Taste and Smell in Mandarin Chinese

Qingqing Zhao, Chu-Ren Huang, and Yat-mei Sophia Lee

Department of Chinese and Bilingual Studies, The Hong Kong Polytechnic University, Hong Kong
zhaoqingqing0611@163.com
churen.huang@polyu.edu.hk
ym.lee@polyu.edu.hk

Abstract. This paper applied the embodiment theory of metaphor to the study of linguistic synaesthesia. In particular, we tried to account for the distribution of synaesthetic uses of Mandarin adjectives for taste and smell in terms of the degree of embodiment of different bodily experiences. We have found that taste is involved frequently both as the source domain and as the target domain in linguistic synaesthesia of Mandarin adjectives, while smell is productive only as the target domain. Besides, the synaesthetic transfer from taste to smell has also been attested to be more predominant than the transfer in a reverse direction, i.e., from smell to taste. We have thus proposed that a finer-grained theory of embodiment is sorely needed to account for the subtle differences in synaesthetic patterns of taste and smell in Mandarin adjectives. That is, the degree of embodiment is not only relevant in terms of the traditional dichotomy of bodily versus non-bodily events in the embodiment theory. The degree of embodiment is also a crucial concept to differentiate physiologically-based events such as those involving sensory modalities, which thus should also be taken into consideration in the theory of embodiment.

Keywords: Linguistic synaesthesia, Embodiment, Taste, Smell, Mandarin.

1   Introduction

The important role of bodies in structuring human language and cognition has been widely recognized (Johnson, 1987; Gibbs, 2005; among others), which is also one of the basic tenets in Cognitive Linguistics (Lakoff and Johnson, 1980; Wang, 2002). Linguistic studies supporting the embodiment theory mainly focus on the conceptualization of non-bodily experiences in terms of concepts representing human bodily perceptions and interactions with surrounding environments (e.g., Sweetser, 1990; Lien, 2005; and so forth). For instance, English verb *see* illustrates the mapping from the visual activity to the mental thinking/understanding in the phrase *to see no reason*, and Mandarin gustatory adjectives 苦 *ku3* 'bitter' and 甜 *tian2* 'sweet' are used to characterize

© Springer International Publishing AG 2018
Y. Wu et al. (Eds.): CLSW 2017, LNAI 10709, pp. 420–427, 2018.
https://doi.org/10.1007/978-3-319-73573-3_38

the situation of life in the idiom 憶苦思甜 *yi4-ku3 si1-tian2* 'recalling the sufferings in the past and contrasting them with happiness at present'.[1] However, as noted by Caballero and Paradis (2015), the relationship and interaction between different bodily experiences concerning embodiment have received less attention in linguistics, although they have been demonstrated to be more challenging and fundamental issues with respect to the theory of embodiment by extensive psychological and neuroscientific studies (e.g., Ramachandran and Hubbard, 2001; Seitz, 2005).

Linguistic synaesthesia, called synaesthetic metaphors alternatively, such as *sweet voice* in English and 冷色 *leng3-se4* 'cold color' in Mandarin Chinese, involves the use of lexical items for the perception in one sensory modality to describe perceptions in others (Ullmann, 1957; Williams, 1976). The associated characteristic of different sensory perceptions in linguistic synaesthesia, thus, would be well-suited to investigate the explanatory power of the theory of embodiment within bodily experiences. Therefore, our study focuses on the application of the embodiment theory to the study of linguistic synaesthesia. Specifically, we will explore: (1) to what extent, adjectives originally for gustatory (and olfactory) perceptions can be employed in linguistic synaesthesia, i.e., used to describe perceptions in other sensory modalities; (2) to what extent, gustatory (and olfactory) perceptions can be characterized by adjectives from other sensory domains; and (3) whether synaesthetic representations of gustatory and olfactory experiences in Mandarin adjectives can be predicted by the embodiment theory.

2   Method: A Corpus-based Approach

Our study adopted a corpus-based approach for data collection, which included extraction and classification of Mandarin sensory adjectives from lexical thesauri and sensory uses of these adjectives from a balanced corpus.

Specifically, two Chinese lexical thesauri were employed, namely, HIT-CIR Tongyici Cilin (Extended) (Che et al., 2010) and HowNet (Dong and Dong, 2003), to extract sensory words. Then, each morpheme in the extracted sensory words was manually examined to identify morphemes that are used for specific senses etymologically. To ensure that correct etymology was identified, we consulted both 說文解字 *Shuo1-wen2 jie3-zi4* (Xu, 1963 [156]) and 說文解字注 *Shuo1-wen2 jie3-zi4 zhu4* (Duan, 2007 [1735–1815]) through the online interface of 漢典 *Han4-dian3*[2] and Hantology (Chou and Huang 2010).[3] Besides, an additional Chinese philological resource, i.e., 漢語大字典 *Han4-yu3 da4 zi4-dian3* (Xu, 2010), was also consulted to double-check the original meaning of the morphemes and to identify the original meaning of the morphemes that are not included in 說文解字 *Shuo1-wen2 jie3-zi4* or 說文解字注 *Shuo1-wen2*

---

[1] Examples used in this paper are from two balanced corpora, of which English expressions were extracted from the BNC corpus (accessed at: http://www.natcorp.ox.ac.uk/) and Mandarin expressions from the Sinica corpus (accessed at http://app.sinica.edu.tw/kiwi/mkiwi/, Chen et al., 1996).

[2] Accessed at: http://www.zdic.net/.

[3] Accessed at: http://hantology.ling.sinica.edu.tw/.

jie3-zi4 zhu4. In principle, we only included adjectives composed of morphemes with the same and attested uses for senses etymologically. Adjectives, such as 苦澀 *ku3-se4* 'bitter', were thus excluded, since in the example word 澀's etymological meaning of 'not flowing smoothly' is related to the tactile sense, while 苦 originally meaning 'bitter vegetable' indicates the gustatory modality.

We then extracted sensory usages for the Mandarin adjectives obtained in the last step from the Sinica corpus, by manually checking the distributions of the adjectives in five senses (i.e., touch, taste, smell, vision, and hearing). For example, the adjective 酸 *suan1* 'sour' was identified to have distributions in the tactile domain, such as 腰酸腿 疼 *yao1 suan1 tui3 teng2* 'feeling sore in the waist and pain in the legs'; the gustatory domain, such as 酸菜 *suan1-cai4* 'the sour vegetable (pickles)'; the olfactory domain, such as 酸臭味 *suan1 chou4 wei4* 'the sour and smelly odor'; and the auditory domain, such as 酸酸…一聲 *suan1-suan1…yi1 sheng1* 'the sour (...) sound'.

3   Synaesthetic Representations in Mandarin Adjectives for Taste and Smell

3.1   Synaesthetic Representations in Adjectives for Taste

There are 24 Mandarin adjectives attested with constituent morphemes all related to taste etymologically, as shown in Table 1, such as 鮮 'tasty' and 甜美 *tian2-mei3* 'tasty'. The distribution of these adjectives in the Sinica corpus shows that adjectives originally for taste can also be used for touch, smell, vision, and hearing. Precisely speaking, the olfactory domain is the highest target concerning the synaesthetic transferability, where 15 of 24 (62.5%) gustatory adjectives can be utilized to characterize olfactory perceptions, such as 淡淡的花香 *dan4-dan4 de hua1-xiang1* 'the slight fragrance of flowers'. By contrast, the tactile domain is the lowest target for Mandarin gustatory adjectives, with the synaesthetic transferability of 20.8% (5/24). Therefore, it can be concluded that taste is a productive source domain in Chinese synaesthesia, as adjectives originally conceptualizing gustatory experiences can be employed to describe perceptual experiences in all other four sensory modalities. In addition, the synaesthetic transferability from taste to other four senses is all over 20%.

Taste can not only be the source domain in linguistic synaesthesia of Mandarin adjectives, but also can be the target domain, based on the sensory usages of adjectives etymologically for other senses. As illustrated in Table 2, except for hearing, gustatory perceptions in Mandarin can be characterized by adjectives from touch (e.g., 澀 *se4* 'not flowing smoothly'), from smell (e.g., 香 *xiang1* 'fragrant'), and from vision (e.g., 厚 *hou4* 'thick'). Among the 18 synaesthetic adjectives for taste, the numbers of adjectives mapping from vision and from touch are close (i.e., nine and eight respectively), while only one adjective transfers from smell.

Mandarin adjectives that can represent gustatory experiences, thus, include two categories: one is adjectives originally for taste, and the other is synaesthetic uses of adjectives from other sensory modalities. In terms of the adjectives composed of morphemes with the same sensory etymology investigated in this study, original adjectives for taste occupy a larger percentage, i.e., with 57.1% (24/42), than synaesthetic adjectives for taste, i.e., with 42.9 % (18/42), with respect to lexical types.

Table 1. Taste as the source domain in linguistic synaesthesia.

Source Domain	Target Domain			
TASTE (24)	TOUCH	SMELL	VISION	HEARING
Number of adjectives	5	15	11	10
Synaesthetic transferability	20.8% (5/24)	**62.5% (15/24)**	45.8% (11/24)	41.7% (10/24)
Examples	一身膩汗 'greasy sweat all over the body'	淡淡的花香 'the slight fragrance of flowers'	鮮黃色 'bright yellow'	甜美的歌聲 the sweet singing'

Table 2. Taste as the target domain in linguistic synaesthesia.

Target Domain	Source Domain			
TASTE (18)	TOUCH	SMELL	VISION	HEARING
Number of adjectives	8	1	9	0
Percentage	**44.4% (8/18)**	5.6% (1/18)	**50% (9/18)**	0
Examples	澀柿子 'puckery persimmons'	口感香 'the taste is appetizing'	酒的厚薄 'thick and thin tastes of wine'	-

3.2   Synaesthetic Representations in Adjectives for Smell

The synaesthetic representation in adjectives for smell exhibits different patterns compared with that for taste in Mandarin. There is only one original olfactory adjective with synaesthetic distributions in taste as discussed above, and one original olfactory adjective in vision (i.e., 臭 chou4 'smelly'), as shown in Table 3. Thus, the synaesthetic transferability of olfactory adjectives to taste and vision is the same, both in 10% (1/10). Smell is, therefore, not as productive as taste to be the source domain in linguistic synaesthesia of Mandarin adjectives.

Table 4, however, can demonstrate that smell is a predominant target domain in linguistic synaesthesia of Mandarin adjectives. There are 42 Mandarin adjectives originally for other senses attested with synaesthetic usages for olfactory perceptions in the Sinica corpus. Among the adjectives, touch is the largest source with 17 adjectives having distributions in smell, and vision is the smallest source with ten adjectives mapping to smell.

Table 3. Smell as the source domain in linguistic synaesthesia.

Source Domain	Target Domain			
SMELL (10)	TOUCH	TASTE	VISION	HEARING
Number of adjectives	0	1	1	0
Synaesthetic transferability	0	10% (1/10)	10% (1/10)	0
Examples	-	鮮香口感 'the tasty and fragrant taste'	一張臭臉 'an unpleasant facial expression'	-

Table 4. Smell as the target domain in linguistic synaesthesia.

Target Domain	Source Domain			
SMELL (42)	TOUCH	TASTE	VISION	HEARING
Number of adjectives	17	15	10	0
Percentage	**40.5% (17/42)**	35.7% (15/42)	23.8% (10/42)	0
Examples	煤味太重 'the odor of coal is too strong'	微苦氣香 'the slightly bitter fragrance of air'	清香 'a slight (delicate) fragrance'	-

The representation of olfactory experiences can also be realized by both adjectives originally for smell and synaesthetic uses of adjectives from other senses in Mandarin. The synaesthetic adjectives for smell, however, are much more than original adjectives for smell in terms of lexical types, where the synaesthetic adjectives occupy 80.8% (42/52) of all collected adjectives conceptualizing the olfactory experience, which is different from the representation of taste in Mandarin adjectives.

It should also be noted that smell is the highest target for Mandarin gustatory adjectives with respect to the synaesthetic transferability, of which 15 adjectives exhibit the transfer from taste to smell in Mandarin. However, there is only one adjective showing the transfer from smell to taste in Mandarin (See Tables 1 and 3).

3.3   From Synaesthetic Patterns of Taste and Smell to Embodiment

Asymmetrical patterns can be observed in the synaesthetic representations of taste and smell in Mandarin adjectives. Specifically, the asymmetries lie in that: (1) taste can be involved in linguistic synaesthesia as both the source domain and the target domain, while smell is only productive as the target domain in linguistic synaesthesia of Mandarin adjectives; (2) gustatory experiences in Mandarin are conceptualized more by adjectives originally for taste than by adjectives mapping from other senses, whereas olfactory experiences in Mandarin are represented overwhelmingly by synaesthetic adjectives originally for other sensory domains (with the percentage over 80%); and (3) the synaesthetic transfer from taste to smell occurs more frequently and predominantly than the transfer in a reverse direction, in terms of both the synaesthetic transferability (i.e., 62.5% vs. 10%) and the number of adjective types (i.e., 15 vs. one).

Such asymmetrical patterns in linguistic synaesthesia of taste and smell are not isolated in Mandarin. That is, two other facts exhibit corresponding asymmetries. Among 24 adjectives originally for taste (see Table 1) and ten adjectives originally for smell (see Table 3), lexical gaps can be found in both the conceptualization of the perceptual intensity and the neutral sentiment. That is, there are lexicalized items representing the gustatory intensity (i.e., 濃 nong2 'of intense taste', 醇 chun2 'of intense taste', and 淡 dan4 'of mild taste') in Mandarin, while there is none for the olfactory intensity. In other words, the olfactory intensity needs to be conceptualized through linguistic synaesthesia in Mandarin, such as 重 zhong4 'heavy' from touch in the expression 煤味太重 mei2-wei4 tai4 zhong4 'the odor of coal is too strong', and 清 qing1 'clear' from vision in the expression 清香 qing1-xiang1 'a slight (delicate) fragrance'. Besides, there are lexical items among adjectives originally for gustatory experiences to represent the positive taste (e.g., 鮮 xian1 'tasty'), the negative taste (e.g., 膩 ni4 'greasy'), and the neutral taste (e.g., 辣 la4 'hot (in taste)'). Mandarin adjectives with etymology in smell, however, only conceptualize the positive odor (e.g., 芬芳 feng1-fang1 'fragrant'), and the negative odor (e.g., 臊 sao1 'of the smell related to urine'), but not for the neutral odor. Therefore, the asymmetries in linguistic representations for taste and smell are systematic in Mandarin, which would in fact indicate the asymmetry of gustatory perceptions and olfactory perceptions in human bodily experiences.

The embodiment theory in Cognitive Linguistics has proposed that experiences with more bodily contact and more bodily interactions with surrounding environments are more embodied, and concepts representing these experiences tend to be used to structure less embodied experiences (Lakoff and Johnson, 1980). Although the theory has been widely supported to account for conceptual metaphors in language (Johnson, 1987), a few researchers, such as Teng (2006) and Gibbs (2011), pointed the potential limitation of the embodiment theory applying to metaphors with domains exclusively for physiological and neural events. Zhao et al.'s corpus-based study (2018, in press), however, demonstrated that the embodiment account could predict most synaesthetic regularities of Mandarin and English gustatory adjectives, since sensory experiences can also be differentiated in different degrees of embodiment. That is, touch and taste necessarily involve physical contact between the sensory organ and the perceived object, while smell, vision, and hearing do not require such physical contact (Shen, 1997; Popova, 2005). In addition, taste is less embodied than touch, since the sensory receptors of the gustatory perception are only in the mouth, while those of the tactile perception are all over the body (Lehrer, 1978). Following these two features, the synaesthetic patterns of taste and smell in Mandarin adjectives could be predicted by the embodiment theory. Specifically speaking, taste productive as both the source domain and the target domain in linguistic synaesthesia, is consistent with the fact that taste is not on the endpoint of the embodiment scale (i.e., neither the most embodied nor the least embodied). Smell, however, is close to the least end of the embodiment scale, which thus motivates the olfactory domain to be more predominant as the target in linguistic synaesthesia than as the source. Additionally, the more frequent transfer direction from taste to smell in Mandarin adjectives is also predictable, since taste is more embodied than smell.

4   Conclusion

This study adopted a corpus-based approach to investigate the embodiment theory within bodily experiences. Based on the asymmetrical patterns of synaesthetic representations for taste and smell in Mandarin adjectives, we have found that embodiment is also supported within bodily perceptions.

One of implications of this study to the embodiment theory is that the traditional dichotomy of bodily versus non-bodily or concrete versus abstract notions are not sufficient to account for metaphors with source domains and target domains both related to physiological or neural experiences. Instead, the degree of embodiment is also a crucial concept, which should be included to enrich the theory of embodiment.

Acknowledgement

The research is supported by the Early Career Scheme (project no. F-PP14) funded by Hong Kong RGC.

References

1. Caballero, R., Paradis, C.: Making sense of sensory perceptions across languages and cultures. Functions of Language 22(1), 1-19 (2015).
2. Che, W., Li, Z., Liu, T.: LTP: A Chinese language technology platform. In: Proceedings of the 23rd International Conference on Computational Linguistics: Demonstrations, pp. 13-16 (2010).

3. Chen, K.-J., Huang, C.-R., Chang, L.-P., Hsu, H.-L.: Sinica corpus: Design methodology for balanced corpora. In: Proceedings of the 11th Pacific Asia Conference on Language, Information and Computation (PACLIC 11), pp. 167-176 (1996).
4. Chou, Y.-M., Huang, C.-R.: Hantology: Conceptual system discovery based on orthographic convention. In: Huang, C.-R., Calzolari, N., Gangemi, A., Lenci, A., Oltramari, A., Prévot, L. (eds.) Ontology and the lexicon: A natural language processing perspective, pp. 122-143. Cambridge University Press, Cambridge (2010).
5. Dong, Z., Dong, Q.: HowNet—A hybrid language and knowledge resource. In: Proceedings of Natural Language Processing and Knowledge Engineering, pp. 820-824 (2003).
6. Duan, Y.: Shuowenjiezizhu [Commentary on explaining graphs and analyzing characters]. Phoenix Press, Nanjing (2007 [1735–1815]).
7. Gibbs, J. R. W.: Embodiment and cognitive science. Cambridge University Press, New York (2005).
8. Gibbs, J. R. W.: Evaluating conceptual metaphor theory. Discourse Processes 48(8), 529-562 (2011).
9. Johnson, M.: The body in the mind: The bodily basis of meaning, imagination, and reason. The University of Chicago Press, Chicago and London (1987).
10. Lakoff, G., Johnson, M.: Metaphors we live by. The University of Chicago Press, Chicago (1980).
11. Lehrer, A.: Structures of the lexicon and transfer of meaning. Lingua 45(2), 95-123 (1978).
12. Lien, C.: Verbs of visual perception in Taiwanese Southern Min: A cognitive approach to shift of semantic domains. Language and Linguistics 6(1), 109-132 (2005).
13. Popova, Y.: Image schemas and verbal synaesthesia. In: Hampe, B., Grady, J. E. (eds.) From perception to meaning: Image schemas in cognitive linguistics, vol. 29, pp. 395-419. Mouton de Gruyter, Berlin and New York (2005).
14. Ramachandran, V. S., Hubbard, E. M.: Synaesthesia--A window into perception, thought and language. Journal of consciousness studies 8(12), 3-34 (2001).
15. Seitz, J. A.: The neural, evolutionary, developmental, and bodily basis of metaphor. New Ideas in Psychology 23(2), 74-95 (2005).
16. Shen, Y.: Cognitive constraints on poetic figures. Cognitive Linguistics 8(1), 33-71 (1997).
17. Sweetser, E.: From etymology to pragmatics: Metaphorical and cultural aspects of semantic sturture. Cambridge University Press, Cambridge (1990).
18. Teng, N.: Metaphor and coupling: An embodied, action-oriented perspective. Metaphor and Symbol 21(2), 67-85 (2006).
19. Ullmann, S.: The principles of semantics. Basil Blackwell, Oxford (1957).
20. Williams, J. M.: Synaesthetic adjectives: A possible law of semantic change. Language 52(2), 461-478 (1976).
21. Wang, Y.: The philosophical basis for cognitive linguistics: Embodied philosophy. Foreign Language Teaching and Research (bimonthly) 34(2), 82-89 (2002).
22. Xu, S.: Shuowenjiezi [Explaining graphs and analyzing characters]. Zhonghua Book Company, Beijing (1963 [156]).
23. Xu, Z.: Hanyudazidian [Great compendium of Chinese characters]. Sichuan Dictionary Publishing Company and Hubei Dictionary Publishing Company, Chengdu & Wuhan (2010).
24. Zhao, Q., Huang, C.-R., Long, Y.: Synaesthesia in Chinese: A corpus-based study on gustatory adjectives in Mandarin. To appear in Linguistics (2018, in press).

A Study on Chinese Vocabulary Learning Strategies of Second Language Learners

Geng Zhi[1] Xiuchuan Lu[2]

[1] Fudan University, Shanghai 200433, China
[2] Fudan University, Shanghai 200433, China
gengzhi@fudan.edu.cn   luxc@fudan.edu.cn

Abstract. This study is to provide insights into how second language learners of Chinese develop their vocabulary learning strategies and explore the differences among beginning, intermediate and advanced learners. The results of investigation indicate that the advanced learners have a wider range of strategies. We also found that learners from different cultures have some specific preferences in using vocabulary learning strategies.

Keywords: Chinese, Second Language, Vocabulary Learning Strategies.

1   Leaning Strategies

One of the main fields of second language acquisition (SLA) studies is on the learning strategies which started gaining prominence in the 1980s. Wenden and Rubin examined learner's strategy in language learning [1]. The very first fundamental issue about learning strategies is its identification: what methods are used by learners. The widest accepted notion was drawn by Oxford [2] who integrated behavioral (direct) and mental (indirect) strategies together.

Table 1. Oxford's Language Learning Strategies

Direct Strategies	Memory strategies
	Metacognitive strategies
	Cognitive strategies
Indirect Strategies	Affective strategies
	Compensation strategies
	Social strategies

International studies on learning strategies were brought into China's English as a foreign language (EFL) field early in the 1990s. Chinese EFL scholars, such as Gui [3] and Wu [4] called these studies "worthy to pay attention". Some scholars later further developed the learning strategies theory. For example, Li [5] proposed a dynamic model of ESL vocabulary learning strategies.

Y. Wu et al. (Eds.): CLSW 2017, LNAI 10709, pp. 428–433, 2018.
https://doi.org/10.1007/978-3-319-73573-3_39

Comparing to numerous English as a Second Language researches, studies on learning strategies of Chinese as a second language lags behind [6]. Although Qian [7] examined the incidental vocabulary learning in Chinese L2 reading, no systemic study on Chinese vocabulary learning has been seen yet and further theoretical explanation for individual differences is also necessary.

2   Project Background

In order to find what strategies are applied by Chinese as a second language learners, we conducted an investigation which was began by designing a scale especially for examining Chinese vocabulary learning strategies. This scale is consisted of 33 items (I1-33) and 7 strategies categories: resource (I1-I2), cognitive (I3-I11), memory (I12-I22), applying (I23-I24), social (I25-26), affective (I27-I28) and meta-cognitive (I29-I32).

With this new scale designed for Chinese vocabulary leaning, thirty Chinese second language learners in different levels from Peking University were investigated in class. Each student was asked to choose a statement from 1(never) point to 5(always) points that best describes how he or she uses the strategy. Following Oxford's explanation, strategies use is identified into 5 levels and 3 frequency levels: Low level frequency 1-2.5 points, High level 3.5-5 points and 2.5 -3.5 points is middle level.

In this investigation, ten subjects from each level were investigated. Among them, there were sixteen European and American students and fourteen Asian students. The gender ratio was also sixteen (male) to fourteen (female). Descriptive and deductive statistical analysis run by the software SPSS 11.0 was applied in data analysis. Considering the limited number of participants, ten subjects were furtherly asked to taken follow up interviews.

3   Results

The uses of strategies in our database are examined in three aspects: (a) the overall uses of different categories of strategy; (b) the variation of participants of different language levels; (c) the influence of culture background of Asian and Westerns learners. These results are shown in table 2, table 3 and table 4.

Table 2. The Overall Uses of Different Categories of Strategy

The frequency of the use of different strategy categories	The high level (HL) strategies items	The low level (LL) strategy items

applying(3.445)	I5: with the help of a	I16:use a word card
affective(3.4),	dictionary(4.03)	(2.03)
resource(3.4)	I32: my own way (3.67),	I9: listen to the tape
meta-cognitive(3.22)	I1: learn out of class	(2.37)
cognitive(3.11)	(3.6)	I10: only learn the
memory(2.92)	I3: guess the meaning	meaning and usage in
social(2.645)	through context (3.57)	the textbook (2.4)
	I6: translating (3.57)	I26: group member
	I24: learn in use (3.57)	check (2.43)

Table 3. The Variation of Participants of Different levels

Group level	The use of different strategy category	The high level (HL)strategy items	The low level (LL)strategy items
Beginning	Affective (3.7)	I15 (3.9)	I10 (2)
	Metacognitive(3.37)	I32 (3.8)	I9 (2.1)
	Applying (3.35)	I27 (3.7)	
	Resource (3.2)	I28 (3.7)	
	Memory (3.1)	I1 (3.6)	
	Social (2.8)	I21 (3.5)	
	Cognitive (2.7)	I31 (3.5)	
Intermediate	Metacognitive (3.48)	I5 (4.5)	I16 (2)
	Resource (3.45)	I31 (3.8)	I19 (2.4)
	Applying (3.35)	I3(3.7)	
	Affective (3.25)	I32 (3.6)	
	Cognitive (3.21)	I24 (3.6)	
	Memory (2.95)	I6 (3.5)	
	Social (2.9)	I2 (3.5)	
Advanced	Applying (3.65)	I5(4.4)I3(4)	I16 (1.4)
	Resource (3.55)	I4(4)I6(4)	I26 (1.9)
	Cognitive (3.4)	I22(4)I17	I15 (2)
	Affective (3.25)	(3.9)I1(3.8)	I12 (2.1)
	Metacognitive (2.85)	I24(3.7)I7	I9 (2.1)
	Memory (2.7)	(3.6)I23(3.6)	I18 (2.2)
	Social (2.25)	I32(3.6)I13(3.5)	I29 (2.4)

Table 4. The Overall Use of Each Strategy Category of Western and Asian Culture Group

	Resource	Cognitive	Memory	Applying	Social	Affective	Metacognitive
Western	3.24	3.84	2.98	3.24	2.78	3.49	3.43
Asian	3.57	3.42	2.86	3.67	2.49	3.28	3.00

4   Discussion

The overall strategy use in the table 2 shows that the most frequently used strategy categories are applying, affective, resource and meta-cognitive while the most infrequent ones are social, memory and cognitive strategies. To be more specific, the data shows that the most frequently applied strategy items are I5, I32, I1, I6, I 24, I13 and I3 while the most infrequent ones are I16, I9, I26 and I10.

It is interesting to find that although strategies as I9 and I16 (using word card and listening to tape/CD) are very common teaching techniques used by teachers, students, in contrast, seem to seldom apply these strategies. A reason to explain this may be that making words card and tape/CD could be quite time-consuming and expensive. At the same time, we can see that "lower cost" strategies such as I5 (consulting dictionary) and I6 (translating into first language) are among the most frequently used ones. As an implication, it is necessary to be aware that the reality of learning settings could make great influence on learners' choice of learning strategies. More implications could be drawn for language instruction. For example, textbook writers could design word card and encourage its publication with textbooks. Teachers could share teaching resources including listening materials with students to encourage learning by creating a friendly environment.

In order to find the features of the advanced level learners, we analyzed the dynamic development process of the use frequency of the seven different categories strategy from level 1(beginning, the fist column) to level 2(intermediate, the second column) and to level 3(advanced, the third column). See Fig 1.

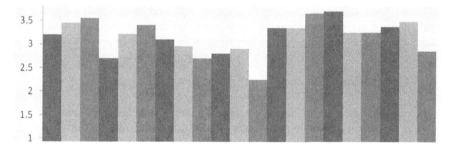

Fig. 1. Strategy use frequency of different language levels.

From this figure, it could be generally told that students of advanced level developed their use of resource, cognitive, social, and applying strategies while they are using less memory, affective and meta-cognitive strategies compared to the beginning level. We can also see that intermediate learners are in a clear transferring stage in the use of strategy from beginning to advanced level.

This general trend has a reflection in the use of single strategy item. Deductive statistical analysis found significant differences between advanced learners and beginning or intermediate learners on I4, I5, I15 and I31. Both I4 (guessing the meaning from character) and I5 (consulting a dictionary) require a potential ability to identify and deconstruct Chinese characters which are language learning device oriented strategies. An increasing use of these strategies indicate that advanced learners have developed this kind of strategy to a certain extent. I15 (repetition) and I31 (arranging the learning time and amount), are considered as general cognitive ability oriented strategies. A decreasing use of these strategies also supports the idea that advanced learners become freer from basic simple strategies that are more likely to be resorted to by beginning learners.

Does the culture background have influence on learner's strategy? To answer this question, comparisons between the Western group and the Asian group were made. We found that Western students seem to be more active in applying learning strategies. The western group applies more strategies in almost every strategy category and the amount of their strategy items in both high level and low level also exceed that of the Asian group.

Specifically, Western learners used more cognitive, memory, social, affective and meta-cognitive strategies while Asian learners used more resource and applying strategies. These two groups show discrepancies in some aspects of language background and learning styles. For example, Asian learners make better use of Chinese characters (I4) and dictionary (I5) in learning Chinese vocabulary while Western learners have no better way except boring repetition (I15). This reminds our teachers to keep in mind that there are extra difficulties that Western learners face in learning Chinese. These difficulties are also pointed out by one male Spanish student in the follow-up interview who had learned Chinese for three years and was at the intermediate level: "Since different students in my class have different cultural backgrounds and learning styles, I think my teacher should be more aware of this diversity, and better coordinate the pace of teaching, encouraging us learn together and improve together".

5   Conclusion

Making clear the use of Chinese vocabulary learning strategies, this study recomposes an existing scale lead to the conduct of quantitative research. This investigation finds that, the most commonly used strategies by all learners are applying, affective, re-source and meta-cognitive while the least commonly used are social, memory and cognitive strategies. Analysis also shows that students at different levels have significant differences in applying strategies of "consulting dictionaries" "simply reciting" "guessing the meaning from Chinese characters" and " arraigning properly the time and amount of learning". The results indicate that the advanced learner has a wider range of better developed language learning device oriented strategies. This study also found that learners of different culture background have some specific preferences in using vocabulary learning strategies. Asian learners more frequently resort to resource and applying strategies, while Western learners more frequently resort to cognitive, memory, social, affective and meta-cognitive strategies.

Besides the discrepancy between learners from different level and culture, a comparison between genders was also examined. No significant difference was found between male and female in analysis. However, the raw data hints that female learners are tending to use more strategies of all kinds which implies that females are normally more active than male in learning language.

Overall, the result of this study leads us to a further understanding of the necessary of conducting special studies on learning strategies of different languages and different systems in a language. It also implicates that learning strategy should be treated as an important part of teaching content, and that language educators and teachers should apply more techniques to give a better environment for encouraging the development of the learner's strategy competence.

Although some valuable results and suggestions have been drawn from this investigation, this study is far away from perfect. Weak-nesses of this research includes a low number of participants, an immature scale and a superficially analyzed data. Future researches into Chinese language learning strategies are expecting.

Acknowledgement.
This research is supported by China's National Office for Education Planning. Project name: the study of international second language textbook's ideology and Chinese textbooks discourse. (全国教育科学规划课题教育部青年课题世界范围内第二语言教材中的意识形态问题及汉语国际教育的教材话语体系研究). Project Number: EGA150360.

References

1. Wenden, Rubin (1987) Learner strategy in language learning. Prentice Hall, New Jersey
2. Oxford. R. L (1990) Language learning strategies: What every teacher should know. 1st edn. Heinle, Boston
3. Gui Shichun (1992) The psychology of Chinese ESL learners (in Chinese). Hunan Education Press, Changsha
4. Wu Yongyi, Chen Yu (2005) Analysis on successful Chinese second language learners' learning strategies (in Chinese) In: Zhao Jinming. (Ed.) Exploring the Teaching of Chinese as a Foreign Language in An Omni-bearing Manner. Commercial Press, Beijing, pp 440-458.
5. Li Songhao (2003) The design of a scale for middle school English vocabulary learning strategies (in Chinese). Journal of school of foreign languages of Shandong Normal University 1: 15-17.
6. Jiang Xin (2000) A tentative study on Chinese second language learning strategies (in Chinese). Language teaching and linguistic studies 1: 61-68.
7. Qian Xujing (2003) On incidental vocabulary learning in Chinese L2 reading (in Chinese). Journal of Peking University (Humanities and Social Sciences) 4: 135-142.

A Study on the Distribution Differences of Sentence Group Coherence in Chinese Texts of Different Genres

Tianke Wei[1][0000-0001-9621-3542], Qiang Zhou[2*][0000-0001-7369-3598], Xuejing Zhang[1][0000-0002-8613-3327], Xueqiang Lv[1][0000-0002-1422-0560]

[1] Beijing Key Laboratory of Internet Culture and Digital Dissemination Research, Beijing Information Science and Technology University, Beijing 100101, China
[2] Tsinghua National Laboratory for Information Science and Technology (TNList) Center for Speech and Language Technologies, Research Institute of Information Technology, Tsinghua University, Beijing 100084, China
18237176870@163.com

Abstract. Chinese sentence group plays an important role in text coherence analysis. Because of the complexity and the diversity of Chinese language, the sentence groups of different genres often show different coherence distribution characteristics. This paper analyzed the coherence of four different corpora in news, application, prose and encyclopedia based on the different statistical features of two independent annotators. In this work, the coherence distribution characteristics of sentence groups in four corpora are analyzed, and the differences of sentence group coherence in different genres are compared in detail. The study lays a good foundation for the automatic segmentation of the boundary of sentence group and automatic analysis of the relation between sentences in the future.

Keywords: Chinese sentence group, coherence annotation, text structure analysis

1 Introduction

The sentence group (SG) is a unit which has logical connection in semantics and structural relation in grammar [1]. Each sentence group generally has only one clear theme. In coherent text, the sentence group is an independent unit which combines both syntax and semantics, it plays an important role in the study of text analysis and machine translation. In addition, it can lay the foundation for the

---

Foundation Project: Supported by the National Natural Science Foundation of China (Project Number: 61433018, 61373075, 61411130162). Supported by the National Key Basic Research and Development Foundation (Project Number: 2013CB329304). National Natural Science Foundation of China (Project Number: 61671070). Beijing Science and Technology High-Tech Innovation Center Project (Project Number: BAICIT - 2016003). National Social Science Foundation Major Project (Project Number: 14 @ ZH036,15ZDB017). National Language Committee Major Project (ZDA125-26).

© Springer International Publishing AG 2018
Y. Wu et al. (Eds.): CLSW 2017, LNAI 10709, pp. 434–447, 2018.
https://doi.org/10.1007/978-3-319-73573-3_40

automatic analysis of text coherence by analyzing the structural characteristics of sentence group in different genres texts.

In order to summarize the distribution of sentence group in different genres texts, we need to annotate the sentence group in different genres texts. Dutch linguist van Dijk [2] made a great contribution to the text structure analysis. He pointed out that the creation of a text must have a theme at first, and then it gradually evolved into the specific meaning expressed by the various sentences. This idea is also applicable to the sentence group. In other words, the composition of a sentence group must define its theme firstly, and then analyzes the relation among the various sentences. Yingtian Wu [3] explored the basic elements and structural patterns of exposition, narration and argumentation, and explained the connection and difference of the different texts structure. TED SANDERS [4] made a detailed description and distinction between semantics and pragmatics, and drew the conclusion that the text of describing objective information is dominated by semantics, and the text of describing argument information is dominated by pragmatics. American linguist Robert Longacre [5] put forward the theory of text analysis clearly and comprehensively, he divided the text into different categories, such as exposition, narration, description, persuasive writing and so on. He put forward a method of sentence relation analysis, linked the sentence within paragraph or between paragraphs with the sentence group, and stressed that the text type, contour, macro structure, text templates and other abstract problems were closely linked with the form, syntax and other specific issues. Wangqi Jiang [6] deeply analyzed the structure of argumentation and summarized that the argumentation was composed by the theme, the positive argument, the negative argument and the conclusion. Weizhang Wu, Xiaolin Tian made a very detailed description about the sentence group on its function, category, composition, segmentation and so on. These researches provide the basic theoretical support for the construction of text coherence annotation system.

At present, there are few studies on the analysis of text structure and content coherence from the level of sentence group, and it also lacks researches on the analysis of different genres texts structural characteristics which use sentence group. The work of the previous period[2] had already pointed out that the sentence group has a certain influence on the difficulty of text cognition, and the relevant data of news corpus had showed that the difficulty of narration and prose is quite different. The main reason for the difference is the boundary and category of sentence group. On the basis of the analysis above, we can draw a conclusion that the sentence group has a great influence on the difficulty of different genres texts, and the relation between the sentences is inextricably linked with the sentence group. Therefore, it is a suitable choice to study the different genres texts by combining the sentences relation with the sentence group.

On the basis of the work in the last stage, this paper has expanded the corpus to narration, application, prose and argumentation. This paper analyzes the

---

[2]A Research on the Difficulty of Chinese Text Annotation. Technical Report of Beijing Key Laboratory of Internet Culture and Digital Dissemination Research, Beijing Information Science and Technology University.

distribution differences of the sentence group coherence in different genres texts, and deeply analyzes the influence of inter-sentence coherence on the sentence group boundary and category, structure and the overall coherence of text. The difference of structure and content coherence of different genres texts is compared by using two different annotation versions, and analyzes the internal relations between sentence group boundary and the functional category with inter-sentence coherence. Using this relation to mine the specific reason why the sentence group is difficult to identify.

The rest of the paper is organized as follows. In Second 2, we analyze the structural characteristics of the sentence group in different genres texts through several annotation examples, and put forward the basic hypothesis of this paper. Section 3 gives the experimental results and the related evaluation methods. The final section is the conclusion and the prospect.

2   Annotation Examples of SG in Different Genres Texts

In order to observe the structural characteristics of sentence group in different genres text, we annotate the sentence group from various angles. According to the principle of a sentence group only has one theme to segment the sentence group. The category of the sentence group need to be defined based on the expression of the sentences in the sentence group. When a sentence can't be associated with other sentences, there will be a single sentence. And then we annotate the coherence between sentences in sentence group, making the two sentences to be a coherent pair. Finally, the coherent form and connection of the coherent pairs are annotated.

The format of the annotation is as follows[3]. The first column is the Sentence Number. The second column is the Sentence. The third column is the Sentence Group (SG) label, which is used to annotate the boundary of each SG and its category. The fourth column is the Coherence, it is used to annotate the sentence which is associated with the current sentence. The fifth column is the Coherent Form, that is, how the sentences are coherent. The last column is the Connection, which is used to specifically annotate the coherent relation between sentences.

In this paper, we use four corpora, the news corpus and application corpus mainly explain the objective facts and describe the specific things, while the prose corpus and encyclopedia corpus describe things based on the author's evaluation information. The following will use some examples in application corpus and prose corpus to compare the distribution differences of sentence group in different genres texts.

---

[3] Annotation Scheme of Chinese Texts Coherence Analysis. Tsinghua National Laboratory for Information Science and Technology.

Table 1[4]. Annotation example of application corpus.

Number	Sentence	SG	Coherence	Form	Connection
1	Wang Jianzhong is chairman and director of Weiyang Rainbow Electronic Parts Factory. 威阳彩虹电子配件厂董事长兼厂长王建中。	1	0		
2	The factory is a large-scale township enterprise, it is a professional factory producing color picture tube. 该厂是全国大型一档乡镇企业，是生产彩色显像管零部件的专业性工厂。	SG-2	0		
3	It has fixed assets of 57.4 million yuan, and can produce two series of 23 varieties of CPT supporting parts. 拥有固定资产5740万元，可生产两大系列23个品种的彩管配套零部件。		1	1	1-1
4	The annual output value of more than 1 billion, profits and taxes 19 million yuan. 年产值1个多亿，利税1900万元。		1	1	1-1
5	In 1995 the factory was rated as "Technology Demonstration Enterprise" by Township Enterprise Bureau of Shaanxi Province, passed the ISO9002 quality system certification in 1996, and has achieved the China Classification Society quality system certification. 1995年该厂被陕西省乡镇企业局评为"科技示范企业"，1996年顺利通过了ISO9002质量体系认证，并取得了中国船级社质量体系认证证书。		1	1	1-1
6	Welcome customers to contact, and agents wanted, all letters will return. 欢迎广大客户前来联系，并诚征各地代理，有函必复。	SG-2	0		
7	TEL：0910－69644471		1	X	2-3

This is an application consists of a title and two expository SGs. The two sentence groups are obviously distinguished from the themes, so the boundary of the sentence group is easier to distinguish. And most of the inter-sentence relations are contract and parallel, making the category of sentence group easy to identify. The news corpus is similar to application. Most of sentence groups are simple and clear, their themes are definite, and the graininess of sentence group is more uniform. The coherence between the sentences is more obvious. In general, the boundary and category of news corpus or application corpus are easier to identify, and the whole text structure is distinctive.

---

[4] The third column: 1 indicate the title. 3 indicate subtitle. SG-2 indicate exposition sentence group. SG-3 indicate argumentation sentence group. The fifth column: 1 indicate topic chain. X indicate other. The last column: 1-1 indicate contract. 2-3 indicate affiliation. 7-2 indicate comment. 6-1 indicate explanation.

Table 2. Annotation example of prose

Number	Sentence	SG	Coherence	Form	Connection
1	"Gang of four" finally stepped down. "四人帮"终于下台了。	SG-3	0		
2	I didn't expect them to collapse so fast. 他们垮得这样快，我没有想到。		1	1	1-1
3	This is a good lesson. 这是一个很好的教训。		1	X	7-2
4	The building on the sand will not be strong, and the power of building on lies will also not last long. 沙上建筑的楼台不会牢固，建筑在谎言上面的权势也不会长久。		1	X	6-1
5	Those who listen to lies and love to lie are punished, and I have not escaped. 爱听假话和爱说假话的人都受到了惩罚，我也没有逃掉。		1	X	1-1

The prose is not so long. It has a wide range of themes and fragmented form, and its writing style is various. The theme of the prose is very concentrated, and the clue is close. These characteristics of the prose make the boundary and category of the sentence group very difficult to distinguish. The transition between sentence groups is not obvious. And each sentence can basically find a closely related sentence to form a sentence group, making the prose rarely appear single sentence. The sentence groups categories in prose are mainly narrative, there is also argumentative SG, descriptive SG or dialogue SG, which makes the identification and annotation of sentence group is more difficult. In Figure 2, the connection is more summary and explanatory. These connections require the annotators to deeply think about what the author has expressed. Relative to the parallel relation, they need to put more energy. So the difficulty of the category identification of sentence group has increased. The encyclopedia is also similar to the prose, it uses narrative SG and argumentative SG to describe an event. The distribution of the sentence group is irregular, and its boundary and category are more difficult to identify.

Through the qualitative analysis of the above two fragments, we can draw a conclusion that the news corpus and the application corpus are very different from the prose corpus and the encyclopedia corpus in the sentence group structure, content coherence and annotation difficulty. This distinction is particularly evident in the category of sentence group and inter-sentence connection. When the inter-sentence connection changes, the category of the sentence group also changes, indicating that there is a certain relation between the inter-sentence connection and the category of sentence group. And such a relation will affect the segmentation of the sentence group and the annotation difficulty of text coherence from a certain perspective.

3   Experimental Results

3.1   Experimental Dataset

Four corpora are used in this paper. The news corpus is taken from People's Daily annotated by the Peking University, and the application, prose, encyclopedia are taken from Tsinghua Chinese Treebank [7]. The basic data can be seen in the Table 1.

Table 3. Basic data of corpus.

Corpus	News	Application	Prose	Encyclopedia
Text	147	196	25	20
Sentence	4775	3433	1990	5549
Word	111950	66820	39078	132558
Average sentence length[5]	23.44	19.46	19.63	23.89

3.2   Evaluation Method

All texts in this paper have two annotation versions, the differences between the two versions are the key to analyze the problem, so it is necessary to design the evaluation method to calculate the difference. The differences on the boundary of the sentence group are divided into inclusion and overlapping. The boundary difference evaluation methods[6] are shown below.

$$\text{macro absolute consistency} = \frac{\text{coincident boundary and identical category SGs in corpus}}{\text{The SGs in corpus}} \quad (1)$$

$$\text{macro fuzzy consistency} = \frac{\text{coincident boundary SGs + inclusion SGs}}{\text{SGs in corpus}} \quad (2)$$

$$\text{micro strict average consistency} = \left(\frac{\text{every text of CBIC SGs in version 1}}{\text{text number in version 1}} + \frac{\text{every text CBIC SGs in version 2}}{\text{text number in version 2}}\right) \div 2 \quad (3)$$

$$\text{micro fuzzy average consistency} = \left(\frac{\text{every text of CIBIC SGs in version 1}}{\text{text number in version 1}} + \frac{\text{every text CIBIC SGs in version 2}}{\text{text number in version 2}}\right) \div 2 \quad (4)$$

The difference evaluation methods of coherence, form or connection are calculated using the macro average consistency and the micro average consistency. The formulas are shown below.

---

[5] Average sentence length = Total number of words / Total number of sentences.

[6] CBIC - coincident boundary and identical category. CIBIC - coincident and inclusion boundary and identical category.

$$\text{macro average consistenc y} = (\frac{\text{consistent total}}{\text{total in version 1}} + \frac{\text{consistent total}}{\text{total in version 2}}) \div 2 \tag{5}$$

$$\text{micro average consistenc y} = (\frac{\text{every text of consistent total in version 1}}{\text{text number in version 1}} + \frac{\text{every text of consistent total in version 2}}{\text{text number in version 2}}) \div 2 \tag{6}$$

3.3 Data Analysis

We segment the sentence group according to the theme. Fay [8] pointed out that there are three main objects that influence the theme of paragraph. They are grammar, semantics and vision. And the understanding difficulty of sentence group in the different genres texts is different. Williams [9] pointed out that the structure of exposition is complicated, the theme of paragraph is more hidden, so it is more difficult to understand than narration. There is no absolute boundary in the sentence group, so it can't be considered incorrect when there is an inclusion difference. The differences on the sentence group boundary are shown in the Table 4.

Table 4. The difference data of sentence group boundary.

Corpus	Application	News	Prose	Encyclopedia
Total SGs in version 1	543	776	190	625
Total SGs in version 2	529	771	147	584
Consistent SGs	440	620	88	291
Inclusion SGs	92	128	46	211
Overlapping SGs	11	28	56	123
A/B[7] macro absolute consistency %	79.55/81.66	78.22/78.72	31.05/40.13	46.48/49.82
A/B macro fuzzy consistency %	97.97/97.92	96.39/96.36	70.52/61.91	80.28/78.93
micro absolute average consistency %	80.11	79.15	32.32	49.73
micro fuzzy average consistency %	98.47	97.84	79.16	83.22

The following is a histogram to compare the sentence group boundary differences in different genres texts.

---

[7] A: use version 1 as the benchmark. B: use version 2 as the benchmark.

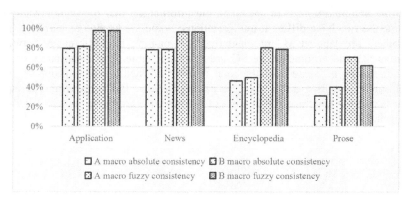

Fig. 1. Sentence group boundary differences

The Figure 1 shows that the fuzzy or absolute consistency of application is the highest, followed by the news corpus. And the corpus of the encyclopedia and prose is almost the same. The macro absolute or fuzzy consistency of the prose is the lowest, the text structure is flexible and the content is more complicated. Each annotator needs to read carefully, and their understanding of the text has a certain deviation, these deviations lead to the lower consistency. Similarly, these differences provide a reference for a variety of relations that may exist among sentences. This is also the original intention of using two annotators to annotate the corpora. In the Figure 1, the encyclopedia macro or fuzzy consistency is between the news and the prose. Analysis the structure of the encyclopedia we can conclude that it is very long, like a combination of narration and argumentation. It is not as objective as narration, and not like the prose to express the author's views and feelings. This data is echoed with the structure, confirming the assumptions that we made before.

According to the Figure 2, the distribution of the four corpora presents a significant difference. It should be noted that the dialogue SG does not exist in the application, the descriptive SG and the dialogue SG does not exist in the encyclopedia, so there is no consistency. In contrast, there are expository SG and dialogue SG in prose corpus, but the consistency rate is zero.

The Figure 2 shows that the consistency of descriptive SG and the dialogue SG in news corpus is high, the main reason is the total number is small. The vast majority of sentence groups in application are expository. And there is a small part of the narrative SG, these SGs hidden in the expository SGs, sometimes difficult to identify, so the consistency is not very high. There are many narrative SGs in the news corpus, the argumentative SG and the explanatory SG cross appear in the text, but the number is not much. The distinction among the three in the news is not obvious, although the crossings of narrative SG and argumentative SG affect the consistency, but the overall consistency is close to 80%.

In the encyclopedia corpus, the consistency of narrative SG, expository SG and argumentative SG are relatively low, indicating the complexity of the overall structure. The consistency of argumentative SG is the lowest, indicating that when the annotators need to speculate the information that the author wants to express, the two have different interpretations. Some are labeled as narrative SG, and others are labeled as argumentative SG, making the differences between narrative SG and argumentative SG are relatively large. The consistency of the prose is not high, because of the total number of each sentence group is very small, once there is a difference, consistency is low. But in general, the main factor is that the structure and content of the sentence group are more difficult to understand.

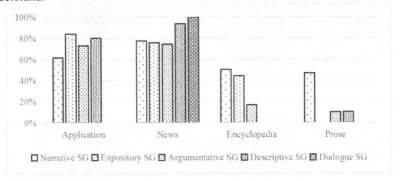

Fig. 2. Sentence group category differences

In order to analyze the structure of the sentence group from multiple angles, the differences of the coherence and the connection are calculated, as shown in Figure 3.

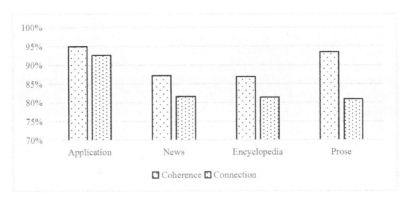

Fig. 3. Coherence and connection differences

From the Figure 3 we can see that different genres texts present a trend, that is, the coherence on the consistency is greater than the connection. Indicating that the more in-depth analysis of the inter-sentence coherence, the lower the consistency. About the coherence, due to the relative distance between the coherent sentences in the sentence group is more stable, the consistency of the application corpus and the prose corpus are higher. The distance between coherent sentences is unstable in news corpus and encyclopedia corpus, and the distance between the two coherent sentences is far, so the consistency is low. About connection, the consistency of the other three corpora is relatively low except application.

We suspect that the connection is closely related to the sentence group category, we divide the connection relation into eight categories, but in many connection relations, linguists pay more attention to the semantics and pragmatics. The coherence between the two sentences connected by semantics can be judged by its propositional content or intralingual meaning, they reflect the coherence between the external events described by the sentences. And the coherence between the two sentences connected by the pragmatics need to be judged by its inference of illocutionary meaning. Sanders analyzed the characteristics of semantics and pragmatics connection in causality. Through the analysis of small-scale corpus, it was found that narration mainly uses semantics, while the argumentation and application mainly use pragmatics. We map all kinds of connection relations to semantics and pragmatics so that we can better analyze the inner relation between coherence and sentence group category. The inner relations are shown in Figure 4.

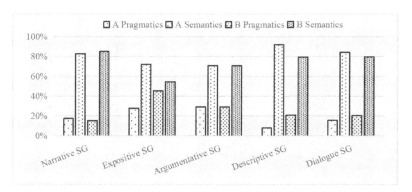

Fig. 4. The influence of connection on SG category in news corpus.

In Figure 4, the A semantics of the narrative SG, descriptive SG and argumentative SG is gradually declining, while the A pragmatics is gradually increasing. According to the consistency of the sentence group category in news corpus, when the total number of pragmatics in the sentence group increases, the consistency of the sentence group category is reduced.

From the data of the Figure 5, the pragmatics proportion of the argumentative SG is the highest, and the category consistency of the argumentative SG is the lowest, which is consistent with the situation in the news. This shows that the increase of the total number of pragmatics makes the identification of the sentence group rise more difficult, resulting in a decrease in the consistency of the sentence group category.

The prose data is shown in Figure 6, and the pragmatics of the argumentative SG and expository SG is higher than other SGs. The consistency of the two sentence groups categories are more consistent. There are few pragmatics in the descriptive SG and dialogue SG, so there is less influence on the sentence group category. The data in Figure 7 shows that the narrative SG, expository SG, and argumentative SG are similar to the news corpus.

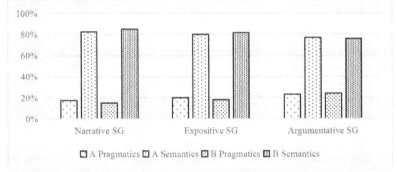

Fig. 5. The influence of connection on SG category in encyclopedia corpus.

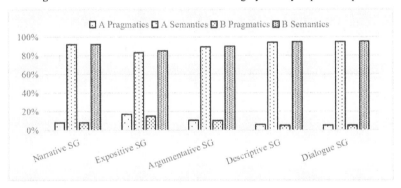

Fig. 6. The influence of connection on SG category in prose corpus.

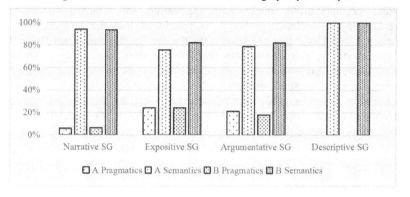

Fig. 7. The influence of connection on SG category in application corpus.

Analysis of the data in the four corpora can be obtained that the narrative SG and expository SG, argumentative SG semantics account for the vast majority, while pragmatics accounts for the fraction. However, the news and application are very different from the prose and encyclopedia in sentence group category. Depth analysis of the reasons can be found that when the pragmatics and semantics appear together in the sentence group, the sentence group category consistency has declined. Most of this situation appears in the expository SG and the argumentative SG. For example, when the inter-sentence connection in the sentence group is a structure of summary + multiple contract relation or parallel relation, the sentence group category is the expository SG or argumentative SG. But when the connections in the sentence group are all contract relation or parallel relation, the sentence group category is generally narration. Although the two sentence groups have only one difference in the total number of inter-sentence connection, the difficulty of recognition in the sentence group is very different, which indicates that the recognition of the sentence group with the pragmatics is more difficult.

In summary, the pragmatics and semantics have a certain influence on the difficulty analysis of the sentence group. When the total number of pragmatics in the sentence group increases, the difficulty of identifying the sentence group category increases. This also shows that the argumentative SG and the expository SG are more difficult to identify than the narrative SG. This is consistent with the conclusion that the consistency of the argumentative SG and the expository SG are relatively low.

4 Conclusion and Future Work

The segmentation of the sentence group boundary and the identification of its category play a vital role in the analysis of text coherence, and the distribution of text coherence of different genres texts is also very different. In this paper, we use narration, argumentative, prose and application to compare the various differences of the sentence group. It is concluded that the boundary of the conclusion group has a great relation with the text genre, and when the text is mostly based on the objective information, the boundary consistency of sentence group is relatively high, such as news corpus and application corpus. And when the annotator need to speculate the author's implication in text, the boundary consistency of sentence group is relatively low, such as the prose corpus and encyclopedia corpus. For the sentence group category, through the relation between the inter-sentence connection and sentence group category, we found that when the pragmatics relation occurs in the sentence group, the consistency of the sentence group category decreases. And the pragmatics relation generally appears in the exposition sentence group and argumentation sentence group. Finally we analyze the distribution of pragmatics and semantics in sentence group category of different genres texts, which confirms the close relation between the inter-sentence connection and the sentence group category.

The final experimental results show that the distribution of the consistency of sentence group in different genres texts is quite different. The determination of the sentence group boundary needs to be considered in many ways, and its graininess is also flexible. The recognition of the category is inseparable from the inter-sentence connection, and the coherent distribution of the sentence group in different genres texts is different. The results of the above researches on the sentence group provide important clues for the sentence group automatic segmentation, and provide a reference for the automatic identification of the sentence group category, which provides a new idea for the text coherence analysis.

References

1. Weizhang Wu, Xiaolin Tian (2000) Chinese Sentence Group [M]. Beijing: Commercial Publishers. (in Chinese)
2. De Beaugrande R, Dressler W U. Introduction to Text Linguistics [J]. Rocky Mountain Review of Language & Literature, 1981:334.
3. Yingtian Wu. Article Structure [M]. Renmin University of China Publishers, 1989. (in Chinese)
4. Sanders T. Semantics and pragmatics sources of coherence: On the categorization of coherence relations in context [J]. Text processes, 1997, 24(1): 119-147.
5. Longacre, R. E. 2003 Holistc Text Linguistics [A]. SIL Electronic Working Papers 2003-2004.
6. Wangqi Jiang. Discourse Structure. [J]. contemporary rhetoric, 2012 (4): 10-19. (in Chinese)
7. Qiang ZHOU. Annotation Scheme for Chinese Treebank [J]. Journal of Chinese Information Processing. 18(4), 1-8. (in Chinese)

8. Williams J P. Instruction in Reading Comprehension for Primary-Grade Students [J]. The Journal of Special Education, 2005, 39(1):6-18.
9. Fay K, Whaley S. Becoming One Community: Reading and Writing with English Language Learners [J]. Stenhouse Publishers, 2004.

The Construction and Application of The Legal Corpus

Huiting Luo and Shan Wang*

The Education University of Hong Kong, Hong Kong
eduhk2018@gmail.com

Abstract: With the development of Teaching Chinese as an International Language and the professionalization trend of Chinese learning, legal Chinese becomes more and more important. To support the legal Chinese teaching and provide Chinese learners, Chinese teachers and other legal workers with authentic data, this paper constructs a legal corpus, which contains 35 legal texts of Mainland China. This study automatically segments the texts into words and manually checks all the segmentation results. Besides, through using the quantitative and qualitative analysis methods, this paper analyzes the common vocabulary of legal Chinese, analyzes the features of legal Chinese, compares the differences between the common vocabulary of legal Chinese and that of the international Chinese teaching, and compares the differences of the common meaning between legal Chinese words and common words in international Chinese vocabulary syllabus. This study also makes reference to the classification of Chinese word level in *The Syllabus of Chinese Vocabulary and Characters Levels* [18] to classify the words in the legal corpus and explores the application of this corpus in international Chinese teaching. This study finds that there are many differences between legal Chinese and general Chinese, in terms of the common vocabulary and the common meaning of words. So, it can be seen that the legal vocabulary has particularity in the teaching. We cannot directly utilize the existing vocabulary teaching methods to the teaching of legal Chinese vocabulary. Therefore, this paper puts forward several solutions for solving this problem.

Keywords: the legal corpus, the legal language, legal vocabulary, teaching Chinese as an international language

1   Introduction

In recent years, Teaching Chinese as an International Language (it is abbreviated as TCIL hereinafter) shows the trend of professionalization [1]. The status of professional Chinese teaching gradually increases. In accordance with this trend, Chinese learners' demands for legal Chinese learning are gradually highlighted. According to a survey, as early as in 2006 there are more than three thousand foreign students studying law in China [2]. However,

Y. Wu et al. (Eds.): CLSW 2017, LNAI 10709, pp. 448–467, 2018.
https://doi.org/10.1007/978-3-319-73573-3_41

there are few studies on legal Chinese teaching and most of them are directed at native law students. There are only two articles in the study of legal Chinese teaching in the field of international Chinese teaching, one is *Course Design and Textbook Writing for Chinese learning beginner of American legal profession* [3], and the other one is *A Study of Legal Vocabulary in Teaching Chinese as a Foreign Language* [4]. The first article mainly elaborates on the status of legal Chinese courses, analyzing the characteristics and learning needs of Chinese learners in the American legal circle through questionnaires. It designs the legal Chinese courses and teaching materials based on these characteristics and learning needs, but it does not specifically analyze the characteristics of legal Chinese, or point out what problems the teachers should pay attention to in the legal Chinese teaching process. The second article finds out the legal Chinese vocabulary from *The Graded Chinese Syllabics Characters and Words for The Application of Teaching Chinese to The Speakers of Other Language (National Standard • Application and Interpretation)*[5] by manual checking, classifies these legal vocabularies according to their meaning, and compares the differences of the words' meaning between modern Chinese dictionary and legal Chinese [4], but does not analyze the legal Chinese words which are not in *The Graded Chinese Syllabics Characters and Words for The Application of Teaching Chinese to The Speakers of Other Language (National Standard • Application and Interpretation)*[5], so its findings can only be applied to general Chinese vocabulary teaching.

Due to the increasing needs of legal Chinese learning, this study constructs a legal corpus for international Chinese teaching. Legal language includes legislative language and judicial language, in which the legislative language is the language used in the normative legal texts, while the judicial language refers to the language used by the legal workers during the enforcement process according to the legal requirements [6]. Besides, legal practice, including judicial practice, is based on normative legal texts, so legislative language is the focus of legal language. Therefore, this study selects 35 typical legal texts in Mainland China and adopts "man-machine combination" approach. That is, we first utilize computer automatic word segmentation and then manually check and correct the results. After that, we calculate the word frequency in this corpus and order them according to their frequency, to get the common vocabulary of legal Chinese. At the same time, the characteristics of the legal language are analyzed, the differences between the common vocabulary of legal Chinese and the vocabulary of the international Chinese teaching are compared, and the differences between the common meaning of legal vocabulary and that of general Chinese are also compared. This paper draws the key points, difficulties and countermeasures of legal Chinese teaching, and the findings can be applied not only to general Chinese teaching, but also to the professional legal Chinese teaching. In addition, in order to meet the needs of international legal Chinese learning, the findings of this paper can also provide references for the legal workers of other fields.

2   Literature Review

The studies on legal corpora in China can be classified into three types according to the purpose of the research. (1) The principles, methods and difficulties of constructing the legal corpus. This type of study includes: *The Construction of Corpus in the Study of Legal Linguistics* [7], *Compilation of Forensic Corpus* [8], *A Review of Corpus-based Legal Languages Studies* [9]. They only put forward the construction idea, but did not establish the real corpus.

(2) Construct the parallel corpus which is used for legal language translation. This type of study includes: *Construction of Parallel Corpus of China's Legal Documents: Philosophy, Processes and Functions* [10], *A Corpus Basic Study of Modal Verbs in Chinese Legislative Language* [11]. In the first study, the Parallel Corpus of China's Legal Documents was released, which is a collection of laws and regulations, but it does not segment the words in the documents, so it cannot intuitively reflect the common vocabulary of legal Chinese. In the second study, both the CLR (China Law Retrieval System) and SLD (UK Statute Law Database) corpus are not published, and they are English texts, which can only be applied in very few areas.

(3) Construct the legal corpus which can be applied in all types of legal practice activities. This type of study includes: *The Construction of the First "Legal Chinese Corpus" in China* [12], *Information-Based legal corpus and Its Use in Legal Discourse Analysis* [13]. Although they mention how the corpus can be applied in legal Chinese learning, it is not entirely applicable to international legal Chinese teaching. For example, the corpus constructed in the first study is still under construction, and its main application is to retrieve discourse information [13]. The teaching role mentioned in this study mainly aims at Chinese native law major or translation major students, and thus it is not fully applicable to Chinese learners.

To solve the problems in the existing research, this study takes the following measures: (1) Construct a legal corpus; (2) In order to intuitively reflect the common vocabulary in legal Chinese, this study segments the words in the documents and orders the words according to their frequency; (3) All the texts selected in this study are the original texts of 35 laws in Mainland China, in which the language is Chinese, and the corpus can be used as a reference for Chinese learners, Chinese native law major or translation major students, legal workers and staff working in other relevant fields, and thus it can be applied in more areas.

3   Construction Procedures of The Legal Corpus

3.1   Select Documents for the Legal Corpus

The constitution and other laws of Mainland China can be classified into seven categories according to the classification criteria set up by The National People's Congress of the People's Republic of China. The categories include: constitution, administrative law, criminal law, civil and commercial law, economic law, social law and procedural law [14]. The legal corpus selected in this study is broadly related to the above seven categories, and all the legal texts are the most important laws of the above seven categories referring to the *National Judicial Examination Outline* [15] and the textbooks of law major. All the texts are the latest revision of above categories [16], as shown in Table 1.

Table 1. 35 legal texts in The Legal Corpus

Categories	The name of legal documents	First time of enactment	Latest release date
Constitution	Constitution of the People's Republic of China (中华人民共和国宪法)	1982	2004
Administrative Law	Law of The People's Republic of China on Administrative Penalty (中华人民共和国行政处罚法)	1996	2009
	Administrative License Law of the People's Republic of China (中华人民共和国行政许可法)	2003	–[1]
	Administrative Reconsideration Law of the People's Republic of China (中华人民共和国行政复议法)	1999	2009
	Administrative Supervision Law of the People's Republic of China (中华人民共和国行政监察法)	1997	2010
Criminal Law	Criminal Law of the People's Republic of China (中华人民共和国刑法)	1979	2015
Civil and Commercial Law	General Principles of the Civil Law of the People's Republic of China (中华人民共和国民法通则)	1986	2009
	Contract Law of the People's Republic of China (中华人民共和国合同法)	1999	–
	Property Law of the People's Republic of China (中华人民共和国物权法)	2007	–
	Marriage Law of the People's Republic of China (中华人民共和国婚姻法)	1980	2001
	Law of Succession of the People's Republic of China (中华人民共和国继承法)	1985	–

---

[1] The symbol"-" in Table 1 means that there are not yet an updated version since the first release.

	Company Law of the People's Republic of China (中华人民共和国公司法)	1993	2013
	Enterprise Bankruptcy Law of the People's Republic of China (中华人民共和国企业破产法)	2006	–
	Negotiable Instruments Law of the People's Republic of China (中华人民共和国票据法)	1995	2004
	Maritime Law of the People's Republic of China (中华人民共和国海商法)	1992	–
	Insurance Law of the People's Republic of China (中华人民共和国保险法)	1995	2015
	Copyright Law of the People's Republic of China (中华人民共和国著作权法)	1990	2010
	Patent Law of the People's Republic of China (中华人民共和国专利法)	1984	2008
	Trademark Law of the People's Republic of China (中华人民共和国商标法)	1982	2013
Economic Law	Law of the People's Republic of China on the Protection of Consumer Rights and Interests (中华人民共和国消费者权益保护法)	1993	2013
	Product Quality Law of the People's Republic of China (中华人民共和国产品质量法)	1993	2009
	Individual Income Tax Law of the People's Republic of China (中华人民共和国个人所得税法)	1980	2011
	Enterprise Income Tax Law of the People's Republic of China (中华人民共和国企业所得税法)	2007	–
	Land Administration Law of the People's Republic of China (中华人民共和国土地管理法)	1986	2004
	Urban Real Estate Administration Law of the People's Republic of China (中华人民共和国城市房地产管理法)	1994	2009
	Environmental Protection Law of the People's Republic of China (中华人民共和国环境保护法)	1989	2014
	Anti-Unfair Competition Law of the People's Republic of China (中华人民共和国反不正当竞争法)	1993	–

	Auction Law of the People's Republic of China (中华人民共和国拍卖法)	1996	2015
	The Bidding Law of the People's Republic of China (中华人民共和国招标投标法)	1999	–
	Law of the People's Republic of China on Commercial Banks (中华人民共和国商业银行法)	1995	2015
	Banking Supervision Law of the People's Republic of China (中华人民共和国银行业监督管理法)	2003	2006
Social Law	Labor Law of the People's Republic of China (中华人民共和国劳动法)	1994	2009
Procedural Law	Administrative Litigation Law of the People's Republic of China (中华人民共和国行政诉讼法)	1989	2014
	Criminal Procedure Law of the People's Republic of China (中华人民共和国刑事诉讼法)	1979	2012
	Civil Procedure Law of the People's Republic of China (中华人民共和国民事诉讼法)	1991	2012

The legal texts selected in this study have the following characteristics:

(1) They are normative. The legal documents written or utilized in the legal practice must comply with the law texts, and the legal language used in the inferior legislation should be similar to that in the superior legislation. Therefore, the legal texts enacted or passed by the National People's Representative Meeting are the "source" of legal language [12], which are the most important and most typical embodiment of legal language, and also the standard specification of legal language. Thus, this study chooses the legal texts which are enacted or passed by the National People's Representative Meeting.

(2) They are accurate. Legal language includes legislative language and judicial language. This study chooses legislative language as the source of data, because the standardization of legislative language is critical to the development of legalization. China is still in the legal society construction process, so the judicial language still has some non-standard terms. For example, some legal staff use non-standard simplified characters, illegible writing in the legal documents, and some judicial staff use their dialects in the courts [17]. Considering the problems above, all the corpus in this study is taken from legal texts, reflecting the character-istics of legislative language.

(3) They are balanced. These texts widely involve various types of legal texts. This study at least selects one legal text in each legal category, and thus the seven legal categories have covered all aspects of the Mainland Chinese legal system.

(4) They are representative. First, all the selected law texts are enacted or passed by the National People's Representative Meeting and are the latest revision. They are used across

the country. Second, all the selected law texts are the most important laws in China and can reflect the most typical embodiment of legal language. Third, this study combines the comprehensive and representative corpus sampling principles. The corpus includes all the legal texts of the constitution category and criminal law category, while selects the representative legal texts in other five categories. The selection criteria refers to the key legal texts listed in the outline of judicial examination and the legal textbooks. For example, in the administrative law category, this study selects *Law of The People's Republic of China on Administrative Penalty, Administrative License Law of the People's Republic of China, Administrative Reconsideration Law of the People's Republic of China* and *Administrative Supervision Law of the People's Republic of China* as the texts, referring to the legal textbook *Administrative Law and Administrative Litigation Law*, which is published by Peking University Press and High Education Press [18]. The selected texts cover the laws most often executed by the government, and involve the executive behaviors, which have great influence on the Chinese people's life.

(5)   They are for specialized use. This study selects the legal texts of Mainland China as corpus. The word segment processing and manual correction in the corpus construction process are based on the legal vocabulary form, collocation and semantics. For example, 法人 *fǎrén* 'corporation' is rarely used in general Chinese, but it is a technical term in legal Chinese, so it is treated as a word in this corpus. The frequency of words listed in the corpus is only based on the frequency in the corpus, rather than the frequency in general Chinese, so this corpus is dedicated to legal language research, learning and application.

3.2   Word Segment Processing and Manual Correction

This corpus uses ICTCLAS, automatic word segmentation software developed by the Institute of Computing Technology Chinese Academy of Sciences, to segment the words in the legal texts. Based on the principle of not contrary to the original meaning of the legal texts, and keep the word segmentation criteria consistent, this study corrects the segmentation results by manual work. In general, ICTCLAS correctly segments the words, however, there are also many errors, and thus ICTCLAS is not entirely applicable to legal Chinese texts, and word segmentation software aiming at legal Chinese should be developed in the future. The segmentation errors include following types.

(1)   Some of the segmentation units (分词单位) are sometimes inconsistently divided as a whole or multiple words. This type of error mainly occurs in the division of noun phrases, like 人民检察院 *rénmínjiǎncháyuàn* 'People's Procuratorate', 诈骗罪 *zhàpiànzuì* 'crime of fraud', 申请人 *shēnqǐng rén* 'proposer' and so on. All these phrases are the common phrases in legal texts, and contain more than two words. In the word segmentation results, these phrases sometimes are divided into multiple words. For example, divide the 人民检察院 *rénmínjiǎncháyuàn* 'People's Procuratorate' into 人民 *rénmín* 'people' and 检察院 *jiǎncháyuàn* 'procuratorate', but sometimes they are regarded as a whole and no further seg-

mentation. This paper corrects this type of errors based on the meaning, the commonness, and the major segmentation results of this segmentation unit, as well as the segmentation results of other similar segmentation units.

(2)   The segmentation units containing numbers and quantifiers are sometimes divided as a whole, while sometimes are divided into two words. For example, the phrase 十五日 *shíwŭ rì* 'fifteen days/ the 15th', sometimes is divided into 十五 *shíwŭ* 'fifteen' and 日 *rì* 'day', while sometimes it is regarded as a whole. After comprehensively analyzing the word segmentation results of such time words, this paper divides the time words as a whole, when such words are used as dates. For example, we segment 1999年12月5日 *1999 nián 12 yuè 5 rì* 'December the 25th, 1999' into 1999年 *nián* 'year', 12月 *yuè* 'month' and 25日 *rì* 'day', but in the phrase 请求之日起十五日内 *qǐngqiú zhī rì qǐ shíwŭ rì nèi* 'within fifteen days from the date of the request', we segment 十五日 *shíwŭ rì* 'fifteen days' into 十五 *shíwŭ* 'fifteen' and 日 *rì* 'day' . Other similar classifier phrases such as 两个 *liǎng gè* 'two' and 第三十六条 *dì sānshíliù tiáo* 'article 36 of the law', we segment them into 两 *liǎng* 'two', 个 *gè* 'Chinese measure word' and 第三十六 *dì sānshíliù* 'the 36th', 条 *tiáo* 'Chinese measure word' .

(3)   Some word segmentation results change the original meaning, because the character in the word can also combine into another word or phrase with other characters next to the word, and it leads to a matching error of the software. For example, the character 行 *xíng* in the phrase 执行人 *zhíxíngrén* 'executor' can combine with 执 *zhí* to be a word 执行 *zhíxíng* 'execute', while it can also combine with 人 *rén* to be a word 行人 *xíngrén* 'pedestrian', so the software sometimes divides 执行人 *zhíxíngrén* 'executor' into 执行 *zhíxíng* 'execute' and 人 *rén* 'person' , while sometimes divides it into 执 *zhí* 'hold' and 行人 *xíngrén* 'pedestrian', which changes the original meaning. There are other similar errors in the segmentation results such as segmenting 收款人名称 *shōukuǎnrén míngchēng* 'The name of the payee' into 收款 *shōukuǎn* 'take the money', 人名 *rénmíng* 'person's name' and 称*chēng* 'weigh'. To correct this kind of errors, we consider the meaning of the original, rather than the major segmentation results.

3.3 The Size of The Legal Corpus

The legal corpus includes a total of 35 legal texts, of which 3 are procedural and 32 are substantive. It contains a total of 460,451 characters (including Arabic numerals and Chinese characters; excluding punctuations and spaces). After the segmentation and manual checking processing, the corpus contains 253,287 tokens (the total number of words) and 6,411 types of word (only count the repeated words once). The words mentioned here can be words or morphemes, but do not contain punctuations and spaces. The number of words' types and its proportion corresponding to each word frequency category are shown in Table 2.

Table 2. The number of words' types corresponding to each word frequency

Word Frequency	The Number of Word's Types	Percentage
>100	453	7.066%
51-100	347	5.413%
11-50	1311	20.449%
6-10	846	13.196%
5	274	4.274%
4	339	5.288%
3	501	7.815%
2	862	13.446%
1	1478	23.054%
Total	6411	100.000%

4   The Application of The Legal Corpus in TCIL

4.1   Divide the Frequency Level of the Words in The Legal Corpus

The Syllabus of Chinese Vocabulary and Characters' Levels (it is abbreviated as SCVCL hereinafter), which is published by the Examination Center of The National Chinese Proficiency Test Committee, is compiled for general Chinese teaching, the preparation of general Chinese teaching materials, general Chinese proficiency assessment and so on [19]. In order to analyze whether SCVCL is applicable to the legal Chinese teaching, and to analyze the characteristics of legal Chinese vocabulary, this paper divides the frequency level of the words in the corpus (the level is named according to the frequency), referring to the proportion of the number of words in each frequency level of SCVCL and the actual frequency of each word in the corpus. According to the actual frequency of the word frequency in the legal corpus and avoiding the error of dividing the word with same frequency into different frequency levels, we make an adjustment to the dividing proportion. After the level division, we compare the words in the corpus and the words in SCVCL.

In general, it is accidental when the words with low frequency appear in a large-scale corpus, and thus these words are not representative in such a corpus. However, in the legal corpus, though some words have very low frequency, they show that the legal texts have the characteristics of specialty. Some social phenomena are usually regulated by only one or very few articles. For example, the legal provision about the description of Chinese national emblem, appears only in Article 137 of the Constitution of the People's Republic of China, so the word 齿轮 *chǐlún* 'gear' which is used for descripting the national emblem, appears only once in this corpus. Similarly, the legal provision about the description of the elements of the trademark is only found in Article 8 of the Trademark Law of the People's Republic of China, so the word 颜色 *yánsè* 'color' which is one of the trademark elements, only presents once in this corpus. After the study of the low frequency words, we find it necessary to have them in when dividing their levels, as shown in Table 3 below.

Table 3. The word frequency level of the legal corpus with reference to SCVCL

SCVCL			The Legal Corpus				
Level	The number of words	Proportion（%）	Level	The number of words	Ranking label（from high frequency to low frequency）	Proportion（%）	The lowest frequency
The first level	1033	11.709%	High frequency	754	1st -754th	11.761%	56
The second level	2018	22.874%	Medium frequency	1357	755th -2111st	21.166%	11
The third level	2202	24.960%	Low frequency	1960	2112nd-4071st	30.572%	3
The forth level	3569	40.455%	Extreme low fre-	2340	4072nd-6411st	36.499%	1

			quency				
Total	8822	—	Total	6411	—	—	—

4.2   The Differences Between Legal Vocabulary and SCVCL

There are 8,822 word tokens and 8,606 word types in SCVCL. Comparing the word types in the legal corpus and SCVCL, this study classifies all the words in the legal corpus and SCVCL into 3 categories: common vocabulary, legal corpus unique vocabulary and SCVCL unique vocabulary. Common words: a total of 2,946 words both appear in the legal corpus and SCVCL; legal corpus unique words: a total of 3,465 words are the words in legal corpus but not in SCVCL; and SCVCL unique vocabulary: a total of 5,660 words are the words in SCVCL but not in the legal corpus.

Table 4. The differences between the legal word types and SCVCL word types

Categories	The number of word types
Common words	2946
The Legal Corpus unique vocabulary	3465
SCVCL unique vocabulary	5660

(1)   The unique vocabulary in the Legal Corpus

There are a large number of words in the legal texts, which do not belong to SCVCL. As shown in Table 5, there are 177 words in the high frequency, 638 words in the medium frequency, 1,120 words in the low frequency, and 1,530 words in the extreme low frequency in the legal corpus. The number of legal corpus unique words types belonging to the high and medium frequency is 815, accounting for all word types in the high and medium frequency of more than 38%.

The top six unique words which with the highest frequency are: 人民法院 *rénmínfǎyuàn* 'court' (repeat 1,266 times in the legal corpus), 本法 *běn fǎ* 'this law' (repeats 955 times in the legal corpus), 有期徒刑 *yǒuqítúxíng* 'set term of imprisonment' (repeats 843 times in the legal corpus) , 依法 *yīfǎ* 'according to law' (repeats 770 times in the legal corpus), 约定 *yuēdìng* 'agreement' (repeats 671 times in the legal corpus) and 罚金 *fájīn* 'fine' (repeats 488 times in the legal corpus).

According to different classification criteria, unique vocabulary in the legal corpus has the following classifications:

a)   According to the different sources of the words, unique words in the legal corpus can be divided into legal terms and legal basic words. Legal terms refer to the words having special legal meanings, and legal basic words are the words in legal fields which are borrowed from general Chinese [20]. The legal terms with high frequency include 罚金 *fájīn* 'fine', 送达 *sòngdá* 'service', and so on. The legal basic words with high frequency include

委员会 *wěiyuánhuì* 'committee', 全国*quánguó* 'the whole country', 责令 *zélìng* 'instruct', and so on.

b)   According to the different parts of speech, unique words in the legal corpus can be divided into nominals, predicates and numerals. The nominals with high frequency include 人民法院 *rénmínfǎyuàn* 'court', 罚金*fájīn* 'fine', 标的 *biāodì* 'object', and so on. The predicates with high frequency include 撤销 *chèxiāo* 'cancel', 没收 *mòshōu* 'confiscate', 责令*zélìng* 'instruct', and so on.

Table 5. The number and proportion of legal corpus unique words in each frequency level

All word types in The Legal Corpus			Unique words in The Legal Corpus	
Frequency level	Amount	Ranking label（from high frequency to low frequency）	Amount	Proportion （%）
High frequency	754	1st -754th	177	23.475%
Medium frequency	1357	755th -2111st	638	47.015%
Low frequency	1960	2112nd-4071st	1120	57.143%
Extreme low frequency	2340	4072nd-6411st	1530	65.385%
Total	6411	—	3465	54.048%

(2) Common vocabulary

The existence of common words indicates that there are similarities between the legal corpus and SCVCL, but there are still some frequency differences between their common words. There are 238 words which within the high frequency level of the legal corpus, in the third or fourth frequency level of SCVCL, accounting for more than 31% of all high frequency words in the legal corpus.

According to different classification criteria, common vocabulary has the following classifications:

a)   According to the different sources of the word, the unique words in the legal corpus can be divided into legal terms and legal basic words. The legal terms with high frequency include 当事人 *dāngshìrén* 'party', 民事 *mínshì* 'civil', and so on. The legal basic words with high frequency include 规定 *guīdìng* 'regulations', 和 *hé* 'and', 公司 *gōngsī* 'company', and so on.

b)   According to the different parts of speech, the common vocabulary of the legal corpus and SCVCL can be divided into nominals, predicates, numerals, measure words, adverbs and function words. The nominals with high frequency include 法律 *fǎlǜ* 'law', 财产 *cáichǎn* 'property', 机构 *jīgòu* 'institution', and so on. The predicates with high frequency include 管理 *guǎnlǐ* 'manage', 申请 *shēnqǐng* 'apply' , 执行 *zhíxíng* 'execute', and so on. The numerals with high frequency include 二 *èr* 'two', 三 *sān* 'three', 十 *shí* 'ten', and so on. The measure words with high frequency include 条 *tiáo* 'used for articles', 张 *zhāng* 'piece', 元 *yuán* 'measure word used for money', and so on. The function words with high frequency include 的 *de* 'auxiliary word, usually be used after attribute', 和 *hé* 'and', 但 *dàn* 'but', and so on.

c)   Comparing the frequency level of the words in the legal corpus and that in SCVCL, the words can be classified into frequency matched words and frequency unmatched words. Frequency matched words refer to the common words, which conform to the rule that if it is in the high frequency level of the legal corpus then it is also in the first frequency level of SCVCL; if it is in the medium frequency level of the legal corpus then it is also in the second frequency level of SCVCL; if it is in the low frequency level of the legal corpus then it is also in the third frequency level of SCVCL; if it is in the extreme low frequency level of the legal corpus then it is also in the fourth frequency level of SCVCL. By contrast, frequency unmatched words refer to the common words which do not conform to the rule above.

Frequency matched words include 的 *de* 'auxiliary word, usually be used after attribute', 条 *tiáo* 'measure word used for articles', 或者 *huòzhě* 'or', 人 *rén* 'person', and so on. Frequency unmatched words include 应当 *yīngdāng* 'should' (a high frequency word in the legal corpus, but in the second frequency level of SCVCL), 权 *quán* 'power' (a high frequency word in the legal corpus, but in the fourth frequency level of SCVCL）, 其 *qí* 'pronoun' (high frequency word in the legal corpus, but in the third frequency level of SCVCL).

To sum up, SCVCL is not applicable to the legal Chinese teaching. If we only take SCVCL vocabulary as a reference, the students will encounter a lot of words that have not been learned, while reading legal provisions or other legal documents. Some of the high frequency words in the legal texts may also be overlooked due to their low frequency level in SCVCL, leading to the reduction of students' reading effect.

5   The Linguistic Features of the Legal Corpus

The linguistic features of this legal corpus are embodied in two aspects: one is that it is particular in comparison with foreign legal languages other than Chinese, and the other is that it also has particularity compared with general Chinese.

(1) Compared to foreign legal languages, the particularity of legal Chinese is embodied in the following areas:

a)   Legal Chinese is different from foreign legal languages, because different country has different social phenomena and social problems. For example, according to the legal corpus, 计划生育 *jìhuàshēngyù* 'birth control' repeats 7 times in the Constitution of the People's Republic of China and Marriage Law of the People's Republic of China. This word appears due to China's specific restrictions on population policy, which is set up to solve the large population problem, and there is no corresponding word in foreign laws.

b)   Legal Chinese is different from foreign legal languages, because the guidance concept is different. For example, 社会主义 *shèhuìzhǔyì* 'social democracy' repeats 78 times and 马克思列宁主义 *MǎKèSī LièNíng zhǔyì* 'Marxism-Leninism' repeats 2 times in the legal corpus. These words reflect that China carries out the spirit of socialism and Marxism-Leninism during the enactment of law, while the legal texts of Anglo-American legal system will not use these words.

c)   Legal Chinese is different from foreign legal languages, because the legal terms are different. For example, China generally names the legal texts that are passed by the National People's Congress 法 *fǎ* 'Law', while the Anglo-American law system generally uses the "Act" to name the legal texts enacted by the parliament, and 法*fǎ* 'Law' refers to all normative documents with legal effect in the Anglo-American laws [21].

(2)   Compared to general Chinese, the particularity of legal Chinese is embodied in the following areas:

Compared to general Chinese, the legal Chinese has the characteristics of appropriateness, generality, ambiguity and standardization [22]. In addition, it is also concrete.

a)   Legal Chinese must be appropriate, because the legal texts are the references to solve the disputes. They are required to be directly quoted by judicial and administrative workers, so as to achieve social justice and to avoid personal discretion as far as possible. For example, the corpus contains a large number of words such as 应当 *yīngdāng* 'should', 必须 *bìxū* 'must', and so on, with clear direction and the command tone, requiring the judicial and administrative personnel that must be in strict accordance with the law when dealing with the cases.

b)   Legal Chinese sometimes is ambiguous, due to the society's evolving reality and the complexity of social phenomena. Once the law text has been enacted and implemented, it should remain relatively constant for a certain period of time. It must not be often changed. Without such stability, it will undermine the seriousness and authority of the law [23]. There are also certain ambiguous words in the legal corpus, such as the word 有关 *yǒuguān* 'about' which repeats 789 times. It usually appears in the last of the clauses, to compensate for the shortcomings of the precise language that cannot mention all the complex social phenomena.

c)   In the book *New Theory of Legal Linguistics*, the concept of generality is basically related to the concept of ambiguity [22]. But in our opinion, generality is different from ambiguity. The purpose of generalization is to streamline the legal chapter, and reduce costs. It is generally reflected by short legal terms. There are many legal terms used for generalization in the legal corpus, such as 有期徒刑 *yǒuqítúxíng* 'set term of imprisonment' , 债务人 *zhàiwùrén* 'obligor', and 法人 *fǎrén* 'corporation'.

d)   In order to provide legal workers with clear guidelines, the legal language is required to be concrete. There are a large number of numeral words in the legal corpus, such as 一 *yī* 'one', 五 *wǔ* 'five'; there are many measure words such as 年 *nián* 'year', 日 *rì* 'day' following the numeral, to precisely restrict the behavior times and amounts.

e)   The national laws are standardized. From the macro perspective, legal Chinese's standardization reflects that the legal documents written or utilized in the legal practice must comply with the law texts and the legal language used in the inferior legislation, which should be similar to that in the superior legislation. From the micro perspective, in the same legal provisions, the concepts and expressions should be consistent, and cannot change them with synonyms, so as to ensure the seriousness of the law. From the words in the legal corpus, we can see the legal texts generally use only one word when expressing the same meaning. For example, the word 应当 *yīngdāng* 'should' repeats 2,911 times in the legal corpus, while its synonym words 应该 *yīnggāi* 'have to' and 理应 *lǐyīng* 'ought to' are not used even once.

It is important to note that the appropriateness does not contradict with ambiguity, because appropriateness is not equal to accuracy, while it requires the legal texts to be accurate when it should be accurate and to be ambiguous when it should be ambiguous [22]. It is not contradictory between generality and being concrete either, because the legal texts are intended to give legal practitioners a clear guideline, and thus the generalized words are the generalization of the relevant concepts, while the words about specific case-handling are concrete.

6   Difficulties and measures in Legal Vocabulary Teaching

With the continuous development of the globalization process, the international legal business is increasing day by day, and foreign students' demands for legal Chinese teaching are also increasing. Two textbooks named *Legal Chinese - Commercial Orientation* [24] and *Chinese Legal Chinese Course* [25] are published in China, which aim at the legal Chinese teaching, and there are a number of universities offering legal Chinese courses [3]. For the legal Chinese learners, the main learning objective is to understand the Chinese legal provisions and Chinese legal instruments, and vocabulary mastery is one of the important factors affecting the reading effect, so legal vocabulary teaching is the key of legal Chinese teaching. On the other hand, because China is in the process of legalization, the high frequency of legal vocabulary use, that is, the trend of legal vocabulary's being daily used is an important feature of the times [4]. According to the statistics of this study, the common words account for more than 34% of the total number of SCVCL, which contain some legal terms. It can be seen that legal vocabulary teaching is necessary for both general Chinese teaching and legal Chinese teaching.

Form the procedure and the achievement of the construction of the legal corpus, targeting at the difficulties in legal vocabulary teaching, this paper gets the following inspiring measures.

(1)   There are a large number of unique words in the legal texts, and many high frequency words in the legal corpus are only the third or fourth frequency level words of SCVCL, increasing the difficulty of the legal texts' reading. Therefore, in the process of teaching Chinese, it is not enough to master the common vocabulary of general Chinese, and SCVCL is not applicable to the legal Chinese teaching. The compilers of Teaching materials and Chinese teachers should refer to the vocabulary and frequency of the legal corpus to confirm the key of vocabulary teaching or set up an appropriate vocabulary outline, considering different curriculum design and students' learning purposes.

(2)   In the process of legal texts reading, word segmentation is a difficult problem. For Chinese learners, word segmentation is always a difficult problem during reading the articles written even in general Chinese. In Chinese reading, students often have the problem of words segmentation and meaning understanding, which lead to the reduction of the reading speed and the misunderstanding of the article [26]. During the construction of the legal corpus, the word segmentation result which is produced by the automatic word segmentation software has many segmentation errors, due to the reason that some Chinese characters in the word or phrase can also be combined into another words or phrases with other characters next to the word. For example, the original meaning of the phrase 活动物 *huó dòngwù* 'live animal' in the Maritime Law of the People's Republic of China is live animal, so we divide the phrase into 活 *huó* 'live', 动物 *dòngwù* 'animal' in the legal corpus, but if the students mistakenly divide this phrase into 活动 *huódòng* 'active', 物 *wù* 'things', then they will misunderstand the meaning of the phrase, so we can see the difficulty of the word segmentation in the legal texts. In this regard, Chinese teachers should take the words as the teaching unit, and they can refer to the word frequency order in the legal corpus, to determine the teaching focus and teaching order, so that the students will be familiar with the common legal vocabulary.

(3)   There are a large number of legal terms, and the meaning of some words is different with that in the daily use, which increases the difficulty of understanding the legal text. For legal terms, Chinese learners may misunderstand the meaning of words by simply combining the meaning of Chinese characters. For the legal basic words, Chinese learners may misunderstand the words due to the meaning of common use. In this regard, the international Chinese teachers should emphasize the meaning of the legal terms in the classroom, and the difference between the meaning of the words in the legal texts and that in the daily use. For example, the word 第三人 *dìsānrén* 'third party' refers to the person neither the complainant nor the defendant but the one who is actually related to the case. However, students may think that the meaning of the word is the third person according to the meaning of the characters in the words. The word 回避 *huíbì* 'avoiding system' refers to a specific litigation activity, if the students understand the word 回避 *huíbì* 'avoiding system' with its common

meaning which is get out of the way and escape, they will not understand the legal texts correctly. Therefore, teachers should tell the students the limitations of deducing the meaning of legal vocabulary by characters and common meanings.

7   The Application of The Legal Corpus

Because of the various characteristics of Chinese legal language, we need to construct a legal corpus for the implementation of the law, the research of legal texts, the legal Chinese learning and other related areas.

For the area of TCIL, the contributions of a legal corpus construction lie in the following points:

(1)   To provide a reference for the Chinese teaching, and to promote the establishment of the specific Chinese vocabulary outline [27], the legal corpus constructed in this study reflects the word frequency in our legal texts, thus reflecting the common language of our legal language, these commonly used vocabulary is the focus of legal Chinese teaching.

(2)   The legal corpus facilitates the study of legal Chinese. It can help us scientifically extract the vocabulary in the legal language and facilitate the analysis of its characteristics. The results provide practical and theoretical guidance to Chinese teaching.

(3)   Provide practical and learning references for Chinese learners. On one hand, this study segments the words in the legal texts, while words segmenting is an important process during reading, so the legal corpus is conducive to the Chinese learners to read the legal texts. On the other hand, because of the differences between legal Chinese and general Chinese, Chinese learners cannot refer to ordinary characters or words dictionaries, when they are learning legal materials, and writing legal instruments, or other instruments that involve legal terms. The Legal corpus can act as a legal words dictionary, to help learners choose the normative legal terms.

The construction of legal corpus also has important significance for other fields, for example:

(1)   The compilation of legal dictionaries. Legal Chinese is different from the general Chinese, so the legal Chinese learners and legal workers need specialized dictionaries when reading and using legal Chinese. The writing of the legal dictionary needs to be based on the legal corpus which conducted the words segmentation, to provide the words, word frequency and other information [28].

(2)   To support the developing of legal Chinese word segmentation software. There are many errors in the word segmentation results produced by ICTCLAS, the software developed to segment the general Chinese words. Word segmentation software developed aiming at general Chinese is not entirely applicable to segment the professional Chinese words.

(3)   The standardization of legislative language. The establishment of a law society depends on the standardization of legislative language, and a legal corpus is conducive to check

whether the language used in the legal texts is normative. For example, some scholars suggest that the legislator should use 对 *duì* 'to' instead of 对于 *duìyú* 'to' as far as possible in legal texts [29], however, according to the ranking results of the words frequency of the legal corpus, the word 对于*duìyú* 'to' repeats 127 times. Besides, according to the ranking results of the words in the legal corpus, the word 但*dàn* 'but' and 但是*dànshì* 'but' are used both in the proviso clauses and the non-proviso clauses, which sometimes leads to the ambiguity between these two clauses [30]. So we can see that legislative language still needs to be improved.

(4)   The standardization of the language in legal practice. This corpus contributes to the legal practitioners in various areas to write legal instruments with legal terms. For example, according to legal corpus, the word 合同 *hétóng* 'contract' repeats 1,224 times in the corpus, while its synonym word 合约 *héyuē* 'agreement' only repeats 3 times. It shows that the normative legal instruments should normally use 合同*hétóng* 'contract' rather than 合约 *héyuē* 'agreement', and according to the results of the search, the term 合约*héyuē* 'agreement' appears only in the phrase 期货合约 *qíhuò héyuē* 'futures agreement', so the legal practitioners can properly use the two words above according to the legal corpus.

8   Conclusions and Further Work

This project has constructed a legal corpus of 35 representative legal texts of Mainland China. We did automatic word segmentation and corrected the segmentation results by manual work, in order to avoid the problem of being contrary to the original meaning of the legal text, and keep the criteria of word segmentation consistent. Then the words are ordered according to the frequency in this corpus. The legal corpus constructed in this study can be applied not only to the legal Chinese teaching, but also to other areas. According to the words in the legal corpus, this study analyzes the characteristics of legal Chinese and the vocabulary differences between legal Chinese and general Chinese. Targeting at the difficulties in the legal Chinese teaching, this paper puts forward some relevant solutions for solving them.

Acknowledgement:

This project is funded by Internal Research Grant of The Education University of Hong Kong. Project No.: 15214, Activity Code: R3733, Reference Number: RG 92/2015-2016.

* Corresponding Author

References

1. Quan Li: Teaching Chinese for Specific Purposes and Its Textbook Compilation (论专门用途汉语教学). Applied Linguistics Journal 8(3), 111–112(2011).
2. Yue Zhao: Design of Business Chinese Course System Based on Target and Object Differences (基于目标与对象差异的商务汉语课程体系框架设计). International Chinese Language Education Development and Research Journal (4), 30-37(2007).
3. Yaofeng Yue: Course Design and Textbook Writing for Chinese learning beginner of American legal profession (针对美国法律界零起点汉语学习者的课程设计与教材编写). Minzu University of China Professional master 's degree thesis (2013).
4. Dan Yang: A Study of Legal Vocabulary in Teaching Chinese as a Foreign Language (对外汉语教学中的法律词汇研究). Heilongjiang University master 's degree thesis (2012).
5. China National Leading Group for Teaching Chinese as a Foreign Language: The Graded Chinese Syllabics Characters and Words for The Application of Teaching Chinese to The Speakers of Other Language (National Standard, Application and Interpretation) (汉语国际教育用音节汉字词汇等级划分（国家标准应用解读本）). Beijing Language and Culture University Press, Beijing China (2010).
6. Yihua Sun, Guangran Zhou: Legal linguistics (法律语言学). China University of Political Science and Law Publisher, Beijing China, 2-3(1997).
7. Yun Liu: The Construction of Corpus in the Study of Legal Linguistics (语料库在法律语言学研究中的构建设想). Journal of Language and Literature studies 3(3), 9-11(2015).
8. Haiyan Yang: Compilation of Forensic Corpus (法律语料库建设设想). Terminology Standardization & Information Technology Journal 3(1), 40-43(2007).
9. Ruina Chen: A Review of Corpus-based Legal Languages Studies (基于语料库的法律语言研究述评). Journal of Guandong University of Foreign Studies 7(4), 20-25 (2015).
10. Hongren Sun, Jianding Yang: Construction of Parallel Corpus of China' s Legal Documents: Philosophy, Processes and Functions ("中国法律法规汉英平行语料库(PCCLD)" 创建的思路、过程与功能). Journal of Shaoxing University 3(2), 48-51 (2010).
11. Ting Jiang, Jin Wen: A Corpus Basic Study of Modal Verbs in Chinese Legislative Language (语料库视野下中国立法语言中的情态动词翻译研究). Journal of Southwest University for Nationalities 1(1), 195-199 (2012).
12. Beiping Song: The Construction of the First "Legal Chinese Corpus" in China (我国第一个 "法律语言语料库" 的建设及其思考). Contemporary Rhetoric Journal 1(1), 25-29 (2008).
13. Jinbang Du, Hongxiu Luo: Information-Based Legal corpus and Its Use in Legal Discourse Analysis (信息型法律语料库及其在法律语篇分析中的作用). Journal of Yunmeng 1(1), 135-140 (2013).
14. Jingwen Zhu: The Socialist Legal System with Chinese Characteristics : Its Structure, Features and Trends (中国特色社会主义法律体系：结构、特色和趋势). Social Sciences

15. Ministry of Justice of the People 's Republic of China: National Judicial Examination Outline (国家司法考试大纲). Law Press China, Beijing China, 1-231(2016).

16. Huiting Luo, Shan Wang: The Construction and Application of The Legal corpus of Mainland China (中国大陆法律语料库建设及其应用研究). Paper presented at The 18th Chinese Lexical Semantics Workshop (CLSW2017), Leshan Normal University, Leshan, Sichuan, China, (2017).

17. Yan Zhang: An Analysis of the Present Situation of the Use of Judicial Language in China (试析我国司法语言使用之现状). Edge Law Forum (边缘法学论坛) (2), 76-80 (2007).

18. Ming'an Jiang: Administrative Law and Administrative Litigation Law (行政法和行政诉讼法). Peking University Press & High Education Press, Beijing China (2015).

19. Examination Center of The National Chinese Proficiency Test Committee: The Syllabus of Chinese Vocabulary and Characters' Levels (汉语水平词汇与汉字等级大纲). Economic Science Press, Beijing China (2001).

20. Hongying Liu: Legal linguistics (法律语言学). Peking University Press, Beijing China (2003).

21. Falian Zhang: Cultural Factors in Legal Translation (法律英语翻译中的文化因素探析). Chinese Translators Journal (6), 48(2009).

22. Zhenyu Li: New Theory of Legal Linguistics (法律语言学新说). China Procuratorate Press, Beijing China (2006).

23. Wenxin Zhang: Jurisprudence (法理学). China Renmin University Press, Beijing China (2008).

24. Taiping Zhang: Legal Chinese - Commercial Orientation (法律汉语——商事篇). Peking University Press, Beijing China (2007).

25. Ruojiang Wang: Chinese Legal Chinese Course (中国法律专业汉语教程). Peking University Press, Beijing China (2007).

26. Jian Zhou, Haiyan Xie: On Chinese Word Boundary Parsing Ability of Foreign Students (留学生汉语阅读分词和语义提取能力研究). Chinese Language Learning 4(2), 70-71(2007).

27. Naigang Zhai: The Construction of Special Chinese System (试论专门用途汉语体系的构建). Shanghai University of Engineering Science Research on Education (2), 44 (2009).

28. Donghai Wang, Jie Wang: Construction for Research Resources of Legal Linguistics ("一库三典"的法律语言学研究资源建设). Journal of CUPL (4), 115-116 (2008).

29. Jie Wang: The Research of Legal Language in Chinese Mainland from the Legislative Era to the Era of Amendment to Law (从"立法时代"到"修法时代"的中国大陆法律语言研究). Applied Linguistics 11(4),6-7 (2010).

30. Huiting Luo, Shan Wang. The Transitional Sentences in the Language of Law – Take "dàn/dànshì" Sentences for Example (立法语言的转折句研究——以"但/但是"句为例). Paper presented at The International Linguistic Association 62nd Annual Conference, City University of Hong Kong, Hong Kong, (2017).

Research on the Lexicography Based on the Corpus of International Chinese Teaching Materials

Yinbing Zhang[1,2], Jihua Song[1(✉)], Weiming Peng[1(✉)], Dongdong Guo[1] and Tianbao Song[1]

[1]College of Information Science and Technology, Beijing Normal University,
Beijing 100875, China
{songjh, pengweiming}@bnu.edu.cn
{zhangyinbing, dongdongguo, songtianbao}@mail.bnu.edu.cn
[2]School of Mathematical Science, Huaibei Normal University, Huaibei 235000, China

Abstract. With the development of computer science and corpus technology, corpus use has been widely accepted in the field of lexicography. However, corpus application has been greatly restricted because of the lack of relevant information regarding the traditional corpus. Through the comparison of research situations at home and abroad, this paper analyses the reasons why the Chinese corpus is inadequate in assisting lexicography. Additionally, through the analysis of data processing for the diagrammatic Chinese syntactic Treebank based on the international Chinese teaching materials constructed by Beijing Normal University, this paper identifies how the diagrammatic Chinese syntactic Treebank can avoid the shortcomings of the traditional Chinese corpus in assisting lexicography. Additionally, according to the HSK lexical syllabus and Modern Chinese Dictionary, we have attempted lexicography of example sentences dictionary assisted by the diagrammatic Chinese syntactic Treebank. Finally, illustrations are provided for the problems encountered, and the important role of corpora in lexicography is emphasized.

Keywords: ·HSK, Treebank, International Chinese teaching, Lexicography

1   Introduction

In recent years, with the development of computer technology and corpus-based study, the application of corpus in lexicography has been paid more attention. The technology of lexicography based on corpus has been one of the most important methods of contemporary lexicography. Corpus has a great significance in the theoretical research and practical application of Lexicography, and it has become a consensus that corpus can assist lexicography greatly [1]. It is beneficial in that corpora can provide a large number of real example sentences for lexicography, which overcomes past issues of overreliance on editors' experience, and greatly improves lexicography quality. Additionally, the combination of corpus and computer technology can greatly reduce the lexicography workload, and improve the lexicography efficiency. As Xiaojun Yang and Saihong Li noted, during the process of lexicography, the

© Springer International Publishing AG 2018
Y. Wu et al. (Eds.): CLSW 2017, LNAI 10709, pp. 468–478, 2018.
https://doi.org/10.1007/978-3-319-73573-3_42

corpus shows great superiority in the ordering of lexical meanings and the source of example sentences [2].

In addition, with the development of corpus resources and language acquisition theory, researchers are paying more attention to the influence of language facts on language acquisition, and suggest acquiring knowledge of a language through authentic language materials [3]. Although the value of corpora to lexicography has been widely accepted, the application of traditional corpora has been greatly restricted because of the lack of relevant information [1]. A diagrammatic Chinese syntactic Treebank (hereafter the Treebank) based on the international Chinese teaching materials have been constructed by the Research Center of Language and Resources, Beijing Normal University (hereafter the center). During the Treebank construction, syntactic structure is annotated, and the POS (part of speech) and lexical meaning are annotated at the same time. Thus, this Treebank can make up for the shortage of traditional corpora to some extent.

2   Analysis of the Research Situation

The use of corpus-assisted English language lexicography started earlier than that for the Chinese language. The COBUILD corpus, established in the 1970s by a team led by Professor John Sinclair, is the model corpus for the lexicography of the modern dictionary. With the assistance of the COBUILD corpus, Collins publishing company has published ten kinds of dictionaries. Today, a considerable number of monolingual or bilingual dictionaries based on this corpus have been compiled by British Dictionary Publishing, such as Longman Dictionary of Contemporary English, Cambridge International Dictionary of English, MACMILLAN English Dictionary for Advanced Learners and Longman Language Activator [4].

Compared with the application of English corpus in lexicography, the study of Chinese corpus in lexicography is relatively lagging behind in China. The main reasons are as follows:

1) Compared with English, the characteristics of Chinese create difficulties in Chinese information processing. As Chinese sentences are composed of a string of characters without spaces to mark word boundaries, issues of segmentation disambiguation, word segmentation granularity and unknown word identification have not been well-addressed.

2) The distinction between Chinese words and phrases is a "persistent" problem in Chinese. In Chinese, a word is a grammatical unit between morpheme and phrase; there is no uniform standard for the definition and collection of words, and this is inconvenient to the collection of words in lexicography.

3) Existing Chinese corpora lack detailed information about internal tagging, most of which only provide simple retrieval functions, and it is by no means an easy task for the compiler to find the required information in the vast amount of data. Therefore, the contribution of these corpora to lexicography is limited [1].

For these reasons, the number of Chinese corpora that serve the lexicography well is relatively small.

3   Exploration of Lexicography

In the process of Chinese lexicography, the data source is mainly composed of three parts. The first part is the eight sets of teaching materials sponsored by NOCFL (National Office for Teaching Chinese as a Foreign Language); the second is 5000 words specified in the new HSK lexical syllabus; and the third is 91897 records from the Modern Chinese Dictionary.

3.1 Annotation of Materials

The Treebank is an annotated corpus, and the annotation work of 29465 sentences (498965 words) has been completed in the Center. The tool used during the annotation process is the "Diagrammatic Analyzing Platform Based on Sentence Pattern Structure" [5, 6, 7, 8] (www.jubenwei.com, hereafter the Platform), developed by the Center, and the interface of the Platform is shown in Fig. 1.

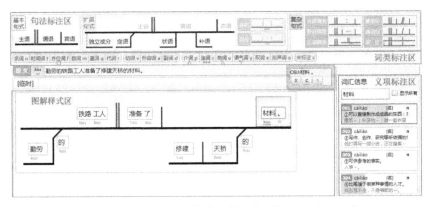

Fig. 1. Diagrammatic Analyzing Platform Based on Sentence Pattern Structure

The Platform adopts the formal design scheme of the Diagrammatic Analyzing Method to analyze Chinese sentences, and the conversion between syntactic structure and XML storage structure has been realized. There is a relationship of encoding and decoding between syntactic structure and XML storage structure.

3.1.1 Annotation of Syntactic Structure and Word Segmentation

First, we divide a sentence into different components according to the formula of basic sentence pattern, extended sentence pattern and complex sentence pattern, as shown in the area of syntax annotation in Fig. 1. During the annotation process, the produced structure is as follows: the subject, predicate and object as three main components are located above the long line; the attributive, adverbial and complement are located below the long line as additional components; and the vocatives and parentheses that do not affect the sentence structure as independent components are also located below the long line. For each component, the word segmentation with spaces can be continued until the corresponding POS and sense of every unit can be found in the Modern Chinese Dictionary.

In the Treebank, the syntactic information is annotated in detail, and the precise word segmentation is realized at the same time. To some extent, this solves the previously identified problems of word segmentation.

3.1.2 The POS and Sense Annotation of Words

As the key step in the construction of the Treebank, the POS and sense tagging play an important role in information extraction and semantic research. The Platform uses the Modern Chinese Dictionary as the foundational lexicon, and it can be used to assist the annotator to segment words and annotate their POS and sense information. An example of "材料 [cailiao] (material)" is given in "The Area of Sense Annotation" in Fig. 1. [9].

To improve the efficiency of the annotation, some annotation intelligent functions are added to the Platform. During the annotation process, if the sense of a word is singular, or a specific sense frequency is more than 80%, or a word is a function word with single POS and sense, then the POS and sense of the word will be annotated automatically by the Platform. However, if the annotation does not match the current context well, you need to manually modify the annotation. In this way, it can not only improve the efficiency of annotation, but also ensure annotation accuracy.

During the process of the Treebank construction, while annotating the syntactic structure, the lexical structure is also annotated. This has addressed a previous issue with traditional large-scale corpora, in that they lack the necessary micro structure information in the annotation process, and do not match the need well in lexicography, which lays the foundation for the lexicography with accurate semantic information. More detailed information of the annotation can refer to He Jing and Song Tianbao [10, 11].

3.1.3 Dynamic Word Structure

During the annotation process, there are many divergences in the distinction between words and phrases, which are mainly reflected in the different word segmentation of "Dynamic Words" outside of the Modern Chinese Dictionary. However, these "Dynamic Words" are often treated as whole concepts in the international Chinese teaching. Based on the practical experience of the Treebank construction and the reality of international Chinese teaching, we advocate that this kind of combination structure with high cohesion is separated from syntactic analysis and treated with lexical analysis (Weiming Peng et al., 2014). The range of dynamic words is extensive, including temporary word formation, configuration, a large number of proper nouns, and some idioms. For example: "全校[quan xiao] (School) ", "桌椅[zhuo yi] (desk and chair) ", "张老师[zhang lao shi] (teacher Zhang) ", "北京师范大学[bei jing shi fan da xue] (Beijing Normal University) ", "家里[jia li] (at home) ","看清[kan qing] (see clearly) ", "举起[ju qi] (raise up) ", "每天[mei tian] (every day) ", and "五六年[wu liu nian] (five or six years) " [12].

To make dynamic words better suited to teaching practice and ensure the standard-ization of the Treebank, we have presented a method to describe the structural mode of dynamic words [13], and set up a dynamic word structural mode knowledge base for the international Chinese teaching. Parts of modes of dynamic words are shown in Fig. 2.

id	mod	example	pos	xml_mod	repath	char_num
1	a↗a↗n	小白兔	n	a↗a↗n	(Null)	3
2	n↗a↗n2	邓副主席	n	n↗a↗n2	(Null)	4
3	v·了·一·v	看了一看	v	v·u·m·v	(.)了\1	4
4	v←来·v←去	飞来飞去	v	v←v·v←v	(.)来\1去	4
5	r2-q	多少个，若干次	r	r2-q	(多少|若干).	3
6	a↗n↗n	黄眉怪，大字报	n	a↗n↗n	(Null)	3
7	m-a-q	一小块，一整箱	m	m-a-q	.+[大小整满长].	3
8	n2↗v2↗n	群众接待站	n	n2↗v2↗n	(Null)	5
9	v|n↗n	安家费，拔秧机	n	v|n↗n	(Null)	3
10	r||v...r||v	你争我夺	v	r||v...r||v	(Null)	4
11	v·不·v	看不看	v	v·d·v	(.)不\1	3
12	n2-之-n	华山之巅	n	n2-u-n	..之..	4
13	v-诸-v2	付诸实践	v	v-p-v2	.诸..	4
14	v-而-d→v	失而复得，笑而不语	v	v-c-d→v	.而..	4
15	v←上·v←下	跑上跑下	v	v←v·v←v	(.)上\1下	4

Fig. 2. Parts of Dynamic Words Structural Mode Knowledge Base

These dynamic words fit actual needs in the international Chinese teaching. Be-cause of the large number of words existing in Chinese language, it is difficult for second language learners to master them. Generally, by using some Chinese word-formation rules can they produce a standardized and customary Chinese expression, which makes learning easier. In addition, dynamic words are helpful for learners to quickly search and extract a linguistic unit, thus further reducing the difficulty of language learning. Therefore, it is necessary to deal with the problem of dynamic words in the teaching of Chinese as a foreign language [2].

3.2 Standard Processing of New HSK Lexical Syllabus and Modern Chinese Dictionary

3.2.1 Standard Processing of the New HSK Lexical Syllabus

Lexicography entries are determined by the new HSK lexical syllabus. There are 5000 words commonly used in the international Chinese teaching, which are included in the new HSK lexical syllabus and divided into levels 1–6. The 5000 new HSK vocabu-lary entries are stored in the "syllabus" table in the database after standard processing, in which "id", "content" and "level" are included as three fields. The field of "id" cor-responds to the serial number of the words, "content" corresponds to the words them-selves and "level" corresponds to the word level.

3.2.2 Standard Processing of Modern Chinese Dictionary

During the lexicography process, the POS and word senses refer to the Modern Chinese Dictionary. This study uses the 6th edition of the Modern Chinese Dictionary published in 2012. There are 91897 records stored in the table of "xianhan" in the database after standard processing, in which the five fields of "id", "ciyu", "pos", "yima" and "shiyi" are included. The specific format is shown in Fig. 3.

id	ciyu	pos	yima	shiyi
1	吖	(Null)	001	见【吖嗪】。
2	吖嗪	n	001	有机化合物的一类，呈环状结构，含有一个或几个氮原子，如吡啶、哒嗪、嘧啶等。
3	阿	u	001	①前缀。用在排行、小名或姓的前面，有亲昵的意味。
4	阿	u	002	②前缀。用在某些亲属名称的前面。
5	阿鼻地狱	n	001	佛教指最深层的地狱，是犯了重罪的人死后灵魂永远受苦的地方。
6	阿昌族	n	001	我国少数民族之一，分布在云南。
7	阿斗	n	001	三国蜀汉后主刘禅的小名。阿斗为人庸碌，后多用来指懦弱无能的人。
8	阿尔茨海默病	n	001	老年性痴呆的一种，多发生于中年或老年的早期，因德国医生阿尔茨海默(AloisAlzheimer)最先描述
9	阿尔法粒子	n	001	某些放射性物质衰变时放射出来的氦原子核，由两个中子和两个质子构成，质量为氢原子的4倍，带
10	阿尔法射线	n	001	放射性物质放射出来的阿尔法粒子流。通常写作α射线。

Fig. 3. Modern Chinese Dictionary Information

3.3 Lexicography Method

The central idea of the lexicography method is as follows. For each word in the new HSK lexical syllabus, we first determined whether it appears in the Modern Chinese Dictionary. If the word appears in the Modern Chinese Dictionary, we recorded the corresponding information and traversed the Treebank to count the frequency of the records and store the set of the example sentence "id". Otherwise, we set the POS and senses of these words to NULL temporarily and dealt with them alone later, and counted the frequency of the records and the set of the example sentence "id" directly.

The detailed description of the lexicography method is shown in the algorithm .

Algorithm： The Method of Lexicography

Input:
29465 annotated international Chinese teaching sentences of the Treebank, 5000 vocabularies in the new HSK lexical syllabus and 91897 records from the Modern Chinese Dictionary.

Output：
There are 10815 records, which includes the word information as "word", word level as "level", part of speech as "POS", sense code as "sen", word sense as "shiyi", frequency as "freq" and the set of example sentences labels as "sentids", as shown in Fig. 4.

Algorithm Flow:
1) By scanning the Modern Chinese Dictionary, we established the corresponding relationship between the word and the set of word "id". We thusly establish the rela-

tion between the word and its "id" in the Dictionary. For example, when the id of 16230, 16231, 16233 and 16234 all correspond to the word "东西 [dong xi] (things)" in the table of "xianhan", we can establish the corresponding relationship between "东西 [dong xi] (things)" and the serial number "16230#16231# 16233#16234".

2) By scanning the new HSK lexical syllabus, the existence of the serial number corresponding to each word is determined. If the serial number exists, it is then split by the character "#". For the former example "东西 [dong xi] (things)", the result is "16230, 16231, 16233, 16234".

3) For each id of the results from the last step, we can take the corresponding record from the Modern Chinese Dictionary and store the POS information, the sense code and the sense. For "东西 [dong xi] (things)", the results are as shown in Fig. 5. If the serial number does not exist, then we set the POS, sense code and sense to NULL.

4) On the basis of the above steps, we scan the Treebank, aim at each word and its "pos", "sen" and "shiyi", get the "freq" and "sentids", and store the information in the table "wordsenfre". The results are as shown in Fig. 4.

id	word	level	pos	sen	shiyi	freq	sentids
110	电脑	1	n	001	指电子计算机。	24	5495 5694 5449 5459 5526 782 154 781 5435
111	电视	1	n	001	①利用无线电波或导线把实物的活动影像和声音变成电	1	843
112	电视	1	n	002	②用这种装置传送的影像。	25	5509 828 5166 5504 5510 1067 1335 1554 38
113	电视	1	n	003	③指电视机。	3	10539 11137 8913
114	电影	1	n	001	一种综合艺术，用强灯光把拍摄的形象连续放映在银幕	33	10925 10921 10923 10949 10957 31801 811 2
115	东西	1	f	001	①东边和西边。	1	30371
116	东西	1	f	002	②从东到西(距离)。	0	
117	东西	1	n	101	①泛指各种具体的或抽象的事物。	84	10555 2179 2324 813 8 59 61 171 189 295 30
118	东西	1	n	102	②特指人或动物(多含厌恶或喜爱的感情)。	0	

Fig. 4. Final Result Information

id	ciyu	pos	yima	shiyi
16230	东西	f	001	①东边和西边。
16231	东西	f	002	②从东到西(距离)。
16233	东西	n	101	①泛指各种具体的或抽象的事物。
16234	东西	n	102	②特指人或动物(多含厌恶或喜爱的感情)。

Fig. 5. Examples of word items

From Fig. 5 we can see that "id" is the identification number used to uniquely distinguish the records, "word" is the word of new HSK lexical syllabus, "level" is the level of the word in the new syllabus vocabulary, "pos" is the word POS, "sen" is the sense code in the Modern Chinese Dictionary, "shiyi" is the interpretation of the word corresponding to the "sen", "freq" is the frequency of record, and "sentids" is the set of the example sentence "id".

Combined with **Perl** programming, the algorithm flow chart corresponding to algorithm 1 is shown in Fig. 6.

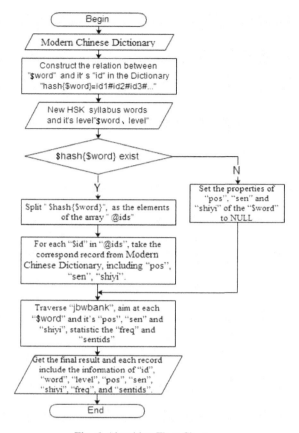

Fig. 6. Algorithm Flow Chart

4   Some Explanations of Lexicography

4.1 Processing of Those Words Appearing in the New HSK Lexical Syllabus but not in the Modern Chinese Dictionary

We identified those words appearing in New HSK lexical syllabus but not in Modern Chinese Dictionary by comparing the new HSK lexical syllabus with the Dictionary entries. There are 113 such words, and these words can be divided into the categories of dynamic words, idioms and fixed collocations, and parts of them are as follows:

1) Dynamic words

Nouns: "凹凸[aotu] (concave convex) ", "大象[daxiang] (elephant) ", "羊肉 [yangrou] (mutton) ", "鸡蛋[jidan] (egg) ", "证书[zhengshu] (certificate) ", "亚洲 [yazhou] (Asia) ", "黄河[huanghe] (the Yellow River) ", "中国[zhongguo] (China) ",

"端午节[duanwujie] (Dragon Festival) ", "公安局[gonganju] (public security bureau) ".

Verbs: "唱歌[changge] (sing) ", "摔倒[shuaidao] (fall) ", "下雨[xiayu] (rain) ", "养成[yangcheng] (develop) ", "油炸[youzha] (fried) ", "遇到[yudao] (encounter) ", "涮火锅 [shuanhuoguo] (hot pot) ", "不客气[bukeqi] (impolite) ", "弹钢琴[tangangqin](play the piano) ".

Adjectives: "好吃[haochi] (delicious) ", "候选[houxuan] (candidate) ", "聋哑[longya] (deaf-mute) ", "兴隆[xinglong] (prosperous) ", "不耐烦[bunaifan] (impatient) ".

Adverbs: "不得不[budebu] (be obliged to) ", "迄今为止[qijinweizhi] (so far) ".

Numerals: "百分之[baifenzhi] (Percent) ".

Quantifiers: "分钟[fenzhong] (minute) ".

Localizers: "之际[zhiji] (when) ".

2) Idioms： " 不 屑 一 顾 [buxieyigu] (beneath contempt) ", " 朝 气 蓬 勃 [zhaoqipengbo] (full of vigour and vitality) ", "称心如意[chengxinruyi] (have sth. as one wishes) ", "东张西望[dongzhanxiwang] (look this way and that) ".

3) Fixed collocations："不但…而且…[budan…erqie…] (not only…,but also…) ", "虽然…但是…[suiran…danshi…] (although) ", "因为…所以…[yinwei…suoyi…] (because) ", "只有…才…[zhiyou…cai…](only) ".

When the program is used to process these words, we can set the POS, sense code and sense to NULL temporarily, and supplement this information manually later. As to the statistics of the example sentences, we can directly compare these words with the annotated corpus. In **Perl** programming, combining the XML form of the corpus, we can compare "$word./" with the annotated corpus. That is to say, **"$word=$word.'/'; $sentag=~/ $word/|^$word;"**.

In addition, there are four fixed collocations in the 113 words, similar to the phrase "不但…而且… [budan…erqie…] (not only…,but also…)". The statistical element would be processed later with the help of **"SELECT * FROM `jbwbank` WHERE sentence like '%不但%而且%';"**, and complement the corresponding information in the final results manually.

4.2 Example Sentences Selection and Sorting

Some words have too many example sentences. For example, "我们 [women] (we)" has 422 example sentences, "什么 [shenme] (what)" has 273 and "现在 [xianzai] (now) " has 195. For these words, it is impossible to list all the example sentences in the lexicography. Therefore, some examples are selected manually from the options, whereas all are included if they have no more than 10 example sentences.

In general, there are several records corresponding to one word in the lexicography. With the assistance of statistics and computer sorting functions, we can sort these records in descending order according to the frequency of the example sentences, which better fits the learner's cognitive law.

4.3 Sense Combination

For the specific purpose of assisting the international Chinese teaching, it would have a negative effect on learners if the sense has been divided into too tiny parts. Some words from the new HSK lexical syllabus with too many senses are listed as follows (The digital in brackets means the sense number of the word in the Modern Chinese Dictionary): "上 [shang] (up) (27)"; "点 [dian] (spot) (26)"; "下 [xia] (down) (24)"; "干 [gan] (dry) (23)"; "开 [kai] (open) (21)"; "行 [xing] (go)"; "正 [zheng] (just) (20)".

The final determination of the word entry needs the manual intervention with the help of the statistical results of example sentences. To reduce the interference for Chinese second-language learners, the following senses should be deleted from the final results: those without example sentences, used senses, classical senses, dialectal senses and some professional senses.

In addition, we can focus on monosyllabic and disyllabic words, and merge those senses with similar meanings. For example, "没有 [mei you] (no)" has seven senses in the Modern Chinese Dictionary, and the distribution of the example sentences is shown in Table 1.

Table 1. Distribution of the Sense, Frequency Statistics of "没有 [meiyou] (no)"

POS	Verb					Adverb	
Sense	001 negative of "领有 [lingyou](possess)具有[juyou](have)"	002 negative of "存在 [cunzai](exist)"	003 use in front of "谁[shui](who), 哪个[nage](which)", indicate "全都不 [quandoubu](none)"	004 not as good as	005 lack, not enough	006 negative of "已然 [yiran](already)"	007 negative of "曾经 [cengjing](ever)"
Frequency	167	18	0	3	1	90	18
Percentage	56.23%	6.06%	0	1.01%	0.34%	30.30%	6.06%

According to Table 1, we find that the difference between sense 001 and 002 is minor, so we can combine them into "verb, negative of the statement". Sense 003 has not been seen in the corpus, so we can delete this sense during the lexicography process. We can also combine sense 004 and 005 into "verb, not enough or not as good as, it indicates that the degree is not enough", and sense 006 and 007 can be combined into "adverb, negative of already or ever". Then the senses number changes from 7 to 3, and this makes it easier for Chinese second language learners to learn.

5   Conclusions

Corpus-assisted lexicography is necessary and inevitable owing to the ongoing development of computer technology and lexicography. The annotated corpus based on the international Chinese teaching materials constructed by the Center lays a resource foundation for theoretical research and application, and this paper has made a significant attempt at lexicography. However, further investigation is needed for the corpus to have an improved auxiliary role in lexicography.

Acknowledgement. Supported by: Natural Science Foundation of the Anhui Higher Education Institutions of China (No: KJ2016B002); Anhui Provincial Natural Science Foundation (No:1608085MF143).

References

1. Yihua, Z.: A Trend of Corpus Development and Its Significance in Lexicography: The Characteristics of COCA in Datamation[J]. Lexicographical Studies, 05:1-8+93 (2015)
2. Xiaojun, Y., Saihong, L.: Advantages of Corpora in Lexicography-Review on OALD (6th edition)[J]; Foreign Languages and Their Teaching, 04:47-51 (2003)
3. Hongbing, X.: Corpus-based Lexical Knowledge Extraction and Foreign-learner Oriented Dictionary Compilation. Lexicographical Studies, 03: 36-41+94 (2013)
4. Junsong, W., Jianguo, T.: Corpus-based Lexicography and Key Issues Concerned. Journal of Zhengzhou Institute of Aeronautical Industry Management (Social Science Edition), 01:71-73 (2013)
5. Weiming, P., Jihua S., Ning, W.: Design of Diagrammatic Parsing Method of Chinese Based on Sentence Pattern Structure. Computer Engineering and Applications, 50(06): 11-18 (2014)
6. Weiming, P., Jihua, S., Shiwen Y.: Lexical Issues in Chinese Information Processing: in the Background of Sentence-based Diagram Treebank Construction. Journal of Chinese Information Processing, 28(02): 1-7 (2014)
7. Weiming, P., Jihua, S., Zhifang, S., Dongdong, G.: Formal Schema of Diagrammatic Chinese Syntactic Analysis. In: Lu, Q., Gao, H. (eds) CLSW 2015. LNAI, vol. 9332, pp. 701-710. Springer, Heidelberg (2015)
8. Tianxin,Y., Weiming, P., Jihua, S.: High Efficiency Syntax Tagging System Based on the Sentence Pattern Structure. Journal of Chinese Information Processing, 28(04):43-49 (2014)
9. Min, Z., Weiming,P., Jihua, S., Tianxin, Y.: Development and Optimization of Syntax Tagging Tool on Diagrammatic Treebank. Journal of Chinese Information Processing, 28(06):26-33 (2014)
10. Jing, H., Weiming, P., Jihua, S., Hongzhang, L.: Annotation Schema for Contemporary Chinese Based on JinXi Li's Grammar System. In: Liu, P., Su, Q. (eds.) CLSW2013. LNCS, vol.8229, pp. 668-681. Springer, Heidelberg (2013)
11. Tianbao, S., Weiming P., Jihua, S., Dongdong, G., Jing, H.: The Construction of Sentence-based Diagrammatic Treebank. In: Dong M., Lin J., Tang X. (eds) CLSW2016. LNCS, vol.10085, 306-314. Springer, Heidelberg (2016)
12. Dongdong, G.: Analyzing on Dynamic Words and Their Structural Modes in Building the Sentence-based Treebank. Beijing Normal University, Beijing (2016)
13. Dongdong, G., Shuqin, Z., Weiming P., Jihua, S., Yinbing,Z.: Construction of the Dynamic Word Structural Mode Knowledge Base for the International Chinese Teaching. In: Dong M., Lin J., Tang X. (eds) CLSW2016. LNCS, vol.10085, pp. 251-260. Springer, Heidelberg, (2016)

Research on Dynamic Words and Their Automatic Recognition in Chinese Information Processing

Dongdong Guo, Jihua Song$^{(\boxtimes)}$, and Weiming Peng

College of Information Science and Technology, Beijing Normal University,
Beijing 100875, China
dongdongguo@mail.bnu.edu.cn, {songjh,pengweiming}@bnu.edu.cn

Abstract. Many of words in Chinese sentences are dynamic construction of "temporary words". Dynamic words are sentence units which are generally not included in the lexicon and should not be done further analysis as phrase structures in the syntactic analysis. The dynamic word problem is one of the key problems in Chinese information processing. On the one hand, it is conducive to the unity of granularity sizes of word segmentation results; on the other hand, it is an important basis for the realization of efficient and accurate automatic lexical and syntactic analysis. This paper summarizes dynamic words in Chinese information processing, analyzes the structural modes of dynamic words and establishes a relatively scientific and complete dynamic word structural mode knowledge base by means of annotating structural mode information of dynamic words in a certain scale corpus. At last, the problem of automatic recognition of dynamic words is preliminarily explored. This paper provides a new idea and way for the study of lexical analysis in Chinese information processing.

Keywords: Dynamic word · Dynamic word structural mode · Automatic recognition · Chinese information processing

1 Introduction

Chinese is a kind of language which is lack of developed forms, and a lot of grammatical phenomena often change gradually rather than change suddenly. Therefore, it is easy to encounter various intermediate states in grammar analysis. In fact, it is difficult to divide the boundaries between words and non-words (smaller than words, larger than words), the limits of the parts of speech and the limits of various sentence components [1].

At present, the mainstream Chinese tree banks in the division of word granularity have basically accepted the standard of Chinese word segmentation directly, that is, all of the word segmentation results are used as leaf nodes, and there are no intermediate transition states [2]. In theory, the analysis of the internal structure of a word should not be expressed in the syntactic tree, and the leaf node of the syntactic tree should be a word. However, many of words in Chinese sentences are dynamic construction of "temporary words". The basic lexicon generally doesn't include these words, such as temporary nouns (大树[da shu], 语文课[yuwen ke], 铁路工人[tielu gongren]), verb-resultative verbs or verb-trending verbs (听清[ting qing], 升高[sheng gao]), quantifiers (一块[yi kuai], 十多个[shi duo ge]), reduplicated forms (看看[kan kan], 走一走[zou yi zou]), etc. If the temporary words are syntactically segmented and handled as phrase structures, the structure of the syntactic tree will grow exponentially. This will undoubtedly increase the burden of syntactic analysis, make the implementation of automatic syntactic analysis more complex and difficult, and have a significant negative impact on the accuracy of analysis results. In addition, ignoring the temporary words will also result in the problem that granularity sizes of the word segmentation results are not uniform. Based on the reality of Chinese information processing, we advocate that this kind of temporary word, which belongs to "intermediate state" with cohesion, is separated from syntactic analysis and treated as a dynamic word [3].

2   Dynamic Word

Dynamic words are sentence units which are generally not included in the lexicon and should not be done further analysis as phrase structures in the syntactic analysis. The combination of words or morphemes in the dynamic word is not a free combination of pure syntactic level, and it is restricted by the degree of significance cohesion, the structural stability, and the syllable prosodic features [4]. The range of dynamic words is very extensive, including temporary word formation, morphology, a large number of proper nouns, as well as part of idioms and locutions and so on.

Dynamic words almost cover all types of parts of speech (POS). According to the research results and practice in the fields of linguistics and Chinese information processing, some typical noun dynamic words, verb dynamic words and adjective dynamic words are summarized as follows:

2.1   Noun Dynamic Words

1. Temporary nouns

- attributive structure nouns: 全校[quan xiao], 本国[ben guo], 满腹[man fu], 群雁 [qun yan]
- combined structure nouns: 师生[shi sheng], 桌椅[zhuo yi], 医患[yi huan], 校企 [xiao qi]

2. Proper nouns

- personal name: 老王[Lao Wang], 张老师[Zhang laoshi], 刘副主席[Liu fu zhuxi], 陈毅市长[Chenyi shizhang]
- place name: 山西省[Shanxi Sheng], 南京路[Nanjing Lu], 赵州桥[Zhaozhou Qiao], 花园小区[Huayuan Xiaoqu]

- organization name: 北京大学[Beijing Daxue], 中国驻巴西大使馆[Zhongguo zhu Baxi dashi guan]

Whether other attribute-head noun combinations are proper nouns depends on whether or not they are conceptualized in the current context. Conceptualized nouns which have upper and lower concept relations with the central nouns can be regarded as a fine classification of the central noun concepts according to a certain attribute, and be associated with the opposite or the same series of sibling combinations in the concept hierarchy, such as 语文课[yuwen ke], 数学课[shuxue ke], 英语课[yingyu ke] and so on (According to the teaching content of the course).

3. Some words with "affix" will form noun dynamic words, such as 强者[qiang zhe], 消费者[xiaofei zhe], 画儿[hua er], 饭馆儿[fanguan er] and 同学们[tongxue men].

2.2   Verb Dynamic Words

1. Verb-resultative verbs or verb-trending verbs

- verb-resultative verbs: 看清[kan qing], 听懂[ting dong]
- verb-trending verbs: 举起[ju qi], 拿下[na xia]

2. Additional morphology

- V+了: 打了[da le], 打击了[daji le]
- V+着: 想着[xiang zhe], 思考着[sikao zhe]
- V+过: 去过[qu guo], 访问过[fangwen guo]

3. Verb reduplicated form

- AA: 看看[kan kan], 试试[shi shi]
- AAB: 帮帮忙[bang bangmang], 散散步[san sanbu]
- ABAB: 锻炼锻炼[duanlian duanlian], 鼓励鼓励[guli guli]
- AABB: 修修补补[xiu xiu bu bu], 打打闹闹[da da nao nao]
- V了V: 想了想[xiang le xiang], 问了问[wen le wen]
- V一V: 谈一谈[tan yi tan], 走一走[zou yi zou]
- V了一V: 听了一听[ting le yi ting], 转了一转[zhuan le yi zhuan]
- V不V: 去不去[qu bu qu], 会不会[hui bu hui]
- V没V: 有没有[you mei you], 买没买[mai mei mai]
- V着V着: 想着想着[xiang zhe xiang zhe], 睡着睡着[shui zhe shui zhe]
- V来V去: 想来想去[xiang lai xiang qu], 看来看去[kan lai kan qu]

4. Other (usually containing non-free morphemes): 极具[ji ju], 相遇[xiang yu], 喊道[han dao], 择日[zhe ri]

2.3   Adjective Dynamic Words

Adjective reduplicated form:

- AA: 高高[gao gao], 冷冷[leng leng]
- ABB: 冷清清[leng qing qing], 亮堂堂[liang tang tang]
- AABB: 白白胖胖[bai bai pang pang], 孤孤单单[gu gu dan dan]
- ABAB: 高兴高兴[gaoxing gaoxing], 轻松轻松[qingsong qingsong]
- A不A: 对不对[dui bu dui], 好不好[hao bu hao]
- A里AB: 古里古怪[gu li guguai], 糊里糊涂[hu li hutu]
- A不XY: 酸不溜丢[suan bu liu diu], 灰不叽叽[hui bu ji ji]

3   Dynamic Word Structural Mode

Table 1. Symbols of Structural Relationship

Structural Relationship	Symbol	Samples	Notes
Coordination	…	花…草[hua cao]; 中[zhong]…小学[xiaoxue]	including reduced coordination
Attribute-head	↗	鸡[ji]↗蛋[dan]; 文字[wenzi]↗改革[gaige]; 北京[Beijing]↗师范[Shifan]↗大学[Daxue]; 刘[Liu]↗队[dui]; 周[Zhou]↗副[fu]↗主席[zhuxi]	including "name-appellation" structure
Adverbial-head	→	极[ji]→其[ju]; 深[shen]→感[gan]; 代[dai]→写[xie]; 改[gai]→用[yong]	including auxiliary verb and serial verb construction
Verb-complement	←	赶[gan]←跑[pao]; 看[kan]←清[qing]; 拿[na]←下[xia]; 举[ju]←起[qi]	verb-resultative structure; verb-trending structure
Verb-obj	|	调[tiao]|酒[jiu]↗师[shi]	usually use with other symbols
Sbj-prd	‖	你[ni]‖争[zheng]…我[wo]‖夺[duo]	
Reduplication	·	看·看[kan kan]; 研究·研究[yanjiu yanjiu]; 看·一·看[kan yi kan]; 看·了·看[kan le kan]; 看·不·看[kan bu kan]; 看·没·看[kan mei kan]	except AABB and ABB forms of adjective
Other	-	桌[zhuo]-上[shang]; 一[yi]-只[zhi]; 一[yi]-大[da]-碗[wan]; 看[kan]-了[le]; 看[kan]-着[zhe]; 看[kan]-过[guo]; 同学[tongxue]-们[men]; 学习[xuexi]-者[zhe]; 拿[na]-得[de]-起[qi]; 华山[Huashan]-之[zhi]-巅[dian]; 付[fu]-诸[zhu]-实践[shijian]; 翩然[pianran]-而[er]-至[zhi]	locative structure; quantitative structure; affix/auxiliary word structure; other fixed format

Automatic recognition of dynamic words is an important part of automatic lexical analysis in Chinese information processing, and it is also an important basis for realization of automatic syntactic analysis. In order to realize automatic recognition of dynamic words, we first need to obtain typical features of various types of dynamic words, which are summarized as the dynamic word structural mode. Dynamic words are restricted by the degree of significance cohesion, the structural stability, and the syllable prosodic features. Four types of information including the whole POS of a dynamic word, the POS of each internal component, the syllable number of each internal component and structural relationship between the internal components can distinguish various types of dynamic words well, so they are used to describe the dynamic word structural mode [5]. The structural relationships between the internal components are shown in Table 1.

Examples of the dynamic word structural mode are shown in Table 2.

Table 2. Dynamic Word Structural Mode

Dynamic Word	Structural Mode	Dynamic Word	Structural Mode
木桥 [mu qiao]	n: n↗n	看清 [kan qing]	v: v←a
彩画 [cai hua]	n: a↗n	翻看 [fan kan]	v: v→v
画儿 [hua er]	n: n-儿	看着 [kan zhe]	v: v-着
阅览室 [yuelan shi]	n: v2↗n	聊聊天 [liao liaotian]	v: v·v2
小白兔 [xiao bai tu]	n: a↗a↗n	城市化 [chengshi hua]	v: n2-化
制药厂 [zhi yao chang]	n: v ǀ n↗n	听了听 [ting le ting]	v: v·了·v
铁路工人 [tielu gongren]	n: n2↗n2	休息休息 [xiuxi xiuxi]	v: v2·v2
专家学者 [zhuanjia xuezhe]	n: n2...n2	翩然而至 [pianran er zhi]	v: a2-而-v

The structural mode of "阅览室[yuelan shi]" is "n: v2↗n". In "n: v2↗n", the "n" before the colon indicates the whole POS is a noun; the "v2" indicates the POS of "阅览[yuelan]" is a verb and its syllable number is 2; the final "n" represents "室[shi]" is a noun and its syllable number is 1 (The syllable number is the default value 1 when it is NULL); the "↗" represents attribute-head relationship.

The structural modes of "画儿[hua er]", "看着[kan zhe]", "城市化[chengshi hua]", "听了听[ting le ting]" and "翩然而至[pianran er zhi]" contain fixed internal components "儿[er]", "着[zhe]", "化[hua]", "了[le]" and "而[er]". The fixed internal components in the structural modes can be uniquely identified or are several determinate types. The appearance of these components in the structural modes can reflect the characteristics of dynamic words more directly and effectively.

In order to obtain structural modes of various types of dynamic words systematically and comprehensively, we annotate structural mode information of dynamic words in international Chinese textbooks (29465 sentences and 498965 words) and select the Modern Chinese Dictionary (Sixth Edition) as the basic lexicon to annotate POS and senses [6,7,8]. After statistical analysis of the annotated result, the dynamic word structural modes which are not typical are removed, and a knowledge base with 672 kinds of dynamic word structural modes for Chinese information processing is finally established, as shown in Table 3.

Table 3. The Dynamic Word Structural Mode Knowledge Base

id	mode	example	pos	syllable	sequence	rule	frequency
1	n: n2↗n	八股文[bagu wen], 棒球场[bangqiu chang]	n	3	n2n		1786
2	n: a↗n2	矮个子[ai gezi], 白瓜子[bai guazi]	n	3	an2		813
3	n: v2↗n	爱国心[aiguo xin], 搬迁户[banqian hu]	n	3	v2n		506
4	n: n↗n2	癌细胞[ai xibao], 丁先生[ding xiansheng]	n	3	nn2		488
5	n: n2-们	同学们[tongxue men]	n	3	n2u	..们	254
6	n: a2↗n	好奇心[haoqi xin], 烦心事[fanxin shi]	n	3	a2n		184
7	n: v | n↗n	安家费[an jia fei], 拔秧机[ba yang ji]	n	3	vnn		89
8	n: m↗n2	零利率[ling lilv], 三原色[san yuanse]	n	3	mn2		87
9	n: n↗n↗n	皮鞋油[pi xie you], 蛇皮袋[she pi dai]	n	3	nnn		70
10	n: n2-儿	绝活儿[juehuo er]	n	3	n2u	..儿	53

The "sequence" represents character sequence about the POS and syllable numbers of internal components; the "rule" represents regular expression rules for dynamic words which reflect some restricted information of partial structural modes, such as the fixed internal components, reduplicated forms, syllable number and so on; the "frequency" represents the frequency of dynamic words corresponding to the dynamic word structural mode in the annotated result.

The 672 kinds of dynamic word structural modes in the knowledge base cover almost all POS except auxiliary and interjection. Dynamic word structural modes the whole POS of which are noun and verb have the largest number, accounting for 37.80% and 27.38% of the total number of structural modes respectively. According to the number of syllable, dynamic word structural modes can be divided into double-syllable, three-syllable, four-syllable, five-syllable, six-syllable and seven-syllable, and their numbers are 124(18.45%), 199(29.61%), 248(36.90%), 61(9.08%), 28(4.17%) and 12(1.79%). In addition, dynamic word structural modes with regular expression rules reach 307, accounting for 45.68% of the total number.

4   Automatic Recognition of Dynamic Words

Automatic recognition of dynamic words is based on initial word segmentation, including word segmentation and POS tagging. The Modern Chinese Dictionary (Sixth Edition) is regarded as the standard vocabulary of initial word segmentation, and the granularity sizes of segmentation results would be small. We will use the "sequence" field and "rule" field of the knowledge base to automatically identify dynamic words in the initial word segmentation results.

Automatic lexical analysis is affected by segmentation ambiguity and unknown words, so there are some problems in word segmentation results. Because of the existence of ambiguity words, POS tagging results are also not ideal [9]. In the automatic recognition of dynamic words, the initial segmentation results are obtained by automatic segmentation method and manual proofreading. In this way, the error rate of word segmentation and POS tagging can be reduced to minimum, so as to study the automatic recognition of dynamic words more effectively.

4.1 Initial Word Segmentation

First of all, the automatic segmentation method [10] is used to deal with the test text which has 20000 Chinese characters. Then the results are manually checked and initial word segmentation results including the information of word segmentation and POS would be obtained, as shown in Fig. 1.

```
你</r>在</p>哪儿</r>工作</v>? </w>
我</r>在</p>一</m>家</q>韩国</n>公司</n>工作</v>，</w>
我</r>是</v>部门</n>经理</n>。</w>
你</r>也</d>工作</v>吗</u>? </w>
我</r>在</p>一</m>家</q>日本</n>公司</n>工作</v>。</w>
你</r>做</v>什么</r>工作</n>? </w>
我</r>是</v>公司</n>的</u>职员</n>。</w>
菲雅</n>，</w>你</r>做</v>什么</r>工作</n>? </w>
我</r>是</v>一</m>名</q>记者</n>。</w>
你</r>喜欢</v>这个</r>工作</n>吗</u>? </w>
我</r>很</d>喜欢</v>。</w>
玛丽</n>，</w>你</r>工作</v>吗</u>? </w>
我</r>现在</t>不</d>工作</v>。</w>
你</r>喜欢</v>做</v>什么</r>? </w>
啊</e>，</w>你</r>是</v>一</m>个</q>画家</n>! </w>
别</d>大惊小怪</a>，</w>我</r>在</d>化妆</v>呢</u>。</w>
你</r>化</v>的</u>是</v>什么</r>妆</n>? </w>
这</r>是</v>京剧</n>的</u>脸谱</n>。</w>
你</r>没</d>听说</v>过</u>吗</u>? </w>
听说</v>过</u>。</w>
京剧</n>脸谱</n>好像</d>有</v>很</d>多</a>种</q>。</w>
这</r>是</v>谁</r>的</u>脸谱</n>? </w>
这</r>是</v>包公</n>的</u>脸谱</n>。</w>
```

Fig. 1. Initial Word Segmentation Results

4.2 Recognition Process

The process of identifying dynamic words in the initial word segmentation results is as follows:

1. Sort the dynamic word structural modes with regular expression rules according to the number of syllable from large to small and the frequency from high to low. Then, match and recognize dynamic words corresponding to the current dynamic word structural mode in order. The POS and syllable numbers of internal components in the dynamic word which is matched must be consistent with the current structural mode, and the corresponding regular expression rules should be also satisfied. Once dynamic words are identified, they are no longer involved in the following recognition operations.
2. Sort the dynamic word structural modes without regular expression rules according to the number of syllable from large to small and the frequency from high to low.

Then, match and recognize dynamic words corresponding to the current dynamic word structural mode in order. The POS and syllable numbers of internal components in the dynamic word which is matched must be consistent with the current structural mode.

3. Compare automatic recognition results of dynamic words with the results of manual annotation, audit and statistics, and calculate the accuracy rate and recall rate of automatic recognition of dynamic words.

4.3   Experimental Result

According to the above recognition process, the automatic recognition experiment is carried out, and the result is shown in Table 4 and Table 5.

Table 4. Dynamic Words Recognition Result (1)

Dynamic Word	Accuracy Rate	Recall Rate
modes with rules	88.64%	99.97%
modes without rules	61.37%s	87.18%

Table 5. Dynamic Words Recognition Result (2)

Dynamic Word	Accuracy Rate	Recall Rate
double-syllable	79.55%	90.09%
three-syllable	75.62%	93.42%
four-syllable	60.04%	95.68%
more than four syllables	62.32%	99.98%

According to the experimental result, it can be concluded that the dynamic word structural mode knowledge base has a significant effect on automatic recognition of dynamic words. The accuracy rate of automatic recognition is lower than the recall rate. The recognition accuracy rate of dynamic words corresponding dynamic word structural modes with regular expression rules reaches **88.64%**, which is much higher than the identification accuracy rate of those words corresponding structural modes without regular expression rules. There are several reasons for affecting the accuracy rate of automatic recognition:

1. Automatic recognition of many types of dynamic words depends only on the POS and syllable numbers of internal components, thus a large number of non-dynamic words would be matched. For example, various combinations of two adjacent monosyllabic verbs would be matched when identifying the dynamic words whose structural mode is "v: v←v".

2. The regular expression rules of some dynamic word structural modes are not perfect enough. So many error results are obtained in recognition.
3. Some dynamic word structural modes have low frequency, which aren't representative and may only be applicable to individual dynamic words. In the recognition more errors will be produced.
4. In the knowledge base, there are many structural modes whose character sequences about the POS and syllable numbers of internal components are same, such as "a: a2…a2", "a: a2 ‖ a2" and "a: a2→a2" three modes. According to the recognition sequence of frequency from high to low, finally the dynamic words corresponding to the three structural modes would only be assigned to the structural mode which has the highest frequency.

5   Conclusion

The dynamic word problem is one of the key problems in Chinese information processing. It is very urgent and significant to study dynamic words and their automatic recognition systematically. On the one hand, it is conducive to the unity of granularity sizes of word segmentation results; on the other hand, it is an important basis for the realization of efficient and accurate automatic lexical and syntactic analysis. The range of dynamic words is very extensive, and the involved content is very rich. It is a long process to study dynamic words and their automatic recognition comprehensively and deeply. In this paper, although some preliminary achievements have been achieved in the research of dynamic words and their automatic recognition in Chinese information processing, there are still a lot of places to be improved and perfected.

References

1. Shuxiang, L.: Problems in Analyzing Chinese Grammar. Commercial Press, Beijing (1979)
2. Peng, W., Song, J., Sui, Z., Guo, D.: Formal Schema of Diagrammatic Chinese Syntactic Analysis. In: Lu, Q., Gao, H.H. (eds.) CLSW 2015. LNAI, vol. 9332, pp. 701-710. Springer, Heidelberg (2015)
3. Weiming, P., Jihua, S., Shiwen, Y.: Lexical Issues in Chinese Information Processing: in the Background of Sentence-based Diagram Treebank Construction. Journal of Chinese Information Processing 28(02), 1–7 (2014)
4. Jinxia, L.: The Theory and Practice of Distinguish between Words and Phrases. China Social Sciences Press, Beijing (2013)
5. Guo, D., Zhu, S., Peng, W., Song, J., Zhang, Y.: Construction of the Dynamic Word Structural Mode Knowledge Base for the International Chinese Teaching. In: Dong, M., Lin, J., Tang, X. (eds.) CLSW 2016. LNAI, vol. 10085, pp. 251-260. Springer, Heidelberg (2016)
6. He, J., Peng, W., Song, J., Liu, H.: Annotation Schema for Contemporary Chinese Based on JinXi Li's Grammar System. In: Liu, P., Su, Q. (eds.) CLSW 2013. LNAI, vol. 8229, pp. 668–681. Springer, Heidelberg (2013)
7. Tianxin, Y., Weiming, P., Jihua, S.: High Efficiency Syntax Tagging System Based on the Sentence Pattern Structure. Journal of Chinese Information Processing 04, 43–49 (2014)

8. Min, Z., Weiming, P., Jihua, S.: Development and Optimization of Syntax Tagging Tool on Diagrammatic Treebank. Journal of Chinese Information Processing 06, 26–33 (2014)
9. Jihua, S., Erhong, Y., Qiangjun, W.: Chinese Information Processing Tutorial. Higher Education Press, Beijing (2011)
10. Mingji, K.: Research on Chinese Word Segmentation System for the Analysis of International Chinese Textbooks. Beijing Normal University, Beijing (2014)

Matching Pattern Acquisition Approach for Ancient Chinese Treebank Construction

Jing He, Tianbao Song, Weiming Peng, and Jihua Song

College of Information Science and Technology, Beijing Normal University, Beijing, 100875, China
{hejing8, songtianbao}@mail.bnu.edu.cn, pengweiming@bnu.edu.cn, sjh13@163.com

Abstract. Matching Pattern (MP) is a sequence of words or part-of-speech (POS), sampled from clauses, and MP acquisition is an effective approach for ancient Chinese treebank construction. This approach uses the typical characteristics of ancient Chinese short-clauses and strong-patterns, and lays down the syntactic annotation process of the treebank construction in three stages. These stages involve: (1) obtaining weighted MPs with a syntactic skeleton; (2) applying these MPs to match the clauses; and (3) generating syntactic structures of these clauses according to the syntactic skeleton of the MP. The syntactic skeletons are constructed based on the Sentence-based Grammar in our experiments. The MP-based parsing procedures are implemented on both clause and fragment units. Experiments on corpora extracted from *Yili* and *Zuozhuan* show that an integrated algorithm, involving both clause and fragment units, can achieve a performance of 99.07%/82.76% and 97.25%/77.77% for coverage/precision, respectively.

Keywords: Matching Pattern, Ancient Chinese Treebank, Treebank Construction, Sentence-based Grammar

1 Introduction

A treebank is an in-depth processed text corpus, with annotated syntactic structure information. It is widely used in natural language processing (NLP) for automatic syntactic analysis, as well as for teaching grammar and researching corpus linguistics. Usually, Chinese treebanks are constructed for modern Chinese applications. Therefore, modern Chinese texts, especially news items, are the mainstream of raw corpora for Chinese treebanks. However, for Chinese language teaching and research, ancient Chinese treebanks are also important due to their great significance to understanding and exploring Chinese culture and its origins. Given the systematic differences in lexical and syntactical aspects of modern and ancient Chinese, the existing modern Chinese treebanks and their construction methods cannot be directly transplanted to ancient Chinese. Therefore, treebank construction for ancient Chinese lags behind methods for construction of modern Chinese treebank. Hitherto, the annotation of ancient

© Springer International Publishing AG 2018
Y. Wu et al. (Eds.): CLSW 2017, LNAI 10709, pp. 489–498, 2018.
https://doi.org/10.1007/978-3-319-73573-3_44

Chinese mostly is at the stage of word segmentation and Part-Of-Speech (POS) tagging, and research involving treebank construction for ancient Chinese texts remains scarce.

It is crucial to emphasize the following two points, concerned with the process of ancient Chinese treebank construction:

(1) A significant difference between ancient and modern Chinese is that the clauses in ancient Chinese are usually very short and have strong patterns. According to our statistics for 35 books of archaic Chinese, the average word count of its clauses is 4.05. Most of the clauses have simple structure and strong-patterned features; namely, the combinations of syntactic components are limited. Consequently, these features can be used in ancient Chinese treebank construction.

(2) Ancient Chinese differs from modern Chinese in its syntactic system, and traditional sentence-based grammar prevails among ancient Chinese scholars. In view of the aforementioned short-length sentences, the flattening annotation schema using Sentence Component (SC; e.g., subject, predicate, object) is a more intuitive approach to its treebank construction rather than dependency relationship structure or phrase structure.

2   Related Work

The construction of an ancient Chinese treebank relies on a lexical corpus that has word segmentation and POS tagging. The groundwork on ancient Chinese information processing is relatively limited. There are mainly four main institutions that have engaged in these studies and constructed large-scale corpora: (1) The Institute of Linguistics in Academia Sinica, which established the Academia Sinica Ancient Chinese Corpus in the 1990s [7]; (2) The University of Sheffield in Britain, which built the Sheffield Corpus of Chinese for the study of Chinese diachronic changes [1]; (3) Professor Chen Xiaohe's group at the Nanjing Normal University, which constructed an ancient Chinese corpus, including 25 kinds of pre-Qin dynasty literature [5]; and (4) The Research Center of Chinese Language and Character Resources (RCCLCR) at Beijing Normal University (BNU), which constructed a corpus with word segmentation and POS tagging information for *The Thirteen Classics* under the project of ancient and modern Chinese parallel corpus [6]. The POS tagging information of the former two corpora is of fine granularity, some of which have elaborated to the semantic level, and the number of the labels in the tag set is over 50. The latter two corpora adopted the general tag set and the number of the labels is 21 and 15, respectively. The untagged corpus of these four corpora mostly overlap, but there are many differences in the POS tagging. This reflects that there is not yet any universally accepted standard POS tag set for ancient Chinese corpus.

Treebanks using SCs as structure nodes are rare, and the only related research was carried out at the BNU Treebank built by the RCCLCR [2, 8, 3, 4]. The BNU Treebank was built under the guidelines of Li Jinxi's Sentence-based Grammar Theory, and represents the structure of sentence as a syntax diagram, stored in a specific XML format. Various syntactic formula and a case example are shown in Fig. 1.

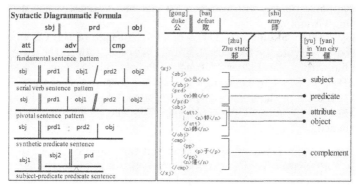

Fig. 1. Various Syntax Formula and an Example Showing Sentence Structure.

3   Parsing Procedure Based on the Clause Unit

We selected the clause as the basic unit for syntactic parsing. Usually, syntactic treebanks use "sentences", which are split by Chinese punctuations — the equivalent of the full stop " 。 ", the question mark " ？ " and the exclamation mark " ！ "—as the parsing unit, whilst clauses are parts of a sentence, divided by commas. It is important to clarify that a clause here is not the same as one defined in linguistics. In other words, not all of the spans separated by commas are strictly linguistic clauses, such as the leading adverbial of a sentence. For example, in the sentence "冬(winter) 十月(October)，不(had not) 雨(rained) 。", "冬十月" is the temporal adverbial of the clause "不雨". In this case, this adverbial should not only be analyzed individually, but also designated as a whole adverbial clause. In this way, the modifier-head relationship between it and the subsequent clause will not be lost during the final merging stage.

Because of the high recurrence rate of syntactic structure in a range of ancient Chinese corpora, we divided all the clauses into several subsets and annotated them in batches according to the specific "Word or POS" sequence, which is referred to here as the "Matching Pattern". Our formalized definitions are as follows (refer to Fig. 3 for details):

- **CS (Clause after word segmentation and POS tagging)**: W_1/P_1 $W_2/P_2 \ldots W_i/P_i \ldots W_n/P_n$, where W_i is the i-th word in a clause and P_i is the POS tag of W_i;
- **MP (Matching Pattern)**: $U_1 U_2 \ldots U_i \ldots U_n$, where U_i is a word or a POS;
- **Match**: For an n-length MP $\{U_i\}$ and an n-length CS $\{W_i/P_i\}$, if U_i is equal to W_i or P_i for $i \in [1, \ldots, n]$, then the MP and the CS Matches;
- **CS_Set (Matching set of a MP)**: $\{CS \mid MP \text{ and } CS \text{ Matches}\}$;

- **MP_Set & Mapping Group**: MP_Set = {MP | the Matching set of a MP equals to a specific CS_Set}, means the Set of MPs that are equivalent. There is a mappable relationship between MP_Set and CS_Set, which defines the Mapping Group;
- **SS (Syntactic Skeleton)**: The syntactic structure of the CS can be abstracted as a Syntactic Skeleton by replacing each word in the diagram and XML file with a placeholder "*" (refer to Fig. 1). The SS can be assigned to the MP of a CS_Set by choosing the one that covers most of the CSs in the CS_Set. If a CS in the testing corpus can be matched by a MP, its syntactic structure can be obtained by replacing "*" in the SS with words in the CS in sequence.

The MPs are generated by all the CSs, and each position in a MP is either a word or a POS from the sampled CS. Among these MPs, the more words adopted, the lower the number of CSs that the MP can Match, and the more likely that the CS_Set shares one SS. In contrast, the more POS adopted, the greater the number of CSs that the MP can Match, and the less likely that the CS_Set shares one SS. The general process for our ancient Chinese treebank construction is shown in Fig. 2:

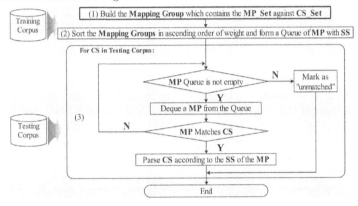

Fig. 2. Parsing Procedure Based on the Clause Unit.

3.1   Building the Mapping Group

The process of building a Mapping Group is shown in Fig. 3:

- **CS → MP**: All the CSs in the training corpus are sampled to generate the MPs. For each position of an n-length CS, either a word or its POS tag is selected. Therefore, there are 2^n combinations, where each one is a MP (refer to step ①). To reduce the computation complexity in the generation of MPs, a restriction is added, as follows: when selecting at a given position, if the frequency of the word (from the statistics in the corpus) is less than 3, then the corresponding position in the MP will always be the POS tag, rather than the word.

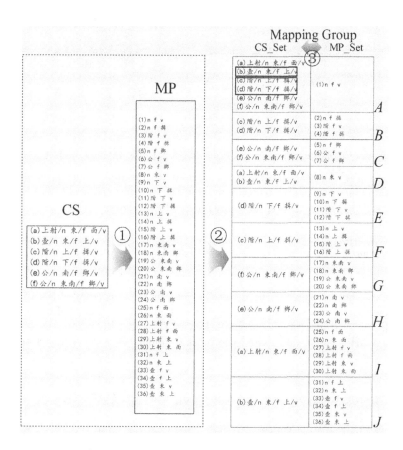

Fig. 3. Example of Building of Mapping Groups.

- **MP → CS_Set**: In step ①, a MP can be generated from multiple CSs. Therefore, for each MP, combine its matching CSs to form a CS_Set (refer to step ②).

- **CS_Set → MP_Set**: In step ②, a CS_Set may be formed by multiple MPs. Therefore, for each CS_Set, combine its corresponding MPs to form a MP_Set (refer to step ③). Each pair of CS_Set and MP_Set defines a Mapping Group, labeled A to J in Fig. 3.

3.2 Sorting the Mapping Groups by Weight

Some of the MP_Set have structural ambiguities. Take group A as an example, (a), (e) and (f) share one SS, (c) and (d) share another SS, while (b) has a third SS (refer to Fig. 4 for details). Accordingly, MP(1) in this MP_Set is structurally ambiguous.

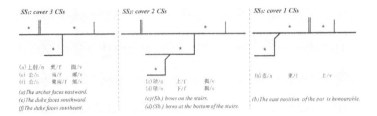

Fig. 4. Syntactic Skeleton (SS) Distribution of CS_Set of Mapping Group A in Fig. 3.

The weight of a Mapping Group is calculated to evaluate the consistency of its syntactic structure; this is decided using the entropy of the SS distribution of the CS_Set. The weighting formula is defined as follows:

$$W(Mapping\ Group) = H(SS\ of\ the\ CS\_Set) = -\sum_{SS} p(SS)\log_2 p(SS) \quad (1)$$

The smaller the weight, the higher the structural consistency of the CS_Set. Consequently, we can sort the Mapping Groups in ascending order of weight. For each Mapping Group, we choose the MP with the most POS from the MP_Set to form a MP Queue, and assign the most frequent SS of the CS_ Set to this MP.

3.3   Parsing by Scanning the Matching Pattern (MP) Queue

For a CS in the testing corpus, we first dequeue a MP from the MP Queue. If they match, then we parse the CS, according to the SS of the MP. If none of the MPs in the Queue match the CS, then we mark it as "unmatched".

4   Parsing Procedure Based on the Fragment Unit

The "unmatched" CSs from section 3 result from the fact that MPs generated from the training corpus cannot completely cover the range of CSs in the testing corpus. To boost this coverage, we apply the matching procedure described above to Fragment (FM) units of the CS, as shown in Fig. 5:

4.1   Obtaining Fragment Units (FMs) and Forming a Type_Seq_Bank

Given the sentence-based syntactic structure, we split each training CS into a sequence of fragments. The gestalt structure of a CS is:

- **CS ::= ADV + SBJ + PS$_1$ + ... + PS$_n$ + MODAL**
- **PS ::= ADV + PRD + CMP + OBJ**

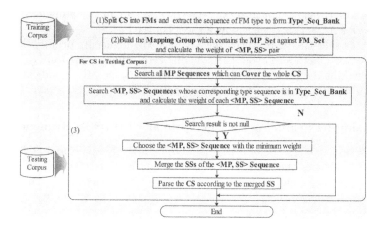

Fig. 5. Parsing Procedure Based on the Fragment Unit.

The CS can be composed of four FMs: the ADV, SBJ, PS and MODAL which represent adverbial, subject, predicate section and modal particles, respectively. The PS which is a kind of FM consists of four parts: adverbial, predicate, complement and object.

All the leading adverbials (if they exist) are merged as one FM, while adverbials after the subject, as well as complements and objects, remain with their predicates to form several PSs. Each PS corresponds to one FM. All attributes remain with their head-words, and are merged to form corresponding FMs. The modal particle is a standalone FM.

Each FM has a type, such as ADV, SBJ, or MODAL, known as its FM_Type. To disambiguate the syntactic relationship between successive PSs, we subdivide the PSs into three types: GEN-PS (general PSs), PVT-PS (the leading PS in a pivotal sentence, which contains the causative verb), and SYN-PS (the leading PS in a synthetic predicate sentence, which contains the auxiliary verb).

When splitting the CS into a FM sequence, we record the corresponding FM_Type sequence and its frequency. Finally, all the FM_Type sequences, with their probabilities are stored in a Type_Seq_Bank.

4.2 Building the Mapping Group and Its Weighted <MP, SS> Pairs

We used the method described in section 3.1 to build Mapping Groups. In this case, we map the MP_Set against the FM_Set. Thus, the only difference in this mapping procedure is that we replace the CS unit with a FM unit.

Similarly, we select the MP with the most POS from the MP_Set, and combine it with each distinct SS of the FM_Set to form a <MP, SS> pair. We also add the FM_Type to the SS to obtain general structural information. Hence, we redefine the weighting formula, as follows:

$$W(<MP, SS>) = \frac{(H(SS_{1..n} \ of \ FM\_Set) + 1) * (length \ of \ MP)}{(FM \ num \ of \ SS)^{0.1} * (Word \ num \ of \ MP + 1)} \quad (2)$$

Now, a lower weight indicates that the <MP, SS> pair has a higher priority. $H(SS_{1..n}\ of\ FM\_Set)$ is the entropy of the SS of the FM_Set. $\frac{length\ of\ MP}{Word\ num\ of\ MP+1}$ demonstrates that the more words the MP has, the higher its priority. We add one to these two factors to avoid them having zero values. $(FM\ num\ of\ SS)^{0.1}$ is used to weight the priority of different SSs for the same MP; it indicates that the more FMs the SS possesses, the higher priority its <MP, SS> pair.

4.3   Parsing by Searching for the Optimal <MP, SS> Sequence

During the testing stage, we omit the SS in the <MP, SS> pair, and first search for all MP sequences that can "cover" the whole CS. Here, "cover" means the MPs in the sequence can match the FMs in the CS in succession. The search algorithm uses the following steps: generate all the substrings (namely word/POS sequences) of the CS; try to match each substring with MPs of the same length; using the result of this matching, search for valid match sequences that can be concatenated to cover the whole CS.

For each valid match sequence (namely each MP Sequence), we add the omitted SSs back to the MPs, extract the FM_Type of the SS, and filter out any <MP,SS> sequences that do not have a FM_Type sequence in the Type_Seq_Bank. For each remaining <MP,SS> sequence, we calculate its weight, as follows:

$$W(< MP, SS > Seq) = \sum_{<MP,SS>} W(< MP, SS >) - P(FM\_Type\ Seq) \quad (3)$$

Similar to equation (2), here a lower weight indicates a higher priority. The former part is the sum of the weight of the <MP, SS> pairs in the sequence, while the latter part is the probability of the corresponding FM_Type sequence stored in the Type_Seq_Bank.

Next, we select the <MP, SS> sequence with the minimum weight, merge its SSs to form an integral SS, and perform a final parse of the CS, according to the integral SS. If the search result after this filtering step is null, then this CS is ultimately marked as "unmatched".

5   Experiments and Results

Experiments were carried out to evaluate the two procedures using CS or FM units individually, and as an integrated procedure. All the experiments were performed on two corpora, selected from the *Yili* and *Zuozhuan* in the BNU Ancient Chinese Treebank built by RCCLCR. There are 8,251 clauses in the *Yili* corpus, 5,786 of which were used for training and 2,465 for testing. Likewise, there were 6,791 clauses in the *Zuozhuan* corpus, of which 4,356 were used for training and 2,435 for testing. The detailed size of each chapter in the two corpora are shown in Table 1 and Table 2.

Two metrics were used to evaluate the three experiments:

$$Accuracy = RC/MC \quad (4)$$

Table 1. The Size of the *Yili* Corpus.

Chapter Name	Sentence number	Clause number	Type
士冠礼 [Shi Guan Li]	207	528	Training corpus
士昏礼 [Shi Hun Li]	310	712	
士相见礼 [Shi Xiang Jian Li]	113	260	
乡射礼 [Xiang She Li]	675	1736	
大射 [Da She]	539	1779	
既夕礼 [Ji Xi Li]	333	771	
聘礼 [Pin Li]	568	1457	Testing corpus
士丧礼 [Shi Sang Li]	400	1008	

Table 2. The Size of the *Zuozhuan* Corpus.

Chapter Name	Sentence number	Clause number	Type
僖公 [Xi Gong]	2181	4356	Training corpus
文公 [Wen Gong]	1174	2435	Testing corpus

$$Coverage = MC/AC \tag{5}$$

In the above equations, RC denotes the number of the clauses parsed correctly, MC denotes the number of the matched clauses, and AC denotes the total number of clauses in the test corpus.

Experiments 1 and 2 were carried out using the parsing procedure based on the CS unit and the FM unit, respectively. In contrast, experiment 3 used clause-based parsing, then a fragment-based parsing for any "unmatched" clauses arising in the former procedure. Their results are shown in Table 3, Table 4, and Table 5, respectively.

Table 3. Results of Experiment 1

Metric	Results for the *Yili* corpus	Results for the *Zuozhuan* corpus
MC	2150	1937
RC	1931	1713
Accuracy	**89.81%**	**88.44%**
Coverage	87.22%	79.55%

The clause-based parsing outweighed the fragment-based parsing in terms of the accuracy, but was inferior in terms of its coverage. The high accuracy of Experiment 1 shows the effectiveness of the MP acquisition approach, while the highest RC value obtained in Experiment 3 shows that fragment-based parsing can be used as a complementary procedure to improve overall performance of our method.

6   Conclusions

Constructing a treebank for ancient Chinese is an important objective that would result in a highly valuable resource for linguistic study and research. This pa-

Table 4. Results of Experiment 2

Metric	Results for the *Yili* corpus	Results for the *Zuozhuan* corpus
MC	2442	2368
RC	1774	1675
Accuracy	72.65%	70.73%
Coverage	**99.07%**	**97.25%**

Table 5. Results of Experiment 3

Metric	Results for the *Yili* corpus	Results for the *Zuozhuan* corpus
MC	2442	2368
RC	**2021**	**1844**
Accuracy	82.76%	77.77%
Coverage	99.07%	97.25%

per proposes an effective approach for treebanking of ancient Chinese based on Matching Patterns.

Our Matching Pattern acquisition relies on the consistency of the syntax and lexicon between training and testing corpora. Such consistency usually exists in the classical works of ancient Chinese, especially among different chapters of the same works. Consequently, our approach can greatly reduce the manual annotation involved in ancient Chinese treebank construction.

References

1. Hu, X., Williamson, N., McLaughlin, J.: Sheffield corpus of chinese for diachronic linguistic study1. Literary and Linguistic Computing 20(3), 281–293 (2005)
2. Peng, W., He, J., Song, J.: The design and implement of diagrammatical sentence-based grammar parsing system. In: 4th International Conference of Digital Archives and Digital Humanities. Research Center for Digital Humanities, National Taiwan University (2012)
3. Peng, W., Song, J., Sui, Z., Guo, D.: Formal schema of diagrammatic chinese syntactic analysis. In: Workshop on Chinese Lexical Semantics. pp. 701–710. Springer (2015)
4. Peng, W., Song, J., Wang, N.: Issues on formalization of chinese syntactic analysis. Journal of Chinese Information Processing 30(3), 175–180 (2016)
5. Shi, M., Chen, X., Li, B.: Crf based research on a unified approach to word segmentation and pos tagging for pre-qin chinese. Journal of Chinese Information Processing 2(24), 39–45 (2010)
6. Song, J.h., Hu, J.j., Meng, P.s., Wang, N.: The construction of corpora in a classic-cotemporary chinese parallel corpus. Modern Educational Technology 1, 027 (2008)
7. Wei, P.c., Thompson, P., Liu, C.h., Huang, C.R., Sun, C.: Historical corpora for synchronic and diachronic linguistics studies. Computational Linguistics and Chinese Language Processing 2(1), 131–145 (1997)
8. Zhao, M., Peng, W., Song, J., Yang, T.: Development and optimization of syntax tagging tool on diagrammatic treebank. Journal of Chinese Information Processing 28(6), 26–33 (2014)

Annotation Guidelines of Semantic Roles for Semantic Dependency Graph Bank

Xinghui Cheng[1], Yanqiu Shao[1*]

[1] Information Science School, Beijing Language and Culture University, Beijing, China
mulin17@163.com ,yqshao163@163.com

Abstract. During the process of annotating the corpus of Semantic Dependency Graph, we found that each semantic role contains tinier semantic characters which are easy for annotators to tag them in different ways. So we set a whole set of annotation guidelines to keep the annotation process objective and identical. There are 3 types of guidelines: paradigmatic relations, syntagmatic relations and semantic features. From the annotation guidelines of subject roles, object roles and some groups of circumstanced roles, a more scientific annotation system was gradually founded, and so that we can make the manual annotation less confused. By means of this, we can make a high-quality corpus and make the computer understand nature language better.

Keywords: annotation guidelines, paradigmatic relations, syntagmatic relations, semantic features

1   Introduction

Semantic Dependency Graph Bank (SDGB) is a corpus which was jointly constructed by Beijing Language and Culture University and Harbin Institute of Technology for the goal of semantic dependency research. The theoretical base is the dependency grammar (DG) [1]. Inheriting and developing the previous theory, a new semantic analysis system named Semantic Dependency Graph (SDG) was put forward. SDG system aims to find all the word pairs with real semantic relations and link up each word pair with a dependency arc with a semantic label on it [2]. Analyzing the dependency relationship of sentences means the deconstruction and recombination of all the words in the sentence. In order to build a high-quality tagged corpus, a complete processing specification must be worked out [3]. Therefor combined with the annotation experience, we found that each semantic tag may have the smaller distinctions, which made the boundaries among them ambiguous. Yuan Yulin [4] summarized that "semantic roles set by different scholars may have a big disparity .The conceptions of each role may have a big disparity too.'' In order to ensure the objectivity of the consistency of the annotation process and the annotation results. And also in order to

---

* Corresponding Author

© Springer International Publishing AG 2018
Y. Wu et al. (Eds.): CLSW 2017, LNAI 10709, pp. 499–509, 2018.
https://doi.org/10.1007/978-3-319-73573-3_45

make the computer understand natural language more accurately, it is necessary to make sure the boundaries of the different semantic roles.

There are three parts of the tagging system in SDGB: semantic roles, semantic constructions and semantic marks. Considering the core semantic labeling is semantic roles, so we make distinguishes among them only. A semantic role refers to the participant's role in the semantic event that the statement is expressed by the language components [5]. Our semantic roles in SDGB are based on the system of Dong Zhendong's Hownet [6] and the parataxis network of Lu Chuan [7] and also united the semantic system of Yuan Yulin [8]. All semantic roles are divided into three types, subject roles, object roles and circumstanced roles. And the former two types refer to the real entities in a semantic event while the latter one refers to some situational factors such as time, space and so on.

Annotation information should be standardized and concise as well as specific and highly recognizable [9]. So based on the roles' characters, the guidelines for labeling that we set are paradigmatic relations, syntagmatic relations and semantic features. And tables of each type of guidelines are made so it can be very clear to present the differences among them. From these 3 aspects the guidelines can be made operational and practical. As for subject roles, there are 4 roles needed to tell the differences: agent role (Agt), experiencer role (Exp), affection role (Aft), and possessor role (Poss). As for object roles there are 5 kinds: patient role (Pat), content role (Cont), dative role (Datv), product role (Prod), belongings role (belg).Besides these above, there are still several groups of easily confused circumstanced roles needed to be distinguished.

2   Paradigmatic relations

Paradigmatic relations means the relations of language units that can be substituted for each other in the same grammatical position. Concretely speaking, paradigmatic relations refer to the semantic role can appear in which kind of sentence patterns and can act as which kind of syntactic components.

2.1   Paradigmatic relations of subject roles

According to the characters of subject roles, we chose 4 items as the paradigmatic relations for annotation. They are respectively "can be subject or not", "can be attributive or not", "can be in adjective predicate sentence or not", or "can be in noun predicate sentence or not". And here is the table to show the paradigmatic relations of subject roles below.

Table 1. The table of paradigmatic relations of subject roles

Paradigmatic relations	Agt	Exp	Aft	Poss
1.be subject	+	+	+	+
2.be attributive	-	-	-	+

3.adjective predicate sentence	-	+	-	-
4.noun predicate sentence	-	+	-	+

From the point of syntactic components, what makes a Poss role special is that it can be attributive. Here are two examples:

1. **老虎·伍兹**的招牌笑容是球迷的最爱。

   The sign smile of *Tiger Woods* is the best love of fans.

2. 她把孩子从**父亲**怀里抢了过去。

   She snatched the son from *father's* arms.

Example (1), the relationship between "老虎·伍兹（Tiger Woods）"and "笑容（smile）" is the relationship of leader and subordinate". And example (2), the relationship between "父亲（father）" and "怀里（arms）" is the relationship of whole and part. So it should be annotated as a Poss role.

From the point of sentence patterns, what makes an Exp role special is that it can appear in adjective predicate sentences. In Chinese, adjectives can act as a predicate to describe the properties and states of subjects. Here are two examples:

1. **宝塔**很高。

   The tower is very tall.

2. **海风**特别凉爽。

   The wind from the sea is very cool.

In the two examples above, "高（tall）" is one of the attributes of "宝塔（tower）" to describe the height of the tower. And the "凉爽（cool）" is one of the attributes of "海风 (the wind from sea)" to describe the temperature of the wind. So it should be annotated as Exp role.

Also, Exp roles and Poss roles can be in the examples with a nominal predicate. In Chinese some nouns can act as a predicate and they are limited to some colloquial examples describing time, weather, native place, age, appearance, and quantity and so on. Their subjects are often Exp roles and Poss roles. Here are two examples.

1. **潘老太太**刚好八十八岁。

   Ms Pan is eighty-eight years old.

2. **她**大眼睛，红脸蛋。

   She has a pair of big eyes and a red face.

Example (1), "八十八岁 (eighty-eight years old)" is a noun phase and it explains the age of "潘老太太 (Ms. Pan)". Also there is no verbs in the example. The function of this noun phase is equal to a verb. So "潘老太太 (Ms. Pan)" should be annotated as an Exp role. Example (2), there are no verbs as predicates, either. Instead, the function of noun phrases of "大眼睛(big eyes)" and "红脸蛋(red face)" is equal to a predicate. They describe the appearances of the subject roles. And the appearances are part of the subject's body. So the subject should be annotated as a Poss role.

2.2   Paradigmatic relations of object roles

An object role is another participant's role of a semantic event. We chose 2 items as the paradigmatic relations. Here is the table to show the paradigmatic relations of subject roles.

Table 2. The table of paradigmatic relations of object roles

Paradigmatic relations	Pat	Cont	Datv	Prod	Belg
1.be objective	+	+	+	+	+
2.adjective predicate sentence	-	-	+	-	-

All the object roles can be objective compared to subject roles. But what makes a Datv role special is that it can be in adjective predicate sentences to act as the comparison objects involved in the semantic event. Here is an example.

1. 月亮比**地球**小。
   The moon is smaller than *the earth*.

In this example, "**地球** (the earth)" is an object to be compared to the subject. So it is a dative participant which is involved in the semantic event. And the adjective is one of results of comparison. So it should be annotated as a Datv role.

2.3   Paradigmatic relations of circumstanced roles

Circumstanced roles are different from subject roles and object roles. They are not the real entities in a semantic event. Instead, they describe the time and space that semantic event happened. Or they introduce the materials and the tools which participant roles used. They are mainly the adverbial components in the sentences and always present in verbal sentences. It is so easy to distinguish them that we don't need to make tables to show the differences of paradigmatic relations.

3   Syntagmatic relations

Syntagmatic relations refer to the combination abilities between semantic roles and some verbs, prepositions and adverbs. Once the syntagmatic relations of semantic roles are determined, which is equal to build the syntax formats with semantic information [10].It is easy to establish the mapping and connection between syntactic structures and semantic structures.

3.1   Syntagmatic relations of subject roles

We chose 9 items to distinguish the subject roles. Here is the table of syntagmatic relations of subject roles below.

Table 3. The table of syntagmatic relations of subject roles

syntagmatic relations	Agt	Exp	Aft	Poss
1.before action verbs	+	-	-	-
2.before psychological verbs	-	-	+	-
3.before statement verbs	-	+	-	+
4.before judge verbs	-	+	-	-
5.before structure of "不(no)+V"	+	+	+	-
6.before structure of " 没有(don't have)+V"	+	+	-	+
7.before structure of "V+(了/一/不)+V "	+	+	-	-
8.before structure of "V +成/完"	+	+	+	-
9.before preposition "把" or after "被"	+	-	-	-

Agt roles usually appear before action verbs and action verbs can be modified by negative words "不 (no)" and "没有 (don't have)". They can also have different overlapping forms such as "V+一+V" or "V +了+V" or "V +不+V". They can also appear in the special sentence patterns and before the preposition "把" or after the preposition "被".

Exp roles usually appear before the statement verbs and judge verbs and these verbs can be described by "不" or "没有", too. And also they can have overlapping forms and they can generate a result. Here are some examples below.

1. **大厦**有30层高。
The building is 30 floors in height.
2. **弟弟**不是中学生。
My brother is not a middle school student.
3. **桌子**上没有灰尘。
There is no dust on the *table*.
4. **水管**锈成实心的了。
The water pipe has rusted into solid.

There are two kinds of Aft roles. One is the subject of "perception" and the other kind is the subject of "emotion". So Aft roles usually appear before the psychological verbs. And some Aft roles can perceive a result. Here are two examples.

1. **他**很崇拜周杰伦。
He adores Jay Chou.
2. **同学们**听完了报告。
The students finished listening to the report.

Example (1), "崇拜(adore)" describes a kind of emotion and "他(He)" is the subject of emotion. Example (2), "听(listen)" describe a kind of perception and "同学们 (the students)" is the subject of perception. So they should be annotated as Aft roles.

Poss roles mainly describe the relationships between the whole and the part or the leader and the subordinate. So they usually appear before statement verbs. For example：

1. **螃蟹**有八条腿。
   A crap has 8 legs.

In this example, the relation between "螃蟹(the crap)" and "腿(legs)" is the whole and the part. So it should be annotated as a Poss role.

3.2   Syntagmatic relations of object roles

We chose 7 items to distinguish the object roles. Here is the table of syntagmatic relations of object roles.

Table 4. The table of syntagmatic relations of object roles

syntagmatic relations	Pat	Cont	Datv	Prod	Belg
1.be in preposition-object structure	-	-	+	-	+
2.be indirect objects	-	-	+	-	-
3.be direct objects	-	+	-	-	+
4.after psychological verbs	-	+	-	-	-
5.after structure of "V +成/完"	-	-	-	+	+
6.after structure of "V+(了/一/不)+V"	+	+	-	-	-
7after preposition "把" or before "被"	+	-	-	-	-

Pat roles can appear in the syntactic contexts No.6 and No.7 above. Here are two examples. Example 1 shows that a Pat role can appear after the overlapping forms of a verb and the example 2 shows that a Pat role can also exist after the preposition "把".

1. 英子写不写**作业**?
   Whether does Yingzi do her *homework* or not?
2. 英子把**作业**写了。
   Yingzi has done her *homework*.

Cont roles can appear in the syntactic contexts No.3, No.4 and No.6. They can act as an indirect object in a sentence or appear after a psychological verb. And also, they can be after the overlapping forms of a verb. Here are some examples below.

1. 张老师给学生讲**历史**。
   Teacher Zhang teaches students *history*.
2. 姐姐喜欢**文学作品**。
   My sisters likes *literary works*.
3. 主席给大家讲了讲今年的**工作任务**。
   The chairman told everyone about *the tasks of the year*

Datv roles can appear in the syntactic contexts No.1 and No.2 above. They can appear in the structure of preposition-object and be direct objects. For example:

1. 张老师给**学生**讲历史。
Teacher Zhang teaches *students* history.

Prod roles can appear in the syntactic context No.5. They can be after the structure of "成/完". "成/完" shows the states which have been completed. So the participants in the semantic event after them should be annotated as Prod roles. For example：

1. 姐姐写完了一本**小说**。
My sister finished *a novel*.

Belg roles can appear in the syntactic contexts No.1, No.3 and No.5. Here are two examples:

1. 新厂长拜老厂长为**师**。
The new director takes the old one as *a teacher*.
2. 阿姨把旧窗帘撕成了**抹布**。
The aunt ripped the old curtains into *rags*.

3.3   Syntagmatic relations of circumstanced roles

What makes some circumstanced roles confused is the syntactic contexts they show up. According to the annotation experience before, there are some groups of confused circumstanced roles. The key to annotate them is to make clear the relationships between each role and the typical prepositions [11]. Prepositions mainly act as the functions of marking, modifying and adding predicate words to indicate the time, place, manner, reason, purpose of the semantic events [12]. So we decided to set the collocations of roles and prepositions as the annotation guidelines.

There are 43 kinds of circumstanced roles in the annotation system. It is meaningless to make comparisons all of them. Therefore we chose several easily confused groups of circumstanced roles to make comparisons.

Group 1: Mann (manner), Tool (tool), Matl (material), Sco (Scope), Reas (Reason)

Table 5. The table of syntagmatic relations of circumstanced roles

syntagmatic relations	Mann	Tool	Matl	Sco	Reas
1.after preposition "用(by)"	+	+	+	-	-
2.after preposition "在(at)"	-	-	-	+	-
3.after preposition " 为 (wei)"	-	-	-	-	+

"在+Sco" and "为+Reas" are easy to distinguish because of the different prepositions. While the Mann roles, Tool roles and Matl roles can all appear after "用". "用" can act as a preposition to import the manners or the tools of semantic events. So these three are not very easy to distinguish. They still need other useful information in certain situations to differentiate.

Group 2: Stat(state), Sini(initial state) ,Sfin(final state),Sproc(process state)

Table 6. The table of syntagmatic relations of circumstanced roles.

syntagmatic relations	Stat	Sini	Sfin	Sproc
1.after preposition "在(at)"	+	-	-	-
2.after preposition " 自 / 从 (from)"	-	+	-	-
3.after preposition "到(to)"	-	-	+	-

From the table above, it is very clear to tell the differences from each other. And also this table can be extended into the circumstanced roles of Time(Time,Tini,Tfin,Tdur) and Space(Loc,Lini,Lfin,Lthru) and Measure(Quan,Nini,Nfin,Qp.)

4   Semantic features.

The semantic features refer to the characters of predicates that govern the semantic roles. We didn't choose the features of semantic roles because there is no exact relations between the words and the roles. For example, the word "teacher" can be a subject role or an object role, which is not confirmed. And also it is the verbs' features that decide a certain word to be a certain kind of roles.

4.1   Semantic features of subject roles

According to the features of verbs which can govern subject roles, we chose 6 items as semantic features. These items are arranged in descending order according to their importance.

Table 7. The table of semantic features of subject roles

semantic features	Agt	Exp	Aft	Poss
1.active	+	-	+	-
2.cause	+	-	-	-
3.attribution	-	+	-	-
4.psychology	-	-	+	-
5.change	-	+	-	-
6.correlation	-	+	-	+

[Active] refers that the subject participant is able to exert action and influence on the object. [Cause] refers that the subjects request or order objects and makes the objects change the state. [Attribution] refers that the predicate describes some features of subjects. [Psychology] refers to the subjects' inner mental activities or likes and dislikes about something. [Change] refers to the changes or improvements from one state to another state. [Correlation] refers to the relationship between subjects and objects governed by predicates.

Agt roles possess the features of [active] and [cause]. Here is an example. "吃 (eat)" is a verb with autonomy. So it has the active attribute and can make some influence on the objects. :

1. **齿鲸**主要吃大鱼和海兽。
   Odontocetis mainly eat big fish and sea animals.

Exp roles possess the features of [attribution], [change] and [correlation]. For example:

1. **骄傲**是他垮台的原因。
   Arrogance is the reason of his failure.

Aft roles possess the features of [active], [psychology]. Here is an example. The subject of "忘(forget)" means a subject of perception. So it should be annotated as an Aft role.

1. **他**把那件事给忘了。
   He forgot that thing.

Poss roles possess the feature of [correlation]. In the example below, "感觉 (feeling)" belongs to "我们(we)". So we annotated it as a Poss role.

1. **我们**今天仍有这种感觉。
   We still have this kind of feeling.

4.2   Semantic features of object roles

According to the features of verbs which can govern object roles, we chose 6 items as semantic features. They are: [Passive], [change], [result], [correlation], and [origin].

Table 8. The table of semantic features of subject roles

Semantic features	Pat	Cont	Datv	Prod	Belg
1.Passive	+	+	-	-	-
2.change	+	-	-	+	-
3.result	+	-	-	+	-
4.correlation	-	-	+	-	+
5.origin	-	-	+	-	-

[Passive] refers that object roles are dominated by other participants in semantic events. [Result] refers that object roles got the things done or produced a result after the domination actions. [Origin] refers to the initial owner of the actions.

Pat roles possess the features of [Passive], [change] and [result]. Here is an example below. "笔(pen)" is a noun with no active attribute. And its owner changed from "他(he)" to "弟弟(brothter)".

1. 他赠弟弟一只**笔**。
   He gave his brother a *pen*.

Cont roles possess the features of [Passive]. In the example below, "历史(histrory)" is an objective existence. And it has kind of an attribute of passive to present that it can't be changed or moved by the subject roles. So it should be annotated as a Cont role.

1. 张老师给学生讲**历史**。
   Teacher Zhang teaches students *history*.

Datv roles possess the features of [correlation] and [Origin]. For example:

1. 张老师给**学生**讲历史。
   Teacher Zhang teaches *students* history.

Prod roles possess the features of [change] and [result]. In this example, "小说(novel)" is a result of "他(he)". And its existence changed from "nothing" to "a book". So it is a product of the subject role and it should be annotated as a Prod role.

1. 他写了一本**小说**。
   He has written *a novel*

Belg roles possess the features of [correlation]. In this example, "朋友(friends)" are from "小宋(Ms. Song)" . So it should be annotated as a Belg role to show semantic features of correlation.

1. 小宋有很多**朋友**。
   Mr. Song has many *friends*.

4.3   Semantic features of circumstanced roles

The semantic features of circumstanced roles are mainly about the adverbial semantic features. And there are 10 kinds of roles in total: manner, material, tool, scope, reason, time, space, measure, state and modifier. Their semantic boundaries are very different from each other. So we don't need to make forms to distinguish them.

5   Conclusion

There are 3 types of guidelines of semantic roles mentioned above all in total. Paradigmatic relations and syntagmatic relations are related to the roles' grammatical power in one sentence. While the semantic features are connected with the predicative and adverbial features of the predicates which are related to the roles. When comes to a certain type of roles, guidelines for different types are made in different ways. Therefore, we observed the most unique characters of each semantic role and make a set of targeted guidelines to instruct the operations of annotation.

This paper focuses on the guidelines of ambiguous semantic roles of Semantic Dependency Graph Bank. Also this paper is a summary of previous work of the establishment and annotations of Semantic Dependency Graph Bank. On the base of conclusions we aim to improve the accuracy and consistency of the corpus annotation process and also build a high-quality corpus on the theory of Semantic Dependency Graph.

6   Acknowledgements

Thanks for National Natural Science Foundation of China (NSFC) No.61170144 and No.61371129.Major Program of China's National Linguistic work Committee during the twelfth five-year plan (ZDI125-41). Young and middle aged academic cadre support plan of Beijing Language and Culture University (501321303).Supported by the Research Funds of Beijing Language and Culture University (No. 17YCX136)

References

1. Robinson, Dependency Structures and Transformation Rules. Language, 1970.
2. Shao Yanqiu, Zheng Lijuan., "Deep Semantic Analysis: from Dependency Tree to Dependency graph," International Journal of Advanced Intelligence，Vol. 8, No.1, May, 2016.
3. Yu Shiwen, Zhu Xuefeng,Duan Huiming,A Guideline for segmentation and Part of Speech Tagging on Very Large Scale of Corpus of Contemporary Chinese,Journal of Chinese Information Processing, Vol.14, No.6,2000.
4. Yuan Yulin, A set of grammatical guidelines to the semantic roles in Chinese,No.3, Chinese Teaching in the World,2003.
5. Chai Yumei,Zhang Kunli, Artificial Intelligence, Beijing,China Machine Press, 2012.
6. Qiang Dong, Zhendong Dong, Hownet and Computation of Meaning. Singapore: World Scientific Publishing Company, 2006.
7. Lu Chuan,The parataxis Network of Chinese Grammar, The Commercial Press, 2001.
8. Yuan Yulin,The hierarchical relationship and semantic features of meta roles,No.3, Chinese Teaching in the World,2002.
9. Aihua Dong,A discussion to annotation of the corpora, Journal of Beijing Institute of Graphic Communication,Vol.24,No.5,2016.
10. Lu Chuan. Prepositions are important symbols of the semantic components of Chinese sentences: Language teaching and research, 1987.
11. Huang Borong, Liao Xudong,Xiandai Hanyu,Higher Education Press,2007.
12. Shao Jingmin, Zhou Shao, Definition and Isolation of Semantic Features, Foreign Language Teaching and Research, vol.37, No.1, Jan.2005.

Chinese Conjunctions in Second Language Learners' Written Texts

Jia-Fei Hong

National Taiwan Normal University, Taiwan
jiafeihong@ntnu.edu.tw

Abstract. In Chinese texts, cohesion refers to grammatical or lexical relationships within sentences and texts. Through these relationships, a series of sentences are connected to form unified texts that are intelligible and meaningful. Various studies have found that cohesion is a crucial factor in readability and reading comprehension, and thus have maintained that cohesion in a text influences comprehension [1]. Among the recent studies on Chinese readability [2], [3], [4], [5], most have overlooked the function of discourse connectives for better reading comprehension. In this study, five Chinese conjunction types taken from a Chinese Written Corpus (CWC) were analyzed to determine their semantic features and structures and the reasons for learners' usage errors. The results of this study will contribute to the development of teaching Chinese writing by using Chinese conjunctions to improve learners' writing abilities.

Keywords. Chinese conjunctions, semantic features, semantic structures, teaching Chinese writing

1   Introduction

Learning Chinese has been a trend in recent years. The development of language learning involves four dimensions: listening, speaking, reading, and writing. In researches of second language learning, learners reported that listening and reading tasks were easier than speaking and writing tasks. Because of the specific grammars and vocabularies in the texts, some studies also found that it is difficult for second language learners to improve their writing ability in a short period of time [6]

In Chinese, cohesion plays a significant role in word/grammar relationships in the context of sentences. The cohesion of words and sentences facilitates the understanding of the meaning of the whole context. Researches have shown that the cohesion of conjunctions is a key point of logical thinking and understanding [1], which helps readers to achieve better comprehension of sentences, paragraphs, and the full context of the written text. Cohesion here refers to using conjunctions properly in sentences.

© Springer International Publishing AG 2018
Y. Wu et al. (Eds.): CLSW 2017, LNAI 10709, pp. 510–522, 2018.
https://doi.org/10.1007/978-3-319-73573-3_46

The current research used a Chinese Writing Corpus (CWC) as the database from which five categories of associated conjunctions were chosen. The conjunctions were analyzed to determine their semantic characteristics and structures and the learners' usage errors. The aim of this research was to discern the writing patterns of Chinese second language learners, the results of which will provide evidence for the current proposal, which in turn will contribute to the development of teaching Chinese writing to improve learners' writing skills using proper conjunctions.

2   Research Motivation and Goal

The development of language learning includes four dimensions: listening, speaking, reading, and writing. Previous research has found that second language learners experience more difficulties in speaking and writing tasks than in listening and reading tasks. Moreover, it was found that teachers encountered difficulties in teaching second language learners to improve their writing abilities, especially among learners at different proficiency levels. As such, teaching structures and materials should be designed to be in line with learners' different proficiency levels.

In teaching Chinese writing, the goal is for learners to be able to write a logical and well-organized text, and conjunctions play a significant role in its comprehension and cohesion in the context of Chinese writing. Based on the Input Hypothesis Model [7], if the message conveyed to learners is too difficult, they might become frustrated and give up, and if it is too easy, they might lose motivation and interest [8]. Therefore, designing teaching materials according to learners' proficiency level will help learners to achieve the best learning outcomes [9], [10], [11].

The current research aimed to analyze the error distribution of conjunctions in five categories taken from a CWC, the results of which will be used to design ideal teaching materials and courses to improve the teaching of Chinese writing.

3   Data Collection

This study used a CWC of collected compositions to analyze the conjunction errors made by learners at different proficiency levels, the results of which will contribute to the amelioration of the Automated Essay Scoring for Han (AES-Han) and related researches [12]. The compositions in the CWC were collected from September 2010 to March 2016. The research team recorded detailed information from each composition, including the topic, the author's name (both in English and Chinese), nationality, mother tongue, and school, which were filed as a text (.txt) and as a scanned file (.jpeg).

In the current research, four different topics from the database were collected: "一個值得去的地方 (*yīgè zhídé qù dì dìfāng*, A place worth a visit.)," "夏天的海邊 (*xiàtiān de hǎibiān*, Summer seaside.)," "寫給家人的一封信 (*xiě gěi jiārén de yī fēng xìn*, A letter to my family.)," and "介紹我的國家 (*jièshào wǒ de guójiā*, Introduce my country.). The total number of compositions collected was 2,683, of which there were 784, 722, 646, and 544 for each topic, respectively [12]. The compositions, which were collected from the MTC (Mandarin Training Center, National Taiwan Normal University) and 10 other language centers in Taiwan,[1] were written by Chinese language learners from 37 countries.

4   Data Analysis

4.1   Selection of Five Conjunction Types

The writing style of the compositions in the CWC were narratives. In a narrative, associated conjunctions play an indispensable role; therefore, associated conjunctions were the target of our research. From the various kinds of associated conjunctions, we chose five categories as the research goal: "concessive," "causal," "hypothesis," "condition," and "purpose." Using the CWC, we first collected the conjunctions and errors found in these five categories. After collection and classification, the five categories were analyzed in terms of their semantic components to determine the cause of the writers' errors. The data collection and categorization steps are shown in Figure 1 below:

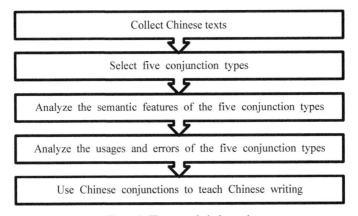

Figure 1: The research design and steps

In the five categories, certain Chinese conjunctions were chosen to exemplify the research target, as shown below:

---

[1] The 10 other Chinese Language Centers are as follows: National Chengchi University, Private Chinese Culture University, Kainan University, National Cheng Kung University, Tunghai University, National Chung Hsing University, Ming Chuan University, Providence University, Feng Chia University, and Fu Jen Catholic University.

(i) Concessive: 虽然 (*suīrán*), 虽 (*suī*), 虽说 (*suīshuō*), 尽管 (*jǐnguan*), 固然 (*gùrán*), 但 (*dàn*), 但是 (*dànshì*), 可 (*kě*), 可是 (*kěshì*), 而 (*ér*), and 然而 (*ránér*)

(ii) Causal: 因为 (*yīnwèi*), 因此 (*yīncǐ*), 所以 (*suǒyǐ*), and 由于 (*yóuyú*)

(iii) Hypothesis: 如果 (*rúguǒ*) and 要是 (*yàoshì*)

(iv) Condition: 不管 (*bùguan*), 只要 (*zhǐyào*), and 除非 (*chúfēi*)

(v) Purpose: 以 (*yǐ*), 以便 (*yǐbiàn*), 以免 (*yǐmiǎn*), and 为了 (*wèile*)

4.2 "Concessive" Category

The "concessive" category included 然 (*sunclu*), 虽 (*sun*), 虽说 (*sunclud*), 尽管 (*jǐnguan*), 固然 (*g然anl*), 但 (*d然a*), 但是 (*d是anlu*), 可 (*k是*), 可是 (*k是anl*), 而 (*é是*), 然而 (*ránér*), etc. First, we found the semantic definitions of each conjunction according to "online dictionaries—the Ministry of Education Chinese Word Dictionary Revised" and Chinese Wordnet. The semantic characteristics of "concessive" conjunctions are "to connect the turning tone of the sentence," "to represent the possibility of the case described in the main clause and the situation described in the subordinate clause," and "to introduce the opposite situation of the previous sentence." The semantic structure of sentences containing concessive conjunctions is as follows:

(1) proposition A + concessive conjunction + proposition B (opposite meaning of A)

(2) 那家店的位子虽然很多，但是早已坐满了用餐的客人。

Nàjiādiàn de wèizi suīrán hěnduō, dànshì zǎoyǐ zuòmǎn le yòngcān de kèrén.

Even though there are a lot of seats in the restaurant, it has been already filled with guests.

Then, we analyzed the distribution of the compositions in the CWC based on the writers' ACTFL scores, with 2 indicating low proficiency and 10 indicating high proficiency [13]. The results demonstrated that the frequency of using concessive conjunctions increased in accordance with the writers' ACTFL scores, as did the frequency of using all kinds of conjunctions, as shown in Figures 2 and 3. This clearly shows that as the learners' writing skills improved, they were more likely to use concessive conjunctions.

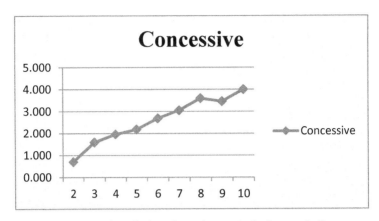

Figure 2: Average number of tokens for each score in the "concessive" category

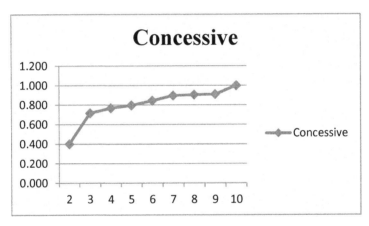

Figure 3: Average number of texts for each score in the "concessive" category

4.3   "Causal" Category

The "causal" category included 因为 (*yīnwèi*), 因此 (*yīncǐ*), 所以 (*suǒyǐ*), 由于 (*yóuyú*), etc. According to the "Ministry of Education Chinese Word Dictionary Revised" and Chinese Wordnet, the semantic characteristics of "causal" conjunctions are "to connect causes or reasons," "the causal relationship of two propositions," and "to demonstrate the result or conclusion based on the reason mentioned before." For causal conjunctions, the semantic structures of the sentence are as follows:

(3) causal conjunction + proposition A (cause or reason) → proposition B (result/conclusion)

(4) proposition A (cause or reason) + causal conjunction → proposition B (re-
     sult/conclusion)

(5) 放假时我不想待在台北，所以我就买机票回国了。
     Fangjiàshí wǒ bùxiǎng dāizài táiběi, suǒyǐ wǒ jiù mǎi jīpiào huíguó le.
     (i) I don't want to stay in Taipei during the holidays, so I bought a ticket and flew
     back to my country.
     (ii) Because I don't want to stay in Taipei during the holidays, I bought a ticket
     and flew back to my country.

Looking back at the compositions in the CWC, the results of the analysis are
shown in Figures 4 and 5 below. The frequency of using causal conjunctions increased for
writers who scored between 2 and 7 on the ACTFL, but this was not the case for those who
scored between 8 and 10, as the counts of causal conjunction use decreased, although the
number of compositions that used causal conjunctions increased. These results propose that
even if second language learners at higher proficiency levels can manage the use of causal
conjunctions, they are not likely to use them in their writing. It can be assumed that learners
at higher proficiency levels preferred to use other parts of speech, instead of conjunctions, to
represent causal relationships.

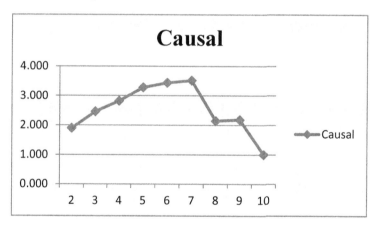

Figure 4: Average number of tokens for each score in the "causal" category

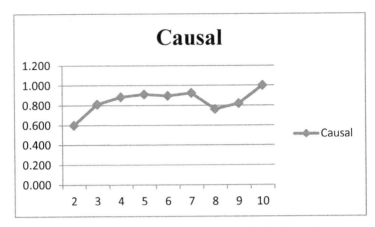

Figure 5: Average number of texts for each score in the "causal" category

4.4   "Hypothesis" Category

The "hypothesis" category included 如果 (*rúguǒ*), 要是 (*yàoshì*), etc. According to the online dictionaries and Chinese Wordnet, the common semantic characteristic of "hypothesis" conjunctions is "to connect hypothesis conditions." For hypothesis conjunctions, the semantic structure of the sentence is as follows:

(6) hypothesis conjunction + hypothesis proposition A → hypothesis B (event in the future)

(7) 如果去海边玩后脸黑了的话，可以使用鸡蛋的蛋白来敷脸。
Rúguǒ qù hǎibiān wán hòu liǎnhēile dehuà, kěyǐ shǐyòng jīdàn de dànbái lái fūliǎn.
If you get a tan after going to the beach, you can use egg whites to alleviate the pain.

In the CWC, we discovered that the distribution of hypothesis conjunctions reached the highest point at score 5, as shown in Figures 6 and 7. Thereafter, it changed corresponding with the learners' proficiency level. It can be assumed that learners at different proficiency levels preferred to use a variety of similar parts of speech or words to describe the same hypothesis meaning.

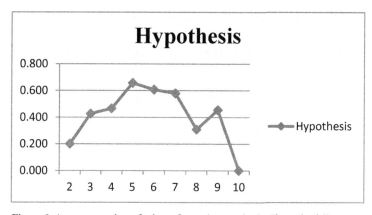

Figure 6: Average number of tokens for each score in the "hypothesis" category

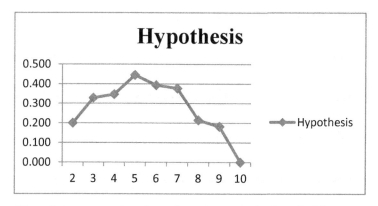

Figure 7: Average number of texts for each score in the "hypothesis" category

4.5   "Condition" Category

The "condition" category included 不管 (*bùguan*), 只要 (*zhǐyào*), 除非 (*chúfēi*), etc. According to the "Ministry of Education Chinese Word Dictionary Revised" and Chinese Wordnet, the semantic characteristics of "condition" conjunctions are "to connect the only condition to the target mentioned in the following clause" and "to be provided with the following condition." For condition conjunctions, often shown with "就 (*jiù*), 都 (*dōu*), or 便 (*biàn*)," the semantic structure is as follows:

(8) target proposition A, condition conjunction + the only condition proposition B to achieve the target

(9) 到那個鄉下，只要搭一個小時的火車就可以到達。

Dào nàge xiāngxià, zhǐyào dā yíge xiǎoshí de huǒchē jiù kěyǐ dàodá.

To go to the countryside, you only need to take the train for an hour.

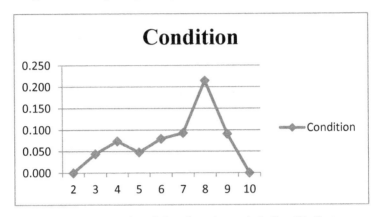

Figure 8: Average number of tokens for each score in the "condition" category

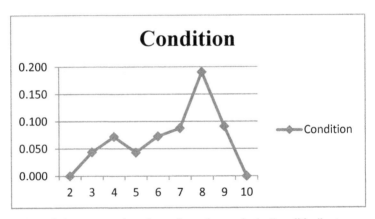

Figure 9: Average number of texts for each score in the "condition" category

4.6 "Purpose" Category

The last category, "purpose," included 以 (*yǐ*), 以便 (*yǐbiàn*), 以免 (*yǐmiǎn*), 为了 (*wèile*), etc. According to the "the Ministry of Education Chinese Word Dictionary Revised" and Chinese Wordnet, the semantic characteristics of "purpose" conjunctions are "to connect purposes," "to serve as the continuation of the previous clause," and "to show that the previous description can achieve the purpose." The semantic structure of purpose conjunctions is as follows:

(10) proposition A → purpose conjunction + proposition B that can achieve the previous purpose

(11) 先准备好所有配备，以便大家可以开心在海边玩耍。

Xiān zhǔnbèi hǎo suǒyǒu pèibèi, yǐbiàn dàjiā kěyǐ kāixīn zài hǎibiān wánshuǎ.

Please prepare all the equipment so that everybody can have a great time at the beach.

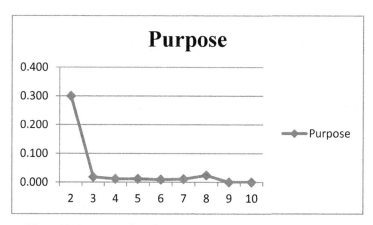

Figure 10: Average number of tokens for each score in the "purpose" category

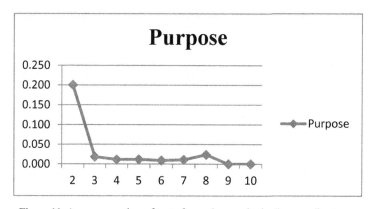

Figure 11: Average number of texts for each score in the "purpose" category

4.7   Using Chinese Conjunctions to Teach Chinese Writing

Figures 2 through 11 show the distribution of the five conjunction categories from the CWC. Figures 12 and 13 show that learners performed better when they used concessive and causal conjunctions. However, there were still many errors among all levels, including adding the wrong conjunction, omitting a conjunction, and misinformation. This suggests that second language learners still had trouble dealing with the "concessive" and "causal" relationships between two relative propositions, which led to their misunderstanding of the semantic meanings of these two propositions. The other three types of conjunctions (hypothesis, condition, and purpose) appeared less frequently in the compositions in the CWC. This suggests that the learners were not familiar with the semantic characteristics and structures of these conjunctions, so they were not likely to be used in their writing. Hence, this might be a focal point for Chinese writing courses in the future.

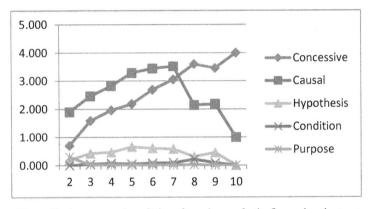

Figure 12: Average number of tokens for each score for the five conjunction types

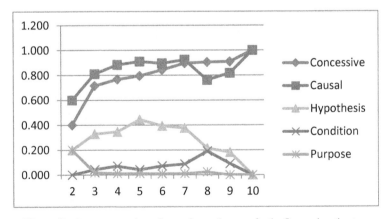

Figure 13: Average number of texts for each score for the five conjunction types

5   Conclusion and Future Work

Based on compositions in a CWC, this research aimed to analyze the error distributions of five categories of Chinese conjunctions. After analyzing the semantic structures and characteristics of the different conjunctions in the compositions, we found that learners at all proficiency levels were more likely to use concessive and causal conjunctions in their writing, although they still made errors when using them. These results will contribute to the development of teaching Chinese writing in real classrooms, as well as the development of specific teaching materials for learners at different proficiency levels to improve their writing skills using proper Chinese conjunctions.

Acknowledgement

This research is supported by the Ministry of Science and Technology, Taiwan, R.O.C., under Grant no. MOST 106-2410-H-003-061.

References

1. Benjamin, Rebekah George. 2012. Reconstructing readability: Recent developments and recommendations in the analysis of text difficulty. *Educational Psychology Review*, 24:63-88.

2. Wang, Lei. 2008. Some concepts of readability formula and relevant research paradigm as well as the research tasks of formula in TCFL. *Language Teaching and Linguistic Studies*, 6: 46-53.

3. Yu, Peng. 2009. Eye movement of Korean college students when reading Chinese texts of different styles. *Journal of Tianjin University (Social Sciences)*, 11(4): 362-366.

4. Fu, Gan. 2012. Eyemovement study in reading of different difficulty of Chinese sentences. *Psychological Research*, 5(5): 39-45.

5. Ma, Yan-Hua. 2005. 高年级留学生汉语阅读理解难易语句分析. *Applied Linguistics*, S1: 45-47.

6. Buckingham, Thomas, and William C. Pech. 1976. An experience approach to teaching composition. *TESOL Quarterly*, 10(1):55-65.

7. Krashen, Stephen D. 1985. *The Input Hypothesis*. London, UK: Longman Group UK Ltd.

8. Chall, Jeanne S., Scott Conrad, and Susan Harris-Sharples. 1991. *Should textbooks challenge students? The case for easier or harder textbooks*. New York, NY: Teachers College Press.

9. Kintsch, Walter. 1994. Text comprehension, memory, and learning. *American Psychologist*, 49(4):294-303.

10. McNamara, Danielle S., Eileen Kintsch, Nancy Butler Songer, and Walter Kintsch. 1996. Are good texts always better? Interactions of text coherence, background knowledge, and

levels of understanding in learning from text. *Cognition and Instruction*, 14(1):1-43.

11. Wolfe, Michael B., Maureen Elizabeth Schreiner, Bob Rehder, Darrell Laham, Peter W. Foltz, Walter Kintsch, and Thomas K. Landauer. 1998. Learning from text: Matching readers and text by Latent Semantic Analysis. *Discourse Processes*, 25(2&3):309-336.

12. Hong, Jia-Fei, and Yao-Ting Sung. 2017. *Chinese written corpus development and analysis*. High Education Press. 197-222, Taipei. [In Chinese]

13. ACTFL Proficiency Guidelines 2012 – Writing. 2012. Retrieved August 18, 2014, from http://actflproficiencyguidelines2012.org/writing .

Study on Lexical Gap Phenomenon at the Primary Stage of Vocabulary Teaching in TCFL[*]

Jingyi Xie

Fujian Normal University, Fuzhou, Fujian, 350007, China
Beijing Normal University, Beijing,100875, China
xjybnu@qq.com

Abstract : Recently, the study on lexical gap phenomenon has not been only the study on whole-word gap and hypernym-hyponym gap, but also the research on word formation gap and lexical development mode gap, etc. However, recent vocabulary teaching in Teaching Chinese as a Foreign Language (TCFL) is still based on language comparison, which leads to the ignorance of the systematicness of this phenomenon. This study will reveal the importance of lexical gap phenomenon at the primary stage of vocabulary teaching in TCFL with the common word "Apple". The rational use of the systematicness of the lexical gap phenomenon will help learners increase morphological awareness.

Keywords: Lexical Gap, Vocabulary Teaching, Morphological Awareness

1   Introduction

In Chinese lexical teaching, teachers often face some questions: "Sir/Mam, what's the meaning of 'Fu'? I checked Fu in the New Words List, which is translated as 'good luck'. So what's the difference between 'Fu' and 'Yunqi'?" "Sir/Mam, why we say 'Pingguo' instead of 'Pingzi' or 'Taoguo'?" "Sir/Mam, what is the difference between 'guo' in 'Ruguo' and 'Pingguo'?" These questions seem to have nothing to do with each other. In fact, they are reflecting of lexical gap in TCFL.

Lexical gap (lexical vacancy) refers to the vacancy of the position in a lexical field(Li, 2007)[1]. There are two sides of the research on this phenomenon: vacancy inside a language and vacancy between languages. Vacancy inside a language refers to a language point which could has been in that language but not yet appeared(Li, 2007)[2]. Some scholars name it "potential word" （Wang，2012）[3]. Vacancy between

---

[*] Sponsored by Beijing Municipal Education Commission social sciences Foundation, ID:SM201610028010

[1] Li Fuyin, F.: Introduction to Semantics. Peking University Press, Beijing (2007)
[2] Li Fuyin, F.: Introduction to Semantics. Peking University Press, Beijing (2007)
[3] Wang Xijie, F.: The Re-recognition of the Potential Words and Vacant Symbols Semiotics. Culture and Communication 1(8), 51–57 (2012)

ⓒ Springer International Publishing AG 2018
Y. Wu et al. (Eds.): CLSW 2017, LNAI 10709, pp. 523–532, 2018.
https://doi.org/10.1007/978-3-319-73573-3_47

languages refers to some language points exist in one language but not in the other language(Zhao, 1998) [4]. The vacancies not only exist in the word meaning, but also in the word context, word distribution, and word frequency. This kind of vacancy will only appear in the comparison of different languages(Hu,2011, quoted from Ю.С.Степанов, 1996)[5].

In TCFL, especially at the primary stage of lexical teaching, teachers often focus on the abstract nouns/concepts based on language comparison or filling in the vacancy by translation/explanation, which ignore the systematicness of the lexical gap phenomenon. The research will start from the category and expression of lexical gap and analysis of the expression and usage at the primary stage of lexical teaching in TCFL.

2   Related Research on the Lexical Gap Phenomenon

2.1   Related Research on the Lexical Gap Phenomenon inside One Language

There are three kinds of vacancies in synchronic level research on the lexical gap phenomenon inside one language: signifier vacancy, signified vacancy and potential word vacancy. Signifier vacancy (Vacant Symbol) is the vacant or absent symbol, which only has concept but no Signifier. For example, we don't have the appellation to address "the husband of female teacher". Signified vacancy refers to the word coinage which language users can make following the word formation rules. But in the meanwhile, the words never exist cause the signified it refers to never exist or it's feature is too weak to emerge[6]. Potential word vacancy refers to the words have both signifier and signified, but the signified is not stable, which limits the spread of the word. Sometimes it's just a temperate use. [7]

On the other hand, in the diachronic view, there is a historical lexical vacancy phenomenon. The vacancy not only exists in comparison with one other language, but also in comparison with other historical periods in the same language(Li, 2002, quoted from Мура-вьев, 1974)[8] For example, there was a developed wine culture in Chinese history, which resulted tens of words referring to different types and status of wine, such as "醇/醨/酤/醅/醴" etc. These monosyllabic words are not in common use in

[4] Zhao Wenxue, F., Wu Boxiang, S.: Culture Difference and Lexical Gap. Jilin University Journals 2(5), 99–110 (1998) (3)

[5] Hu Guming, F, Shenman, S.: Translation Strategy of Culture Vacancy Words in Chinese-Russian Translation. Teaching Russian in China 1(4), 17–21 (2011)

[6] Wang Xijie, F.: The Re-recognition of the Potential Words and Vacant Symbols Semiotics. Culture and Communication 1(8), 51–57 (2012)

[7] Zhao Yiheng, F.: Research on Semiology Culture: Current Situation and Trend of the Future. Journal of Southwest University for Nationalities (Humanities and Social Science) 12(8), 37–39 (2009) (12)

[8] Li Xiangdong, F.: Phenomenon and Research of Vacancy. Teaching Russian in China 4(18), 91–96 (2002)

modern Chinese language, which are replaced by disyllable words and phrases(Yu, 2011)[9]. It is the reason of the historical vacancy of the "Wine" kind of words.

2.2   Related Research on the Lexical Gap Phenomenon between Languages

Research on lexical gap phenomenon between languages involves six aspects as follows:

First, whole word vacancy caused by concept absent. There are a great quantity of cultural words and gramma words related to Chinese culture/gramma features such as "客气" involved value system,   "阴/阳" involved philosophical thought , "地主" involved history events,   measure words like "张/辆",   gramma auxiliary words like "了/着/过" etc. These words are easily cause vacancy phenomenon while compared to other languages (Pan, Li, 2000)[10]. Sometimes, words which represent the same concept differ in concept range will cause part vacancy. For example, color word "青" in Chinese refer to blue\green\black these three different colors while in English there are three color words for them separately.

Second, sense vacancy caused by similar concept meanings. Cause the various lexical development ways and national cultures, similar basic concept meanings in different languages will develop different extended meanings which caused sense vacancy of same words. For example, "娘" in Japanese can either refer to daughter or a general appellation for young females. While in Chinese, it always refers to mother. (Wang, 2006)[11] Another example is the "黄色" in "黄色电影". In   *The Contemporary Chinese Dictionary*   ,   its sense is "the indecent publications", while there is no such sense of yellow in English.

Third, connotative sense vacancy caused by connotative sense difference in the same words.

This phenomenon refers to same or similar words with different value meanings. For example, cat/dog, dragon/bat have totally different connotative senses in English and Chinese.

Forth, word-making approach vacancy caused by Chinese unique disyllable word-making approach.

Taking word-making approach vacancy into lexical gap research is a hot spot recently. For example, although there are composite and derivative ways to form new compound words, their range of application and frequency are different in English and Chinese. First, the disyllable and compound words are main parts of new Chinese words, while in English, they are loan words from foreign languages. For example, "红宝石 --ruby"/"关系 --guanxi" etc. Second, cause of the Chinese characters and monosyllabic word morpheme differentiation, one morpheme with multiple meanings

---

[9]   Yu Haikuo, F., Li Rulong, S.: A Contrastive Approach to Vocabulary Teaching in TCSL. Journal of Shanxi University (Philosophy & Social Science) 5(12), 71–78 May, (2011)

[10]   Pan Huixia, F., Lihui, S.: Research on Culture Vacancy in Chinese-English Translation. Foreign Language Education 4(15), 74–77 (2000)

[11]   Wang Lingling, F.: Analyses on Vacancy Phenomenon between Chinese and Japanese. Foreign Languages and Their Teaching 6(6),18–20 (2006) (6)

phenomenon is very popular in Chinese language. That's the reason for less word-making morphemes and more multiple meaning morphemes in Chinese than in English.

"*Common word-making Character Dictionary*" includes 325 compound words structured by "水" and 272 compound words structured by "手" (Fu, 1982)[12]。 In English, there are water-/hydro-/aqua- and so on to refer to water in a word. (Yu, 2011)[13]

Fifth, form-pronunciation relationship vacancy caused by Chinese characters particularity. Chinese characters often suggest its meaning, which doesn't appear in alphabetic writing.

Sixth, hypernym/hyponym vacancy caused by lexical system development path.

Hypernym/hyponym is a word set which concepts are include/included by each other, which show the subsidiary unit relationship. In different languages, hypernym/hyponym are often different. This phenomenon is called "Meaning Exist while Forms Absent". For example, in English, there is the concept of "笔", while the words are pencil, pens but not the direct hypernym representing this meaning.

In conclusion, lexical gap phenomenon includes six kinds: whole word vacancy, sense vacancy, connotative sense vacancy, word-making approach vacancy, form-pronunciation relationship vacancy and hypernym/hyponym vacancy.

3   Analysis of Lexical Gap Phenomenon in Primary Stage of TCFL

In ordinary TCFL, emphasis on lexical gap phenomenon often starts from the intermediate stage of TCFL. (In general thinking, 800/2000 Chinese learning hours is the bounds of primary/ intermediate/high stage of TCFL. (Zhang, 2006)[14]) And teachers often focus on whole word vacancy caused by concept vacancy. Actually, lexical gap phenomenon is a systematic lexical phenomenon. We especially need to pay more attention to those widely used words with long history and strong word-making ability. Those words are always in the basic level of Chinese lexical system and are the most important words in language which should be learned first in TCFL.(Yang, 2014)[15] For example, color words with multiple culture meanings and action words like "打/吃" with complicated senses, whose senses and usage are with different difficulty, are hard to leant at the same time. Although those words which look like with no ambiguity also

---

[12] Fu Xingling, F.: Commonly Used Word Formation Dictionary. Renmin University of China Press, Beijing (1982)

[13] Yu Haikuo, F., Li Rulong, S.: A Contrastive Approach to Vocabulary Teaching in TCSL. Journal of Shanxi University (Philosophy & Social Science) 5(12), 71–78 May, (2011)

[14] Zhang Hesheng, F.: A Quantitative Study of Vocabulary Development of Foreign Students Learning Chinese as a Foreign Language. Chinese Teaching in the World 1(6), 70–76(2006) (1)

[15] Yang Jichun, F.: Theories and Methods on the Construction of Basic-level Category Lexicon for International Chinese Teaching. Applied Linguistics4(14), 68–76 (2014) (4)

will relate to lexical gap phenomenon. In a word, lexical phenomenon is various and closely related to the vocabulary learning strategy and morphological awareness. We will take "苹果" as an example to analyze the lexical phenomenon in primary stage of TCFL as follows.

3.1   Lexical Gap Phenomenon inside One Language of "苹果"

According to article above, there are four kinds of vacancies in synchronic level research of the phenomenon of lexical gap inside one language: signifier vacancy, signified vacancy, potential word vacancy and historical vacancy.

(1) Signifier vacancy: In real concept world, there are different kinds of apple. But Chinese lexical system doesn't develop that many signifiers for each kind of apple while add modifier before the word "苹果" instead, such as "红苹果"/ "青苹果"etc.

(2) Signified vacancy: The word-making approach for "苹果" is to add affix "-果" after "苹"。 "ShuoWenJieZi" (A book on glosses of etymology of ancient Chinese characters) records: "the character '果' refers to fruits of a tree. Its form looks like a fruit on a tree. Its pronunciation is 'guo'. " This shows, actually, "果" is a hypernym which becomes an affix means fruit category. "芒果", "无花果", "奇异果" all follow this kind of word-making approach. But actually fruit names with "-果" are limited. If learners make "梨果", "桃果" follow this word-making approach, they can't get correct words in Modern Chinese lexical system.

(3) Potential word vacancy: With the introduction of imported fruits, the morpheme "-果" is becoming more and more active, which developed "百香果", "鸡蛋果", "青柠果" and other words in recent years. But these words are often "Multiple Forms with Multiple Meanings" or " One Form with Multiple Meanings ". For example, "百香果" and "鸡蛋果" refer to the same fruit, while "青柠果" can either be immature little lemon/ green lemon or cyan。 As a result, these words are still "potential word" category. Either they will move into modern Chinese vocabulary or not remains to be tested by time.

(4) Historical vacancy: In history, the word "苹果" actually referred to the Chinese flowering crabapple fruit, whose ancient name was "柰". In Yuan dynasty, we used Buddhist words "频婆果" to refer to "柰," then simplified it as "苹果". Because of "柰" 's low sweetness, poor taste, compared to the "梨" and "桃", it's not widely cultivated in ancient times. Until one hundred years ago, with modern apple introduced from western world to coastal areas of China, this kind of fruit's planting area increased and gradually accepted by people. Therefore, in Chinese, there are sayings like "孔融让梨/望梅止渴/二桃杀三士", while idioms and allusions associated with apple are much less. In a word, there is a certain historical vacancy with the word "苹果" either in the specific form or the culture concept.

3.2   Analysis on Lexical Gap Phenomenon between Chinese and English of "苹果" and "apple"

According above, there are six kinds of lexical gap phenomenon between languages: whole word vacancy, sense vacancy, connotative sense vacancy, word-making approach vacancy, form-pronunciation relationship vacancy and hypernym/hyponym vacancy. According to this classification, our analysis results to the words "苹果" and "apple" are as follows:

(1) Whole word vacancy: "苹果" and "apple" appear both in English and Chinese, there is no whole word vacancy here.

(2) Sense vacancy: In English, the word "Apple" also refers to the grenades and bomb. The Big Apple is used to refer to New York (recorded in "the 21st century Big English-Chinese dictionary"[16]). In contrast, in Chinese, there is no such extended meaning of the word "苹果".

(3) Connotative sense vacancy： As a result of the same pronunciation of "苹" in "苹果" and "平" in "平安" in Chinese, "苹果" in Chinese has gradually obtained the meaning of "peace" recently. In English, "apple" is associated with health, so there is a saying "one apple a day, keep doctor away".

In addition, in English culture, "apple" is often associated with "temptation": Snow White died from eating poisoned apple; Adam and Eve lured by a snake because of an apple. While in Chinese, there is no such cultural meaning in "苹果".

(4) Word-making approach vacancy: The word "apple" is made by "苹" and "-果". While "apple" in English is a single morpheme word.

(5) Form-pronunciation relationship vacancy: The word "苹果" is formed by "苹" and "-果". "苹" in "苹果" is a pictophmetic character while phonetic radical "平" only suggests its pronunciation and semantic radical "艹" indicates the plant category attributes. "Apple" in English only records the pronunciation.

(6) Hypernym/hyponym vacancy: In Chinese, "苹果" is a hypernym, there are no specialized words for different kinds of apples respectively. While in English there is a word "pearmain" specifically for a kind of red apple.

4   Lexical Gap Theory Application at Primary Stage of TCFL

According to the analysis in previous chapter, most of types of vocabulary vacancies can be embodied in the word "apple". In fact, "apple" is only a representative content of the vocabulary teaching at the primary stage of TCFL.

These words have been acquired by students at the primary stage. But they often only get core meaning of the word, while other resources of the word are not utilized effectively.

Core meaning acquisition and morphemes consciousness have certain inspiration function in cultivating learners' ability to guess the meaning of words. But if they ignore

---

[16]   Li Huaju, F.: 21 Century English-Chinese Dictionary. Renming University of China Press, Beijing (2005).

the multilayered feature of word meaning and lexical gap phenomenon, they will overuse the word-making rule which will lead them to the vocabulary development bottleneck period. Therefore, at the primary stage of Chinese vocabulary teaching, the lexical vacancy phenomenon should be paid more attention as a whole system.

(1) Teachers should pay attention to the internal vacancy of one language and guide the formation and development of learners' morpheme consciousness correctly.

At the primary stage of vocabulary teaching, analogy is the main method that teachers will adopt when guiding learners to form morpheme consciousness. The empirical research shows when the morpheme are commonly used, teaching effect of morpheme pedagogics is obvious. However, at the primary stage of the development of morpheme consciousness, if learners ignore the rule, they will export the incorrect analogy. For example, the "桃子", "梨子" will lead to "苹子", or "苹果" will lead to "桃果", etc.

This requires teachers paying attention to the use scope and conditions of morpheme in morpheme teaching. To the words with limited transparency corporeality of lexical meaning (especially abstract words), teachers should also provide a more adequate context. [17]

In addition, the historical lexical vacancy also suggests teachers in teaching should also ask students to pay attention to word's different meanings in different context. As mentioned at the beginning of the article, "福" and "运气" were clearly made and used in the different historical period. They also have different usage in modern Chinese. And the word "青", for example, which is often used as a morpheme in modern Chinese in word formation, means "blue", "green" and "black". For example, "青天" generally refers to the blue sky ; "青草" refers to the green grass while "青丝" refers to the black hair. These words were formed in different eras, their morpheme collocation was relatively fixed. In the teaching, on the basis of the awareness of difference between word meaning and usage, teachers should ask students to take the whole word as a unit for memory and introduce the history and cultural knowledge at a right time.

Primary stage of TCFL is the period of forming morpheme consciousness. Until intermediate stage, learners won't have a certain structure and morpheme formation (Feng ,2002)[18]. At the primary stage of Chinese vocabulary teaching, therefore, teachers should guild learners correctly to distinguish the applicable conditions of whole word memory/part word analogy etc., which will finally help learners to form the correct morpheme awareness.

(2) Teachers should attach great importance to the lexical vacancy phenomenon between languages, compare words appropriately on the basis of the right word meaning, carry on teaching design and enhance learning interest.

Lexical gap phenomenon between languages teaching can be divided into three categories and targeted to adopt corresponding teaching strategies.

---

[17] Zhao Wei, F.: A Study on the Applicability of the Morphemic Vocabulary Teaching Method to Learners of Chinese as a Second Language. Chinese Teaching in the World 2(3), 16–22(2016) NO.2

[18] Feng Liping, F.: The Role of Lexical Structures in Words Processing of Chinese and Foreign Chinese learners, Ph.D. Thesis of Beijing Normal University (2002)

First category includes the whole word vacancy, sense vacancy, connotative sense vacancy. For this category of vacancy, teachers can try to use the class explanation, footnotes, translation and other ways to make up for the vacancy, and make corresponding teaching design based on learner's native language background. Especially words like "苹果" which have simple culture meaning in Chinese but complex culture meanings in other languages, even more, should be treated with caution to avoid cross-cultural conflict.

Second category is form-pronunciation relationship vacancy caused by Chinese characters particularity. The particularity of Chinese characters shows in form, function and word-making approach. From the point of form, comparing with English, Chinese characters form a two-dimensional square, that's why how to combine and distinguish the configuration unit is one of difficulties in learning Chinese characters. How to recognize radicals of Chinese characters and confirm the connection and usage of them is another difficulty in learning Chinese characters. The function of Chinese characters is varied. The record of language units sometimes is a word, sometimes morpheme, sometimes syllable. The relationship between word unit and language unit is also not a one-to-one relationship. Phenomenon like same character with different words (morpheme) or same word (morpheme) with different characters is widespread, which seriously impacts on the proper use of Chinese characters and the understanding of the written literature. This is the main reason for Chinese characters learning difficulty which should be the focus of the teaching of Chinese characters. (Li Yunfu, 2014)[19] For this kind of vacancy, teaching should be combined with Chinese characters teaching content to form a recess interaction, which will connect the Chinese characters teaching and vocabulary teaching. For example, in learning the word "苹果", the characteristics of the pictophmetic character "苹" can at the same time be both Chinese characters and vocabulary teaching materials. If students can study with the help of related software, they can achieve twice result with half effort. (Gong, 2014)[20]

Third category is word-making approach vacancy caused by Chinese unique disyllable word-making approach. To make up for this kind of vacancy relies on the emphasis on frequency difference and mode of word-formation polysemy morpheme.

In terms of word formation frequency difference, taking English and Chinese language for example, it does exist dual compound word formation in both languages. But in Chinese, dual tone word-formation dominates, there are frequency differences between these two languages. Such differences will naturally bring certain difficulties to learners to identify the composition of compound word semantic. Compound words "邻居" and "选择", for example, the corresponding words in English is a whole word "neighbor" and "choose" respectively. The composition and structure of these two words are totally not corresponding, which makes students use the whole word memorization method to remember meanings of these two Chinese words, and ignore

[19] Li Yunfu, F.: Characteristics of Chinese Characters and Chinese Character Teaching. Chinese Teaching in the World 3(6), 356–367(2014).

[20] Gong Tianran, F.: Design and Implementation of Chinese Pictophmetic Characters Teaching Software. Journal of Capital Normal University (Social Sciences Edition) 5(15), 145–150 (2014)

the understanding and mastering of morpheme. (Xu, 2016) [21] In order to solve this situation, comparison and conscious guidance are needed to avoid foreign students from going to a supermarket to find "鸡蛋的妈妈".

The key to solve polysemy morpheme problem is the analysis from the angle of combining rule of dual tone words. Teachers should point out the key role of word-making approach in the meaning explain. This is helpful to activate the second language learners' perception of dissyllabic words semantic relations, so as to guide adult learners accurately grasp dissyllabic words in Chinese words. (Zhi, 2006) [22] Teachers should guide the learners to pay attention to polysemy morpheme and pay attention to flexibility and variability of polysemy morpheme meaning in different compounds （Zhang, 2010） [23], which requires Chinese teachers in class instruction to form the polysemy morpheme meaning into a rules-based system, rather than individual, scattered memory units. This can help students master the meaning of dual tone words system, which will develop Chinese morpheme awareness of vocabulary learning.

5   Conclusion

Lexical gap phenomenon is an organic ensemble, which not only contains the concept vacancy and explicit meanings vacancy, but also contains historical vacancy, disyllable word vacancy and so on. Only if we regard the phenomenon as a whole at the primary stage of Chinese vocabulary teaching and pay more attention to the using scope and conditions of using morpheme, we can help learners to distinguish the using conditions of whole word memory, word parts memory methods correctly. When faced with a gap phenomenon between languages, explanations in the classroom, footnotes, after-school translation methods and so on are effective ways to make up for the vacancy. Teachers also need to connect the Chinese characters teaching and vocabulary teaching by using characteristics of Chinese characters and word-formation theory based on the individual meaning of polysemy morpheme to form the meaning of the rules-based system. This system is the best way to help students form the correct morpheme awareness, develop the foundation for students' vocabulary learning and make a real breakthrough at the advanced vocabulary learning stage.

References

1. Feng Liping, F.: The Role of Lexical Structures in Words Processing of Chinese and Foreign Chinese Learners, Ph.D. Thesis of Beijing Normal University (2002) (In Chinese).

---

[21] Xu Xiaohua, F.: A Study on Foreign Students' Understanding of Chinese Semi-free Morphemes. Language Teaching and Linguistic Studies1(5), 40–47 (2016)
[22] Zhu Zhiping, F.: Analysis of How Morphemes Combined a Disyllable Compound Word and its Application in Second Language Teaching. Chinese Teaching in the World 1(10), 83–90 (2006) (1)
[23] Zhang Jiangli, F.: Effects of the Relationship between the Meaning of Words and Morphemes on Inferring the Meaning of Chinese Words. Language Teaching and Linguistic Studies 2(5), 99–110 (2010) (3)

2. Fu Xingling, F.: Commonly Used Word Formation Dictionary. Renmin University of China Press, Beijing(1982) (In Chinese).
3. Gong Tianran, F.: Design and Implementation of Chinese Pictophmetic Characters Teaching Software. Journal of Capital Normal University (Social Sciences Edition) 5(15), 145–150 (2014) (In Chinese).
4. Hu Guming, F, Shenman, S.: Translation Strategy of Culture Vacancy Words in Chinese-Russian Translation. Teaching Russian in China 1(4), 17–21 (2011) (In Chinese).
5. Li Fuyin, F.: Introduction to Semantics. Peking University Press, Beijing (2007) (In Chinese).
6. Li Huaju, F.: 21 Century English-Chinese Dictionary. Renming University of China Press, Beijing (2005). (In Chinese).
7. Li Xiangdong, F.: Phenomenon and Research of Vacancy. Teaching Russian in China 4(18), 91–96 (2002) (In Chinese).
8. Li Yunfu, F.: Characteristics of Chinese Characters and Chinese Character Teaching. Chinese Teaching in the World 3(6), 356–367(2014). (In Chinese).
9. Pan Huixia, F., Lihui, S.: Research on culture vacancy in Chinese-English Translation. Foreign Language Education 4(15), 74–77 (2000) (In Chinese).
10. Wang Lingling, F.: Analyses on Vacancy Phenomenon between Chinese and Japanese. Foreign Languages and Their Teaching 6(6),18–20 (2006) (6) (In Chinese).
11. Wang Xijie, F.: The Re-recognition of the Potential Words and Vacant Symbols Semiotics. Culture And Communication 1(8), 51–57 (2012) (In Chinese).
12. Xu Xiaohua, F.: A Study on Foreign Students' Understanding of Chinese Semi-free Morphemes. Language Teaching and Linguistic Studies1(5), 40–47 (2016) (1) (In Chinese).
13. Yang Jichun, F.: Theories and Methods on the Construction of Basic-level Category Lexicon for International Chinese. Teaching. Applied Linguistics4(14), 68–76 (2014) (4) (In Chinese).
14. Yu Haikuo, F., Li Rulong, S.: A Contrastive Approach to Vocabulary Teaching in TCSL. Journal of Shanxi University (Philosophy & Social Science) 5(12), 71–78 May, (2011) (In Chinese).
15. Zhang Hesheng, F.: A quantitative Study of Vocabulary Development of Foreign Students Learning Chinese as a Foreign Language. Chinese Teaching in the World 1(6), 70–76(2006) (1) (In Chinese).
16. Zhang Jiangli, F.: Effects of the Relationship between the Meaning of Wordsand Morphemes on Inferring the Meaning of Chinese Words. Language Teaching and Linguistic Studies 2(5), 99–110 (2010) (3) (In Chinese).
17. Zhao Wei, F.: A Study on the Applicability of the Morphemic Vocabulary Teaching Method to Learners of Chinese as a Second Language. Chinese Teaching in the World 2(3), 16–22(2016) NO.2(In Chinese).
18. Zhao Wenxue, F., Wu Boxiang, S.: Culture Difference and Lexical gap. Jilin University Journals 2(5), 99–110 (1998) (3) (In Chinese).
19. Zhao Yiheng, F.: Research on Semiology Culture: Current situation and trend of the future. Journal of Southwest University for Nationalities (Humanities and Social Science) 12(8), 37–39 (2009) (12) (In Chinese).
20. Zhu Zhiping, F.: Analysis of How Morphemes Combined a Disyllable Compound Word and its Application in Second Language Teaching. Chinese Teaching in the World 1(10), 83–90 (2006) (1) (In Chinese).

Study on Chinglish in Web Text for Natural Language Processing

Bo Chen[1,2], Lyu Chen[2], Ziqing Ji[2]

Department of Chinese, Hubei University of Art & Science, Xiangyang, China
Computer School, Wuhan University, Wuhan, China

{chenbo, lvchen1989}@whu.edu.cn, 1163539719@qq.com

Abstract. Recently, Chinglish in Web Text is one of new language phenomena, and has brought some problems for automatic analysis of natural language processing. This paper builds a small-scale open Chinglish corpus for NLP, then analyzes the linguistic characteristics of Chinglish in Web Text from two aspects: vocabulary and grammar, as well as Chinese-English translation of phrases and sentences. The study can be helpful for natural language processing, such as machine translation, sentiment analysis and information extraction.

Keywords: Chinglish in Web Text, natural language processing, machine translation, linguistic characteristics

1   Introduction

Chinglish is a kind of Chinese-style English with Chinese vocabulary, Chinese grammar and Chinese expression of habit. Chinglish in Web Text (CWT), the combination of the network and Chinglish created by netizens and widely disseminated on the network, is a new lingual phenomenon of Chinglish. For example: "*geliva-ble*"(*awesome*) and "*ungelivable*" created from Chinese word "给力"(*pinyin: geili*), "*zhuangbility*"(*pretentious, ostentatious*) and the new synonym "*drunbility*" created from Chinese word "装逼"(*pinyin: zhuangbi*). As a polysemous or polymorphic phenomenon that possesses a variety of forms including characters, words, phrases, clauses, sentences [1-4], CWT has brought difficulties for Natural Language Processing (NLP).

Currently in linguistic fields, systematic research on CWT is not abundant. Wang (2016) studied this phenomenon in microblogging text, and applied it to machine translation system [5].

This paper systematically studies CWT based on the web text in the past three years, constructs an open small-scale CWT corpus, and analyzes its linguistic features for machine translation, sentiment analysis and other related natural language processing areas.

© Springer International Publishing AG 2018
Y. Wu et al. (Eds.): CLSW 2017, LNAI 10709, pp. 533–539, 2018.
https://doi.org/10.1007/978-3-319-73573-3_48

2   Construction of CWT Corpus

We have built several Chinese semantic annotation corpus based on semantic dependency graph for NLP from 2008 to 2015 [6-7]. The task of this paper is to solve the problems that exist in identification and semantic analysis of CWT.

2.1   Corpus Source

The raw texts of the corpus are from real-time web text. Considering the typicality, timeliness, coverage and completeness of the corpus, we crawled data from seven categories of representative websites, such as: news, WeChat public accounts, Q & A, blog, microblogging, forum and twitter. Up to June 2016, we got 2449 typical texts (see Fig.1).

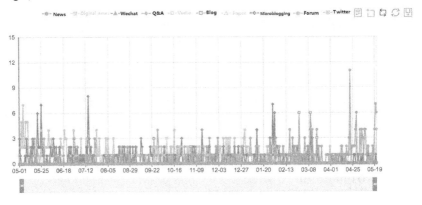

Fig. 1. CWT distribution in 2015-2016

Examples of corpus are as follows:

(1) Stupig (*stupid pig*)

（from Sina Microblogging, 2015/11/24 01:21:18）

(2) no dashouji (*do not take a phone call*)

too how (*rich man*)

togayther (*gays get married*)

（from Sohu, 2015/7/23 09:56:24）

2.2 Corpus Construction

Based on the web data, we built an open small-scale language resources of CWT in constant expansion. The current labeled resources include 55 words, 105 common phrases, 68 common sentences. As for vocabulary corpus, we designed 8 columns: entry, interpretation, part of speech, other forms, corresponding Chinese word, corresponding English translation, word formation and example sentences. As shown in Table 1:

Table 1. Examples of vocabulary corpus

Entry: **zhuangbility**	
Corresponding Chinese Word	装逼
Corresponding English Translation	pretentious, ostentatious
Interpretation	To show off or deceive others to get self-satisfaction
Part Of Speech	V, Adj
Other Forms	Drunbility, drunb, drunbee, drunby, drunber
Word Formation	affixation
Example Sentences	-

3   The Lexical Features of CWT

The vocabulary of CWT contains words and phrases. They are mainly from some buzzwords and current social events in China, such as: "*suihide*" (from "躲猫猫", *a social security incident*), "*vegeteal*" (from the QQ game "*stealing vegetables*"); "*stupig*" (from the existing Chinese word "*stupid pig*"), "*a knife in the smile*" (from the existing Chinese phrase "笑里藏刀(*with murderous intent behind one's smiles*)") [8]. The lexical features of CWT can be analyzed by word formation [9].

The word formation method of CWT follows the standard English word formation method, such as: affixation, blending and compound method. Netizens have created some new word formation methods, such as the embedded method and homophonic method. These word formation methods also have Chinese characteristics.

3.1 Affixation Method

By adding the affixes to the root of the word, the affixation forms a new word. It contains the prefix method and the suffix method (except for the very few infixes in English). The affixation of CWT also contains the prefix method and the suffix method, and the prefixes in Chinglish words are mostly "un", such as:

(3) un   +   geli   +   able   =   ungelivable
(prefix)   (the Pinyin deformation of "给力")   (suffix)   (not so good as you think)

(4) un   +   ding   +   able   =   undingable
(prefix)   (pinyin of "顶")   (suffix)   (unbearable)

(3) - (4) are direct transliteration of Chinese vocabulary. A new Chinglish word is created by combining the Chinese pinyin and the English affix.

3.2 Blending Method

The blending method operates on two original words, chooses the former part or the latter part, and then merges them into a new word. There are three categories, as shown in Table 2:

Table 2. The classification of blending method of CWT

Classification	Word Composition
keeping the former part of the first word + the latter part of the second word	Sprother=***Spr***(spring)+***other***(brother)
	Chinsumer=***Chin***(China)+***sumer***(consumer)
	vegeteal=***veget***(vegetable)+***eal***(steal)
keeping the original form of the first word + deleting the former part of the second word	smilence=***smile***(smile)+***nce***(silence)
	shitizen=***shit***(shit)+***izen***(citizen)
	sexretary=***sex***(sex)+***retary***(secretary)
keeping the original form of the second word + deleting the former part of the first word	divoice=***di***(divorce)+***voice***(voice)
	animale=***ani***(animal)+***male***(male)
	suihide=***sui***(suice)+***hide***(hide)

3.3 Compound Method

The compound method merges two or more words into a new word in a certain order. It is a common word formation method in English, such as:

(5) free + damn　=　freedamn
　　　　　　　　　(*freedom*)
(6) egg + ache　=　eggache
　　　　　　　(蛋疼, *an existing Chinese word*)

"*Freedamn*" is composed of the English words "*free*" and "*damn*". The pronunciation of "*freedamn*" is very similar to the English word "*freedom*". "*Freedamn*" reflects netizens' ridicule on freedom.

"*Eggache*" is composed of the English words "*egg*" and "*ache*", which means people do unreasonable things when they are too bored.

3.4 Homophonic Method

The harmony method is a new word formation method created by netizens. A part of the word is replaced by a similar pronunciation unit, such as:

(7)　　　newb　　　　　　+ ity　=　newbility
　　(*The homophonic of Pinyin niubi*)　　　(*great*)
(8)　　　drunb　　　　　　+ ity　=　drunbility
　　(*The homophonic of Pinyin zhuangbi*)　(*pretentious, ostentatious*)

In (7) -(8), after creating the Chinglish word "*niubility*" and "*zhaungbility*", netizens replace "*niubi*" , "*zhuangbi*" with their homonyms "*newb*", "*drunb*" in order to make the words more normative, respectively.

(9)　Z　+　turn　=　Z-turn
　　　　　　(*tossing, zhe teng*)

In (9), the Pinyin of "折腾" is "*zhe teng*". On one hand, the pronunciation of the letter "*Z*" is similar with the Chinese pinyin "*zhe*", and the pronunciation of the word "*turn*" is similar with the Chinese pinyin "*teng*". On the other hand, "*Z*" and "*turn*" let people easily think of the winding road. So the Chinglish word "*Z-turn*" vividly expresses the meaning of the word "折腾".

3.5 Embedded Method

The embedded method is also a new word formation method created by netizens. Unlike the compound method, this method embeds a complete word into another complete word, such as:

(10) together + gay = to**gay**ther
                       (get married)
(11) property + poor = pro**poor**ty
                       (real estate)

A new Chinglish word "*togayther*" is composed by embedding the word "*gay*" into the word "*together*", and "*togayther*" becomes an alternative English translation of "终成眷属, *get married*". It reveals the increasing tolerance of Chinese young people towards homosexuality.

Another new Chinglish word "*propoorty*" is created by embedding the word "*poor*" into the word "*property*". It indicates that people feel "*poor*" when confronting the mounting house prices.

From these different methods, the word formation methods of CWT not only have some traditional English methods, by also possess their own specific methods, which reflect the abundant imagination and creativity of netizens.

4   The Grammatical Features of CWT

CWT includes vocabulary and sentences. The vocabulary is self-created by netizens and mostly follows the rules of English word formation methods. However, most of the sentences of CWT directly ignore English grammar, such as word order, tense, etc. There are three grammatical characteristics of CWT.

4.1 POS Transfer

Part-of-speech(POS) transfer is one of characteristics of CWT, such as: from noun to verb, or from verb to noun.

(12) Let's **niubility**!
(13) If you **tiger** me,I will **moutain** you!
(14) You give me **stop**!

In (12) - (13), *niubility, tiger, moutain* are nouns, transferring to verbs as the predicate. In (14), *stop* is a verb, transferring to a noun as the object.

4.2 Mainly with Simple Sentences and Exclamation Sentences

From syntactical structure, the sentences are short and conform to the principle of linguistic economy. Many sentences are directly translated from Chinese common syntactical structure or idiomatic phrase. Simple sentences are much more than complex sentence, such as (15). Exclamation sentences are more than 60% in whole corpus, such as (16).

(15) five talk, four beauty, three lover

五讲　　四美　　三热爱

Wu jiang　simei　san reai

five stresses, four points of Beauty and three aspects of love

(16) Release your horse and come!

放　　　马　　　过来！

Fang　　ma　　　guolai

bring it on!

4.3 Types of Translation Methods

The translation methods of the sentences of CWT mostly have five types, as Table 3.

Table 3. The 5 types of translation methods of CWT

Type	Examples
Literally word for word translation, following Chinese word order	People mountain people sea *(huge crowds of people)*
Translating homonymously	Even game win, even so whole. *(no pain, no gain.)*
Very few according to English grammar	Many people think they are full of niubility *(great, awesome)*, and like to play zhuangbility*(pretentious)*, which only reflect their shability*(stupid)*.
Combination of English grammar and literally word for word translation	I will give you some colour to see see. *(I will teach you a lesson)*
Combination of Chinese pinyin and English	no zuo no die. *(If you do not do the stupid thing, you will not die)*

5　Conclusion

Before CWT is properly standardized, many NLP tasks, such as machine translation, sentiment analysis and information extraction, have encountered the problems of CWT. This paper builds a small open corpus based on real-time web data, and analyzes the linguistic characteristics of the phenomena from lexical and grammatical features.

Acknowledgment. The work is funded by the following projects: the Humanities and Social Science Foundation of Ministry of Education of China No.16YJCZH004.

References

1. Xue, J.J.: On CWT from the perspective of memetics. Journal of Yangtze University 37(7), 108-110(2014). (in Chinese)
2. Zhang, K.: Study on microblog language characteristics. Shannxi normal university (2012). (in Chinese)
3. Chen, J.W.: Study on buzzwords. Guangxi University (2008). (in Chinese)
4. M, Z.Y.: On the Characteristics and causes of CWT. Journal of Chongqing Technology and Business University 28(5), 115-120(2011). (in Chinese)
5. Ling W, Marujo L, Dyer C, et al.: Mining parallel corpora from sina weibo and twitter. Computational Linguistics 42(2), 1-37(2016).
6. Chen, B. Ji, D.H., Chen, L.: Building a Chinese semantic resource based on feature structure. International Journal of Computer Processing of Languages 24(1),95-101 (2013).
7. Chen, B. Lyu, C. Wei, X.M. Ji, D.H.: Chinese Semantic Parsing Based on Feature Structure with Recursive Directed Graph. Wuhan University Journal of Natural Sciences 20(4).318-322 (2015).
8. Yang, X.G., Liu X.Q.: On the Characteristics of Emerging Chinglish. Journal of Nanjing Forestry University 11(3), 49-52(2011). (in Chinese)
9. China internet network information center.: The 39th China Statistics Report on Internet Development (2017). (in Chinese)

Construction of a Database of Parallel Phrases in Chinese and Arabic

Alaa Mamdouh Akef[1], Yingying Wang[1], Erhong Yang[1(✉)]

[1] School of Information Science, Beijing Language and Culture University, Beijing 100083,
China
alaa_eldin_che@hotmail.com

Abstract. Parallel Corpora are a basic resource for research in bilingual and
multilingual Natural Language Process (NLP), comparative linguistics, and
translational studies. The basic unit of semantics in natural language is the
phrase with fixed form and meaning. Phrasal alignment is a very important application for a parallel corpus. The current paper adopts a "analyze-analyze-
match" strategy to select phrases for alignment from a parallel corpus of Chinese and Arabic. An aligned phrase database is built and the verbal phrases are
compared between Chinese and Arabic. Verbal phrases in Arabic typically have
three categories: Verb + Noun Phrase, Verb + Prepositional Phrase, and Particle
+ Verb. When aligned to Chinese phrases, each category of Arabic verb phrase
corresponds to a number of phrase categories, including verb phrases, as well as
noun phrases and prepositional phrases. The translational examples and rules
derived from the aligned Arabic and Chinese phrases can have important supporting role in translational studies and comparative linguistics research.

Keywords: Chinese-Arabic, phrase alignment, analyze-analyze-match, verbal
phrase, parallel corpus.

1 Introduction

Parallel corpora can serve as a basis for empirical research, comparative linguistics,
and translation theories, and have applications for bilingual information retrieval,
bilingual word bank extraction, and bilingual dictionary compiling (Liu Chaoming,
2007). Processing of parallel corpora is important for the field of machine translation,
both practically and theoretically. Most researches on parallel corpora foucs on aligning discourses, paragraphs, and sentences, but ignore alignment at phrase level.
Phrasal alignment reveals the matching relations between a pair of translated sentences at the level of sentence phrases, and is an important processing step for bilingual
corpora. During the early phases of the present research, it was discovered that parallel corpora research for Chinese and Arabic relied on English as an intermediary.
Because Arabic has limited corpora resources and there are few large scale public
resources in which Chinese and Arabic appear in parallel, there is all the more need
for a deep level of processing on a Chinese-Arabic parallel corpus.

© Springer International Publishing AG 2018
Y. Wu et al. (Eds.): CLSW 2017, LNAI 10709, pp. 540–551, 2018.
https://doi.org/10.1007/978-3-319-73573-3_49

To meet the needs for Chinese-Arabic phrase aligned parallel corpus, the current research first establishes the parallel corpus, then conducts phrasal alignment to create a database of parallel Chinese-Arabic phrases. The phrasal structure distributions of the two languages as represented in the database are statistically analyzed, and using verbal phrases as an example, we summarize the corresponding phrasal structures between Arabic and Chinese. Real examples are extracted from natural linguistic data to provide illustrations for translation and comparative linguistics of Chinese-Arabic research.

2   Linguistic Sources and Pre-processing

2.1   Corpus Source

We first created an Arabic-Chinese parallel corpus drawn from the United Nations Parallel Corpus. The corpus includes 7,125 pairs of aligned sentences and a total of 827,500 words (265,427 words in Chinese).

2.2   Pre-processing

To ensure accuracy of the linguistic source, and make the Arabic and Chinese texts more suitable for the Stanford parser, we conducted the following few modifications.

    a.   Misspellings.
    b.   A small number of ungrammatical Arabic sentences or misaligned sentence
          pairs.

Stanford's Syntax Parser is unable to provide syntactic tagging on ungrammatical sentences in Arabic. Misalignment will also influence the results of the syntactic analysis and accuracy.

    c.   Punctuation.

When the Stanford Parser encounters a sentence with a comma, it does not independently parse each clause, but attempts to analyze the entire sentence. This often leads to memory overflows and interruption of the parser. Therefore, we change commas to periods in the Chinese at appropriate places to best match the Arabic sentence structures.

    d.   Titles.

Because subject headings and titles typically do not end with a period, batch processing by the Stanford parser will mistakenly append titles to the following sentence. To prevent this and ensure maximum amount of parallel sentences for phrasal alignment, we added periods to the ends of titles.

3   Parallel Phrasal Database Construction

3.1   Construction Process of the Phrasal Database

To create the Chinese-Arabic parallel corpus based on UN Proceedings, it needs first a semiautomatic alignment at sentence level, then aligment at word level with the help of GIZA++, and then syntactic analysis, for which we used the Stanford parser for

Chinese and Arabic sentences. A strategy of "analyze-analyze-match" was applied to select matching phrases from the results of the word alignment and parsing. The selects aligned phrases constitute the Chinese-Arabic parallel phrase database, and the entire process is illustrated by the following graph:

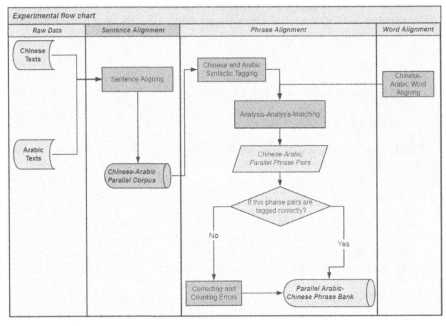

Fig. 1.   Chinese-Arabic Parallel Phrase Database Construction Flow Chart.

3.2   Phrasal Alignment Difficulty Analysis

The purpose of phrasal alignment across the two languages after separately conducting syntactic parsing is to obtain phrasal translation matches for a closer examination of the interaction between syntactic parse trees and phrasal machine translation. Phrasal alignment is not only an important step in machine translation, but also an unsolved problem in natural language processing. For years, researchers have focused on syntactic alignment and word alignment as the basis for bilingual corpus phrasal alignment, which occurs in one of two main ways: directly using word alignment for phrasal alignment or indirectly using word alignment results for phrasal alignment.

The current research adopts the former approach, first conducting a syntactic analysis of the source and target languages before using word alignment as the basis for selecting aligned phrases. This way of alignment is sometimes called "analysis-analysis-matching" strategy (Zhang & Gao, 2012). Kaji first used the method in 1992 to extract aligned phrases between Japanese and English, and it has been widely used since. The strategy can be implemented in different ways with variations in syntactic analysis format and heuristics used in the alignment process. Some methods consider grammatical rules of the source and target languages during the alignment process, such as using dependency grammars to analyze both languages. However, these methods are applied to the results of word alignment, that is, looking for target language segments of equivalent value to the source language segment on the way to word alignment, and thus are an alignment method which directly uses word alignment results. Use of this strategy for Chinese-Arabic phrasal alignment presents the following problems:

a.   Word alignment is relatively difficult, and the accuracy of word aligment is very low.

Chinese and Arabic are very different languages with no similarities between their vocabulary systems, which creates the essential difficult for word alignment. Secondly, extant word alignment tools have low accuracy rates, and phrasal alignment directly relies on word alignment.

b.   It's very difficult to achieve robust and precise monolingual syntactic parse results.

Syntactic parsing technology for Chinese and Arabic is not as mature as that for English, and it is difficult to find a reliable parsing tool. Though Stanford has parsers for Chinese and Arabic, the accuracy rates are low. Parsing in each language is a basis for the entire alignment process following the "analysis-analysis-matching" strategy, and has a direct impact on the final phrasal alignment results.

c.   Results of syntactic analysis across languages may not have direct matches.

Two languages with completely different grammatical systems mean that even if the output of the individual syntactic parsers was completely accurate, there may still be difficulty in matching the results. Structural differences across Chinese and Arabic make it impossible to perfectly align the parse trees of the source and target languages. Syntactic analysis relies on the various grammatical peculiarities and associated syntactic theories for each language, and it is impossible to completely avoid this problem.

d.   Disambiguation among multiple candidates of structural alignment carries subjectivity.

When a phrase in Arabic has several potential candidate phrases in Chinese for alignment, there is a structural alignment ambiguity. The "analysis-analysis-matching" strategy typically uses heuristic formulas or rules to resolve the ambiguity, but this contains a degree of subjectivity.

3.3   Chinese-Arabic Phrasal Alignment, Word alignment, and Syntactic Analysis

The data for the current research is already aligned texts of Chinese and Arabic. After automatically segmenting by sentences, it was clear that the number of sentences was different, with Arabic having 7,125 sentence and Chinese having 7,523. A sentence in Arabic often amounts to two Chinese sentences in length, and this 1-2 correspondence occurred 398 times in the corpus. To ensure an equal number of sentences for sentence alignment, the Chinese sentences in question were merged by substituting a comma for a period.

GIZA++ (Och & Ney; 2003) was used to perform word alignment on the aligned sentences. GIZA++ performs statistical word alignment using an IBM-developed source channel model. During alignment, every source language vocabulary item is restricted to a single corresponding target language word and unmatched words are assigned a NULLWORD category. Running the Chinese and Arabic sentences through GIZA++ resulted in quite a number of NULL word alignments. To understand why, and ignoring the NULL alignments stemming from free translation methods, the majority of the NULL alignments were caused by differences in the Chinese and Arabic vocabulary systems. For example:

Sentence in Chinese: 中国 倡议 建立 东亚 自由 贸易 区。

Sentence in Arabic: تدعو الصين لبناء منطقة التجارة الحرة في شرق آسي آسيا.

	中国	倡议	建立	东亚	自由	贸易	区	。
تدعو		■						
الصين	■							
لبناء			■					
منطقة							■	
التجارة						■		
الحرة					■			
في								
شرق				■				
آسيا								
.								■

Arabic is a VSO language, where sentences begin with a verbal predicate, which is followed by the subject and then the object. Thus, the Arabic sentence begins with 'advocate', but Chinese as a SVO language begins the sentence with 'China', so there is a significant difference in ordering across the sentences. Furthermore "倡议" does not take an object, so " لبناء(build)"must begin with a preposition. When locations are referenced in Arabic, they are usually preceded by a location marking preposition "في (in, at)." Neither of these prepositions has a corresponding word in Chinese, so both are aligned with NULL. This example illustrates the differences between Chinese and Arabic. The word alignment results of GIZA++ will have a strong influence on the final Chinese-Arabic phrasal results.

The Arabic sentences were processed by Stanford's Arabic language parser arabicFactored.ser.gz (Gree & Manning, 2010) and xinhuaFactoredSegmenting.ser.gz (Levy & Manning, 2003) was used for the Chinese parsing. Glancing over the output of both parsers, it was clear that a number of part of speech tags were wrong, the most glaring examples of which were when empty elements were tagged with a part of speech or syntactic component. For example, in (NP (NN)), the NN is clearly an empty component, but the entire noun phrase has no content. To circumvent this error, we deleted sentences pairs afflicted with empty components, removing 738 sentence pairs all together, and leaving 6,387 for further processing.

The steps of the "analyze-analyze-match" phrasal alignment strategy are proceed as follows:

a. Apply the word alignment tool to bilingual sentence input (A, C), where A and C respectively refer to the Arabic and Chinese sentences. Select all aligned vocabulary items from the results.

b. Run sentence parsers on A and C, and let TA and TC refer to the outputted parse trees.

c. Traverse Arabic parse tree T_A, extracting all nodes except the root to create a parse tree forest $\{ST_A^1, ST_A^2, \cdots, ST_A^m\}$; do the same for T_C ing $\{ST_C^1, ST_C^2, \cdots, ST_C^n\}$.

d. For each Arabic sub-parse tree, ST_A^i, compute the degree of matching by traversing each Chinese sub-parse tree and select the best matching ST_C^j as the aligned phrase. Repeat this step until the best matching Chinese sub-parse tree has been found for every Arabic sub-parse tree.

e. Repeat steps 1-4 for each pair of sentences until bilingual phrasal alignment is complete.

The formula for degree of matching between parse (sub) trees A and C is:

$$LinkScore(A, C) = \frac{Link(A,C)}{Num(A)+Num(C)} \tag{1}$$

Link(A,C)is the number of matching words spanned by Arabic and Chinese parse trees A and C. Num(A) is the number of words spanned the parse tree A.

This algorithm was applied to the 6,387 pairs of sentences to extract 19,586 aligned phrases.

3.5   Error Marking and Adjustment

When looking through the aligned phrases obtained through the methods described above, it was discovered that the parses for each language contained a number of tagging errors. A semiautomatic method was used to correct the labeling errors. First, aligned phrases containing only a single word (or character) were deleted automatically (see example 2). Second, the remaining aligned phrases were systematically inspected, and any errors noticed were corrected or deleted. For statistics on parse error analysis of Chinese and Arabic, refer to Akef et al. (2016).

Example 2: Single element tagging error:

(NP (DT ذلك))

The noun phrase only contains one word and is thus not a phrase. This is a classic tagging error.

Example 3: Human corrected tagging error:

(NP (DNP (NP (NN 罹患哮喘)) (DEG 的)) (ADJP (JJ 最大)) (NP (NN 风险) (NN 因素)))

"罹患哮喘" is tagged as a noun phrase, but it should be a verb phrase, i.e. (VP (VV 罹患) (NN 哮喘)). Applying this correction, the Chinese-Arabic aligned phrases are as follows.

(NP (DNP (VP (VV 罹患) (NN 哮喘)) (DEG 的)) (ADJP (JJ 最大)) (NP (NN 风险) (NN 因素)))

(NP (الاختطار DTNN) NP (NP (عوامل NN) NP (اقوى JJR) ADJP) (وتتمثل VBD) VP
(للاصابة NNP) (به NNP)))))))

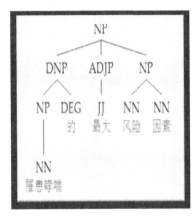
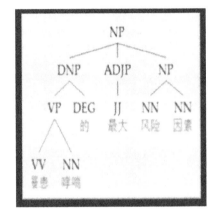

Fig. 2. Syntax trees of the Chinese sentence in Example 3 before and after being corrected tagging errors.

Applying these tagging error corrections, resulted in a total of 15,352 aligned phrases, which serve as the basis for the Chinese-Arabic aligned phrase database.

4   Experiment Results and Analysis

4.1   Chinese-Arabic Aligned Phrase Database Phrase Structure Distribution

Descriptive statistics for the phrasal structure of the Chinese and Arabic phrases in the database are captured in the following table.

Table 1. Aligned Phrase Database Phrasal Structure Distribution.

Phrasal Structure	Functional Category	Chinese	Arabic
NP	Noun Phrase	5203	4972
IP/S	Simple Sentence	2056	2198
VP	Verb Phrase	1584	4833

ADVP	Adverbial Phrase	1239	102
ADJP	Adjective Phrase	1050	735
PP	Prepositional Phrase	955	1543
QP	Quantifier Phrase	805	0
DNP	Possessive Phrase using"的"	788	0
CP	Modifier Phrase using"的"	665	0
LCP	Locational Phrase	483	0
DP	Determinative Phrase	317	0
DVP	Possessive phrase using"地"	207	0
SBAR	Subordinate clause with a conjunction	0	579
FRAG	Sentence Fragment	0	367
WHNP	Noun Phrase with Question Word	0	23
	Total	15352	

From Table 1, it should be clear that phrase structure categories do not have a one-to-one relationship between Arabic and Chinese. There are six categories exclusive to Chinese and three exclusive to Arabic. However, the most common phrase structures are common, with the top three being noun phrase, verb phrase, and simple sentence.

The following sections will use verb phrases as an example and explore the correspondence between Chinese and Arabic with the internal structure.

4.2   Chinese-Arabic Verbal Phrase Internal Structure

Within the aligned phrasal database, Arabic had 4,833 verb phrases, which can be subcategorized as in the following table:

Table 2. Arabic Verb Phrase Structure.

Internal Structure	Example	Number	Proportion
VBD+NP	(VP (VBD صارت) (NP (DTNN التجارة) (DTJJ الخارجية)))	3032	69.10%
VBP+NP	(VP (VBP يمثل) (NP (DTNN السلام)))	869	19.80%
RP+VBP	(VP (PRT (RP لا)) (VBP يستغني))	136	3.10%
VBN+NP	(VP (VBN وتوسعت) (NP (NN حصة) (NP (NN وصادراتها) (JJ وارداتها))))	71	1.62%
VBD+PP	(VP (VBD ورفعت) (PP (IN من) (NP (NN مستوى) (NP (NN ادارة) (NP (DTNNS المؤسسات))))))	67	1.53%
VBP+PP	(VP (VBP تحافظ) (PP (IN على) (NP (CD 100) (PUNC %))))	62	1.41%

VBN+PP	(VP (VBN وشاركت) (PP (IN في) (NP (DTNN الثِّمار (DTJJ النَّاتِجة))))	61	1.39%
VN+PP	(VP (VN ويحتاج) (PP (IN إلى) (NP (NN بذل) (NP (NN جهود) (JJ شاقة)))))	59	1.34%
VBD+ADJP	(VP (VBD وقع) (ADJP (JJR اكثر) (PP (IN من) (NP (NP (CD 150) (NP (NN بلدا)))))))	31	0.71%
Total	4388		

Arabic verb phrases can mostly be broken down into three categories: verb + noun phrase, verb + prepositional phrase, and particle + verb. The verbs in each category can fall into a number of different tenses.

4.3   Chinese Phrasal Structure for Aligned Verb Phrases

For each of the three main categories of Arabic verb phrase structure, we look at the phrasal structures of the aligned Chinese phrase.

a.   Verb + Noun Phrase (Arabic)

There are basically five phrasal structures in Chinese which correspond to V + NP in Arabic.

Table 3. Arabic V+NP and the aligned Chinese phrasal structures.

Chinese Phrase Structure	Arabic Verb Phrase Example	Aligned Chinese Phrase
PP(P+NP)	(VP (VBP يصيب) (NP (DTNN والنساء) (DTJJ الرجال)))	(PP (P 对) (NP (DNP (NP (NN 男性) (CC 和) (NN 女性)) (DEG 的)) (NP (NN 影响))))
VP(VV+NP)	(VP (VBP يعرقل) (NP (NN عملية) (NP (DTNN التنفس) (DTJJ العادية))))	(VP (VV 减缓) (NP (DNP (NP (NN 疾病)) (DEG 的)) (NP (NN 发展))))
VP(NP+VP)	(VP (VBP تتولى) (NP (NN منظمة) (NP (DTNN الصحة) (DTJJ العالمية))))	VP((NP (NN 世卫) (NN 组织)) (VP (VV 领导)))
VP(ADVP+VP)	(VP (VBP يركز) (NP (NN تحديدا)))	(VP (ADVP (AD 具体)) (VP (MSP 来) (VP (VV 说))))

b.   Verb and Prepositional Phrase

The Chinese phrases aligned to an Arabic V+PP phrase can also be placed into five categories.

Table 4. Arabic V+PP and the aligned Chinese phrasal structures.

Chinese Phrase Structure	Arabic Verb Phrase Example	Aligned Chinese Phrase
VP(VV+NP+VP)	(VP (VBP يسيطر) (PP (IN على) (NP (DTNN المرض) (DTJJ ويمكن))))	(VP (VV 使) (NP (NN 疾病)) (VP (VV 得到) (NP (NN 控制))))
VP(VV+VP)	(VP (VBP تساعد) (PP (IN على) (NP (NN توسيع) (NP (DTNN الهوائية) (DTJJ المسالك) (DTJJ الرئيسية))))))	(VP (VV 帮助) (VP (VV 扩张) (NP (NP (NN 肺部)))))
VP(VV+NP)	(VP (VBP يؤدي) (PP (IN الى) (NP (NP (NN تضييق) (NP (DTNN المسالك) (DTJJ التنفسية))))))	(VP (VV 导致) (NP (NN 气道狭窄)))
VP(V+PP)	(VP (VBP يظهر) (PP (IN في) (NP (NOUN_QUANT جميع) (NP (DTNN البلدان)))))	(VP (VV 发生) (PP (P 在) (NP (DP (DT 所有)) (NP (NN 国家))))
NP(NP+ADJP+NP)	(VP (VBP تختلف) (PP (IN في) (NP (NP (NN شدتها) (JJ وتواترها)))))	NP((NP (PN 其)) (ADJP (JJ 严重)) (NP (NN 程度)))

c.   Particle and Verb

Finally, the RP+V structure in Arabic has three corresponding structures in Chinese.

Table 5. Arabic RP+V and the aligned Chinese phrasal structures.

Chinese Phrase Structure	Arabic Verb Phrase Example	Aligned Chinese Phrase
VP	(VP (RP لا) (VBP يرقبان))	(VP (VA 不足))
NP(ADJP+NP)	(VP (PRT (RP قد)) (VBP تظهر) (NP (NN فورا)))	(NP (ADJP (JJ 直接)) (NP (NN 并发症)))

Functional words are a unique linguistic phenomenon of Arabic (Zhou & Lu, 2011). The Stanford parser follows the tagging system of the Penn Treebank which labels each of the three distinct functional words as a particle (RP):

a.   "كان" is a special word form in Arabic, called the broken verb. It does not have a definite meaning on its own, but has a grammatical function to emphasize the past condition of the subject.

b.   Some functional words added to the front of present tense verbs to make the accusative case.

c.   Functional words which act as verbal prefixes to indicate case.

Looking over the three phrasal alignment tables, when Arabic verb phrases are translated into Chinese, they do not always stay verb phrases, but are often rendered as noun phrases or prepositional phrases. Furthermore, the subcategories of verb phrases in Arabic have a one-to-many relationship with their aligned Chinese phrases.

5   Conclusion

This paper used a phrasal alignment method, called "analyze-analyze-match" strategy, which directly utilized the output of word alignment and syntactic parsing for both the source and target languages, to construct a Chinese-Arabic aligned phrase database. The specific steps taken include: first, aligning 7,125 sentences of Chinese and Arabic from a parallel corpus. Using GIZA++ to conduct vocabulary alignment, and using localized Stanford syntactic parsers to obtain parse trees. After manual error correction including deletion of erroneous parses, there were 6,387 aligned sentences available for the "match" step which attempts to align phrases based on the aligned vocabulary and the parse trees. An additional round of error correction yielded the final Chinese-Arabic aligned phrase database of 15,352 phrase pairs. Statistical analysis of the phrase structures found that most phrases in the database are noun phrases, verb phrases, or simple sentential phrases. Using the Arabic verb phrases for an example, additional analysis of the 4,388 phrases found a variety of internal phrase structures which corresponded to different structures in Chinese. Specifically, Arabic verb phrases are typically categorized as verb + noun phrase (V+NP), verb + prepositional phrase (V+PP), and particle + verb (RP+V), each of which is subject to different verb tenses. V+NP accounted for nearly 90% of the Arabic verb phrases, and could correspond to a verb phrase or a prepositional phrases in Chinese. V+PP Arabic verb phrases aligned to noun phrases or verb phrases in Chinese. RP+V corresponded to noun phrases or verb phrases in Chinese. "Analyze-Analyze-Match" strategy is highly dependent on the accuracy of the vocabulary alignment and parsing, and currently available open source tools have relatively low accuracy in Chinese and Arabic domains. Therefore, the results of the current study have some limitations. Further research is needed to address the specifics of Chinese and Arabic to increase the overall results of phrasal alignment methods for Chinese and Arabic.

Acknowledgment. This paper is supported by the Major Project of the National Language Committee of the 13rd Five-Year Research Plan in 2016 (ZDI135-3).

References

1. Akef, A. M., Yang E., Wang Y.: An analyzing of Arabic phrases for Chinese Arabic syntax phrase database study. In: The 12th China Workshop on Machine Translation (2016) (in Chinese).
2. Green S., Manning C. D.: Better Arabic parsing: Baselines, evaluations, and analysis. In: Proceedings of the 23rd International Conference on Computational Linguistics (2010).

3. Levy R., Manning C. D.: Is it harder to parse Chinese, or the Chinese Treebank? In: Proceedings of the 41st Annual Meeting on Association for Computational Linguistics (2003).
4. Liu C.: Overview of Parallel Corpus study. Journal of Yanshan University, 31(6), 120-121 (2007).
5. Och F J, Ney H.: A systematic comparison of various statistical alignment models. Computational linguistics, 29(1), 19–51 (2003).
6. Zhang C., Gao X.: The Translation Knowledge Acquisition Based on Phrase Evaluation. Harbin Institute of Technology Press (2012).
7. Zhou W.: Arabic Grammar Course. Shanghai Foreign Language Education Press (2011).
8. Homepage of the United Nations Parallel Corpus:
https://conferences.unite.un.org/uncorpus, last accessed 2017/7/1.

A Study on the Discourse Connectives in *Analects of the Sixth Chan Patriarch Huineng*

Haifang Guo [1,2], Tao Liu [3], Wenhe Feng [1*], and Yi Yang [4]

[1] Laboratory of Language Engineering and Computing, Guangdong University of Foreign Studies, Guangzhou 510006, China

[2] Department of Chinese Language and Literature, Henan Institute of Science and Technology, Xinxiang 453003, China

[3] College of Uyghur Language and Culture, Northwest Minzu University, Lanzhou 730030, China

4 Laboratory of Computer Lexicography, Ural Federal University, Ekaterinburg 620000, Russia

wenhefeng@gmail.com

Abstract. By labeling the structure of *Analects of the Sixth Chan Patriarch Huineng*, this paper is devoted to study of the explicit and implicit connectives, their semantics and usage. We examine the following results: 1) Implicit connectives (2067,84.9%) are more than explicit connectives (369,15.1%). Among 17 discourse relations, only in 2 Hypothesis and Concession explicit connectives are used more than implicit. 2) There are different ways to use synonymous connectives to represent the same relation. On the one hand, the connectives are used most frequently in Continuity – 14 times. On the other hand, Summary-elaboration and Background relations can be set up without any connectives. 3) Among 60 kinds of connectives, the monosemous connectives are more than the polysemous. Polysemous connectives ("ruo(若), ji(即), yi(亦)") contain at most 4 meanings which are used in different ways in sentences. Besides, we analyze the usage of synonymous connectives in Hypothesis and the polysemous connective ("ji(即)") for case studies.

Keywords: Analects of the Sixth Chan Patriarch Huineng; Discourse structure; Connective; Semantic analysis

1   Introduction

Analects of the Sixth Chan Patriarch Huineng (《六祖坛经》) is known as the only "sutras" of Chinese buddhistic scriptures, which records Liuzu Huineng's speech and behavior about getting dharma, imparting the dharma and share them with his disciples. *Analects of the Sixth Chan Patriarch Huineng* is "the first vernacular Chinese work", in which the language is popular and simple to understand that takes an important part in Chinese language studies.

---

* Corresponding author.

© Springer International Publishing AG 2018
Y. Wu et al. (Eds.): CLSW 2017, LNAI 10709, pp. 552–563, 2018.
https://doi.org/10.1007/978-3-319-73573-3_50

Existing studies of *Analects of the Sixth Chan Patriarch Huineng* are mainly concentrated on the syntax and lexicology: the syntactic aspect mainly studies on interrogative sentence[1], determinative sentence[2], passive sentence[3] and verb-complement structure[4]. The lexical aspect studies on the morphological derivation of double-syllable compounds[5], and auxiliary verbs[6]. Besides, there is a paper named *Language Studies about Analects of the Duhuang Version of Sixth Chan Patriarch Huineng* by Li Jing[7]. Based on a self-annotated corpus, this paper studies on the connectives from the discourse perspective: explicit and implicit forms of the connectives, relation types, and their usage in natural text.

2   Discourse Annotation of *Analects of the Sixth Chan Patriarch Huineng*

Selected text for building the corpus is the Zongbao version of *Analects of the Sixth Chan Patriarch Huineng* [1] (in the following - «*Analects*»), which includes 24559 words. According to an existing discourse structure analytical framework[8], we annotate the discourse structure of «*Analects*», which includes clause segmentation, hierarchical structures, identifying the discourse connectives and relations. Examples (1-2) give the main annotated information.

The main terms in this paper are defined as the followings:

1. Explicit and implicit connectives: Connectives are the units which play a connection role in utterances and represent logic relations. They can join words, phrases, clauses, sentences and others. Connectives can be divided into explicit and implicit, grouped according to status of visible connective in clauses. As shown in (1) and (2), "yi(亦)" "dan...ji(但...即)" are the explicit connectives.

2. Relation types: According to the functional semantic of connectives, relation types can be grouped into four categories and 17 subclasses. Relations Continuity, Transition and Parallel relations are shown in examples (1) and (2).

(1) 法海等闻，//(顺承)悉皆涕泣。/(转折)惟有神会神情不动，//(并列)亦无涕泣。

Fahai Deng Wen, //(Shuncheng)Xi Jie Tiqi. /(Zhuanzhe)Weiyou Shenhui Shenqing Budong, //(Binglie)Yi Wu Tiqi.

Author's translation[2]: Sea of Dharma and other disciple heard about that，//(Continuity) they are beginning to cry. /(Transition)Only Shen Hui is quietly, //(Parallel relation) and he do not cry.

(2) 但持《金刚经》，//(条件)即自见性，//(顺承)直了成佛。

Dan Chi<Jin Gang Jing>,/(Tiaojian)Ji Zi Jian Xing, //(Shuncheng)Zhi Liao Chengfo.

---

[1] *Analects of the Sixth Chan Patriarch Huineng* mainly contain four versions which are Dunhuang Ben, Hui Xin Ben, Ming Zang (Qi Song) and Zongbao. Among them, the most popular versions are Dunhuang and Zong Bao. Zongbao version is also named *the Sutra Spoken by the Sixth Patriarch* ,which is adapted by Zongbao in Yuan Dynasty Zhiyuan twenty-eight years. The version is edited by monks Zongbao, including a volume of ten products. The Zongbao version is used in our analysis.

[2] All the English parts in the following instances are the author's translations.

As long as we practice Diamond Sutra，/(Condition) we can find our own Buddha nature，//(Continuity) and we can immediately become a Buddha.

The corpus contains 2436 annotated discourse relations. All the annotations are added in the platform for annotating Chinese discourse structure analysis [8]. The annotated data is saved in XML format, example (1)' is a segment of annotated data of example (1).

(1)' <R ID="1" Structure Type="逐层切分" Connective Type="隐式关系" Layer="1" Relation Number="单个关系" Connective="" Relation Type="转折关系" Connective Position="" Connective Attribute=" 不 可 添 加 " Role Location="normal" Language Sense="true" Sentence="法海等闻，悉皆涕泣。|惟有神会神情不动，亦无涕泣。" Sentence Position="1…10|11…24" Center="2" Child List="2|3" Parent Id="-1" Use Time="14"/>

3   Connectives and Relations

3.1   Explicit and Implicit Connectives

The statistics on distribution of explicit and implicit connectives are given in Table 1. From Table 1 it can be seen that there are 369 explicit connectives, accounting for 15.1%, and 2067 implicit connectives, accounting for 84.9% in «*Analects*». Implicit connectives are five times more than the explicit connectives.

Table 1. Explicit and implicit connectives of *Analects of the Sixth Chan Patriarch Huineng*.

Relation type	Frequency	Percentage
Implicit Relation	2067	84.9
Explicit Relation	369	15.1
Total	2436	100

3.2   Explicit and Implicit Connectives and Relations

We then focus on explicit connectives and study on their semantics that represent different discourse relations. There is an inseparable contact of connectives and discourse relations (Table 2).

The following Table 2 shows that:

1) There are 11 types of discourse relations, in which implicit connectives are more than explicit, accounting for 64.7% of all the relations. They are Continuity (687>61), Parallel relation (358>42), Interpretation (191>47), Transition (180>26), Progressive(178>2), Causality (173>40), purpose(89>3), Condition(69>18), Correlation (38>2), Inference (17>1) and Evaluation (14>3).

2) There are 2 types of discourse relations, in which explicit connectives are more than implicit, accounting for 11.8% of all the relation types. They are Hypothesis (99>28) and Concession (21>16).

3) There is only one discourse relation, in which explicit and implicit connectives are equal to each other, accounting for 5.9% of all the relation types: Preference (2=2).

4) There is only one discourse relation, in which only use the explicit connectives, accounting for 5.9% of all the relation types: Exemplification (2, 100%).

5) There are 2 discourse relations, in which only implicit connectives can be used, accounting for 11.8% of all the relation types. They are Background (17, 100%) and Total and separation relation (10, 100%).

Table 2. The explicit and implicit connectives and relation types.

Explicit contrast	Types	The implicit		The explicit	
		Frequency	Percentage	Frequency	Percentage
	Continuity	687	91.8	61	8.2
	Parallel relation	358	89.5	42	10.5
	Interpretation	191	80.3	47	19.7
	Transition	180	87.4	26	12.6
The explicit more and	Progressive	178	98.9	2	1.1
implicit	Causality	173	81.2	40	18.8
less(11, 64.7%)	Purpose	89	96.7	3	3.3
	Condition	69	79.3	18	20.7
	Correlation	38	95	2	5
	Inference	17	94	1	6
	Evaluation	14	82.4	3	17.6
The implicit more and	Hypothesis	28	22	99	78
explicit less (2, 11.8%)	Concession	16	43.2	21	56.8
The same of explicit and implicit (1, 5.9%)	Preference	2	50	2	50
Implicit only(2, 11.8%)	Background	17	100	0	0
	Total and separation	10	100	0	0
Explicit only(1, 5.9%)	Exemplification	0	0	2	100

4   Synonymous Connectives

4.1   Types of Synonymous Connectives

The discourse connectives can represent the discourse semantics. The synonymous connectives refer to the different explicit discourse connectives which represent the same discourse relation. The Table 3 gives the relation types and their synonymous connectives.

Table 3. Synonymous connectives for relations.

Frequency	Types	Connectives (Frequency, Percentage)	Species	Total
numerous (≥10) 54.1%	Continuity	ji(即)(19,31.1), sui(遂)(11,18), ze(则)(10,16.4), bian(便)(8,13.1), nai(乃)(7,11.5), que(却)(2,3.3), ci(次)(1,1.6), fu(复)(1,1.6), hou(后)(1,1.6), shi(使)(1,1.6), xian...hou(先...后)(1,1.6), yu shi(于是)(1,1.6), zai(再)(1,1.6), sui(遂)(1,1.6)	14	61
	Interpretation	ji(即)(28,59.6), ru(如)(5,10.6), youru(犹如)(4,8.5), piru(譬如)(2,4.3), yi(亦)(2,4.3), you(犹)(1,2.1), pi(譬)(1,2.1), ru...ru(如...如)(1,2.1), ru shi(如是)(1,2.1), shi wei(是谓)(1,2.1), si(似)(1,2.1)	11	47
	Parallel relation	yi(亦)(19,45.2), you(又)(9,21.4), ji(及)(3,7.1), bing(并)(2,4.8), er(而)(2,4.8), yi...yi(亦...亦)(2,4.8), geng(更)(1,2.4), huo(或)(1,2.4), qie(且)(1,2.4), yi...yi...yi(亦...亦...亦)(1,2.4), yi...yi...yi...yi(亦...亦...亦...亦)(1,2.4)	11	42
	Causality	gu(故)(21,52.5), suo yi(所以)(7,17.5), wei(为)(3,7.5), sui(遂)(2,5), yin(因)(2,5), nai(乃)(1,2.5), ruo(若)(1,2.5), sihyi(是以)(1,2.5), yi(以)(1,2.5), you(由)(1,2.5)	10	40
medium (≥5, <10) 31.8%	Concession	sui(虽)(11,52.4), dan(但)(2,9.5), ji(即)(1,4.8), ji(既)(2,9.5), zong...yi(纵...亦)(2,9.5), nai(乃)(1,4.8), sui...er(虽...而)(1,4.8), ye(也)(1,4.8)	8	21
	Condition	dan(但)(7,38.9), ji(即)(5,27.8), ruo(若)(2,11.1), dan...que(但...却)(1,5.6), fang(方)(1,5.6), yi(以)(1,5.6), yin...yin...fang(因...因...方)(1,5.6)	7	18
	Transition	er(而)(8,30.8), que(却)(7,26.9), dan(但)(6,23.1), nai(乃)(2,7.7), ran(然)(2,7.7), ze(则)(1,3.8)	6	26
	Hypothesis	ruo(若)(79, 79.8), ruo...ji(若...即)(16, 16.2), que(却)(1,1), ruo...bian(若...便)(1,1), ruo...ze(若...则)(1,1), tang(倘)(1,1)	6	99
few (<5) 14.1%	Purpose	Ling(令)(1,33.3), wei...wei(为...为)(1,33.3), wu(勿)(1,33.3)	3	3
	Evaluation	you ru(犹如)(2,66.7), yi(亦)(1,33.3)	2	3
	Exemplificatin	pi ru(譬如)(1,50), ru(如)(1,50)	2	2
	Correlation	wu(勿)(1,50), yi(亦)(1,50)	2	2
	Progressive	geng(更)(2,100)	1	2
	Preference	shi...bu shi(是...不是)(2,100)	1	2
	Inference	ruo(若)(1,100)	1	1
Total			85	369

As shown in Table 3, there are various explicit connectives in different discourse relations:

1) There are 4 types of discourse relations which are represented by numerous (≥10) explicit connectives: Continuity (14 kinds), Parallel (11 kinds), Interpretation(11 kinds) and Causality(10 kinds).

2) There are also 4 discourse relations which are represented by medium (≥5, <10) explicit connectives: Concession(8 kinds), Condition(7 kinds), Transition (6 kinds) and Hypothesis(6 kinds).

3) There are 7 discourse relations which are represented by few (<5) explicit connectives: Purpose (3 kinds), Evaluation(2 kinds), Exemplification(2 kinds), Correlation(2 kinds), Progressive(1 kind), Preference(1 kind) and Inference(1 kind).

4.2   Distribution of Synonymous Connectives

The Table 3 also shows that:

1) Explicit connectives are most frequently used in: Hypothesis(99 times), Continuity(61 times), Interpretation(47 times), Parallel relation(42 times) and Causality(40 times).

2) Explicit connectives are used for a medium frequency in: Transition (26 times), Concession(20 times), and Condition(18 times).

3) Explicit connectives are used for a few frequency in: Evaluation and Purpose(3 times), Preference (2 times), Exemplification (2 times), Correlation(2 times), and Inference(1 time).

4) Sometimes the relations can be represented by unique connectives but sometimes they can not. For example in the Continuity, "ji(即)" are used for a high frequency(31.3%), "sui(遂),ze(則),bian(便) and nai(乃)" are used for a middle frequency, but "que(却) and ci(次)" are used for a low frequency (less than 4%).

There are two factors which mainly influence the frequency of connective using: first, it is associated with existent number of synonymous connectives. The more synonymous connectives in the relation, the more frequent connective using in this relation. As shown in the Table 3, the relation Continuity contains the most kinds of synonymous connectives, correspondingly in Continuity the connectives are used for a high frequency. Second, it is associated with the style features of the connectives and relations. The relations, such as Continuity, Interpretation, Parallel and Causality (16.5%, 12.7%, 11.4%, 10.8%), are represented many connectives relating to the buddhistic scriptures.

5   Polysemous Connectives

5.1   Monosemous and Polysemous Connectives

Connectives can be monosemous and polysemous. Monosemous connectives can represent only one meaning and represent one type of discourse relation. Polysemous connectives can represent more than one meaning and represent multiple relations. Their meanings and usage can be completely different.

As shown in the following Table 4:

1) The connectives can represent at least one meaning, while at most 4 meanings. Each connective has an average of 1.4 (85/61) meaning items.

2) There are 46 monosemous connectives and 6 polysemous connectives. Among them, there are 9 connectives that have 2 meaning items. There are 3 connectives that have 3 meaning items. Besides, there are 3 connectives that have 4 meaning items.

Table 4. Distribution of monosemous and polysemous connectives.

	Singler connectives	Polysemous connectives		
Meaning items	1	2	3	4
Connectives	bian(便), que(却), ci(次), fu(复), hou(后), shi(使), xian...hou(先...后), yu shi(于是), zai(再), you(犹), pi(譬), ru...ru(如...如), ru shi(如是), shi wei(是谓), si(似), you(又),ji(及), bing(并), yi...yi(亦...亦), huo(或), qie(且), yi...yi...yi(亦...亦...亦), gu(故), suo yi(所以), yi...yi...yi...yi(亦...亦...亦...亦), wei(为), yin(因), shi yi(是以), you(由), sui(虽), ji(既), zong...yi(纵...亦), nai(乃), sui...er(虽...而), ye(也), dan...que(但...却), fang(方), yin...yin...fang(因...因...方), ran(然), ruo...ji(若...即), ruo...bian(若...便), ruo...ze(若...则), tan(倘), ling(令), wei...wei(为...为)	sui(遂), er(而), ru(如), youru(犹如), ze(则), pi ru(譬如), geng(更), yi(以), wu(勿)	que(却), nai(乃), dan(但)	ruo(若), ji(即), yi(亦)
Total	46(80%)	9(15.3%)	3(3.4%)	3(5%)

Table 5. The Semantic Distribution of polysemous connectives.

Connectives	Types(Frequency,Percentage)	Kinds	Total
ruo(若)	Hypothesis (79,95.2), Condition (2,2.4), Inference (1,1.2), Causality (1,1.2)	4	83
ji(即)	Interpretation (28,52.8), Continuity (19,35.8), Condition (5,9.4), Concession (1,1.9)	4	53
yi(亦)	Parallel relation (16,80), Interpretation (2,5), Correlation (1,5), Evaluation (1,5)	4	20
que(却)	Transition (7,70), Continuity (2,20), Hypothesis (1,10)	3	10
nai(乃)	Continuity (7,70), Transition (2,20), Causality (1,10)	3	10
sui(遂)	Continuity (11,84.6), Causality (2,15.4)	2	13
er(而)	Transition (8,80), Parallel relation (2,20)	2	10
ru(如)	Interpretation (5,83.3), Exemplification (1,16.7)	2	6
dan(但)	Condition (7,46.7), Transition (6,40), Concession (2,13.3)	3	15
you ru(犹如)	Interpretation (4,66.7), Evaluation (2,33.3)	2	6
ze(则)	Continuity (3,75), Transition (1,25)	2	4
pi ru(譬如)	Interpretation (2,66.7), Exemplification (1,33.3)	2	3
geng(更)	Progressive (2,66.7), Parallel relation (1,33.3)	2	3
yi(以)	Condition (1,50), Causality (1,50)	2	2
wu(勿)	Purpose (1,50), Correlation (1,50)	2	2

5.2   Semantic Distribution of Polysemous Connectives

The Table 5 gives the statistics on the semantic distribution of polysemous connectives:

1) The statistics show that there is only one common meaning item of the connective to be used. The common meaning of the connective develops to the specific meaning of the connective, and represent a fixed type of relation. For example, "ruo(若)" is used in Hypothesis more often than in Condition, Inference and Causality. Nowadays connective "ruo(若)" is a specific sign of Hypothesis.

2) From the aspect of the relationship between the number of meaning items and the frequency of appearance, the more number of meaning items of a connective, the more often it can be used. Such as the connectives "ruo(若)" "ji(即)"and "yi(亦)".

6   Case studies of Connectives and Relation Types

Based on the annotated corpus, for case studies we choose the synonymous connectives in Hypothesis and polysemous connective "ji (即)".

6.1   Synonymous Connectives in Hypothesis

The Hypothesis is chosen to be a case study of synonymous connectives because of that in this relation the explicit connectives are used more than implicit. There are 6 explicit connectives to represent Hypothesis. These connectives are evenly distributed in text, and retain a certain characteristic of significance. The connectives for Hypothesis in «*Analects*» are: ruo(若), que(却), ruo…bian(若…便), ruo…ji (若…即), ruo…ze (若…则), tang (倘). The followings show the characteristics of their usage:

i. To represent Result. Connectives "ruo(若)" and "tang(倘)" can't represent Result, while the other four connectives can represent Results. For examples:

(3)若自不悟，|需觅大善知识，解最上乘法者，直示正路。(如果)

Ruo Zi Buwu, |Xu Mi Da Shan Zhishi,Jie Zui Shangcheng Fa Zhe, Zhishi Zhenglu.(Ruguo)

If you can't digest, | you must find the Maha kalyanamitta, which means to understand the most superior people, directly indicating the way.(if)

(4)修道之人，倘不以智慧照破烦恼，无始生死，|凭何出离? (假使，如果)

Xiudao Zhi Ren, Tang Bu Yi Zhihui Zhaopo Fannao,Wu Shi Shengsi, |Ping He Chu Li? (Jiashi, Ruguo)

Those who practice the Buddha, if not using the wisdom to break the trouble, that no beginning and death of life and death cycle, | and how can free?(suppose, if)

(5)起心著净，|却生净妄。(就，那么)

Qi Xin Zhu Jing, |Que Sheng Jing Wang.(Jiu, Name)

Deliberately view the Sukhavati, | it just produced an improper thought to fixate on the Sukhavati.(just, then)

ii. Location. These connectives can appear at the beginning of the clauses, except connective "tang(倘)".

(6) 若闻开示，|便能悟入。(如果...就，那么)

<u>Ruo</u> Wen Kai Shi, |Bian Neng Wu Ru.(Ruguo...jiu,Name)

<u>If</u> one listens to enlightenment, you can get consciousness.（just then）

(7) 若不听更生，|则永归寂灭，同于无情之物。(如果...就，那么)

<u>Ruo</u> Buting Geng Sheng, |Ze Yong Gui Jimei,Tongyu Wuqing Zhi Wu.(Ruguo...Jiu,Name)

<u>If</u> you do not let them regenerate, |then everything is perished, and it is the same as ruthless things.（just then）

iii. Typical connectives for Hypothesis. These connectives are the typical connectives for relation Hypothesis, except connectives "ruo(若)" and "que(却)".

iv. To join independent sentences. In examples (4), connective "bian(便)" joins complex sentences, and it cannot join independent sentence.

v. Frequency ≥10. Connectives "ruo(若)" and "ruo...ji(若 … 即)" are used more than 10 times in the corpus. Other connectives are used less than 10 times. In summary, statistics on connectives for Hypothesis are shown in the following Table 6.

Table 6. Analysis of the connectives for Hypothesis.

Features / Connectives	Mark the results	At the beginning of the clauses	Typically represent Hypothesis	To connect a single sentence	Frequency ≥10
若	-	±	-	+	+
却	+	+	-	+	
若...便	±	+	+	-	-
若...即	±	±	+	+	+
若...则	±	+	+	+	
倘	-	-	+	-	-

(Sign "+" indicates that the connectives have the feature. Sign "-" indicates that the connectives has not the feature. Sign "±" indicates that the connectives can have or not have the feature.)

6.2   Polysemous connectives: "ji(即)"

Polysemous connectives represent different relations in utterances. We choose the connective "ji(即)" for a case study. In Table 5, the connective "ji(即)" in the *«Analects»* appears 53 times, which, in Interpretation appears 28 times, in Continuity appears 19 times, in Condition appears 5 times, and in Concession appears 1 times. From the frequency of appearance can be seen, connective " ji(即)" is mainly used for the Interpretation and Continuity. For example:

(8) 一切处所，一切时中，念念不愚，常行智慧，|即是般若行。(解说关系)

Yiqie Chusuo, Yiqie Shizhong, Nian Nian Buyu, Chang Xing Zhihui, |<u>Ji</u> Shi Banruo Xing.(Jieshuo Guanxi)

All the locations, all in the time, every thought will not fall into the state of ignorance. Often with wisdom to consider things. | namely this is the highest wisdom. (Interpretation)

(9)"慧能一闻经语，|心即开悟。"(顺承关系)

Huineng Yi Wen Jingyu, |Xin Ji Kai Wu.(Shuncheng Guanxi)

Huineng heard the scriptures that he read, | and his heart immediately was understood. (Continuity)

(10)愚人忽然悟解心开，|即与智人无别。(条件关系)

Yuren Huran Wujiexinkai, |Ji Yu Zhiren Wu Bie.(Tiaojian Guanxi)

Stupid people suddenly hear the awakening of consciousness, then having no difference with wise people . (Condition)

(11)即对面千里，|何勤远来？(让步关系)

Ji Duimian Qianli, |He Qin Yuan Lai?(Rangbu Guanxi)

Though it's a thousand miles away, |it's like me. (Concession)

The Interpretation refers to the explanatory or supplementary information to previous mentioned item or words. In the corpus, the Interpretation is mostly represent a contrary relation to refer explanatory of supplementary information to the latter item or words. From the analysis, we found that in the «*Analects*», connective "ji(即)" for Interpretation is always located at beginning of the latter clause of a sentence (clause 2). It reflects the major feature about buddhistic language: for Interpretation relation, the previous clause always explain the latter one, and the center is located in the latter clause.

7   A related comparison

7.1   A Subsection Sample

Under the same discourse structure analytic framework, we annotated the *Canonical Scripture of a Hundred Parables* (in the following – «*Canonical Scripture*») which is similar to the «*Analects*». Comparing the discourse connectives between these two buddhistic works can examine the following differences:

1) Explicit and implicit relations: connectives in the «*Canonical Scripture*» contain 1958 implicit connectives (88.1%) and 263 explicit connectives (11.8%). In general, explicit connectives in «*Analects*» are higher than in the «*Canonical Scripture*» up to 3.3%. Taking into account for a low proportion of the explicit connectives, there are extreme differences of explicit and implicit connectives. Besides, we found that in the «*Canonical Scripture*» there is not a relation that has explicit connectives more than implicit.

2) Synonymous connectives: in the «*Canonical Scripture*», there can be 11 kinds of synonymous connectives in one relation (Parallel and Causality), but in the «*Analects*» there can be 14 kinds of synonymous connectives in one relation (Continuity).

3) Polysemous connectives: there are 61 kinds of connectives in the «*Analects*», which has 46 monosemous and 15 polysemous. Among the polysemous there are 4 meaning items at most, and each connective has an average of 1.4 meaning items (85/61). While in the «*Canonical Scripture*» 56 kinds of connectives, which has 51 monosemous and 5 polysemous. Among the polysemous there are 6 kinds meaning items at most, and each connective has an average of 1.4 meaning items (85/61).

The *Canonical Scripture of a Hundred Parables* and *Analects of the Sixth Chan Patriarch Huineng* are both buddhistic works. However, there are differences between these two books of study on the explicit and implicit connectives and relations. The nature of these differences is necessary to further study.

8   Conclusion

This paper annotates the discourse connectives of *Analects of the Sixth Chan Patriarch Huineng*. Based on the corpus, we study the explicit and implicit connectives, the relation types and their specific usage.

1) By comparing the number of explicit and implicit connectives, we access the fact that the implicit connectives (2067, 84.9%) are much more than explicit (369, 15.1%). Among the defined 17 relations, only in Hypothesis (99>28,78%>22%), Concession (21> 16,56.8%> 43.2%) and Exemplification (2> 0) explicit connectives are used more than implicit.

2) A relation can be represented by at most 14 kinds of different synonymous connectives (Continuity) and at least without connective (Background, total and separation). Each relation is represented by 5 (85/17) synonymous connectives on average. Synonymous connectives in each relation can be used in different ways. A connective can have at most 4 kinds meaning items ("ruo(若),ji(即),yi(亦)"), while most of the connectives represent 2 meaning items. Each connective has 1.4 meaning items on average (85/61). There are also differences in the frequency of using connectives, generally 1 or 2 of all the meaning items are used more frequently.

3) We study the synonymous connectives in Hypothesis and the polysemous connective "ji(即)" for case studies. Compare the similarities and divergences of 6 kinds of synonymous connectives in the Hypothesis relation, and also analyze the polysemous connective "ji(即)" and the relations (4 kinds).

4) A comparison of the connectives in two buddhistic works *Analects of the Sixth Chan Patriarch Huineng* and *Canonical Scripture of a Hundred Parables*.

Generally, in this paper we have analyzed the usage of the connectives in the buddhistic scripture *Analects of the Sixth Chan Patriarch Huineng*. At the same time, we are annotating many other Chinese Classics which contributed in developing language under the same discourse structure analytic framework [9]. Based on the coming large number corpora, we will eventually construct the history of development of Chinese connectives and Chinese discourse grammar. We believe that our annotation works will make a specific contribution to the study of Chinese discourse grammar.

Acknowledgments

This paper was supported by Ministry of Education Humanities and Social Sciences Project(15YJC740021 、 16YJC74005), Major Projects of Basic Research in Philosophy of Henan Province(2015-JCZD-022), China Postdoctoral Fund(2013M540594), National Natural Science Foundation of China(61502149, 61273320), Key Laboratory of Language Engineering and Computing Laboratory, Guangdong University of Foreign Studies 2016 (LEC2016ZBKT001), China Scholarship Council (201508090048) and Programs to Improve Competitiveness of Russia (02.A03.21.0006).

References

1. Ruan, Shipai: Study of Interrogative Sentences in the Stutra of Hui Neng. Master 's Thesis, Guangxi Normal University, Nanning (2002).
2. Xuanzong Nv Guilian: Study of Judgment Sentences in the Stutra of Hui Nengs. Master 's Thesis, Guangxi Normal University, Nanning (2000).
3. Chen, Niangao: Passive Sentence of the Word "bei" about Dunbo Version of the Stutra of Hui Neng. Journal of Huaiyin Normal University (6), pp. 784-786. Huaiyin (2010).
4. Chen, Niangao: Verb-complement Structure about Dunbo Version of the Stutra of Hui Neng. Journal of Huaiyin Normal University (3), pp. 389-393. Huaiyin (2010).
5. Lv, Pei: The Study of Semantic Word-formation about Two - syllable Compound Words about Analects of the Sixth Chan Patriarch Huineng. Master 's Thesis, Shanxi Normal University. Taiyuan (2014).
6. Zhang, Zening: The Study of Auxiliary Verbs "de,xu,ke,gan,neng" Use about Analects of the Sixth Chan Patriarch Huineng. Journal of Guangzhou Open University, Guangzhou (2014).
7. Li, Jing: Language Studies about Analects of the Sixth Chan Patriarch Huineng of Duhuang Version. Master 's Thesis, Shanghai Normal University. Shanghai (2010).
8. Li, Y., Feng, W., Sun, J., Kong, F., Zhou, G.: Building Chinese discourse corpus with connective-driven dependency tree structure. In: Emporical Methods in Natural Language Processing, pp. 2105-2114. Doha, Qatar (2014).
9. Feng, W., Guo, H., Li, Y., Ren H.: Studies on the Discourse Connectives in *Shishuoxinyu*. Journal of Chinese Information Processing (01), 212-220 (2017).

Transitivity Variations in Mandarin VO Compounds

--- A Comparable Corpus-based Approach

Menghan Jiang[1] and Chu-Ren Huang[2]

[1, 2] Department of CBS, The Hong Kong Polytechnic University
menghan.jiang@connect.polyu.hk,
churen.huang@polyu.edu.hk

Abstract. This paper adopts a comparable corpus-based statistical approach to VO compound Variations in two varieties of Mandarin Chinese and examines the variations from a transitivity perspective. In recent years, more and more VO compounds are observed to have transitive usages. Previous studies categorize the transitivity of VO compound in a dichotomy way, while we argue that each VO actually differs in their degree of transitivity, especially when the variations between different variants of Mandarin are taken into consideration. The degree of transitivity can be measured by both transitivity frequency and its semantic/syntactic properties (follow the theory of Hopper and Thompson [1]). In our study, we compare the transitivity difference between Mainland and Taiwan Mandarin by adopting a corpus-based statistical approach. For both transitivity frequency and semantic/syntactic properties study, the results clearly show that Taiwan VO compounds have a higher degree of transitivity than the Mainland counterparts. We further argue that the higher transitivity degree in Taiwan also illustrates the conservatism of Taiwan Mandarin. This observation is consistent with the earlier study of transitivity variations of light verbs (Jiang et al. [2]) and follows the established null hypothesis in language changes that peripheral varieties tend to be more conservative.

Keywords: VO Compound, transitivity, Language Variation.

1 Introduction

In Mandarin Chinese, some VO compound verbs are observed to have transitive usages, i.e. these VO compounds can take external objects and yield expressions in the configuration of $[VO_1+O_2]$. The interesting thing for this phenomenon is that the verbal morpheme V in VO_1 has already taken an object. Syntactically it is not allowed to take another object. However, in fact, this kind of configuration has become more and more popular in the actual usage, and numbers of VO compounds began to be used transitively.

The transitivity of VO compound has attracted the interests of many linguists. Most of the studies categorize VO in a dichotomy way: VO compound is either transitive or intransitive (e.g., Liu and Li [3]). Her [4] has made a tripartite division in terms of the transitivity: VO can be intransitive (e.g., 得意 'be proud'); semi-

© Springer International Publishing AG 2018
Y. Wu et al. (Eds.): CLSW 2017, LNAI 10709, pp. 564–575, 2018.
https://doi.org/10.1007/978-3-319-73573-3_51

transitive (e.g., 在行 'be good at') and transitive (e.g., 留意 'pay attention to'). However, in our study, we have observed that the VOs which are considered to be transitive actually are very different in their degree of transitivity. Hence, it is more appropriate to view the transitivity of VO in a continuous way. For example, for the word 关心 'be concerned with' and 留心 'be careful', it is very natural for them to take another object, as in the construction 关心别人/留心他的表现 'be concerned with someone/be careful about his performance'. For the word 观光 'tour', it is not very natural if we say 观光意大利 'tour Italy' but it is still comprehensible without ambiguity. Nevertheless, it is not acceptable when the word like 出丑 'make a fool of oneself' is used transitively.

The degree of transitivity of VO compound becomes more complicated if the variations between different variants of Mandarin Chinese are considered. It has been observed that the transitivity of VO compound is likely to differ in different varieties of Chinese. Wang [5] lists about 50 VO compounds (e.g., 登陆 'landing', 涉嫌 'be suspected of', 加盟 'join in', 入围 'finalist') which are commonly used as transitive verbs in Singapore and climes that the transitivity degree of VO compounds in Singapore is much higher than that of in Mainland Mandarin. Diao [6] also points out that the reason behind the increasing popularity of VO_1+O_2 is the influence of Taiwan Mandarin. Although some previous studies have already observed the variation difference, they investigate the issue by only listing some examples extracted from daily newspapers or novels. In addition, their studies are still at the descriptive level. Hence, there lacks of systematic and comprehensive study for the VO compounds variations between different variants of Mandarin, especially based on large corpora. A similar problem is, in previous studies, the variation differences are also examined in a dichotomy way (i.e. Taiwan or Singapore VO can be used transitively while Mainland VO cannot). As the communication between different variants become more and more frequent, the variation differences tend to be a tendency/preference difference instead of the dichotomy difference. For example, although 中意 'like' has also become transitive in Mainland usage, the frequency of being used transitively is much lower than that of in Taiwan or Hong Kong Mandarin. Moreover, Taiwan and Mainland VO compounds can also differ in the type of objects they are taking (e.g., 帮忙他 'do him a favor' can only be observed in Taiwan Mandarin) or the context they can occur in (e.g., 曝光 'exposure' can only be used in negative context in Mainland but not necessary in Taiwan), this kind of variations are not easy to be observed by a traditional methodology.

2 Methodology and research questions

In our current study, in order to investigate the syntactic variations between different variants of Mandarin Chinese in actual usages, a comparable corpus-based statistical approach is applied. The variants we focused on are Mainland and Taiwan Mandarin.

171 VO compounds collected from previous studies (e.g., Wang, 1997; Diao, 1998; Liu and Li, 1998) were examined. The corpus used in this paper is the annotated Chinese Gigaword corpus, which contains over 1.1 billion characters, including 700 million characters from Taiwan Central News Agency and 400 million characters from Mainland Xinhua News Agency (Huang [7]).

In our study, two research questions are addressed:

1). For each VO compound, does its Mainland and Taiwan usages differ in their transitivity frequencies (i.e. the frequency of being used transitively)? What is the pattern of the tendency?

2). What kind of distributional differences in terms of semantic/syntactic features do they have between Mainland and Taiwan Mandarin? Does this refer to their differences in transitivity? (According to Hopper and Thompson [1])

3   Variations between Mainland and Taiwan Mandarin

3.1   Variation in transitivity frequency

To investigate the transitivity frequency differences of VO compounds between Mainland and Taiwan Mandarin, we calculated the relative frequency for each VO in each variant (relative frequency=transitive tokens/all the tokens). The 171 VO compounds were first intersected with the wordlist of Gigaword corpus and Sinica Corpus, in order to exclude the words that are only used in Mainland or Taiwan Mandarin. 16 words such as Mainland unique words 叫板儿 'challenge', 试水 'test the water' were excluded after the intersection. A list of 155 VO compounds was used for further analyses. To test whether the transitivity frequencies of Mainland and Taiwan have significant difference or not, Z-test is utilized. When P-value < o.o5, the difference between two varieties is considered to be significant.

The result of Z-test shows that among all the 155 VO compounds, 33 words show non-significant transitivity differences between Mainland and Taiwan (e.g., 驰誉 'be famous'/调任 'be transferred' /放眼 'expand one's horizon'). 46 words are actually used as intransitive verbs in both varieties (the transitivity frequencies in both variants are smaller than 1‰, e.g., 参展 'join an exhibition'/出丑 'make a fool of oneself'/对话 'have a dialogue with'/联网 'networking'). Therefore, about half (76/155) VO compounds show statistically significant difference in transitivity frequency between these two variants.

Among these 76 words, 53 Taiwan VO compounds show significant higher transitivity frequency than their Mainland counterparts, while 23 VO compounds have significantly higher transitivity frequency in Mainland. Obviously, Taiwan VO compounds tend to be more likely to have higher transitivity usages.

It should also be noted that, although all these 76 words show statistically significant frequency differences, their degrees of differences vary. The degrees of differences can be measured by the likelihood ratio (=higher frequency/lower frequency), meaning that the higher the ratio is, the more obvious variation differences they have. For example, the transitivity frequency of 过境 'transit' in Taiwan is 0.341 (=341/1000) while in Mainland is 0.033 (=33/1000). The likelihood ratio of Taiwan to Mainland is 10.33, meaning that Taiwan 过境 'transit' is about 10 times more likely to be used as a transitive verb than the Mainland counterpart. If the 76 words are further filtered by the likelihood ratio, the transitivity tendency between Mainland and Taiwan becomes more obvious. When the ratio>=10, it is considered to have prominent significant difference in transitivity frequency between Mainland and Taiwan. Table 1 shows that for all the 8 words whose ratio is larger than 10, their frequencies in Taiwan are all prominently higher than that of in Mainland. Combined with the result of Z-test, it can be summarized that in terms of their transitivity frequency, Taiwan VO compounds are more likely to be used in a transitive way, especially when the variation difference is prominent significant.

Table 1. Words have prominent difference (ratio>=10).

Words	Taiwan	Mainland	Ratio
媲美	727/1021	28/1030	26.19
中意	192/540	8/1337	59.42
把关	182/743	11/1547	34.45
过境	341/1000	33/1000	10.33
献计	6/84	2/1000	35.71
移民	455/2000	1/1000	227.5
接壤	34/922	1/2269	83.67
撤军	23/1000	1/1000	23

More importantly, 7 words have been observed to have contrast transitivity difference (i.e. transitivity usages only detected in one variety) between Mainland and Taiwan. For these 7 words (as shown in Table 2), all of them are used as transitive words frequently and naturally in Taiwan while no transitive usages can be detected in Mainland corpus.

Table 2. VOs have contrast frequency difference

Words	Taiwan	Mainland	**Examples in TW**
撤兵	1/197	0/46	撤兵**西岸地区**
垂爱	5/37	0/2	老天特别垂爱**钟岳岱**
领航	76/810	0/169	有能力领航**国家发展**
观光	4/1000	0/5224	观光**意大利**
转行	18/392	0/167	转行**影视界**
失望	3/1000	0/1000	我很失望**他未全力处理问题**
过目	22/317	0/65	过目**所有的展品幻灯片**

Therefore, referring to the transitivity frequency, Taiwan VO compounds are more likely to be used in a transitive way, and the differences between Mainland and Taiwan are obvious.

3.2   Variation in semantic/syntactic properties

To address the 2nd question, the distributional differences in terms of syntactic and semantic properties should be examined. As mentioned above, we argue that the variation differences usually lie in the presence/absence of a kind of trend; thus, a statistical method based on annotated data is carried on to investigate their preference differences in collocation. 9 features which help to characterize Mainland and Taiwan variants are selected. These features cover semantic (e.g., the semantic role of the taken object), syntactic (e.g., POS of the object; take aspectual marker or not), as well as discourse levels (e.g., the polarity of the context it occurs in; structural parallelism). The detailed annotated schema is shown in Appendix.

The 109 VO compounds used for Z-test are also included in this step. About 200 transitive tokens are randomly collected for each VO compound, half from the Mainland Gigaword Xinhua Agency sub-corpus and the other from the Taiwan Gigaword Central News Agency sub-corpus. It should be noted that some of the VO compounds do not have enough 100 transitive tokens. In that sense, we collect all their transitive usages for annotation. The selection principle is to check whether it can cover all different uses of each VO compound. All examples collected for analysis are manually annotated based on these 9 features. The annotator is a trained expert on Chinese linguistics. Any ambiguous cases were discussed with another two experts in order to reach an agreement.

To examine the variation differences between Mainland and Taiwan, Chi-square test is used to determine the significance of the co-occurrence of each feature with each variety for each individual VO compound. The tool we used is SPSS v. 22. The two variables are considered to have significant difference at P<0.05 level. 24 words which violate the assumption of Chi-square test are first excluded for further analyses (the cells do not have expected counts greater than or equal to five).

Among all the 85 (=109-24) VO compounds, 14 words show no significant distributional difference in any of these 9 features: 入境 'enter a country', 驰誉 'be famous', 留学 study abroad', 入籍 'naturalize', 定都 'establish a capital', 登场 'come on stage', 迁居 'move', 中意 'like', 操心 'worry about', 满意 'be satisfied with', 致函 'write to', 出土 'be unearthed', 变身 'shape shifting', 更名 'rename'. For other 71 words which show significant variation differences in at least one feature, we will discuss their tendency differences in details by each feature.

1) Syntactic type of object

First, about the syntactic type of the object taken by VO compound: among 85 words, 30 words demonstrate significant differences in this feature. Among these 33 words, 15 words present the tendency that the Taiwan VO tends to take event-denoting objects (deverbal noun, VP and clause) while the Mainland counterpart prefer to take common NP as the object (投身 'throw oneself into', 插手 'have a hand in', 动员 'mobilize', 投诉 'complain', 控股 'hold controlling interest', 寄语 'send word', 寄望 'depend on', 签约 'sign a contrast', 参选 'stand for election', 接手 'take over', 聚焦 'focus', 插足 'participate' and 涉嫌 'be suspected'). Only 4 words (立足 'base oneself upon', 起诉 'sue' and 帮忙 'do a favor') display the opposite tendencies (Mainland is more likely to take the event-denoting objects). Several examples are shown in Table 3:

Table 3. Example of syntactic difference

Words	Taiwan	Taiwan Examples	Mainland	Mainland examples
插手	VP	插手经营家族企业	NP	插手地方事务
投诉	Clause	投诉本地导游所提供的服务欠佳	NP	投诉有关部门
接手	VP	日本接手举办这项比赛	NP	他很愿意接手这个职务

Therefore, in terms of the syntactic type of the taken object, Taiwan VO compounds present a very strong tendency of taking event-denoting objects while Mainland have more preference of taking common NP as the object.

Another tendency which is not very strong but still can be seen from the result is that, when VO compounds can take both common NP and quantity NP or time NP as the object (撤军黎巴嫩/三十万 'troop withdrawal from Lebanon/withdrawal 30000 troops'; 执教中国男篮/五十年 'coach Chinese National Basketball team/coach for fifty years'), Taiwan VO compounds more prefer the common NP (e.g., 撤军黎巴嫩 'troop withdrawal from Lebanon') while the Mainland may have more preference for the quantity and time object (e.g., 投资三千万 'invest 30 million').

2) Pronominality

For the pronominality property, only 4 words (接手 'take over', 起诉 'sue' and 获赠 'be awarded') display significant differences in this feature. But variation differences still exist, although sometimes are not statistically significance. In general, Taiwan VO are more likely to take person pronoun as the object, the constructions as 帮忙他 'do him a favor', 满意他 'be satisfied with him' can only be detected in Taiwan corpus.

3) Structural parallelism

Referring to the feature of structural parallelism, the tendency between Mainland and Taiwan is quite clear. Among all the 10 words, which show significant differences, 7 of them (把关 'guarantee, 取信 'win trust', 称霸 'seek hegemony', 聚焦 'focus' and 挑战 'challenge') demonstrate the tendency of using structural parallelism strategy in Mainland while only 3words (立足 'base oneself upon' and 放眼 'expand one's horizon') display the opposite trend. In other words, Mainland VO+O construction is more likely to be appeared in the parallelism structures (e.g., 他们坚持把关审核、强化责任、规范操作、配套协调 'They insist on guarantee the checking, strengthen the responsibility, standardize the operation and supporting the coordination).

4) Headline

For this feature, the tendency is very obvious that Mainland VO+O construction is more likely to appear in the headline while the Taiwan ones prefer the normal texts (15 words). For example, 16 out of 104 VO+O constructions of 登陆 'land' (e.g., 登陆上海 'landing Shanghai') are shown in the headline in Taiwan while in Mainland the frequency is 36/104.

5) Complexity of object

Here, the complexity of the object is measured by "whether the object has modifier or not". The variation difference between Mainland and Taiwan is quite clear. Among 27 words which show significant difference in this feature, 18 words show preference over this feature in Taiwan (e.g., 媲美 'rival with', 放眼 'expand one's horizon', 致力 'devote oneself to'). Complicated examples as 任职国界委员会与大陆礁层委员会所辖海洋事务部 'hold a post in Boarders Committee and Ministry of Ocean Affairs under the jurisdiction of the Continental Reef Commission' are not very commonly used in Mainland Mandarin. In contrast, Mainland VO prefers the bare object.

6) Polarity of context

8 words show variation difference in this feature. The difference in preference between Taiwan and Mainland is not very obvious. For Taiwan variety, 2 words prefer neutral context, 3 words have preference for negative context and 4 words favor the positive context (words can show significance in more than one polarity). While in Mainland, only 3 words prefer the negative context, and the other 5 all prefer the neutral context. For instance, 插手 'have a hand in' in Mainland are very likely to be shown in negative context (e.g., 各方势力经常插手流通环节，造成市场秩序十分混乱 'the parities often intervene in the flow of links, resulting in the disruption of market order'), while Taiwan 插手 'have a hand in' are frequently used in both neutral (e.g., 她很少插手姐姐的事情，鼓励她自己做决定 'she rarely intervene the business of her sister, and encourage her to make decision by herself') and positive context (e.g., 各个部门热切希望他可以插手运营，稳定市场秩序 'Every departments are intent on his intervenes on the business operation and help to stabilize the market order').

7) Proper noun

Although more than half (37) words show significant variation difference in this feature, there is no obvious preference difference observed. Among these 37 words, 18 VO compounds in Taiwan show the preference of choosing a proper noun as the object, while in Mainland the other 19 words present the same tendency.

8) Aspectual marker

Aspectual marker taken by VO compounds is also considered. Only 6 words display significance variation difference in this feature, but the difference of tendency is absolute. All of the 6 words (出席 'attend', 出版 'publish', 得罪 'offend', 命名 'name' and 执教 'coach') show significant favor of aspectual marker (either "了" LE or "过" GUO) in Mainland while their Taiwan counterparts show dis-favor over aspectual marker. This tendency is consistent with the findings showed in light verb variation study (Huang et al. [8]).

4   Transitivity in VO Variations

Based on their distributional differences between Taiwan and Mainland Mandarin, we argue that the VO compound itself may differ in its degree of transitivity. Taiwan VO compound have a higher degree of transitivity compared to its Mainland counterpart. The most obvious evidence is that Taiwan VO compounds tend to have higher transitivity frequency (as the result of Z-test presented in Section 3.1), and also Taiwan VO compounds have the tendency of taking more types of NPs and VPs as the complements with less collocation constraints (as has shown in section 3.2). It is more transitive in the sense that it is more likely to be used transitively in different contexts.

Besides this, some other properties as we discussed in section 3.2 also demonstrate the higher transitivity of Taiwan VO compounds. According to Hopper and Thompson [1], 10 parameters can be used to identify the degree of transitivity. VO compounds in two varieties do show variations in some of the parameters (mainly in individuality and affectedness of object). There are mainly three evidences supports this argument.

As mentioned in section 3.2, Taiwan VO compound has the preference of taking VP or clause as the complement (e.g., 投诉澳娱分红不公平 'complain that the dividends of STDM are not unfair'; 插手经营家族企业 'intervene the management of family enterprise') while the Mainland counterparts may prefer deverbal noun (e.g., 插手电商的经营 'intervene the management of electricity business') or common NP (e.g., 插手中亚问题 'intervene the issue of Central Asia'). VP, compared to deverbal noun, is obviously higher in individuality as the patient is overt. Also, as the patient is already in the construction, the affectedness of the objects in Taiwan is also higher than that of in Mainland. The higher individuality and affectedness of object both indicate the higher transitivity of Taiwan VO compounds.

We have shown that Taiwan VO compounds more prefer common NP (e.g., 撤军黎巴嫩 'troop withdrawal from Lebanon') while Mainland may have more preference for quantity and time object (e.g., 投资三千万 'invest 30 million'; 执教五十年 'coach for fifty years'). This should be considered as another evidence to show the higher transitivity of Taiwan VO compounds. Common NP, compared to the object denoting time and quantity, is obviously higher in individuality, and of course, higher in transitivity.

The third evidence is, the Chi-square test shows that Taiwan usages tend to prefer complicated object (object has modifier with DE) while Mainland may prefer bare object. This contrast actually corresponds to the distinction of endurant/perdurant variations (proposed by Huang [9]). According to Huang [9], DE-insertion is allowed only when the object has perdurant properties (a perdurant is an entity which has a time element crucially associated with its meaning). On the contrary, bare object without DE, which is preferred by Mainland Mandarin, may refer to a generic concept, which is endurant (an endurant, is an entity that has spatial component but does not depend on a specific time of occurrence). Therefore the referentiality of bare object is less, which demonstrates a lower individuality, and also indicates a lower transitivity of VO compound in Mainland.

By showing that Taiwan VO has higher degree of transitivity, we further argue that the higher transitivity of Taiwan VO may indicate the conservatism of Mandarin in Taiwan, since Taiwan VO compounds remain more verbal properties, especially the ability of taking the object. Remaining the transitivity is an evidence of being conservative. In contrast, Mainland VO is introducing a new verb class that can take the object, which is transferring from the intransitive to transitive verbs. The evidence of Mainland usages being innovative is that, we have found for the VO_1+O_2 construction, the frequency of being appeared in headline is much higher in Mainland than in Taiwan Mandarin. The headline, as the summaries of a normal text, has length limit and also has more flexibility. It is usually forced to be innovative and new constructions often emerge from the headline.

The observation that Taiwan VO compounds are being more conservative is consistent with Jiang et al.'s [2] finding in Light Verb Variations.

5   Conclusion

In our current study, a corpus-based statistical approach is adopted to compare the transitivity difference between Mainland and Taiwan Mandarin. Different from previous researches, our study clearly shows that in both frequency and distributional constrains, Taiwan VO compounds have a higher degree of transitivity. We further argue that the higher degree of transitivity is the consequence of attempting to preserve the transitive nature of the verbal construction during incorporation. In this interpretation, Taiwan Mandarin is more conservative, hence consistent with the null hypothesis in historical linguistics that peripheral varieties away from the main speaking community are more conservative.

Appendix

Appendix. Annotation schema of VO_1+O_2 construction

Feature	Values (example)	Feature	Values (example)
1. syntactic type of the object taken by a VO compound	Common NP: 获赠一部手机 Event noun: 投身大游行	6. The semantic polarity of context	Polarity: 各方都热切期盼他能插手 Neutral: 她一般不插手妹妹的事

	Deverbal noun: 插手电商的运营 Clause: 投诉澳娱分红不合理 VP:插手经营企业 Quantity: 驻军十万 Time: 执教五十年		Negative: 多方插手农资流通，市场秩序混乱
2. proper noun or not:	Yes: 移民美国 No: 移民发达国家	7.Whether the object of VO has modifier	No: 媲美中亞 Yes: 媲美这个世界一流名声大噪的科技新产品
3. Whether the VO compounds are followed by pronouns	Yes: 帮忙他 No: 帮忙家人	8.Whether the VO compound is affixed with zhe.le.guo	ASP.le: 出版了一套系列丛书 ASP.zhe: 媲美着世界闻名的技术 ASP.guo: 执教过中国队
4. Whether the VO+O construction has parallel structure or not	Yes: 经委协调控制，厅局把关审批，铁路监督保证 No: 把关服务质量	9. Semantic role of the object	Patient; theme; result; target; beneficient; goal; location
5. Whether the constructions are appeared in headline	Yes: 海地警察头目要求出国避难太子港 No: 当年避难上海的3万多犹太人		

References

1. Hopper, P. J., and Thompson, S. A. 1980. Transitivity in grammar and discourse. *Language*, 251-299.

2. Jiang, M. H., Shi, D. X., and Huang, C.R. 2016 Transitivity in light verb variations in Mandarin Chinese- A comparable corpus-based statistical approach. *Proceedings of the 30th Pacific Asia Conference on language, information and computing.* Seoul, Korea.

3. Liu, Y., and Li, J. X. 1998. The transformation of VO_1+O_2 construction and the semantic type of O_2 （"动宾式动词+ 宾语" 的变换形式及宾语的语义类型）. *Journal of Jinghan University (江汉大学学报)*, 5, 011.

4. Her, O. S. 1997. Interaction and variation in the Chinese VO construction. Crane Publishing Company.

5. Wang, H. D. 1997. The rule of VO_1+O_2 construction ("动宾式动词+ 宾语" 规律何在?). *Language Planning (语文建设)*, (8), 30-31

6. Diao, Y. B. 1998. Discussion on VO_1+O_2 construction (也谈 "动宾式动词+ 宾语" 形式). *Language Planning (语文建设)*, (6), 39-41.

7. Huang, C. R. 2009. *Tagged Chinese Gigaword Version 2.0.* Philadelphia: Lexical Data Consortium, University of Pennsylvania. ISBN 1-58563-516-2

8. Huang, C. R., Lin, J. X., Jiang, M. H., and Xu, H. Z. 2014. Corpus-based Study and Identification of Mandarin Chinese Light Verb Variations. *COLING Workshop on Applying NLP Tools to Similar Languages, Varieties and Dialects.* Dublin, August 23.

9. Huang, C. R. 2015. Notes on Chinese grammar and ontology: the endurant/perdurant dichotomy and Mandarin DM compounds. *Lingua Sinica, 1*(1), 1.

Entrenchment and Creativity in Chinese Quadrasyllabic

Idiomatic Expressions

Shu-Kai Hsieh[1] Chiung-Yu Chiang[1] Yu-Hsiang Tseng[2] Bo-Ya Wang[1] Tai-Li Chou[12]
Chia-Lin Lee [12]

[1] Graduate Institute of Linguistics, National Taiwan University, Taiwan
[2] Department of Psychology, National Taiwan University, Taiwan
shukaihsieh@ntu.edu.tw

Abstract.

This paper aims to explore a special type of idiomatic expressions of even length called Quadrasyllabic Idiomatic Expressions (QIEs) in Chinese, and explain their variations with reference to semantic and structural constraints on the elements imposed by the construction of QIEs on the one hand, and its interplay with individual semantic elements in semantic space in the comprehension task of QIEs variants. Results of human ratings and behavioral experiment both show that semantic distance affects the speed of comprehension with the construction entrenchment. For those QIEs with idiomaticity, semantic distance leads to no major effect. We show that Chinese QIEs provide an ideal testing ground for the empirical investigation of the functional linguistic notion of entrenchment in processing multi-morphemic strings.

Keywords: Idioms, Prefabs, Semantic Distance, Construction Grammar.

1   Introduction

As an idiosyncractic and indispensable part of language, idioms/idiomatic expressions have gained increasing attention. From the usage-based emergentist perspective, idioms as one type of *Multi-Word Expressions* (MWEs) are characterized by a holistic storage format that reveals high-level entrenchment and constructionist accounts of complex linguistic strings in the minds of language users.

Traditionally, idioms are defined as MWEs for which the semantic interpretation is not a compositional function of their composing units. The idea of schematicity in idiomatically combining expressions have a different status across linguistic theories. Usage-based accounts (incl. construction grammar, pattern grammar, emergentist and alike) have reasonably shown that idiomatic expressions as pairings of form and meaning are entrenched in a speaker's mind [3,4], and the defining properties of them singling them out from other MWEs are their conventionality and metaphoricity.

© Springer International Publishing AG 2018
Y. Wu et al. (Eds.): CLSW 2017, LNAI 10709, pp. 576–585, 2018.
https://doi.org/10.1007/978-3-319-73573-3_52

However, it is also noted that corpus evidence and acceptability ratings support that idioms are subject to variation too [6]. As we will discuss in later section, assuming the usage- based/constructionist view of idiomatic expressions does not necessarily preclude their being compositionally analyzable. In order to have a deeper understanding of them, both aspects - chunking in representation and fluidity in processing - need to be keep tracked of and well-justified [1]. The large number of idiom variants identified in corpus demonstrates that we need a systemic theory to account for this universal linguistic phenomenon.

In this paper, we will focus on a special type of idiomatic expressions of even length in Chinese called **Quadrasyllabic Idiomatic Expressions** (QIEs, 四字格), which have pervasive presence in the Sinosphere (e.g., Japan, Korea, Vietnam, and other ethnic groups like the Nasi) due to the influence of emblematic logographic writing system [11]. We divide QIEs into two main types: *idioms* ('chengyu') and *prefabs*. Idiom-QIEs often involves Locus Classicus and awareness of cultural background with classical Chinese, they are formed through ages of constant use, well-compiled in dictionary and learned in school (e.g., 化險为夷 hua4 xian3 wei2 yi2, 'turn danger to safety'); while prefabs-QIEs are direct results of language use, can be understood as four-character lexical bundles (e.g., 好久不見 hao2 jiu3 bu2 jian4 'long time no see'). With their archaic origins, idiom-QIE in particular, are still prevalent in modern use and behaves more vividly than its synonyms represented by common lexemes. Tsou [11] observes some defining characteristics of QIEs which cannot find direct equivalents in English: they consist of four syllables or logographs, have relatively fixed structure and patterns, and carry figurative meaning and semantic opacity. The overarching question of this study is whether and how the processing of QIEs and their (nonce) variations reflect the interplay of structural influences and semantic flexibility.

2   Literature Review

There has been a proliferation of research in the past about Chinese idioms, mostly centering around the discussion on their preserved parallel, symmetrical and other structures, as well as their connotative meanings. Recent neurolinguistic works also debate on the bilateral hemispheric involvement in processing idioms [15]. Three major models are proposed to account for processing idioms. The lexical representation model [13] maintains that idioms are stored and processed as lexical items; however, retrieving the idiomatic meaning is faster than literal meaning. In the Configuration Hypothesis [7], the stand in hold is that literal meanings need not be activated at all. The activation is based on the weights of lexical nodes. For instance, even though 'bucket' and 'jar' are both types of containers, in the idiomatic expression 'kick the bucket,' the three words are more connected than the three words in 'kick the jar.' [11]. The Graded Salience Hypothesis [8], on the other hand, discusses both when and where the process happens. In stronger RH view, the literal meaning activates 'broad semantic fields', but in stronger LH view, the idiomatic meaning activates 'narrow semantic fields.' The fMRI study on Chinese idioms done by Shaoqi et. al [2] show that real QIEs and false idioms are related to left inferior frontal gyms (BA47), and the amount of grey matter right orbito-frontal cortex as well as right hippocampus play an important role in processing QIEs. Yang et al [15] also discusses about how left and right hemispheres involve in processing idioms.

Recent constructionist linguists also argues that idioms are not different from normal lexical units, namely, they are also form-meaning pairing. The idioms, as meaning-bearing symbolic units, are with concrete cognitive status rather than the epiphenomena from the computation of generative syntax. The language performance does not come from word-by-word computation, but from the retrieval of prefabricated chunks of discourse. For example, Wulff [14] recognizes the multifactorial significance of construction, which includes semantic composition, frequency effect, and syntactic flexibility. In line with that, corpus-based and experimental studies on the processing mechanism of 'idiomaticity' naturally lead to the constructionist and usage-based linguistic explanation, where its chunk-like status can be seen as a result of high token frequency in use. This frequency effect further results in a tightening of syntagmatic bonds, as well as a loosening of paradigmatic bonds, which means that 'individual component parts become disassociated from their paradigmatic alternatives or semantically related items' [1]. However, this view has been lacking of solid experimental support in the sense that it has been still considered as a rather di cult task to distinguish between holistic and compositional processing of 'formulaic sequences' such as idioms [16,17]. We will argue that the formulaic sequences of even length like QIEs can provide a suitable testbed.

It is noted that, in contrast with idioms of English idiomsm, Tsou [12] shows that Chinese QIEs are different in that they are phonologically composed of four syllables, syntactically fixed structure, and semantically intransparent. Besides, in addition to being symbolic unit of the constructions, its quadrasyllabic structure, unique semantic representation carried by Chinese characters, and rich cultural background embedded in all involve deep cognitive processing.

To sum, in line with the cognitive-constructionist proposal that the notions of schematicity and compositionality are not mutually exclusive [1,9], we investigate how QIEs as entrenched construction impose constraints on the 'open slot' it contains, and how individual lexemes exert their preferential cognitive-paradigmatic semantic space under such constraints through the comprehension task of QIEs and their variants.

3   Methods

This section describes the experimental methods we employed in this study. With QIEs and its variants as targets, we aim to probe how constructions in QIEs set constrain the semantic elements composing the QIEs. Given the specific construction controlled, by replacing one character in the target QIE with other characters of difference semantic distances to the original one, we assume that we can understand how individual elements with different semantic relations interact with constraints set by the constructions. Three hypothesis are made: 1. Idiom-QIEs are processed faster than prefab-QIEs. 2. QIEs with near-semantic neighborhood replacements are processed faster than with far-semantic neighborhood replacements. 3. The effect of entrenchment in idiom-QIEs is more obvious than that in prefab-QIEs, so the reaction time of the replacements of the former will be slower than the reaction time of the replacements of the later.

Liu [18] indicates that numerical idioms (i.e., idioms contain at least one composing character with numeric meaning) count 10.07% among all types of idioms. Besides, symmetric numerical idioms - nAnB and AnBn type-, account for one third of the total idioms. So we choose idioms of the nAnb pattern as our first target. To set the stage for the experiments, we have created required language resources tailored for Chinese QIEs.

We collected and pre-processed ((e.g., word segmentation, and QIE reservation) the texts from two newspapers and the largest online forum in Taiwan for the past ten years (2006-2016), yielding a large corpus with size of 875,473,424 word tokens. 39,845 idioms from the open source dictionary (Moedict) as well as 149,522 numeral idioms extracted from the corpus we build are used to create wordlists of QIEs. Second, the most frequent 96 idioms in nAnB construction are then selected as stimuli. 36 construction patterns were extracted from these idioms. Then, we take these 36 patterns as our standard to select the 96 top frequent prefab-QIEs. Third, we create replacements for these 192 expressions. The replacements are either replaced the second position of the expression or the fourth position of the expression. Semantic distance of these replacements, namely, they are near or far in semantic distance of the original one, are manipulated and evaluated by three native speakers. The amount of replacements for two types of QIEs (idiom-QIEs and prefab-QIEs) as well as the quality of the created replacements (to be near or to be far) is counterbalanced. Thus, there are 96 idiom-QIEs, 48 near idiom-QIEs, 48 far idiom-QIEs, 96 prefab-QIEs, 48 near prefab-QIEs, and 48 far prefab-QIEs. There are 384 QIEs in total.

Table 1. Information about Experimental Stimuli

QIEs					
Type	idiom-QIEs		prefab-QIEs		Total
Number	96		96		192
Examples	一模一樣、七嘴八舌、四平八穩…		半工半讀、一家三口、四捨五入…		
Type of Alternatives	Near Semantic Distance	Far Semantic Distance	Near Semantic Distance	Far Semantic Distance	192
Number	48	48	48	48	
Examples	一年一度 >> 一年一次 一麟半爪 >> 一鱗半爪	三更半夜 >> 三更半刀 一板一眼 >> 一看一眼	一箭二鵰 >> 一箭二看 一胖一瘦 >> 一肥一瘦	一體兩面 >> 一體兩酒 三戰兩勝 >> 三對兩勝	
				Total	384

Two empirical methods are conducted in our research: questionnaire and behavioral experiment. To control the individual familiarity, semantic distance and comprehension, a paid questionnaire was conducted online in which all the selected stimuli were evaluated by a normative group of forty participants (gender balanced) with the 7-point-Likert Scale (1 = strongly disagree, 2 = agree .... 7 = strongly agree). In Familiarity rating, participants are asked to rate how often the presented QIEs are used in daily life. In comprehension rating, the evaluators rate the comprehensible level the presented QIEs are. To judge semantic distance, the replaced characters, semantically related (near condition) or with far semantic relationships (far condition), are paired up with the original character. Then, the participants are invited to score the degree of correlation the paired characters are with. The total items in each rating parts are more than 400, so the questionnaires are divided into version A and version B. Lexical items in one version do not re-occur in another one. Results of questionnaires are used to choose appropriate experimental stimuli as well as to be compared with corpus data and results of behavioral experiment.

E-Prime 2 is used for behavioral experiment. Instruction of behavioral experiment is, "Can you comprehend if someone uses the following QIE?" There are 8 practice trials before the real experiment, which includes 240 trials. The 240 trials are divided into three blocks. There are 8 conditions (2 types of idioms x 4 types of semantic manipulation) in our experiment, and we design 10 trials for each condition, so each block contains 80 trials. The order of presented stimuli is randomized by computer program. In every trial a fixation cross (300 ms) is first presented, then followed by a 200 ms blank, a QIE (1500 ms), and a "?" as a reminder for reaction. After the question mark is presented, participants have at most 1500 ms to press buttons. The answers and reaction time are automatically recorded by the computer.

4   Discussion and Analysis

40 native speakers (10 male and 10 female for each version) are paid to complete the questionnaires. The results confirm our assumptions on the influence of semantic distance. It reveals that participants rated original idiom-QIEs and original prefab-QIEs as highly comprehensible (M= 6.13, SD= 0.91) and frequently used (M= 4.76, SD= 1.19). Near semantic neighborhood replacements were, though less than the original ones, generally comprehensible (M= 4.88, SD= 1.27), and were less frequently used in daily life (M= 2.38, SD= 1.01). Far semantic neighborhood replacements were not comprehensible according to the rating results (M= 1.82, SD= 0.49), and are judged as being seldom used in daily life (M= 1.27, SD= 0.18).

The upper part in Figure 1 shows the by-subject average scatter plot for ratings on familiarity frequency and comprehension. The bottom part in Figure 1 further indicates the correlation between semantic distance and comprehensibility. The nearer the semantic distance is, the more comprehensible the QIE is. In addition, as shown in the left part of Figure 2 the group average distribution of comprehensibility is similar for all of the original ones, all of the near replacements, and all of the far replacements. Responses to semantic distance judgement test also reveal the consistent result: words used in near replacements (M= 5.58, SD= 0.83) are viewed as more semantically correlated than words used in far replacements (M= 1.69, SD= 0.59). The result of the questionnaire also indicates that it is hard to comprehend any type of replacements of the idioms that are highly correlated to Chinese cultural background or traditional classics (e.g. 三生有幸、班門弄斧) no matter whether these replacements are near or far related to the original ones.

20 native speakers are paid to participate in the behavioral experiment. Among the 20 participants, one of whom has taken the questionnaire, four of whom fail to make responses within 1.5 seconds, and four of the participants have reaction time longer or shorter than 1.5 IQR of the median reaction time in at least one experimental condition, namely, their reaction time belongs to extreme value, so these data are not taken into analysis. The results of the rest 11 participants are analyzed for discussion.

We then probe further whether our manipulation on different types of QIEs (idiom-QIEs and prefab-QIEs) and semantic replacements (original idiom-QIEs/prefab-QIEs set, near replacements, far replacements, and random combination set) influence participants' comprehension and reaction time or not. Thus, we focus on the reaction time when participants made right responses. In other words, in original idiom-QIEs/prefab-QIEs set and near replacements, participants are expected to respond with the answer "comprehensible," but in far replacements, and random combination, participants are expected to respond with the answer "incomprehensible." In our data, 86% participants did make expected responses as shown in Table 2.

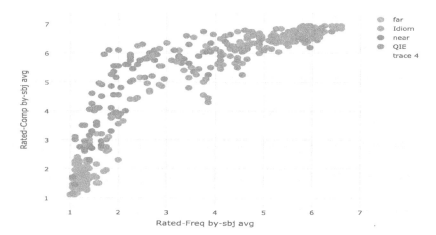

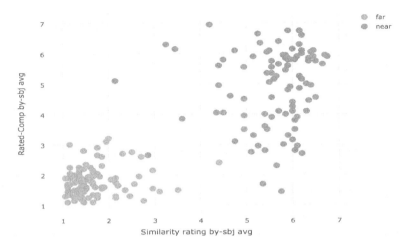

Fig. 1. Upper: Familiarity and Comprehensibility   Bottom: Correlation and Familiarity

Table 2. Results of Behavioral Experiment

	Item type	group name	Number	M	SD		Item type	group name	Number	M	SD
com	idiom-QIEs	Original	443	377.3341	178.3066	inco	idiom-QIEs	Original	5	459.4	155.2669
preh		Near	334	425.9162	231.9069	mpre		Near	99	547.6869	304.1041
ensi		Far	63	484.3016	201.6937	hens		Far	374	449.492	235.5625
ble		Control	30	616.9	175.5015	ible		Control	409	448.1785	230.6231
	prefab-QIEs	Original	401	402.9277	209.6604		prefab-QIEs	Original	38	470.9737	213.5874
		Near	324	446.2407	246.093			Near	106	564.8962	316.5363
		Far	37	543.8919	261.6695			Far	405	436.7185	230.4273
		Control	25	494.96	158.1614			Control	415	416.9398	207.2863

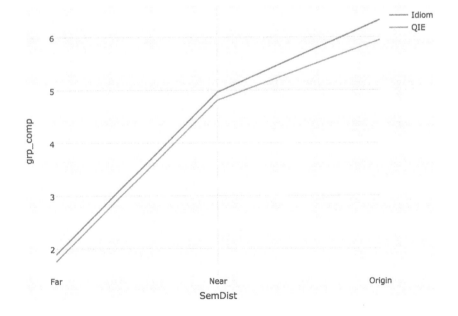

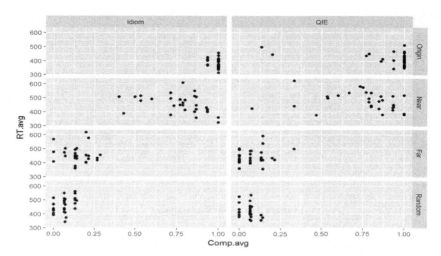

Fig. 2. Upper: Average Distribution of Comprehensibility Bottom: Reaction Time of all Types

As shown in the upper part of Figure. 2, when comparing the comprehensibility and reaction time, we find that the results of behavioral experiment correspond to the results of questionnaire: the most comprehensible original idiom-QIEs and original prefab-OIEs are the two fastest reacted conditions in behavioral experiment (idiom-QIEs, M=356.59 ms, SD= 43.86 ms; prefab-QIEs, M=376.88 ms, SD=68.98 ms). Similarly, the most incomprehensible ones are reacted slower (idiom-QIEs, M=418.85 ms, SD= 76.95 ms; prefab-QIEs, M=408.46 ms, SD=85.39 ms). In the comprehensible part, the reacting order is as following: the original idiom-QIEs (377 ms) > the original prefab-QIEs (402 ms), but in the incomprehensible part, the control group and the far-replacements are with close reaction time (400 ms ~ 450ms).

According to ANOVA analysis as shown in Figure 3, semantic manipulation is found to have significant effect; namely, participants' reaction time changes as the manipulating factors change (F(3,30)=3.18, p=.038). On the other hand, both the results of behavioral experiment and the results of questionnaire indicate that there is no significant effect from types of OIEs, idiom-QIEs or prefab-QIEs, (F(1,10)=0.667,p=.433). However, the interaction between types of QIEs and semantic manipulation shows significant effect (F(3,30)=3.05, p=.043). This interaction implies that different types of QIEs are with different qualities, and different manipulations on different types of QIEs achieve different effects.

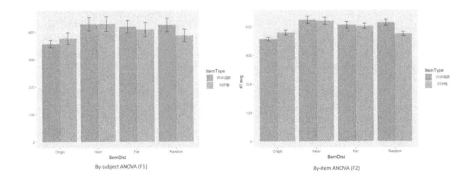

Figure 3   ANOVA analysis

5   Conclusion

In this paper, we have examined the semantic properties of Chinese numeral constructions both in stabilized forms and variations around the stabilities. Corpus evidence
and human ratings suggest that the comprehension and processing of nonce QIEs
emerges from the interaction of construction and lexical semantics. In the rating part,
the most comprehensible ones (the original idiom-QIEs and the original prefab-QIEs)
are the fastest reacted ones in experimental conditions. Besides, semantic manipulation also achieves significant effects. In other words, reaction time of participants
changes according to different semantic manipulations. Studies on variants of QIEs
can help us understand the dynamic procedure language users operate when processing verbal and non-verbal information.

We believe the study of Chinese QIEs variations will shed more light on our understanding of cognitive dynamics that underlie natural linguistic and non-linguistic
pro- cessing and understanding model. The results gained from this empirical study
have set the stage for our follow-up neuro-imaging experiment in the future.

References

1. Blumenthal-Dramé, A.: Entrenchment in Usage-based Theories: What Corpus Data do
and do not Reveal about the Mind, volume 83. Walter De Gruyter (2013).
2. Chen, S., Y. Zhang., Z. Xio, X. Zhang.: Specific Neural Basis of Chinese Idioms Processing: An Event-related Functional MRI Study. Chinese Journal of Radiology 41(9),
930-933 (2007).
3. Croft, W. and D. A. Cruse.: Cognitive Linguistics. Cambridge University Press. Cambridge (2004).
4. Croft, W.: Verbs: Aspect and Causal Structure. Oxford University Press, Oxford (2012).

5. Erman, B., Warren, B.: The Idiom Principle and the Open Choice Principle. Text 20(1), 29–62 (2000).

6. Geeraert, K., J. Newman., H. Baayen.: Idiom Variation: Experimental Data and a Blueprint of a Computational Model. Topics in Cognitive Science (2017).

7. Gibbs, R.: Literal Meaning and Psychological Theory. Cognitive Science 8(3), 275-304 (1984).

8. Giora, R., Eran, Z., Nachum, S., Gila, B., Asa, K.: Differential Effects of Right-and Left-Hemisphere Damage on Understanding Sarcasm and Metaphor. Metaphor and Symbol 15(1-2), 63-83 (2000).

9. Goldberg, A.: Constructions at work: The Nature of Generalization in Language. Oxford University Press (2006).

10. Liina, P.: Studying the Neural Bases of Semantic Composition with MEG. invited speech, (2015).

11. Marshal, N. M. Faust, T. Hendler, and M. Jung-Beeman.: Hemispheric dif- ferences in processing the literal interpretation of idioms: Converging evidence from behavioral and fmri studies. cortex, 44(7):848–860 (2008).

12. Tsou, B.: Idiomaticity and Classical Traditions in Some East Asian Languages. In: 26th Pacific Asia Conference on Language, Information and Computation (PACLIC 26), pp. 39. (2012).

13. Swinney, D., A. Cutler.: The Access and Processing of Idiomatic Expressions. Journal of Verbal Learning and Verbal Behavior 18(5), 523-534 (1979).

14. Wulff, S.: Rethinking Idiomaticity: A Usage-based Approach. Continuum (2008).

15. Yang, J., P. Li, X. Fanga, H. Shu, Y. Liu., L.Chen.: Hemispheric Involvement in the Processing of Chinese Idioms: An fMRI Study. Neuropsychologia. 87: 12-24 (2016).

16. Wray, A.: Formulaic Language and the Lexicon. Cambridge University Press (2005).

17. Wray. A.: Identifying Formulaic Language: Persistent Challenges and New Opportunities. Formulaic language, 1:27–51 (2009).

18. 劉美芸. 數詞成語形式結構的計量分析. 東吳線上學術論文2, 199-228 (2008).
Liú, M.Y.: shù cí chéng yǔ xíng shì jié gòu de jì liáng fēn xī. dōng wú xiàn shàng xué shù lùn wèn 2, 199-228 (2008).

A Study on Chinese Synonyms:
From the Perspective of Collocations

Tsinghua University, Beijing 100084, China.
echin_001@hotmail.com

Abstract. Words are often considered to be synonyms when they share the same meaning. However, there are subtle differences of synonyms appear in actual language use and expressions. Compared to previous approaches mostly based on invented instances, this study uses a corpus-based approach which provides a more comprehensive method to investigate the synonymy through their collocations. This paper examines three pairs of synonyms expressing the concept of something not being "real" with 伪 *wěi*-假 *jiǎ* being the etymological root, as well as their derivatives 伪装 *wěi zhuāng*-假装 *jiǎ zhuāng* and 虚伪 *xū wěi*-虚假 *xū jiǎ*, words in each pair are often used to simply mutually define one another in dictionaries and do not further explain their differences. Using the statistical method namely Mutual Information to compute data collected from corpus, this paper analyzes the relation between each word and their collocates by looking at the register in which they appear as well as their semantic features and prosody.

Keywords: corpus-based, collocation, mutual information, semantic prosody.

1 Introduction

Previous studies mostly rely on subjective intuition to analyze words and meanings, which is hardly objective. Modern technology has allowed scholars to widen the scope of study of semantics by using large digitalized corpora. Not only can they gather large amount of natural occurring textual data within a short time, but also select the computer assisted method of text and corpus analysis according to their objective. This in turn has increased the accuracy and reliability of their results considerably. Syntagmatic relation between words is considered as a key element in order to discuss their attributes and characteristics [1], [2], [3], [4]. Since its structure is consistent with the sentence in Chinese, phrasal structure has been the main focus in the research of Chinese language [5]. It is necessary to study and interpret subtle distinctions between the patterns hidden under the general structure of Chinese.

In Chinese lexicology, the words '伪(*wěi*)' and '假(*jiǎ*)' denote a similar meaning under the concept of something being 'not-real'. *The Contemporary Chinese Dictionary* (7th edition) defines both of them being the antonyms of the concept of 'realness' (真(*zhēn*)), in which '假(*jiǎ*)' is categorized as an adjective whereas '伪(*wěi*)' is uncategorized. In addition, verbs like '伪装(*wěi zhuāng*)' and '假装(*jiǎ zhuāng*)' are often used to mutually explain one another in the dictionary. To Chinese

© Springer International Publishing AG 2018
Y. Wu et al. (Eds.): CLSW 2017, LNAI 10709, pp. 586–600, 2018.
https://doi.org/10.1007/978-3-319-73573-3_53

language learners, this circular interpretation only brings further confusion if they do not understand any of them.

The main approach used so far to examine the relation between words pertaining to the concept of 'not-real' has been from an etymological perspective. Studies show that '伪(wěi)' has been replaced by '假(jiǎ)' through a chronological process which prove that these words are evidently similar on meanings and denotation [6], [7], [8]. However, the subtle differences between them has yet to be further defined because they sometimes can be used exclusively in different contexts. Therefore, this study proposes a more objective approach, to investigate the following pairs of synonyms (伪(wěi)-假(jiǎ), 伪装(wěi zhuāng)-假装(jiǎ zhuāng) and 虚伪(xū wěi)-虚假(xū jiǎ)) by using corpus-based approach.

First, this paper presents the methodology used to compare the differences in their similarity by looking at the register of language in which they appear. Second, it examines their collocational patterns using statistical calculation. Finally, this study attempts to identify the context in which they are used and the semantic prosody.

2   Methodology

2.1   Corpus data and analysis tools

This study is using data extracted from the Chinese Linguistics Corpus (CCL) [9] developed by Peking University. Data collection focused on written genres which are newspapers and novels. Two kind of tools were used in this study, namely ICTCLAS [10] for word segmentation and annotation, and AntConc [11] for statistical analysis.

2.2   Collocations and statistical calculation

In order to study and compare words meaning, this paper investigate the concordances of a node word and collocates according to their probability to co-occur under a specified span. A span is a condition where a node word treated as the pivot, and its distance with other words in a sentence. For example, if '伪 (wěi)' is set as the node word with span 0:1, it means that we are looking for its immediate right collocates. It is highlighted that the span between words unfolds the discontinuous collocations in which concordance data can be summarize in a wider scope [12]. For instance, span 5:5 means that a node word is observe in line with five words to the left and five words to the right, shown as below:

N-5, N-4, N-3, N-2, N-1, (Node word), N+1, N+2, N+3, N+4, N+5

In general, all the collocations are expected to be co-occur at a rate higher than chance, which is refer as 'collocability' [13]. The collocability of a node word and other words can be calculated in some standard statistical procedures. Mutual information (MI) is used as the statistical test to measure the collocational strength in this study. Mutual Information formula is as Fig. 1.

$$MI\ (w_1, w_2) = \frac{P\ (w_1, w_2)}{P(w_1)\ P\ (w_2)} \tag{1}$$

Fig. 1. w_1 is the node word and w_2 is the collocates word

Calculations for the MI compare the probability of observing the two words together with the probability of observing each word independently based on the frequencies of the words. A score beyond 0 shows that the words tend to co-occur at a rate greater than chance. The higher the score, the stronger the association between words [4].

Words do not randomly combines each other. In fact, they are required to be grammatically as well as semantically acceptable in order to express meaning in language use. Therefore, it is quite possible to observe evidence of the meaning of a word by looking at its repeated patterns of co-occurrence [14]. In addition, words with similar semantic preference tends to form collocation to maintain a cohesive expression. Semantic preference is part of a word's meaning which is called 'semantic prosodies' in most of collocational studies. The idea of sematic prosody is highly identical to the concept in Chinese saying '物以类聚 (*wù yǐ lèi jù*)' (like attracts like). Semantic prosody is defined as a "consistent aura of meaning with which a form is imbued by its collocates [15]. Words may be further distinguished as positive, neutral or negative semantic prosody.

3   Results and discussions

3.1   Register variations of group '伪(*wěi*)' and group '假(*jiǎ*)'

This study focuses on two registers, i.e. newspapers and novels. Table 1 shows the occurring frequency of the three pairs of synonyms in each register. The group '伪 (*wěi*)' (including 伪(*wěi*), 伪装(*wěi zhuāng*) and 虚伪(*xū wěi*)) consists of 5741 tokens, whereas the group of '假(*jiǎ*)' (including 假(*jiǎ*), 假装(*jiǎ zhuāng*) and 虚假(*xū wěi*)) consists 5852 tokens.

Table 1. Register variations of group '伪 (*wěi*)' and group '假 (*jiǎ*)'

	Group '伪(*wěi*)'			Group '假 (*jiǎ*)'		
	伪	伪装	虚伪	假	假装	虚假
Newspapers	849	143	106	2341	12	288
Novels	3424	549	670	2697	416	98
Total	4273	692	776	5038	428	386

The figure below show the frequency distribution in percentage. It is clearly that the use of '伪 wěi ' and '假(jiǎ)' vary from a register to another. The group '伪(wěi)' is predominantly used in novels, while ' 假 (jiǎ)' does not seem to be significantly preferred in either register.

Fig. 2. Registers variation of '伪(wěi)'、'假(jiǎ)'

As illustrated in figure 2, the group '伪'(wěi)' is typically used in novels and exhibit a stronger narrative feature whereas the group '假(jiǎ)', with a distribution of 55% in newspapers and 45% in novels, does not have any predilection. Although both newspapers and novels are under written genre, they are defined by their situational of use, such as communication purposes and content, thus they are clearly different in targeted readers, topics, setting etc. Control of a range of registers is crucially important for any competent speakers of language [4]. Normally newspapers' focus is to convey information about facts and truths to its readers, therefore doesn't use the same style of writing as in novels [16]. Literary work is mostly fictional, thus affective words and phrases are more frequently used.

3.2　The pair of synonyms '伪(wěi)' and '假(jiǎ)'

First, this paper examines the first pair – '伪 (wěi)' and '假 (jiǎ)'. '伪 (wěi)' occurs 4273 times whereas '假 (jiǎ)' occurs 5038 times. This discussion is based on the immediate right collocates of '伪 (wěi)' and '假 (jiǎ)' that retrieved by using the MI calculation method, among which only those showing significantly strong collocation with the condition of a MI score of 6.0 and above, and with a minimum co-occurrence frequency of 5 times and above were selected.

Immediate right collocates of '伪 (wěi)'.

Table 2. Immediate right collocates of '伪 (wěi)'

Collocate	f(n,c)	MI	Collocate	f(n,c)	MI
满洲国(mǎn zhōu guó) Manchukuo	42	7.84458	币 (bì) coin/money	120	7.43858
省长 (sheng zhǎng) provincial governor	74	7.78724	警官 (jǐng guān)	7	7.33000

			police officer		
君子 (*jūn zǐ*) noble man	117	7.76075	县长 (*xiàn zhǎng*) county magistrate	13	7.29709
军 (*jūn*) troop	1904	7.68208	政权 (*zhèng quán*) regiment	46	7.19821
保长 (*bǎo zhǎng*) head of safeguard	69	7.59555	总队 (*zǒng duì*) corps	5	7.16650
公务员 (*gong wù yuán*) civil officer	5	7.58154	县政府 (*xiàn zhèng fǔ*) county government	8	7.14414
工会 (*gong huì*) labour union	15	7.50354	村长 (*cūn zhǎng*) village head	33	7.10761
誓 (*shì*) promise	7	7.48201	警备 (*jǐng bèi*) guard	22	7.01861
自卫 (*zì wèi*) self defense	31	7.47684	满 (*mǎn*) abbr. of Manchukuo	33	6.98718

Table 2 shows that collocates of '伪(*wěi*)' are mainly nouns and can be grouped under the semantic field of law and order, country governance. '伪 (*wěi*)', which functions as a attributive word in a phrasal structure denies the legality of these collocates. As a result, phrases of '伪(*wěi*) + noun' denote the meaning of the illegal status of the person, professions or country. Some examples of '伪(*wěi*) + noun' :

1. 长春曾是**伪满洲国**首都，日伪时期大批日本人在此居住过……
   cháng chūn céng shì wěi mǎn zhōu guó shǒu dū，rì wěi shí qī dà pī rì běn rén zài cǐ jū zhù guò
   During the alleged era of the Japanese occupation, a number of Japanese lived in Changchun, the pseudo capital city of Manchuria.
2. 他自己规定一天画3张，一年多时间内，这种制作极其粗糙的**伪币**居然流通到了河南、湖北、陕西、甘肃等省。
   tā zì jǐ guī ding yì tiān huà 3 zhāng，yī nián duō shí jiān nèi，zhè zhǒng zhì zuò jí qí cū cāo de wěi bì jū rán liú tōng dào le hénán、húběi、shǎn xī、gān sù děng sheng
   He made himself draw three pieces a day. In about more than a year, these raw counterfeit bills surprisingly made it to Henan, Hubei, Shanxi, Gansu and other provinces.

From the above examples, '伪 (*wěi*)' displays two layers of meaning. First, '伪 (*wěi*)' denotes the idea of not complying with the law and order. Second, it expresses resentment or disapproval from the speaker. For instance, '日伪军 (*rì wěi jūn*)' not only does it deny the status of the troop but it also implies the resentment of the speaker towards them.

From table 2, it also shows a combination with words that refer to a misconduct such as '伪誓 (*wěi shì*)'(deceit) and '伪君子 (*wěi jūn zǐ*)'(hypocrite).

3. 你杀人的凶手，你用**伪誓**欺人的骗子……

nǐ shā rén de xiōng shǒu, nǐ yòng wěi shì qī rén de piàn zi

You are a murderer that killed people, you deceived people by making fake promises…

4. 善于透过甚至诿罪于人却又自诩清白、道德卑下、道貌岸然的**伪君子**。

shàn yú tòu guò shèn zhì wěi zuì yú rén què yòu zì xǔ qīng bái、dào dé bēi xià、dào mào àn rán de wěi jūn zǐ

A low morality, sanctimoniously hypocrite who is good at bragging about his own innocence by blaming other.

Immediate right collocates of '假 (*jiǎ*)'.

Table 3. Immediate right collocates of '假(*jiǎ*)'

Collocate	f(n,c)	MI	Collocate	f(n,c)	MI
洋鬼子 (*yáng guǐ zi*) foreign devil	14	7.64415	老婆(*lǎo pó*) wife	76	7.07189
钞 (*chāo*) bill	101	7.62993	牙(*yá*) tooth	34	7.05918
肢 (*zhī*) limb	69	7.62339	球 (*qiú*) ball	19	7.03409
币 (*bì*) coin/ money	164	7.59231	银元 (*yín yuán*) money	5	6.96607
山石 (*shān shí*) rocks	5	7.38111	文凭 (*wén píng*) certificate	8	6.94371
警报 (*jǐng bào*) alarm/ alert	9	7.22911	合资 (*hé zī*) joint investment	38	6.93788
睫毛 (*jié máo*) eyelashes	6	7.22911	货 (*huò*) stock	92	6.92930
徐宝生 (*Xú Bǎoshēng*) (a person's name)	6	7.22911	发票 (*fā piào*) receipt	165	6.90194
药 (*yào*) medicine	235	7.17193	正经 (*zhèng jīng*) decent	22	6.81817

Table 3 shows that collocates of '假(*jiǎ*)' are mainly entity nouns, referring to concrete objects or humans. As a result, the combination of "假(*jiǎ*) + collocate" denotes the meaning of being an imitation of an original. '假(*jiǎ*)' is rather used generally to express the replication of something or someone, yet in contrast to '伪 (*wěi*)', does not necessarily imply that it violates the law and order. For example, '假币(*jiǎ bì*)' (fake coin/ money) violates the law but '假牙(*jiǎ yá*) (false tooth) ' does not. Overall, '假(*jiǎ*)' collocates with entity nouns to express that they are an imitation or artificial.

5. 一些人怕戴"假集体"、"假国营"、**"假洋鬼子"**之类帽子，犹豫观望。

yì xiē rén pà dài "jiǎ jí tǐ"、"jiǎ guó yíng"、"jiǎ yang guǐ zi" zhī lèi mào zi，yóu yù guān wàng

Some people are afraid to be associated with a 'fake collective', 'fake state-run business', 'fake foreign devil', so they hesitate.

6. 你真的认为我们只要盯住刘志彬就能找着**假徐宝生**吗？

nǐ zhēn de rèn wéi wǒ men zhǐ yào dǐng zhù liú zhì bīn jiù néng zhǎo zhe jiǎ xú bǎo sheng ma

Do you really think we could find the fake Xu baosheng by keeping an eye on Liu Zhibin?

7. 既然可以有**假药**、假酒、假金银首饰之类，为什么就不能再有假字画！

jì rán kě yǐ yǒu jiǎ yào、jiǎ jiǔ、jiǎ jīn yín shǒu shì zhī lèi，wèi shén me jiù bù néng zài yǒu jiǎ zì huà

Since there is counterfeit medicine, counterfeit wine, counterfeit jewelries, why can't there be counterfeit calligraphy and paintings!

In the light of these findings, this paper concludes that although both '伪(*wěi*)' and '假(*jiǎ*)' are synonym and modify nouns, they however cannot be used interchangeably in every context. While '假(*jiǎ*)' exhibit a wider scope of usage, '伪(*wěi*)' has been used predominantly in the semantic field law and order to express the non-compliance to legality.

Grammatically speaking, '假(*jiǎ*)' is an adjective that can function as an attribute by modifying its collocates (ex. fake coin). It can also act as a predicate modified by an adverb of degree (ex. '非常假 (*fēi cháng jiǎ*)' (extremely fake), '有点假 (*yǒu diǎn jiǎ*)' (a little fake), expressing how fake or close the imitation is to the real thing. While '伪 (*wěi*)' can only be used as an attribute before nouns. Thus '伪 (*wěi*)' is an attributive word rather than a predicative word. The former is called '区别词 (*qū bié cí*)' (distinguishing word) [17].

3.3   The pair of synonyms '伪装(*wěi zhuāng*)' and '假装(*jiǎ zhuāng*)'

Next, this study will look at the pair of synonyms of '伪装 (*wěi zhuāng*)' and '假装 (*jiǎ zhuāng*)' by looking at 692 and 428 tokens respectively. In order to compare the collocates of '伪装(*wěi zhuāng*)' and '假装 (*jiǎ zhuāng*)', their immediate right collocates are obtained within span 0:1, a minimum MI score of 2.0 and its co-occurrences at least 5 times and above.

Immediate right collocates of '伪装 (*wěi zhuāng*)'.

Table 4. Immediate right collocates of '伪装 (*wěi zhuāng*)'

Collocate	f(n,c)	MI	Collocate	f(n,c)	MI
服 (*fú*)	5	7.50551	部队 (*bù duì*)	9	5.68108

uniform			troop		
成 (chéng)	74	7.26892	起来 (qǐ lái) (complement)	11	4.85511
into					
进步 (jìn bù)	5	6.92055	技术 (jì shù)	5	4.59862
progress			technique		
物 (wù)	5	5.95092	得 (de)	17	4.34921
item			(particle)		
分子 (fēn zǐ)	5	5.92055	自己 (zì jǐ)	10	3.95477
member			self		

From a syntactic perspective, the verb '伪装(wěi zhuāng)' can form a noun phrase by modifying its collocating noun (ex. '伪装服(wěi zhuāng fú)' (camouflage clothing), '伪装部队(wěi zhuāng bù duì)' (camouflage unit).

8. 陆军航空兵，第一次露面，就落在对手一个**伪装部队**的陷阱中去了……

lù jūn háng kōng bīng, dì yī cì lòu miàn, jiù luò zài duì shǒu yī gè wěi zhuāng bù duì de xiàn jǐng zhōng qù le

When ground and air force armies showed up for the first time, they fell right into the trap set by the improvised troop…

9. 偷猎取名人的镜头时，我很少穿绿色的**伪装服**，要是不慎被逮到，我便假装走错路。

tōu liè qǔ míng rén de jìng tóu shí, wǒ hěn shǎo chuān lǜ sè de wěi zhuāng fú, yào shi bú shèn bèi dǎi dào, wǒ biàn jiǎ zhuāng zǒu cuò lù

Whenever I secretly snap pictures of famous people, I seldom wear green camouflage clothing; if I were to be caught by incident, I could just pretend that I was lost.

Furthermore, it can also be followed by another verb which in Chinese could function as a particle/marker introducing a complement of degree.

10. 为了保密，令士兵穿着中国便衣，**伪装成**一般中国码头工人搬运。

wèi le bǎo mì, lìng shì bīng chuān zhuó zhōng guó biàn yī, wěi zhuāng chéng yì bān zhōng guó mǎ tóu gong rén bān yùn

For the sake of confidentiality, soldiers were ordered to wear normal Chinese clothing to pretend to be working as an ordinary Chinese dockman.

11. 假药劣药常常**伪装得**很像。

jiǎ yào liè yào cháng cháng wěi zhuāng dé hěn xiàng

Fake and bad medicine often look genuine.

12. 他揭露慷慨常常只是一种**伪装起来**的野心。

tā jiē lù kāng kǎi cháng cháng zhǐ shì yī zhǒng wěi zhuāng qǐ lái de yě xīn

He revealed that a generous act often hides an ulterior motive.

Immediate right collocates of '假装 (jiǎ zhuāng)'.

Table 5. Immediate right collocates of '假装 (*jiǎ zhuāng*)'

Collocate	f(n,c)	MI	Collocate	f(n,c)	MI
生气 (*sheng qì*) angry	10	7.71542	什么 (*shén me*) what	8	3.99224
关心 (*guān xīn*) concern	5	7.59512	看 (*kàn*) see	6	3.35736
特 (*tè*) extremely	6	7.37273	自己 (*zì jǐ*) self	5	3.16484
没 (*méi*) to not have	26	5.68971	去 (*qù*) to go	5	2.40135
没有 (*méi yǒu*) to not have	13	4.18078	着 (*zhe*) (particle)	5	2.24321

On the other hand, '假装(*jiǎ zhuāng*)' tends to collocate with negative adverbs such as '没(*méi*)' and '没有(*méi yǒu*)' (to not have), and seem to have a tendency to collocate verbs expressing a state (ex. '看(*kàn*)' (to see)), or an emotion (ex. '关心 (*guān xīn*)' (to care for)).

13. 奉行多一事不如少一事的态度；**假装没**看见、不置可否的回答为7.4%。

 fēng xíng duō yī shì bù rú shǎo yī shì de tài du, jiǎ zhuāng méi kàn jiàn bú zhì kě fǒu de huí dá wéi 7.4%

 7.4 % of the people answer randomly because they can't be bothered and therefore pretend they haven't seen anything.

14. 我就是这样儿。用不着不好意思**假装关心**别人。

 wǒ jiù shì zhè yang er。 Yòng bu zháo bù hǎo yì si jiǎ zhuāng guān xīn bié rén.

 I am just like this. There is no need to feel embarrassed and pretend to care about others.

15. 领导者的优秀素质和才能，不但**假装生气**地在早会上批评了刘唐一番……

 lǐng dǎo zhě de yōu xiù sù zhì hé cái néng, bú dàn jiǎ zhuāng sheng qì de zài zǎo huì shàng pīpíng le liú tang yì fān , ér qiě……

 The leader is skillfull man, not only he pretended to be angry to criticize Xiaoliu at the meeting this morning, but also…

In the light of this analysis, '伪装(*wěi zhuāng*)' and '假装(*jiǎ zhuāng*)' can both act as verbs function as a predicate and be modified by another verb or a particle introducing a complement such as a result or a degree. They differ in the following cases: 1) '伪装(*wěi zhuāng*)' cannot be followed by a negative adverb whereas '假装 (*jiǎ zhuāng*)' can; 2) '假装(*jiǎ zhuāng*)' cannot form a noun phrase as opposed to '伪 装(*wěi zhuāng*)'. From a semantic perspective, '伪装(*wěi zhuāng*)' seems to focus on the intention or result of the word it modifies as an entity, whereas '假装(*jiǎ zhuāng*)' rather emphasizes on specific action verbs or parts of a whole.

3.4   The pair of synonyms '虚伪 (*xū wěi*)' and '虚假 (*xū jiǎ*)'

In this section, this paper examines the following pair of synonyms '虚伪(*xū wěi*)' and '虚假(*xū jiǎ*)' which appear respectively 776 and 386 tokens in the data. Table 6 and table 7 show the 20 top collocates for each under the conditions of locating at most 5 words to the right (f(R)) and to the left (f(L)) of the node word.

Analysis of semantic prosody of '虚伪(xū wěi)'.

Table 6. Discontinuous collocates of '虚伪(*xū wěi*)'

Collocate	f(n,c)	f(L)	f(R)	MI	collocate	f(n,c)	f(L)	f(R)	MI
礼节(*lǐ jié*) courtesy	5	0	5	10.04266	散布(*sàn bù*) To spread	5	5	0	9.45770
冷酷(*lěng kù*) unfeeling	9	8	1	10.01619	爱情(*ài qíng*) love	7	5	2	9.30570
残忍(*cán rěn*) cruel	5	3	2	9.820270	半点(*bàn diǎn*) slightly	6	6	0	9.30570
做作(*zuò zuo*) overdo	6	2	4	9.720730	笑容(*xiào róng*) smile	5	1	4	9.16819
热烈(*rè liè*) warmly	7	1	6	9.653620	自私(*zì sī*) selfish	11	8	3	9.12127
谦虚(*qiān xū*) modest	5	2	3	9.62763	真诚(*zhēn chéng*) sincerity	14	8	6	9.11305
讨厌(*tǎo yàn*) disgust	10	9	1	9.62763	捏造(*niē zào*) to make up	5	5	0	9.04266
礼貌(*lǐ mào*) manner	8	5	3	9.60526	多么 (*duō me*) extremely	18	13	5	9.01619
狡诈(*jiǎo zhà*) cunning	8	2	6	9.60526	暴露(*bào lù*) to reveal	6	4	2	8.98377
假象(*jiǎ xiàng*) false impression	8	7	1	9.4577	罪恶(*zuì è*) sin	11	7	4	8.95777

Majority of the collocates of '虚伪 (*xū wěi*)' show a negative connotation in expression. For instance, '残忍(*cán rěn*)' (cruel), '做作(*zuò zuo*)'(overdo), '狡诈(*jiǎo zhà*)' (cunning), etc. It can affirm that words with a negative connotation tend to combine with each other in order to emphasize the idea of negativity. Therefore, this reinforce the fact that '虚伪(*xū wěi*)' is negative in semantic prosody and it is used normally to express hypocritical attitude as opposite to 'realness'.

1. 英国上流社会的享乐腐化、穷奢极侈、**虚伪**、**狡诈**、勾心斗角作了一定程度的揭露。
   yīng guó shàng liú shè huì de xiǎng lè fǔ huà、qióng shē jí chǐ、xūwěi、jiǎo zhà、gōu xīn dòu jiǎo zuò le yí ding chéng dù de jiē lù

It was revealed that the extravagant, hypocrite and cunning British upper class society practices hedonism.

2. 他写了不少揭露现实社会的自私、**冷酷**、**虚伪**、欺诈的诗篇。

    tā xiě le bù shǎo jiē lù xiàn shí shè huì de zì sī、lěng kù、xū wěi、qī zhà de shī piān

He wrote many poems describing how selfish, cold-blooded, hypocrite and deceitful society is.

Nevertheless, some collocates show a positive connotation, such as 热烈 (*rè liè*)(warmly), 谦虚 (*qiān xū*) (modest), etc.

3. 要知道**谦虚**客气也含有**虚伪**欺骗的成份……

yào zhī dào qiān xū kè qi yě hán yǒu xū wěi qī piàn de chéng fèn

Under every modest and polite face, there is a touch of hypocrisy and cheating…

4. 臃肿的四奶奶脸上，恶毒的神情和**虚伪**的**笑容**交织在一起。

yōng zhǒng de sì nǎi nai liǎn shàng，è dú de shén qíng hé xū wěi de xiào róng jiāo zhī zài yì qǐ

The evil look and hypocrite smile both showed on the fat face of the 4th mistress.

Although all the above collocates have a positive meaning, '虚伪(*xū wěi*)' is used to shed a negative light on them. Therefore '虚伪(*xū wěi*)' is proved to have a negative semantic prosody.

Analysis on semantic prosody of '虚假(*xū jiǎ*)'.

Table 7. Discontinuous collocates of '虚假(*xū jiǎ*)'

Collocate	f(n,w)	f(L)	f(R)	MI	Collocate	f(n,w)	f(L)	f(R)	MI
捏造 (*niē zào*) to make up	7	6	1	10.98775	半点(*bàn diǎn*) slightest	6	6	0	10.12793
陈述(*chén shù*) statement	10	0	10	10.86490	宣传(*xuān chuán*) publicity	20	2	18	10.05754
繁荣(*fán róng*) prosperity	12	0	12	10.76536	出具(*chū jù*) to show	9	9	0	9.876390
误解(*wù jiě*) misunderstanding	5	3	2	10.67225	数据(*shù jù*) data	5	0	5	9.86490
广告(*guǎng gào*) advertisement	61	9	52	10.65170	文件(*wén jiàn*) document	11	4	7	9.80976
散布(*sàn bù*) to spread	9	7	2	10.61336	证券(*zhèng quàn*) securities	9	6	3	9.71289
误导(*wù dǎo*) misleading	14	1	13	10.51382	资料(*zī liào*) Material	10	0	10	9.67225
泡沫(*pào mò*) bubble	6	0	6	10.35032	串通(*chuàn tōng*) to gang up	5	3	2	9.67225
信息(*xìn xī*) information	13	1	12	10.24341	内容(*nèi róng*) content	11	6	5	9.56183

需求 (xū qiú)					隐瞒 (yǐn mán)				
needs	9	2	7	10.19832	to conceal	7	4	3	9.51382

Unlike '虚伪 (xū wěi)', the collocates of '虚假 (xū jiǎ)' as listed in table 7 do not exhibit a clear strong negative connotation. Most of them are rather neutral semantically.

5. 同实体资本和实业部门的成长脱离越来越远，便会造成社会经济的**虚假繁荣**，形成**泡沫**经济。

   tóng shí tǐ zī běn hé shí yè bù mén de chéng zhǎng tuō lí yuè lái yuè yuǎn, biàn huì zào chéng shè huì jīng jì de xū jiǎ fán róng, xíng chéng pào mò jīng jì

   The more the physical capital grows apart from the industrial sector, the more the society will fall into an illusionary prosper economy, turn into a bubble economy.

6. **泡沫**经济引致的**虚假繁荣**景象扭曲了消费者的消费行为……

   pào mò jīng jì yǐn zhì de xū jiǎ fán róng jǐng xiàng niǔ qū le xiāo fèi zhě de xiāo fèi xíng wéi

   A bubble economy leads to an illusionary prosper situation which affects the consuming behavior of the consumer...

Example (5) shows a collocation of '虚假 (xū jiǎ)' with positive words i.e. '繁荣 (fán róng)' (prosperity) and example (6) shows collocation with neutral word '泡沫 (pào mò)' (bubble). However, the context in which they appear is negative. Therefore, this study concludes that '虚假 (xū jiǎ)' also sheds a negative light on the sentence in which it appears.

Nevertheless, there is a situation in which the use of '虚假 (xū jiǎ)' does not shed such a light. In fact, the sentence exhibits a rather neutral connotation. Based on the following examples, this paper discovers that the presence of a negation adverb or verb that denotes the idea of denial or rejection cancels the negative meaning expressed by '虚假 (xū jiǎ)'.

7. 第14条中更明确，经营者**不得**捏造、散布**虚假**事实损害竞争对手的商业信誉。

   dì 14 tiáo zhōng gèng míng què, jīng yíng zhě bù dé niē zào、sàn bù xū jiǎ shì shí sǔn hài jìng zhēng duì shǒu de shāng yè xìn yù

   As clearly stated in line 14, the management is not allowed to falsely create or spread facts that could cause damage to the reputation of their competitors.

8. 董事必须保证公开披露文件内容**没有虚假**、严重误导性陈述……

   dǒng shì bì xū bǎo zhèng gong kāi pī lù wén jiàn nèi róng méi yǒu xū jiǎ、yán zhòng wù dǎo xìng chén shù

   The trustees must guaranty publicly that the documents do not contain false or severely misleading statements…

9. **拒绝**传播**虚假**的科学技术信息和广告。

   jù jué chuán bō xū jiǎ de kē xué jì shù xìn xī hé guǎng gào

   Do not share false scientific and technological information and advertisement.

3.5   Interchangeability of '伪(wěi)-假(jiǎ)', '伪装(wěi zhuāng)-假装(jiǎ zhuāng)' and '虚伪(xū wěi)-虚假(xū jiǎ)'

Despite the differences between these synonyms described above, they are after all synonyms because they share similarities in meaning and expressions. The pair of synonym '伪(wěi)' and '假(jiǎ)' share a common collocate, i.e. '币(bì)' (coin/ money) (refer to table 2 and 3). On a more general level, they both express the fabrication of an imitation of money. While '伪币(wěi bì)' undeniably refer to illegal counterfeit money, '假币(jiǎ bì)' could either refer to counterfeit money or money used in board games such as Monopoly.

1. **假币**使用者能够屡屡得手，不仅仅在于他们的狡猾，更在于他们使用的**伪币**制作得越来越精细，足可以以假乱真，令专家也一时难辨真伪。

   jiǎ bì shǐ yòng zhě néng gòu lǚ lǚ dé shǒu, bù jǐn jǐn zài yú tā men de jiǎo huá, gèng zài yú tā men shǐ yòng de wěi bì zhì zuò dé yuè lái yuè jīng xì, zú kě yǐ yǐ jiǎ luàn zhēn, lìng zhuān jiā yě yì shí nán biàn zhēn wěi

   The use of counterfeit money has increased considerably not only because criminals are smart, but also because techniques have allowed the production of fake bills true to the real ones, so true that even experts can hardly distinguish them.

In addition, '伪(wěi)' and '假(jiǎ)'also shows interchangeability on some phrasal structure such as 防伪打假 (fáng wěi dǎ jiǎ) and 打假防伪 (dǎ jiǎ fáng wěi), both structure denote the similar meaning of anti-forgery and prevent fraud. Also, they are interchangeable in 假冒伪劣(jiǎ mào wěi liè) and 伪劣假冒(wěi liè jiǎ mào) that denote to forgery and shoddy product.

As for the pair of verbs '伪装 (wěi zhuāng)' and '假装 (jiǎ zhuāng)', this study also found the reflexive pronoun i.e. '自己(zì jǐ)' as their common collocate (refer to table 4 and 5). From a semantic perspective, they both refer to the meaning of 'someone is pretending him/herself' to avoid recognition by others.

2. 丧服与我们日常服饰不相同，因此古人穿丧服的目的在**伪装自己**，以避免死神认出来。

   sāng fú yǔ wǒ men rì cháng fú shì bù xiāng tóng, yīn cǐ gǔ rén chuān sang fú de mù dì zài wěi zhuāng zì jǐ, yǐ bì miǎn sǐ shén rèn chū lái

   Mourning clothing differs from normal clothing for people in ancient times believed that disguising oneself in such clothes would help them avoid being caught by the God of death.

3. 假装什么事情也没发生，**假装自己**还像孩子一样纯洁，那也太做作了。

   jiǎ zhuāng shén me shì qíng yě méi fā shēng，jiǎ zhuāng zì jǐ hái xiàng hái zǐ yí yang chún jié，nà yě tài zuò zuo le

   To pretend that nothing happened or that one is still as innocent as a child is way too pretentious.

Finally, as for the adjectives '虚伪(*xū wěi*)' and '虚假(*xū jiǎ*)' , the following common collocates were listed: "半点(*bàn diǎn*), 捏造(*niē zào*), 散布(*sàn bù*)" (refer to table 6 and 7). There doesn't seem to be a significant difference in meaning when either or is used.

4. 科学来不得**半点虚伪**，事关祖国尊严和人格，因此他据理力争。

   kē xué lái bu de bàn diǎn xū wěi, shì guān zǔ guó zūn yán hé rén gé, yīn cǐ tā jù lǐ lì zhēng

   Science cannot be improvised in any circumstances because it affects a country's honour and dignity, and therefore he should defend it.

5. 科技成果鉴定是一件科学性很强的工作，来不得**半点虚假**。

   kē jì chéng guǒ jiàn dìng shì yī jiàn kē xué xìng hěn qiáng de gong zuò，lái bu de bàn diǎn xū jiǎ

   Technological achievements are the fruits of hard scientific labor, therefore fake ideas should not be tolerated.

6. 禁止**捏造、散布虚假事实**，损害竞争对手的商业信誉和商品声誉。

   jìn zhǐ niē zào、sàn bù xū jiǎ shì shí，sǔn hài jìng zhēng duì shǒu de shāng yè xìn yù hé shāng pǐn sheng yù

   It is prohibited to falsely create or spread inaccurate facts that could harm the reputation and credibility of any competitors.

7. 依法查处商业诋毁行为,对**捏造、散布虚伪事实**,损害他方商业信誉的,将责令其停止违法行为。

   yī fǎ chá chǔ shāng yè dǐ huǐ xíng wéi，duì niē zào、sàn bù xū wěi shì shí，sǔn hài tā fang shāng yè xìn yù de，jiāng zé lìng qí tíng zhǐ wéi fǎ xíng wéi

   An investigation upon the false creation or spreading of inaccurate facts causing damage to the reputation of a business shall be conducted and sanctioned according to the law.

As shown as above, '半点虚伪 (*bàn diǎn xū wěi*)'and '半点虚假 (*bàn diǎn xū jiǎ*)' are exchangeable in examples (4) and (5) without any change in meaning. So as in (6) and (7), they are expressing the same meaning of fake truth.

4   Conclusion

Using a corpus-based approach, this study determines the differences within the similarities of three pairs of words, pertaining to the concept of something being an imitation, a pretention or a false, unreal, counterfeit copy, by reinforcing researcher's intuitive analysis (qualitative) of the language with statistical data (quantitative). The corpus-based methodology provides a more objective and concrete results. These findings provide important insights and information for future work in lexicology studies and in writing dictionaries. As a matter of fact, it defines precisely the signification of each word, their context of usage and what makes them different although they are similar in meaning.

References

1. Sinclair, J.: Corpus, Concordance, Collocation. Oxford University press, Oxford (1996).
2. McEnery, T., Wilson, A.: Corpus Linguistics. Edinburgh University Press, Edinburgh (2001).
3. Stubbs, M.: Words and Phrases: Corpus Studies of Lexical Semantics. Blackwell, Oxford (2001).
4. Biber, D., Condrad, S., Reppen, R.: Corpus linguistics. Foreign Language Teaching and Research Publisher, Beijing (2000).
5. Zhu, D.: Handouts on Grammar. Commercial press, Beijing (1982). [In Chinese]
6. Wang, F.: Ancient words analysis. Jilin literature and history publisher, Jilin (1993). [In Chinese]
7. Qi, Y.: Distinguish 'jia', 'wei'. Journal of Changzhi institute 24(1), 46&57 (2007). [In Chinese]
8. Yang, M.: A study on the change of meaning of the common words 'wei', 'jia'. Journal of Liuzhou professional institute 10(3), 84-89 (2010). [In Chinese]
9. CCL corpus: http://ccl.pku.edu.cn
10. Zhang. H. ICTCLAS [Computer software]. Beijing, China: Beijing Institute of Technology (2014). Available from http:// http://ictclas.nlpir.org/
11. Anthony, L. AntConc (Version 3.4.3) [Computer Software]. Tokyo, Japan: Waseda University (2014). Available from http://www.antlab.sci.waseda.ac.jp/
12. Yang, H.: Introduction to corpus linguistic. Shanghai Foreign Language Teaching Publisher, Shanghai (2002). [In Chinese]
13. Firth, J. R.: A synopsis of linguistic theory, 1930-1955. Studies in Linguistic Analysis. Special Volume, Philological Society, pp.1-32. Blackwell, Oxford (1957).
14. Stubbs, M.: Text and corpus analysis. Oxford: Blackwell (1996).
15. Louw, B. Irony in the text or insincerity in the writer? The diagnostic potential of semantic prosodies. Text and technology: In honour of John Sinclair, pp.240-251 (1993).
16. Crawford, W.J., Csomay, E.: Doing corpus linguistics. Routledge, New York (2016).
17. Zhu, D.: Questions and answers on grammar. Commercial press, Beijing (1985). [In Chinese]

Author Index

Printed in the United States
By Bookmasters